Time Out
Dublin

Penguin Books

PENGUIN BOOKS

Published by the Penguin Group
Penguin Books Ltd, 27 Wrights Lane, London W8 5TZ, England
Penguin Books USA Inc., 375 Hudson Street, New York, New York 10014, USA
Penguin Books Australia Ltd, Ringwood, Victoria, Australia
Penguin Books Canada Ltd, 10 Alcorn Avenue, Toronto, Ontario, Canada M4V 3B2
Penguin Books (NZ) Ltd, 182-190 Wairau Road, Auckland 10, New Zealand

Penguin Books Ltd, Registered Offices: Harmondsworth, Middlesex, England

First published 1998
10 9 8 7 6 5 4 3 2 1

Copyright © Time Out Group Ltd, 1998
All rights reserved

Colour reprographics by Precise Litho, 34-35 Great Sutton Street, London EC1
Mono reprographics, printed and bound by William Clowes Ltd, Beccles, Suffolk NR34 9QE

Edited and designed by

Time Out Magazine Limited
Universal House
251 Tottenham Court Road
London W1P 0AB
Tel + 44 (0)171 813 3000
Fax + 44 (0)171 813 6001
Email net@timeout.co.uk
http://www.timeout.co.uk

Editorial

Managing Editor Peter Fiennes
Editor Nicholas Royle
Consultant Editor Orlaith O'Sullivan
Deputy Editor Louise Gray
Researcher Bruce O'Connor
Indexer Jackie Brind

Design

Art Director John Oakey
Art Editor Paul Tansley
Designer Mandy Martin
Design Assistant Wayne Davies
Picture Editor Catherine Hardcastle
Picture Researcher Michaela Freeman

Advertising

Group Advertisement Director Lesley Gill
Sales Director Mark Phillips
Advertisement Sales (Dublin) John Paul Duignan

Administration

Publisher Tony Elliott
Managing Director Mike Hardwick
Financial Director Kevin Ellis
Marketing Director Gillian Auld
Production Manager Mark Lamond
Accountant Catherine Bowen

Features in this guide were written and researched by:

Introduction Emma Donoghue. **History** Orlaith O'Sullivan (**Mum's the word** Katy O'Dowd). **Architecture** Luke Dodd. **Literary Dublin** David Wheatley (**Lite bite** Ian Cunningham). **Dublin by Area** Bridget Hourican (**Park life** Clare Lapraik Guest). **Sightseeing** Bridget Hourican. **Dublin by Season** Paul Delaney (**The Liffey Swim** Rachel Andrews). **Museums** Clare Lapraik Guest. **Art Galleries** Louise Kidney. **Restaurants** John McKenna. **Bistros, Cafés & Coffee Shops** John McKenna. **Pubs & Bars** John McKenna. **Shopping & Services** John Boyne & Dylan Cotter (**Molly's mussels** Rachel Andrews). **Accommodation** Sean Sheehan. **Clubs** Declan Long. **Children's Dublin** Orlaith O'Sullivan. **Film** Emily Hourican. **Gay & Lesbian Dublin** Neil Hegarty. **Media** John Boyne & Dylan Cotter. **Music: Classical & Opera** John O'Mahony. **Music: Rock, Folk & Jazz** Ann-Marie Hardiman (**Mass appeal** Louise Gray). **Sport & Fitness** Paul Delaney. **Theatre, Dance & Comedy** Emily Hourican (**Comedy** John Boyne & Dylan Cotter; **Stand up** Ardal O'Hanlon Rachel Andrews). **Trips Out of Town** Sean Sheehan & Pat Levy (**Where to eat** John McKenna; **Belfast additional material** Gus Grew). **Directory** Orlaith O'Sullivan. **Further Reading** Louise Gray, Nicholas Royle, Peter Fiennes, Ian Cunningham.

The Editor wishes to thank the following: Chris Bohn, Ian Cunningham, Peter Fiennes, Louise Gray, Sarah Guy, Oisin Murphy-Lawless, Bruce O'Connor, Orlaith O'Sullivan, Mike Rogers, Caro Taverne.

Maps by JS Graphics, 17 Beadles Lane, Old Oxted, Surrey RH8 9JG.

Photography by Alan O'Connor except for: page 4 **BBC**; pages 5, 12 **Trinity College Library**; pages 59, 192, 193, 196, 197, 198, 200, 201, 202, 203, 206, 207, 208, 209 (top), 210, 215, 217, 218, 219, 221, 222, 224, 226, 227, 228, 229, 230, 232, 235, 237, 238 (left), 240, 241, 243, 244 **Bord Failte/Irish Tourist Board**; page 13 **Hulton Deutsch**; pages 15, 16 **Hulton Getty**; page 18 **Frank Miller**; page 155 **Helen Rose**; page 156 **David Appleby**; pages 145, 147, 148, 159, 160, 161 **Trish Brennan**; page 178 **Simon Bruty/Allsport**; page 187 **Amelia Stein**; page 188 (left) **Dermot Bolger**; page 188 (right) **Tom Lawlor**; page 189 **Kip Carroll/Colsceim Dance Theatre**; pages 194, 205, 209 (bottom), 212, 216, 220, 223, 231, 233, 234, 235 (bottom), 236, 238 (right), 239, 246, 249, 250. Photographs on following pages provided by featured establishments: pages 167, 169.

Contents

About the Guide

This is the first edition of the *Time Out Dublin Guide*, one in a series of 17 city guides that also includes London, New York, Paris, Amsterdam, Rome, Prague, Los Angeles, Miami, Barcelona, Berlin, Brussels, Budapest, Florence & Tuscany, Madrid, San Francisco and Sydney. Our team of resident writers has striven to provide you with all the information you'll need to tackle what is currently one of the most popular travel destinations in Europe. Those heading out from Dublin to the south-west of Ireland, the west coast or even the north will require **Trips Out of Town**, now the longest such section in the series.

CHECKED & CORRECT

Above all, we've tried to make this book as useful as possible. Addresses, telephone numbers, transport details, opening times, admission prices and credit card details were all checked and correct at the time of going to press. All of these, however, are liable to change at any time, so it would be advisable to check opening times, admission prices and other key details before setting out for whichever bar or gallery or Thai restaurant or museum or festival.

ADDRESSES & PHONE NUMBERS

Dublin is divided into Northside and Southside by the River Liffey. Throughout this guide we have used the numbered postal districts – Dublin 1, Dublin 2 and so on. Telephone numbers are seven-digit numbers. To dial a Dublin number from the UK, you need to use the prefix 00 353 1. Always assume that any number listed in the guide is a Dublin number, to be prefixed by 01 if you are calling from within Ireland but outside Dublin. Numbers listed for restaurants and hotels et cetera in the **Trips Out of Town** section are prefixed by the local code.

PRICES

The prices we have supplied should be treated as guidelines, not gospel. All prices given are in Irish punts, but for simplicity's sake we have used the symbol £ rather than IR£. Fluctuating exchange rates and inflation can cause prices, in shops and restaurants particularly, to change rapidly. If prices vary wildly from those we've quoted, ask whether there's a good reason. If not, go elsewhere. Then please write and let us know. We aim to give the best and most up-to-date advice, so we always want to know if you've been badly treated or overcharged.

CREDIT CARDS

The following abbreviations have been used for credit cards: **AmEx**: American Express; **DC**: Diners' Club; **JCB**: Japanese credit cards; **MC**: Mastercard (Access); **V**: Visa (Barclaycard).

RIGHT TO REPLY

It should be stressed that the information we give is impartial. No organisation has been included in this guide because its owner or manager has advertised in our publications. We hope you enjoy the *Time Out Dublin Guide*, but we'd also like to know if you don't. We welcome tips for places that you think we should include in future editions and take notice of your criticism of our choices. There's a reader's reply card at the back of this book.

There is an online version of this guide, as well as weekly events listings for several international cities, at http://www.timeout.co.uk.

Introduction

The seagulls will probably wake you, but don't get up all at once. Lie in bed trying to read the first chapter of James Joyce's *Ulysses* till your arm goes numb. Your first meal should be a dirty great fry-up. The toast should be brown stone-ground bread; the jam should be rhubarb and ginger.

Go out now and get rained on. Huddle in your coat and don't much care. Instead of buying a newspaper, get your taxi driver or anyone in the bus queue to give you a scurrilous run-down on Church scandals and political corruption, all on first-name terms. Marvel at the sheer number of babies and nuns; wonder about a possible connection between the two.

To feel like a real Dubliner, do not get around to seeing the Book of Kells. Feel mildly, slothfully guilty. There's nothing you really have to do, or see, or take pictures of. After the best weekends in Dublin, no one can remember what they did.

Mooch at random through the streets, past redbrick terraces, past Georgian mansions with gaudily painted doors. Watch out for weird bronzes at every street corner (Molly Malone falling out of her bodice, a four-foot cinema usher, a giantess in a fountain known as 'the floozy in the jacuzzi' or 'the hoor in the sewer').

Everything is near enough, small enough (much too small, the locals would say). Any gallery can be done in half a morning; you can whip round the Celtic gold collection in an hour. Which leaves you with lots of time for easygoing consumption of Dublin's pleasures. Lunchtime plays (where else are the lunches long enough?), gossip, a slowly drawn pint in an empty pub with stained-glass windows at two in the afternoon, more gossip, the best chips in the world (made by Italians, eaten out of newsprint, preferably in the rain).

Walk down Grafton Street to sample six different styles of busking, from fresh-faced girls with cellos to silver-painted mimes. Buy an apple from a fearsome woman's wheelbarrow; shake hands with a medieval skeleton in a crypt, count the bullet holes from the 1916 Rising in the breasts of the stone angels on O'Connell Street.

The city is more than a thousand years old, built on a Viking rubbish-heap; it is not easily impressed, known for its 'begrudgery', in fact. And certainly some things never change: the litter, the eight-year-old beggars. But the city is booming, becoming fashionable, as any Dubliner will tell you with a slight curl of the lip. Beside the leprechaun souvenir shops are springing up scores of ethnic restaurants and cyber-coffeehouses.

The River Liffey gave Dublin its name, literally 'black pool'; it cuts the city like a belt. Ask a Northsider (traditionally working class) about Southsiders (traditionally middle class), and vice versa, but don't believe a word of what they tell you. Keep crossing and recrossing the river, especially by the Ha'penny Bridge, which bounces under your feet.

But the very best thing about Dublin is that you can get out of it fast. Climb on to the green DART train that hugs the shore, and take your pick of green hills and bare beaches less then half an hour away.

Come back into the city at twilight, feeling faintly, enjoyably sad. Be late for things; everyone else will, so you might as well get used to it.

Find a free-for-all music session in a pub where you are only two feet away from the bodhrán drummer and nobody is uncool enough to clap. Eavesdrop on Dubliners slagging their friends as if they're enemies.

The cobbled lanes of Temple Bar, a tongue-in-cheek Left Bank, swarm with clubbers by night. A hundred yards away, the dark, slick river swallows all the lights.

Oh, and don't talk too loudly on the buses: somebody will put you in their next book.

Emma Donoghue, like James Joyce, is a Dubliner in self-imposed exile; there the resemblance ends. Her Dublin novels are Stir-Fry *and* Hood, *both in Penguin paperback.*

Irish Museum of Modern Art

Image: **John Kindness**
Scraping the surface 1990
Etched painted steel,
taxi-cab fragment

An exciting and wide-ranging cross-section of Irish and international art of the 20th century, housed in one of Ireland's most beautiful buildings.

Admission Free
Museum & Bookshop open
Tues - Sat 10 - 5.30 Sun & Bank Hol 12 - 5.30
Free guided tours of exhibitions
Wed & Fri 2.30 Sat 11.30
Coffee shop open
Mon - Sat 10 -5 Sun & Bank Hol 12 -5

Áras Nua Ealaine na hÉireann
Royal Hospital, Military Road
Kilmainham, Dublin 8
Telephone 01 612 9900
Fax 01 612 9999

In Context

Key Events

432 St Patrick arrives in Ireland.
841 Vikings settle in Dublin area; build *longphort*.
902 Vikings driven out.
917 Vikings reoccupy Dublin; build *dun*.
1014 Boru defeats Vikings at Clontarf.
1038 Christchurch founded.
1170 Arrival of Strongbow.
1171 Arrival of Henry II; Dublin becomes capital of English colony.
1191 St Patrick's Cathedral founded.
1348 Plague hits Dublin.
1530s Dissolution of the monasteries under Henry VIII.
1558 Elizabeth I crowned.
1560 Ireland proclaimed an Anglican country.
1562 Elizabethan wars in Ireland begin.
1575 Plague kills 30 per cent of Dublin's citizens.
1591 Monastery of All Saints refounded as Trinity College.
1597 140 barrels of gunpowder explode on Dublin quays.
1601 Hugh O'Neill defeated by Mountjoy in Kinsale.
1607 The Flight of the Earls: O'Neill and O'Donnell flee, forfeiting their lands to the Crown.
1608 Plantation of Ulster begins.
1641 Great rebellion over land.
1649 Arrival of Oliver Cromwell.
1690 (14 July) William of Orange defeats James II at Battle of the Boyne.
1695 Legislation of the penal laws begin.
1713 Jonathan Swift becomes Dean of St Patrick's Cathedral.
1726 Swift's *Gulliver's Travels*.
1742 Handel's *Messiah* at the New Music Hall, Fishamble Street.
1782 Ireland granted Legislative Independence
1796 Wolfe Tone rebellion.
1800 Act of Union revokes Legislative Independence.
1803 Robert Emmet's rising.
1829 Catholic Emancipation Act.
1845-59 The Great Famine.
1858 James Stephens founds Fenian Brotherhood.
1867 Fenian rising.
1879 Land League founded.
1886 First Home Rule Bill introduced.
1890 Parnell deposed.
1893 Gaelic League founded.
1897 Bram Stoker's *Dracula*.
1900 Queen Victoria visits Dublin.
1904 Abbey Theatre founded by Yeats, Lady Gregory and Synge.
1911 Irish Women's Suffrage Federation founded.
1912 Third Home Rule Bill.
1913 UVF, Irish Citizen Army and Irish National Volunteers founded.
1915 *Lusitania* sinks off the Old Head of Kinsale: 1,198 lives lost.
1916 Easter Rising.
1918 WWI ends. Sinn Fein wins election.
1919 Dail Éireann meets in Dublin.
1920 Black & Tans, Auxiliaries arrive. Bloody Sunday in Dublin.
1921 Collins signs Anglo-Irish Treaty.
1922 Civil War. Collins killed. James Joyce's *Ulysses*.
1923 WB Yeats wins Nobel Prize for Literature.

In 1931, **Orson Welles** *played at the Gate.*

1925 George Bernard Shaw wins Nobel Prize for Literature.
1926 De Valera founds Fianna Fail.
1931 Orson Welles plays in Chekov and Ibsen at the Gate Theatre.
1937 Constitution of Eire drawn up.
1939 IRA bombing campaign in Britain. Fine Gael/Clann na Poblachta elected.
1949 Republic of Ireland declared.
1951 Ernest Walton wins Nobel Prize for Physics.
1963 JFK visits Ireland.
1966 Nelson's Pillar (built 1808) blown up.
1967 Northern Ireland Civil Rights Association founded.
1969 Provisional IRA formed. Samuel Beckett wins Nobel Prize for Literature. Dublin Arms Trial: future Taoiseach Haughey acquitted on gun-running charges.
1972 Bloody Sunday in Londonderry. Parliament at Stormont suspended.
1974 Sean MacBride wins Nobel Peace Prize.
1976 Founders of the Northern Ireland Peace Movement Mairead Corrigan and Betty Williams win Nobel Peace Prize.
1978 Four Dublin musicians form U2.
1982 Northern Ireland Assembly opened at Stormont.
1983 Abortion referendum defeated.
1987 Roddy Doyle's *The Commitments*.
1988 Ireland qualify for the first time in a major soccer tournament. Dublin City celebrates its millennium.
1990 Mary Robinson elected as President of Ireland. *Italia '90:* Ireland get through to the quarter-finals of the World Cup, where they are beaten by Italy.
1993 Roddy Doyle wins the Booker Prize for *Paddy Clarke, Ha Ha Ha.*
1994 (31 August) IRA announce ceasefire.
1995 Seamus Heaney wins Nobel Prize for Literature. Divorce referendum: majority votes in favour of divorce.
1996 Divorce Act becomes law. (Feb 9) IRA end ceasefire.
1997 (20 July) Latest IRA ceasefire begins at midday...

History

Everyone but the Romans: how Dublin assimilated Gaels, Vikings and Anglo-Saxons to create its own unique character.

In the beginning

Although the city of Dublin celebrated its millennium in 1988, the area has been inhabited since 8,000 BC. Ireland survived wave after wave of invaders, but with the arrival of the Gaels (shortly before the birth of Christ) the language and the culture of the native people were irrevocably changed. The modern names of the capital city – 'Baile Átha Cliath' and 'Dublin'– derive from two distinct settlements in early Gaelic Ireland.

Ath Cliath ('the ford of the hurdles') is thought to be the older settlement, a fortified secular enclosure dating from the sixth century. It was most likely a trading post, marking the junction of the long-distance routeways from the four provinces (Ulster, Leinster, Connaught and Munster). The importance of Ath Cliath as a meeting of the ways is debatable, but it was certainly of some value, for its ale was renowned in the early Christian period. It appears that the Guinnesses are only continuing a long tradition of brewing in Dublin.

Dubhlinn ('the black pool') takes its name from a tidal pool in the estuary of the river Poddle. It was a monastic community in the area now known as the Liberties, comprising several churches, religious houses and holy wells. Ireland received Christianity early: Saint Patrick arrived in 432 AD and soon extinguished the rites of the pagans. A golden age of Gaelic Christianity followed, which produced such magnificent works of religious art as the Book of Durrow, the Ardagh Chalice and the **Book of Kells**. Dubhlinn bears the imprint of the great missionary: legend holds that **St Patrick's Cathedral** (founded 1191) marks the site where the saint himself baptised the heathen Irish.

It was only with the arrival of the Norse that the Dublin area became urbanised. After an attack in 839, Norwegian Vikings established themselves in Dubhlinn in 841 with the construction of a harbour or *longphort.* In the decades that followed, they used Dublin as a base from which to raid and plunder the surrounding regions. The invaders were unimpeded by any unified resistance and the area became the focal point of Scandinavian settlement in Ireland, developing into an important port and market place for the trade of slaves (men and women captured during the raids).

Dublin gained mention in the Viking sagas, and a wealth of artefacts have been preserved in its soil, including the largest Viking burial site outside of Scandinavia (at Islandbridge-Kilmainham). Although politically united during the early years of their reign, after the death of Ivar the Boneless in 873, there was considerable internal dissent amongst the Scandinavians, and, in 902, they were driven out by the joint forces of Brega and Leinster.

A second invasion began in 914 and Dublin was reoccupied in 917. This time, their settlement was not described as a *longphort*, but as a *dun* or stronghold. It was a period of great construction, during which Wood Quay was developed and permanent dwellings constructed in the area now flanked by Christchurch and Dublin Castle. Yet the leadership remained radically unstable, as consecutive Scandinavian kings attempted to rule both Dublin and their English centre, York, concurrently.

The Dublin Vikings concentrated their efforts on Ireland only after the collapse of the Scandinavian

The **Book of Kells** – *Trinity College Library.*

kingdom of York in 954. From this point, their status changed: they established the first Irish towns, intermarried with the Irish and chose Gaelic names for their children. Yet although it was during this period that the Norsemen became absorbed into the Gaelic world, all was not peaceful. The Vikings continued to plunder the countryside; monasteries took to building 'round towers' (which may still be seen, for example, at Monasterboice) to keep watch.

Dublin came under regular attack from the Irish after 936. When the king of Meath was declared high-king in 980, the Norse leader Olaf challenged him. Their forces clashed at Tara, with the Christian Mael Sechnaill emerging victorious. In the following years, Sechnaill laid siege to Dublin a further four times and his high-kingship (980-1002, 1014-22) marks the transition between Viking and Hiberno-Norse Dublin. The Scandinavians were defeated by King Brian Boru at Clontarf on Good Friday 1014, the year in which Dublin became a Christian vassal state. After King Sitric Silkbeard's pilgrimage to Rome (1028), there was considerable activity in the religious lives of Dubliners, resulting in the foundation of **Christchurch Cathedral** and the westward expansion of the town. Sitric was deposed in 1036, and Dublin was ruled by Irish over-kings until 1170, when the town (indeed, the whole country) underwent another massive upheaval as the English arrived.

Strongbow – **Christchurch Cathedral**.

The medieval city

In 1169, a small Norman troop landed in County Wexford, sent over by the earl of Pembroke (better known as Strongbow). They helped the king of Leinster, Diarmait Mac Murchada, in his war, then returned to England to gather more men. By 1170, Strongbow had taken Dublin from the Hiberno-Norsemen (or Ostmen). He rebuilt the wooden Christchurch with a stone foundation, married Mac Murchada's daughter, and inherited the kingship of Leinster on the death of Diarmait. The English king Henry II then sent in his own army to keep an eye on Strongbow. These Anglo-Normans, like the Vikings before them, became 'more Irish than the Irish themselves', and so began the pattern of invasion, resilience and assimilation which would characterise Irish history.

In 1171, Henry II proclaimed that Dublin was under his rule. The Vikings were expelled, and the city became the capital of the English 'colony' in Ireland, with its own Parliament and Exchequer. In fact, the only area brought under English control was 'the Pale', consisting of a few hundred square miles around Dublin (thus 'beyond the Pale', meaning one who is uncontrollable). As the decades progressed, even this small area began to shrink, and the English focused their attentions on Dublin itself. Under Henry II and his son, John, the city was established in legal terms, and during the following century expanded rapidly as a port and merchant centre. Trade became standardised with the gradual development of the craft guilds, which were strictly monitored to exclude any Gaelic elements, only allowing men and women 'of English name and blood'.

In many respects, Dublin was a medieval city like any other. It was overcrowded, with its population (estimated at 5,000) crammed into a small, walled area. Fire had a tendency to rage through the enclosed space, full of thatched roofs. The burgesses were diligent in establishing water supplies (usually limited to the wealthy, in true medieval fashion). There was a large population of poor, who suffered especially in times of famine and sickness. Fortunately, Dubliners were generous: their wills are filled with bequests to the needy, and the citizens founded a massive leper hospital (which was allowed the rents from the present-day St Stephen's Green). Still, there was great strife: in 1295, it was reported that there was such a shortage of food that the poor actually ate the criminals hanged on the gallows; 1317 saw the worst famine of the Middle Ages, when mothers supposedly devoured their own children.

In 1348, the plague hit Dublin. Infectious diseases were at their most lethal in medieval cities. By modern Western standards, even the wealthy lived in disgusting conditions, coping with open sewers, flea-infested beds, rats, floors covered with

*Fifteenth-century pilgrims were drawn to **Saint Patrick's** cathedral, among other shrines.*

soiled straw and filthy streets. The Black Death returned regularly, restricting the growth of the city for the next century. In times of disease, all beggars were banished from the city and regulations concerning health and hygiene increased. In 1489, the focus was on the city's pigs. Royal letters ordered the swine of Dublin to be contained, complaining that they 'infect the air and produce mortality, fevers and pestilence throughout the city'.

But such mortal dangers did not dissuade the hordes of pilgrims journeying to the shrines of Dublin each year. There was a plethora of churches and religious houses within the city, where the main crowd-pullers were the two cathedrals: **St Patrick's**, and the church of the **Holy Trinity (Christchurch)**, among whose relics was the *bacall Iosa* ('staff of Jesus'). The highlight of Dublin religious life was the Corpus Christi pageant, a spectacular procession of Biblical plays, funded by the guilds of the city. Each Bible story was designated to an appropriate guild, so the tale of Noah was performed by the mariners, the fishermen played the 12 apostles and so on.

Corpus Christi was not the only time for celebration: the Church calendar contained so many feast-days (on which it was forbidden to work) that there remained around only 200 working days in a year. For the other 165 days, the citizens were left to their own devices. The wealthier people could afford harpers, minstrels or troubadours, but the common people entertained themselves with dancing, cock-fighting, bull-baiting, 'galbardy' (a form of football), hurling and wrestling.

The staple element of a Dubliner's diet was fish, and – because the major fishing areas were on private land – poaching was common. Salmon were so plentiful that the citizens complained and insisted on a change of menu. Shellfish were also popular: oysters were cheap, and a favourite, but often caused fights, since people ate them in pubs and carelessly threw away the shells, sometimes blinding fellow-customers. Alcoholism had already become a problem by the Middle Ages: taverns were plentiful, with beer and ale inexpensive. This favourite pastime of Dubliners, in an age where most people went armed, made the medieval city a violent one, where a stray oyster-shell could mean serious trouble.

Tudors & Stuarts

By the Tudor period, Dublin had expanded beyond its medieval walls and won some considerable privileges from the English government. The rest of Ireland persisted in tribal kingdoms. In 1534, Henry VIII attempted to quell their anarchy, ordering the surrender of all lands to the English Crown. When Elizabeth inherited the crown, she set about 'civilising' the primitive people of Ireland. As the loyalties of Anglo-Normans resident in Ireland were unreliable, the queen exported true Englishmen to conquer Ireland. The idea was to reform the country through breaking its will utterly; the Irish savages were 'only by force and fear to be vanquished'. One deputy lined the path leading to his tent with the heads of those killed. Unarmed citizens and children were slaughtered, and quite apart from the Gaelic, the Anglo-Irish rebelled six times against their queen.

Despite such resistance, Elizabeth's resolve to bring Ireland to its knees prevailed. The final Gaelic battle was on Christmas Eve 1601, when a Spanish fleet landed in Kinsale to aid Hugh O'Neill's rebellion. He lost and was forced to make a formal submission to the Crown. England had won.

During this century of strife, England kept the capital on a tight rein. Dublin became a place of relative stability, although the Gaelic Irish were always suspect. One way to demonstrate power was through control of religion: by 1540, the monasteries of the city had been dissolved, and the urban landscape began to change. The *bacall Iosa* was ritually burned in Skinner's Row outside Christchurch in 1558, and the following year the removal of all 'superstitious' relics and images was ordered. When the English proclaimed Ireland an Anglican country in 1560, the country split on religious grounds. Protestants took over the Catholic churches, leaving those of the old religion to worship in cellars and back rooms.

The English newcomers settled in Dublin in a climate of acquisition and opportunity and so began the royal expansion of the city. For the latter half of the century, Dublin was run by a war administration, whose heavy military expenditure encouraged economic growth. During this period Dublin changed from being a medieval provincial centre to an Elizabethan stronghold, with its role as a centre of trade and administration increasing dramatically over the course of the century.

But while merchants amassed wealth, the public utilities degenerated. The Liffey bridge and Dublin Castle were both teetering, and in 1562, the south wall and roof of Christchurch collapsed. In addition, the problem of the poor had worsened with the closure of the monasteries, and the 1575 plague claimed up to 34 per cent of the city's population. In response, an initiative was begun to clean up the city: streets were widened and dilapidated buildings reconstructed. The religious institutions were appropriated: St Andrew's church became a stable; St George's was turned into a bakery; and, in 1591, the defunct monastery of All Saints became **Trinity College**.

Further hardship came in the final decades of the century, when the citizens were ordered to fund the new troops of the royal army. Almost every Dublin family had to 'diet' a soldier to fight in the Nine Years War which began in 1594. The calamity of the century occurred on 11 March 1597, when 140 barrels of gunpowder exploded on the quays. They had been left unattended, the clerk having gone for a pint. The explosion killed 126 men, women and children, and caused massive damage, wiping out much of the medieval city. The century ended bleakly: the citizens of the city had suffered

terrible personal and financial losses, and were being daily threatened with invasion. In London, where rumours abounded that Dublin was run by papists, Elizabeth ignored the pleas of her deputies across the sea.

'This gorgeous mask'

Under James I, the English government paid more attention to Ireland. In 1607, Hugh O'Neill and his comrade, the earl of Tyrconnell, fled to Europe. Their lands (the counties of Donegal, Tyrone, Derry and Armagh) were declared forfeit to the Crown, and the 'Plantation of Ulster' began. This involved shipping loyal Protestants in from England and Scotland to colonise the land. (The plantations have current ramifications: the plantation of Derry, for instance, was followed by an alliance between the new city and the Corporation of London, which involved both county and city in a name change. Londonderry city and county were born and their titles remain contentious. People use the names of Derry or Londonderry to show where their allegiances lie. Some, with a tired irony, refer to the place as Stroke City.)

Dublin boomed as a garrison town. By 1640, it was overwhelmingly Protestant and remained so for over a century, which further widened the gulf between the Anglicised capital and the rest of the country. Inevitably, discontent grew as the oppressed Catholic majority congregated in ruined churches or in open fields to practice their religion. Rebellion broke out in 1641, followed in 1649 by Oliver Cromwell's personal retribution. But these upheavals did not infringe greatly upon the city of Dublin. The most significant effect was the collapse of suburbia, which had been flourishing for 50 years. Now the citizens moved back to the centre of the city, closer to the heart of the colony. Dublin entered into its architectural heyday.

From the reign of Charles II, the city expanded rapidly, both in terms of population and construction. Most of present-day Dublin dates from this period of magnificent growth and expansion, during which a neoclassical city was built by the upper-classes. The Anglo-Dutch phase dates from the Restoration (1660) to about 1720, after which time the Georgian style dominated. The two centuries saw a phenomenal amount of work undertaken. Urban initiatives salvaged **Dublin Castle**, and started construction on the **Royal Hospital** at Kilmainham, **Phoenix Park**, and **Temple Bar. Marsh's Library** was built in 1702, and the library at Trinity College was begun in 1712. In 1664, St Stephen's Green was set out as an urban square, becoming a central focus for the construction of new streets. There was a plan (inspired by Paris and Amsterdam) to develop the land along the river, and work on the quays began. The earl of Drogheda, Henry Moore, purchased a large

*James Gandon built the marvellous **Custom House** towards the end of the eighteenth century.*

Built by Luke Gardiner in 1720, **Henrietta Street** *was named after the Duchess of Grafton.*

area of land north of the river, developing Henry Street and its environs.

In 1705, Joshua Dawson bought a plot between Trinity College and St Stephen's Green. He set out the aristocratic boulevards of Dawson Street and Grafton Street, interconnected by Anne Street and Duke Street. Dawson built a grand house for himself, which in 1715, became the **Mansion House**, home of the Lord Mayor of Dublin. In 1720, Luke Gardiner built Henrietta Street (named after Henrietta, Duchess of Grafton). This area was a prime aristocratic quarter, and Gardiner had further success with Gardiner Street, a stunning line of terraced houses overseen by James Gandon. The Wide Street Commissioners were established and began regulating the thoroughfares. They created one of the widest streets in Europe – O'Connell Street (then called Sackville Street).

The new Parliament House was opened in 1731, and, 20 years later, building began on the impressive façade of Trinity College – the largest piece of collegiate architecture in Europe.

The aesthetic influence of the Age of Enlightenment merged with the increased wealth and the growing awareness of Dublin as a capital city. Upper-class life reached the height of extravagance between 1770-80. The intense construction showed no signs of abating: from the Fitzwilliam Estate emerged the Georgian lines of Merrion Street, Merrion Square, Baggot Street and Pembroke Street, all intended as residential areas for the Protestant ascendancy. Gandon designed Beresford Place and the Custom House and Kings Inns. He took over Inns Quay (set in the bourgeois quarter) for the Four Courts, and one block of the North Quay for the **Custom House** in 1782.

In this atmosphere of growth, the city thrived. The first American ship arrived in 1785. Dublin was second only to London in terms of music, theatre, publishing and service industries. The names of those born, educated, or living in the city read as a *Who's Who* of the arts. Handel lived in Abbey Street in 1741-42, and it was in Fishamble Street that his *Messiah* had its début. Swift was born in Dublin in 1667, and attended Trinity, as did the Dublin-born political philosopher Edmund Burke (born 1729), and playwrights William Congreve and Oliver Goldsmith. Other Dubliners include the founder of *The Tatler,* Richard Steele (born 1672), and the dramatist Richard Sheridan (born 1751).

However, underneath the glorious Protestant façade of the city, dissatisfaction grew. Dublin was called 'this gorgeous mask of Ireland's distress'. Although the penal laws enforced under William III did not outlaw the practice of Roman Catholicism, it was actively discouraged. No Catholic could hold any office of state or stand for Parliament. They could not join the armed forces or practice law. Most crucially, Catholics could neither vote nor buy land. By the third quarter of the eighteenth century, barely 5 per cent of the land of Ireland remained in Catholic hands. Because of rural migration, by the mid-eighteenth century the capital city had a clear Catholic majority. As an economic and artistic centre, Dublin began to spearhead new movements of a more dissenting nature.

The sectarian animosity was translated inevitably into violence and Protestant-Catholic riots became common. In the early 1700s, they went under Whig-Tory factions, but soon the gang-war was between the (mostly Protestant) Liberty boys and the (mostly Catholic) Ormond boys.

But, apart from the multitude of popular disturbances, there was a growing awareness of being 'Irish', regardless of religion. Henry Grattan won legislative independence for Ireland in 1782 and some of the penal laws were repealed. Catholics were finally allowed to practice law, but were excluded from any municipal role. Deeply affected by the French revolution, the oppressed Irish were inspired to take matters into their own hands.

In 1796, a fleet of French republican troops arrived to help in a revolution, which failed. Two years later, Dubliner Protestant Wolfe Tone harnessed urban discontent and orchestrated his own rebellion of 'United Irishmen'. This was unsuccessful in all but convincing the English government that they had given Ireland too much slack. The reins had to be tightened.

A blight on the land

The Act of Union (1800) dissolved Ireland's Parliament and transferred its power to the English Crown. In 1803, the Protestant Robert Emmet led a nationalist uprising, whose aim was to take over Dublin Castle. Emmet failed (dismally), but the lawyer Daniel O'Connell continued the fight. The 'Liberator' O'Connell initiated a campaign for Catholic Emancipation – the dissolution of the remaining penal laws discriminating against Catholics. He ran for Parliament in 1828, winning by a landslide, but, as a Catholic, he could not take his seat. Faced with this organised display of resistance,

Mum's the word

'The expectant mother should avoid all violent motion, and abstain from hard labour. Beware sharp and cold winds… excessive heat, anger, perturbations of the mind, affright and terrors… whilst eschewing leaping, dancing, running, riding, tight-lacing, intemperate eating and drinking and over-much venery… But surely, sleep is very fit for her.' James Wolveridge, *Speculum Matricis*, c1671.

Born in 1712, the second son of Reverend Thomas Mosse, Dr Bartholomew Mosse settled on man-midwifery as a career – not that elegant a choice in the 1700s, being lower in rank than physicians, barber-surgeons and apothecaries.

During the previous half century, Dublin's population had risen from about 45,000 in 1685 to 112,000 in 1744. What had not changed were the squalid conditions in which the city's poor lived.

To Mosse, the most distressing aspect of this was the pitiable state in which women lived and suffered before, during and after pregnancy. And so, armed with more compassion than capital, he set up the first ever lying-in, or maternity, hospital in Great Britain and Ireland on South Great George's Street on 15 March 1745. The 24-bed house relied on charity, and provided the women – mostly widows and the wives of poor tradesmen – with a more sanitary environment, as well as postnatal care, an outpatients' clinic and apothecary shop, although the last two were subsequently disbanded due to lack of funds.

In the first 15 months of the hospital's existence, from 25 March 1745 to 1 July 1746, 209 women were received; 191 were discharged, with 105 boys and 85 girls.

Mosse's plans for his hospital grew, helped no doubt by its success and public demand, and on 15 August 1748 he acquired four acres of land on Great Britain Street (now Parnell Street) on which to build new premises. Richard Castle, whose previous work included designing Leinster House, was chosen as architect and the new hospital was opened on 8 December 1757.

Along with continuing care for women, it also became a teaching institution and the remainder of the land was converted into public pleasure gardens. The success of previous classical music concerts as a form of fund-raising inspired Mosse, and the new gardens became the setting for Dublin's illustrious and fashionable to hear the 18 musicians who had been hired by the hospital, alongside the best available soloists, performing 60 concerts per year, three times a week, from April to September. From the time the gardens were opened in 1749, there began a period of nearly half a century where the Governors of the Hospital became the foremost and most consistent promoters of regular concerts, fancy dress parties and balls in Dublin.

Bartholomew Mosse died in 1759 at the age of 46. The Rotunda remains in use today, while a cluster of other activities take place in adjacent sections which are now used by the Ambassador cinema and the Gate theatre.

the British government passed the Emancipation Act in 1829, and O'Connell became the first Catholic Lord Mayor of Dublin in 1841. By the 1840s, when O'Connell began to call for a repeal of the Act of Union, Ireland was wholly concerned with another problem: famine.

In 1845, a fungus ravaged potato crops in Ireland, destroying the staple food of the poor. The Great Famine began. On hearing the pleas for help, Prime Minister Robert Peel remarked that the Irish had a tendency to exaggerate, but soon the government were forced to act. They began importing Indian corn, but the food was not to be given out as emergency aid – the people would have to work for it. Concerned that food subsidies would undermine the Irish economy and encourage laziness, the government established workhouses. A multitude of projects were thought up to consume the time and energy of the starving Irish.

The evidence of the pointless labour enforced during the famine years (1845-49) may still be seen: roads begin in a field and go nowhere, perhaps ending on a beach. Again, for fear of damaging the economy, the wages for the 'moving skeletons' on the public works were to be lower than average. The reality was that they were often not paid at all; many died from starvation and exhaustion.

The terrible irony was that there was plenty of food in Ireland; it was simply not available to the poor. Cargo-loads of imported corn sat in depots for months, until the government felt that releasing the corn for sale would not adversely affect food prices. The Head of the Treasury Charles Trevelyan actually refused food en route to Ireland, claiming that the cargo was not wanted. Huge quantities of cattle, pork, sheep, oats, eggs and flour were all being exported from Ireland.

One of the only options available to the poor was emigration. During the famine, about 1.5 million people left Ireland for good; 75 per cent of these took the long voyage to the United States. In 1841, Ireland's population was estimated at 8 million. Cut by death and migration, it had fallen to 6.5 million in 1851.

Dublin's famine experience was different. It was here that the wealth of the country was focused, and in many respects, life continued as normal for the upper classes. Balls were held at the **Mansion House**, and plans were made to establish a Library, Museum, Natural History Museum and Gallery for the people of Ireland (constructed 1852-1871 at Merrion Square). But its population had surged from some 10,000 in 1600 to approximately 247,000 in 1851. The city limits were strained: the quality of water, air and housing was degenerating. The mortality rate was high, due to the epidemics spreading from 'fever nests' throughout Dublin. Gerald Manley Hopkins was one more famous victim; he contracted his fatal dose of typhoid while living at St Stephen's Green.

Civic funding was practical and sought to establish a modern infrastructure for the deteriorating city. A commercial rail network was set up, the tramways were completed, the Grand and Royal Canals were built, and hospitals opened. New bridges across the Liffey were erected, and the GPO was finished in 1818. The system of policing was completely overhauled, and the Dublin Metropolitan Police set about cleaning up the city. Public baths and wash-houses were opened to help contain the grime of the poor, thought to spread disease. Finally, there was an initiative to supply permanent social housing for the poor of Dublin.

The middle and upper classes simply moved away from the filth, building sumptuous homes in suburbia. The once-fashionable Henrietta Street and other aristocratic areas became derelict and ended up as over-crowded slum tenements. The only advantage of this period was that the classical city was left practically untouched, stagnating in squalor.

The fight for independence

The horrors of the famine left many in Ireland convinced of the need for total independence. The next nationalist movement was the Fenian Brotherhood, formed by James Stephens and James O'Mahony. Named after the Fianna, the

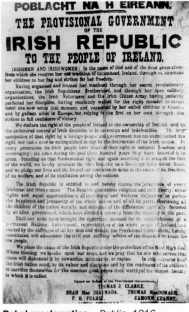

Rebel proclamation – *Dublin, 1916.*

*Interior of the **General Post Office** or GPO burnt out in the Easter Rebellion of 1916.*

ancient Gaelic warrior elite, the society soon had the support of thousands of Irish at home and in America. A 1867 rebellion was thwarted and the Fenians had only minor success. Despite this, many remained active within the Irish Republican Brotherhood.

In the late 1870s, with famine threatening once more, Michael Davitt (a Fenian) persuaded Charles Stewart Parnell – a Protestant landowner from Wicklow – to join him in the struggle of the Land League of Ireland. The Land League aimed to help Irish farmers struggling with increasing rents and forced evictions. Its top officials were all Fenian men. Parnell took on the cause, and, in the 1880s, came to dominate British parliamentary life, battling against William Gladstone for the Land League. The Land Acts introduced by Gladstone enabled tenants to buy their land, and, by 1920, 11 million acres had changed hands.

Parnell's second cause was Home Rule, with which Gladstone agreed. The Home Rule Bill (1886) was defeated and its further progress impeded when news broke of Parnell's long-term affair with Mrs Katharine (Kitty) O'Shea. He was deposed from his party and he died in 1891.

One of Parnell's successes was the tapping of the burgeoning feelings of pride in 'Irishness', and the appeal of the nationalist cause. The movement to distinguish and preserve things distinctly 'Irish' gained momentum. The Gaelic Athletic Association (GAA) was set up in 1884 to promote Irish games (*see chapter* **Sports & Fitness**). In 1893, the Gaelic League was founded to champion the

(dying) Irish language, and encourage Irish arts. Its influence is evident in writers such as WB Yeats, whose poetry is steeped in Irish myth.

In Dublin, the standard of living continued to be appallingly low. The slums of the capital city were the worst in Europe. In 1913, there were, on average, five families per house, with almost 90,000 people living in tenements. In such an atmosphere, political freedom seemed to promise better times. Jim Larkin and James Connolly fought against low wages and corporation corruption, forming the Irish Citizen Army to protect the workers. During the 'Great Lockout' of 1913, a public meeting which had been prohibited by the authorities went ahead. Over 200 people were batoned by British forces and the day became known as Bloody Sunday.

In the first decade of the twentieth century, the Irish Republican Brotherhood was revived. Arthur Griffith, who worked on nationalist newspapers *The United Irishman* and *Sinn Fein* ('Ourselves Alone'), called for the Irish MPs to form their own government in Dublin. Home Rule was a live issue again. By 1910, it seemed a foregone conclusion, despite vigorous protests from northern Irish Orangemen (so called because their forefathers had supported William of Orange in his victory over the Catholic king, James II, at the Battle of the Boyne in 1690). In January 1913, the Home Rule Bill was read for its third time.

In Belfast Town Hall, half a million men and women signed a covenant to affirm that they would resist Home Rule, with many signing in their own blood. There were threats of establishing a Protestant province of Ulster from senior MP Sir Edward Carson. He demanded the exclusion of six counties (Derry, Antrim, Tyrone, Down, Armagh and Fermanagh), and had an Ulster Provincial Government standing by. The Ulster Volunteer Force (UVF) was established, consisting of 100,000 men from Orange lodges. The nationalist Irish Volunteers were formed as a reaction to the UVF and both societies set about gun-running to arm themselves.

The outbreak of World War I put the Home Rule issue on hold. Around 180,000 Irish signed up with the British forces, hoping that their loyalty would win them favour. But others felt that Ireland needed to be free from British rule altogether. Old members of the IRB met with younger reactionaries like the trade unionist James Connolly, Belfast barman Sean MacDermott and schoolteacher Padraig Pearse. They planned their revolt for Easter 1916. Strategic centres were chosen: the Four Courts, Jacob's Biscuit Factory, St Stephen's Green, Boland's Flour Mill, and Liberty Hall. Their headquarters were to be the GPO.

The rising was planned for Easter Sunday, but this ended in confusion. The official leader of the Irish Volunteers, Eoin MacNeill, had been kept in the dark about the rebellion. When he finally found out, he put an advertisement in the *Sunday Independent* announcing that the 'manoeuvres' planned for the day were cancelled. The leaders rescheduled for Monday and about 1,000 men turned up to fight. Pearse, Connolly and Clarke marched to the GPO where Pearse declared Ireland to be a republic. The general public saw an opportunity for disorder and looted Clery's department store. Reinforcements were sent from London, and the British troops slowly enclosed the Irish. By Friday evening, the GPO was ablaze, and had to be evacuated. The centre of Dublin was ravaged.

The casualties were estimated at 300 civilians, 130 British troops and 60 rebels. Pearse, horrified by the bloodshed, eventually surrendered on Sunday evening. He was imprisoned in Kilmainham, and shot, along with Tom Clarke. In all, 77 death sentences were issued, although many were commuted. Last to be killed were Sean MacDermott and James Connolly, who, because of a broken ankle, was unable to stand to face the firing party and had to be shot sitting in a chair.

Two nationalists filled the power vacuum left in the wake of the rising. Eamon De Valera was a mathematics teacher who had led the garrison at Boland's Mill. Michael Collins was a west Cork man who had emigrated to England, but returned home for the Rising. Collins trained and organised the Irish Republican Brotherhood. In 1917, the society won several by-elections – one candidate was a sentenced prisoner, still jailed in Britain. When released in July, 1917 (with the rest of the rebels), De Valera ran for election and won.

The new party went by the name of Sinn Fein. In the general election of 1918, Sinn Fein won nearly 75 per cent of all Irish seats. (However, voting was rigged, and some supporters cast as many as 20 votes.)

The new MPs met in Dublin at Dail Éireann (the Irish Parliament) and declared a sovereign independent Irish Republic. De Valera went to the US to rally support among the emigrants and have the Irish Republic recognised. Collins took a different route. Officially, he was Minister of Finance, but his main energies were spent as director and overseer of the Irish Volunteers, later to be called the IRA. The killing of policemen and informers began. The Royal Irish Constabulary fought back. Disguising themselves in civilian clothes, they murdered the nationalist Lord Mayor of Cork and targeted other Sinn Fein supporters. There were not enough uniforms to accommodate the new recruits imported from England, who instead wore military khakis and became known as the Black and Tans. The poet Austin Clarke wrote: 'No man can drink at any public-house/In Dublin but these roarers look for trouble/And break an open door in…'.

Anti-British feeling was fanned by the list of martyrs from 1916 and rumours of conscription for the Irish. The ruthlessness of the Tans and the Auxiliaries did much to encourage nationalist resentment. They posted bills declaring that for every Crown servant killed, two Sinn Feiners would be shot; house-burning became a standard way of targeting suspects. Dublin was badly hit: entire sections were cordoned off as suspects were rounded up. Ambushes and street shooting made life dangerous for civilians.

The second Bloody Sunday was on 21 November 1920. At dawn, Michael Collins had 14 undercover British intelligence officers executed in their beds. That afternoon, British troops opened fire on a crowd of football spectators at Croke Park. Twelve were killed. Later that day, two senior IRA men and an innocent Sinn Fein supporter were put to death in Dublin Castle. Michael Collins came out of hiding to lay a wreath at their funeral.

The terrorism continued on both sides. In December, the Auxiliaries torched the centre of Cork city in a show of retaliation. The IRA's biggest initiative came in May, 1921. During working hours, 120 men took over the Custom House – the centre of the British administration. They set it alight, but were surrounded and eventually surrendered, with their artillery supplies drained. Presumably unaware that the IRA had few men or arms left, British representatives met with De Valera on 9 July 1921. Two days later a truce was signed, and on 6 December the Anglo-Irish Treaty was settled. Michael Collins remarked, 'I have signed my death warrant.'

Michael Collins *became head of the provisional government ten days before he was killed.*

From Free State to Republic

The terms of the treaty gave limited independence to 26 counties of Ireland. It was not called the Irish Republic, but the Irish Free State. The remaining six counties refused to join. Britain's authority was still evident: members of the Dáil would have to swear allegiance to George V and his heirs. Chaos erupted. Eamon De Valera dissociated himself from the Treaty. The IRA split, the Treaty was ratified by a small majority and nationalist Ireland was torn asunder. In Northern Ireland, the death toll for the first half of 1922 was 264 people; some 65 per cent were Catholic.

Civil war broke out in June between the pro- and anti-Treaty factions. Again, O'Connell Street and the Four Courts provided the battle grounds. After eight days of fighting, De Valera's supporters were forced to surrender. Emergency anti-terrorist legislation was enacted: any republican carrying arms would be shot by the Free State troops. Within seven months, 77 people had been executed and 13,000 were in prison, many on hunger strike. Michael Collins was killed near Bandon in west Cork on 22 August.

The civil war dominated Irish politics. De Valera reformed Sinn Fein as Fianna Fail ('Warriors of Ireland'), and spoke out against the Free State's betrayal of the country. In 1927, FF won as many seats as the government party. They refused the oath of allegiance and, for a period, were locked out of the Dáil before joining the government. In 1932, they took the majority: again, the voting was

rigged and the IRA were 'encouraging' voters. They remained in power for 17 years, widening the gap between England and Ireland. The enforced oath of allegiance was scrapped, IRA prisoners were released with some offered commissions in the state army. However, when the IRA refused to disarm, De Valera declared them illegal. The 1937 constitution declared the state's name as Eire; Roman Catholicism was prioritised as the majority religion.

During this time, the Four Courts and O'Connell Street were slowly rebuilt (again). IRA terrorist activities remained sporadic in Ireland, but extended to the English mainland, with London targeted for a bombing campaign in 1939. When WWII broke out, Eire remained neutral (although the IRA aided the German war effort, including bombing Belfast docks). But the government focused on abstract republican ideals, paying little attention to social welfare and the stagnating slums. In 1948, FF were ousted by a coalition of Fine Gael and Sean MacBride's Clann na Poblachta. In 1949, Ireland was declared a republic.

The coalition government tackled the enormous problem of tuberculosis, attempting to introduce 'radical' health care legislation which would provide pre- and post-natal care for mothers. The Catholic Church took umbrage, and the government fell over the issue. In 1955, Ireland joined the UN. It was a significant step, in stark contrast to the insular, isolationist beliefs of De Valera's party. The 1950s were a time of tremendous emigration and immigration, with rural communities dying

Eamon De Valera *(1882-1975).*

out as young people moved to urban centres, especially the capital.

Dublin began growing and never stopped, its radius increasing with each year as villages on the outskirts of the city became engulfed in the sprawling suburbia. By 1957, FF were back in power, with De Valera leading until 1959, when he swapped the role of Taoiseach (prime minister) for that of President of Ireland. Sean Lemass took over FF, and became Ireland's first true economic manager. His expansionist policies brought about the first moves away from an agrarian economy crippled by emigration. International trade grew and Ireland began to compete tentatively on the world market. In 1966, Lemass was succeeded by Jack Lynch. As the fiftieth anniversary of the Easter Rising, 1966 was the last gasp of the romantic republican spirit. Rallies and celebrations were held all over the country and Nelson's pillar on O'Connell Street was blown up.

But the high-flown ideals were soon to be overshadowed by reality. To the north, where Catholics were, in effect, second-class citizens, the Northern Ireland Civil Rights Association was founded in 1967, drawing inspiration and methods from the American Black civil rights movement. The British government banned all civil rights marches and the Royal Ulster Constabulary baton-charged the peaceful demonstrations. The ensuing

riots were horrific: in Londonderry, the RUC fired machine guns and tear gas at Catholic protesters. A few months later, in the winter of 1969, the IRA split in two, leading to the formation of the Provisional IRA.

The third Bloody Sunday occurred in Londonderry in January 1972 when 13 civilians were shot by British paratroopers during a protest march. The Belfast Parliament at Stormont was suspended and direct rule from Westminster imposed. In 1973, the 'Sunningdale agreement' offered concessions: every adult was allowed a vote in local elections, and the RUC was disarmed. The measures were rejected by extreme unionists, and the fighting continued.

Meanwhile, several members of FF were accused of gun-running for the IRA. Charles Haughey (who was later acquitted) was one of the Cabinet sacked by Jack Lynch in 1970. On 1 January 1973 Ireland joined the EEC, the decision passed only by a narrow margin. FF were booted out later that year, the FG/Labour coalition ruled under Liam Cosgrave until 1977. Ireland was feeling the effects of the worldwide oil crisis and the industrial unrest resulted in large-scale structural unemployment. Interest rates were high, inflation soared, at one stage reaching 25 per cent. In 1977, FF roared back, again led by Lynch. They promised voters the world in their manifesto, and the National Debt Crises shortly ensued. Two years later, Haughey assumed the leadership of the party on resignation of Lynch.

The political situation remained dangerously unstable. In 1981, FF lost to the coalition, which in turn fell in February 1982. The result of the election was inconclusive, and FF formed a minority government. After a further election in November, Garret Fitzgerald became Taoiseach, leading a FG/Labour coalition. Left with a legacy of debt, the government struggled to regain economic control. In 1985, the first Anglo-Irish agreement was signed; the unionists were outraged and the covenant of 1913 was appropriately re-enacted. Emigration increased dramatically, except now the emigrants were highly educated graduates. In 1987, FF took over leadership, although with no majority. Haughey was finally ousted around three years later.

There were other fracture lines. The issue of abortion split the country in 1992. In 1983, a fanatical campaign had been initiated by a 'pro-life' movement to get the prohibition of abortion enshrined in the constitution. Strenuously encouraged by the Church, the referendum was passed. Then, in 1992, came the 'X Case' – a young Dublin girl who was pregnant as a result of rape was restrained from travelling to England to have an abortion. The Supreme Court ruled that, not only was it legal for her to travel, but that under those circumstances it was not unconstitutional for her to have an abortion in Ireland. The right-wing element were incensed, organising a further referendum to declare abortion illegal, to prohibit pregnant women leaving the country with the intention of procuring an abortion, and to ban the dissemination of information concerning abortion. The first was passed, but the others were defeated, leaving Ireland in something of a hypocritical no-man's land.

There were other issues traditionally considered to be under the jurisdiction of the Catholic Church. Contraception was outlawed altogether until the late 1970s, when it was available on prescription only. Recently retail outlets have been allowed to stock contraceptives. The most recent controversy concerned divorce, which was finally passed by referendum in 1995.

The day of the all-powerful voice of the Church has passed, chronically weakened by various well-publicised scandals concerning acute mismanagement of clerical funds, numerous priests' children, sexual abuse and paedophilia. In 1994, Labour pulled out of coalition with FF as a result of allegations of possible collusion between the government, Church and the Attorney General's office. The matter concerned the case of Father Brendan Smith, a paedophile priest wanted in Northern Ireland, who was currently at liberty in the republic. The extradition request made by the NI authorities was allegedly ignored in Dublin; Labour were outraged and collapsed the government, reforming with FG and the Democratic Left.

By then, the Celtic tiger was stretching its claws. Ireland, which had always lagged socially and economically, began to make its mark on the economic map. Dublin served as European City of Culture in 1990, becoming rejuvenated in the process. Temple Bar was revitalised as the 'left bank' of the city, and tax breaks attracted home-buyers back to central Dublin. It was once more a place in which to work and to live.

But Dublin's crime rate and drug problems have also grown, curtailing its casual, relaxed atmosphere. On 26 June, 1996, the journalist Veronica Guerin was murdered while investigating the crime lords of Dublin. Her death shocked the

Damned education

Women's entrance into Trinity College, Dublin was relatively painless. After a few years of campaigning, the university opened its doors to the female sex in 1904 – well before either Oxford or Cambridge dared so a radical step. At first, women were subject to stringent rules and banned from college after 6pm. However, as women proved themselves academically, the 'Cinderella hour' was moved further back. Eventually, women shared the privileges of male scholars (although it was not until 1964 that the first female fellow of the college was elected). Catholics had it much tougher.

Elizabeth I's original foundation of TCD declared its intention to provide 'our people' (good practising Anglicans) with 'knowledge and civility'. It was motivated by the fact that scholars were returning from continental universities 'infected with Popery and other ill qualities'. The establishment was fundamentally anti-Catholic, and remained so for a long time. Even when the college lightened up on such matters, the Catholic Church focused on the Protestant (and therefore inherently bad) nature of the university. If they couldn't control the institution, they could at least boycott it. The great synod of 1927 decreed that, since there were three colleges in Ireland 'sufficiently safe as regards faith and morals', no reason existed to warrant a Catholic attending TCD. When John Charles McQuaid became archbishop of Dublin in 1941, he took the moral danger of attending TCD very seriously, and set about enforcing the legislation of 1927. His disapproval was long-standing: in 1914 he had declared it 'a proximate occasion of sin' for Catholics to attend Trinity, and deemed those who studied there to be 'guilty of grave violation of the natural law'. The warnings were soon turned into an outright ban, from which only McQuaid could grant a dispensation. Trinity reacted by relaxing the college statutes and forced attendance at (the Anglican) chapel was abolished in 1957. McQuaid's zeal grew more ardent, and in his Lenten pastoral of 1961, he asserted that UCD was safe to attend, but that Catholics were forbidden 'under pain of mortal sin' to frequent Trinity.

The resolution of the century-long debate was simple: the Archbishop died. In 1970, the Church lifted the ban and it was no longer a mortal sin to attend TCD. One of the primary reasons given was that only Trinity offered courses in veterinary medicine and dentistry, therefore Catholics would be severely disadvantaged (and we all know how many eager Catholic wannabe vets and dentists there were lining up). The Church of Ireland gave up its rights to the college chapel, and opened it up to all other Christian denominations. The dust has yet to settle.

nation, and catalysed a tremendous movement to root out the drug barons and racketeers of the city. A new initiative of 'zero tolerance' has just been introduced: time will tell if it proves as effective as in New York.

Dublin's problems are not limited to drugs and petty theft, since it is also the seat of the government. The chronically embarrassing political fiascos of the last two decades were topped in 1997 by the allegation that Haughey received £1.3 million from magnate Ben Dunne and allegedly laundered it through the Cayman Islands. The money was pooled in a Cayman bank account for Ireland's obscenely rich, holding more than £40 million. Investigations are currently under way.

Despite such phenomenal tax evasion, the economy of the country seems to be doing well. Today, for the first time in history, the per capita income in Ireland exceeds that of the UK. There is further progress: in 1990, Mary Robinson changed the presidency from a retirement home for superannuated politicians into a vital, active post. In 1997, she was appointed UN High Commissioner for Refugees. However, politics remain divided along the De Valera/Collins lines set by the civil war, and the Northern Ireland troubles show little sign of abating. Ireland's past remains unfortunately all too present.

O'Connell Bridge – *wider than it is long.*

Dublin today

Dublin is an unusual capital city. Since 1921, it has grown at an unprecedented rate, and it now houses well over one million people. Yet it has no skyscrapers. First impressions are of spaciousness and there seems an unusual amount of sky visible. Since the 1960s, there has been continuous construction in the suburbs, and until recently the inner city was a place to work, not to live. By 1986, less than 17 per cent (83,204) of Dublin's population lived in the city centre. However, in the last decade there has been a huge initiative to revive it as a residential environment and thousands of people have returned. Prices of apartments continue to rise, with run-down areas being overhauled. Students now occupy the four-story Georgian town houses – the landlords simply halve or quarter the old bedrooms. In 1991, Dublin was the European City of Culture. Rejuvenation projects such as the revitalisation of Temple Bar have been an outright success, and the area is now filled with galleries, pubs and restaurants.

But changes are hard-won. Northside and Southside are still at loggerheads. The inflammatory subjects remain; religion and politics are still taboo. The issues of divorce and abortion have violently split the country. When Madonna did her Pepsi ads, pubs in certain areas received memos from the Catholic Church asking them not to stock the soft drink. But given that the Catholic Church no longer preaches that attending TCD is a mortal sin, there has been some progress. Headway in politics is more difficult to discern, with one official tribunal after another investigating alleged misconduct.

The poet Louis MacNeice spoke of Dublin's 'seedy elegance': 'The glamour of her squalor,/The bravado of her talk.' Roddy Doyle traces a similar character for the city, which highlights its paradox. Some aristocratic boulevards are now grimy streets, serving as reminders of a bygone age. Dublin distinguishes itself from the rest of Ireland, yet has separated itself utterly from England.

In many ways, the city has a unique character, greater than the sum of its parts. It retains much that is 'Irish', although the presences of its various invaders and overlords are still felt. A multitude of influences converge in this melting-pot: the resulting vibrant dichotomy nurtures artistic sentiments, as testified to by the staggering range of writers and musicians bred in Dublin.

However, you don't have to be poetic to enjoy Dublin. It's still a small, fairly mellow town. You can saunter from the medieval to the Georgian city in a matter of minutes. If you're lucky, the smell of the Guinness brewery at James' Gate will be pervading the streets. It's an eclectic place, and much of its history is still very much alive, clearly visible in its architecture. Perhaps, above all, Dublin is a survivor, but a friendly one.

Architecture

Don't be fooled by Dublin's Georgian elegance: there's much more in a city unafraid to make some modern ventures.

The relationship of Irish people to their architectural heritage is complex. Any country which emerges from an extended colonial experience is at best dubious about, or at worst hostile to, what are viewed as remnants of an alien, imposed order. Throughout the eighteenth century, Dublin was regarded as the second capital of the British Empire, and until the 1960s, Dublin remained the most intact Georgian city in either England or Ireland. Over the past three decades, much has been lost through a mixture of prosperity, and a desire to break free from the past which that prosperity has made possible for the first time. There are few legislative provisions, and little state funding, to safeguard Ireland's architectural heritage, but attitudes have, largely, changed for the better. However, debates about the preservation of the built environment are often as divisive, in Ireland, as those relating to social issues such as divorce.

century, although significant sections of the original medieval parts survive. The crypt of Christchurch is the oldest intact building in the city, dating from the twelfth century. The tomb of its most famous dean, Jonathan Swift, can be visited in St Patrick's.

The thirteenth century and the first half of the fourteenth were times of prosperity and expansion for Dublin. From this period to the Reformation, much effort was expended by the city population on keeping the native Irish out, as they were excluded from the economic and political life of the city. Relatively little is known about Dublin's architecture during this period, except that it marked a transition from timber to brick construction. After the Reformation, when the Tudor monarchy confiscated substantial church property, the urban structure was consolidated. This marked the transition from medieval to modern times.

Viking & medieval Dublin

Dublin is bisected by the River Liffey which flows from west to east. The Vikings, who founded Dublin, first sailed their longboats up the river in the ninth century. The city, which grew to international importance in the Viking world, was established in an area between the Liffey and Christchurch Cathedral. Viking Dublin is known about today through rich archaeological remains, but nothing survives by way of an intact dwelling. The building materials employed by the Vikings – timber and mud – do not make for permanence. Although the Vikings were ousted in the Battle of Clontarf in 1014, they were soon replaced by the Normans who took the city in 1171. The Normans accepted the basic design inherited from the Vikings, adding new walls, streets and lanes, and suburban monasteries. Although **Dublin Castle** (started 1204) provided the administrative centre of medieval Dublin, it is now a largely eighteenth-century complex of buildings.

The only substantial remains of the Norman city walls are at Cook Street; **St Andrew's Arch** was completed in 1275. The reason for the proximity of Dublin's two great medieval cathedrals, **Christchurch** (founded 1038), and **St Patrick's** (consecrated in 1192), is that the former formed part of the walled city while the latter did not. Both buildings were heavily restored in the nineteenth

The Neoclassical tradition

After the Restoration of Charles II in the 1660s, Dublin experienced an economic boom period. The city became a permanent seat of parliament, viceroy and university. This coincided with the introduction of Neoclassicism to Ireland. Contemporary Dublin owes more to the Georgian period than any other in its past. The **Royal Hospital** in Kilmainham (1680) is the first great classical building in Ireland. Built as a home for retired soldiers, it was modelled on Les Invalides in Paris. This large scale quadrangular building was completely restored in the 1980s by the Irish government, and subsequently converted into the **Irish Museum of Modern Art**. An earlier proposal to convert the building into additional exhibition space for the National Museum might have been a more successful use of the interconnected, modest internal spaces which are eminently more suitable for the display of small artefacts than for contemporary art.

Other examples of early classical buildings include **St Michan's Church** (1683-86), although the interior is largely early nineteenth-century, and **Marsh's Library** (1705) which was built to house the library of Archbishop Narcissus Marsh. The exterior has been changed, but the interior with its book-lined aisles remains largely untouched, and is one of the most magical places in Dublin.

As with England, the pure classicism of Palladianism was the preferred architectural style in Ireland throughout the first half of the eighteenth century. Sir Edward Lovett Pearce introduced the style to Ireland. He was related to Vanburgh, the English Baroque architect, and worked under his tutelage. Although his time in Ireland was short – seven years – his dozen or so commissions while here transformed the face of Irish architecture. His **Parliament House** (1720s), now the Bank of Ireland, was the first public building built in the Palladian style in either Ireland or England. The unity and grandeur of its design belies the fact that it was reworked by several architects throughout the eighteenth and nineteenth centuries. It is one of the great public buildings of Europe and is a tangible expression of Irish colonial independence. More than a century after it was started, it provided the inspiration for the British Museum in London. The original House of Lords chamber is open for viewing, on request, by bank security staff at the door.

Another Lovett Pearce project, **Castletown House** (1720s) on the outskirts of Dublin in Celbridge, County Kildare, is certainly worth a visit, as it is the grandest 'big house' in the entire country. Although he worked on Castletown with an Italian architect, the wings and entrance hall are by his hand. The most intact Dublin streetscape from this period is **Henrietta Street**. This imposing terrace of town houses (1725-30), some of which were also designed by Lovett Pearce, is often used as a location for period films.

Dublin Castle, the centre of British colonial power in Ireland for 700 years, is worth a visit. Arranged around two quadrangular yards, the original state apartments (1685, with later additions) are open to the public. Dublin's other important complex of eighteenth-century buildings is **Trinity College**, actually founded in 1592. The red-brick **Rubrics** (1700) is one of the few surviving examples, in Dublin, of the once very popular Dutch-influenced gabled style of the late seventeenth and early eighteenth centuries. The **Old Library** (1712) was designed by Thomas Burgh and houses the world-famous Book of Kells (*see chapter* **Museums**). Inside is the magnificent, barrel-vaulted, first-floor library which rises through two floors and was created in the nineteenth century by the architectural partnership of Deane and Woodward.

Another early eighteenth-century building in Trinity College is the temple-like **Printing House** (1734) designed by Richard Castle, a German, who after the death of Lovett Pearce dominated the Irish architectural scene until his death in 1751. Another follower of Palladio, his **Leinster House** (1745), now home to the Dáil Éireann (or House of Representatives), is a good example of his Dublin work. It looks more like a country than a town

house as it was originally prefaced by a forecourt similar to, and no doubt inspired by, Burlington House in London.

The construction of the **Casino** at Marino, a short ride from the city centre, heralded the arrival in Ireland of Neoclassicism. It was commissioned by Lord Charlemont from the British architect Sir William Chambers in 1758. Throughout the rest of his career, Chambers never again equalled the elegance and sophistication of this early conceit. From the outside, the building appears to be little more than a one-roomed structure. The inventive, multi-roomed interior is an entirely different matter. The Casino is fully restored and open to the public, and despite the unsympathetic surroundings, it would be difficult to think of a more perfect building, anywhere.

James Gandon dominated Dublin's architectural scene in the latter half of the eighteenth century. Although the interiors of his two great public buildings, the **Four Courts** (1786) and the **Custom House** (1791) suffered greatly during the politically turbulent years at the beginning of this century, both are beautifully balanced, supremely accomplished exercises in Neoclassicism. Another fine example of the style can be seen in the sadly neglected **St Catherine's Church** (1769), designed by John Smyth. It was outside this church in 1803 that Robert Emmet was hanged, following his abortive uprising against the Crown forces in Ireland.

One feature more than any other, the Georgian square, distinguishes Dublin from other eighteenth-century cities. The most intact squares are **Merrion Square** (1760s), and **Fitzwilliam Square** (1790s). The external decoration of the individual houses is usually confined to the doorway and surround, and often belies exuberant internal plasterwork. The overall domestic character of these sombre, red-brick squares has altered little since they were built. The once-private parks in the centre of these squares are now, mostly, open to the public (except Fitzwilliam Square).

Regency & Victorian

In 1800, the Act of Union dissolved the independent Irish Parliament, and, as a consequence, the wealth, power and sophistication of Dublin diminished greatly. However, the classical tradition lasted well into the nineteenth century, particularly in the design of many Roman Catholic churches erected after the granting of Catholic Emancipation in 1829. The identity of the architect of the Catholic **St Mary's Pro-Cathedral** (1814) is unknown, although it's generally believed that it wasn't the man who won the competition to design it. The overall design was compromised by the insertion of a dome, but nothing takes from the sublime Greek revival exterior.

National Botanical Gardens *at Glasnevin.*

The **General Post Office** was started in the same year and designed by Francis Johnston, an Irish-born architect, who was for the nineteenth century what James Gandon had been for the previous one. The building was entirely gutted during the 1916 Rising, but the exterior retains all of its original elegance. A short distance away is one of Dublin's most familiar landmarks, the graceful **Halfpenny** (or Ha'penny) **Bridge** (1816), a pedestrian walkway over the Liffey which, as the name suggests, operated as a toll-bridge until 1919.

With the advent of the railway, some fine railway stations were constructed, including **Heuston Station** (1845) designed by Sanction Wood. The main block is derived from an Italianate palazzo, while the low façade is more traditionally Neoclassical. The healthy ecleticism employed here informs the work of most late-nineteenth-century architects.

One of Dublin's most beautiful nineteenth-century buildings is the **Museum Building** (1850s) in Trinity College. John Ruskin called this building the embodiment of all his ideals, and indeed his writings had been influential on the architects, Deane and Woodward. Ruskin's influence is evident in the naturalistic carving, and the use of polychromy, notably in the fine central stair hall presided over by the skeleton of the now extinct giant Irish deer.

All of Dublin's national cultural institutions were constructed in the latter half of the nineteenth century, but the most distinctive is the **Natural History Museum** (1850s). The architecture is pedestrian enough, but the interplay between it and the collection, and the fact that it remains virtually untouched since the last century, conspire to make it the very embodiment of nineteenth-century museology. Another national institution, the **National Botanical Gardens** (1840s) at Glasnevin, has a wonderful example of the work of Richard Turner, a Dubliner who was one of the nineteenth century's great innovators in the use of iron and glass. As with his Palm House at Kew Gardens in London, his curvilinear range at Glasnevin has been splendidly restored, and can be seen to best advantage at the moment before the new plants have fully matured.

As with the Georgian squares of the previous century, another distinctive feature of Dublin's architecture is the endless, late-nineteenth-century terraces of modest red- or yellow-brick houses. The tiny, accompanying gardens are a poignant reminder of the optimism with which the suburban attempts to forestall the urban.

With all nineteenth-century architecture, it is wise to lift the eyes above the streetscape. Sometimes, the most ordinary, seemingly modern shopfront is crowned by something exotic. **Westmoreland Street** is a prime example: a site where many wonderful Victorian buildings, inserted into the eighteenth-century streetscape, can only be appreciated by their upper floors.

The modern

A distinct strain of classicism also informs much Dublin architecture of the twentieth century. However, improved building technology and increasing foreign influence slowly began to change the city's face. The classical tradition is very obvious in **Government Buildings** (1920s), an exercise in Edwardian Baroque. Classicism of a very different order informs Edwin Lutyens' **Irish National War Memorial** (1930-40) on the banks of the Liffey. The austere beauty of the design, with its sunken circular gardens, pergolas, fountains, and pavilions, is unaffected, despite the inappropriate planting and extensive tarmacadam.

The other important early twentieth-century influence, the Arts and Crafts Movement, is obvious in the **Iveagh Trust Buildings and Baths** (1894-1915). This ambitious rehousing programme by a Guinness family trust, while dilapidated, still functions as housing. The exuberance of the scheme is in marked contrast to the pedestrianism of the contemporary Dublin Corporation housing which surrounds it. However, in recent decades, much contemporary Corporation housing, which can also be seen in and around the Iveagh

*Designed by Michael Scott, the central bus station, **Busáras**, is a great modernist landmark.*

Buildings, has been internationally recognised for the quality of its design.

Busáras (1940s), the central bus station, is undoubtedly a landmark in Dublin's twentieth-century architecture. It is internationally recognised as one of Ireland's great modernist buildings. It was designed by the Irish architect, Michael Scott, and is influenced by Le Corbusier and the early International Style. Apart from a bus terminus, the complex also originally housed government offices and a theatre.

In 1967, Trinity College's pioneering **New Library** by Paul Koralek heralded a new dynamism in Dublin architecture. It was followed by a number of innovative projects which include the former **Bord na Mona Headquarters** (1977) at Baggot Street Bridge by Sam Stephenson, and the same architect's very controversial **Civic Offices** (1986) at Wood Quay. The 'Bunkers', as these gaunt, bleak twin towers came to be known, aroused controversy less for their appearance than for their location. They were erected on a Viking archaeological site of international significance. The banality of Stephenson's design has been much modified by Scott Tallon and Walker's design for new Civic Offices at Wood Quay (incorporating the original buildings) which were erected in the mid-1990s. It is a splendid example of integrating the best in modern design with a prime site which has a strong architectural character.

In the early 1990s, the Irish Government initiated an important venture by designating Temple Bar, an area sandwiched between the Liffey and Dame Street, as a cultural quarter. A competition was held in 1991 for an architectural framework plan for how that aim might be achieved. It was won by Group 91, and most of the original framework has now been completed. The various projects which were built include the **Irish Film Centre**, **Arthouse** (a multi-media centre), the **Music Centre**, the **National Photographic Archive**, the **Gallery of Photography**, the **Ark** (a children's cultural centre), two squares, and one curved street. The Irish Film Centre (1992), designed by O'Donnell and Twomey, is housed in a former eighteenth-century Friends' (Quaker) Meeting House. Because the complex has no significant street frontage, the glazed internal courtyard with its bar, restaurant, shop and cinemas, is a wonderful surprise. This is a good example of how a new and appropriate use can be found for an old building while at the same time consciously acknowledging the modern interventions.

The Temple Bar development is the most tangible expression of the vibrant Dublin which emerged during the economic boom of the late 1980s and early '90s. Although few would regard the 'cultural quarter' as a complete success – the high ratio of bars to retail outlets has caused some problems, and some significant buildings have been destroyed – the overall approach, and the integration of the very new with what already existed is refreshing. As in the eighteenth century, the ability to foster innovative architecture practice still relies heavily, it seems, on Dublin's economic fortunes.

Literary Dublin

Maybe it's something in the water. Whatever, Dublin has raised so many Nobel literature winners that the prize virtually belongs to it.

In his poem 'Dublin', Louis MacNeice describes the city as a:

> 'Fort of the Dane,
> Garrison of the Saxon,
> Augustan capital
> Of a Gaelic nation.'

The Danes may not have left too many literary remains, but in more recent centuries, Dublin's unique mix of cultures has produced a peerless collection of writers for which the city is known throughout the world. Modern Irish writing begins with Jonathan Swift (1667-1745). His birthplace at Hoey's Court has not survived but is marked by a plaque on Little Ship Street by Dublin Castle.

After an undistinguished career at Trinity College, Swift was ordained a clergyman and served in Antrim and Meath. Failing to secure advancement in England, he returned to Dublin where he became Dean of St Patrick's Cathedral in 1714. His *Drapier's Letters*, a series of pamphlets denouncing British attitudes to Ireland, gained him a reputation as an Irish patriot. His satirical masterpieces are *The Tale of a Tub* and *Gulliver's Travels*. A bequest in his will helped found St Patrick's Hospital for the treatment of mental illness, or as Swift put it: *'He gave the little wealth he had,/To build a house for fools and mad,/And showed by one satiric touch,/No nation wanted it so much.'* If visiting St Patrick's Cathedral, where he is buried, drop in to Marsh's Library (*see chapter* **Museums**), the oldest public library in Ireland and little changed since Swift's time.

The statues on either side of Trinity College's front gate commemorate political philosopher Edmund Burke (1729-97) and Oliver Goldsmith (1728-74). Arguably (although unintentionally, for he was a Whig) the forefather of British Conservative thought, Burke was born on Arran Quay on the north side of the Liffey, and was baptised in nearby St Michan's church. On completing his degree, he left Dublin for England. He became MP for Bristol in 1774; his best-known work is *Reflections on the Recent Revolution in France* (1790). Goldsmith, too, did not stay very long in Dublin. Much of his childhood was spent in County Roscommon, which inspired his great poem 'The Deserted Village'. After studying at Trinity College, he went to London, where his plays *The Good Natur'd Man* and *She Stoops to Conquer* were huge successes.

James Clarence Mangan (1803-49).

Ireland's foremost poet of the nineteenth century, James Clarence Mangan (1803-49), was born in historic Fishamble Street, also the site of the first performance of Handel's *Messiah* in 1742. His colourful appearance and prodigious drinking at taverns such as the Bleeding Horse on Camden Street (still in business today) made him a notable Dublin character of his time. He worked as a legal scrivener and, later, in the library of Trinity College. Mangan produced almost a thousand poems and translations, of which the most famous include 'Dark Rosaleen', 'Siberia' and 'The Nameless One'. He died of malnutrition and is buried in Glasnevin cemetery.

Novelist Joseph Sheridan Le Fanu (1814-73) came from a Huguenot background (make time to visit the Huguenot cemetery on St Stephen's Green). After legal studies, he became the editor of a series of Dublin magazines and began to publish his distinctive ghost stories. His *Ghost Stories* and *Tales of Mystery* appeared in 1853. *The House by the Churchyard* (1863), a novel, is set in the suburb of Chapelizod and was a central influence on Joyce's *Finnegans Wake*. After his wife's death, Le Fanu rarely left his home in Merrion Square, devoting his time to the study of magic and demonology. One of his most famous stories, 'Carmilla', anticipates Bram Stoker with its exotic theme of lesbian vampirism.

Bram Stoker (1847-1912) is best remembered as the author of *Dracula (see **Lite bite** page 25)*. He was born at 15 Marino Crescent, Clontarf and worked as a civil servant in Dublin Castle. He attended the salons of Lady Wilde (mother of the playwright), and later married a former girlfriend of Oscar's. A great theatre enthusiast and drama critic, he acted as manager for the celebrated Victorian actor Henry Irving. *Dracula* appeared in 1897. A long list of macabre volumes followed, including *The Jewel of the Seven Stars* (1903) and *The Lair of the White Worm* (1911). Bram Stoker died in London.

Oscar Wilde (1854-1900), or Oscar Fingal O'Flaherty Wills Wilde to give him his full name, was born at 21 Westland Row. His father was the surgeon and architect Sir William Wilde and his mother the nationalist poet 'Speranza', whose conservatory can be seen at 1 Merrion Square. Wilde was educated at Trinity College, where he won a gold medal for Greek and became a protégé of the classicist and wit Sir John Pentland Mahaffy. He won a scholarship to Magdalen College, Oxford in 1874 and, thereafter, seldom returned to Dublin. His brilliant conversation and plays, including *Lady Windermere's Fan, An Ideal Husband* and *The Importance of Being Earnest*, helped him conquer London, but an ill-considered libel action led to his downfall and prosecution for homosexuality. 'The Ballad of Reading Gaol' and 'De Profundis' are painful records of his time in prison. Bankrupt and homeless, he died in Paris in 1900.

Another playwright who left Dublin for London is George Bernard Shaw (1856-1950), born at 33 Synge Street in the south inner city (*see chapter **Museums***). Between 1866-73, he lived at Torca Cottage in Dalkey, where the picturesque views of the bay impressed him greatly. He worked as a clerk, cashier and estate manager before leaving for London in 1876. His return visits were brief and infrequent. Among his many successful plays are *John Bull's Other Island*, exploring Anglo-Irish relations, *Man and Superman, Saint Joan* and *Pygmalion*. He was awarded the Nobel prize for literature in 1925, and left a third of his royalties to the National Gallery, where a statue of him stands.

Ireland's greatest poet, William Butler Yeats (1865-1939), was born at 5 Sandymount Avenue (easily accessible by DART), but spent much of his childhood in Sligo and London. His father JB Yeats

William Butler Yeats *(1865-1939).*

and brother Jack were both painters of note. With Lady Gregory he founded the Irish Literary Theatre, which found a home in the Abbey Theatre in 1904. This building burned down in 1951, to be replaced by the current theatre in 1966. Among his early plays are *The Countess Cathleen* and *Cathleen ni Houlihan*, in which his great love Maud Gonne played the lead. The poem 'Easter 1916' is his response to the Easter Rising and contains the famous line, 'A terrible beauty is born'. He was made a senator of the Irish Free State and was awarded the Nobel prize for literature in 1923. His best work was yet to come and it included such late masterpieces as 'Sailing To Byzantium', 'Among School Children' and 'The Circus Animals' Desertion'. He died in France in 1939, and was reinterred in Sligo in 1948 with these lines on his headstone: *'Cast a cold eye/On life, on death./Horseman, pass by!'* In more recent times his native Sandymount has become the address of another Nobel laureate, Seamus Heaney.

Playwright John Millington Synge (1871-1909) was born to an old clerical family in the suburb of Rathfarnham. Family holidays in County Wicklow gave him a first taste of the country life depicted so vividly in his plays. After studies at Trinity College, he spent several years on the continent before his first visit to the Aran Islands in 1898. Returning to Dublin, he became associated with Yeats and Lady Gregory's Irish Literary Theatre. His early plays include *Riders to the Sea* and *The Well of the Saints*, but his masterpiece is *The Playboy of the Western World*, which caused riots when first produced at the Abbey in 1907. He died of Hodgkin's disease in a Lower Mount Street nursing home and is buried in Mount Jerome cemetery.

Another playwright, Sean O'Casey (1880-1964), was born at 85 Upper Dorset Street in the north inner city. His working-class childhood and experiences in the Irish labour movement are described in his multi-volume autobiography. Working for many years as a labourer, he did not become a full-time writer until in his forties. His three great plays of Dublin life are *The Shadow of a Gunman* (1923), *Juno and the Paycock* (1924) and *The Plough and the Stars* (1926), which, liked Synge's *Playboy*, caused a riot at the Abbey. In later years he lived in Devon, where he died in 1964.

Supreme among literary chroniclers of Dublin is James Joyce (1882-1941). Joyce was born at 41 Brighton Square, Rathgar. John Joyce, his colourful, anti-clerical father, was a strong influence who fecklessly dissipated his family's wealth: by the time Joyce left Ireland in 1904, his family had occupied 14 different rented addresses. Joyce was educated at the Jesuit colleges of Clongowes and Belvedere, and later University College, Dublin. An early pamphlet, 'The Day of the Rabblement', bore witness to his cosmopolitan sympathies and distrust of Catholic nationalism. Among the last of his Dublin addresses was the Martello tower in Sandycove, where he was a guest of Oliver St John Gogarty (Buck Mulligan in *Ulysses*) in September 1904. In October, he left Dublin with his lifelong companion Nora Barnacle for Paris, Pola and Trieste, where he taught English. His earliest writings were poetry, collected as *Chamber Music* in 1907, and short prose sketches or 'epiphanies', some of which appear in his early novel *Stephen Hero* (unpublished in his lifetime). His first prose

book to appear – though not before lengthy wrangling with his publishers – was *Dubliners* (1914), a collection of short stories. John Huston made a film of the last and longest of these, *The Dead*, in 1987. *A Portrait of the Artist as a Young Man* (1916) is an autobiographical novel charting the growth of Joyce's mind and his decision to abandon Ireland and Catholicism for the 'silence, exile and cunning' of his artistic vocation. He visited Ireland again in 1909 to help establish the country's first cinema, on Mary Street, but never returned after 1912.

He began his masterpiece *Ulysses* in Trieste in 1914 and published it under the imprint of Shakespeare & Co in Paris in 1922. It is set on June 16, 1904, in memory of Joyce's first date with Nora Barnacle, and charts a day in the life of Stephen Dedalus, a student, and Leopold Bloom, an advertising canvasser. The novel closely follows the structure of Homer's *Odyssey*, with Bloom representing Ulysses and Stephen his son, Telemachus. Many of the novel's locations can be visited today (*see* **On the Ulysses trail** *page 27*).

Having finished off the daylight world in *Ulysses*, Joyce plunged into the netherworld of

Lite bite

Dracula was a Dubliner. Well, nearly. Certainly his creator was and, without the influence of Irish folklore, it is doubtful whether Bram Stoker's 1897 classic would ever have been written.

Stoker was born at 15 Marino Crescent in Clontarf. Close to his home was an unconsecrated graveyard where, until only a few years before his birth in 1847, suicides had regularly been buried with wooden stakes through their hearts in order to prevent their spirits from returning to haunt the living. The Stokers themselves had a family crypt at St Michan's church (*see chapter* **Sightseeing**) near the Four Courts, where, even then, visitors would pay to see the perfectly preserved, mummified corpses.

Nor was vampirism a new theme in Irish literature. In one folk tale, the castle of Dún Dreach-Fhola is inhabited by the undead, who feed on the blood of unwary travellers. Other tales, from Waterford, Kerry and Antrim, tell of *dearg-diúlai* – blood suckers – who seduce their victims before killing them. More recently, in 1872, another Dubliner, Joseph Sheridan Le Fanu, had published 'Carmilla', a vampire story with lesbian undertones.

How much of this was in Stoker's head when he sat down to write *Dracula*, we'll never know for sure. It's possible to read almost anything into

his gory tale, from sexual anxiety and oral sex to menstruation. Stoker's own sexuality remains shrouded in mystery. As a student at Trinity College, he discovered Walt Whitman's homoerotic anthology *Leaves of Grass* and immediately became, in his own words, 'a lover' of the American poet, although it was years before the two men met. In the meantime, Stoker married Florence Balcombe, pinching her from her then boyfriend Oscar Wilde. (Oscar, then being treated for syphilis, was under medical instructions to remain celibate for two years.) The Stokers left Ireland for London, where Bram became righthand man to the actor Henry Irving. Is there something of the demanding, charismatic Irving in the blood-sucking, seductive figure of the Count?

Stoker wrote his masterpiece painstakingly over five years, though he never went anywhere near Transylvania, getting all the background detail he needed from guide books. Henry Irving himself would later play the title role on stage. Stoker's other works, mainly dashed off for money, are all but forgotten. He died in 1912, so we cannot know what he would have thought of the film portrayals of his neck-nibbling hero. However, his widow, Florence, devoted much of her latter years to suppressing them, on grounds of breach of copyright.

dreams in his last novel, *Finnegans Wake* (1939), which took him 17 years to write. The novel is 'set' in the Mullingar Inn, Chapelizod, in the dreams and dream-language of publican Humphrey Chimpden Earwicker and his wife and children Anna Livia Plurabelle, Shem the Penman, Shaun the Post and Issy. Its last sentence is unfinished ('along the'), connecting with its first ('riverrun…'), suggesting the novel's theme of resurrection and eternal recurrence. Joyce was highly indignant at war breaking out in the same year that the novel was published, and did not live to see it hailed as *Ulysses* had been. It remains a uniquely daunting book, but also a uniquely rewarding one. Driven out of Paris by the German occupation, Joyce died in Zürich in 1941.

Poet Austin Clarke (1896-1974) was born at 83 Manor Street in Stoneybatter. *Twice Round the Black Church* (1962) is an affectionate memoir of his early years. He was hospitalised in St Patrick's for a nervous breakdown, an event he describes in his long poem 'Mnemosyne Lay in Dust'. After many years in London, he moved back to Dublin, living by the banks of the Dodder in Templeogue. A satirical portrait of him, as 'Austin Ticklepenny', can be found in Beckett's novel *Murphy*.

Although more strongly associated with County Cork, novelist Elizabeth Bowen (1899-1973) was born at 15 Herbert Place in the city centre. Her Dublin childhood is recalled in *Seven Winters* (1943). Her finely drawn novels of middle-class life include *The Last September* (1927), *The Death of the Heart* (1938) and *The Heat of the Day* (1949). She inherited an ancestral 'big house' in County Cork in 1930 and died in Kent in 1973.

Dublin's third Nobel laureate, Samuel Beckett (1906-89), was born in the well-heeled suburb of Foxrock and educated at Trinity College. He travelled to Paris in 1928, where he became a friend of Joyce, who dictated some of *Finnegans Wake* to him. His collection of stories, *More Pricks Than Kicks* (1934), was written in a garret in Clare Street and promptly banned by the Free State government. Perhaps in revenge for this, a character in *Murphy* (1938) assaults the buttocks of national hero Cuchulainn's statue in the General Post Office – careful observers will notice that the statue does not, in fact, possess any buttocks (*see chapter* **Sightseeing**). He moved to Paris in 1937 and spent much of the war on the run from the Gestapo in the south of France. Returning to Paris, he produced the clutch of masterpieces that would bring him international fame, including the play *Waiting for Godot* (1955). Dublin and its environs never disappear from his work, however, with Dalkey Island, Dun Laoghaire pier and Foxrock railway station all easily recognisable in *Malone Dies*, *Krapp's Last Tape* and *All That Fall*.

A canal bank statue off Baggot Street commemorates Patrick Kavanagh (1904-67). Born in Inniskeen, County Monaghan, he described his country childhood in *The Green Fool* and *Tarry Flynn*. He moved to Dublin in the 1930s, where he wrote his long poem 'The Great Hunger'. Never financially secure, he started his own newspaper, *Kavanagh's Weekly*, which soon collapsed. Many of his best poems celebrate the tranquillity of the canal where his statue now sits.

Brian O'Nolan (1911-66), aka Flann O'Brien or Myles na gCopaleen, was born in County Tyrone but brought up in Dublin. He worked as a civil servant. *At Swim-Two-Birds* (1939) is a burlesque novel about a Dublin student writing a book whose characters turn on their author; it won the praise of James Joyce. It also contains the poem 'A pint of plain is your only man', to be recited over a round of drinks in the Palace or any of the other bars associated with O'Nolan. *The Third Policeman* (completed in 1940, not published until 1967) is darkly surrealist, while *An Béal Bocht* (*The Poor Mouth*, 1941) is a brilliant satire of Gaelic autobiography. O'Nolan's satirical column in the *Irish Times* was a feature of Irish life for almost three decades before his death on April Fools' Day, 1966.

Playwright, drunkard and general hellraiser, Brendan Behan (1923-64) was born in Holles Street Hospital and brought up in Russell Street, off the North Circular Road. He was arrested for republican activities while still in his teens, and after a second arrest, spent five years in prison, an experience which shaped his plays *The Hostage* (1958, written circa 1941) and *The Quare Fellow* (1954). Too much time spent in McDaid's pub on Harry Street and other watering holes undermined his talent and hastened his early death.

Among the writers who continue to make Dublin a vibrant literary capital are Seamus Heaney, John Banville, Derek Mahon, Roddy Doyle and Eavan Boland. Of the city's many bookshops, Waterstone's, Hodges Figgis and Fred Hanna's cluster together on Dawson Street and Nassau Street (*see chapter* **Shopping & Services**). The excellent Books Upstairs on College Green stocks a mixture of new and secondhand books, while the multi-storey Winding Stair on Ormond Quay is a browser's delight, offering food and a lively calendar of poetry readings, too. Poetry Ireland, the national organisation for poetry, can be found in the impressive surroundings of Dublin Castle (Bermingham Tower, Dublin Castle, Dame Street, Dublin 2; 671 4632). Other venues for literary events include Waterstone's, Bewley's Oriental Café on Grafton Street (*see chapter* **Bistros, Cafés & Coffee Shops**) and the Irish Writers' Centre at 19 Parnell Square, Dublin 1 (872 1302) beside the Dublin Writers' Museum. For the more bibulous visitor, the Jameson Dublin Literary Pub Crawl offers tall tales and liquid relief. It sets off from the Duke pub in Duke Street, Dublin 2, and you can book on 454 0228.

On the *Ulysses* trail

Bloom's house at 7 Eccles Street in the north inner city was demolished to make way for the Mater Hospital, but many other locations associated with the novel survive, some of them marked by pavement plaques laid down in Dublin's millennium year, 1988. They include:

The Martello Tower, the Forty Foot. Beside the 'snotgreen scrotumtightening' sea in Sandycove, Stephen, 'stately, plump Buck Mulligan' and the Englishman Haines enjoy a fried breakfast in the Martello Tower in chapter one ('Telemachus'), before walking to the forty foot pool, still a popular bathing place. Mulligan and Haines bathe naked: get there before 9am if you feel like doing the same.

Sandymount strand where Stephen takes a philosophical stroll ('Am I walking into eternity along Sandymount strand?') in chapter three ('Proteus'). Later the same day, Gerty McDowell watches a fireworks display here and flirts at a distance with Leopold Bloom, who discreetly masturbates (chapter 13, 'Nausicaa').

St Andrew's Church, Sweny's chemist. Though Jewish, Bloom looks in on mass at St Andrew's church on Westland Row and buys a bar of lemon soap from Sweny's chemist (still in business today) in chapter five ('Lotuseaters').

Glasnevin cemetery. Bloom travels to Glasnevin with Stephen's father Simon to attend Paddy Dignam's funeral.

The Oval, Mooney's. After a visit to the offices of the *Freeman's Journal* and the *Evening Telegraph* on Prince's Street North (now a branch of British Home Stores), Bloom stops at two pubs in chapter seven ('Aeolus'): the Oval and Mooney's (now the Abbey Mooney) on Lower Abbey Street.

Thomas Moore statue, Davy Byrne's. In chapter eight ('Lestrygonians') Bloom passes the statue of poet Thomas Moore on College Green, enjoying the irony by which the author of 'The Meeting of the Waters' now stands over a urinal. Homer's cannibals are transformed by Joyce into the lunchtime clientèle of Davy Byrne's 'moral pub' on Duke Street, where Bloom lunches on a cheese sandwich and a glass of wine.

National Museum, National Library. Bloom continues down Molesworth Street in chapter nine ('Scylla and Charybdis') to the National Museum and National Library on Kildare Street. Stephen is in the library too, where he engages Æ (poet George Russell) and other literary types in a debate on *Hamlet*.

Ormond Hotel. Chapter 11 ('Sirens') is a musical fantasia set in the Ormond Hotel, Ormond Quay, where Bloom hears Stephen Dedalus and Ben Dollard sing.

Holles Street Hospital. Mrs Purefoy gives birth to a son in Holles Street Hospital in chapter 14 ('Oxen of the Sun') while Stephen carouses with students and meets Bloom, come to pay his respects.

Railway Street, Olhausen's. The climactic chapter 15 ('Circe') is set in nighttown or the 'kips', Dublin's former red-light district. Visiting one of its most famous brothels, that of Bella Cohen on present-day Railway Street, Stephen confronts the ghost of his mother and has to be rescued by Bloom from a skirmish with a soldier. Bloom also buys a pig's trotter and a sheep's hoof from Olhausen's, a pork butcher on Talbot Street that is still in business. The area was cleared of its prostitutes by the Catholic Legion of Mary after Irish independence.

Amiens Street, North Star Hotel, Butt Bridge. Leaving nighttown, Bloom and Stephen make their way in chapter 16 ('Eumaeus') to a cabman's shelter by Butt Bridge. To get there, they walk down Amiens Street, passing Dan Bergin's pub (now Lloyd's), the North Star Hotel and the Dublin City morgue on the corner of Amiens Street and Store Street.

Gardiner Street, Mountjoy Square, Eccles Street. Bloom and Stephen make their way back to Bloom's home by way of Gardiner Street, Mountjoy Square, St George's church (now refurbished as a theatre), Temple Street, Hardwicke Place. The novel ends with Molly Bloom's soliloquy as she drifts to sleep in the now-demolished house on Eccles Street.

Visit the **Joyce Museum** in Sandycove (accessible by DART) and the **James Joyce Centre** (*see chapter* **Museums**) to get a fuller flavour of the writer's life.

Dublin by Area

Dublin by Area

Southside, Northside and the bits on the edges.

Dublin is in flux – cafés, restaurants and clubs appear almost overnight, and, if they go bust, reappear under a different name. So although it makes it difficult to pin the city down in any definitive way, it also means that now is an exciting time to visit. Dublin has been a Viking fort, elegantly Georgian, a dirty old town, a revolutionary hot bed, a seaside port, a European city of culture, a Celtic tiger. Whatever its future guise, it will still be all these things. Dublin will for ever be an amalgam of all that is past, passing and yet to come.

There are a number of good ways to see Dublin; driving around is not one of them, nor is availing yourself of the buses. Unfortunately, despite ambitious plans, there are as yet neither metro nor trams, so the entire city centre is congested with traffic. There are three ways to see Dublin. The DART (Dublin Area Rapid Transport), following the curve of the sea, is the perfect way to see the coastal area from Dalkey to Howth. Bicycles are always good and everyone uses them. But the proper way to see Dublin is to walk. Even before Joyce changed twentieth-century literature by sending Leopold Bloom off to walk around Dublin, it was a famous city for walking. In fact, Joyce sent Bloom out walking because that is what you do in Dublin. As Richard Ellmann, celebrated biographer of Joyce, Wilde and Yeats, has it: 'To walk in Dublin is to meet with friends.' Walking in Dublin may be compared to sitting at the cafés in the Champs-Elysées in Paris – sooner or later, you will bump into everyone you ever knew.

Dublin has three assets which make it unique among Europe's crowded capitals – it is on the sea, with a bay of harbours and bathing spots, it is surrounded by hills and mountains, and it has the largest park in Europe. Although the centre is congested, escape is always easy. And that is as it should be in an island famed for remote and wild greenery.

Boundaries are difficult in Dublin, one area merging into another. The city centre is roughly bounded by four corners: St Stephen's Green, the top of O'Connell Street, Trinity College, and Christchurch. That is a wide, though not homogeneous, area. Like all city centres, it's saturated with places to visit. The whole area is extremely crowded, except for very early in the morning.

Around St Stephen's Green

Grafton Street, Baggot Street, Leeson Street; these are the busiest of the Southside's streets and they all radiate from St Stephen's Green – but mind, Dubliners rarely use the 'Street'. Usually packed, the Green is a necessary rest place for shoppers and workers. It is famous for summer lunches, its bewildering array of statues and courting couples. Until the seventeenth century, it was common ground used for hangings and whippings. Then it was fenced off and acquired gravel paths. For a brief period from 1814, its gates were locked and an annual entrance fee of one guinea was demanded. Lord Arthur Guinness then pushed through an Act of Parliament in 1877 opening the gates to the public. He financed the design of the park that you see today.

It remains a graceful, though formal, park. Nature is kept in control; there's a pretty pond. To the left of the central area (with its large flower beds) is a curious place of stone circles. Here is

Grafton Street – *Dublin's busiest for shops.*

Re Joyce

You cannot escape Joyce in Dublin even if you didn't know who he was when you came here. There are statues to him in St Stephen's Green and, looking on to O'Connell Street, in North Earl Street Street, there's his museum in Sandycove, another in North Great George's Street, there's Newman House and mostly there's *that* book. The city currently resembles a Joycean theme park as quotations from *Ulysses* have appeared in large fluorescent writing over various monuments of national importance, such as Trinity College. The best of the quotations is over the bookies in Fleet Street and reads, 'I hate an unlucky man.' These quotations are on a seasonal or trial basis and it's uncertain how long they'll last, although the pervasiveness of Joyce's presence is not, in any case, dependent on them.

Joyce was censored in Ireland in his lifetime and, as is often sardonically noted, it took American and European veneration to force him to the front of Irish attention. It's also noted, somewhat savagely, that nobody's read him all the way through, anyway. This misses the point. Joyce literally put Dublin on the map. It was not there before. And that is a remarkable achievement which no other author can claim for his city, not even Dickens for London, since London had its own literary creations long before Dickens. People still arrive in Dublin with maps of the city carefully constructed from *Ulysses* and, as Joyce had what he described as a grocer's assistant's mind, these maps are wonderfully accurate. So Dublin may as well pay belated homage and make some money while it does so.

---

probably the finest statue in the park: WB Yeats by George Moore. In a city where statuary realism rules with an iron hand, this one has the witty curve of expressionism. Others beg to differ and the piece is now covered with graffiti.

In Dublin, statues of historical figures are more than just moribund memorials to past greatness; because of the continuing problems in Northern Ireland they are loaded with significance for the present. As a consequence, they are seldom left alone. Nelson's Pillar in O'Connell Street, blown up in 1966, is only the most famous victim. On the southwest corner of the Green is a statue of **Theobold Wolfe Tone**; hailed as the father of Irish Republicanism, he is one of those brilliant figures from Irish history now tainted by being venerated by the IRA. The statue was blown up by the UVF (Ulster Volunteer Force) in 1979; the head was found by the Shelbourne Hotel, and the pieces put back together again.

The Georgian houses lining the square are now put to public use. On the north side is the spacious **Shelbourne Hotel**. Sumptuous in presentation, it is dedicated to solid comfort over glitz. The bar tenders have intimate knowledge of what makes a good cocktail. Of its two bars, the Horseshoe is more elegant than the Shelbourne; between about six and nine every evening it fills up with barristers. Otherwise, both bars are emptier than others in the city, probably because the imposing hotel entrance acts as a deterrent.

On the south side, at 85-86, is **Newman House** and, beside it, **Newman University Church**. These are named after Cardinal Newman, who founded the Catholic University here, and left his rigorous mark on generations of Irish thinkers. Gerard Manley Hopkins was professor of Classics here from 1884 till his death in 1889, and Joyce was a student between 1899-1902. There are quotations from Newman and Hopkins in the Church, but nothing from Joyce, whose comments about the Catholic Church would have been considered unprintable. His presence around these buildings is an uneasy one, given his contempt for the Church and, to some measure, the University, but it is he who draws most visitors judging from the comments in the visitors' book.

The interior of Newman House belies its sombre exterior, being spacious, extravagant and lavish. However, the most interesting room here – the study-bedroom of Hopkins – is distinctly sober, and it's well worth the climb up flights of back stairs to it. Hopkins was depressed in Dublin and you feel this as soon as you enter his room; the mattress is as hard as a board and the sheer number of crucifixes invokes desperation.

Newman House backs on to the **Iveagh Gardens** which, visible from Hopkins' room, can only be entered from Earlsfort Terrace. This is a small street almost entirely taken up by a building that used to be the main premises of **University College Dublin** (UCD), but is now the **National**

Concert Hall. UCD has been banished to the suburbs of Belfield, where it has made up for in space what it has certainly lost in architectural merit. Part of UCD's engineering faculty still remains beside the hall, and if you go to the back of this building you can enter the gardens. These are open to the public, but access is hidden and they give the impression of being private, so are generally almost empty. Quiet, peaceful and romantic, the gardens have long lawns and a delicate stone fountain. There is no better place to sit awhile before going into a concert.

On the west side of the Green is the elegant and imposing **Royal College of Surgeons**, beside it the glass-domed **St Stephen's Green Shopping Centre**, the interior of which relies on clever use of space and natural light. The centre mounts redbricked, pedestrianised **Grafton Street**, one of Dublin's key streets. Once extremely fashionable, it was the main shopping thoroughfare of the Anglo-Irish Ascendancy. It has somehow held on to this reputation and still boasts Dublin's most upmarket shops, although it is nowhere near as exclusive as it was. Fast-food places have slipped in, as have British high-street names such as Marks & Spencer and Miss Selfridge. Two buildings remain as the soul of the street: **Bewley's Oriental Café** (*see chapters* **Bistros, Cafés & Coffee Shops** and **Museums**) and the lavish department store **Brown Thomas** (*see chapter* **Shopping & Services**). Bewley's three cafés have a special position in Dublin, which, in the past few years, has acquired an astonishing and quite unforeseen reputation as a coffee capital. Every week, a new café appears with an extravagant menu inviting you to try an amaretto-flavoured double cappuccino or a light Colombian blend. In a country where the only coffee you could ever get used to be instant, this may be seen as a revolution. It remains to be seen if it is sustainable. New cafés come and go, but Bewley's is a steady presence. Founded in the nineteenth century, with its distinctive stained-glass windows and its numerous rooms, it is certainly an institution, though currently deserted by the younger crowd who prefer more intimate surroundings.

Brown Thomas is a fine, spacious, three-storey store where you can acquire everything from Irish linen sheets to designer knitwear. At Christmas, children are brought to see its window display. On Christmas Eve, the pubs shut at 6pm and, by 5pm, they are overflowing with people and parcels. This is the time when you meet everyone you ever went to school with who left for America to make their fortune. There are a good number of pubs off Grafton Street. **McDaid's, Kehoe's** and the **International** (*see chapter* **Pubs & Bars**) are three of the best. These are pubs that could only be found in Dublin. A good Dublin pub is not too large, has both bar and lounge, lots of polished dark wood

Temple Bar – *strikes a chord with the young.*

and mirrors with brand names on them, and never, ever, has piped music.

Running parallel is **Dawson Street**, where the great bookshops of Hoggis Figgis and Waterstone's eye each other uneasily from their positions on opposite sides of the street. Both have wonderful premises and offer remarkable bargains. Also here is **Café en Seine** (*see chapter* **Pubs & Bars**), a very recent addition to the city; it's a place of unexpectedly wild art nouveau beauty, with huge dulled chandeliers and a long copper-tinted bar. It is much better to visit in the daytime; at night it fills up with yuppies and a depressingly conventional door policy is in operation.

Trinity College

All streets lead to Trinity College or TCD. Home to priceless treasures such as the **Book of Kells** (*see chapter* **Museums**), this is the biggest tourist attraction in the city and, founded in 1591 by Elizabeth I, one of the oldest universities in the British Isles. It is also of great importance to those who are neither tourists nor students. The Front Gate is a famous meeting place. The Pavilion Bar (or Pav) on the cricket pitch is one of the best places to drink outdoors in the summer. Trinity is so artfully constructed that it cuts out all the noise of the city. As soon as you get inside its walls, the sound of traffic recedes. If you want peace and quiet, come here rather than to one of the central parks. Trinity's students are a laid-back bunch, who speak a variation of Dublinese known as the Trinity accent. If you have a good ear for these things, you will notice that it is slower and more drawling then the language of the streets.

A roll call of Trinity's graduates reveals some of the strongest names in literature: some, such as Jonathan Swift, author of *Gulliver's Travels*, Bram Stoker, creator of *Dracula*, Oscar Wilde and Samuel Beckett, need little in the way of introduction. Collectively, they brewed a storm in the Jane Austen teacup of English literature, and their writings have shocked generations from positions of comfortable complacency.

The front gate of Trinity is on College Green, a triangle with a fine conjunction of buildings. Unfortunately, it is now a traffic crossroads and it is almost impossible to cross the road, let alone stand and take it in. Opposite Trinity is the classical building of the **Bank of Ireland** (*see chapters* **Museums** and **Sightseeing**), which began life as the seat of the Irish parliament, established in 1729 and voted out of existence in 1800. Open only to the Protestant minority, it was exclusive even in eighteenth-century terms, which is probably why its demise is never painted in the tragic colours of other Irish defeats. The bank seems unwilling to push itself as a tourist attraction, but go inside and ask for the **House of Lords**. Panelled in Irish oak, it is filled with treasures such as the eighteenth-century crystal chandelier made from 1,223 pieces.

From Trinity, you can go north up O'Connell Street, or west up the more fashionable Dame Street. O'Connell Street is grander and has more historical associations. Take your pick.

Dame Street to Temple Bar

Dame Street is a street of banks. The most obvious of these is the **Central Bank**, a famous eyesore. Halfway up the street and acting as a gateway to Temple Bar, it looms over the area like a huge concrete bunker. Its interest lies solely in its architectural design: it is not constructed from ground to sky, but suspended around a central axis.

The recently renovated **Temple Bar** proved itself a huge success. More surprisingly, it's a vibrant place that has withstood the death knell sounded by that dread phrase, 'urban renewal project'. It slots neatly in behind Dame Street, leading down through Crown Alley, to fine views of the river Liffey.

Its eighteenth-century cobbled streets are pedestrianised and completely given over to fun. This means lots of restaurants, bars and clothes shops. Most interesting are the new cultural enterprises, including the **Irish Film Centre** (*see chapter* **Film**) which shows an impressive range of rare films, the Art House, a multimedia centre where you can rent time to surf the Net; the Temple Bar Gallery and the Original Print Gallery (*see chapter* **Art Galleries**), both of which have exhibition spaces and rooms upstairs in which artists can work. These ensure that Temple Bar is not just dependent on tourism.

Temple Bar is also U2 territory, the superstar rock group whose investment created **Kitchen** nightclub and revamped the **Clarence Hotel**. The Kitchen is a cavernous place with quirky touches, such as the moat around the dance floor. Music changes nightly from ambient to hardcore; big names are consistently attracted. There are any number of good-value restaurants in Temple Bar, the best of these is the Indonesian restaurant Chameleon (*see chapter* **Restaurants**). Unfortunately, it's very small with erratic opening hours, so you can spend weeks trying to get in. The most charming sight in Temple Bar is the housing development on **Asdil's Row**, where little red-brick houses are grouped around a courtyard.

On the other side of Dame Street, is **George's Street**, home to two of the most popular bars in the city, the **Globe** and **Hogan's**. Both of these are very recent and they do not follow the Dublin pub formula. They have fine big windows on to the street, allowing punters to be observed sipping bottled beer. Always packed, they play funky music, although with varying degrees of success, and operate a door policy. If you want a more traditional pub, the **Long Hall**, opposite Hogan's, has a bar the length of the pub. Another choice is the **Stag's Head**, just around the corner on Dame Lane. This is one of the most beautiful pubs in the city. It goes through peaks and troughs; a few years ago you could never get inside and everyone drank outside. Now it's suddenly gone quiet. But its star will rise again.

Towards Christchurch

Up past George's Street is **Dublin Castle** (*see chapter* **Museums**), former seat of British power in Ireland, now a benign tourist attraction and diplomatic function room. Dating from the thirteenth century, it has had a turbulent history. You can walk into the peaceful open courtyard, but to get inside you will have to pay for a guided tour. Like Trinity College and other Dublin sites, the Castle keeps acquiring additional functions. There is now a small theatre – the Crypt – also a restaurant and the ubiquitous heritage centre.

Dublin is famous for its Georgian architecture, but little other architecture besides. It has, in truth, few houses which make you stop and stare. But across the road from the Castle, on Parliament Street is the lovely **Sunlight Chambers**, a rare, ornate building in a city of plain exteriors. It has faintly Gothic columns and windows; the fresco around the edges tells the story of Sunlight soap.

Dame Street ends at Christchurch. This is a good position to stop and look back. There is the lovely redbrick curving block of shops on Dame Street. There is the whole view down Dame Street with the Central Bank glowering over it. There is a street to the left called **Fishamble**, the oldest street in Dublin, where Handel's *Messiah* was first performed in 1742. On Fishamble, is the huge **Dublin Corporation Building**. Making good use of space, natural light and undulating curves rather than static blocks, it is one of the more successful of Dublin's modern buildings. However, its existence is still the centre of a huge controversy, with many maintaining that it should never have been built at all. Excavations which preceded building on Wood Quay revealed remains of a huge early Viking settlement. The Corporation pushed on with their project, despite a huge protest march in 1978.

You are now in church territory, with three of the oldest churches in the city within chiming distance of each other: **Christchurch**, **St Patrick's** and **St Audoen's** on High Street. These are all Norman medieval churches dating from the twelfth century. All have been Church of Ireland since the seventeenth century, belonging to that time when Dublin was the second city of Britain. In St Patrick's, there are military memorials to the Royal Irish Regiments including a depiction of British forces storming Rangoon. This is a Victorian alliance of God and Empire at total odds with modern Ireland.

Jonathan Swift was Dean of St Patrick's from 1713-45 and his tomb is in the church. Behind Christchurch towards the Guinness Brewery is **St Patrick's Hospital** for the mentally ill, established with money left by Swift in his will.

Christchurch is on the edge of glossy, well-heeled Dublin. Immediately around it are poorer areas. Here are also great street markets selling junk; the best of these was in the covered red-brick **Iveagh Market** on **Francis Street**, established by Lord Iveagh of the Guinness family in 1907. Once it was good for Adidas T-shirts at 50p, but proximity to the centre drag these areas up quickly, and change happens fast. This has already happened around St Patrick's in the area known as the **Liberties**, the gateway to which is at the junction of Kevin Street and Francis Street. This was a district outside the walls of the medieval city, run by local courts and free of the city restrictions on trade. With the introduction of British trading restrictions in the eighteenth century, it became a famously vibrant, colourful slum. Its tiny red-brick houses have now been yuppified and Francis Street does a golden trade in expensive antiques. Even the Iveagh Market has been suspiciously shut for some time. **Thomas Street**, up from Christchurch, has so far resisted gentrification, but with the high-tech National College of Art and Design and a pub favoured by art students, the Clock, it may be a matter of time. Only the proximity of the flats on **Oliver Bond Street**, notorious for crime and drugs, may prevent this.

O'Connell Street & environs

O'Connell Street is certainly the finest street in the city, imperially wide, with grand buildings and a great collection of statues. It is also currently the most disfigured. Two fatal mistakes were made this century when the stylish trams were removed and it was opened up indiscriminately to fast-food

places. It's tacky and noisy, with huge double-decker buses roaring up and down. One wonders if it is because this street falls on the Northside that it has been allowed to go under. There's certainly never been any talk of selling St Stephen's Green off to multinationals.

O'Connell Street has been through many names. It began life in 1700 as Drogheda Street; after being widened by Luke Gardiner in 1740 it became Gardiner's Mall. In 1794, it became the main street in Dublin after the completion of Carlisle Bridge (later O'Connell Bridge). It was then known as Sackville Street, and, in 1924, was renamed after Daniel O'Connell. A street of statues, it is bound top and bottom by the imposing figures of **Daniel O'Connell** and **Charles Stewart Parnell**. O'Connell's statue is the gateway to the street. Built in 1854, it's a fine bronze statue of the stout man, flanked by four winged victories. Slap bang in the nipple of one of them is a bullet hole, sustained in the fighting of 1916 (*see chapter* **Dublin History**). It can only have enraged the ghost of O'Connell who famously said, 'The price of Irish freedom is not worth the shedding of one drop of blood.' O'Connell Street gains much of its historical importance from the Easter Rising of 1916.

Much of the street was destroyed during the fighting and had to be rebuilt in the 1920s. The **General Post Office (GPO)** is the heart of the street. It was here that **Patrick Pearse**, **James Connolly** and five others proclaimed the Irish Republic on Easter Monday, 1916. The text of their proclamation can be seen in the GPO window, likewise a sculpture of the *Death of Cuchulainn*. The way in which Pearse used Cuchulainn, the legendary hero of ancient Ireland, to romanticise the Irish struggle was made explicit by Yeats in his poem 'The Statues': '*When Pearse summoned Cuchulainn to his side/What stalked through the Post Office?*' Yeats wrote a series of poems on 1916, the finest being 'Easter 1916.'

Near the GPO was Nelson's Column. This had stood in the street since 1815, predating that in Trafalgar Square, London. In 1966, on the fiftieth anniversary of the Easter Rising, it was blown up by the IRA and the head now sits in the **Dublin Civic Museum**. Just outside the GPO is a marvellous statue of the trade unionist **Jim Larkin**. He is associated with 1913, the year of the general strike which he organised. Caring more for the welfare of the people then the status of the country, he was universally loved. Here he is seen throwing his arms in the air in a characteristically vigorous pose.

The most recent statue in the street is the 1988 **Anna Livia Millennium Fountain**, a homage to Anna Livia, spirit of the Liffey, in Joyce's *Finnegans Wake*. Dubliners mock their statues and this grotesque fountain is known as the 'Floozy in the Jacuzzi' or the 'Whore [whoo-er] in the Sewer'.

Moore Street – *home to one of Dublin's lively pedestrianised street markets.*

Joyce himself appears in bronze on the corner of North Earl Street, gazing sardonically across at his fountain. (*See also chapter* **Sightseeing: Bombs away** and **Pedestal japes.**)

Besides statues and fast food joints, O'Connell Street has theatres and cinemas. On Abbey Street and Marlborough Street is the **Abbey Theatre**. Founded in 1904 by WB Yeats and Lady Gregory, the Abbey has enjoyed a distinguished history, having premièred radical plays by JM Synge and Seán O'Casey which refused to pander to the myth of Gaelic Catholic Ireland and so caused riots. An incensed Yeats ventured on stage to reprimand the audience. The plain people of Ireland never did measure up to Yeats' lofty notions of them. The Abbey has never regained the excitement of old and it is now seen as an establishment theatre mounting safe productions of classics, though you still see the odd great performance. The Peacock, the fringe theatre on the same premises, presents new, experimental pieces.

At the top of O'Connell Street, on Parnell Square, is the other great Dublin theatre, **The Gate**. It, too, lies in the shadow of former greatness. It was founded in 1929 by two remarkable characters, **Hilton Edwards** and **Micheál MacLiammoir**, who were both in fact English (MacLiammoir changed his name and learnt fluent Gaelic) and openly homosexual (MacLiammoir would walk around Dublin in full drag) in the most Catholic country in Europe. MacLiammoir gave his last performance in his one-man show, *The Importance of Being Oscar* in 1975.

O'Connell Street is renowned also for its lively pedestrian market streets – **Moore Street** and **Henry Street**. Here are cheap fruit and vegetable stalls, as well as numerous other bargains offered by street traders.

O'Connell Street gives way to **Parnell Square**, a large Georgian Square with museums and public buildings. The south side of the square is taken up by the imposing **Rotunda Hospital** (*see chapter* **History: Mum's the word**), built by Richard Castle in 1755 as the first maternity hospital in Britain or Ireland. On the north side is the Garden of Remembrance, established in 1966 on the fiftieth anniversary of the Easter Rising, to commemorate all those who died for Irish freedom. It is dominated by a huge sculpture of the Children of Lir. A tale of four children changed into swans by their evil stepmother, the children form one of Ireland's oldest legends.

Beside the garden is the **Hugh Lane Municipal Gallery of Modern Art**. It, too, has had an interesting history in which Yeats is involved again. Sir Hugh Lane owned an important collection of Impressionist paintings which he promised to leave to the nation if a suitable gallery could be built for them. Unfortunately, Dublin Corporation could not be persuaded to part with any money. Their philistinism, like the rioting in the Abbey Theatre aroused Yeats' ire and he wrote a bitter poem entitled, 'To a Wealthy Man Who Promised a Second Subscription to the Dublin Municipal Gallery if it Were Proved that the People Wanted Pictures'. Sir Hugh sank, along with the *Lusitania* in 1915, before it had been proved that the people wanted pictures. In his will, he left his collection to London. There was, however, an unwitnessed codicil which allowed the pictures go to Dublin if a gallery was built. In 1933, the Municipal Gallery moved to its present fine premises, the former eighteenth-century townhouse of Lord Charlemont. Then began a legal tussle over the collection between Dublin and London, with the latter holding the legal high ground and the former the moral. In 1979, a final settlement was reached, giving Dublin most of the paintings, but allowing London to keep eight. Exhibits include works by Rodin, Degas, Monet, Manet, Jack B Yeats.

Next door is the **Dublin Writers' Museum**, established in 1991 in a house once belonging to the Jameson whiskey distilling family.

Phoenix Park & along the quays

The quays follow the river Liffey from **Phoenix Park** (*see* **Park life** *p39*) in the west to **Dublin Harbour** in the east, encompassing the city centre at **O'Connell Bridge**. They are the oldest part of the city and have distinct characters of their own.

The Liffey comes from the Wicklow hills down to Dublin Bay. It divides the city into the prosperous Southside and the poorer Northside. Twenty years ago, it had a fine stench, although it has been somewhat cleaned up since then. It was immortalised by James Joyce in *Finnegans Wake* as Anna Livia, and the river gives the book its marvellously cyclical beginning and ending – 'riverrun past Eve and Adam's from swerve of shore to bend of bay' – which is the only passage from that impenetrable work that everyone knows.

The Liffey flows into central Dublin past the vast expanse of Phoenix Park. At 1,752 acres, it takes half a day to walk around, but there is a road cutting through the centre allowing you to drive, cycle or skate. The only time it has been filled in recent memory was when a million people gathered to see the Pope in 1979; a papal cross at the centre commemorates the event. Phoenix Park incorporates **Dublin Zoo**, Ashtown Castle, and Áras an Uachtaráin, the residence of the president, but these are really incidental pleasures in an area that is more of a nature reserve than a city park. You can move from the order of well-laid football pitches to untamed spaces where deer roam.

On the south bank of the Liffey is **Kilmainham Gaol** (*see chapter* **Museums**) and the **Royal Hospital**. The Gaol is remarkable because it housed every famous Irish felon from 1798 until 1924, when the Free State government closed it. Along the way, it was home to Robert Emmet, Parnell (whose cell looks more like a country house bedroom), de Valera and all the men of 1916 who were executed in the prison yard. The Royal Hospital, brilliantly restored in 1986, is now the

Irish Museum of Modern Art. It dates from 1684, when it was built as a hospital for military veterans. Constructed around a large inner courtyard, it is classically proportioned and the oldest secular non-military building in Ireland.

The first of the Liffey's 14 bridges, **Frank Sherwin Bridge** goes from Victoria to Wolfe Tone Quay. The whole of Victoria Quay is taken up by the **James' Gate Guinness Brewery** where the smell of the beer mingles with that of the Liffey. The brewery, also called the hop store, has been producing Ireland's world-famous black brew since 1759; it can now be visited as a museum and as a bar. Behind it are tiny red brick houses which once housed its workers, but are now prime yuppy residences.

Leading off from Arran Quay is **Smithfield**, with its network of tiny Victorian streets of redbrick houses converging on a small square. It has the nineteenth-century urban charm which developers are unable to resist: it's currently undergoing renovation. There are good fruit markets here, but, best of all, on the first Sunday of every month there is still a **horse market** in the small square. There are urban horse markets all over Ireland, but this is the only one in Dublin; it should not be missed. If you go out to the Northside suburbs of Tallaght and Ballyfermot, you can see kids riding around on horses much as in the films *The Commitments* and *Into the West*.

The central part of the quays is bounded by the **Four Courts** in the west and the **Custom House** in the east (*see chapter* **Architecture**). These are both eighteenth-century masterpieces by **James Gandon**, Dublin's greatest architect. These buildings remain Dublin's finest, in spite of the ravages of time, war and the Office of Public Works. Gandon's extraordinary and original techniques included constructing the foundations of the Custom House on wooden supports over a bog. To this day they haven't shifted an inch, enduring even the fire of the independence war of 1921, which blazed for five days courtesy of the IRA, reducing the building to a shell and immobilising British administration. The Four Courts cupola is also supported on wood; it survived being shot at in 1916 by the British, and then, during the civil war, a defence against the forces of Michael Collins' army which did far more damage than the actual attack. Both buildings fell into the hands of the OPW, and it is great testimony to their original design that they survived their restoration processes so well. But it is a shame that neither the King's Inns nor the Custom House is ever open to the public, although the latter has a visitors' centre.

The 1922 occupation of the Four Courts marked the start of the civil war. Led by de Valera, the IRA forces took it over for two months and were besieged by the forces of the new Free State government lead by Michael Collins. The government

The enduring image of the **Ha'penny Bridge**.

eventually starting shelling and the building was destroyed, being rebuilt in 1932. The Four Courts houses the Supreme and High Courts, so only the entrance hall beneath the great dome is open to visitors.

The Liffey continues on to **Ormond Quay**, which dates from 1678. The Ormond Multimedia centre is a great space which still needs much development. But in a city of mostly basement clubs, its huge warehouse space is a welcome place to dance. It's only an occasional venue, attracting one or two big names every month. Otherwise, it holds art exhibitions.

Across from Ormond Quay is **Wood Quay**; dating from 1200, it's the oldest of all the quays. It was a site of major Viking excavations, which have since been reburied by the unlovely Dublin Corporation building.

The **Ha'penny Bridge** goes from Temple Bar to the **Winding Stair**, best-loved of all Dublin's secondhand bookshops. The Ha'penny Bridge is a charming pedestrianised arched structure, built in 1816. It's officially known as the Liffey Bridge but, as there used to be a halfpenny toll crossing charge, its common name endures. The next bridge is the most important one – **O'Connell Bridge**, formerly Carlisle Bridge. Designed in 1794-98 by Gandon, it is wider than it is long.

Just beyond O'Connell Bridge, the distinctive copper-domed Custom House, topped with a sculpture of Commerce, is a landmark in the city. It is best viewed from across the river at George's Quay. It is classically proportioned and stretches for 114 metres along the quays. Along the portico are busts representing the gods of Ireland's 14 major rivers (only the Liffey is a goddess – even before Joyce, Dublin's river was taken as being female). Across the river from the Custom House, on Moss Street, is the **City Arts Centre**. Nearby is **Windmill Lane**, made famous by the Windmill Lane studio where U2 recorded many albums. There's a U2 wall, covered in fans' graffiti.

The rest of the quays stretch for miles along derelict sites until reaching Dublin Harbour where ferry services depart and arrive from Holyhead in Wales. It's a seedy, old-fashioned harbour with oily smells and dockside pubs. It's wonderful if you like the trappings of shipping. On the south bank is an empty, haunting view across to the **Pigeon House Fort,** now used as a power station, and out to **Poolbeg Lighthouse**.

The banks of the **Grand Canal**, *not used commercially since 1960, are ideal for a stroll.*

Georgian Dublin & Grand Canal

From St Stephen's Green to Ballsbridge lies the well-preserved heart of Georgian Dublin. It was not always so: Georgian building actually began on the Northside and the greatest single Georgian square in Dublin was **Mountjoy Square**, now sadly in decline. This area is also, unsurprisingly, the wealthiest quarter of the city. Close to the centre, it is a peaceful self-contained place, except for **Baggot Street** which is given over to lively shops and restaurants.

The Georgian buildings are WB Yeats' 'grey eighteenth-century houses'. Generally four storeys high over large basements, they line squares and streets and have no front gardens of their own. They are absolutely without exterior ornament except for the flamboyant colours of their doors. Well-bred, they keep their extravagance exclusively within, where beautifully proportioned spacious rooms have wild stucco plasterwork on walls and ceilings.

Merrion Square, whose former residents read like a *Who's Who* of nineteenth-century Ireland, is almost exclusively occupied by offices, clubs and organisations. Small oval plaques by the houses recount the names of former occupants. It is best to walk down **Merrion Square South**, as this is where many congregated. **WB Yeats** lived at No

Merrion Square – Georgian doors galore.

82 from 1922-28. Two doors down, at No 84, lived the poet and mystic, **George Russell**, also known by his cipher, Æ. The great horror story writer, **Joseph Sheridan Le Fanu** lived at No 70; the Austrian **Erwin Schrödinger**, co-winner of the 1933 Nobel Prize for physics, lived at No 65, and best loved of all, O'Connell lived at No 58, where a plaque, reading 'The Liberator' is situated. The British embassy used to occupy Merrion Square East, until it was burnt down in 1972 in protest against Bloody Sunday.

There are pretty gardens in the centre of the Square which seem labyrinthine until you get to the open space at the centre. There is a bust of Michael Collins at the south end. Now the subject of Neil Jordan's 1996 film, he was the architect of Irish independence.

At the west side of Merrion Square turning into Merrion Street Upper are two of the most important buildings in the city – **Leinster House** and the **National Gallery**. Leinster House is the Irish parliament, made up of the **Dáil** or lower house and the **Seanad** or upper house. It was built by Richard Castle in 1745-48 for the Earl of Kildare, who became Duke of Leinster in 1766. It was the premises of the Royal Dublin Society from 1814-1925, until the new government of independent Ireland decided to establish parliament there. The main entrance to Leinster House is on Kildare Street. In front of the Merrion Square entrance is an obelisk dedicated to Arthur Griffith, Michael Collins and Kevin O'Higgins, founders of independent Ireland.

The **National Gallery** is a small gallery with an excellent collection which is beautifully housed. The recently refurbished rooms are a pleasure to walk through. The gallery has major works by Caravaggio, Goya and Vermeer, and not to be missed is the room of Irish painters, including many canvases by Jack B Yeats, younger brother of the poet. He and Paul Henry, also shown here, evolved an impressionistic style uniquely suited to the Irish landscape.

At No 24 Merrion Street Upper, the Duke of Wellington was born. He was a self-made man, routing Napoleon and rising to a dukedom. He coined the great epitaph of self-made men from Christ onwards: 'Just because you're born in a stable, doesn't make you a horse.'

Merrion Square East used to run into Fitzwilliam Square in the longest unbroken line of Georgian houses in the world. Then, in 1961, the Electricity Supply Board knocked down 26 of them to build its hideous offices. Because all its finest houses were built by the British, the new Irish state had scant respect for its heritage and only in recent years has come around to protecting it. **Fitzwilliam Square**, completed in 1825, is the smallest, most discreet and most residential of the Georgian squares. It is immensely charming.

Park life

Given the organisation of Georgian buildings along carefully controlled vistas, and around squares, it is not surprising that parks and gardens play a prominent role, and that at almost any point within the city centre there is some oasis of greenery relatively close at hand. The largest park in the city – indeed within any city in Europe – is the Phoenix Park at 1,752 acres, which stands just beyond the end of the quays on the Northside.

As well as containing the presidential residence, Áras an Uachtaráin, the enormous extent of the park is staked out in monuments which reflect Ireland's history as an object of imperial interest; the presidential residence (formerly the Viceregal Lodge) stands opposite the residence of the American ambassador, while the Wellington Obelisk and the Papal Cross, proclaimers of the British and of the Catholic imperium, play pendant to one another. At the central crossroads of the Park is the Phoenix monument, a Corinthian column with the mythical bird emerging from a nest of flames, but even this monument, which commemorates the opening of the Park to the people of Dublin by Lord Chesterfield in 1747 has its own narrative of appropriation – the Park has little, if any, relation to the iconography of the bird, and the name 'phoenix' is a transliteration of the ancient name of the land 'fionn uisce', meaning 'bright waters'. Set out in grand avenues, the Park unfolds itself as a sequence of vistas, each of which which make very emphatic – and very diverse – statements about the scenographic creation of a landscape as a theatre for the symbols of colonialism.

The symbolic tensions of the Park are eased, or complicated by the fact that to the west it overlooks two burial grounds, one the monumental War Memorial gardens at Islandbridge, designed of all people by the colonial architect Edwin Lutyens, and the other being the land now in the area of Heuston Station, which is thought to contain Viking Burial Fields.

The Park itself lies in the area of the Dubh Linn, the site of the earliest monastic and Viking settlements, and it is to this area, and to the Park that Joyce keeps returning in *Finnegans Wake*, where the renamings and the real and symbolic appropriations of history become part of the universalising play of the mind.

Only residents have access to the lovely central garden. Protective shrubs are carefully grown around the gates.

Fitzwilliam Square leads on to **Leeson Street**, one of the nicest streets to walk down in Dublin. Wide, long and sloping, it has largely kept shops out and it cuts the canal with a buoyant bridge. Until very recently, all the basements from Leeson Bridge up to St Stephen's Green – an area known as the **Strip** – housed clubs. Since they only had wine licences, entrance was free and, dependent on the whim of the bouncer, once inside you might be forced to buy a bottle of plonk at a minimum of £25. It was sleazy, the music was dire and every Sunday morning Leeson Street was a debris of hot dogs and other regurgitated food. Slowly, new clubs began to open; U2 founded Kitchen and the rest is history. An evening walk down the new Leeson Street past the empty club premises induces immediate joy among Dubliners.

The busiest street in the area is **Baggot Street**, which has cheerfully knocked down many of its Georgian houses to make way for banks. Lower Baggot Street is a good place to eat. Notably, it has **Ayumi-ya** (good Japanese food) and, best of all, on James' Place, is **Restaurant Patrick Guilbaud**, which recently acquired a second Michelin star. It is the cheapest two-star restaurant in the world, which doesn't make it cheap. The food is exquisite and the décor beautifully simple with paintings by modern Irish masters Phelim Egan and Roderick O'Conor.

Both Baggot Street and Leeson Street cut the **Grand Canal** which connects Dublin to the river Shannon. It goes through south Dublin to Ringsend, while the **Royal Canal** heads off through north Dublin. Built between 1756-96, the Grand Canal was the longest canal in the British Isles. It has not been used commercially since 1960. Its pleasant grassy banks are used for leisure activities – lunching, walking and cycling. In summer, boys swim when the locks are full.

The pleasantest stretch of the canal is probably between Mount Street and Leeson Street. This is the territory of the poet **Patrick Kavanagh** who wrote 'The Great Hunger' about Catholic sexual repression. Famous in Ireland (though less so elsewhere) for his bleak themes, he also wrote a beautiful love song called 'Raglan Road' (it's just up from the canal in Ballsbridge), which has been sung by Irish singers from the Dubliners to Van Morrison and, more recently, Sinéad O'Connor. In his older years, he left off the themes of dejection and took to writing nature poems by the canals. There is a statue of him reclining on one of the benches here.

Howth harbour – *fishing and yachting centre, easily reached by DART from Dublin.*

If you take the ferry from Holyhead to Dublin, you see from afar the lovely horseshoe curve of Dublin Bay, with **Killiney Head** at the south end and **Howth Head** at the north. It is still a poignant sight, the last view the nineteenth-century emigrants had of their native land. All the best sights in Dublin outside the centre are along this curve and the way to get to them is by the DART. Make sure to sit on the side looking out to sea.

North

The Northside has fewer pretty seaside towns than the Southside, possibly because the coastline does not lend itself so well to swimming and there are fewer convenient coves. However, views at Howth Head are spectacular. **Howth** was once the main harbour in Dublin, and it was here that Erskine Childers' boat, the *Asgard*, landed German guns for the Irish Volunteers in 1914. The harbour is now a centre for fishing and yachting. The DART lets you off at the pretty town on the waterfront with steep, winding streets. It's not overdeveloped for tourism; most people make straight for Howth Head. This is a steep, clifftop walk where you are rewarded by dramatic views of the bay. You can rest on the way at the Summit pub.

Off Howth lies the tiny rocky island known as **Ireland's Eye**. This sea bird sanctuary incorporates the ruins of a sixth-century monastery and a distinctive Martello tower. Round, granite, with thick walls and slits for windows, Martello towers are a distinctive sight along the bay. Built as lookouts during the Napoleonic wars, they line the coast from Howth to Dalkey.

Further north from Howth is **Malahide**, which was built first as a summer seaside resort, but is now residential. It has kept its air of being a village a long way from the centre. It is not even accessible by DART, though you can take an intercity train from Pearse Station, or get a 42 bus from Beresford Place, besides Busáras.

Malahide town has small charming streets and comfortable houses in a variety of styles. The seashore is never far away (some 42s go along the coast road and deliver you straight to the beach) and it's not strikingly pretty when you get there, but you can swim in the eye of Ireland's Eye. However, watch out for the sea's strong pull. If you fancy a longer walk, start at Malahide and strike out along the strand for Portmarnock.

The town rests in the shadow of **Malahide Castle**, which is on a 300-acre site also containing the **Talbot Botanic Gardens** and the **Fry Model Railway**. The most remarkable thing about the Castle is that it remained in the Talbot family from the twelfth century until 1973 apart from the brief Cromwellian period (1649-60). The Castle was not open to the public until the 1970s, so many of the current residents of Malahide grew up circumventing this vast estate.

The Castle, with its Great Hall, its oak room, its family portraits and minstrel's gallery, should be visited. The grounds contain the fifteenth-century church of St Sylvester, where lie generations of Talbots. The Fry Model Railway is in a museum of its own. The layout is spread over 240 square metres and illustrates Ireland's rail system.

If you want to see a murder of crows, go to Malahide. The number of crows here is remarkable, even sinister. At twilight, the sky is black with them.

South

The Southside is punctuated with bathing spots. **Booterstown** is not a place to stop, but there's a good view from the DART. The marshy bird sanctuary with ducks, grebes, snipe, dunlin, tern and gulls is situated here. The marshlands hide the birds, but if you look towards the coast you see great flocks of them. The sands here go on for many miles, so that even when the the tide is in, it never comes up to the wall and the birds always have somewhere to cluster.

Two stops from Booterstown is **Seapoint**, an elegant Victorian bathing place which is still used for swimming. It has a group of hardy faithfuls who swim all year round; these are either fine old ladies or middle-aged men who hang around all day doing exercises between swims. Only on very hot days is it at all crowded.

Dún Laoghaire is the main port of call on the Southside. Although an important harbour, it has the slightly seedy, depressed air of a once-bustling nineteenth-century shipping town. This doesn't apply to the harbour itself with its two great piers, new state-of-the-art ferry depot, yachting clubs and pretty sailing boats. However, the main street is grim enough to make you stick to the shore.

Settled for over 1,000 years, Dún Laoghaire is named after a fifth-century king who was converted to Christianity by St Patrick. In 1821, it was renamed Kingstown to mark George IV's visit; in 1922, the Free State reverted to the town's old name. Construction of the harbour began in 1815 and rapidly grew into one of the biggest building endeavours in the British Isles. By the time the piers were completed, the project had cost over £1 million, an enormous sum for its time.

Dún Laoghaire – *sea breeze on the east pier.*

Two great piers encircle the harbour. The east pier is good for a walk. A stout sea breeze encourages you along to the lighthouse and gun-saluting station. On Sunday, families with children eating whipped ice-creams are out in force. There is a Victorian bandstand in the centre where you are more likely to catch puppet shows then bands.

Walk along the seafront and scramble over rocks to **Sandycove**. Here is a tiny sandy beach and beyond it the most famous bathing spot in Dublin, the **Forty Foot**. It takes its name from the the Fortieth Foot regiment, who were stationed at the Martello tower here during the nineteenth century. You can always get a swim here, whatever the tide. The Forty Foot used to be a (nude) gents-only venue. Now open to everyone, there is a sign warning 'Togs must be Worn'. Nude men still lurk resentfully behind rocks a little way from the main changing area. James Joyce lived for less than a week in 1904 in the Martello tower at the Forty Foot, which was time enough for him to set the great opening sequence of *Ulysses* here and to describe unforgettably 'the snotgreen scrotumtightening sea'. The Martello tower now houses the Joyce museum (*see chapter* **Literary Dublin**).

Behind the Forty Foot is **Caviston's**, the best delicatessen in the city, famous for its seafood. They now serve lunches which should not be missed. Get there before 3pm.

Continue along the coast to **Bullock Harbour**, the first of Dalkey's two harbours. Bullock Castle, built by St Mary's Abbey in the twelfth century, overlooks this. Five minutes' walk from this is **Dalkey**. This is a village of great charm which retains the feel of a small fishing town. There are magnificent views from Killiney Hill and lovely beaches below. These advantages have made Dalkey so attractive that it is now known, rather unoriginally, as 'Dalkeywood' by reason of its celebrity inhabitants who include Neil Jordan, Lisa Stansfield, Damon Hill and members of U2.

From Dalkey village, you walk down Coliemore Road and along the coast where you pass **Dalkey Island**. There are boats available from Coliemore Harbour out to the island, which is like a Southside version of Ireland's Eye. It's a bird sanctuary and home to wild goats. It has a Martello tower and the ruins of the medieval **St Begnet's Oratory**.

If you continue up Coliemore Road, you reach the most exclusive address in Dublin, Sorrento Terrace, where the great houses seem carved out of the hill and face across to a view that has been compared to the Bay of Naples. Carry on to Vico Road where there are more spectacular views. A lane at the end brings you up to the top of Killiney Hill. There is a wishing stone here and an obelisk which was built for the arrival of Queen Victoria to Kingstown. Stop here to take in the myriad views, north to Dublin, south to Wicklow before returning down the opposite side to Dalkey village.

Where do you find out what's happening in London?

http://www.timeout.co.uk

Time Out

Your weekly guide to the most exciting city in the world

Sightseeing

**IRELAND.
JET PROPELLED JOURNEYS IN HALF THE TIME.**

Take a trip from Holyhead to Dun Laoghaire on the Stena HSS and you'll fly there in style in just 99 mi
On board, you'll find a great choice of bars, restaurants, shopping, movies, games and children's play
Together, they make your crossing the most relaxed imaginable. Add our speedy Stena Lynx and Superf
and you'll see why no-one offers you more routes, more ships and more sailings to Ireland. So whether
going just for the day, a short break, or on holiday, call **0990 70 70 70** or see your Travel Agent. And di
why Stena Line leads the way to Ireland.

Stena Li

The next generation of ferry com

Sightseeing

Gape at mummified bodies or linger by St Valentine's bones: small wonder, then, if Bram Stoker hatched his Dracula idea here.

*Built in time to incarcerate the leaders of the 1798 Uprising – **Kilmainham Gaol** – see p47.*

Two attitudes will certainly increase your enjoyment of Dublin's sights – a sense of history and a sense of literature. The banknotes and statues give it away: Ireland has an inexhaustible supply of self-styled freedom fighters and writers. This is still the case. However, although it is wise to pick up some rudimentary history, and it is less bewildering if you know something of *Ulysses* before being exposed to the city's flourishing Joyce industry, you can nevertheless come to Dublin cold and enjoy it immediately. There's much to see.

Georgian houses have opened their doors to reveal the sumptuousness behind their stern exteriors; thirteenth-century castles offer their magnificent grounds and costly fittings for viewing; you can stroll through the elegant city gardens and try to take in all of Phoenix Park, the largest park in Europe. You can even reflect on the Phoenix Park Murders in 1882 and the political consequences that followed: wherever you are in Dublin, its history has a way of seeping through.

Attractions

Dublin Zoo

Phoenix Park, Dublin 8 (677 1425). Bus 10, 25, 26.
Open 9.30am-6pm Mon-Sat; 10.30am-6pm Sun.
Admission £5.80; £3.10 under-16s; £3 OAP; free under-3s; £15-£17 family.
For years famously depressing, Dublin Zoo is finally beginning to brighten up and has once more begun to attract visitors other than first communion children. It is, however, the third oldest zoo in the world (and it shows), but on a sunny day, set in Phoenix Park's 1,752 acres, it is a very pleasant place to be. Check out the new discovery centre. (*See also chapter* **Children's Dublin**.)

Glasnevin Cemetery

Finglas Road, Glasnevin, Dublin 11 (830 1133). Bus 40.
Open 8.30am-5pm daily. **Admission** free.
The anti-Catholic penal laws were so harsh and repressive that, even though there was no actual law forbidding burial in Catholic grounds, popular belief invented one and lived miserably in observance of it until Daniel O'Connell proved it unfounded. Even then, there was no place available in the existing, largely Protestant, cemeteries, so in 1832 he set up Glasnevin, or Prospect, cemetery on nine acres of ground. It

OLIVER PEOPLES

at

○ ○

O P T I (A

by Donal MacNally jnr.

1 ROYAL HIBERNIAN WAY DUBLIN
TEL 6774705 • FAX 6774706

*The Papal Cross, **Phoenix Park** – see p57.*

*The Long Room, **Trinity College** – see p56.*

now boasts 120 acres, with over one million people buried here. The old part of the cemetery is very Dickensian and atmospheric with crumbling walls, worn stone monuments and ivy. This is accessible through the old gates off Curran's Square, where you will also find the famous Gravediggers' pub. Daniel O'Connell's grave is easy to find, imposingly marked by a nineteenth-century version of an early Irish round tower, but it contains his body minus his heart, which is buried in Rome. Parnell is also buried here, in a mass grave among the people of Ireland, as he desired. A large boulder over the grave carries his name. Other famous cadavers include De Valera, Michael Collins, Gerard Manley Hopkins in the Jesuit plot, and Phil Lynott from Thin Lizzy. Different architectural and cultural movements are well represented by the sculptures, monuments and gravestones – many of which bear shamrocks, harps and wolfhounds, remnants of the Young Ireland movement.

Kilmainham Gaol

Inchicore Road, Kilmainham, Dublin 8 (453 5984). Bus 51, 51A, 78A, 79. **Open** *Apr-Sept* 9.30am-6pm daily; 4.45pm last admission. *Oct-Mar* 9.30am-5pm Mon-Fri; 4pm last admission; 10am-6pm Sun. **Admission** by guided tour only: £2; £1 children, students; £1.50 OAPs; £5 family.

This massive landmark of Irish life and history was built just in time to incarcerate the leaders of the 1798 Uprising, a role it repeated during the rebellions of 1803, 1848, 1867 and, most famously, 1916. The huge grey stone building remains fairly gloomy and intimidating. It was redesigned during the Victorian era along the lines of Pentonville prison (where Roger Casement was hanged following the 1916 Rising), to try out some popular theories of the time. The idea was to keep prisoners under constant supervision – hence the open plan arrangement of cells and the still visible strips of padded carpet running alongside them, which allowed

guards to creep up within easy distance of the peephole cut into each door. This new wing will be familiar to anyone who has seen *In the Name of the Father*. The prison catered for men, women and children; in the early part of the nineteenth century an eight-year-old was remanded there for five months' hard labour for stealing a cloak. The list of those who spent time here reads like a role call of Nationalist heroes – Robert Emmet, John O'Leary, Joseph Plunkett, Pearse, De Valera (who had the honour of being the last ever prisoner released from the jail). Even Parnell spent some time here – in a cell that, even now, is in striking contrast to those around it. Noticeably brighter and more spacious than the others, it was positively luxurious while he occupied it. He was allowed his own furniture, received private visits from Kitty O'Shea, and there is even a rumour that he had his own key. The prison chapel has a very melancholy air – it is here in May 1916 that Plunkett married his fiancée, Grace Gifford, just hours before being executed in Breaker's Yard, the scene of 14 executions in just ten days and still a very grim place. The boat in dry dock is the *Asgard*, Erskin Childers' vessel which successfully negotiated the British blockade and landed guns for the Irish Volunteers at Howth in 1912. (*See also chapter* **Museums & Art Galleries**.)
AV presentation. Disabled: access. Group discounts.

Castles

Malahide Castle & Fry Railway Museum

Malahide Castle Demesne, Malahide, Co Dublin (846 3779). Bus 42/rail Malahide. **Castle open** *Apr-Oct* Mon-Fri 10am-5pm; 11am-5pm Sat, Sun, Bank Holidays; *Nov-Mar* 10am-5pm Mon-Fri; 2-5pm Sat, Sun, Bank Holidays. **Closed** 12.45-2pm. **Admission** £2.95; £1.60 3-11 yrs; £2.45 12-18 yrs; £7.95 family. **Railway Museum open** *Apr-Sept* 10am-6pm Mon-Thur; 11am-6pm Sat; 2-6pm

The smoothest whiskey you'll meet on your travels

Before maturing our whiskey for many years, we like to distil it a third time. We think you'll find this rather unique finishing touch gives our whiskey an exceptional smoothness.

JAMESON® The Spirit of Ireland

Sun, Bank Holidays. **Closed** Fri. *June-Aug* 10am-6pm Fri; *Oct-Mar* 2-5pm Sat, Sun, Bank Holidays. **Closed** for tours 1-2pm. **Open** on request (846 2184). **Admission** £2.65; £2 concs; 3-11-yrs £1.50; £7.25 family. Combined Malahide Castle/Newbridge House tickets available.

The castle was only opened to the public in 1975; for 800 years before that it was owned by the Talbot family, bar a small interlude during Cromwellian times, when it was presented to the regicide Miles Corbet. It stands in nearly 300 acres of land and combines an interesting, if haphazard, arrangement of architectural styles. In the grounds is a 20-acre botanic garden laid down by Lord Milo Talbot. The oldest part is a twelfth-century square tower, while the main body of the castle is post-medieval. Inside there is some good rococo plasterwork and some remnants of what was the finest collection of eighteenth- and early nineteenth-century furniture in the country. Part of the National Portrait collection is on loan to Malahide Castle, and the family's own collection is large. In the Great Hall is Van Wyck's magnificent commemoration of the 1690 Battle of the Boyne, a reminder of one of the sadder Talbot family tales; 14 members of the family gathered to breakfast in the hall on the morning of the battle, then rode off together to fight for the Catholic King James. Not one came back. Also in the Great Hall is a small pointed door leading to Puck's Tower. Puck was so misshapen and crooked, he was given the job of watchman, being unequal to greater tasks. Unfortunately, he wasn't much good at that either. Enemies attacked the castle while Puck napped and, in shame, he hanged himself; he comes back to express his displeasure every once in a while – the last sighting was in 1975 when the Castle was being auctioned. Behind the castle are the ruins of the fifteenth-century abbey, dedicated to St Sylvester. The carvings included two Shelia-na-gigs and in the nave is the wonderful effigy tomb of Maud Plunkett who was 'Maid, wife and widow' all in one day. Her husband, Lord Galtrim, was called away to battle on their wedding day, Whit Monday 1429, and killed. This prompted Gerald Griffin to write his maudlin ballad 'The Bridal of Malahide'. In fact, he needn't have bothered; she then married Sir Richard Talbot, and outlived him to marry

a third time. In the Castle grounds, you'll find the **Fry Model Railway**, a delight for children. This is the largest of its kind in Ireland and gives a minutely accurate tour of most of Ireland's rail system and surrounding terrain; trees, houses, stations, bridges, barges, rivers and bus are all lovingly recreated to form a very charming overview of Ireland's transport system. It even includes the DART and Irish Sea ferry services. The models are all painstakingly handmade and many date back to the 1920s (*See chapters* **Children's Dublin** and **Museums & Art Galleries**.)

Bookshop. Disabled: access. Foreign-language tours.

Newbridge House

Donabate, Co Dublin (843 6534/846 2184). Bus 33B. **Open** *Apr-Sept* 10am-5pm Tue-Fri; 11am-6pm Sat; 2-6pm Sun, Bank Holidays. **Closed** 1-2pm. *Oct-Mar* 2-5pm Sat, Sun, Bank Holidays. Open on request outside these hours for groups of 20 plus. **Admission** £2.75; £2.45 concessions; £1.50 3-11 yrs; £7.50 family. Combined Malahide Castle/Newbridge House tickets available.

Although not actually a castle, it was designed by Richard Castle and is definitely a manor; built in 1737 for the Archbishop of Dublin. It has one of the most complete and exquisite Georgian interiors in Ireland, with incredible stucco work is by Robert West. Fingal County Council bought it under much the same circumstances as led to their acquiring Malahide Castle – only this time, learning by their mistakes, they isolated a set of private apartments for the Cobbe family (whose coat of arms bears the evocative motto, 'Dying I Sing'), who still live there, in return for keeping intact the original furniture which would otherwise have suffered the same fate as the contents of Malahide Castle and been dispersed at auction. Each room has its own distinct style, virtually unaltered in 150 years. Of particular note are the Red Drawing Room, ceiling by William Stuccoman, and the Museum of Curiosities. Here, among stuffed birds and snake-skins you can find such rarities as bricks from Babylon, an African chief's umbrella, a mummified head and an Indian dancing-girl's hair-plait. The courtyard has been restored and is surrounded by artisans' workshops filled with their

Unitarian Church, *aka the 'Pepper Canister Church' for obvious reasons – see page 53.*

Car rental in Ireland reaches new levels of professionalism and service with *Access Car Rentals*. Hire a car next time you visit Ireland be it for a holiday driving around the Ring of Kerry or to Dublin on business, be sure to arrange your transport with us. Reasonable rates, immaculately prepared new vehicles and an extremely high level of service are only some of the many benefits our customers enjoy. We are located in the **Dublin International Airport Complex** for your convenience.

All prices include:

▼ **FREE COLLECTION / DELIVERY**

▼ **INSURANCE & C.D.W.**

▼ **GOVERNMENT TAX**

▼ **UNLIMITED MILEAGE**

▼ **24 HOUR BREAKDOWN SERVICE**

Tel: 844 4848

DUBLIN AIRPORT, IRELAND

Telephone: 353-1-844 4848

Approved by:

Bord Fáilte
Irish Tourist Board

E-mail: access@indigo.ie
http://indigo.ie/~accesscr

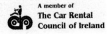
A member of
The Car Rental
Council of Ireland

Malahide Castle *combines an interesting arrangement of architectural styles – see p47.*

nineteenth-century tools. Pay particular attention to the Lord Chancellor's amazing coach in the stables, as it has a claim to being the best ever executed example of carriagework. In the 350 acres of undulating pastureland, watercourses and pleasure grounds is a traditional farm with old fashioned, storybook breeds of goats, sheep, giant hens and an incredibly ugly Vietnamese pot-bellied pig; miniature horses and donkeys can be petted and there is an outdoor aviary full of peacocks and partridges. These grounds are open from 10am-5pm during winter and to 9pm in the summer. (*See chapter* **Museums & Art Galleries.**)
Café. Craft shop. Disabled: no access. Multi-lingual tours.

Churches

Ireland may have the most committed church-going population in Europe, but it is far from having the finest churches. You will find neither exquisite examples of different eras, nor costly fittings. There are good historical reasons for this, both to do with poverty and repression. The few remnants left over from the ransacking of the monasteries suggest that the medieval period must have been glorious, but there has been little of note since then. A few charming Anglican churches were built for the Protestant Ascendancy and today all the most beautiful churches in Dublin are still Anglican (Church of Ireland), an unusual situation given that C of I currently makes up about 3 per cent of the population. Two of the three cathedrals in Dublin and the two oldest and grandest churches in the city, Christchurch and St Patrick's Cathedral, are both Church of Ireland. As these were originally Norman, a strong case might have been made for returning one of them to Catholicism upon independence.

Christchurch Cathedral

Christchurch Place, Dublin 8 (677 8099). Bus 50, 78A. **Open** 10am-5pm Mon-Fri; 10am-4.30pm Sat; 12.30-3pm Sun. **Services** *Eucharist* 12.45pm Mon-Fri (Lady Chapel); *choral evensong* 6pm Thur, 5pm Sat (not July-Aug); *sung Eucharist & sermon* 11am Sun; *choral evensong* 3.30pm. **Donation** £1.
This is a fine Norman church, founded in 1172 by Richard de Clare, known as Strongbow, who has the distinction of being Ireland's first English invader. An earlier wooden church, dating from 1038, had previously occupied the site. Only the south transept, the north wall, the western part of the choir and the huge crypt remain from Strongbow's time. The rest was restored in 1871-78 by the architect George Edward Street. His restoration must have been faithful because the church has kept a rather forbidding Norman feel. It is high, dark and grey inside with stone sculptures, including one of Strongbow, reclining in full armour. The most unique feature is the vast crypt (in the lower church), one of the largest in the British Isles, which extends under the entire church. The charming bridge leads into what was the Synod Hall and is now Dublinia, an audio-visual exhibition recreating both specific moments in Dublin's history and the daily life of medieval Dublin (*see also chapter* **Museums & Art Galleries**). Throughout its long and chequered history, this church has seen many things: Edward VI was crowned king of England here in 1487 and, a hundred years later, Henry VIII burned it, after which, it was turned into law courts and even, during the time of James II, became Catholic for a while. Almost the best way to appreciate Christchurch's dramatic architectural qualities is to view it from the nearby quays where it looms upwards, impressive against the hills.

Newman University Church

87A St Stephen's Green South, Dublin 2 (478 0616). Bus 10, 11, 13, 14, 14A, 15A, 15B. **Open** 8.45am-2pm daily. **Admission** free.
This is the Catholic Newman University Church, and University College Dublin's answer to the privileged tradition of Trinity College. A favourite place for society weddings, its opulent, neo-Byzantine interior found little favour when

it was built in 1854-56, but time has mellowed such objections and its extravagant décor now makes it one of Dublin's most fashionable churches.

Disabled: access.

St Michan's Church

Church Street Lower, Dublin 7 (872 4154). **Open** 10am-4.45pm, 2-2.45pm, Mon-Fri; 10am-1pm Sat. **Admission** £1.20; 50p children.

Reasons to visit here range from the general interest to the grotesque. Rumour has it that Handel gave the first ever performance of his *Messiah* on the church organ, which dates from 1724. Below the church are seventeenth-century vaults composed of magnesium limestone, which dries the atmosphere so much that the bodies buried there have been preserved. It makes a gruesome, but hugely popular, attraction. St Michan's occupies the site of the first suburban church of Norse Dublin (1096), although little remains from this era. The current building dates from 1685-86, but was drastically restored in 1828 and again, following the civil war, giving the whole place a somewhat inconclusive air.

St Patrick's Cathedral

Patrick's Close, Dublin 8 (475 4817). Bus 50, 54A, 56A. **Open** *Apr-Oct* 9am-5pm Mon-Sat; *Nov-Mar* 9am-4pm Mon-Sat; 10am-4.30pm Sun. **Services**

Pedestal japes

Dublin has few statues of intrinsic aesthetic beauty and most are made interesting only by association and by historical context. An exception to this is Oisin Kelly's lovely 1966 sculpture of the **Children of Lir** in the Garden of Remembrance. Made on the fiftieth anniversary of the Easter Rising, its subject – the four children turned into swans by the evil stepmother – is one of the most famous and tragic of Ireland's ancient legends.

O' Connell Street is the main thoroughfare of statues. At the bottom of the street, on O'Connell Bridge, is a fine statue of **O'Connell** himself, made by John Henry Foley in 1854. Around its base are four winged Victories – Patriotism, Fidelity, Eloquence, Courage. These represent O'Connell's special virtues and were made by Thomas Brock in 1882, eight years after Foley's death. Bang in the middle of one Victory's nipple is a bullet hole, sustained during the 1916 Rising.

The street is bordered at its Parnell Square end by a monument to **Charles Stewart Parnell** as seen by the American sculptor Augustus St Gaudens, in 1911. Parnell is throwing his arm flamboyantly to the right and above him is the quotation, 'No Man has the Right to set a Boundary on the March of a Nation. No Man has the Right to say Thus far shalt thou Go and No Further.' In the middle of the street, just outside the GPO, stands Oisin Kelly's attractive statue of **Jim Larkin**, trade unionist and instigator of the 1913 general strike. He, too, displays an energetic pose; made in 1979, it is a fitting tribute to a man who was so loved by his people.

On the corner of O'Connell and North Earl Streets, a natty and nonchalant **James Joyce** appear in bronze, looking like the dandy he was. Made in 1991 by the writer's nephew, Ken Moynihan, Joyce is sardonically facing the dreadful statue of the 'Floozy in the Jacuzzi', a work supposed to represent his **Anna Livia**, the spirit of the River Liffey in *Finnegans Wake*.

Children of Lir – *Garden of Remembrance.*

In fact, Dublin's famously caustic and irreverent wit has applied itself, with zeal, to the city's statues. The **Molly Malone** statue on College Green quickly became 'the Tart with the Cart', while 'the Hags with the Bags' can be found on Liffey Street, commemorating the area's long trading tradition. In 1996, huge sums of National Lottery money were spent designing a millennium countdown clock and installing it in the Liffey at O'Connell Bridge. Within days it was known as 'the Time in the Slime'.

Eucharist 8.30am daily; *choral matins* 9.40am Mon-Fri (school term only); 11.15am Sun; *choral evensong* 5.45pm Mon-Thur; 5.30pm Fri; 3.15pm Sun. **Donation** £1.20.

St Patrick's Cathedral is the oldest Christian site in Dublin. St Patrick himself is supposed to have baptised the Irish pagans in a well beside the building; there has been a church here since 450. The present building dates from 1191. Like Christchurch, it was extensively restored in the nineteenth century. Although St Patrick's doesn't share the same commanding position as Christchurch, it has the more interesting associations. It is for ever linked with Jonathan Swift, who was Dean here between 1713-45. His tomb is in the church beside that of his companion, Stella, and its Latin inscription translates as *'Here He Lies, Where Savage Indignation Can No Longer Lacerate His Heart'.* Swift gave himself this epitaph, an oddly gloomy one for a Christian dean, but a most appropriate one for the greatest satirist in the English language. Swift's servant, Alexander McGee, is also buried here, in the south-west corner. A hole cut in the old door of the chapter-house is the result of a quarrel between the two great Norman earls, Kildare and Ormond, in 1492. During a duel, Ormond took refuge inside the chapter-house. Later the dispute was settled and a hole cut in the door so that the two men could shake hands safely, hence the expression 'chancing your arm'. In the north choir aisle is the stone with which Swift marked the grave of the Duke of Schomberg, who was William III's general and who died at the Battle of the Boyne in 1690. The cathedral choir school dates back to 1432. These days it performs on Tuesdays and from Thursday to Sunday in July and August.
Disabled: access.

Unitarian Church

St Stephen's Green West, Dublin 2 (478 0638). DART Pearse Station/bus 7, 7A, 8, 45, 63, 84. **Open** 12.30-2.30pm Mon-Fri. **Services** *Eucharist* 11am Sun; 11.30am Wed. **Admission** free.

Throughout Dublin this is known as the 'Pepper Canister Church', an apt nickname which precisely captures its appearance and Greek revival-style architecture. Better outside than in, it is best seen from the far end of Merrion Square, near Leinster House. At night, it is well-lit and appears enigmatic. Unfortunately, its position on a traffic island has recently made it a very popular beat for prostitutes. Nevertheless, it manages to be a fully functioning Anglican church, although it specialises in Christmas carol singing, weddings and concerts. Shape and location have made this church an endlessly popular location for films – it features three times in *Michael Collins* alone. East of the church is Huband Bridge, one of the most attractive canal bridges.

Whitefriar Street Carmelite Church

Whitefriar Street, off Aungier Street, Dublin 8 (475 8821). Bus 16, 16A, 19, 19A, 22, 22A. **Open** 8am-6.30pm Mon, Wed-Fri; 8am-9.30pm Tue; 8am-7pm Sat; 8am-7.30pm Sun; 9.30am-1pm Bank Holidays. **Admission** free.

The church stands on the site of a thirteenth-century Carmelite Priory zealously suppressed by Henry VIII in 1537. Its lands and wealth were seized and the Priory itself fell into complete ruin; now nothing at all remains of the original building. But it was not forgotten; three centuries later the Carmelites returned and opened a new church largely designed by George Papworth, architect of St Mary's Pro-Cathedral, Dublin's only Catholic cathedral. The church is the scene of many romantic pledges as its altar contains the remains of St Valentine, the patron saint of lovers. These were donated by Pope Gregory XVI in 1835. Also worth checking is the life-sized oak figure of Our Lady of Dublin, believed to be the only wooden statue to escape the ravages of the Reformation.

Focal points

Dublin Castle

Dame Street, Dublin 2 (677 7129). Bus 49, 50, 54A, 77, 77A. **Open** 10am-5pm Mon-Fri; 2-5pm Sat, Sun. **Admission** £2; £1 student.

Once the seat of British power in Ireland, the Castle is constructed on the foundations of a Viking fortress, parts of which can be seen in the subterranean undercroft. The oldest surviving visible building is the thirteenth-century Record Tower, from which the flamboyant Red Hugh O'Donnell escaped in 1591 and, again, in 1592. Other buildings have been gradually added over the centuries so that there is now a grand mixture of styles. The guided tour is much recommended as you get to hear the colourful history of the castle and see the great state apartments, which are among the finest interiors in the country. (*See also chapter* **Museums & Art Galleries**.)
Café. Disabled: access to state apartments. Guided tours. Multi-lingual tours. Shop. Theatre.

General Post Office

O'Connell Street, Dublin 1 (705 7000). DART Connolly Station/all cross city buses. **Open** 8am-8pm Mon-Sat. **Admission** free.

A landmark which is as much physical as it is historical, the GPO was designed by Francis Johnston and opened in 1818. In 1916, Patrick Pearse read his proclamation of an Irish republic from its steps, then barricaded himself and his army inside. During the ensuing siege the building was completely burnt out. Six years later, the outbreak of civil war did further damage and it was not reopened until 1929. You can still put your fingers in the bullet holes which riddle the columns and façade. The steps of the GPO are still used as a rallying-point for demonstrations and protests of every kind. The inside is wonderfully spacious and tends to trap what light

Death of Cuchulainn *in* **General Post Office**.

Subscribe now to i-D to receive 12 issues
full of the latest i-Deas, fashion, clubs, music and people.

SUBSCRIPTIONS

| annual subscription rates (please choose) | uk ☐ (£30.00) | europe ☐ (£40.00) | world(airmail) ☐ (£60.00) |

Access/Visa number:

☐☐☐☐☐☐☐☐☐☐☐☐☐☐☐☐

Signature:_____

Expiry date:_____

Name:_____
Address:_____
_____
_____

Tel:_____
Date:_____

If you do not have a credit card send a cheque/ postal otder in pounds sterlingmade payable to Levelprint Ltd. Do not forget to fill in your name and address. Return the above form to i-D, Universal House, 251-255, Tottenham Court Road, London, W1P 0AE. For enquiries please call 0171 813 6170

James Gandon's **Custom House** *– see page 65 – most distinguished river front in the city.*

there is; most of the features and fittings have been respectfully preserved. Near a window and visible from the outside is the beautiful *Death of Cuchulainn*, a statue by Oliver Sheppard commemorating the building's reopening. Cuchulainn, legendary knight of the Red Branch and admired heroic ideal, is said to have died at the age of only 27. Such was the awe and terror he inspired in his enemies that even after killing him none dared approach his body until some ravens landed on his shoulders, proving that he was dead.

Leinster House

Kildare Street, Dublin 2 (618 3000). DART Pearse Station/bus 5, 7, 7A, 7X, 8, 10, 18, 45, 63, 84. **Open** by prior arrangement with the Public Relations office. **Admission** free.

Open to the public only when parliament is not sitting, this is the seat of Oireachtas na hÉireann, Ireland's legislature. Both the Dáil (lower house) and the Seanad (senate or upper house) meet here, in the first of Dublin's great eighteenth-century houses to be built south of the Liffey. The Seanad meets in the sumptuous north wing saloon, the Dáil in a rather grubby room added on as a lecture theatre in 1897. The house was begun by Richard Castle for the earl of Kildare in 1745, and changed its name with him in 1766 when he became Duke of Leinster. It is jealously guarded by the National Library on one side and the National Museum (*see chapter* **Museums & Art Galleries**) on the other, both the result of enthusiastic activity by the Royal Dublin Society who owned the house between 1815-1922, when the Irish Free State government bought them out. The house has two formal fronts: the Kildare Street frontage, designed to look like a townhouse, and the other on Merrion Square. Like a country house, they are connected by a long central corridor. The house has been claimed as the prototype for the White House in the United States, which was built by James Hoban who was born in 1762 in County Carlow. The entrance hall and principal rooms were redecorated towards the end of the eighteenth century with the help of James Wyatt and are fine, noble chambers. On Leinster Lawn there stands an obelisk dedicated to the founders of the Irish Free State – Michael Collins, Arthur Griffith and Kevin O'Higgins. A statue of

Bombs away

In Dublin, few statues have escaped the rebel's bomb. The most notorious bombing was of **Nelson's Column** which stood in the middle of O'Connell Street. Built in 1817, it predated Nelson's Column in Trafalgar Square. The IRA blew it up in 1966 on the occasion of the fiftieth anniversary of the Easter Rising. Nelson's head is now in the Dublin Civic Museum. **William of Orange** (still the most important figure for Ulster Unionists) used to sit on his white horse in College Green. He was bombed in 1836, and then again in 1929. Another keen equestrian, **George II**, formerly situated on St Stephen's Green, was blown off his horse in 1937, and **Field Marshal Gough**, previously of Phoenix Park, had his head and sword sawn off in 1944 before being bombed in 1956 and, then again, conclusively, in 1957.

Not only figures of the British imperialist past have fallen victim to the bombing mania. Edward Delaney's statue in St Stephen's Green of the great Republican, **Wolfe Tone**, was blown up by the UVF in 1989. The head was found by the Shelbourne Hotel. The statue was reconstructed and still stands guard on the corner of the Green.

*Students working flat out at **Trinity College**.*

Prince Albert by John Henry Foley has been retained, although Queen Victoria's statuesque likeness was removed in 1948. No cameras or recording equipment allowed.
Free tours.

Trinity College

Trinity College, Dublin 2 (677 2941). Entrances at Nassau Street, College Green, Pearse Street. DART Pearse Station/all cross city buses. **Open** *Old Library & Book of Kells 9.30am-5pm Mon-Sat; Oct-May noon-4.30pm Sun; June-Sept 9.30am-4.30pm Sun.* **Closed** 10 days over Christmas & New Year. **Admission** £3.50; £3 students; £7 family; under-12s free.

All the great streets of Dublin lead off from Trinity College's grounds. It's a prestigious university of 9,500 students and also one of Ireland's most important historical sites, boasting the finest buildings in the city and displaying, among other treasures, the **Book of Kells**. Trinity College Dublin (TCD) was founded in 1592 by Elizabeth I as the Oxbridge of the Anglo-Irish Ascendancy. Catholics were admitted in 1793, but until 1970 they had to get a special dispensation from the Archbishop of Dublin to be allowed to attend (*see chapter* **History**). Of particular note is Lanyon's 30-metre **Campinile** in Library Square, with beautiful old maple trees beside it. Also check out the multi-denominational chapel in Front Square; Pomodoro's **Sphere within a Sphere** in front of the **Berkeley Library**; the cricket pitch and the new state-of-the-art **Samuel Beckett Theatre**. There are often lunchtime and evening plays showing here during term time. Dating from the eighth century, the **Book of Kells** (in TCD's Colonnade gallery) is an extraordinary testament to the early Christian monks' passion and learning. Reading the Gospels would be a slow business, however: only one page is turned each day. (*See also chapter* **Museums & Art Galleries**.)
Café. Disabled: access located in Arts Block. Group discounts available. Multi-lingual brochures. Shop. Tours.

Notable buildings

Bank of Ireland & House of Lords

2 College Green, Dublin 2 (677 6801). All cross city buses. **Open** 10am-4pm Mon-Wed, Fri, 10am-5pm Thur. **Tours** 10.30am, 11.30am, 1.45pm, Tue. **Admission** free.

Obviously, banks always get the best buildings in a city, but it is not just on its architectural merit that you should visit the Bank of Ireland's headquarters. It has seen more exciting debates than those centred around the fall of the Irish pound. Constructed in 1729 as the seat of the Irish Parliament, it kept this role for only 70 short years. In 1800, it voted for its own abolition and the Act of Union made Ireland part of Great Britain. The former House of Commons has been subsumed into the bank, but the oak-lined House of Lords has been kept intact. Its eighteenth-century tapestries depict the 1689 Siege of Londonderry and the 1690 Battle of the Boyne, both Protestant victories which are celebrated noisily every year by Orangemen in the north. (*See also chapter* **Museums & Art Galleries**.)
Disabled: access. Free guided tours.

Casino at Marino

Malahide Road (entrance opposite Clontarf Golf Club), Dublin 3 (833 1618). Bus 20A, 20B, 27, 27A, 27B, 32A, 42, 42B, 42C, 43. **Open** *May-mid-June, Nov* noon-4pm Sun, Wed; *mid-June-Sept* 9.30am-6.30pm daily; *Oct* 10am-5pm daily. **Admission** £2; £1 concs; £5 family.

This little-visited house is actually one of the best and most unusual sights in the city. It is an architectural conceit in a no-nonsense Georgian city. It is not, of course, a casino, but a small house designed by Sir William Chambers for the Earl of Charlemont in the eighteenth century. From the outside, it looks like a folly: you imagine one largish room within. In fact, it's a magical complex of tiny rooms spread over three floors and has in miniature everything one would expect to find in a house of that time, including a butler's pantry and servants' hall. The windows are deliberately blackened to conceal the presence of these convoluted and cunning rooms, and the huge, imposing front door is nothing but a trick – entry is actually via a small panel. Inside, there are all the fairytale tricks of concealment, disguise and deception: columns that act as drains, huge urns inside which lurk heaters, wall drapes that turn out to be carved. There is a zodiac room and a Chinese room, and even an underground tunnel leading to Charlemont House. Charlemont's estate did not long survive his death; the townhouse on Parnell Square, also designed by Sir William Chalmers, became the Municipal Art Gallery and the Casino, despite its rare and exquisite interior, was neglected for many years. Restoration of it only began during the 1970s. In 1919-21, its large underground out-buildings were used as a soundproof arms training school by the IRA. Charlemont's eccentricities clearly irritated some people, and, in 1792, the painter Charles Folliot contrived to insult him by building a terrace of rather beautiful houses, Marino Crescent, just where they would obscure his view of the sea. No 15 is where Bram Stoker was born. (*See also chapter* **Museums & Art Galleries**.)

Newman House

85-86 St Stephen's Green, Dublin 2 (706 7422/706 7419). Bus 10, 46A. **Open for guided tours** noon, 2-4pm Tue-Fri; 2-4pm Sat; *June-Aug* 11am, noon Sun. **Admission** £2; £1 concs.

The original premises of University College Dublin, founded by Cardinal Newman, taught in by Gerard Manley Hopkins and attended by James Joyce. Although these names are draw enough for most, Newman House is also probably the finest example of eighteenth-century Georgian architecture open to the public, with lavish reception rooms and superb plasterwork by the Swiss stuccodores Paolo and Fillipo Lafranchini. All this makes it one of the best sights in the city, but for years it lay neglected and restoration only

Sir Robert Smirke's Wellington Monument in **Phoenix Park**, *the largest city park in Europe.*

began in 1989. This is still on-going and the interior has a rather pleasant, unfinished feel. Newman House is actually two houses. No 85 was built in 1738 for Hugh Montgomery, an Irish MP, and purchased in 1865 by the Catholic University of Ireland. The classical plasterwork was found then to be too outrageous and the fine female nudes were covered up. Juno's curves are still hidden by a rough costume but other figures have been returned to nature. No 86 was begun in 1765 by Richard Whaley, father of the notorious gambler and founder of the Hell-Fire Club, 'Buck' Whaley. It, too, was later purchased by the Catholic University. Here, perfectly preserved, at the top of the house is Hopkins' bedroom/study. (*See chapter* **Museums & Art Galleries**.)

Parks

These stay open during the hours of daylight, but be careful towards twilight – not much warning is given and it is possible to get locked in.

National Botanic Gardens

Finglas Road, Glasnevin, Dublin 9 (837 7596/837 4388). Bus 13, 19, 134. **Open** *summer* 9am-6pm Mon-Sat; 11am-6pm Sun; *winter* 10am-4.30pm Mon-Sat; 11am-4.30pm Sun. **Admission** free.
Usually virtually empty, these gardens are magical, with just the right mix of the exotic and the dilapidated. At eight acres they are big enough, and untidy enough, to get lost in. The glasshouses were built between 1843-69 by Richard Turner, who is responsible for the Belfast Botanic Gardens'

glasshouse and the Palm House in Kew Gardens. The yew-walk beside the river Tolka has trees dating back to the early eighteenth century and is particularly lovely.

Phoenix Park

Dublin 7. Bus 25, 26, 66, 67, 51.
This is a really wonderful place, at 1,752 acres the largest city park in Europe, with an invigorating mixture of formal, elegantly laid-out gardens, huge expanses of casual fields, wild undergrowth and beautiful, mature trees. The land which makes up the park was seized from Kilmainham Priory during the Reformation; a viceregal residence, the Phoenix, was built and a royal deer park established – indeed, there are still plenty of easy-going deer around. The huge **Wellington Monument** is well worth a look; by Sir Robert Smirke, it stands on the south side of the main road. The towering **Papal Cross** is definitely not to be missed; it was put up in 1979 and marks the gathering of one million people who came to hear Pope John Paul II say, 'Young people of Ireland, I love you.' The residence of the Irish President, **Áras an Uachtaráin**, formerly that of the Lord Lieutenant, is near the beautiful **Phoenix Column**. Within sight of this residence on May 6 1882, the Phoenix Park Murders took place. Lord Frederick Cavendish, recently-arrived Chief Secretary of Ireland, and TH Burke, the Under-Secretary, were stabbed to death in an episode which poisoned and embittered Anglo-Irish relations for years to come. The home of the American ambassador, a gracious eighteenth-century house, is also in the Park. The **Phoenix Park Visitor Centre**, on the grounds of the old papal nunciature, has both a castle and an information centre. (*See also chapter* **Dublin by Area: Park life**.)

*Fortunately, hangings, whippings and burnings are things of the past at **St Stephen's Green**.*

St Stephen's Green

Dublin 2. All cross city buses.

If it's sunny in Dublin city centre, this is the place to be. Ponds, rustling trees and ducks set against formal walks and fine statues make it pleasant, restful and very popular. Originally, it was mucky common ground and the site of such spectator sports as public hangings, whippings and burnings. Sir Arthur Guinness (Lord Ardilaun) made it what it is today by financing the laying out of the ponds and gardens in 1880, so, in respectful commemoration, there is a statue of him by John Henry Foley, who also made the statue of Sir Benjamin Lee Guinness in St Patrick's Cathedral. Nearby is one of Robert Emmet which has a twin in Washington DC. In the centre of the park, dotted around a fountain stand busts of Countess Marcievicz and James Clarence Mangan, and a very odd sculpture of WB Yeats by Henry Moore. James Joyce is to be found by Queen Victoria's Jubilee Bandstand, while the Three Fates, a gift from the German people thanking Ireland for aid given in the aftermath of World War II, are in the corner near to Leeson Street. In 1916, the park was occupied for a short time by a contingent of the Citizen Army; its main entrance, the Fusilier's Arch commemorating the Irish dead in the Boer War, was riddled with bullets in the exchange of fire between the Irish Nationalists who had occupied the Royal College of Surgeons, and the British army, based in the Shelbourne Hotel. However, the damage is quite uneven –

the side facing the Nationalist rebels is virtually unmarked, their bullets were so precious that none was fired randomly, while the British could afford to blast away extravagantly. This arch is at the north-west corner, opposite Grafton Street.

Tours of Dublin

On foot, by horse-drawn carriage or in open-topped double-decker bus, there is a big selection to choose from. Some concentrate on historical Dublin, others favour its literary, Georgian, musical or revolutionary aspects. Some take the form of pub crawls and others follow a prescribed physical route. It's up to you to mix and match. Most will cost £5-£6 (if the price is considerably more than this it probably includes admission fees) and last about two hours. Contact the Dublin Tourism Centre on Suffolk Street, Dublin 2 (605 7799). Lots of fun is the **Jameson Literary Pub Crawl** which meets during the evening at the Duke, Duke Lane, Dublin 2. You can book on 454 0228. (*See also chapter* **Literary Dublin**.)

Dublin by Season

A seasonal guide to the traditions and the celebrations.

As a country famous for music, sports, the arts and drink, it is hardly surprising that most of Ireland's, and indeed Dublin's, festivities should strive to mix these different ingredients into a single cocktail. What is curious, however – though in keeping with the capital's ambivalent relationship to the rest of the country (*see chapter* **History**) – is the extent to which most of Dublin's celebrations are unique to the city. That said, Dublin continues to share 17 March with the rest of Ireland (and with Irish communities all over the world), remembering it as the most important date in the annual calendar. In Dublin, St Patrick's Day is enjoyed in a wide array of colour (usually green), which has both secular and religious overtones: the historic parade and dog show, a three-day fleadh, the Railway Cup Final (*see chapter* **Sport & Fitness**) and Church celebrations all contribute something to the celebration of the day. In doing so, they also bear witness to the extraordinary flavour of Dublin's festivals.

St Patrick's Day Parade – *every 17 March.*

Spring

Dublin Film Festival

1 Suffolk Street, Dublin 2 (679 2937 information/679 2939 fax). **Date** 3-12 Mar 1998; phone for 1999 details. **Admission** £3-£5.

First run in 1986 and an annual event ever since, the Dublin Film Festival provides the occasion for a celebration of Irish and overseas cinema. In addition to screening a wide ranging programme of premières, new releases, low-budget films and classics, the Festival also invites guest speakers to introduce and debate relevant topics. Events are spread across the city, with films shown in most of the cinemas in the city centre, as well as in some of the larger multiplexes in Dublin's suburbs. The festival is extremely popular, so it is advisable to book well in advance. (*See chapter* **Film**.)
E-mail: dff@iol.ie
Web site: http://www.iol.ie/dff/

St Patrick's Day Parade

Christchurch Cathedral to O'Connell Street. **Date** noon 17 Mar.

Although parades are held in every major town throughout Ireland, by far the largest celebration of the Bank Holiday is enjoyed in the capital city. The St Patrick's Day Parade begins at midday, and features a wide display of imaginative floats, marching bands, street entertainers and famous faces. Traditionally, the route from Christchurch Cathedral to O'Connell Street is lined with huge crowds, so it is advisable to arrive early to secure a good vantage point. In recent

years, the parade has been supplemented with a large open-air carnival in the city centre, with rides and entertainments of all sorts adding to the atmosphere of this special occasion.

Irish Kennel Club's St Patrick's Day Championship Show

National Show Centre,Cloghran, Co Dublin (840 0735 information). **Date** 16-17 Mar. **Admission** £2; £1 OAPs, children; £5 family.

For many years, the dog show held a unique status as the only place in Dublin where one could get a drink on St Patrick's Day. Naturally, this temptation proved too great for too many people, and the show itself seemed overshadowed. According to the playwright Brendan Behan, the bar in the RDS was a great place to go, but a terrible place to bring a dog. In recent times, things have changed: laws on alcohol consumption on Ireland's national feast-day have been relaxed, and the show has moved from its traditional arena in the RDS. More popular than ever, it has become a two-day event, and is now held in the National Show Centre in Cloghran, County Dublin (just beside Dublin airport). The personalities and crowds from all walks of life continue to assemble for this famous show. Judging commences at 9am, and continues until about 5.30pm.

Guinness Temple Bar Fleadh

Temple Bar Information Centre (671 5717). **Date** St Patrick's weekend.

In celebration of St Patrick's Day, a three-day fleadh or traditional music festival has been held in the Temple Bar area of Dublin for the last few years. It's proved a major success, always packed to the gills with revellers attracted by the party atmosphere. A wide range of musical styles are incorporated by traditional musicians and dancers, and can be enjoyed at over 20 venues free of charge. Most of these venues are indoor, with many of the gigs being played in the neighbouring pubs. However, sessions are also performed in the open air, in Meeting House Square.

Music in the Park

(679 6111 information from Dublin Corporation). **Date** June-Aug. **Admission** free.

During the summer months, open-air concerts can be enjoyed in a number of alternating venues. **St Anne's Park** in Raheny, **Bushy Park** in Terenure, **Fairview Park**, **Sandymount Green**, **Herbert Park** in Ballsbridge, and the **Civic Offices Park** all provide for a pleasant afternoon's recital. Brass, reed and swing bands perform on different dates, and can be enjoyed free of charge courtesy of Dublin Corporation. In addition to this, jazz concerts are performed most Tuesdays and Thursdays during the summer between 1-2pm. Again, venues alternate with concerts generally being held in the **Civic Offices Park**, **Herbert Park** or **Herrion Square Park**.

Meeting House Square Events

Temple Bar Information Centre (671 5717). **Date** June-Aug. **Admission** free.

Throughout the summer months, this special outdoor venue hosts a wide variety of events which are to be enjoyed at no cost. Concerts are held on Tuesday lunchtimes and on Friday evenings; games and other family events are held every Sunday afternoon. What's more, outdoor screenings of classic films are shown every Saturday night in the Square during June and July. Although these films are free of charge, tickets are required for admission and must be obtained from the Temple Bar Information Centre. Facing the Information Centre on Eustace Street is the Ark, a recently designed cultural centre for children aged between 4 and 14. Complete with theatre, gallery, and workshop, the Ark hosts a number of events which include plays, exhibitions, workshops, concerts, readings, and performances of various kinds. Admission prices are modest, and donations are always gratefully received.

Adidas/Evening Herald Women's Mini Marathon

(670 9461 information). **Date** 2nd or 3rd Sun in June.

Organised by Dundrum South Dublin Athletic Club (DSDAC), the Women's Mini Marathon attracts incredible numbers of competitors – over 28,000 women competed in 1997 – and is now firmly established as the largest all-women sports event in the world. The celebratory atmosphere of the race, as crowds cheer on the thousands of women who walk and run the ten-kilometre course for charity, has contributed much to its overwhelming popularity and success.

Bloomsday

James Joyce Centre, 35 North Great George's Street, Dublin 1 (878 8547). **Date** 16 June.

Every year, the writings of James Joyce are celebrated on 16 June or 'Bloomsday' – the day named for the central character of *Ulysses*, certainly the most famous book about Dublin.

The Liffey Swim

If you have ever had the urge to swim in the murky, icy waters of Ireland's most famous river, you should join with Leinster's finest swimmers as they complete a series of qualifying sea races taking place over the summer and, certification in hand, head off for Dublin to compete in one of the most important contests in the city's sporting and social calendar, the Liffey Swim. A 14-mile swim upstream, this has been an annual event in the city every September for the last 75 years.

The initial inspiration for the swim came from a Dublin archivist named Fagin, who had the idea while crossing O'Connell Bridge one evening after a swimming meeting. The idea gathered momentum and, with some associates, Fagin managed to enlist the support of the *Irish Independent* Newspaper Group, which went on to sponsor the race for the next 70 years. The first race took place in 1920 and, that year, the organisers were delighted to welcome as many as 50 entrants to the start line at Watling Street Bridge. Then an exclusively male competition, it was to be another 70 years before women were allowed to participate.

The swim became enormously popular among Dubliners and, in its heyday, spectators would stand ten deep. This excitement and drama is perhaps best illustrated by painter Jack Butler Yeats' famous 1923 rendition of the event. The picture (which hangs in the National Gallery) is set at the height of the action and captures all the intensity of the race, the swimmers in full flow and the crowd surging forward, some standing on trams, each straining for the best view.

Spectator attendance of the swim has decreased while the turn-out of swimmers is more impressive than ever. In 1996, about 235 men and 120 women took part. Women have been allowed to participate in the race since 1990, when the Electricity Supply Board took over its running. Intent on raising the swim's profile, this was also the year that the ESB changed the scheduled day of the event from midweek to Saturday, thus encouraging more support. In 1996, the organisers changed the finishing point from Burgh Quay, near O'Connell Bridge, to opposite the Custom House, where the river is broader and there is more room on the Quays to hold crowd-enticing activities.

Dubliners will use any excuse to throw a party and attractions and festivities are traditionally laid on in full force for the day. The organisers are hoping that clowns, face painters, trumpeters, marching bands and thousands of balloons will attract big crowds.

It's an uniquely Dublin event, giving the city a chance to celebrate its capital status. The participants are not all super-athletes, just strong swimmers with strong stomachs – the latter a necessity for the Liffey's less than pristine waters.

And the best way to celebrate? By walking the streets of Dublin, in the footsteps of Leopold Bloom. The James Joyce Centre organises a week of activities, to commemorate Bloom's 'walking out' and prepare for the events of Bloomsday itself. Readings, performances, excursions and meals help to recreate the atmosphere of Dublin, circa 1904. All are welcome to participate, and encouraged to dress in Edwardian style. However, it is advisable to book in advance to avoid disappointment.

Web site: http://www.joycecen.com

National Concert Hall Open Day

(475 1666 information). **Date** 3rd Sun in June. **Admission** free.

Since 1993, the doors of the NCH (home to the National Symphony Orchestra) have been open free to the public for a day's celebration of music. Sponsored by Bus Éireann and Fête de la Musique, this annual event attracts over 1,000 musicians and promises something for everyone's taste. Traditional music, jazz, classical music and rock are enjoyed throughout the NCH and its grounds, and combine with face-painters and brass bands in the neighbouring Iveagh Gardens, to provide a wonderful day's entertainment. The celebrations are officially launched by Dublin's Lord Mayor at 1pm. Music commences at 1.30pm, with the ever-popular family concert in the main auditorium, and then continues through the day until about 8pm.

Guinness Blues Festival

(497 0381 information/fax 497 0631). **Date** 3rd weekend in July. **Admission** free.

Since 1992, the streets and pubs of Dublin have been home to an international blues festival. More than 50 artists and bands converge annually upon the Temple Bar area, from all over Ireland, UK and the US, and have recently been joined by such greats as BB King, Buddy Guy and Taj Mahal. Immensely popular with the punters, the festival aims to celebrate the history and diversity of the blues, and includes samples of Delta blues, R&B, rockabilly blues, New Orleans blues and, of course, Chicago style, in addition to hosting a number of talks and workshops. Most of the gigs are free to the public, although it is advisable to arrive early to beat the crowds. However, several of the late-night shows have a small cover charge of about £6.

Kerrygold Horse Show

RDS, Anglesea Road, Ballsbridge, Dublin 4 (668 0866 information). **Date** 1st week in Aug, Wed-Sun. **Open** 9am-6.30pm. **Admission** £6-£12.

The equestrian showpiece of the year, the Kerrygold Horse Show offers spectacular entertainment for those interested in international show jumping. Spread across five days, it features an array of events, and attracts audiences and competitors from around the world. Some of these events (the National Jumping competitions) are of national importance,

Kerrygold Horse Show *– jump to it in August.*

while others (the Kerrygold Puissance and the Kerrygold Nations' Cup) are of international renown. The Nations' Cup, where international teams compete for the prestigious Aga Khan Trophy presented by the President of Ireland, is traditionally held on Friday, with Thursday being remembered as Ladies' Day, when prizes are offered to the best dressed, and a special prize is awarded for the most stylish hat.

Autumn

All-Ireland Hurling & Football Finals

Gaelic Athletics Association, Croke Park (836 3222). **Hurling** 2nd Sun in Sept. **Football** 4th Sun in Sept.

The two great titles in Gaelic sports are decided on separate Sundays in September, in Croke Park. *(See chapter* **Sport & Fitness.***)*

Web site: http://www.gaa.ie

Dublin Theatre Festival

(677 8439 information). **Date** 5-17 Oct 1998.

Since its formation in 1957, the Dublin Theatre Festival has been a showcase for the best of Irish and overseas theatre, providing a welcome stage for emerging local talent, while also attracting productions of international stature. Its programme of events is generally varied, and encompasses most of the major theatrical venues in Dublin. Shows are normally very popular, drawing both Irish and international audiences. Many are heavily booked, so it is advisable to book tickets well in advance. *(See also chapter* **Theatre, Dance & Comedy.***)*

Web site: http://www.istm.ie/dublinfestival

98FM Dublin City Marathon

(676 4647 information). **Date** last Mon in Oct.

First run back in 1980, the Dublin City Marathon continues to enjoy tremendous success, attracting a field of several thousand competitors from all over the world. Traditionally, the 26.3-mile course starts at O'Connell Bridge and runs through many of Dublin's historic streets and suburbs. The response of thousands of Dubliners who come out to cheer on the field has been largely responsible for its enduring success, and continues to make it one of the great events in the city's year.

Web site: http://www.internet-Ireland.ie/Dublin-Marathon

Winter

Christmas Eve Vigil

St Mary's Pro-Cathedral, Marlborough Street, Dublin 1 (874 5441). DART Connolly Station. **Date** 24 Dec.

The Christmas vigil is celebrated in the Catholic St Mary's Pro-Cathedral every year by the Archbishop of Dublin. Perhaps the most important event in the church calendar, the mass service begins at 10pm, and is preceded by the sounds of the Palestrina Choir. The choir themselves begin singing at 9.30pm, and are well worth an audience.

Christmas Day/St Stephen's Day

Date 25, 26 Dec.

Although there is great activity on the streets of Dublin in the lead up to Christmas time, with trees, cribs, Santa Claus and carol singers all combining together with the famous windows of Brown Thomas' on Grafton Street, to produce a special festive atmosphere, Dublin remains pretty much asleep for Christmas Day itself. Shops, pubs, restaurants and clubs are all shut, and the public transport system shuts down for the day. Places begin to reopen on St Stephen's Day, as Dublin reawakens to partake in the celebration. St Stephen's Day also sees the beginning of the historic Christmas Racing Festival at Leopardstown *(see chapter* **Sport & Fitness***).*

Irish Museum of Modern Art

Image: **John Kindness**
Scraping the surface 1990
Etched painted steel,
taxi-cab fragment

An exciting and wide-ranging cross-section of Irish
and international art of the 20th century, housed
in one of Ireland's most beautiful buildings.

Admission Free
Museum & Bookshop open
Tues - Sat 10 - 5.30 Sun & Bank Hol 12 - 5.30
Free guided tours of exhibitions
Wed & Fri 2.30 Sat 11.30
Coffee shop open
Mon - Sat 10 -5 Sun & Bank Hol 12 -5

Áras Nua Ealaine na hÉireann
Royal Hospital, Military Road
Kilmainham, Dublin 8
Telephone 01 612 9900
Fax 01 612 9999

Museums & Art Galleries

From the sublime to the ridiculous: exquisite manuscripts, 'True Bugs' and exceptionally large scallops... while on the walls and in the streets, Irish art is bubbling with a new-found confidence.

Museums

The museums of Dublin are numerous and frequently specialised, while the two largest collections, those of the **National Museum** and the **Chester Beatty Library**, put only a fraction of their collections on display at any time. Three collections of international importance stand out – the Chester Beatty Library, the insular manuscripts in **Trinity College** and the Bronze Age and medieval Irish metalwork in the National Museum. Of these three, it is the first, with its outstanding collection of Oriental, Islamic and European art with an emphasis on manuscripts, illuminated books and scrolls, and graphic arts, which is the least known, the least visited and the most exceptional.

On the whole, the finest collections in Dublin tend to be archaeological or scholarly, and sometimes require some background reading to yield their full fruit. As information is not always plentiful, this may have to be supplied yourself, although the Chester Beatty has recently started to use very effective, low-key multimedia aids to put exhibits in their context.

Alongside these important collections, there are a number of historic sites and museums which are important buildings in their own right. **Bishop Marsh's Library** and the **Royal Hospital** at Kilmainham, home of the **Irish Museum of Modern Art**, are fine examples of Irish neoclassical architecture; while in the **Custom House**, the **Casino at Marino**, the **Hugh Lane Municipal Gallery**, the **James Joyce Centre** and **Newman House** we can see the richness and variety of Irish Georgian building.

It is also interesting to consider which items of Ireland's past have been recontextualised and which ones have been abandoned as the detritus of history. The statues of mounted generals, monarchs and bishops that once peppered British-ruled Dublin are now gathered together like gigantic and discarded chess pieces under the guard of the Office of Public Works.

The plethora of museums in Dublin means that, in place of one all-embracing history, there are omissions and overlaps, while the larger picture remains vague, or becomes the subject of conflicting narratives. Irish history is too often depicted as archaeology or propaganda. As well as this, the tourist boom has created a heritage industry that's often more interested in the prettification of past events than any profounder exploration.

In addition to the main museums, there are a number of buildings which, though not museums, can be visited by private arrangement. If you have a passionate interest in eighteenth-century building and decoration, or you have some academic or professional reason for wishing to visit sites not maintained as museums, contact the **Irish Georgian Society** at 74 Merrion Square, Dublin 2 (676 7053), who should be able to furnish a comprehensive list of sites of interest. As for buildings themselves, Gandon's two other masterpieces are the **Four Courts** on the north quays, and the **Kings Inns** on Henrietta Street.

Like North Great George's Street, Henrietta Street was one of the most fashionable and architecturally noteworthy streets in Dublin before the city's social centre of gravity shifted south of the Liffey. And, as with North Great George's Street, Henrietta Street has become one of the most active conservation battlegrounds in the city, with slums and painstakingly restored eighteenth-century dwellings existing cheek by jowl. Not far from Henrietta Street is Dominick Street Lower, in a similar state of dilapidated grandeur; No 20, now the headquarters of the National Youth Federation, was the home of the stuccadore Robert West and contains some of his most flamboyant and inventive plasterwork. Visits to the building can be arranged through the Irish Georgian Society.

Bank of Ireland & House of Lords

2 College Green, Dublin 2 (677 6801). All cross city buses. **Open** 10am-4pm Mon-Fri; 10am-5pm Thur. **Closed** Sat, Sun, Bank Holidays. **Admission** free. **Guided tours of Lords** 10.30am, 11.30am; 1.45pm Tue only. **Tours** free. Actually a talk, rather than a tour, in the former upper chamber of the former parliament. It was a stipulation of the Bank

Chester Beatty Library – *superb collection.*

of Ireland's purchase of the parliament building in 1803 that the House of Commons be demolished to discourage political activism. The House of Lords is a fine wood-panelled and vaulted chamber, more sober in style than the stucco extravaganzas of contemporary residential and institutional Dublin buildings, although the fireplace shows the robust inventiveness of eighteenth-century Irish wood carving. The principal ornament of the chamber is a pair of eighteenth-century tapestries commemorating Protestantism triumphant and heroic at the Battle of the Boyne and the Siege of Londonderry respectively, and a reminder of the allegiance of the Lords. Not surprisingly, the House of Lords appears to have been relatively staid compared to the Commons: from contemporary depictions the public gallery of the latter appears packed, especially with women, suggesting the dynamism of the short-lived Irish parliament.

Museum of Banking

Bank of Ireland Arts Centre, Foster Place, Dublin 2 (671 1488/670 7555). All cross city buses. **Open** 10am-4pm Tue-Fri; weekends by arrangement; groups free. **Admission** £1.50; £1 OAPs, students; free children.
The Bank of Ireland Arts Centre, round the corner from the main bank in Foster Place, is the venue for concerts of classical music, and houses the Museum of Banking, an interactive museum which covers the history of 200 years of banking in Ireland. The museum is most interesting at the points where banking and politics interface; it was here that the ill-fated parliament voted itself out of existence in 1800. Exhibits include the eighteenth-century mace of the House of Commons, and correspondence from the Abbey Theatre bearing the signatures of Yeats, Synge and Lady Gregory. *AV presentation. Café. Disabled: access.*

Bewley's Café Museum

Bewley's, 78 Grafton Street, Dublin 2 (677 6761). All cross city buses. **Open** 10.30am-5pm daily. **Admission** free.
The only thing immediately striking as a museum piece is the Jugendstil stained glass by Harry Clarke in the atmos-

pheric gloom of the main café (*see chapter* **Bistros, Cafés & Coffee Shops**), for which it was commissioned. The café museum, one of the quieter spots in Bewley's, deserves commendation more as an idea than for the somewhat motley array of items relating to bygone confectionery manufacture and tea trading. Nevertheless, it is partially redeemed by a few attractive Chinese tea canisters.

Casino at Marino

Malahide Road (entrance opposite Clontarf Golf Club), Dublin 3 (833 1618). Bus 20A, 20B, 27, 27A, 27B, 42. **Open** *mid-June-Sept* 9.30am-6.30pm daily. **Admission** £2; £1.50 OAPs, students; £1 children; £5 family.
One of the finest neoclassical buildings in Ireland, and as elegant a Palladian pleasure villa as can be found anywhere. The Casino was built for the patriotic Italophile Lord Charlemont by William Chambers, architect of Somerset House in London, whose other work in Ireland includes the Chapel and Examination Hall in Trinity College, Lucan House and Lord Charlemont's townhouse in Rutland (now Parnell) Square, which is today the Muncipal Gallery of Modern Art. The Casino is a building of extraordinary architectural ingenuity, which appears to be no bigger than a tem-'ple or folly from without, but whose interior spaces seem to unfold through Chambers' manipulation of symmetry, and where every element, down to decorative details, is put to use; the four columns at the corners of the building are hollow to carry water off the roof, and the rococo urns conceal chimney pots. As well as the sculptural character of the Casino, the crisp, rich quality of the decoration both outside and within is striking. The salon carries an Apollonian theme (as, incidently, does the stucco in the earlier Apollo Room in Newman House), while in the study, the celestial theme is represented by a domed ceiling banded by a zodiac which lifts and opens the tiny space of the room. Upstairs, Lord Charlemont's bedroom betrays a heavier touch with an opulence reminiscent of a Greek temple precinct; by the time this room was decorated, Chambers had abandoned the Casino because he wasn't being paid. The interior of the Casino is compromised by the presence of unsympathetic Victorian additions, in the form of carved panelling in the china closet and red flock wallpaper in the study, and the fact that the original furnishings are long since dispersed. The replacements are not always of the fine quality that the building demands and do not reflect the high standards of contemporary Dublin cabinet making.

Chester Beatty Library

20 Shrewsbury Road, Ballsbridge, Dublin 4 (679 2777). All cross city buses. **Open** 10am-5pm Tue-Fri; 2-5pm Sat. **Admission** free. **Guided tours** 2.30pm Wed, Sat; free.
Once the Chester Beatty Library moves (sometime in 1998) to its new premises in a restored eighteenth-century barracks at Dublin Castle, there will be the opportunity to see a little more of this outstanding collection, which its curators calculate will take 55 years to display in its totality on a rotating exhibition basis. The collection was bequeathed to the people of Ireland by Sir William Chester Beatty, an American connoisseur, who died in 1969. It comprises Japanese prints, Chinese furniture, oriental painted scrolls, ceramics and snuff bottles, Mogul and Persian manuscripts and illuminations, Tibetan mandalas and Buddhist scrolls and statuary, Arabic scientific instruments and scriptures, Biblical and Egyptian papyri, Coptic and Armenian icons, medieval and renaissance illuminated manuscripts, German renaissance woodcuts (including an important collection of Dürer's works), precious bookbindings and eighteenth-century prints, and even this list just scratches the surface of the collection. It's impossible to do justice to the quality and the rarity of the objects themselves, which is never less than breathtaking in any area of the collection. Even with enlarged exhibition space, only a fraction of the collection will be on show at once, although there is discussion of producing a CD ROM. While an informed appreciation of even an area of the collection

may require a specialist, the beauty and fineness of the objects needs no introduction, and makes the Chester Beatty Library one of the best collections of its kind in the world. *Café. Disabled: access. Tours. Shop/bookshop.*

Custom House Visitor Centre

Custom House Quay, Dublin 1 (878 7660). All cross city buses. **Open** *mid-Mar-Oct* 10am-5pm Mon-Fri; 2-5pm Sat, Sun, Bank Holidays. *Nov-mid-Mar* call for details. **Admission** £2; £1 children; £5 family.

Built in 1791 by James Gandon, architect of the Four Courts and the Kings Inns, the Visitor Centre (opposite Tara Street DART station) gives access to the small area of the building – two spaces on the ground and first floor – which remains as planned by Gandon. Displays and a video relate to the history of the building, to its uses, and to Gandon. Unless you have a passionate interest in the administration of customs and excise duties in eighteenth-century Ireland, the main reason for visiting the building is architectural, as it has the most distinguished river front in the city, and the interior open to the public culminates in a beautiful octagonal space on the first floor, the only place where the original elegant ornamentation remains. The view from the windows to the corporate edifices on the other side of the Liffey reveals how much the quality of riverside development has deteriorated in the last 200 years.

AV presentation. Disabled: access (telephone first).

Drimnagh Castle

Long Mile Road, Drimnagh, Dublin 12 (450 2530). Bus 22, 22A, 123, 50, 56A, 77, 77A. **Open** noon-5pm Wed, Sat, Sun; 4.15pm last tour; open other days by appointment. **Admission** £1.50; 50p OAPs, students, children.

Drimnagh Castle is a Norman keep with later additions, in a state of partial, though careful, restoration, surrounded by a moat with a very picturesque seventeenth-century-style formal garden – almost a physic garden, from the presence of medicinal herbs and plants. Behind the garden is a collection of colourful squabbling farmyard hens and ornamental birds, including peacocks. The place is a lovely and peaceful oasis (if you don't mind the squawking), all the more so as it lies in a faceless industrial suburb.

Café. Multi-lingual information.

Dublin Castle

Dame Street, Dublin 2 (677 7129). Bus 49, 50, 54A, 77, 77A. **Open** 10am-5pm Mon-Fri; 2-5pm Sat, Sun, Bank Holidays. **Admission** £1-£2.

A guided tour takes in the state apartments and the excavations of one of the towers of the Norman stronghold which predated the present eighteenth-century administrative complex. The state chambers contain a fine enough assortment of antiques, but lack the elegance and delicacy of the buildings erected by the Dublin-based ruling class of the time. Artistically speaking, the finest thing to be seen on the tour are the sprightly rococo ceilings which were removed from Mespil House on the south side of the city when it was demolished. For the rest, the heavy hand of an empire in a seat of colonial administration culminates in the ponderous Victorian ornament of the throne room. The archaeological part of the tour reveals the lower reaches of the Norman castle at a point where the river which once fed the moat emerges above ground. There are depictions of Norman Dublin, a sizeable settlement, still largely Viking in appearance. At the back of the castle lie the Dubh Linn gardens, which adjoin the new premises of the Chester Beatty Library. The gardens are attractive and well-planted, with an interlaced brick pattern laid in the lawn which apparently depicts two entwined eels. The gardens and the rehoused Chester Beatty Library represent an attempt to embellish Dublin Castle as a cultural, rather than a predominantly administrative centre.

Café. Disabled: access to state apartments. Foreign language tours/information. Shop. Theatre.

Dublin Civic Museum

58 South William Street, Dublin 2 (679 4260). All cross city buses. **Open** 10am-6pm Tue-Sat; 11am-2pm Sun. **Admission** free.

Exhibitions and a collection of artefacts and memorabilia which fail to do justice to the city's rich history. It's worth visiting for two documents which depict Dublin at the beginning and the end of the eighteenth century: Charles Brooking's map of 1728 and a set of 26 James Malton aquatints of 1793 which show the city at the culmination of the Georgian expansion, illustrated as an amalgam of merchant town, garrison city and Neopalladian utopia. The museum also houses Nelson's head, blown from his column in O'Connell Street when the monument fell foul of an IRA explosion in 1966. The statue of the 'one handled adulterer' was chiefly celebrated for featuring in an anecdote in *Ulysses* when it is climbed by two 'Dublin vestals', who spit plum stones from its summit. The museum inhabits a Georgian building which bursts into occasional flourishes of decoration but otherwise has an air of slight neglect.

Dublinia

St Michael's Hill, Christchurch, Dublin 8 (679 4611). Bus 49, 50, 54A, 56A, 77. **Open** *Apr-Sept* 10am-5pm daily; *Oct-Mar* 11am-4pm Mon-Sat; 10am-4.30pm Sun. **Admission** £2.90-£3.95; £10 family; under-5s free.

Very tourist-orientated multi-media presentation of medieval Dublin, possibly most useful for subduing boisterous school parties. The ground floor features a sequence of waxwork-style tableaux to the accompaniment of a blarneying audio commentary. Upstairs, things get more serious with a model of Dublin circa 1500, and artefacts from the Wood Quay site, thought to be one of the largest Viking archaeological sites in the world, and now filled in by the behemoth Corporation offices, where those inside the building reputedly enjoy superb views. Something that does emerge from the exhibition is the antagonism between the Pale and those beyond it, and Dublin's paradoxical status as a chartered royal city. The ticket includes admission to Christchurch Cathedral.

AV presentation. Café. Disabled: access. Multi-lingual self-guided tours. Shop.

Dublin Writers' Museum

18 Parnell Square North, Dublin 1 (872 2077). Bus 3, 10, 11, 13, 16, 19, 22. **Open** 10am-5pm Mon-Sat; 10am-6pm Sun. **Admission** £2.90; £2.40 OAPs, students; £1.20 under-12s.

Two crowded rooms with displays relating to Irish writers from the seventeenth century to around 1970, with a 'gallery' upstairs containing images of a selection of literary notables, the room itself being an extravagant nineteenth-century concoction of cherubs. The museum is useful for providing an introduction to Irish literature, with first editions, correspondence and memorabilia, and it pays a fair amount of attention to Dublin theatre which has formed so vital a part of the city's cultural life since the days of Congreve. The display stops abruptly with Behan, with no information about the liveliness or international standing of Irish literature over the last 25 years. The question of what is intended by a museum of Dublin writers is also sidestepped, as many of the writers featured were not born in the city, nor was their work particularly inspired by it. The museum adjoins the Dublin Writers' Centre, and is active in hosting a wide range of public lectures and receptions. On the first floor is Tara's House, an enormous doll's house which features an Indian colonial room and what appears to be a Chinese opium den.

Café. Disabled: access limited to ground floor, cafe & bookshop. Exhibition rooms. Foreign-language self-guided tours/information. Shop/bookshop. Zen garden.

Earth Science Museum

Merrion Row, Dublin 2 (660 1117).

Currently closed for renovation, this houses geological collections, fossils and the odd bit of dinosaur.

Ireland's first public library, built in 1701, now fully preserved – **Marsh's Library** *– see p69.*

Freemasons' Hall

17 Molesworth Street, Dublin 2 (679 5465). Bus 10. **Open**
June-Aug only 11.30am-2pm Mon-Fri. **Admission** £1.
Video presentation and exhibition relating to the symbolism
of freemasonry and its history in Ireland since the foundation of the Irish Lodge in 1725, housed in the Irish Grand
Lodge. Upstairs is a tour of the four principal chambers used
for various ceremonies and degrees in the order; all of them
decorated in diverse styles in the latter part of the nineteenth
century, some with considerable flamboyance. A testimony
to the lengths to which Victorian historicism could go, perfectly preserved and in full working order.

Guinness Hop Store

Crane Street, Dublin 8 (453 6700). Bus 68A, 78A, 123.
Open *Jan-Sept* 9.30am-5pm Mon-Sat; 10.30am-4.30pm
Sun, Bank Holidays. *Oct-Dec* ring for details. **Admission**
£3; £2 students; £1 children.
Your ticket entitles you to a pint of Guinness. On the whole,
the visitors' centre is tourist-geared, although quite enjoyable with enormous copper vats and lots of wiggly pipes.
The emphasis is on audio-visual presentation (a video is
shown every 20 minutes between 10am-3.30pm), and a small
selection of publicity posters fails to do justice to Guinness's
consistent excellence in advertising. The exhibition focuses
on the process of brewing, but has little to say about the relationship between Dublin and its most famous product. There
is also a dearth of information on the Guinness family themselves, who had a long and distinguished history as liberal
employers and as patrons, giving support to Trinity College
and other institutions. Look out for the strange brick tower
with a copper onion dome close to the Guinness breweries,
which is one of the most distinctive shapes in the Dublin
skyline — an old distilling tower for whiskey manufacture.
AV presentation. Bar. Disabled: access. Group discounts.

Heraldic Museum

*2 Kildare Street, Dublin 2 (677 7444). Bus 10, 11,
13.* **Open** 10am-4.30pm Mon-Fri; 10.30am-12.30pm
Sat. **Admission** free.

The museum houses a number of intriguing artefacts, including seals, thirteenth-century coins of Dublin, the insignia of
Roger Casement and British and papal decorations, as well
as a small display of objects sporting armorial bearings. The
museum itself shares the rooms of the former Kildare Street
Club with the Alliance Française; the social standing of
the club members is evident from the size of the building, a
substantial Ruskinian-Venetian pile which has stylistic
cognates in the Old Museum Building in Trinity College, the
only edifice in the university commended by Ruskin.

Irish Jewish Museum

*3-4 Walworth Road, Portobello, Dublin 8 (453 1797).
Bus 16, 16A, 19, 19A, 22, 22A.* **Open** *May-Sept*
11am-3.30pm Sun, Tue, Thur; *Oct-Apr* 10.30am-3.30pm
Sun only or by appointment (467 0773/475 8388).
Admission donation.
A collection of documents relating to the Jewish community,
including a reconstruction of a turn-of-the-century kitchen
typical of a Jewish home in the neighbourhood, while upstairs the Walworth Road synagogue is preserved with all
its ritual fittings. The museum was opened in 1985 by Dr
Chaim Herzog, President of Israel, and son of the first chief
rabbi of Ireland. Rabbi Herzog's home at 55 Bloomfield
Avenue is commemorated by a plaque, while at 52 Upper
Clanbrassil Street, a few minutes' walk away, another plaque
pays homage to Ireland's most famous fictional Jew: 'Here
in Joyce's imagination was born in May 1866 Leopold Bloom
Citizen Husband Wanderer, Reincarnation of Ulysses.'

Irish Museum of Modern Art

*Royal Hospital, Military Road, Kilmainham, Dublin 8
(612 9900). Bus 68, 69, 79.* **Open** 10am-5.30pm Tue-Sat;
noon-5.30pm Sun, Bank Holidays. **Admission** free.
One of the most important seventeenth-century buildings in
Ireland and, more recently, a vital exercise in cultural regen-
eration. The Royal Hospital was founded in 1684 as a home
for retired soldiers, and designed by Sir William Robinson
in a style loosely based on Les Invalides in Paris. In 1991,
the restored Hospital was opened as the Irish Museum of

Irish Museum of Modern Art – *housed in the Royal Hospital at Kilmainham – see page 67.*

Modern Art, the year which also saw the launch of the Irish Film Centre in Temple Bar, another flagship in the cultural rebirth of the city. The most striking feature of the building is the courtyard, with its arcades which run around three walls, relieving a massive and potentially austere space, with a play of depth, light and shadow. Inside, the museum has superb exhibition spaces; the displayed work generally takes the form of a number of shows and a select exhibition from the museum's permanent collection. There are shows by internationally recognised artists, work by local artists and a showcase highlighting pieces by a contemporary artist. The museum also runs a number of educational and community-based projects, and artists' works programmes, as well as hosting prestigious concerts, frequently chamber music. The museum favours a kind of scrupulous minimalism, and is occasionally accused of being relentlessly conceptual in a country which, for historical and geographical reasons, suffers from an impoverished visual arts tradition. While the setting of the museum is splendid and the art on show often of international importance, and while the museum does engage in a number of outreach activities, there's also a lack of context, so that the elegant, solemn vistas of stone and whitewash often feel empty. The museum is by no means the only attraction at the Royal Hospital, however; apart from concerts, the chapel and banqueting hall can be seen on free guided tours on Wed, Fri, Sat, while the imposing grounds of the museum include a beautifully restored baroque formal garden.

Café. Disabled: access. Free guided tours: 2.30pm Wed, Fri; 11.30am Sat. Foreign-language tours: pre-booking required. Shop/bookshop.

Irish Whiskey Corner

The Old Jameson Distillery, Smithfield, Dublin 7 (872 5566). Bus 25, 26, 39, 37, 68, 69. **Open** 10am-6pm daily. **Admission** £3.50.

Slightly cramped display including an AV presentation which is effectively an advert. The style of presentation concentrates on the manufacturing process. A beautifully crafted model of the distillery vessels and machines made for the 1924 World Exhibition is the most interesting object on show for those without any professional knowledge of whiskey production. The ticket includes a complementary glass of Jameson's. The museum (to which admittance is by tour only) gives plenty of information about the five brand names of Irish Distillers (Bushmills, Jameson, Paddy, Powers and Tullamore Dew), but details are scarce about other, slightly more specialised labels such as Redbreast or Midletons.

AV presentation. Bar. Disabled: access. Multi-lingual information. Shop. Tours.

James Joyce Centre

35 North Great George's Street, Dublin 1 (878 8547). DART Connolly Station/bus 3, 10, 11, 13, 16, 19, 22. **Open** 9.30am-4.30pm Mon-Sat; 12.30-5pm Sun. **Admission** £2.75; £2 OAPs, students; £1 children; £6 family.

One of the most interesting cultural centres in the city, combining Joyce memorabilia and Dublin history in a splendidly restored Dublin townhouse. The house was built in 1784 for Valentine Brown, the Earl of Kenmare, with elegant neo-classical plasterwork by one of the most famous of the Dublin stuccadores, Michael Stapleton. Each room or floor of the house has its own motifs; in the dining room vines and sheaves of corn curl around Maenads; in the restored first-floor rooms sphinxes frame charioteers and zodiacs; while on the upper stairs, stucco infants are linked by festooned swaddling bands under the gaze of delicate gorgons. The building aside, the most attractive feature of the centre is the first floor library which contains editions and translations of Joyce's work, critical and biographical texts, works by other Irish writers, as well as a selection of material relating to Dublin and to Ireland. This reading room is beautifully appointed and tranquil. The centre strikes a nice balance between the historical importance of the building and the archival or biographical character of a writer's museum, while giving visitors space to discover Joyce for themselves. Joyce's link with the house, which he knew as Denis Maginni's dancing academy, is documented, as is Maginni himself (actually not an Italian emigré but a local called

Maginnis) who crops up in the 'Wandering Rocks' episode of *Ulysses*, and the street is dominated by Belvedere College, the prestigious Jesuit school which Joyce attended. The centre owes its existence to the efforts of David Norris – Joycean scholar, Irish Senator and human rights activist – who fought for the preservation and restoration of Georgian buildings of the North Inner City, buying 35 North Great George's Street when it was threatened with demolition.
AV presentation. Bookshop. Café. Foreign-language guided tours. Guided city tours.

Joyce Museum

Joyce Tower, Sandycove, Co Dublin (280 9265). DART Sandycove/bus 8. **Open** *Apr-Oct* 10am-5pm Mon-Sat; 2-6pm Sun, Bank Holidays. **Closed** 1-2pm. *Nov-Mar* by arrangement (872 2077). **Admission** £2.40; £2 OAPs, students; £1.15 under-12s; £7 family.
Contains a collection of memorabilia relating to the great man, but the chief attraction is the Martello tower where Joyce briefly resided with Oliver St John Gogarty (surgeon, man of letters and raconteur, commemorated by more plaques than any other figure in Dublin; he appears to have been born in about three different places). Joyce found Gogarty fairly insufferable, and revenged himself by portraying him as 'plump stately Buck Mulligan' in the opening words of *Ulysses*, whose first chapter is set in the Martello tower. It's from here that Mulligan and Stephen Dedalus look out on the 'snotgreen sea' and muse, somewhat sarcastically, about 'hellenising' Ireland.
Bookshop. Disabled: limited access. Foreign-language tours.

Kilmainham Gaol

Inchicore Road, Dublin 8 (453 5984). Bus 51, 51B, 78A, 79. **Open** *Apr-Sept* 9.30am-6pm daily, 4.30pm last admission; *Oct-Mar* 9.30am-5pm Mon-Fri, 4pm last admission; 10am-6pm Sun, 4.30pm last admission. **Admission** by guided tour only; £1-£2; £5 family.
The most notorious of Irish prisons, it was here that the leaders of the 1916 Rising were executed. The prison also reflects changing attitudes to penal servitude from the eighteenth to the nineteenth century, when the Gaol was partly rebuilt in the model of Pentonville gaol, in accordance with Benthamite ideas on reform and surveillance. The cells of Robert Emmet and Parnell are here, the latter more of a private room in keeping with Parnell's status as a parliamentarian and a landowner. If you are interested in documentation relating to the Easter Rising and its aftermath, or to previous uprisings in Ireland from the eighteenth century onwards, come here rather than to the National Museum in Kildare Street – the active, indeed militant, role of women in the revolutionary period is particularly striking. The most famous of such women was Countess Markievicz, the first woman elected to Westminster for Sinn Fein in 1922 and the first woman cabinet minister in Europe as Minister for Labour in the first Dáil of 1919. There are also displays relating to conditions in nineteenth-century prisons and to the penal theories of Bentham and Howard, and records of the atrocious character of prison organisations and regimes of the time – all grimly informative, although the multi-media display on hanging seems gruesome beyond the call of documentation.
AV presentation. Disabled: access. Group discounts.

Municipal Gallery of Modern Art (Hugh Lane Gallery)

Charlemont House, Parnell Square, Dublin 1 (874 1903). Bus 3, 10, 11, 13, 16, 19, 22. **Open** 9.30am-6pm Tue-Fri; 9.30am-5pm Sat; 11am-5pm Sun. *Apr-Aug* 9.30am-8pm Thur. **Closed** Mon. **Admission** free.
A collection of nineteenth- and twentieth-century paintings and sculpture, which shows some Irish and British art, as well as exhibitions, but is most noted for its collection of French Impressionist works, with Manet's *Le Concert aux Tuileries*, Degas' *Sur la Plage*, and Vuillard's *La Cheminée*

among the works currently on show. The paintings were the bequest of Sir Hugh Lane, who first offered his outstanding collection of Impressionist paintings to Dublin on condition that a suitable gallery was built to house them. Plans for a gallery (including projects by Edwin Lutyens and a design for a structure spanning the Liffey) faded away, and Lane then approached the National Gallery in London, much to the chagrin of Yeats, who wrote a number of poems vilifying his compatriots for their philistinism. Lane later reverted to the original plan of leaving the collection to the city of Dublin, and changed his will, but, as the codicil was not witnessed before his 1915 death on the *Lusitania*, the situation is unresolved, with the masterpieces of the collection remaining generally in London, and works travelling back and forth, rather like a metaphor for the uneasy confusion of Anglo-Irish relations. An agreement has now been reached whereby the most important works rotate between the two galleries. Also interesting is an exhibition of exuberant art nouveau stained glass panels by Harry Clarke, who worked as an illustrator in the style of Aubrey Beardsley, and whose most accomplished work was his mannered and brilliant stained glass – some rather restrained panels can be seen in Bewley's Café in Grafton Street. The museum also has a collection of international and contemporary Irish art, and holds exhibitions. The gallery is located in the townhouse of Lord Charlemont, builder of the Casino at Marino, and like the Casino, was designed by William Chambers – the entrance hall and upstairs galleries show the fine elegance of late eighteenth-century Dublin interiors. The gallery runs free Sunday afternoon concerts (*see chapter* **Music: Classical & Opera**).
Bookshop. Café. Disabled: access. Lectures.

Malahide Castle & Fry Railway Museum

Malahide Castle Demesne, Malahide, Co Dublin (846 3779). Bus 42/rail Malahide. **Castle open** *Apr-Oct* Mon-Fri 10am-5pm; 11am-6pm Sat, Sun, Bank Holidays; *Nov-Mar* 10am-5pm Mon-Fri; 2-5pm Sat, Sun, Bank Holidays. **Closed** 12.45-2pm. **Admission** £2.95; £1.60 3-11 years; £2.45 12-18 years; £7.95 family.
Malahide Castle, seat of the Talbot family from 1185-1973, is a fine stately home with turrets, antiques and the ubiquitous Robert West swooping rococo plaster eagles, set in 250 acres of parkland that include fine botanical gardens. Its grounds contain the **Fry Model Railway**, a collection of handmade models of Irish Trains, beautifully detailed and engineered, and miniature constructions of Dublin's stations and other landmarks (*see chapter* **Sightseeing**).
Bookshop. Disabled: access. Foreign-language tours.

Maritime Museum of Ireland

Mariners' Church, Haigh Terrace, Dún Laoghaire (280 0969). DART Dún Laoghaire/bus 46B. **Open** 1-5pm Tue-Sat. **Admission** £1.50; 80p OAPs, children; £5 family.
Collection of maritime models, documents and other miscellaneous items. If things marine take your fancy, the two arms of the pier at Dun Laoghaire make for an invigorating walk and culminate in somewhat De Chirico-like spaces with carefully posed lighthouses.
Disabled: limited access.

Marsh's Library

St Patrick's Close, Dublin 8 (454 3511). Bus 49, 50, 54A, 77, 77A, 150. **Open** 10am-12.45pm, 2-5pm Mon, Wed-Fri; 10.30am-12.45pm Sat. **Admission** £1; free children.
If you follow the small lane past the entrance of St Patrick's, an unexpectedly picturesque spot in an area of urban deprivation, you come to a handsome Queen Anne box, which stands among mature and fragrant gardens. This is Bishop Marsh's Library; in fact, Ireland's first public library, built in 1701 by Archbishop Narcissus Marsh, and designed by Sir William Robinson, architect of the Royal Hospital,

Kilmainham. Up a flight of ancient stairs is a beautiful, and fully preserved, scholars' library with carved and gabled bookcases and three wire 'cages' into which readers consulting particularly precious works were locked. Apart from its fine architectural qualities, the library also possesses a valuable collection, much of it bequeathed by early librarians, and encompassing classical, liturgical and humanistic material, as well as mathematics, science, music and early Russian, Hebrew, Arabic and Turkish printings. A collection of manuscripts includes a volume of *Lives of the Irish Saints*, written around 1400, an important Irish medieval liturgical drama, and some very fine sixteenth-century music manuscripts. There is also a collection of memorabilia relating to Swift, who, as Dean of St Patrick's, was governor of the library, including books with his extensive (and sometimes insulting) annotations. The library should be considered alongside the Old Library at Trinity College, rather than just viewed as an annex to St Patrick's; both are very fine examples of early eighteenth-century libraries. If in Trinity College's Long Room, we see learning presented in terms of a classicising canon of eminent luminaries, in Bishop Marsh's Library it is the private world of the baroque scholar which is most in evidence.

Museum of Childhood

20 Palmerston Park, Rathmines, Dublin 6 (497 3223). Bus 13. **Open** 2-5.30pm Sun. **Admission** £1; 75p under-12s.

A private collection of dolls' houses, prams and toys including the oldest doll in Ireland and the travelling doll's house of Sissi, Empress of Austria – although quite how the latter found its way from Mitteleuropa to suburban Dublin is a wonder. The Museum is temporarily closed at time of writing, so call for details.

National Museum

Kildare Street, Dublin 2 (677 7444). DART Pearse Station/bus 10, 11, 13. **Open** 10am-5pm Tue-Sat; 2-5pm Sun. **Admission** free.

See **box** *facing page.*

National Print Museum

Garrison Chapel, Beggars Bush, Haddington Road, Dublin 4 (660 3770). DART Lansdowne Road/bus 5, 7, 7A, 8, 45. **Open** May-Sept 10am-12.30pm, 2.30-5pm Mon-Fri; noon-5pm Sat, Sun, Bank Holidays. **Admission** £1.50-£2.50; £5 family.

Contains a fascinating array of presses and apparatus relating to printing technology from nineteenth-century handpresses to early computers, the emphasis being on industrial printing rather than print-making or graphic arts. An informative video on printing and interesting guided tours are available. This is one of the few museums of industrial archaeology that actually succeeds in leaving the visitor stimulated and enlightened. Beggars Bush was originally a barracks – in fact the first barracks handed over by the British Army to the Irish State in 1922. The central garrison building houses the **Irish Labour History Museum**, which is more of an archive and library than a museum, although an interesting display reproduces documents relating to labour and industrial history in Ireland since 1728. *AV presentation. Café. Disabled: limited access.*

National Transport Museum

Howth Castle Demesne, Howth. DART Howth/bus 31, 31B. **Open** 10am-5pm Sat, Sun. **Admission** £1.50; 50p OAPs, students; £3 family.

A chance to see the contents of the Fry Model Railway in the flesh, with shedfuls of trams, buses, commercial, military and fire appliances on display. Given the state of the city transport service today, it will come as quite a shock to discover that Dublin transport was among the most advanced urban networks in the world at the turn of the century, being one of the first cities to introduce electric trams. Howth itself is most famous for its walks, boasting a splendid beach, a pretty harbour and the rugged heathy path that clings round the headland of the peninsula.

National Wax Museum

Granby Row, Parnell Square, Dublin 1 (872 6340). Bus 3, 10, 11, 13, 16, 19, 22. **Open** 10am-5.30 Mon-Sat; noon-5.30pm Sun. **Admission** £2.50-£3.50; £10 family.

Encompasses an eclectic range of figures such as Wolfe Tone, Eamonn De Valera, Snow White, Wolfman and Elvis, but probably most enjoyable for small children or those with an exaggerated appreciation of kitsch. Certainly not recommended for verisimilitude. The entrance lobby is redolent of a slightly camp recreation of an old fashioned picture palace. *Disabled: access limited to ground floor.*

Natural History Museum

Merrion Square West, Dublin 2 (677 7444). DART Pearse Station/bus 44, 48. **Open** 10am-5pm Tue-Sat; 2-5pm Sun. **Admission** free.

Worth a visit as a monument to Victorian taxidermy and as a mausoleum to nineteenth-century museums. All manner of stuffed things are carefully displayed in mahogany cases and glass bottles, some with wonderful captions – 'True Bugs' or 'Exceptionally Large Scallop' – which speak of the days when zoology was the province of gentlemen with tropical helmets and ingenious folding cabinets full of beetles pinned on cards. Irish fauna is downstairs while on the upper floors the visitor wanders through a jungle of Darwinian apes, moth-eaten bison and an Indian elephant which appears to have been dipped in bitumen. *Disabled: limited access. Shop.*

Newbridge House

Donabate, Co Dublin (843 6534/846 2537). Bus 33B. **Open** Apr-Sept 10am-5pm Tue-Fri; 10am-6pm Sat; 2-6pm Sun; Oct-Mar 2-5pm Sat, Sun. **Admission** £2.75; £2.45 OAPs, students; £1.50 children; £7.50 family.

Like **Malahide Castle** (*see above*), Newbridge is a famous Irish stately home, but a coherent eighteenth-century edifice rather than the assortment of styles and turrets that characterises Malahide. Once again, the house boasts stucco by Robert West, and is decorated after the great house manner, with red damask and gilt frames aplenty. The courtyard and various estate buildings have also been restored, including a farm stocked with animals to divert children tortured by antique furnishings. (*See chapter* **Sightseeing**.) *Café. Craft shop. Disabled: no access. Foreign-language tours.*

Newman House

85-86 St Stephen's Green, Dublin 2 (706 7422/706 7419). All cross city buses. **Open for guided tours** noon, 2-4pm, Tue-Fri; 2-4pm Sat; June-Aug 11am, noon, Sun. **Admission** £1-£2.

Two superb Georgian townhouses, bought as the premises of the Catholic University of Ireland and now owned by University College Dublin. If the stucco decorations of Michael Stapleton at 35 North Great George's Street represent the neoclassical delicacy of late-eighteenth-century Dublin plasterwork, in Newman House we see an earlier and more sculptural rococo style. The slightly earlier decorations of No.85 were executed around 1740 by the Swiss La Franchini brothers, those at No.86 by the Irish stuccadore Robert West, whose work can also be seen at Malahide Castle. No.85 contains the famous Apollo Room, whose panels depict Apollo and the Muses, and the magnificent saloon on the piano nobile, where allegories of the virtues of prudent economy and good government are framed by rococo motifs of shells and foliage. The work of the La Franchini tends to be sculptural, with naturalistic and solid modelling. No.86, built about 30 years later, has more inventive and fantastic work. West's work is always graceful, but this is a grace which suggests licence and daring; swooping birds or garlands of

National Museum

From 1998, the National Museum collections will be split between the nineteenth-century museum in Kildare Street and the restored Collins Barracks at Arbour Hill, Dublin 7 (opening times not available at press time), which will principally house decorative art collections. The Kildare Street museum concentrates on archaeological material, chiefly relating to Ireland; the most striking exhibitions will be those of Bronze Age Irish gold and of metalwork from the Iron Age to the Middle Ages, housed in the Treasury. The Bronze Age gold – one of the most comprehensive collections in Europe – shows huge sun discs, collars and lunulae, where the metal is worked into simple, often flat forms and radiates its own splendour.

The objects in the Treasury, on the other hand, both sacred and secular ornaments, show the intricate craftsmanship which we see in the insular manuscripts. It is in the Treasury that the most famous pieces of Irish medieval metalwork can be found, such as the **Tara Brooch** or the **Ardagh Chalice** (both eighth century).

Realistically, the museum can only hope to show a fraction of its vast collections at any one time. In addition to the Bronze Age gold and the Treasury, there are also displays relating to prehistoric and Viking Ireland. A rather cramped display of ancient Egyptian artefacts is on permanent exhibition on the first floor – many of the objects, including a fine mummy portrait, are Romano-Egyptian and show the close links between the two cultures.

An exhibition relating to Irish political history between 1900-21 and entitled 'An Thóir na Saoirse – The Road to Independence' suffers somewhat from being dislocated from the other displays; the presentation at Kilmainham Gaol is more rewarding, since it is better contextualised and more extensively documented.

When fully developed at Collins Barracks, the museum will contain an exhibition of decorative arts, political and military history, science and technology from the late Middle Ages, thus leaving the Kildare Street premises free to concentrate on archaeology and medieval artefacts.

The museum building itself is worth some attention; opened to the public in 1890, it was designed by Thomas Newenham Deane, and squeezed into a site to the side of the impassive facade of Leinster House, with an entrance which appears to be made up of compressed, almost bulging curves. This rather anamorphic sense of space continues in the domed entrance hall, or Rotunda, which looks like a Victorian reworking of the Pantheon, where the mouldings between the windows on the upper gallery have been modelled to jut inwards, so that the space appears to cave in towards the spectator. On the floor is a mosaic pavement depicting the signs of the zodiac.

Once in the main hall, the 'industrial' materials of iron and glass are in slightly uneasy dialogue with rich but slightly heavy historicist styling, in which a very Victorian interpretation of Italian Renaissance design predominates; the ponderous but rather splendid polychrome majolica work around the door frames is especially noteworthy.

Despite fine premises and the outstanding quality of parts of its collections, the National Museum suffers from a fault that could be laid to Dublin museums as a whole; that of fragmentation, or the sense that one is presented with particulars, but that the larger whole is rarely explored.

National Museum, Kildare Street, Dublin 2 (677 7444). DART Pearse Station/bus 10, 11, 13. **Open** 10am-5pm Tue-Sat; 2-5pm Sun. **Admission** free. *A V presentation. Café. Disabled: limited access. Multilingual information/tours. Shop. Tours June-Sept.*

---

fruit transform into complex and asymmetrical configurations of lines: trophies of musical instruments, so finely modelled that their strings could be played, are tied by ribbons that descend from grimacing monkey masks. Yet all this splendid ornamentation is only a part of the interest of Newman House. The names of two celebrated Victorian converts to Catholicism, Cardinal Newman and Gerard Manley Hopkins (who was appointed Professor of Classics and died in Dublin of typhus in 1889), are also associated with it, and James Joyce is possibly its most illustrious alumnus. One of the classrooms where Joyce would have attended lectures is preserved, as is Hopkins' gloomy cell. From the windows of Newman House, you can see a nineteenth-century formal garden; this is the Iveagh Garden which can be entered from Clonmel Street (off Harcourt Street) or from the back of the

National Concert Hall on Earlsfort Terrace, and which is one of the most tranquil parks in the city centre.
Foreign-language tours subject to availability.

Number Twenty Nine

29 Lower Fitzwilliam Street, Dublin 2 (702 6165). Bus 6, 7, 8, 10, 45. **Open** 10am-5pm Tue-Sat; 2-5pm Sun. **Admission** £2.50; £1 OAPs, students, unwaged; free under-16s.

An eighteenth-century merchant house restored by the Electricity Board in recompense for having pulled down the rest of the block to build their offices. The house is presented as a bourgeois dwelling circa 1790-1820, with the effect one of comfort rather than elegance. It's more interesting from a heritage viewpoint than for any artistic or architectural reasons, although there are some quite good examples of Irish Georgian cabinet making scattered through the house. The house is on the corner of one of the most elegant vistas in Dublin, the long neoclassical perspective that stretches from Merrion Square West down Mount Street and culminates in St Stephen's Church, called the 'Pepper Canister' because of its elongated tower.

AV presentation. Café. Multi-lingual information. Shop.

Pearse Museum

St Enda's, Grange Road, Rathfarnham, Dublin 16 (493 4208). Bus 16. **Open** *Nov-Jan* 10am-4pm daily; *Feb-Apr, Sept-Oct* 10am-5pm daily; *May-Aug* 10am-5.30pm daily. Last admission 30 minutes before closing. **Admission** free.

A museum dedicated to Patrick Pearse, one of the most charismatic figures of the 1916 Rising, which occupies the eighteenth-century premises of St Enda's, Pearse's experimental school, and the first to use bilingual Irish-English instruction. Displays document Pearse's life and work, although a little more information on what was taught (and how) would be interesting, as many of Pearse's ideas on education were inspired and his protests against the institutionalism of the schoolroom were eloquent. His enthusiasm for piety and patriotism might not be to present taste, but his emphasis on the personal liberty of the pupil, on sensitivity to the environment and on language acquisition through dialogue and culture, rather than method, remain refreshing, while his discussion of romantic individualism and the 'heroism' of sacrifice comes interestingly close at certain points to the pronouncements of Yeats. If Pearse holds no fascination for you, it's still worth going to the museum for its beautiful gardens and park. The tea-room, in the stable block with a pretty landscaped garden and fountain, is likewise a pleasant spot.

AV presentation. Café. Disabled: access. Guided tours on request. Nature Study Centre. Self-guiding outdoor trail.

Phoenix Park Visitors' Centre

Ashtown Castle, Phoenix Park, Dublin 7 (677 0095). Bus 37, 39. **Open** *mid-end Mar* 9.30am-5pm daily; *Apr-May* 9.30am-5.30pm daily; *June-Sept* 9.30am-6.30pm daily; *Oct-mid Mar* 9.30am-5pm daily; 9.30am-4.30pm Sat, Sun. **Admission** £1-£2; £5 family.

The Visitors' Centre lies a little beyond the Phoenix monument on the right if you stand with Áras an Uachtaráin behind you on the right. The centre deals with the history of the Park and its wildlife, and is housed in the coach house of the former papal nunciature, which was demolished to reveal a seventeenth-century tower house enclosed within the later residence. (*See chapter* **Sightseeing**.)

AV presentation. Café. Group discounts.

Shaw Birthplace

33 Synge Street, Dublin 8 (475 0854). Bus 16,16A, 19, 19A, 22, 22A. **Open** *May-Oct* 10am-1pm, 2-6pm, Mon-Sat; 11.30am-1pm, 2-6pm, Sun. **Admission** £1.15-£2.40; £7 family.

A neat Victorian house, the early home of George Bernard Shaw, Ireland's most overlooked Nobel prizewinner, who is celebrated simply as 'author of many plays' on the plaque outside. Shaw's greatest contribution to Dublin, however, is the National Gallery on Merrion Square which he endowed generously and which commemorates him with a statue in its front garden.

Bookshop. Foreign-language tours. Group discounts.

Trinity College Library

Trinity College, Dublin 2 (677 2941). All cross city buses. **Open** 9.30am-5pm Mon-Sat; noon-4.30pm Sun. **Admission** £3.50; £3 OAPs, students; £7 family; under-12s free.

It's worth trying to get here early, as the Old Library attracts huge crowds, especially in the summer. One ticket covers an exhibition from the library collections, which changes on average once a year, the **Books of Kells**, **Armagh** and **Durrow**, and a visit to the **Long Room**, which contains a smaller display of books and manuscripts. The famous illuminated books themselves have a delicacy of workmanship and colouring that does not always translate in reproduction, perhaps because of the vellum on which they are painted. The Book of Kells, a Latin copy of the Gospels written around 800, is a deservedly celebrated manuscript (although whether it deserves the aggressive marketing it now receives is open to debate). The Book of Durrow (675) and the Book of Armagh (807), although less extraordinary, are still beautiful examples of insular manuscripts and exhibit a similar, if less extraordinary, refinement. The **Long Room** itself is an imposing Georgian library nearly 65 metres long with a lofty barrel-vaulted ceiling added in 1860, and containing about 200,000 of the library's early books. The library was established with the foundation of the University of Dublin in 1592 and, since 1801, has been a copyright library with the right to claim a free copy of every book published in Great Britain and Ireland; its stocks now reach about three million volumes. The library buildings were constructed between 1712-32 to the design of Thomas Burgh, and are the oldest surviving library buildings in the University. The library also houses a collection of marble busts, started in 1743 – that of Jonathan Swift, by Louis François Roubiliac is particularly fine – and the oldest surviving Irish harp, made of oak and willow, dating probably from the fifteenth century; it's the model for the harp which appears on Irish coins. The Long Room is ideally visited out of summer: you'll have more time to gaze along the dark carved wood and rows of leather folios which rise to the vast dim arc of the ceiling; although the effect is somewhat spoiled by the hole punched in the library floor to take tourists back down to the souvenir shop at the entrance to the Old Library. Trinity's grounds are extensive and mature, encompassing three quadrangles, gardens, walks and two leafy sports fields. A large Venetian-style Victorian edifice, the **Old Museum Building**, was commended by Ruskin, but for most visitors the finest buildings are those in Front Square, which is dominated by the twin Palladian façades of the **Chapel** and the **Examination Hall**, both designed by Chambers, the second containing extremely fine stuccowork by Michael Stapleton. Many of the recent buildings in the University are also distinguished: the **Arts Block**, entered from Nassau Street, is criticised for poor light and ventilation, but has attractive terraced gardens from within College; and the **Berkeley Library** has strong rhythmic and sculptural qualities. There are also a few good pieces of sculpture dotted around: in particular, the **Henry Moore** in the lawns to the back of the Campanile in Front Square, the Alexanits decoration.

Café. Disabled: access in Arts Block. Group discounts. Multi-lingual brochures. Shop.

Waterways Visitor Centre

Grand Canal Quay, Dublin 2 (677 7510). Bus 3. **Open** *June-Sept* 9.30am-6.30pm daily; *Oct-May* 12.30-5pm Wed-Sun. Last tour 45 minutes before closing. **Admission** £2; £1.50 OAPs, students, groups (over 20); £1 children; £5 family.

Any visitor to Dublin will be struck by the often picturesque canals that ring the city. The Grand Canal, which curls round the city to the south, flows into the City Basin in the old industrial zone of Ringsend before joining the Liffey at the south docks. Here, the Waterways Visitor Centre has been created to give historical and environmental information on Ireland's inland waterways and canals, many of which are in the course of restoration. The building itself deserves some commendation: it's not the floating Portakabin it resembles at first glance, but an airy space of wood and glass, whose suggestion of mobility and fluidity reflects the water which flows around and under the building.

AV presentation. Disabled: limited access. Group discounts. Guided tours.

Temple Bar Gallery & Studios – *a rich diet of cutting edge exhibitions – see page 75.*

Art Galleries

There is a huge capacity for art in Dublin and it plays a major role in the culture of the city: in the galleries, in magazines such as *Circa, 4d* and *Source*, and on the streets, tied to the railings in Merrion Square, where visitors to the National Gallery can also browse through the city's own open-air gallery, containing an array of striking – and strikingly ghastly – paintings.

Since the development of Temple Bar, where many of the city's contemporary art galleries are located, recent art in Dublin has been given a great boost. The area, and the galleries, are thriving.

Much of Dublin's art is in its buildings, but there are also sculptures placed at various points around the city. Visitors to Trinity College can see a classical sculpture by Henry Moore (1898-1986) and Arnaldo Pomodoro's *Sphere Within Sphere*. Also at Trinity, the Book of Kells, an eighth-century illuminated manuscript, is on view in **Trinity College Library** (*see above* **Museums**).

A selection of works by Ireland's best known nineteenth- and early twentieth-century artists can be found in some of Dublin's galleries, and in the **National Gallery's** collection. The **Municipal Gallery of Modern Art** exhibits art dating from the nineteenth century to the present day. Situated in the Royal Hospital, Kilmainham, the **Irish Museum of Modern Art** (IMMA) concentrates on more contemporary works. Close to IMMA is the **National College of Art and Design,**

Ireland's most prestigious art school. Its graduates include Jacki Irvine, Darragh Hogan and, from the fashion world, hatter Philip Treacy and designer Murray Scallon. The College's degree show, held every June, is the launch pad for each generation of Ireland's new artists.

Celtic Roots Gallery

Parliament Street, Temple Bar, Dublin 2 (677 9127/fax 677 9119). DART Tara Street/all cross city buses. **Open** 10am-1pm, 2-6pm, Mon-Sat. **Admission** free.

In the midst of Temple Bar, the Celtic Roots Gallery houses spectacular sculptural designs created by bog wood sculptor Michael Casey and his team from near Ferbane, Co Offaly. All the pieces are designed and sculpted by hand, using woods which have been buried under the bog for over 5,000 years, and only surfaced as a result of turf-cutting. Works are finished with a natural polish of soft beeswax. Many sculptures are for sale, with prices ranging from £50. Gallery staff are unobtrusive, helpful and informative.

Davis Gallery

11 Capel Street, Dublin 1 (872 6969/fax 872 5580). DART Tara Street/all cross city buses. **Open** 10am-5pm Mon-Sat. **Admission** free.

The Davis Gallery, owned and run by well-known Irish artist Gerald Davis, is a large, bright space in the centre of Dublin. The gallery exhibits a variety of works, media and styles. The main exhibits are by the gallery's own artists, including Gerald Davis, Patrick Cahill, Patrick Viale, Tony Klitz, Mary Hennessey, George Oakley, Olivia Hayes and Dee Crowe. Prices range from £300-£5,000.
Disabled: access.

RHA Gallagher Gallery

15 Ely Place, Dublin 2 (661 2558/fax 661 0762). DART Pearse Street/all cross city buses. **Open** 11am-5pm Mon-Wed, Fri, Sat; 11am-9pm Thur; 2-5pm Sun. **Admission** donations.

Situated just two minutes' walk from St Stephen's Green, the RHA Gallagher Gallery is a modern building built to replace the Royal Hibernian Academy of Art which was destroyed during the 1916 Rising. There are four galleries within, and space for an outdoor sculpture court. The gallery is one of Ireland's main centres for modern and contemporary art hosts the RHA Annual Exhibition. Because of their large spaces, the galleries allow for major and large-scale exhibitions to come to Dublin.
Disabled: access.

Gallery of Photography

Meeting House Square, Temple Bar, Dublin 2 (671 4654/fax 670 9293). DART Tara Street/all cross city buses. **Open** 11am-6pm Mon-Sat. **Admission** donations.

Run in conjunction with the Arts Council and Dublin Corporation, this non-profit-making gallery is Ireland's leading photography venue. A well-lit gallery set on three levels, it houses both Irish and international exhibitions, which are accompanied by talks, seminars and workshops (contact gallery for details). Group visits are welcomed and informal talks on the current exhibition can be arranged through the gallery. A great place to visit, if you can overlook the staff's rather brusque manner.
Bookshop. Disabled: access.

Graphic Studio Gallery

Through the Arch, Cope Street, Temple Bar, Dublin 2 (679 8021). DART Tara Street. **Open** 10am-6pm Mon-Sat; 11am-5pm Sun. **Admission** free.

Run in conjunction with the Graphic Studio Workshop, established in 1962, the Graphic Studio Gallery deals solely in contemporary original prints by established and emerging Irish artists. Planned on two levels, a vast amount of work is on view, including etchings, lithographs, monoprints, screen, relief and carborundum prints. Works are available, both framed and unframed (the gallery will organise framing). Prices range from as little as £75 upwards (for framed works) and from £40 upwards for unframed. But you're welcome to just browse.

Green On Red

58 Fitzwilliam Square, Dublin 2 (661 3881/fax 662 1252). DART Pearse Street/bus 10, 48. **Open** 11am-6pm Mon-Fri; 11am-5pm Sat. **Admission** free.

Filling the first floor of a typical Georgian Dublin house, the Green On Red Gallery is a small, well-lit gallery with a pleasant atmosphere. Twelve exhibitions are held during the year, made up of gallery artists and invited artists from the UK and Europe. The gallery specialises in contemporary Irish and non-Irish art of an abstract, conceptual nature, covering various media, including video and photography. The gallery exhibited at the London Contemporary Art Fair in 1996 and hopes to develop its roster through further involvement in international art fairs. The Green On Red also houses exhibitions at its gallery on Lombard Street East – a brief walk from Pearse Street DART station and a considerably larger space than the Fitzwilliam Square gallery. Generally, exhibitions on show are divided between both venues, although there are plans to run individual shows in both. Access to both galleries is obtained by intercom system.
Disabled: no access.
Branch 26-28 Lombard Street East, Dublin 2 (671 3414).

Douglas Hyde Gallery

Arts Building (entrance Nassau Street gate), Trinity College, Dublin 2 (608 1116). DART Pearse Station/all cross city buses. **Open** 11am-6pm Mon-Wed, Fri; 11am-7pm Thur; 11am-4.45pm Sat. **Admission** free.

Established by the Arts Council and Trinity College Dublin, the Douglas Hyde Gallery is a self-contained unit, planned on two levels, with the main space on the lower level. Introductory talks relating to the current exhibition are held on

Non-profit-making **Gallery of Photography**.

Tuesdays at 1.15pm and at noon on Saturdays. Lunchtime talks are also held on Wednesdays at 1.15pm. Nearby are the lively surroundings of Trinity College's Arts Building, stuffed full of contemporary work.
Bookshop. Disabled: limited access.

Irish Museum of Modern Art

Royal Hospital, Military Road, Kilmainham, Dublin 8 (612 9900). Bus 68, 69, 70. **Open** 10am-5.30pm Tue-Sat; noon-5.30pm Sun, Bank Holidays. **Admission** free. **Guided tours** free 2.30pm Wed, Fri; 11.30am Sat.
See above **Museums**.

Kerlin Gallery

Anne's Lane, South Anne Street, Dublin 2 (670 9093/fax 670 9096). DART Pearse Station/bus 11. **Open** 10am-5pm Mon-Fri; 11am-4.30pm Sat. **Admission** free.

The Kerlin Gallery moved to these premises in 1994, and was designed by John Pawson, an English architect who got the minimalist vote after designing, *inter alia*, Calvin Klein's flagship store in Manhattan. Planned on two levels, the upper is the main space. It is a bright, well-lit place in which is exhibited mainly Irish conceptual, minimalist and abstract art. Most of the time is taken up with solo exhibitions by the gallery artists – among them Dorothy Cross, Willie Doherty, Mark Francis, Kathy Prendergast, David Godbold, Gwen O'Dowd, Stephen McKenna and Brian Maguire – although international contemporary art is also exhibited. One of Dublin's leading abstract art galleries.

Municipal Gallery of Modern Art

Charlemont House, Parnell Square, Dublin 1 (874 1903). Bus 3, 10, 11, 13, 16, 19, 22. **Open** 9.30am-6pm Tue-Fri; 9.30am-5pm Sat; 11am-5pm Sun. *Apr-Aug* 9.30am-8pm Thur. **Closed** Mon. **Admission** free.

Also known as Hugh Lane Gallery. *See above* **Museums**.

National College of Art & Design

Thomas Street, Dublin 8 (671 1377).
A functioning art college; visitors are restricted to the degree shows, held at the end of the first week in June. Graduates range from design and fine art to fashion and film-making.

National Gallery of Ireland

Merrion Square West, Dublin 2 (661 5133/fax 661 5372). DART Pearse Station/bus 5, 6, 7, 7A, 8, 10, 44, 47, 48, 62. **Open** 10am-5.15pm Mon-Wed, Fri, Sat; 10am-8.30pm Thur; 2-5pm Sun. **Admission** donations welcome.
Founded in 1854, Ireland's National Gallery houses a fine collection of European and Old Master works from the fourteenth to the twentieth centuries. George Bernard Shaw was a major benefactor and there's a statue of him outside the gallery. It's a grand, imposing building in the epicentre of Georgian Dublin, exhibiting a number of high-quality works from the likes of Titian, Tintoretto, Goya, El Greco, Monet, Degas and Picasso, as well as a predictably thorough Irish collection. It's here you'll find a roomful of paintings by Jack Yeats, WB's younger brother, as well as works by Roderic O'Conor, William Orpen, Nathaniel Hone, Walter Osborne and others. The smaller British collection is also impressive, with paintings by Hogarth, Landseer and Gainsborough. Every January, a collection of Turner's watercolours is exhibited, drawing art-lovers from all over the world. The bequest of the century was of Carravagio's *The Taking of Christ*, which was rediscovered by Jesuits in 1992 and is now on permanent display. There's a multi-media gallery with a user-friendly computerised system, containing information on 100 of the gallery's most accomplished works.
Bookshop. Disabled: access. Self-service restaurant. Shop.

New Apollo Gallery

17-18 Duke Street, Dublin 2 (671 2609/fax 679 7558). All cross city buses. **Open** 9.30am-6pm Mon-Wed, Fri, Sat; 9.30am-8pm Thur; 1-6pm Sun. **Admission** free.
The New Apollo Gallery is a somewhat cluttered, yet cosy, gallery specialising in nineteenth- and twentieth-century paintings. Among their most acclaimed extant exhibitors is Irish-born Graham Knuttel, whose large, colourful canvases, featuring rather sinister-looking characters, are in great demand among numerous Hollywood celebrities. Other exhibits include works by Joby Hickey, Markey, Alex McKenna and TC Murphy. Marie Carroll, whose work shows the influence of both Impressionism and Romanticism, and still-life paintings by Adam Kos, are also exhibited.
Disabled: access.

Oisín Art Gallery

44 Westland Row, Dublin 2 (661 1315/fax 661 0464). DART Pearse Station/all cross city buses. **Open** 9am-5.30pm Mon-Fri; 10am-5.30pm Sat. **Admission** free.
Just a few doors up from Pearse Station, the Oisín Art Gallery was set up in 1990 and concentrates on contemporary Irish art. Works by Marie Carroll, Markey, Eccles and Rabchinsky are available. They also deal in limited-edition prints.
Art supplies shop. Disabled: access.

Original Print Gallery

4 Temple Bar, Dublin 2 (677 3657/fax 677 3676). DART Tara Street/all cross city buses. **Open** 10.30am-5.30pm Tue, Wed, Fri; 10.30am-8pm Thur; 11am-5pm Sat; 2-6pm Sun. **Admission** free.
Located next door to the **Temple Bar Gallery & Studios** (*see below*), this gallery specialises in limited-edition prints, including etchings, lithographs, woodcuts and silkscreens. Exhibits include works by over 150 artists, both well-known and emerging Irish and international print makers working in every imaginable style. The gallery is purpose-built and in 1996 won the Architectural Association of Ireland award for best design.
Disabled: access.

Jo Rain Gallery

23 Anglesea Street, Temple Bar, Dublin 2 (677 9966). DART Tara Street/all cross city buses. **Open** 11am-5.30pm Mon-Fri. **Admission** free.
A compact, first-floor space, the Jo Rain Gallery was established in 1994 and is the only independently run gallery in Temple Bar. About 16 exhibitions are held each year, mainly solo shows of contemporary work by mostly young Irish painters. Since exhibiting its first solo shows, the gallery now has its own group of painters whose works it exclusively exhibits, including artists such as Michael Coleman, Helena Gorey and Stephen Brandes. Staff are helpful.
Disabled: no access.

Rubicon Gallery

10 St Stephen's Green, Dublin 2 (670 8055/fax 670 8057). All cross city buses. **Open** 11am-5.30pm Mon-Sat. **Admission** free.
Established in 1991, the Rubicon Gallery is a bright and well-lit gallery, overlooking St Stephen's Green. Its exhibitions include paintings by contemporary Irish and international artists. The gallery holds works by up to 40 printmakers, concentrating on monoprints, monotypes and small-edition prints. Generally, works by gallery artists are shown in solo shows, and works by young emerging artists are shown annually. The gallery is in a prime location and has a pleasant atmosphere in which to either browse or buy. Staff are charming.
Disabled: no access.

Solomon Gallery

Powerscourt Townhouse Centre, South William Street, Dublin 2 (679 4237/fax 671 5262). All cross city buses. **Open** 10am-5.30pm Mon-Sat. **Admission** free.
Established in 1981, the Solomon Gallery, on the top floor of the Powerscourt Townhouse Centre, deals in contemporary Irish and international art works. Exhibitions are shown every three to four weeks, and recent ones include works by gallery artists Martin Mooney, Brian Bollard, Peter Collins RHA, Hector McDonnell, Elizabeth Cope, Francis Tansey, Daragh Hogan, Brett McEntagart RHA, Sarah Spackman, Victor Richardson and James Longueville. Exhibitions also include works by well-known Irish and international artists. Early twentieth-century paintings are also available, including works by artists such as Jack B Yeats (brother of the poet), Dan O' Neill, Sir William Orpen, Evie Hone, Sir John Lavery and Maine Jellet. A wide selection of sculpture and contemporary glass is housed by the Solomon, including works by Rowan Gillespie, Linda Brunker, Anna Duncan, Deborah Brown and US glass artist Dale Chihuly.
Disabled: no access but guards will carry wheelchairs upstairs.

Temple Bar Gallery & Studios

5-9 Temple Bar, Dublin 2 (671 0073/fax 677 7527). All cross city buses. **Open** 10am-6pm Mon-Sat; 2-6pm Sun. **Admission** free.
Founded in 1983, the Temple Bar Gallery & Studios was the first cultural organisation to arrive in Temple Bar, an area that's now glutted on galleries (and designer bars). It was set up by artists for artists, so provides a public exhibition space, as well as studio space for working artists. Originally a factory, it was redesigned in 1994, and is now the largest studio and gallery complex in the country, catering for both established and emerging artists, as well as offering exhibition space to artists who have no links with commercial galleries. There's space here for 30 full-time professional artists in which to finish projects, exhibitions and commissions. The gallery promotes the use of all media including painting, printing, photography, mixed media and sculpture. Links with many national and international organisations mean there's a rich diet of cutting-edge exhibitions.
Disabled: access.

TimeOut

Film
Guide

Edited by John Pym

Annually updated, the *Time Out* Film Guide is a comprehensive A-Z of films from every area of world cinema and has stronger international coverage than any other film guide.

Each entry includes full details of director, cast, running time, release date and reviews from the *Time Out* magazine critics. There are also indexes covering films by country, genre, subject, director and actor. So if you want to get the lowdown on a film, pick up the latest edition of the *Time Out* Film Guide - available in a bookshop near you.

'Without doubt, the "bible" for film buffs.'
British Film and TV Academy News

Consumer

Restaurants

Whatever else is on Dublin's menus, the taste of stylish and global confidence is pervasive.

The last decade has seen nothing less than a revolution in Dublin's attitude to eating and drinking. The famous Dublin restaurants of the 1970s and 1980s were elitist and expensive. The best known, and best loved, restaurants of the 1990s are, on the contrary, democratic, fun and creative.

Eating in restaurants, once reserved for special occasions and business entertaining, has been transformed into an everyday experience as a new generation of chefs, determined to make their mark in both a culinary and social sense, discovered that a young population was equally determined to enjoy their work.

This concoction of cook and consumer has been aided by the fact that Dubliners have enjoyed an economic boom in recent years and, like the hedonists they are, they have proceeded to spend their money on the pleasures of the table.

The creation of the Temple Bar area, saved from original plans to turn it into a massive bus station and transformed instead into Dublin's *rive gauche*, is simply the best example of what has been a radical change in the city's appreciation of food.

A more sophisticated attitude has been paralleled by ever-increasing sophistication amongst the best chefs in the city, whose approach mirrors that of London and other capital cities, inasmuch as they plunder the globe for culinary influences, then spin their own twists on the influence, bringing the food back home.

The sense of excitement which one finds now in Dublin's restaurants lies partly in the fact that the culinary revolution is taking place day by day, with new restaurants keen to make their mark with distinctive, delicious food, and also with the fact that Dubs are both relaxed and respectful of restaurant eating. Their long history of socialising in pubs has gifted the city with a laid-back approach to eating out: it is to be enjoyed, first, foremost and above all.

Chapter One

18-19 Parnell Square, Dublin 1 (873 2266). Bus 10, 12. **Lunch served** 12.30-2pm Tue-Sat. **Dinner served** 6-11pm Tue-Sat. **Credit** AmEx, DC, MC, V.
Visitors to the Dublin Writers' Museum often make their way downstairs to Chapter One, a formal restaurant space

*The flavour-drenched cooking at **L'Ecrivain** is definitely something to write home about.*

*Book in advance at **Eden** and try to get a table downstairs or, indeed, outside.*

which can produce some snappy cooking: shallot and soya tarte tatin with goat's cheese, pan-fried cod with pesto and mussels.

The Commons Restaurant

85-86 Newman House, St Stephen's Green, Dublin 2 (475 2597). All cross city buses. **Lunch served** 12.30-2.15pm Mon-Fri. **Dinner served** 7-10.15pm Mon-Sat. **Average** lunch £18 +15%; dinner £32 +15%. **Credit** AmEx, DC, MC, V.

Serenity is the keynote of this exceedingly formal restaurant, where Sebastian Masi's cooking provides a poised and precise cuisine which trades classical dishes off against modern innovations and Irish gestures. A rewarding experience.

Cooke's Café & The Rhino Room

14 South William Street, Dublin 2 (679 0536/7/8). Rhino Room (670 5260). All cross city buses. **Lunch served** 12.30-3.30pm Mon-Sat. **Dinner served** 6-11.30pm Mon-Sat. **Average** lunch £14.95 +12.5%; dinner from £25 + 12.5%. **Credit** AmEx, DC, MC, V.

John Cooke has regained the fashionable high ground with the opening of the Rhino Room, upstairs from his chic café. The food is simple – black bean soup with lime, grilled lobster with citrus dressing, beef arragui with chilli – all superbly executed, with breakfast eliding into lunch, lunch into afternoon tea, and then gently into dinner from 5.30pm on. Downstairs, the cooking is more involved, and equally well delivered. Great people-spotting room.

Le Coq Hardi

35 Pembroke Road, Dublin 4 (668 4130/9070). Bus 18. **Lunch served** 12.30-2.30pm Mon-Fri. **Dinner served** 7-11pm Mon-Sat. **Average** lunch £19; dinner £36. **Credit** AmEx, DC, MC, V.

The quintessential Dublin power-restaurant – clubbable, formal, very pricey – is no longer as fashionable as it once was, but nevertheless has a lot to recommend it, not least

John Howard's elegant and classical cooking: braised oxtail, coq Hardi smokies, soufflé of Dover sole. Famous (and duly expensive) wine list.

Dobbins Wine Bar

15 Stephen's Lane, Dublin 2 (676 4679). Bus 7, 45. **Lunch served** 12.30-3pm Mon-Fri. **Dinner served** 8-11.45pm Tue-Sat. **Average** lunch £14; dinner £25. **Credit** AmEx, DC, MC, V.

Dobbins is one of the great old troopers of the Dublin restaurant scene, masterminded by John O'Byrne and a crack team who have given many years of service to the Wine Bar. It's a fiercely sociable place, with lunches likely to be long and dinners likely to be rowdy, so cancel all appointments.

L'Ecrivain

109A Lower Baggot Street, Dublin 2 (661 1919). Bus 10. **Lunch served** 12.30-2.30pm Mon-Fri. **Dinner served** 6.30-11pm Mon-Sat. **Average** lunch £15; dinner from £28. **Credit** AmEx, DC, MC, V.

L' Ecrivain is a quintessentially Irish restaurant, thanks to the service of Sallyanne Clarke and Ray Hingston, and to the generous, flavour-drenched cooking of Derry Clarke. Mr Clarke loves gutsy, intense flavours, but he also has the skill to make things taste vivid and distinct: chargrilled entrecôte with roasted red peppers and a Café de Paris butter, roasted venison with a star anise fumé, roasted Toulouse sausage with braised red cabbage, baked rock oysters with cabbage and bacon and a Guinness sabayon or the searing assault of seared scallops with garlic, ginger and a chilli dressing.

Eden

Sycamore Street, Meeting House Square, Temple Bar, Dublin 2 (670 5372). All cross city buses. **Open** noon-late Tue-Sun. **Average** lunch £8; dinner £16. **Credit** AmEx, MC, V.

A most vivid, post-modern Dublin restaurant. The design may recall a minimalist feel, but the food is utterly classical – organic sirloin steak with bearnaise sauce and Dingle chips, sole on the bone, chocolate and mint soufflé – and superbly executed by Eleanor Walsh and her team. A hipper-than-hip crowd pack the place out, so book in advance and always try to get a table downstairs.

Elephant & Castle

18 Temple Bar, Dublin 2 (679 3121). All cross city buses. **Open** 8am-11.30pm Mon-Thur; 8am-midnight Fri; 10.30am-midnight Sat; noon-11.30pm Sun. **Average** lunch £7; dinner £12. **Credit** AmEx, DC, MC, V.
Perhaps the most important restaurant in recent Dublin history, the E&C first cracked the idea of serving spirited, capable food at good prices in an informal context. Dubs have had a love affair with it since day one. The specials of the day allow whoever is in the kitchen to show their newest influences; the spicy chicken wings are legend, the soundtrack is fixed at mid-period Miles Davis, and you can't book.

Ernie's

Mulberry Gardens, Donnybrook, Dublin 4 (269 3260). Bus 10, 46A. **Lunch served** 12.30-2pm Tue-Fri. **Dinner served** 7.30-10.30pm Tue-Sat. **Average** lunch £13.95; dinner £25 +12.5%. **Credit** AmEx, DC, MC, V.
Set in a courtyard just off the main strip of Donnybrook, Ernie's is a pampering, perfectionist little place, characterised by a dedication to service which is wholly admirable. The food isn't fashion-foolish – tian of crab with chive mayonnaise, feuillette of duck's livers with caramelised red onions, ragout of monkfish with red peppers, guinea fowl with Puy lentils, prune and Armagnac tart – but instead allows the kitchen to play to their strengths.

Fitzers Cafés

RDS, Ballsbridge, Dublin 4 (667 1301). **Open** noon-3pm; 6-11pm Mon-Sun. **Credit** AmEx, DC, MC, V.
The three rooms of the Fitzers group are startlingly diverse: extra-elegant in the lovely room of the RDS, funky in Temple Bar, and laid back on Dawson Street. The cooking, under head chef Will Fitzgerald, is modern and assured, and value for money. Different menus (and prices, with the RDS costing £5 or so more) at each café reflect the clientèle: seared

calamari with pickled chillies and lemon oil can be had in Temple Bar while the more conventional cookery can be found at of the RDS and Dawson Street.
Branches Dawson Street (677 1155); Temple Bar Square (679 0440).

Les Frères Jacques

74 Dame Street, Temple Bar, Dublin 2 (679 4555). All cross city buses. **Lunch served** 12.30-2.30pm Mon-Fri. **Dinner served** 7.30-10.30pm Mon-Thur; 7.30-11pm Fri-Sat. **Average** lunch £15; dinner £25. **Credit** AmEx, DC, EC, MC, V.
With dishes ranging from French peasant soup, saddle of lamb baked in puff pastry and lobster ravioli with a fillet of turbot, to terrine of river pike, crème brûlée and vanilla bavarois, this is classic French fare.

Hibernian Hotel

The Patrick Kavanagh Room, Eastmoreland Place, Ballsbridge, Dublin 4 (668 7666). Bus 10. **Lunch served** 12.30-2.30pm Sun-Fri. **Dinner served** 6.30-10pm Mon-Sat. **Average** lunch £15; dinner £25. **Credit** AmEx, DC, MC, V.
The Hib has character, thanks to the energy of manager David Butt and the accomplished cooking of David Foley, whose work is a reproach to the staid dullness of most hotel cooking.

Kapriol Restaurant

45 Camden Street Lower, Dublin 2 (475 1235). **Open** 7.30pm-midnight Tue-Sat. **Average** dinner £30. **Credit** AmEx, DC, MC, V.
The Kapriol has been an outpost of good food for so many years that its achievements are in danger of being overlooked. But let their classic Italian cooking seduce you, and you'll soon see why it endures so successfully.

Lobster Pot Restaurant

9 Ballsbridge Terrace, Dublin 4 (668 0025/660 9170). Bus 7, 8, 8A. **Lunch served** 12.30-2.30pm Mon-Fri. **Dinner served** 6-10.30pm Mon-Sat. **Average** £30. **Credit** AmEx, DC, MC, V.

Elephant & Castle – *or the E&C – offers capable food at good prices in an informal context.*

Fitzers Cafés *offer a choice of dishes and prices at the RDS, Dawson Street or Temple Bar.*

As comfy and ageless as a gentlemen's club, the Lobster Pot pays little attention to trite food fashions. They brew bisques, offer the catch of the day cooked whatever way you like (but preferably with a sauce with dollops of wine and cream) and look after you in such a way that every visit is a treat.

Locks

1 Windsor Terrace, Portobello, Dublin 8 (454 3391). Bus 19. **Lunch served** noon-2.30pm Mon-Fri. **Dinner served** 7-11pm Mon-Sat. **Average** lunch £16; dinner £27. **Credit** AmEx, DC, MC, V.

Claire Douglas runs Locks with a precision and prescience which can be almost perfect. In their commodious room, the subtle cooking is enjoyable, serving staples of traditional French-style cooking.

The Mermaid Café

69-70 Dame Street, Temple Bar, Dublin 2 (670 8236). All cross city buses. **Dinner served** 6.30-11pm Tue-Sat. **Average** lunch £14; dinner £22. **Credit** MC, V.

The Mermaid is relaxed and unselfconscious, the perfect space for Ben Gorman's unfussy cooking. New England crab cakes, veal sweetbreads with saffron and jasmine rice, and monkfish with lobster sauce are great favourites, as are their chicken breasts with wild mushroom risotto and great crystallised pecan nuts with Illy coffee. Prices are very keen and service amongst the best in the city.

Morels Bistro

14-17 Lower Leeson Street, Dublin 2 (662 2480). Bus 10, 11, 13, 46A. **Lunch served** 12.30-2pm Mon-Fri. **Dinner served** 6.30-10pm Mon-Sat. **Average** lunch £11.50; dinner £20. **Credit** AmEx, DC, MC, V.

The tearaway success story of the late 1990s, Alan O'Reilly's original southside Morels has found a second home, underneath the Stephen's Hall Hotel, a basement to contrast with the upstairs room, above a pub, out in Glasthule. Bright colours in the rooms match bright flavours on the plate, with John Dunne's cooking beautifully measured. Especially well-favoured are the salad of duck confit with tapenade, angel hair pasta with chorizo, wood pigeon with crispy bacon and roast shallots and monkfish tempura with lime and coriander. Great value, with great wines and great service.

Muscat

64 South William Street, Dublin 2 (679 7699). All cross city buses. **Lunch served** 12.30-2.15pm Tue-Fri. **Dinner served** 6-11pm Tue-Sat. **Average** lunch £15; dinner £22. **Closed** Sun, Mon. **Credit** AmEx, MC, V.

Step off South William Street into this cosy little place where the quality of Brian and Bernie's food is reassuringly good. The sweet-toothed will probably find their Bailey's walnut steamed pudding with toffee sauce irresistible.

The Old Dublin

90-91 Francis Street, Dublin 8 (454 2028). Bus 56A, 77. **Lunch served** 12.30-2.30pm Mon-Fri. **Dinner served** 6-11pm Mon-Sat. **Average** lunch £12.50; dinner £22. **Credit** AmEx, DC, MC, V.

One of the senior citizens of Dublin restaurant life, and the eclectic style of the Old Dub – a strange fusion of Irish food and Scandinavian themes – is unique in the city.

101 Talbot

100-102 Talbot Street, Dublin 1 (874 5011). All cross city buses. **Open** 10am-3pm Mon; 10am-11pm Tue-Sat. **Lunch served** noon-3pm. **Dinner served** 6-11pm. **Average** lunch £9; dinner £15. **Credit** AmEx, DC, MC, V.

A happy, charming space upstairs from grotty Talbot Street, 101 is a place where vegetarian dishes are treated with great care, where you can have a seriously good long lunch, a grand family dinner, or just grab a sandwich.

Pasta Fresca

3-4 Chatham Street, Dublin 2 (679 2402). Bus 6, 7, 8, 10, 46. **Open** 8am-11.30pm Mon-Sat; 12.30-8.30pm Sun. **Average** lunch £5; dinner £10. **Credit** DC, MC, V.

The shop out front sells fresh pasta, oils and sauces, while the restaurant is open all day, selling a familiar range of pastas and Italian dishes.

Peacock Alley

47 South William Street, Dublin 2 (662 0760). **All cross city buses.** **Lunch served** 12.30-2.30pm Tue-Fri. **Dinner served** 6-11pm daily. **Average** lunch £23; dinner £40. **Credit** AmEx, DC, MC, V.

Describing his food as 'Mediterranean provincial cooking', Conrad Gallagher combines ingredients to cater for the subtlest tastes. Recommendations here could be endless, but consider the ravioli with lobster, tomato and goat's cheese, chicken stuffed with organic greens with a red pepper polenta or his gratin of oyster with a blanket of leeks and a shallot and tarragon custard. Very tall cooking, executed with panache and professionalism, which will, no doubt, also be present at his new 100-seater brasserie on Merrion Street, close to the Dáil, which is scheduled for late 1998 opening.

Restaurant Patrick Guilbaud

21 Upper Merrion Street, Dublin 2 (676 4192). **Bus 10.** **Lunch served** 12.30-2pm Mon-Sat. **Dinner served** 7.30-10.15pm Mon-Sat. **Average** lunch £30; dinner £70. **Credit** AmEx, DC, MC, V.

RPG's move to the lavish Merrion Hotel may prove to be a new start for this long-established organisation. Ruthlessly efficient and easily capable of producing food of a stellar standard, RPG is, however, rather too self-conscious for many, and it seems happy to rely on the patronage of its well-heeled clientèle, while the younger set hang out elsewhere in town.

Roly's Bistro

7 Ballsbridge Terrace, Dublin 4 (668 2611). **Bus 7, 7A, 8.** **Lunch served** noon-3pm daily. **Dinner served** 6-10pm Mon-Thur, Sun; 6-10.30pm Fri, Sat. **Average** lunch £10.50; dinner £17.50. **Credit** AmEx, DC, MC, V.

Excellent bistro cooking executed with verve and nerve: salmon trout with fennel and saffron sauce, fluted with sun-dried tomato and pistou vinaigrette, and fricassée of Dublin Bay prawns with vanilla sauce never fails to please. Roly Saul is one of Dublin's great restaurateurs, greeting, meeting and marshalling in his inimitable style.

La Stampa

35 Dawson Street, Dublin 2 (677 8611). **All cross city buses.** **Lunch served** 12.30-2pm Mon-Fri. **Dinner served** 6.30-11.15pm Mon-Thur, Sun; 6.30-11.45pm Fri, Sat. **Credit** AmEx, DC, MC, V.

Mike Benjamin has returned from the UK to take over the kitchens at La Stampa, a former guild hall which is the most gorgeous dining room in the city. His cooking is as assured as the service of Declan Maxwell. Menu highlights include fricassée of warm oysters, baked brill with fennel purée and red wine sauce, honey roast and confit guinea fowl and buttered cabbage and calvados jus.

The Tea Rooms

The Clarence, 6-8 Wellington Quay, Dublin 2 (670 7766). **All cross city buses.** **Lunch served** 12.30-2pm Mon-Fri. **Dinner served** 6.30-10.30pm daily. **Average** lunch £15; dinner £20. **Credit** AmEx, DC, MC, V.

Michael Martin's menu focuses on satisfying a diverse clientèle, from the friends of U2 (the hotel is part-owned by Bono and The Edge) to the ordinary citizens of Dublin who are likely to stroll in at lunch or dinner-time. A variety of tastes is on offer, ranging from the smoked chickens and spring onion and potato pies with Puy lentils to the soufflés of Swiss cheeses roasted in cream and Thai coconut soup. The room is gorgeous, service is professional, and the Tea Room was winner of the second Taste of Temple Bar Award.

Thornton's

1 Portobello Road, Dublin 8 (454 9067). **Bus 14, 15, 15A, 15B, 54A, 155.** **Lunch served** 12.30-2pm Fri. **Dinner served** 6.30-11pm Tue-Sat. **Average** lunch £15.50; dinner £32. **Credit** AmEx, DC, MC, V.

An engaging blend of styles from Kevin Thornton creates plenty of pleasant surprises for guests here. Combing ingredients in truly novel ways (foie gras with marinated salsify and warm brioche or red mullet with squid ink and red pepper sauce, perhaps), his immaculate, adorable food has won every award going in the last two years. The room is elegantly simple, the service sublime, and despite the high prices, Thornton's is actually good value for money.

Truman's

Buswell's Hotel, Molesworth Street, Dublin 2 (676 4013). **DART O'Connell Street.** **Lunch served** noon-3pm Mon-Sat. **Dinner served** 6-11pm Mon-Fri. **Average** lunch £15; dinner £25. **Credit** AmEx, DC, MC, V.

The complete refurbishment of Buswell's Hotel has drawn design brickbats for the elaborate ornateness of Truman's Restaurant, with its clashing colours and cheap reproduction paintings. But Jack Duffy's food has met a better reception, as those who've eaten his oxtail and barley broth, corned beef and cabbage or cod with tomato crust will testify.

Wright's Fisherman's Wharf

Financial Services Centre, Dublin 1 (670 1900). **All cross city buses.** **Lunch served** 12-3pm Mon-Fri. **Dinner served** 6-11pm Wed-Sat. **Light meals served** (downstairs) 9.30am-5.30pm. **Average** lunch £14; dinner £18. **Credit** AmEx, DC, MC, V.

Overlooking the water at the FSC, Wright's is bright and light, with all the modern references we find in purpose-built restaurant spaces: white walls, big windows, lean furnishings, an open kitchen. In short, a space where function and form unite. The food is as of-the-moment as the design: marinated chicken with a lemon grass, chilli and sun-dried tomato dressing; poached sea trout has courgette ribbons, baked haddock with cucumber noodles, herb and garlic boxty with raspberry dressing and organic greens. The choreography of the chefs behind the counter and the girls on the floor works well.

Global flavours

Dublin offers almost all of the cuisines of the world within the embrace of the city, but hunting down true ethnic flavours demands dogged pursuit. There are Chinese restaurants, for example, where the standard cookery is not merely conventional, but utterly compromised for western tastes. And yet, in these same places at different times, you can enjoy dim sum of exquisite, dedicated deliciousness, specialist dishes which offer all the slithery, slippery, squidgy joy that restaurants presume Western tastes cannot appreciate.

In recent years, the arrival of balti houses has encouraged Dubliners to enjoy Indian food in a simpler, more accessible style. The city's Italian restaurants tend, for the most part, to be Italian-Irish restaurants, with a souped-up style of trattoria cooking which is embedded in the 1950s.

The most impressive ethnic restaurants are, as you would expect, those run by people who have moved to Ireland from their original country, whilst the least impressive are those where Irish cooks simply try to replicate a cuisine which they enjoy. This latter situation only delivers the most compromised style of cooking, so do choose carefully, and remember that the simplest rooms often provide the truest food.

*Panache and professionalism are part of the package at **Peacock Alley**, South William Street.*

Cajun/Creole

Tante Zoe's

1 Crow Street, Temple Bar, Dublin 2 (679 4407). **Lunch served** noon-4pm daily. **Dinner served** 5pm-midnight daily. **Average** lunch £6.50; dinner £15. **Credit** AmEx, DC, MC, V.

Tante Zoe's mixture of Creole cooking for Irish tastes has proved enduringly popular, thanks to its emphasis on fun.

Chinese

Fan's Fantonese Restaurant

Dame Street, Dublin 2 (679 4263). All cross city buses. **Lunch served** 12.30-2.15pm. **Dinner served** 6.30pm-midnight daily. **Average** lunch £7; dinner £18. **Credit** AmEx, DC, EC, MC, V.

Accessible, familiar Chinese cooking.

Furama Chinese Restaurant

Ground Floor, Eirpage House, 88 Donnybrook Road, Dublin 4 (283 0522). Bus 10. **Lunch served** 12.30-2pm. **Dinner served** 6-11.30pm Mon-Sat; 6pm-midnight Fri, Sat; 1.30-11pm Sun; 6-11pm Bank Holidays. **Average** lunch £11; dinner £21. **Credit** AmEx, DC, EC, MC, V.

Furama is a Chinese restaurant which makes the minimum of culinary compromises for its clientèle, producing food that has panache. Try the king prawn with minced pork or fine roast duck, otherwise the excellent steamed black sole, great Yuk San and lovely scallops with black bean sauce. It's Chinese cooking for the Dublin 4 bourgeoisie who come here, and it works.

Good World Restaurant

18 South Great George's Street, Dublin 2 (677 5373). **Open** noon-3am Mon-Sat. **Average** lunch £6.50; dinner £14.50. **Credit** AmEx, DC, MC, V.

The Good World is one of the best spots for dim sum in the city, and popular with the Chinese community precisely for this reason. Their expertise with these little dishes is something to relish, and their dim sum cannot be matched in town for its verve and complexity. Go early on Sunday to make sure you get a table upstairs where the action is. Their standard menu is also imaginative.

Imperial Chinese Restaurant

12A Wicklow Street, Dublin 2 (677 2580). All cross city buses. **Open** noon-midnight Mon-Sat. **Average** lunch £10; dinner £22. **Credit** AmEx, MC, V.

The cooking in the Imperial tends towards the familiar notes of Chinese cooking for Western tastes – steamed sea bass with ginger, the beef and black bean sauce – so to see it at its best, go on a Sunday lunchtime, for their sublime dim sum (served daily 12.30-5.30pm). Serving delicacies such as glutinous rice in lotus leaf, prawns in rice paper, shark's fin dumpling with the spicy chicken feet a joy; also squid and pork crackling achieved with finesse. Tremendously keen prices: you can feed the family for half nuthin'.

Kites

15-17 Ballsbridge Terrace, Dublin 4 (660 7415). Bus 10. **Lunch served** 12.30-2pm Mon-Fri. **Dinner served** 6.30-11.30pm Mon-Fri; 6-11pm Sun. **Average** lunch £10; dinner from £15. **Credit** AmEx, DC, MC, V.

Easy-going Chinese food, attracting lots of folk from the nearby hotels.

Orchid Sichuan

120 Pembroke Road, Dublin 4 (660 0629). Bus 7A, 10, 45. **Lunch served** 12.30-2.15pm Mon-Fri. **Dinner served** 6.30pm-midnight Mon-Sat; 6-11.30pm Sun. **Average** lunch £7; dinner £16. **Credit** AmEx, DC, EC, MC, V.

This is quite a formal Chinese restaurant, with a stylish interior and precise service. Good, if familiar, food.

GRAFTON ST. ♦ WESTMORELAND ST. ♦

DUBLIN AIRPORT ♦ GEORGES ST. ♦ DUNDRUM ♦ NUTGROVE ♦

TALLAGHT ♦ OMNI PARK ♦ BLACKROCK ♦ STILLORGAN

Bewley's

EST. 1840

*Bewley's Café,
Grafton St., Dublin.*

*Cafe Society
– Irish Style!*

♦ MARY ST. ♦ BLANCHARDSTOWN ♦

Indian/Pakistani

Bu-Ali

28 Lower Clanbrassil Street, Dublin 8 (454 6505) Bus 54. **Open** 5.30-11.30pm daily. **Average** dinner £9. **Credit** MC, V.

The great thing about the Bu-Ali is its ambience. A counter, some chairs, garish lighting, a bleating telly and scrumptious food. Mostly specialises as a takeaway, though you can eat here if you don't mind the paucity of comfort. Bu-Ali's well-judged, simple tastes will likely make you nostalgic for back-packing days, as you sit with fine chapatis, tikka, karai, dansak and dal.

Eastern Tandoori

34-35 South William Street, Dublin 2 (671 0428). Bus 10, 16, 22, 46, 46A. **Lunch served** noon-2.30pm Mon-Sat. **Dinner served** 6pm-midnight Mon-Sat; 6-11.30pm Sun. **Average** lunch £9; dinner £16. **Credit** AmEx, DC, MC, V.

The Eastern has mushroomed into an empire of restaurants now, with a branch in Cork city as well as the trio of Dublin restaurants. The vision of the owners is one of comfortable surroundings with comfortingly rich food which can please almost everyone, so an evening here mixes the modus of the Western restaurant with the food of the east in an easygoing embrace.

Punjab Balti House

15 Ranelagh Village, Dublin 6 (497 9420). Bus 44, 48. **Open** 5.30-11pm Mon, Sun; 5.30-11.30pm Tue-Sat. **Average** dinner £14. **Credit** MC, V.

Whilst described as a balti house, the menu in Mohammed Latif's increasingly popular spot in Ranelagh village actually includes many familiar dishes – tandoori and tikka chicken, rogan josh, dansak, among others – with the decisive accent of flavouring firmly on the Punjabi Pakistani style. Service is excellent, and their bring-your-own-wine policy means that an evening in the here can be very inexpensive. Friday and Saturday nights it's advisable to book, but

if you come along and can't get a table immediately, you can wait over a pint in the Four Provinces pub until one is free and they will come and get you.

The Rajdoot Tandoori

26-28 Clarendon Street, Dublin 2 (679 4274). All cross city buses. **Lunch served** noon-2.30pm daily. **Dinner served** 7.30-10pm daily. **Average** lunch £6.95; dinner £16.50. **Credit** AmEx, DC, EC, MC, V.

The Rajdoot belongs to that time when Indian restaurants aimed at the upper-end of the restaurant market, before the balti craze introduced simple food, low prices and a canteen ethic to Indian cooking. It doesn't require a second mortgage, however, to explore the delights of vegetable sashlik, channa bunna, the tandoori dishes, the splendid onion kulcha. Vegetarian choices are particularly excellent; service is a byword for professionalism.

Saagar

16 Harcourt Street, Dublin 2 (475 5060). All cross city buses. **Lunch** 12.30-3pm Mon-Fri; **Dinner** 6-11.30pm daily. **Average** lunch £8; dinner £16. **Credit** AmEx, DC, MC, V.

Saagar is a sleek operation, housed in a basement, and the attention to detail is dazzling. The menu aims to explore the regional cooking of India – spicy, hot Colombo fish curry and excellent tandoori chicken – as well as offering novel creations of their own, such as *murgh dumpukht*, a mild chicken dish with a coconut and almond base which is sweet, nutty and delicious. The wine list is good, and the temperateness of most of the Saagar dishes makes them suitable partners for a good bottle. Prices are modest.

The Shalimar

17 South Great George's Street, Dublin 2 (671 0738). All cross city buses. **Lunch served** noon-2.30pm Mon-Sat. **Dinner served** 6pm-midnight Mon-Thur, Sun; 6pm-1am Fri, Sat. **Average** lunch £7.50; dinner £15. **Credit** AmEx, DC, MC, V.

The opening of their basement Balti House allows the Shalimar

*Deserving winner of the Beck's Taste of Temple Bar Award – **Chameleon** – see page 87.*

*The best noodles in town and a variety of steaks, too – **Ayumi-Ya Japanese Steakhouse**.*

to offer further variants of the Pakistani Punjab cuisine in which the restaurant specialises. The simple balti dishes – chicken, seafood, korma, vegetable kofta, cooked, served and eaten from a karahi — are a contrast to the more formal food of the restaurant – such as tandoori specialities, Punjabi dishes and a range of biryanis.

Indonesian

Chameleon

1 Fownes Street Lower, Temple Bar, Dublin 2 (671 0362). All cross city buses. **Dinner served** 5.30-11pm Tue-Sat; 5.30-10pm Sun. **Average** £15. **Credit** MC, V.
Chameleon is the antithesis of the self-conscious coolness and the flash money of Temple Bar. Dominated by the vivacious bonhomie of Carol Walshe, with Vincent Vis in firm control of the cooking, it's Temple Bar's Mom 'n' Pop place, a shrine devoted to the caring work of these two people. Excellent fun, deserving winner of the first Beck's Taste of Temple Bar Award.

Langkawi

46 Upper Baggot Street, Dublin 2 (668 2760). Bus 10. **Lunch served** 12.30-2.30pm Mon-Fri. **Dinner served** 6-11pm Mon-Sat. **Average** lunch £10; dinner £15. **Credit** AmEx, DC, EC, MC, V.
Very popular restaurant whose far eastern mélange of foods attracts office workers and locals.

Japanese

Ayumi-Ya Japanese Steakhouse

132 Lower Baggot Street, Dublin 2 (662 0233). All cross city buses. **Lunch served** 12.30-2.30pm Mon-Fri. **Dinner served** 6-11.15pm Mon-Thur; 6pm-12.15am Fri, Sat. **Average** lunch £6; dinner £11. **Credit** AmEx, DC, MC, V.
A fine basement restaurant, characterised by calm service, excellent cooking – the noodles are the best in town – and by the brilliant bento box takeaway service. Sit at the counter and rub shoulders with the Japanese salarymen or have a table and enjoy the steaks, which come in all varieties, including vegetarian. There is also a sushi menu. Sister to the Ayumi-ya in Blackrock (*see* **Outside the city: Southside**).

Yamamori Noodles

71 South Great George's Street, Dublin 2 (475 5001). All cross city buses. **Lunch served** 12.30-3pm Mon-Sat. **Dinner served** 5.30-11pm Mon-Sat; 5.30-11.30pm Fri, Sat; 2-10pm Sun. **Average** lunch £7; dinner £12. **Credit** AmEx, DC, EC, MC, V.
The Yamamori has acquired cult status, with an increasing stream of devotees who love its noodles, its hipness and its cheapness. The music is fabulous, the Japanese waitresses splendid, and Yoshi Iwasaki's flavour-filled cooking makes dishes such as soba noodles with chicken and spring onion, and udon noodle with seaweed and vegetables, delightful.

Middle Eastern

Sinners

12 Parliament Street, Temple Bar, Dublin 2 (671 9345). All cross city buses. **Open** 5.30pm-midnight daily. **Average** £18. **Credit** AmEx, DC, MC, V.
Friendly, atmospheric middle eastern cooking with mezzes a speciality of the house.

Moroccan

Marrakesh

11 Ballsbridge Terrace, Dublin 4 (660 5539). Bus 11. **Lunch served** noon-2.30pm. **Dinner served** 6-11pm Mon-Sun; 6-11.30pm Fri, Sat. **Average** lunch £9; dinner £15. **Credit** AmEx, DC, MC, V.
Akim Beskri offers the classics of Moroccan food upstairs in the Marrakesh: try harira soup, pigeon and almond pastilla or falafel. Also couscous *royale aux sept legumes* and excellent sweet pastries. Especially good are shebbakia and beghrir with a sauce of honey, orange and butter. Flavours are good, and make for enjoyable and inexpensive food, though the atmosphere can be a little quiet at times.

Thai

The Chilli Club

1 Anne's Lane, South Anne Street, Dublin 2 (677 3721). All cross city buses. **Lunch served** 12.30-2.30pm Mon-Fri. **Dinner served** 6-11pm Mon-

Thur; 6-11.30 Fri, Sat. **Average** lunch £10; dinner £15.
Credit AmEx, DC, EC, MC, V.
The Chilli Club preceded the current boom in all things Thai
which has been sweeping the city in recent years; its satays
are crisply tactile and the curries sweet with coconut milk.
It's very easy to enjoy both food and room, though a little
innovation might be a good thing now and again.

Pad Thai

30 Richmond Place, Portobello, Dublin 8 (475 5551).
Buses 14, 14A, 15, 15A, 83. **Lunch served** 12.30-
2.15pm Mon-Fri. **Dinner served** 6-11pm Mon-Sat; 6-
10pm Sun. **Credit** MC, V.
A funky room with loud music and, when the diminutive
Fon is in the kitchen, snappy Thai cooking. Recommended
dishes include hot and sour clear prawn soup, hot peppers
stuffed with tofu, nuts, coriander and corn; also chicken with
chilli and cashew nuts, and stirfried prawns with ginger,
chilli and Thai fungus. A favourite hanging-out spot.

Outside the city

There was a time when the Northside of Dublin
was the fashionable and prosperous side of the
city, but today its steady loss of status to the
Southside is mirrored especially by the paucity of
good places to eat while, in comparison, the Southside offers a plenitude of good cooking.

The wealthy boroughs of the Southside, such as
Dun Laoghaire, Ballsbridge and Donnybrook, are
all well served by a mix of good places to eat,
though there are few stars amongst the suburban
restaurants, with the really ambitious chefs still
choosing mainly to work in the centre of the city.
Here and there, however, restaurateurs with
panache have created thunderously successful
places, with Morels and Caviston's – two unlikely
spots almost facing each other just south of Dun
Laoghaire – showing that good cooking will
attract an audience wherever it occurs.

Do remember to take recommendations from
locals about their favourite restaurants with a
large pinch of salt: the very worst places are often
spoken about in awed terms by locals who are
blind to their many shortcomings.

Northside

Drumcondra

Il Corvo

*100 Upper Drumcondra Road, Dublin 9 (837 5727). Bus
3, 11, 16, 33, 36, 41, 51.* **Open** lunch Mon-Sat;
12.30-11pm Sun. **Average** lunch £10; dinner £20.
Credit AmEx, MC, V.
A popular little place in Drumcondra, Il Corvo offers familiar food in the Italian style, including very good pizzas.
Relaxing food that's perfect for its suburban location.

Independent Pizza Co

46 Lower Drumcondra Road, Dublin 9 (830 2957).
Bus 3, 11, 16, 33, 36, 41, 51. **Open** noon-12.30am
Mon-Wed, Sun; noon-1am Thur-Sat. **Average** £10.
No credit cards.
An excellent purveyor of classic pizzas, where pizza-making
is an art of its own. A local treasure.

Howth

Adrian's

*8 Abbey Street, Howth (839 1696). DART
Howth/bus 31, 31A.* **Lunch served** 12.30-2.30pm
Mon-Sat. **Dinner served** 6-9.30pm Mon-Sat;
6-7.30pm Sun. **Average** lunch £8; dinner £16.
Credit EC, MC, V.
Adrian's is one of the very best places to eat on the Northside, particularly at the weekends when the pair of rooms
have the buzz they need to be at their best. Catriona Holden
is a good cook, who revels in the challenges and creativity
of the kitchen – her fennel soup is subtle, the splash of
whiskey in her chowder makes it snappy – and she does
wholly lovely things, like pairing Gubbeen cheese with tagliatelle, or adding a fried banana to a chicken fillet in a mild
curry sauce.

Casa Pasta

*12 Harbour Road, Howth (839 3823). DART Howth/bus
31, 31A.* **Open** 6pm-midnight Mon-Sat; 1-11pm Sun.
Average £12. **Credit** MC, V.
Casa Pasta has been the success story of Howth ever since
its 1993 opening, and has recently spawned a sibling restaurant which can be found on the main road close to Clontarf
village. Simple furnishings, keen prices, good views over the
bays and straightforward zappy food: spicy chicken wings,
deep-fried brie, bresaola, Greek salad, fettucine with pesto,
pasta with shrimps, tiramisu.
Branch Clontarf Road, Dublin 3 (833 1402).

King Sitric

*East Pier, Howth (832 5235). DART Howth/bus 31,
31A.* **Open** 6.30-11pm Mon-Sat (also *May-Sept*
noon-3pm Mon-Sat). **Average** £30. **Credit** AmEx,
DC, EC, MC, V.
Aidan MacManus' restaurant is one of the longest established in Dublin, and has always wisely centred its cuisine
around the fish landed at the pier just yards away.

Malahide

Bon Appetit

9 St James Terrace, Malahide (845 0314/2206). Bus 42.
Lunch served 12.30-2.30pm Mon-Fri. **Dinner served**
7-10.30pm Mon-Sat. **Average** lunch £12; dinner £20.
Credit MC, V.
A clever conjoining of the classical and the reliable is at the
heart of both Patsy McGuirk's cooking and of Bon Appetit's
success. Mr McGuirk cooks in the French style and his food
enjoys a comforting familiarity, which is precisely what his
customers appreciate.

Eastern Tandoori

1 New Street, Malahide (845 4155). Bus 42. **Open** 6-
11.30pm Mon-Thur; 6-midnight Fri, Sat; 1-11pm Sun.
Average lunch £10; dinner £16. **Credit** AmEx, DC,
MC, V.
One of a trio of reliable mid-priced Indian restaurants.

Siam Thai Restaurant

Gas Lane, Malahide (845 4698). Bus 42. **Open** 6pm-
midnight daily. **Average** £17.50. **Credit** AmEx, MC, V.
The Siam is a very popular restaurant, its succinct and
expert cooking drawing the crowds from miles around. If
you order soup, watch out for the *tom yum gung* which is
volcanically spicy, whilst *tom kha gai* – chicken breast with
lemon grass in coconut milk – is more sedate. Main courses
are organised under different headings – spicy salads, curries, poultry, meat dishes, sweet and sour, and so on. Stirfried chicken with ginger, chillies, black fungus and spring
onions are good, though there are occasional misses.
Branch Monkstown (284 3309).

Pasta Fresca at any time

Skerries

Red Bank Restaurant
7 Church Street, Skerries, Co Dublin (849 1005). Bus 33.
Lunch served 12.30-2.15pm Sun. **Dinner served** 7-9.30pm Tue-Sat. **Average** lunch £15.75; dinner £24.
Credit AmEx, MC, V.
Terry McCoy is the great fish expert of the east coast and his consummate skill at cooking everything that swims is enough to justify heading all the way northwards out to Skerries. The room is informal, the food is spot on: try seafood selection Paddy Attley or hake with horseradish. There are lots of locally sourced foods to complement these main attractions.

Smithfield

Paddy's Place
Corporation Markets, Dublin 7 (873 5130). All cross city buses. **Open** 6am-2.30pm Mon-Fri; 7am-11am Sat. **No credit cards.**
A lovely little caff in the middle of the Corpo markets, where you can find Dublin coddle, beef stew, and fresh fish, which can, on occasion, be lobster, providing market prices are not too high.

Swords

The Chuck Wagon
N1, north of the Swords dual carriageway. **Open** 8am-7pm Mon-Sat.
This is the best grub-to-go to be found, on the most boring road in the country. The Chuck Wagon makes the very best bacon and sausage soda bread sarnies you can buy, alongside lots of other protein-rich, saturated fat-filled burgers and banger concoctions.

The Old Schoolhouse
Coolbanagher, Swords (840 2846). **Lunch served** 12.30-2.30pm Mon-Fri. **Dinner served** 7-10.30pm Mon-Sat. **Average** lunch £15; dinner £25. **Credit** AmEx, DC, MC, V.
The Old Schoolhouse is a capable, enthusiastic restaurant, founded on a well-understood notion of service, tuned into the demands of its suburban clientèle and very expert at catering to the needs of the ever-growing population of Swords.

Southside
Blackrock

Ayumi-Ya
Newpark Centre, Newtownpark Avenue, Blackrock (283 1767). Bus 45, 46A. **Open** 6-11.30pm Mon-Sat; 5.30-9.45pm Sun. **Average** dinner from £16.50. **Credit** AmEx, DC, MC, V.
The Japanese food in the Ayumi-ya is impressively well understood and delivered and, as its Dublin customers have become more adventurous, the restaurant has been allowed to play to its strengths, serving raw yellow-fin tuna as part of a tantalising, yet restorative, plate of San Francisco sashimi, as well as the easily loved tempura, chargrilled salmon, or the same fish cured with ginger. Also, soba noodles with chicken and the ever present miso soup.

La Tavola
114 Rock Road, Booterstown (283 5101). Bus 45. **Open** 5-10.30pm Mon; 5-11.30pm Tue-Sat. **Average** dinner £18. **Credit** AmEx, DC, MC, V.
The pizza and pasta recipe familiar from so many places is rather better executed in La Tavola than elsewhere, and its

continuing success in an uninspiring location is testament to their care with staples such as penne *all' arrabbiatta* or their much-loved pizzas.

Dalkey

PD's Woodhouse
1 Coliemore Road, Dalkey (284 9399). DART Dalkey/bus 8. **Open** 6-11pm Mon-Sat; 1-9.30pm Sun. **Average** dinner £20. **Credit** AmEx, DC, MC, V.
Populated by a slightly older, but still-determined-to-be-hip crowd, PD's Woodhouse has carved out a neat niche for itself as a place to feast on their speciality chargrilled steaks and baked potatoes with crisp salads.

Al Minar
21 Castle Street, Dalkey (285 0552). DART Dalkey/bus 8. **Lunch served** noon-2.30pm Mon-Sat. **Dinner served** 6pm-midnight daily. **Average** lunch £9; dinner £15. **Credit** AmEx, DC, MC, V.
A quiet little Indian restaurant on the main street of the village of Dalkey. Quietly lit, with quiet service, the Al Minar makes up for this deference by enjoying the demands of customers who ask for dishes to be prepared in the way the staff eat them.

La Romana
The Queen's, Castle Street, Dalkey (285 4569). DART Dalkey/bus 8. **Open** 5.30-11.30pm Mon-Sat; 12.30-10.30pm Sun. **Average** £14. **Credit** AmEx, DC, MC, V.
A room in the big, plush pub that is the Queen's, La Romana offers pasta and pizzas in that style which owes rather more to Ireland than Italy. But the room is bright and busy, and a dinner of simple foods, after a brace of pints, can be enjoyably successful.

Deansgrange

Eastern Tandoori
The Old Parish Hall, Kill Lane, Deansgrange (289 2856). Bus 45A, 46A. **Lunch served** noon-2.30pm Mon-Sat. **Dinner served** 6-11.30pm Mon-Sat; 1-11pm Sun. **Average** lunch £10; dinner £16. **Credit** AmEx, DC, MC, V.
With sibling restaurants in Cork city as well as a trio of Dublin, Eastern Tandoori offers good, spicy food in pleasant surroundings. Their menu contains something which can please almost everyone.

Dún Laoghaire/Sandycove

Bistro Vino
56 Glasthule Road, Sandycove, Co Dublin (280 6097). DART Sandycove/bus 8. **Open** 5pm-late daily. **Average** £13. **Credit** AmEx, DC, MC, V.
Bistro Vino's food is much as one might expect – fresh prawns with faralline; baked field mushrooms with crab meat and fresh prawns, or with blue cheese; a range of seafood dishes, such as monkfish pepperonata, and a variety of meats and poultry. Food has Italian leanings. Good atmosphere in this successful, well-served little local place.

Black Tulip Bistro
107 Lower George's Street, Dún Laoghaire (280 5318). DART Sandycove/bus 7, 8, 46A. **Lunch served** noon-3pm Mon-Fri. **Dinner served** 5.30pm-late Mon-Sat. **Average** £22.50. **Credit** AmEx, MC, V.
An elegant space where they certainly know how to produce a fine rack of lamb with potatoes or a symphony of seafood. The room needs the buzz of a lot of people to be at its best, so weekends see the Black Tulip at its most vital. A promising venture.

Caviston's

59 Glasthule Road, Sandycove (280 9120). DART Sandycove/bus 8. **Open** noon-4pm Tue-Sun. **Average** £10. **Credit** MC, V.

The great ship Caviston have added a little fish restaurant to their great deli, with chef Noel Cusack offering pan-fried cod's roe with crème fraîche, baked oysters with coriander and pine nut topping, marinated tuna with teriyaki sauce, chargrilled salmon with couscous and a balsamic vinaigrette, all precisely and expertly delivered. In summer, they put some tables out on the street. Definitely one of the delights of the Southside.

Krishna Indian Restaurant

1st floor, 47 George's Street Lower, Dún Laoghaire (280 1855). DART Dún Laoghaire/bus 7, 7A. **Lunch served** 12.30-2.30pm Mon-Sat;. **Dinner served** 6-11.30pm Sun-Thur; 6pm-12.30am Fri, Sat. **Average** lunch £8; dinner £16. **Credit** MC, V.

A small, dimly lit upstairs room – there is much to enjoy in the Krishna, with their breads, in particular, proving especially excellent. Their work also enjoys a particular air of authenticity – the cooking is in the buttery, nutty, northern Indian style – and everything works together to make this a genuine little place.

Morels Bistro

18 Glasthule Road, Dún Laoghaire (230 0210). DART Sandycove/bus 8. **Lunch served** 12.30-2pm Sun. **Dinner served** 6-9.45pm Mon-Fri; 6.30-10.30pm Sat; 6.30-9pm Sun. **Credit** AmEx, DC, MC, V.

This Southside success story has spawned a sister restaurant in town, but the original remains a sure-fire bet. Everything about the room and the service is designed to show you the best time possible, so the cooking is terrific, the service excellent and prices fair.

Odell's

49 Sandycove Road, Dún Laoghaire (284 2188). DART Sandycove/bus 8. **Open** 6-10.30pm Mon-Sun; 6-9.30pm Sun. **Average** £16; £12.95 early bird menu. **Credit** AmEx, DC, MC, V.

Odell's is a friendly bistro, with understated, cosmopolitan food – Cajun dishes, Mediterranean stylings, Chinese spicings – served in generous portions by generous staff.

Brasserie Na Mara

The Harbour, Dún Laoghaire (280 6767). DART Dún Laoghaire/bus 7, 7A. **Lunch served** 12.30-2.30pm Mon-Fri. **Dinner served** 6.30-10pm Mon-Sat. **Average** lunch £10.50; dinner £21. **Credit** AmEx, DC, MC, V.

Adrian Spellman's cooking in the stylishly redesigned Bistro is classical and effective. Gravadlax with a buckwheat blini and coriander cream, rilette of duck and foie gras, deep-fried hake in a tortilla crust, fillet of beef with artichoke and wild mushrooms, sautéed chicken with Puy lentils. This is smart, modern cooking, wholly appropriate to this delightful, modern room with its tall white walls and mega-mirrors.

Purty Kitchen

Old Dún Laoghaire Road, Dún Laoghaire (284 3576). DART Salthill/bus 7, 7A, 8. **Open** noon-9.45pm daily. **Average** lunch £5; dinner £16. **Credit** AmEx, MC, V.

This long-lived pub serves well-regarded grub – soups and sandwiches popular at lunch-time, with a variety of simple dishes such as deep-fried cheese, garlic mussels, steaks and regular seafood concoctions available all day. Their fish is all from Caviston's celebrated delicatessen, and so is the smoked duck, which is one of the best choices for a lunchtime open sandwich.

Foxrock

Bistro One

3 Brighton Road, Foxrock, Dublin 18 (289 7711). Bus 64. **Open** 7-10.30pm Tue-Sat. **Average** £20. **Credit** MC, V.

Set above a dry cleaner's shop in this little commercial strip of Foxrock Village, Bistro One is a well-kept secret on the Southside. The one-page menu is abetted by daily specials: crabmeat, coriander and chilli tart, a selection of standards such as deep-fried fish and chips with tartare sauce. Also recommended are Bistro One's Irish stew, smokies with fresh chives, camembert in wafer pastry with a redcurrant jus. There is an open fire, and a calm atmosphere, carved out by the regulars who colonise the restaurant and who regard it as a home from home.

Glencullen

Fox's Famous Seafood Kitchen

Glencullen, Co Dublin (295 5647). Bus 44B. **Open** noon-10pm Mon-Sat; 4-10pm Sun. **Average** lunch £6; dinner £22. **Credit** AmEx, DC, MC, V.

The highest pub in Ireland is also one of the merriest, and can be splendidly raucous at weekends. Lots of entertainment, with well-considered food which is better than most. Perfect for those sunny days, sitting outside with pint in hand.

Monkstown

Empress Chinese & Thai Restaurant

Clifton Avenue, Monkstown (284 3200). DART Salthill/bus 7, 7A, 8. **Open** 6pm-midnight Mon-Sat; 3pm-late Sun. **Average** dinner £20. **Credit** AmEx, DC, MC, V.

The Empress has a décor of black marble and tall mirrors, friendly service, with such typical food as stuffed crab claws, Thai spring rolls, beef with tomato and green pepper in a chilli and herb sauce, pork fillet in Sichuan sauce.

FXB's

3A The Crescent, Monkstown (284 6187). DART Salthill/bus 7, 7A, 8, 46A. **Open** 12.30-11pm Mon-Thur, 12.30-11.30pm Fri, Sat; 12.30-10.30pm Sun. **Average** lunch £10.95; dinner £18.95. **Credit** AmEx, DC, MC, V.

As you would expect from a restaurant owned by the FX Buckley chain of butcher's shops, the emphasis in FXB's is on meat, both here and in their city sister restaurant. But the menus do offer lots of choices, including vegetarian dishes. **Branch** Pembroke Street (676 4606).

Valparaiso

99 Monkstown Road, Monkstown (280 1992). DART Salthill/bus 7, 7A, 8. **Open** 6.30-11pm Mon-Sat; 5.30-10pm Sun. **Average** £18. **Credit** AmEx, DC, MC, V.

Spanish colourings of vivid blue and yellow, and Spanish-accented food – tapas, gambas al ajillo, piperade – are the recipe of the long-established Valparaiso.

Stillorgan

China-Sichuan Restaurant

4 Lower Kilmacud Road, Stillorgan (288 4817). Bus 7, 7A, 8. **Open** 12.30-2.30pm Mon-Fri; 1-2.30pm Sun. **Dinner served** 6-11pm daily. **Average** lunch £9; dinner £18. **Credit** AmEx, DC, MC, V.

David Hui's restaurant easily outpaces its many rivals when it comes to authenticity and the cooking of food with distinct, vital flavours. They can do certain things which are beyond the reach of anyone else, such as monkfish in yellow bean sauce, magnificent shredded pork with garlic sauce or a thrilling almond bean curd. In addition, the service is excellent, as are the vegetarian creations. Fair prices.

Bistros, Cafés & Coffee Shops

Continental cuisine combines with traditional food to create a renaissance in Irish cooking.

Fifteen years ago, the vocabulary of coffee drinking was unknown in Dublin. For a city which now trumpets the names of the great Italian brands with such confidence, which can deliberate on the particular merits of cappuccino and espresso, it seems remarkable that, back then, coffee was simply a black and white matter.

But the arrival of the gleaming Gaggia machines, shining brightly behind every bar, quickly changed all that. Coffee acquired a ceremonial aspect, the order for an espresso or a cappuccino followed by the splutter and cough, the dribble and the whoosh, as steam fired up the milk, and the dark, entrancing lotion fell from the spout of the machine.

Coffee, and the café society, is increasingly becoming a map of the daily life of the city. But if Dubs are now slaves to caffeine, the reason why is actually an ancient one, summarised in one memorable name: Bewley's.

Bewley's, the 'legendary lofty clattery café', is the key to understanding just how and why Dubliners have taken so quickly to the modern café society. Long before it was fashionable to do so, Bewley's was serving good coffee in beautiful rooms, stirring up an addiction for decades before the new interlopers arrived and, today, a cup of brew, drunk as the arcing light streams in through those famous Harry Clarke stained-glass windows, remains a unique pleasure.

Bernardo's
19 Lincoln Place, Dublin 2 (676 2471). All cross city buses. **Open** 12.30-2.45pm Mon-Fri; 6.15pm-12.30am Mon-Sat. **Average** lunch £8; dinner £18. **Credit** MC, V.
Step in the door of Bernardo's and you step back in time. Celebrated for their scampi and their ice creams, the food is otherwise Irish-Italian.

Bewley's Oriental Café
Grafton Street, Dublin 2 (677 6761 switchboard). All cross city buses. **Open** 8am-1am Sun-Thur; 7.30am-5am Fri, Sat. **Credit** AmEx, DC, MC, V.
The Bewley's cafés are undergoing major revisions, which will see them opening for dinner and changing much of the self-service style which they have operated for many years. They are gorgeous rooms, with amazing potential (check out their Café Museum; *see chapter* **Museums**), and it looks as if Dublin's classic cafés are now gearing up for

the new millennium, bringing their glorious history up to date. The Grafton Street branch really does operate these extraordinarily long hours.
Branches Mary Street (closes 6pm); Westmoreland Street (closes 8pm).

The Billboard Café
43 Lower Camden Street, Dublin 2 (475 5047). All cross city buses. **Open** 24 hours Fri, Sat; 7am-7.30pm Mon-Thur, Sun. **No credit cards.**
The Billboard is something of a cult classic, thanks to staying open 24 hours a day over the weekend. Pat and Carol's café boasts a jukebox which brings in the ravers, solid grub which attracts the guards from Harcourt Street's station, a friendly buzz which attracts those with insomnia, an all-day breakfast which attracts the protein fiends and even ordinary, decent folk.

Blazing Salads II
Powerscourt Townhouse Centre, Dublin 2 (671 9552). All cross city buses. **Open** 9.30am-6pm Mon-Sat. **Average** £7.50. **No credit cards.**
A thoughtful, venerable vegetarian restaurant, high up in the attic of the Powerscourt Townhouse, with imaginative gluten-, sugar-, dairy- and yeast-free dishes on offer.

Brown's Bar
Brown Thomas, Grafton Street, Dublin 2 (679 5666). All cross city buses. **Open** 9am-6pm Mon-Wed, Fri, Sat; 9am-8pm Thur; 2-6pm Sun. **Average** £10. **Credit** AmEx, DC, MC, V.
The chic Brown's Bar, downstairs in equally chic Brown Thomas (*see chapter* **Shopping & Services**), is an arm of the Masarella Catering Group, offering a menu of soups, groovy sarnies, salads and drinks, including excellent espresso and cappuchino. They don't actually call any of their creations 'sandwiches', so focaccia and crostini are the order of the day. The loos, incidentally, are excellent.

Ristorante Bucci
7 Lower Camden Street, Dublin 2 (475 1020). All cross city buses. **Open** 12.30-2.30pm Tue-Fri; 6-11.30pm Mon-Sun. **Average** lunch £8; dinner £10. **Credit** MC, V.
Bucci's roll-call of pasta and pizza is well executed, another fashionable variation on that grab-bag modern style of food that has little time for authenticity, but is rather good at delivering food with savour. It's an important player in this neglected part of the city, and a good lunchtime spot. The music is also good.

Leo Burdock's
2 Werburgh Street, Dublin 2 (454 0306). Bus 49, 77. **Open** 12.30-midnight Mon-Fri; 2-11pm Sat; 4pm-midnight Sun. **Average** £4.50. **No credit cards.**

The original and best Dublin chipper. Fish and chips and bottles of pop is what they do, and they do it with no compromises and with good cheer. Traditionalists may mourn the passing of the old coal-powered fryer, but Burdock's remains a classic purveyor of classic fish and chips.

Caesar's

16 Dame Street, Dublin 2 (679 7049). All cross city buses. **Open** 6.30pm-12.30am Mon-Sat. **Average** £25. **Credit** AmEx, DC, MC, V.

Caesar's is the quieter brother of the eternal Nico's, that beloved home of Irish-meets-Italian food just across the road. Caesar's offers more of that Italian-Irish food, unchanging over the years, and as popular as ever. Go for the fettuccine *dopio burro*, toss in some pepperonata and spinach, order a side dish of fried potatoes and *voilà!* – you've just got the best out of Caesar's.

The Cedar Tree

11 Saint Andrew's Street, Dublin 2 (677 2121). All cross city buses. **Open** noon-5pm Mon-Sun; 5.30pm-midnight Mon-Sat; 5.30-11pm Sun. **Average** lunch £9; dinner £18. **Credit** AmEx, DC, MC, V.

The Tree is a restaurant which has built a popularity with a left-field crowd who like its informal way, and it is much enjoyed by vegetarians who appreciate its clever use of pulses and grains, and also by the late-night crew who head in here to munch mezzes and slug wine.

Café Java

145 Upper Leeson Street, Dublin 4 (660 0675). **Open** 8am-6pm Mon-Fri; 9am-5pm Sat; 11am-5pm Sun. **Average** £5. **Credit** MC, V.

The Javas are extremely popular breakfast, lunchtime and coffee-time places, and their clever mix of light food – smoked salmon with bagels, poached eggs with bacon, chicken with yogurt – is confidently handled. Good coffees, and they also offer a selection of wines. The South Anne Street branch opens at 7.45am during weekdays, with an extra hour tacked on in the evenings.

Branch South Anne Street (660 8899).

Café Rouge

1 St Andrew's Street, Dublin 2 (679 1357). All cross city buses. **Open** 10am-11pm Mon-Sat; 10am-10.30pm Sun. **Average** lunch £6.95; dinner £14. **Credit** AmEx, MC, V.

A beautiful, lingersome room, designed by Irishman David Collins, is part of the attraction of the sassy British chain. The food is French grub à l'anglaise, service is good and prices keen.

Canaletto's

69 Mespil Road, Dublin 4 (678 5084). Bus 10. **Open** 8am-late Mon-Sat; 11am-4.30pm; 7pm-late Sun. **Average** lunch £4.25; dinner £20. **Credit** AmEx, DC, MC, V.

They cook good, punchy, soulful food in Canaletto's, and it has considerably greater imagination than many other Dublin eateries. Lunchtime sees speedy counter service – good sandwiches and bakes, lively salads – which then slows down to a more relaxed pace during the evening: pasta with chillies or maybe pesto, lasagne, spicy chicken dishes. It's fashionable and fun.

La Cave

28 South Anne Street, Dublin 2 (679 4409). Bus 10, 11, 13. **Open** 12.30pm-2am daily. **Average** lunch £6; dinner £16.50. **Credit** AmEx, DC, MC, V.

The basement Cave is nostalgically decorated with bistro clichés in terms of posters and prints, and with cleverly agreeable bistro dishes: goose rilettes; lamb with prunes, couscous *aux sept legumes*. Also tarte tatin and good coffee. Atmosphere is everything, and they handle the late-night crew with just the right, indulgent touch.

Chompy's

Powerscourt Townhouse Centre, Dublin 2 (679 4552). All cross city buses. **Open** 8am-6pm Mon-Sat. **Average** lunch £5. **Credit** MC, V.

The great American breakfast is one of the big attractions in Frank Zimmer's popular place, with folk queuing up for the pancakes with maple syrup, the lox and bagels, eggs benedict, and good french toast with icing sugar.

Cora's

1 Saint Mary Road, Ballsbridge, Dublin 4 (660 0585). Bus 10. **Open** 9am-5pm Mon-Fri; 10am-7pm Sat; 10am-3pm Sun. **Credit** MC, V.

Cora's has been run by the Basini family since 1978, and as well as splendid pizzas, the menu might include fillet of trout with duchess potatoes, beef in Guinness or coq au vin and meat balls in tomato sauce. It's a darling, simple place with amazingly low prices. A great place to bring the family for Sunday lunch, and the staff kiss your babies.

Cornucopia

19 Wicklow Street, Dublin 2 (677 7583). All cross city buses. **Open** 9am-8pm Mon-Sat; 9am-9pm Thur. **Average** lunch £5; dinner £13. **Credit** V.

Eddie Bates runs the kitchens in Cornucopia now, which has seen an injection of style and sumptuousness into the cooking of this favourite vegetarian restaurant. He cooks with brio: green lentils, roast tomatoes and leeks with balsamic dressing are good, so too the cashew nut, leek and tarragon loaf and courgette, spinach and feta cheese strudel with broccoli sauce. Table service operates on weekend nights only.

Expresso Bar

Westbury Mall, Dublin 2 (670 7056). All cross city buses. **Open** 7.45am-6pm Mon-Fri; 9am-6pm Sat; 11am-6pm Sun. **Credit** DC, MC, V.

A hip, white space, Ann Marie Nohl's Expresso Bar has become a cult success with a stylish crowd who admire the lightness and elegant control of the cooking. It's very much a lifestyle, feel-good outfit, which wouldn't be out of place in a West End store. All the modern ingredients are here: crostini and bruschetta, fashionable pastas, clever salads, gourmet open sandwiches, 'naughty' desserts plus a terrific range of designer coffees. Their original shop is in Dublin 4.

Branch: Shelbourne Road (660 8632).

Gloria Jean's Coffee Co

Powerscourt Townhouse Centre Dublin 2 (679 7772). All cross city buses. **Open** 8am-7pm Mon-Sat; 8am-8pm Thur; 10am-6pm Sun. **Credit** AmEx, DC, MC, V.

A coffee venture which has been imported from the US, Gloria Jean's offers an enormous array of coffees, of all varieties and prices and a broad range of flavoured coffees. You can drink them here, or buy the coffees and all the paraphernalia to take home.

The Gotham Café

8 South Anne Street, Dublin 2 (679 5266). All cross city buses. **Open** noon-midnight Tue-Thur; noon-12.30am Fri, Sat; noon-10.30pm Sun. **Average** lunch £10; dinner £10. **Credit** MC, V.

For many people, the Gotham produces one of the best pizzas in the city, a fact which rather obscures the other fine things they do in here. Like the pizzas, the food is very Cal-Ital: goat's cheese crostini, chargrilled chicken with peanut sauce or penne with chilli and creole sausage. It's a funky, good-vibes space, bedecked with old *Rolling Stone* covers on the walls, and kids like it.

The Grey Door

22-23 Upper Pembroke Street, Dublin 2 (676 3286). Bus 10, 11. **Lunch** 12.30-2.15pm; **dinner** 6-10.30pm daily. **Average** lunch £11.50 +12.5%; dinner from £20. **Credit** AmEx, DC, MC, V.

Westbury Mall's **Expresso Bar** *has become a cult success with a stylish crowd.*

Newly reborn as an Irish restaurant and chef Michael Durkin has tried to contemporise traditional dishes, so expect spring lamb with boxty and spring vegetables, smoked salmon with vegetable ribbons and mash, guinea fowl with buttered cabbage. Pier 32, downstairs, is more informal. There are also rooms upstairs.

Juice

9 Castle House, South Great George's Street, Dublin 2 (475 7856). All cross city buses. **Open** 8am-2.30pm; 6.30-10.30pm daily. **Average** lunch £8; dinner £11. **Credit** MC, V.
Juice is a restaurant which positively proselytises on behalf of healthy food, offering a wide range of foods which can be eaten raw and adding a fresh juice bar to its roll-call. Their wines are all organically produced while the cooking is happy to tread largely familiar vegetarian themes: goat's cheese in filo, cashew and hazelnut roast; vegetable stir-fry with noodles.

Kilkenny Design

6 Nassau Street, Dublin 2 (677 7066). All cross city buses. **Open** 9am-6pm Mon-Wed, Fri, Sat; 9am-8pm Thur. **Average** lunch £9. **Credit** AmEx, DC, MC, V.
The Kilkenny shop is a vital source of desirable kitchen implements and objects, but don't overlook the careful and enjoyable cooking in the upstairs restaurant. The cold cuts are good, the salads fine, and the stews and bakes hit the spot. It's also a great spot for coffee and for peering out at the grounds of Trinity.

Lane Gallery Restaurant

55 Pembroke Lane, Dublin 2 (661 1829). Bus 10. **Lunch** noon-3pm Mon-Fri; **dinner** 6.30-10.30pm Mon-Sat. **Average** lunch £10; dinner £17. **Credit** AmEx, DC, MC, V.
An atmospheric little restaurant, with occasional live music to enjoy along with the French-styled cuisine and the alternating exhibitions of paintings.

Lord Edward Seafood Restaurant

23 Christchurch Place, Dublin 8 (454 2420). All cross city buses. **Lunch** 12.30-2.30pm Mon-Fri; **dinner** 6-10.45pm Tue-Sat. **Average** lunch £13; dinner from £25. **Credit** AmEx, DC, MC, V.
An old-fashioned restaurant, sort of gentlemen's club meets boarding school. It is upstairs from the pub of the same name, and the speciality is fish cookery, which it does simply and very well, at prices which are affordable by its usual clientèle of barristers.

Little Caesar's Palace

5 Balfe Street, Dublin 2 (671 8714). All cross city buses. **Open** 12.30pm-12.30am daily. **Average** £10. **Credit** AmEx, DC, MC, V.
A boisterous place that fizzles with gung-ho energy, Little Caesar's specialises in pizzas, and specialises especially in the theatrics of spinning the tablets of dough way up in the air, catching it before it plummets to the ground and then speedily dressing it before it is cooked. Great fun, especially if you are 12 years old.

Marks Bros

7 South Great George's Street, Dublin 2 (677 1085). Bus 16, 19, 22A. **Open** 6-11pm Tue-Sun. **Average** £15. **Credit** MC, V.
One of the longest-established places in the city and now under new ownership, Marks Bros has transformed from a daytime sandwich-and-soup place into an evening-time vegetarian restaurant, with familiar food: lentil spicy kofte, wild mushroom risotto, ginger-coated tofu and vegetable tempura and a range of inexpensive wines.

The Mercantile Bar & Grill

27-28 Dame Street, Dublin 2 (679 0522). All cross city buses. **Lunch** noon-3pm Mon-Sat; **dinner** 5-9pm Mon-Wed; 5-9pm Thur-Sat. **Average** lunch £10; dinner £18. **Credit** AmEx, MC, V.
A splendid, if surreal, over-the-top interior is part of the fun of this bank become bar, hotel and restaurant.

La Mère Zou

22 St Stephen's Green, Dublin 2 (661 6669). All cross city buses. **Lunch** 12.30-2.30pm Mon-Fri, Sun; **dinner** 6-10.30pm Mon-Fri; 6-11pm Sat, Sun. **Average** lunch £9.50; dinner £16. **Credit** AmEx, MC, V.

Belgian-orientated cooking with things such as chicken waterzooie, and decent meatballs. Unpretentious and good value. Also open for snacks throughout the afternoon.

Milano

38 Dawson Street, Dublin 2 (670 7744). All cross city buses. **Open** noon-midnight daily. **Average** lunch £10; dinner £14. **Credit** AmEx, MC, V.

Milano, a branch of the UK's Pizza Express chain, occupies a cool space, and the pizzas and pastas attract a cool crowd.

Mitchell's

21 Kildare Street, Dublin 2 (662 4724). Bus 10, 11, 13, 14, 15, 22. **Shop open** 10.30am-5.30pm Mon-Fri; 10.30am-8pm Thur; 10.30am-1pm Sat. **Restaurant** 12.15-2.30pm Mon-Sat. **Closed** *June-Aug* Sat. **Average** lunch £15. **Credit** AmEx, DC, MC, V.

Mitchell's is a handsome wine shop which houses a simple restaurant in the basement with an Irish vernacular style of cooking which has changed little in recent times. It attracts a devoted crowd of civil servants, older ladies who lunch, and a clatter of the professional classes who all know what they are going to get, and who like it like that.

National Museum Café

Kildare Street, Dublin 2 (662 1269). Bus 10, 11, 13. **Open** 10am-5pm Mon-Sat; 2pm-5pm Sun. **Credit** MC, V.

Joe Kerrigan's restaurant offers just the sort of food you want after a traipse around the museum: grilled chicken, Dublin coddle, plus good salads and sweet things.

National Gallery Restaurant

Merrion Square, Dublin 2 (661 5133). Bus 44, 48. **Open** 10am-5pm Mon-Sat; 10am-7.30pm Thur; 2-4.30pm Sun. **Average** £5.95. **Credit** AmEx, DC, MC, V.

Another outpost of the Fitzers' empire, the Gallery restaurant is a reliable source of well-considered food.

No 10 at Longfield's Hotel

Lower Fitzwilliam Street, Dublin 2 (676 1367). Bus 10. **Lunch** 12.30-2.30pm Mon-Fri; **dinner** 6.30-10pm Mon-Thur; 6.30-11pm Fri; 7-11pm Sat; 7-9pm Sun. **Average** lunch £18; dinner £27.50. **Credit** AmEx, DC, MC, V.

Tommy Donovan's cooking is imaginative and enjoyable, a far cry from most hotel food in Dublin. No 10 is a cosy basement room, with tables very close together, and a clubby atmosphere prevails, much as in the hotel itself.

Odessa

13-14 Dame Court, Dublin 2 (670 7634). All cross city buses. **Open** 5-11pm Mon-Wed; 5pm-midnight Thur, Fri; noon-midnight Sat, Sun. **Average** lunch £8; dinner £15. **Credit** AmEx, MC, V.

Odessa's menu is a typical example of the modern Irish style. 'An eclectic mix of freshly prepared food for cosmopolitan palates,' they promise, which in practice means ceviche alongside ciabatta, marinated tofu beside tandoori chicken, Caribbean mussels beside angel hair with pesto. By and large, very fashionable.

The Periwinkle

Powerscourt Townhouse Centre, Dublin 2 (679 4203). All cross city buses. **Open** 11.30am-5pm Mon-Sat. **Average** £9. **Credit** MC, V.

Good chowders and simple fish dishes are the staple of the Periwinkle. They haven't changed very much in the way they do things down here, in the basement of the Powerscourt Centre, since the day they opened.

Il Primo

16 Montague Street, Dublin 2 (478 3373). All cross city buses. **Lunch** noon-3pm; **dinner** 6-11pm Mon-Sat. **Average** lunch £10, dinner £18. **Credit** AmEx, DC, MC, V.

A fine wine list assembled by Dieter Bergman is one of the main attractions of little Il Primo. The food is familiar modern Italian, popular with the local office folk.

QV2

14-15 St Andrew's Street, Dublin 2 (677 3363). All cross city buses. **Lunch** noon-3pm; **dinner** 6pm-12.30am Mon-Sat. **Average** lunch £15; dinner £18. **Credit** AmEx, DC, MC, V.

The most modish of the cluster of restaurants on St Andrew's Street which offer Italian food, QV2 is an efficient operation with voguish Italian food. Le Caprice, just down the street, is more traditional and has a piano player.

The Side Door

The Shelbourne Hotel, St Stephen's Green, Dublin 2 (676 6471). Bus 10, 11, 14A, 15A, 15B. **Open** noon-11pm daily. **Average** lunch £8.50; dinner £17.50. **Credit** AmEx, DC, MC, V.

The Side Door is at the side of the Shelbourne Hotel, although you wouldn't think its vivid décor – limeish greens, purples, wood floors and tables – has anything to do with this sedate old hotel. The menu offers pizzas (with barbecue chicken, Mediterranean vegetables) and focaccia, Thai soup, chocolate brownies, and staples such as chargrilled ribs of beef, baked fillet of cod, and supreme of chicken. In the hotel itself, the food is much more classical and much more expensive.

Senor Sassi's

146 Upper Leeson Street, Dublin 4 (668 4544). Bus 10. **Lunch** noon-2.30pm Tue-Fri; 12.30-4pm Sun; **dinner** 6-11.30pm Mon-Thur; 6-11pm Fri; 6.30-11.45pm Sat; 5.30-10pm Sun. **Average** lunch £12; dinner £20. **Credit** AmEx, DC, MC, V.

The arrival of Paul O'Reilly in the kitchens of Sassi's has gifted these handsome rooms with greater consistency and more imaginative food: angel hair pasta with crab and pesto, lime and ginger soup, brochette of tiger prawns and red peppers, lemon and saffron broth, veal stuffed with black olives, pancetta and spinach.

Smyth's on the Green

Habitat, St Stephen's Green, Dublin 2 (677 1058). Bus 10, 43, 46. **Open** 10am-5.30pm Mon-Wed, Fri, Sat; 9.30am-8pm Thur; noon-6pm Sun. **Average** £8. **Credit** AmEx, MC, V.

An upstairs showcase for the stylish tableware of the shop in which it is housed, Smyth's is rather more than a mere mannequin for Habitat's kitchenware, and has some decent lunchtime cooking.

South Street Pizzeria

South Great George's Street, Dublin 2 (475 2273). All cross city buses. **Open** 11am-1am daily. **Average** lunch £5; dinner £15. **Credit** AmEx, EC, MC, V.

The South Street has become one of the successes of the George's Street's strip of restaurants, its punchy, funky pizzas attracting a cool crowd who like to chill out in here.

Steps of Rome

Chatham Street, Dublin 2 (671 6861). Bus 6, 7, 8, 10, 46. **Open** 10am-midnight Mon-Thur; 10-1am Fri, Sat; 1-10pm Sun. **Average** lunch £5; dinner £8. **No credit cards**.

The Steps of Rome is just a single room with a counter, beside Neary's pub, and folk just love it to bits. The pizzas, especially the potato and rosemary, are widely admired, the charm is intimate and romantic, while the warm nonchalance of the service is perfect. Super-cool.

Tosca

20 Suffolk Street, Dublin 2 (679 6744). **Lunch** noon-
3.30pm; **dinner** 5.30-late daily. **Average** lunch £8;
dinner £16. **Credit** AmEx, DC, EC, MC, V.
Aongus Hanley's food is just right for the lean space of
Tosca, a clever mix of pastas (choose both the pasta and
sauce), salads and familiar staples. They house visiting art
exhibitions, and the buzz is always good.

Trocadero

3 St Andrew's Street, Dublin 2 (677 5545). **Open** 6pm-
12.15am Mon-Sat; 6-11.30pm Sun. **Average** dinner £25.
Credit AmEx, DC, MC, V.
The Troc is a smashing room, timeless, calmly lit, a place of
good times. The food is straight out of the 1970s, but who
cares? Certainly not the night owls, the thespians, the hacks
and the media-movers who fill it up and who sail into the
small hours on a raft of booze and supercharged chat. Unique.

Unicorn Restaurant

*12B Merrion Court, Merrion Row, Dublin 2
(676 2182). Bus 44, 48A.* **Lunch** 12.30-3pm
Mon-Sat; **dinner** 6-11.30pm Mon-Sat; 6pm-midnight
Fri, Sat. **Average** lunch £14; dinner £22. **Credit** AmEx,
DC, MC, V.
The Unicorn's food remains classic trattoria fare – chowder,
baked haddock with aubergine, a buffet from which you can
select a selection of cold dishes and meats. But, truth be told,
the Unicorn is not about the food. It's about the crowd, and
there are few better entertainments in the city than this mix
of suits, shakers, wannabees, politicos and bosses.

The Winding Stair
Bookshop & Café

*40 Ormond Quay Lower, Dublin 1 (873 3292). All cross
city buses.* **Open** 10.30am-6pm Mon-Sat. **Average** £4.
Credit EC, MC, V.
The loveliest, most lingerable bookshop in Dublin has
offered cracking lunchtime food for years now, packing the
place out at lunchtime. To get the best out of the Winding
Stair, arrive at about 11am, browse the shelves, sip some coffee, check out the cool sounds, have lunch, buy some books,
and bliss out. A Dublin institution.

Temple Bar cafés

Bad Ass Café

*Crown Alley, Temple Bar, Dublin 2 (671 2596). All cross
city buses.* **Open** 11.30am-midnight Mon-Sun. **Average**
lunch £5; dinner £10. **Credit** AmEx, MC, V.
A Temple Bar institution, the Bad Ass does what it has
always done (pizzas, salads, wines) the way it has always
done them.

Café Auriga

*Temple Bar Square, Dublin 2 (671 8228). All cross city
buses.* **Open** 5.30-11pm Mon-Sat. **Average** dinner £20.
Credit AmEx, MC, V.
A lovely upstairs room which winds around the corner and
looks down on Temple Bar Square, this is a very stylish
place, with all the right sort of furniture and all the right sort
of modern food: curried cod with smashed potatoes, roasted
tomato and mozzarella with smoked salmon. Hip.

Da Pino

*38-40 Parliament Street, Temple Bar, Dublin 2
(671 9308). Bus 68A, 78A, 123.* **Open** noon-11.30pm
Mon-Sat. **Average** lunch £4; dinner £7. **Credit** AmEx,
DC, MC, V.
Classic Italian food – spaghetti carbonara, pizza caruso,
entrecôte pizzaiola, zuppa di cipolla – in a room that hums
with good character, good cheer and fun. There is a second
branch of Da Pino. In Marbella.

Gallagher's Boxty House

*20-21 Temple Bar, Dublin 2 (677 2762). All cross city
buses.* **Open** noon-11.30pm Mon-Sun. **Average** lunch
£4.95; dinner £14. **Credit** DC, MC, V.
Irish cooking, they call it at Gallagher's Boxty House, which
means boxty and stews and suchlike. Tourists comprise the
bulk of the clientèle.

Nico's

*53 Dame Street, Temple Bar, Dublin 2 (677 3062). Bus
8, 19.* **Lunch** 12.30-2.30pm Mon-Fri; **dinner** 6pm-
12.30am Mon-Sat. **Average** lunch £7; dinner £20.
Credit AmEx, DC, MC, V.
Beloved of lovers, post-theatre parties, innocents on a first
date, your auntie and, it seems, everyone else, Nico's is ageless and for everyman. The food is enjoyable trattoria stuff
– chicken cacciatora, pasta carbonara, zabaglione – but the
theatre of the evening is what really counts.

The Old Mill

*Merchant's Arch, Temple Bar, Dublin 2 (671 9262). All
cross city buses.* **Open** noon-4am Mon-Sun. **Average**
lunch £10; dinner £18. **Credit** MC, V.
A simple place, upstairs at the Merchant's Arch, with enjoyable cooking in classic bistro style, and a romantic ambience.

Il Pasticcio

*12 Fownes Street, Temple Bar, Dublin 2 (677 6111). All
cross city buses.* **Open** 12.30-11pm Mon-Thur; 12.30-
11.30pm Fri, Sat; 5-10pm Sun. **Average** lunch £10.
Credit AmEx, MC, V.
Good pizzas and lots of atmosphere are the formula.

Terrace Café

*Temple Bar Hotel, Fleet Street, Dublin 2 (677 3333).
All cross city buses.* **Open** 7am-noon, 12.30-3pm,
Mon-Fri; 7am-noon, 12.30-3pm, 6-10pm, Sat, Sun.
Average lunch £9.95; dinner £15. **Credit** AmEx,
DC, MC, V.
Part of the Temple Bar Hotel, this is a well-regarded space
where they work hard to get things right.

Thunder Road Café

*Fleet Street, Temple Bar, Dublin 2 (679 4057).
All cross city buses.* **Open** noon-midnight daily.
Average lunch £6.95; dinner from £17. **Credit** AmEx,
MC, V.
Thunder Road Café is Temple Bar's answer to the Hard Rock
Café. Loud and fun.

Trastevere

*Temple Bar Square, Dublin 2 (670 8343). All cross city
buses.* **Open** 12.30-11pm Mon-Wed, Sun; 12.30-11.30pm
Thur-Sat. **Average** lunch under £10; dinner under £15.
Credit MC, V.
Italian food such as crab and shrimp Piemontese, panzarot-
ti, tortellini and so on. Friendly and fun, and a nice room for
people-watching.

Le Vigneron

*6 Cope Street, Temple Bar, Dublin 2 (671 5740).
All cross city buses.* **Open** 12.30-11pm Mon-Sun.
Average lunch £9; dinner £15. **Credit** AmEx, DC,
MC, V.
One of the best wine lists in the city, and French bistro-style
food which enjoys some fine moments.

The Well Fed Café

*Resource Centre, Crow Street, Dublin 2 (677 1974). All
cross city buses.* **Open** 10.30am-8.30pm Mon-Sat.
Average lunch £5. **No credit cards.**
Whole-foody, and often very scrummy, very simple cooking
from a co-operative which has been around from long before
Temple Bar became fashionable.

Pubs & Bars

Dublin's great democratic pursuit still involves Guinness – lots of it – and whiskey, with an 'e'. And strawberry and ricotta bagels.

There are no other pubs like Dublin pubs. Irish bars may be busy conquering foreign drinking territories throughout the world, but what they miss, what they cannot capture, amidst all their sawdust and polished wood and pints of porter, is the ambience of the Dublin pub.

All told, this ambience is a curious thing. You don't find the same quality in pubs outside the capital, splendiferous though they may be. It is a factor composed partly of attitude – friendly, mock-serious, devoted – which you find amongst both the staff and the regular customers, and partly of style. It also has something to do with setting. The architecture and design of the great old Dublin pubs has to be savoured. The clock in the Long Hall. The carved bar in the International. The snug in Kehoe's. These are as distinctive of Dublin culture as any other artefact in the city.

But the strange thing about the ambience of the Dublin pub is that it is shared by the new style of boozers which have become popular in recent years. The Front Lounge may be a million miles away from McDaid's in terms of style and décor,

but the ambience is similar. The Porterhouse, with its brilliant brews, is a new pub, but feels as if it has been there for centuries. There is little in common between the Stag's Head and Café en Seine, save absurdly over-the-top interiors, and yet an almost identical atmosphere pervades them both.

Dublin's pubs are also great levellers. They offer relaxed opening hours – typically, from 10.30am until 11pm, with an additional 30 minutes in summer – and, with all welcome, they are places where everyone's opinion is worth hearing, places where the glass in the hand makes each the equal of the other. Put simply, drinking in Dublin is the city's great democratic pursuit.

Pubs & bars

The Auld Dubliner
17 Anglesea Street, Temple Bar, Dublin 2 (677 0527).
All cross city buses.
Freshly redecorated, though it looks much as it has ever done, the Auld Dub is where you wait if there are no free tables in the Elephant & Castle, just across the street. Busy and lively.

*No need to feel self-conscious if you want a coffee rather than a beer at **Café en Seine**.*

*It's not all strawberry and ricotta bagels at the **Chocolate Bar** – you can shoot pool as well.*

The Bailey

2 Duke Street, Dublin 2 (679 3734). All cross city buses.
A super-trendy part of Dublin's social and cultural history which attracts everybody from record company hipsters, through minor-league musicians and self-conscious thespians, to aspiring journalists and pop scribblers. You enter through the door of Leopold Bloom's house, which is now all that remains of the original building described by James Joyce in *Ulysses* (*see chapter* **Literary Dublin**).

Baggot Inn

143 Lower Baggot Street, Dublin 2 (676 1430). Bus 10, 11, 11A.
The Baggot Inn seems to change its design and orientation as often as punks change the colouring of their hair. Rock music gigs are held here, both upstairs and downstairs. Leather jackets are not compulsory, despite appearances to the contrary.

The Bleeding Horse

Upper Camden Street, Dublin 2 (475 2705/478 2101 restaurant). Bus 16, 16A, 55, 83.
Enjoying a prominent site at the top of Camden Street, the Bleeding Horse has an interconnected series of rooms downstairs, replete with heavy beams, a rather dark, medieval atmosphere and a restaurant above.

The Brazen Head

20 Lower Bridge Street, Dublin 8 (679 5186). Bus 21, 21A.
The haunt of all those foreign students who come to Dublin to learn English, as well as almost everyone else who visits the city and must, just must, visit the oldest bar in town.

Davy Byrne's

21 Duke Street, Dublin 2 (677 5217). All cross city buses.
The pub where Leopold Bloom partook of a gorgonzola sandwich and a glass of burgundy in James Joyce's *Ulysses*. Nowadays, Davy Byrne's gets a swish crowd, most of whom

will not have read Joyce's unique slice of Dublin life, and lots of tourists who will have read the book and are only too keen to discuss it.

Café en Seine

40 Dawson Street, Dublin 2 (677 4369). All cross city buses.
The beauty of Café en Seine can take the breath away: bistro lighting, a long tunnel of a room with high-side seating, and the relentless energy of the super-hip crowd shooting the atmosphere into overdrive. Designed to be like a French café, so there's no need to feel self-conscious if you want coffee rather than alcohol.

The Chocolate Bar

Upper Hatch Street, Dublin 2 (478 0166). Bus 15A, 15B, 15C, 20, 86.
The Choc is impossibly trendy; a vivid Gothic fantasy in twisted metal, with the weirdest loos in the city, and high balcony seating overlooking the main action of the bar. It's so cool they serve strawberry and ricotta bagels. Good cocktails.

The Dawson Lounge

25 Dawson Street, Dublin 2 (677 5909). All cross city buses.
A tiny little downstairs lounge at the bottom of a corkscrew staircase. Cosy in winter, cosy in summer and always, somehow, curiously surreal.

The Dockers'

Sir John Rogerson's Quay, Dublin 2 (677 1692). DART Tara Street.
U2 have made this riverside pub famous, as they hang out here if using nearby Windmill Lane recording studios. Even without the pop stars, it's a neat pub.

Doheny & Nesbitt

5 Lower Baggot Street, Dublin 2 (676 2945). Bus 10, 11, 11A.
At the weekends, this glorious old pub is packed to the gills with lawyers, all of them getting more than squiffy and

quoting Archbold, Blackstone and the hottest law library gossip at each other. Nesbitt's (as it's known) may actually be best during the week for a contemplative sup in the company of barmen who behave like philosophers: silent as Wittgenstein, stoic as Socrates.

The Duke
9 Duke Street, Dublin 2 (679 9553). All cross city buses.
Stalled academics, lesser novelists and Dublin characters, all of them wearing tweed jackets and an appropriate disdain for much of life, pile in here. Refurbishment a few years ago did nothing to alter the charm of a place which is both delightful and infuriating.

The Front Lounge
Parliament Street, Dublin 2 (670 4112). All cross city buses.
Also known as the Back Lounge, depending on which entrance you use, this is the quintessential new Dub pub. Plaster casts, fountains, couches and chaise longues, spot-lighting make it as slick as it gets; packed out with the chardonnay crowd who scrutinise each new arrival with acute eyes.

The Globe
11 Great George's Street, Dublin 2 (671 1220). Bus 12, 16, 16A, 55.
Fashionable, dimly lit pub in the middle of Great George's Street which was one of the earliest amongst the new pubs in the city.

Oliver St John Gogarty
57 Fleet Street, Dublin 2 (671 1822). All cross city buses.
Popular, timeless boozer, which has a restaurant upstairs that offers many 'traditional' dishes – Irish stew, bacon and cabbage and the likes.

Grogan's Castle Lounge
15 South William Street, Dublin 2 (677 9320). All cross city buses.
Creative folk, some of whom who want to be creative but

aren't, and those who bear the brunt of the hard end of the wedge fill up this neat pub just at the back of the Powers-court Centre. Very understated, very fashionable.

GF Handel
165-166 Capel Street, Dublin 1 (872 3247). All cross city buses.
A single, tall room at the river end of Capel Street, Handel's is a popular music venue and attracts a cool young crowd. There is jazz on Sundays.

Hartigan's
100 Lower Leeson Street, Dublin 2 (679 2280). Bus 11, 11A, 13, 46A, 64A.
Spartan, serious pub for real drinkers, which makes it all the stranger that law students gaggle here at the weekend and try desperately to misbehave.

Hogan's
35 George's Street, Dublin 2 (677 5904). Bus 12, 16, 16A, 55.
One of two café bars on George's Street, Hogan's is stylish-ly understated and classical with rather fine drinks.

The Horseshoe Bar
Shelbourne Hotel, St Stephen's Green, Dublin 2 (676 6471). All cross city buses.
If you want to see how the executive, legislative and judicial arms of the Irish government operate, this is perhaps the best place to start. Forget Leinster House: this is the seat of Irish government and a very comfortable seat it is. Affairs of state can get pretty wild late on a weekend evening, when the executive, legislative and judicial arms may get a little woozy. An essential and amusing slice of Dublin life.

Hughes' Bar
19 Chancery Street, Dublin 7 (872 6540). All cross city buses.
During the day, young men contemplating an imminent spell inside may quaff their last drink in freedom here in the company of pitiful relatives and equally pitiless lawyers.

The International Bar – *a good spot for contemplative afternoon drinks – see page 103.*

Porterhouse Brewing Company – *Dublin's only micro-brewery-and-pub – see page 104.*

In the evenings, some sharp rug-cutting generally takes over Hughes' Bar, when excellent sessions and fine set-dancing seizes the place.

The International Bar

23 Wicklow Street, Dublin 2 (677 9250). All cross city buses.
An exuberant, wood-suffused temple which enjoys superb natural lighting. Matt, once one of the bar's great retainers, is now pulling pints in some celestial bar, but Simon is still on hand to dispense calm, crafty advice about any subject you care to mention. A good pub for contemplative afternoon drinks at 4pm, as well as the place for all sorts of blathery rowdiness at 11pm.

Kavanagh's

1 Prospect Square, Glasnevin, Dublin 9 (no phone). Bus 13.
Out at Glasnevin cemetery, a few miles from the city, this famous boozer, known as the Gravediggers', hasn't changed a jot in a century and a half of trading.

Kehoe's

9 South Anne Street, Dublin 2 (677 8312). All cross city buses.
Many drinkers' favourite Dublin pub, with grand old snugs but regrettably difficult-to-get-to loos. The barmen are all existentialists, with appropriately jaundiced views of human morality and motivation.

The Long Hall

51 South Great George's Street, Dublin 2 (475 1590). All cross city buses.
If there is a bar in heaven, it will look like this. One of the most exuberant pieces of design you can find in the town, the Long Hall is a veritable cathedral of booze. You can

Catch all the latest legal gossip at **Doheny & Nesbitt** *on Lower Baggot Street – see page 99.*

sacrifice your brain cells at this shrine without guilt, perhaps chewing the cud about William Morris. Mention him to the staff and they will ask, 'What team does he play for?' A droll bunch, for sure.

McDaid's

3 Harry Street, Dublin 2 (679 4395). All cross city buses.
Popularly known as the Brendan Behan. A major place of pilgrimage for tourists who want to discover the real literary Dublin and are just dying to ask everyone intelligently daft questions about same. Décor is strictly unreconstructed Gothic.

Mulligan's

8 Poolbeg Street, Dublin 2 (677 5582). DART Tara Street.
A legendary pint of Guinness – perhaps the most celebrated and discussed in the entire town – is served by blokes who have seen it all and heard it all. Attracts a curious crowd who boast their authentic Dubliner status by talking loudly and pretending to ignore you. Don't miss either the pint or the regulars.

Neary's

1 Chatham Street, Dublin 2 (677 8596). All cross city buses.
As it enjoys a back door to the Gaiety theatre, Neary's is inevitably a slightly theatrical boozer, but late at night, and especially on rugby weekends, the theatricality tends to affect everyone. Gets mighty crowded late in the evening.

The Norseman

27-8 East Essex Street, Temple Bar, Dublin 2 (671 5135/679 8372). All cross city buses.
This agreeably relaxed pub, just refurbished, should, of course, be called the Norseperson: per unit of trendiness, it is one of the coolest and most credible pubs in town. Theatre folk, a rock 'n' roll element, the Temple Bar art community and, heaven help us, some respectable folk as well come here to chat and quaff. Arty and artisan.

*While away an afternoon in the **Stag's Head**, where time has stood still – see page 106.*

O'Brien's

4 Sussex Terrace, Leeson Street, Dublin 4 (668 2594).
Bus 11, 11A, 13, 46A, 64A.
Even though one is no more than a couple of hundred yards
from the bridge at Leeson Street, O'Brien's, which looks
like a handsome, well-worn city pub, nevertheless has a
vaguely suburban atmosphere, instead of the sharply tuned
frisson of expectation common to a great many of the true
city centre pubs.

Octagon Bar

Clarence Hotel, 6-8 Wellington Quay, Dublin 2 (670
9000). All cross city buses.
The main bar in the U2-owned Clarence Hotel is delightful,
with a central bar surrounded by seating and with good staff,
but the air conditioning should be toned down somewhat.
Good cocktails, especially the dry martinis.

O'Donoghue's

15 Merrion Row, Dublin 2 (660 7194/676 2807 lounge).
All cross city buses.
Good impromptu music sessions can be enjoyed in this
smoky old pub, originally famous as the haunt of musical
mini-legends, the Dubliners. O'Donoghue's draws in actual
Dubliners, visitors and denizens, young and old. Its fame as
a staple of each and every guide book has not made the staff
the slightest bit self-conscious: they just get on with the business of pulling pints and paying precious little attention to
the punters.

O'Dwyer's

7 Lower Mount Street, Dublin 2 (676 2887). Bus 8, 45,
46, 52.
A busy, rather trendy pub which concocts an old-fashioned
appearance from new materials and clever design. Preferred
by the young urban professionals of the town who work
around and about it.

The Old Stand

37 Exchequer Street, Dublin 2 (677 7220). All cross
city buses.
A very professional and very comfortable pub. Droves
of regulars love it, others find it a place that they may visit
only rarely.

O'Shea's Merchant

12 Lower Bridge Street, Dublin 8 (679 6793). Bus
21, 21A.
Perhaps the sharpest traditional dancing to be found in the
city most week nights, when gangly civil servants, energetic
wives, women in, or just past, their bloom and other keepers
of the flame disport themselves with wild abandon.

The Palace

21 Fleet Street, Dublin 2 (677 9290/679 3037 lounge).
All cross city buses.
For many Dubs, their single favourite boozer and a place
they would like to be in when they depart this mortal coil.
A lovely old bar which vaults and swirls with wood and
glass, and a good pint. Also serves the new Dublin brews,
such as Beckett's.

Peter's Pub

1 Johnston's Place, Dublin 2 (677 8588). All cross
city buses.
Peter's Pub is spoken of with touching fondness by many
in this town and, if you pitch in here at 6pm on a bright
day, this airy, simple place will endear itself to yourself as
quickly as any 'first one of the day'.

Porterhouse Brewing Company

Parliament Street, Dublin 2 (679 8847). All cross
city buses.
Dublin's only micro-brewery-and-pub has the best brews in
the city – Wrassler XXXX, An Brainblásta, Oyster Stout,

*Wherever you are in **Temple Bar**, you're no more than a couple of yards from the next pub.*

Porterhouse Porter – created by Belfast man Brendan Dobbin, and all of them show a clean pair of heels to conventional, bland brews: just compare Wrassler XXXX to a pint of Guinness and you will see how insipid popular brewing has become. Nice room.

Thomas Read

1 Parliament Street, Dublin 2 (670 7220). All cross city buses.
For a Dublin pub, Thomas Read's does one hell of a good imitation of a Viennese coffee house, and you could be forgiven for mistaking it for a food and coffee place during the day. Evening time sees the focus switch back to the bar, and then it's a live-wire spot. The food, during the day, is decent pub grub.

Ryan's

28 Parkgate Street, Dublin 8 (677 6097/671 9352 restaurant). Bus 23, 25, 26.
A beautiful old bar, with a beautiful old counter you will have seen a thousand times in photographs and picture postcards. Wonderful snugs at the back of the pub, and some pretty decent food upstairs in the restaurant. A true, well-maintained slice of Victoriana.

Sheehan's

17 Chatham Street, Dublin 2 (677 1914). All cross city buses.
Formerly a comfortable, elbow-patchy, much-loved pub which is now a slightly over-designed and quietly self-conscious watering hole. Irrespective of the changes, Sheehan's continues to attract lawyers, writers and a smattering of the creatively funky classes.

Slattery's

29 Capel Street, Dublin 1 (872 7971). All cross city buses.
Perhaps the best music pub in the city, in the middle of slowly dying, slowly decaying, already desiccated Capel Street.

Stag's Head

1 Dame Court, Dublin 2 (679 3701). All cross city buses.
A very lovely pub which is good for drinking and idling away the afternoon hours, good for motoring through the evening hours and, mercifully, good for eating: the food here may be the best pub food in town. An oaky, smoky bar with relaxed, friendly staff. Perfect.

The Temple Bar

48 Temple Bar, Dublin 2 (677 3807). All cross city buses.
Refurbished a few years back to make it look like an age-old, authentic Dublin boozer, the Temple Bar is permanently stuffed to bursting with raucously trendy types and age-old authentic citizens. Everything and everybody spills out on to the streets in the summertime.

Toner's

139 Lower Baggot Street, Dublin 2 (676 3090). Bus 10, 11, 11A.
Authentic Dublin pub which has been tarted up over the years without removing the necessary character which makes it ever popular: the bar itself is still particularly pleasing. Agreed, by all and sundry, to be a good place.

The Turk's Head

Parliament Street, Dublin 2 (679 2567). All cross city buses.
Stylistically varied: one half of the Turk's Head is completely different from the other, and the whole effect has been succinctly summarised as 'gaudy Gaudi'. Rather fun, with an extra cool crowd.

Whelan's

25 Wexford Street, Dublin 2 (478 0766/476 2420). Bus 16, 16A, 55, 83.
An old pub which looks new, sort of, thanks to careful and clever restoration. Never less than hyper, with droves of foreign students and rock 'n' roll heads who come for the music.

A pub of two halves, **The Turk's Head** *attracts a super-cool crowd to Parliament Street.*

Shopping & Services

Familiar chainstores abound, but so, too, do the small and idiosyncratic shops where all kinds of delights may lurk.

When it comes to shopping, Dublin may not have the reputation of Paris or Milan, but it's still an ever-growing metropolis of department stores, chain stores, shopping centres, independent shops, stalls and street vendors that can make it an always interesting and sometimes expensive experience.

What follows is a guide through every type of purchase you might want to make and the best places to go. A lot of the small independent shops – particularly those around the Temple Bar area – have a tendency to shut down and reopen at an alarming rate, but whatever comes and goes, something new always appears in its place.

OLD-TIMERS

While Dublin, unlike other more rational cities, does not usually devote whole streets or areas to the retail of a specific product or service, the wholly rational world of **antiques** (where you pay more for something the older it is) provides us with our first exception. Some 25 minutes' walk westwards off Grafton Street lies **Francis Street**, the heart of Dublin's antique trade.

From top to bottom and on both sides, Francis Street is lined with small, welcoming shops crammed to the jambs with antiques of varying historical, aesthetic and monetary values. Dealing mainly in later-period furnishings and ornamentation, the shops here exude a dusty, dreamy atmosphere more readily associated with small town dealers, but be not fooled – the façade of easygoingness, with the footstep of the grandfather clock in the corner going nowhere slowly, hides a tad business with a brisk turnover. This stealthy alacrity, combined with the reluctance of individual dealers here to specialise in particular objects or periods, means that the visitor is better off scanning all of the shops rather than focusing on one or two. One thing is certain – if you are serious about antique-hunting in Dublin, a trip to Francis Street is always essential and often fruitful.

At the southern end of Francis Street turn left, and then right at the junction, onto **Clanbrassil Street**. On the left-hand side of this street as you head south, there is a scattering of smaller, junkier antique dealers, where, armed with copious amounts of time and alertness, you might just find that oil-lamp you've always wanted, or that tandem stolen on your first visit here in 1971.

Lovers of finer jewellery and silverware will be better off in the **Grafton Street** area. **South Anne Street** houses several silver merchants, as well as an antique prints dealer and an antique bookshop. Take the tiny left turn off Grafton Street immediately after Bewley's Café into Johnson Court (with a fine antique jeweller on the left-hand side towards the end), and follow the signs for the **Powerscourt Townhouse Centre**. Climb the main stairs in the Townhouse and turn left for a broad selection of antique jewellery, silverware, ornaments and small furnishings, all in beautiful and comfortable surroundings. Finally, opposite the tourist office on **Andrew Street** is a small antique shop called **Rhinestones** with an eclectic selection of curious, colourful paraphernalia from across the spectra of time and taste; it's isolated from all of the above antique-shop clusters but well worth a mention and a visit.

BARGAINS

As in every flourishing city, bargains are rare on the central, pedestrianised shopping streets of Grafton Street and Henry Street, or anywhere within lunching distance of the business districts of St Stephen's Green and surrounds. But, just as typically, the bargain-hunter doesn't have to venture far outside these areas to get the first whiff of prey. From St Stephen's Green, walk west to Camden Street or further to Francis Street and Thomas Street: there's nothing particularly amazing, but everything is cheaper and friendlier.

Or turn off Henry Street on to Liffey Street, which is particularly cheap for clothes and household goods. At the end of Henry Street, keep walking on to Mary Street and Mary's Lane for Capel Street, probably Dublin's best area for hardware, survival gear and practical furniture. Across O'Connell Street at the other end of Henry Street is North Earl Street, which is excellent for cheap luggage among other things. And alongside the

Popular with students at Trinity College and all lovers of the written word – **Books Upstairs**.

river itself, on Crampton Quay and particularly Aston Quay, cheap books, music, videos, and electrical goods can be found in abundance.

Sales in Dublin, as elsewhere, are ongoing in different stores at different times of the year. If you are looking for recorded music, for example, shop around the superstores and you will almost certainly find one of them has a sale on.

The seasonal sales are more predictable: the best ones happen in more or less all shops, great and small, in January and July, with other less universal discounts around halfway between these months.

Books

Dublin has always had a great literary tradition and this is celebrated in the number of bookshops contained within the city. From James Joyce to Roddy Doyle, the city has acted not so much as a backdrop but as a character in the literature of the day. Today, the book-chains, the independents and the specialists co-exist peacefully and profitably in the city.

General

Book Stop

Dun Laoghaire Shopping Centre (280 9917). Bus 7, 8, 46A. **Open** 9am-5pm Mon-Sat. **Credit** AmEx, MC, V.
General titles, children's and a wide range of schoolbooks, new and secondhand.
Branch: Blackrock Shopping Centre (283 2193).

Books Upstairs

36 College Green, Dublin 2 (679 6687). All cross city buses. **Open** 10am-7pm Mon-Fri; 10am-6pm Sat; 1-6pm Sun. **Credit** AmEx, DC, MC, V.
A small, but quality, bookshop opposite Trinity College, it stocks several subject matters (particularly good on Irish literature, drama, women's studies and gay and lesbian material), but in quite modest quantities. Bargains are often to be found on the tables inside the door and there's a range of American editions, too.

Eason's

40 O'Connell Street, Dublin 1 (873 3811). All cross city buses. **Open** 8.30am-6.15pm Mon-Wed, Fri, Sat; 8.30am-8pm Thur. **Credit** MC, V.
Large, busy shop, selling books on the ground floor, along with stationery, art supplies, magazines. Primarily popular fiction, new titles and Irish. Good bargains often available but it doesn't cater for much outside of the mainstream. **Branches** are too numerous to list here. Check the telephone directory for your nearest.

Hodges Figgis

56-58 Dawson Street, Dublin 2 (677 4754). All cross city buses. **Open** 9am-7pm Mon-Wed; 9am-8pm Thur; 9am-6pm Sat; noon-6pm Sun. **Credit** AmEx, MC, V.
A large bookshop with a section for everything. The upside is the huge range of books and ordering facilities; the downside is the dull lighting and the ease with which you can get lost in there. Still, there's a great coffee shop on the first floor which is always worth checking out.

Not necessarily first stop for all your underground literature needs, but **Eason's** *has a good stock of popular fiction.*

Hughes & Hughes
St Stephen's Green Shopping Centre, Dublin 2 (830 4811). All cross city buses. **Open** 9.30am-6pm Mon-Wed, Fri, Sat; 9.30am-8pm Thur; 1-6pm Sun. **Credit** AmEx, DC, MC, V.
Literary chainstore with a good mix of popular titles, Irish titles, fiction and a fine collection of children's books.
Branches: Blackrock Shopping Centre (283 4316); Dublin Airport (704 4034); Rathfarnham (493 6633).

Waterstone's
7 Dawson Street, Dublin 2 (679 1415). All cross city buses. **Open** 9am-8pm Mon-Wed, Fri; 9am-8.30pm Thur; 9am-7pm Sat; 9am-6pm Sun. **Credit** AmEx, DC, MC, V.
Large, bright, open-plan shop with a wide range of books on every possible section, including popular, literary and academic, with particularly good Irish and children's sections. A quality range of titles over two floors makes this probably the best bookshop on the northside of the city. Check out the readings and events programmes in both shops.
Branch: Jervis Centre (878 1311).

Specialist

Forbidden Planet
36 Dawson Street, Dublin 2 (671 0688). All cross city buses. **Open** 10am-6pm Mon-Wed, Fri, Sat; 10am-7pm Thur; noon-5pm Sun. **Credit** AmEx, MC, V.
Science fiction and fantasy bookshop, with a huge range of comics, books, magazines, videos, toys, action figures and posters from all parts of the world. Definitely the best shop of its type in the city. Also stocks a good range of movie stills and posters.

Fred Hanna's
27-29 Nassau Street, Dublin 2 (677 1255). Bus 7, 10, 11, 13. **Open** 9am-6pm Mon-Sat; 9am-8pm Thur. **Credit** AmEx, MC, V.
Well known, family owned shop. Specialists in academic texts, they also stock a good range of other books, particularly popular Irish titles. It's deceptively small from the outside. The extremely high shelves can be intimidating, but the staff are friendly and knowledgeable.

International Books
18 Frederick Street South, Dublin 2 (679 9375). Bus 7, 10, 11, 13. **Open** 9am-5.30pm Mon-Sat. **Credit** MC, V.
Language specialists with books, cassettes, videos and CD ROMs for most of the world's languages.

Veritas Bookshop
7-8 Abbey Street Lower, Dublin 1 (878 8177). All cross city buses. **Open** 9am-6pm Mon-Fri; 9am-5.30pm Sat. **Credit** AmEx, MC, V.
Specialists in religious books and paraphernalia. Probably the best shop of its kind in the city.

Secondhand/rare

Cathach Books
10 Duke Street, Dublin 2 (671 8676). All cross city buses. **Open** 9.30am-6pm Mon-Sat. **Credit** AmEx, MC, V.
Specialists in rare Irish titles and worth checking out if only to inspect the signed editions of everyone from Yeats to Heaney. They also buy books secondhand and stock a good range of rare maps and prints.

Greene's
16 Clare Street, Dublin 2 (676 2554). All cross city buses. **Open** 9am-5.30pm Mon-Fri; 9am-5pm Sat. **Credit** AmEx, DC, MC, V.
A large, sprawling bookshop, mostly secondhand and Irish

titles with a range of rare books, too. A great place for endless browsing, but it can sometimes be difficult to find that specific book you're looking for.

Winding Stair
40 Ormond Quay Lower, Dublin 1 (873 3292). All cross city buses. **Open** 10am-6pm Mon-Sat. **Credit** EC, MC, V.
A great, old fashioned bookshop over two floors; cheap paperbacks and bargains downstairs and up, but with the added bonus of a great café upstairs, overlooking the Liffey. A great place for lunch or a coffee, the tables are surrounded by books and it's a fine place to while away some time.

Clothes
Designer

Though Naomi, Kate, Claudia, Helena and all the other skinny girls and boys upon whom the international designers drape their creations have been partying and holidaying here for several years, the big shots of the fashion business have been strangely tardy in setting up their own stores in Dublin. But though there are as yet no Armani, Klein, Versace or Mugler shops, this is not to say that their clothes are unavailable in Dublin.

Dawson Street boasts two magnificent shirt emporia – **Smyth & Gibson** at the north end, which caters particularly well for the more understated, not-too-racy businessman; and **Pink**, at the southern end, which targets the riskier and zestier young upstart.

Acquiesce
31 South Anne Street, Dublin 2 (671 9433). **Open** 9am-5pm Mon-Sat. **Credit** AmEx, MC, V.
Well-tailored women's clothing: pastel-shades, traditional cuts from popular British and European designers.

Alias Tom
Duke House, Duke Street, Dublin 2 (671 5443). **Open** 9am-5.30pm Mon-Sat. **Credit** AmEx, MC, V.
Currently Dublin's most popular men's designer clothing store. The emphasis is on European- rather than American-influenced designs, and the range is mouth-watering. The prices are, as you might expect, on the high side.

A-Wear
26 Grafton Street, Dublin 2 (671 7200). **Open** 9am-6.30pm Mon-Sat. **Credit** AmEx, MC, V.
For a cheaper but more limited range of Irish designs, try downstairs in A-Wear on Grafton Street, where the highly acclaimed work of Quin and Donnelly make up a large part of the stock on show.

Boutique Homme
2 South Anne Street, Dublin 2 (671 5122). **Open** 9am-5.30pm Mon-Sat. **Credit** AmEx, MC, V.
The place to go for exclusive men's clothing of a conservative, well-cut variety.

Brown Thomas
88-95 Grafton Street, Dublin 2 (605 6666). All cross city buses. **Open** 9am-6pm Mon-Wed, Fri, Sat; 9am-8pm Thur. **Credit** AmEx, MC V.
For top-flight designers, Brown Thomas is best. After its major redesign and rebirth three years ago, the store now oozes a truly cosmopolitan and sophisticated air, as well as stocking all the more popular designers. As electric and capitalist as any major city could offer.

*Stylish, sophisticated **Brown Thomas** stocks all the most popular designers – see page 111.*

Louis Copeland

39-41 Capel Street, Dublin 1 (872 1600). All cross city buses. **Open** 9am-5.45pm Mon-Wed, Fri, Sat; 9am-8pm Thur. **Credit** AmEx, MC, V.

Match your latest shirt purchase to a suit from Louis Copeland – one of Europe's most highly acclaimed tailors and suitmakers. You'll be as ready to walk the length of Dublin's unofficial catwalk – alongside the bar in Dawson Street's Café en Seine.

Platform

16 Creation Arcade, Lemon Street, Dublin 2 (677 7380). **Open** 9am-6pm Mon-Sat. **Credit** MC, V.

Platform stocks a small but eclectic mix of designer brands, with a bias towards sensual fabrics and flowing lines.

Powerscourt Townhouse Centre

Design Centre, 59 South William Street, Dublin 2 (679 4144). **Open** 9am-6pm Mon-Wed, Fri, Sat; 9am-7pm Thur. **Credit** MC, V.

For the best of Ireland's designers, and by far the most popular of Dublin's designer stores, climb the stairs in the Powerscourt Townhouse on Clarendon Street and enter the Design Centre. Its enduring popularity is understandable when you look around: here you'll find clothes by innumerable gifted designers of national and international renown in every fabric and style, for every taste. Louise Kennedy, Sharon Hoey and Mary Gregory are just some of the people whose latest works are represented here, in simple and spacious surroundings. The prices are generally high, though sales and 'seconds' are well worth keeping an eye out for.

Mid-range

In a city where half of the population is under 25 years of age, it comes as no shock to discover that the strongest element of Dublin's fashion culture

Dublin's main shopping thoroughfare, **Grafton Street***, on a sunny Saturday afternoon – an agoraphobic's nightmare.*

is the mid-price, mass-produced retailer, with a speedy turnover in ultra-fashionable clothing. The city has dozens and dozens of these shops – from small single-outlet stores in the suburbs and back streets to the instantly recognisable branches of large British and European fashion franchises and the larger Irish department stores and fashion chains. And there is little doubt that as the market for this type of store has grown, so too, has the quality of clothing on offer.

Interesting and trendy women's stores to look out for include **Oasis** (one outlet near each end of Grafton Street, at St Stephen's Green and on Nassau Street), probably the market leader when it comes to achieving a balance of cost and fashionable originality; branches of British chains **Warehouse**, **Miss Selfridge** and **River Island** (all on Grafton Street) which target the young, hip, and modestly financed.

Alternatively, try the more upmarket, but equally cool, **Kookai** and **Morgan** on Wicklow Street. For acceptably striped or ticked sportswear, **Champion Sports** and **Marathon Sports** (each with branches on both Grafton Street and Henry Street) are market leaders.

Less clubby but of excellent quality and still aimed squarely at the younger end of the market, are shops such as **Next**, **Benetton**, **Monsoon**, **Principles**, **Airwave** and **Jigsaw** (all on Grafton Street). For high quality, mass produced clothes, **Marks & Spencer** (Grafton Street and Mary Street) and **Debenhams** in the Jervis Centre are always a safe bet.

For men, upstairs in **Jigsaw** (on Grafton Street) offers exceptional quality and originality, but

Film
Institute
of Ireland

TheIrishFilmCentre=2Cinemas+IrishFilmArchive+EducationDepartment+Library+Shop+Bar+Restaurant

Irish Film Centre, 6 Eustace St, Temple Bar, Dublin 2. Tel: 679 5744 Fax: 677 8755 Email: info@ifc.ie Website: http://www.iftn.ie/ifc

stretches the definition of mid-price to its upper limit. More accessible ranges may be found on the same street in **Next**, A-Wear, River Island, and the **Levi's Store**. **O'Connor's** (opposite Bewley's) is well worth a visit if the latest and grooviest clubwear is what you're after.

Budget

The best-value clothing in Dublin is often to be found in the large Irish department stores, such as **Dunnes Stores** and **Penney's**. The former is particularly cheap and quick to mass-produce the latest fashions at a fraction of the original labels' costs. Dunnes have branches in the St Stephen's Green Centre, Grafton Street, Henry Street and in the Ilac Centre. Penney's are located on O'Connell Street and Mary Street. Single-outlet low price women's clothing stores can be found downstairs in the St Stephen's Green Centre and all along the Henry Street/Mary Street mile: names to look out for are **Extrovert**, **Japan**, **Zero** and the **No-Name Depot**. For men's clothes, a saunter along Upper and Lower Liffey Street can be rewarding.

For the best in used clothing, the George's Arcade and Temple Bar areas are strongest: particular names to look for here are **Jenny Vander's** (in the Arcade) and **Harlequin** (nearby on Castle Market) and the **Eager Beaver**, **Damascus**, **Flip**, and **Sésí** (in Temple Bar). The **Cerebral Palsy** and **Oxfam** charity shops on George's Street are madly erratic but worth a flying visit.

Shoes, hats & accessories

There are several well-stocked, reasonably priced accessory shops and stalls on the ground floor of the St Stephen's Green Centre – the most obvious being **Accessorize** (also found in Monsoon on Grafton Street). A few minutes away on St Stephen's Green itself, **Oasis** has a particularly strong in-house line of sunglasses, jewellery, watches, bags and other paraphernalia.

For specialist stockists of socks, ties and lingerie, look no further than the **Sock Shop** (both ends of Grafton Street and in **Clery's** on O'Connell Street), **Tie Rack** (Grafton Street, St Stephen's Green Centre and the Jervis Centre) and **Knickerbox** (St Stephen's Green Centre and Henry Street) respectively. For men's suit and tuxedo hire, **Black Tie** outlets can be found throughout the city (140 Lower Baggot Street, Dublin 2; 676 3711).

Aspecto
South Anne Street, Dublin 2. All cross city buses. **Open** 8.45am-6pm Mon-Sat. **Credit** MC, V.
Strong on Birkenstocks and offensively colourful runners.

Black Boot
28 Wicklow Street, Dublin 2 (679 5795). All cross city buses. **Open** 9am-5.30pm Mon-Sat. **Credit** MC, V.
A must for Doc Martens lovers.

Carl Scarpa
25 Grafton Street, Dublin 2 (677 7846). All cross city buses. **Open** 9am-6pm Mon-Sat. **Credit** MC, V.
As well as many of Grafton Street's fashion houses, Carl Scarpa offers higher quality footwear at reasonable prices.

Debenhams
Jervis Centre, Dublin 1. All cross city buses. **Open** 9am-6pm Mon-Wed; 9am-9pm Thur; 9am-7pm Fri; 9am-6.30pm Sat. **Credit** AmEx, MC, V.
Where Ireland's own headgear sensation, Philip Treacy, is well represented.

DV8
4 Crown Alley, Dublin 1 (679 8472). All cross city buses. **Open** 9am-5.30pm Mon-Sat. **Credit** MC, V.
Undoubtedly Dublin's hippest shoe shop. With Docs in every colour, shape and flavour, alongside an ever-changing array of the most popular contemporary designs – from Shelley's to Booga's, Red or Dead and Nose, and many more – this store has something for every cobble-weary pedestrian; be prepared, on occasion, to ask where your foot goes in.

Hat Shop
St Stephen's Green Centre, Dublin 2. All cross city buses. **Open** 9am-6pm Mon-Sat. **Credit** MC, V.
Stocks an affordable selection of informal and semi-formal head-toppings.

Hat Stand
5 Temple Bar Square, Dublin 2 (671 0805). All cross city buses. **Open** 9am-7pm Mon-Sat; 11am-6pm Sun. **Credit** MC, V.
Offers an interesting range of headwear, from the traditional to the zany.

Hat Studio
33 Clarendon Street, Dublin 2 (679 7988). All cross city buses. **Open** 9am-5.30pm Mon-Sat. **Credit** MC, V.
Boasts one of the largest ranges of hats for all occasions, both for sale and hire.

Korky's
47 Grafton Street, Dublin 2 (670 7943). All cross city buses. **Open** 9am-5.30pm Mon-Sat. **Credit** AmEx, MC, V.
Mid-priced fashion footwear.

Natural Shoe Store
25 Drury Street, Dublin 2 (671 4978). All cross city buses. **Open** 9am-5.30pm Mon-Sat. **Credit** MC, V.
As close as conservationists can get to going barefoot in the city.

Sneaker Stadium
St Stephen's Green Centre, Dublin 2. All cross city buses. **Open** 9am-7pm Mon-Sat. **Credit** AmEx, MC, V.
Has a diverse, though not quite stadium-sized stock.

Zerep
57 Grafton Street, Dublin 1 (677 8320). All cross city buses. **Open** 9am-5.30pm Mon-Sat. **Credit** AmEx, MC, V.
Mid-priced fashion footwear.

Crafts

There are two types of crafts available in Ireland – the 'traditional' stuff (that is, woolly jumpers, shillelaghs, anything indigenous and big enough to bear a shamrock, a harp or the word 'Guinness'), and the more creative, 'modern' crafts, which, being less stereotyped, are more genuinely Irish. While it is a commonly made mistake (propagated

in airport shops all over the country) to believe that all Irish crafts are of the traditional variety, it is an equally dangerous error to think of all of these traditional crafts as necessarily tacky. The stores below have been chosen for high quality across a broad range.

Traditional

Nassau Street (running along the south side of Trinity College) is home to a number of large, well-stocked, traditional craft shops. The **House of Ireland** (38 Nassau Street, Dublin 2; 671 6133) carries expensive cut-glass, porcelain, leather, wool and linen products from around the country. Eastwards, on the same side of the street, is Dublin's branch of the **Blarney Woollen Mills**

(Nassau Street, Dublin 2; 677 7066). The Mills, situated in Cork, have a long-standing reputation for producing the finest hand-woven garments (though the designs are fairly staid) and the Dublin branch stocks a full range at relatively reasonable prices. **The Kilkenny Shop**, a further few doors along (6 Nassau Street, Dublin 2), stocks the usual range of traditional knitwear, some expensive Irish designer wear, and an excellent selection of Irish-made pottery, from delicate Belleek porcelain to more robust and earthy Shanagarry.

Near the St Stephen's Green end of Dawson Street (perpendicular to Nassau Street at the House of Ireland) is **Needlecraft** (27 Dawson Street, Dublin 2; 677 2493), which specialises in finished Irish linen as well as all of the raw materials and literature you will need to knit, sew or torture

Not to be missed

Dublin has a compact and easily navigable city centre: with a little map and a little energy, there is no reason why a broad selection of the best shops from these cannot be visited with ease in a single day. What follows is such a selection: a sample of stores of various kinds, intended to cater for various tastes and interests. The shops are listed in a south-to-north direction, starting at St Stephen's Green.

The **St Stephen's Green Shopping Centre** won several international architectural awards when it first opened in the late 1980s, and it remains strikingly different from other centres. But while it is spacious, bright, and visually appealing (with a brilliantly situated café on the top floor), as a practical shopping experience it has always been a little less exciting than its quantity and quality of shops lead you to expect. Nevertheless, for shopping mall buffs, it is an absolute must.

Brown Thomas of Grafton Street may lack the visual impact of St Stephen's Green, but it more than compensates with its broad and glamorous stock and its strong cosmopolitan vibes. Dublin's leading stockist of international designer clothing, BT also offers the very best of everything else one would expect in a department store – lots of groovy household goodies, electrical equipment, watches and jewellery, and countless perfume and beauty counters, as well as two terrific in house cafés. The **Kilkenny Shop** (Nassau Street) is unbeatable as a large, all-encompassing but comfortable traditional Irish clothing and craft store - and upstairs is popular for lunch.

The **Powerscourt Townhouse Centre** on Clarendon Street is Dublin's most exclusive and luxurious shopping complex – it's worth a visit for the pianist alone – and a flight of stairs brings you to the Design Centre's magnificent collection of the best in Irish fashion, craftwork and jewellery.

Across the street from here, the **George's Arcade** may be less luxurious but is just as atmospheric, with a rich clutter of shops and stalls (trading in everything from secondhand jeans and bean-bags) gathered under one high roof. While only the unluckiest of antique-lovers will miss a trip to **Francis Street**, **Rhinestones** of Andrew Street is sure to offer some fascinating consolation prizes.

No visitor should miss **Whichcraft** of Lord Edward Street. Loaded with all kinds of beautiful crafts gathered from around the country, and sold with friendly advice and at fair prices, Whichcraft cannot disappoint.

Moving towards the river via Parliament Street will bring you past **Thomas Read & Co**, reputedly Dublin's oldest extant shop and a cutler of great distinction. Cross the river on the Ha'penny Bridge and immediately to your left you will find one of Dublin's finest and most inviting second-hand bookstores, the **Winding Stair**. The focus is strongly (though not exclusively) on Irish works; what makes it most attractive is its small café on the first floor, where you can watch over the Liffey, and the amusing portraits of Ireland's best-known scribes can watch over you.

And finally, no trip to Dublin would be complete without a stroll down **Moore Street**, where the senses are bombarded by the city's liveliest street market.

Grafton Street *offers the shopper a bewildering variety of ways of parting with their cash.*

imaginatively at home. Five minutes north-west from here on Clarendon Street and, good for brass- and tack-fetishists, is **Treasure Ireland** (37 Wicklow Street, Dublin 2; 679 4560); right next to this is the small but excellent **Irish Crystal** shop and around the corner on Wicklow Street is the popular **Sweater Shop**.

Around the corner on St Stephen Street Lower is the **Foko** store (Drury Street, Dublin 2; 475 5044), with quirky furniture for the ideal post-nuclear home and filled with ingenious and strik-ing gimmicks for the gadget-lover. The fare here is rarely Irish-made and not strictly 'craftwork', but the gimmicks in particular are fairly priced and worth a look.

Halfway along Dame Street, **Gurteen Country Interiors** (50 Dame Street; 679 9668) stocks a range of country-style furnishings, while further along on Lord Edward Street (between the City Hall and Christchurch Cathedral) is another good spot for craft shops, both traditional and modern, with its **Irish Celtic Craftshop** (12 Lord Edward Street; 679 9912) and, around the corner, the **Christchurch Craftshop** (though the latter is tinged with tack).

Over the nearby Ha'penny Bridge, a few stalls of handmade jewellery usually front the **Dublin Woollen Mills** (41 Lower Ormond Quay; 677 5014), which are as similar to the Blarney Woollen

Mills as the name would suggest (though the standards and prices are slightly lower). And finally, if you have either a penchant for porcel-ain and crystal or a pet bull in tow, the **China Showrooms** on 32 Lower Abbey Street (878 6211) may make an interesting pitstop.

Modern

By far the greatest of Dublin's modern craft shops is **Whichcraft**, at 5 Castlegate, on Lord Edward Street (670 9371). A new shop relative to most of those mentioned above, it has, through hard work, rapidly become Dublin's most exciting and com-prehensive stockist of contemporary work of all kinds from all counties – even more remarkable given its tiny size. From wooden bowls and rock-ing chairs to jewellery, ceramics, and terrific iron-work, it is essential for visitors interested in the crafts of modern Ireland.

Moving down Dame Street and left into Temple Bar, Essex Street East is home to the **Design Yard**, another showcase for leading Irish crafts-people (though be warned – you'll need a 24-carat gold card to walk out with anything other than your head in your hands). On the upper floors of the **Powerscourt Townhouse Centre** (Drury Street) the **Crafts Council of Ireland** (679 7383) also gathers together an expansive and expensive selection of the work of Ireland's most droppable names in crafts (but if you do drop it, you'll have to be prepared to pay for it).

The Kilkenny Shop (*see above*) is probably Dublin's most reliable stockist of ceramic crafts from around the country. **Natural Interiors** at 46 Dawson Street (677 1666) does not restrict itself to Ireland in its quest for beautiful natural fabrics, wood and rope mirrors, cane furniture and so on.

Last, but by no means least: if you find yourself in Dublin in early December, disregard all of the above and make your way to the **Craft Fair**, where a small admission fee will grant you access to the broadest range of Irish crafts (traditional, modern, iron, linen, wood, wax) under one roof. For many years it was held in the Mansion House on Dawson Street but, in 1996, too big for its handcrafted leather boots, it moved to the RDS in Ballsbridge.

Dry cleaning & repairs

Baggot Cleaners
33 Baggot Street, Dublin 4 (668 1286). **Open** 7.45am-6.30pm Mon-Wed; 7.45am-7.00pm Thur, Fri; 9-6pm Sat. **Credit** MC, V.
Specialists in leather, suede and sheepskin, with a same-day service available. Collection and delivery facilities available. Just off the main city centre area and surrounded by offices, it's relatively peaceful at weekends.

Crown Dry Cleaners
81 Lower Camden Street, Dublin 2 (475 3584). **Open** 8.30am-6pm Mon-Fri; 9am-6pm Sat. **No credit cards**.
Cleans most garments.
Branches are too numerous to list here. Check the telephone directory for your nearest.

Grafton Cleaners
32 South William Street, Dublin 2 (679 4309). **Open** 8.30am-6pm Mon-Fri; 8.30am-1.30pm Sat. **No credit**.
Suede, sheepskin, fur and leather cleaning. They also do repairs and alterations.

Jeeves Dry Cleaners
16 Main Street, Blackrock (288 1391). **Open** 8.30am-6.30pm Mon-Wed; 8.30am-8.30pm Thur; 8.30am-6pm Fri; 9am-6pm Sat. **Credit** MC, V.
Dry cleaners and launderers with branches throughout the city. Check the telephone directory for full listings.

Prescott's Cleaners
Dundrum Shopping Centre, Dublin 14 (298 3005). **Open** 9am-6pm Mon-Sat. **No credit cards**.
Standard laundry services. Same-day service possible sometimes but it's more usual to wait a day or two. Still, if you're in a hurry, they'll do what they can.
Branches are too numerous to list here. Check the telephone directory for your nearest.

Department stores

Argos
12 Jervis Centre, Dublin 1 (878 1160). All cross city buses. **Open** 9am-6pm Mon-Wed, Fri, Sat; 9am-8.30pm Thur. **Credit** AmEx, MC, V.
An Argos by any other name is still an Argos. Big catalogues

of all their goods, fill 'em in and bring 'em to the counter. Quick, efficient service, but you never get a chance to inspect anything or ask a question. Still, the prices are always good and you can save a lot of browsing time there.

Arnotts
12 Henry Street, Dublin 1 (872 1111). All cross city buses. **Open** 9am-5.30pm Mon-Wed, Fri, Sat; 9.30am-8pm Sat. **Credit** AmEx, DC, MC, V.
A large department store in the heart of Henry Street, Arnotts holds a vast range of goods, but specialises in ladies' and gents' clothing. They also have a restaurant. It gets very busy there at lunchtimes and weekends so be prepared for a lot of pushing and shoving, and stressed staff.

Brown Thomas
88-95 Grafton Street, Dublin 2 (605 6666). All cross city buses. **Open** 9am-6pm Mon-Wed, Fri, Sat; 9am-8pm Thur; 2-6pm Sun. **Credit** AmEx, DC, MC, V.
Probably the most upmarket of the department stores, bring a credit card or chequebook with you, no matter what you're after. Plush surroundings, thick carpets, expert staff all lend the shop a Harrods-like atmosphere for the well-heeled, but don't let that put you off; BT has a long history in Dublin and caters also for the less well-off.

Clery & Co
O'Connell Street, Dublin 1 (878 6000). All cross city buses. **Open** 9am-6.30pm Mon-Wed; 9am-9pm Thur; 9am-8pm Fri; 9am-5.30pm Sat. **Credit** AmEx, DC, MC, V.
Perhaps the most famous of the department stores, Clery's has pride of place in the centre of O'Connell Street and its famous clock has been, for decades, the regular meeting place for dates. It stocks everything from clothes to carriage clocks, computers to chastity belts (well, maybe), operates over many floors and is generally quite reasonably priced. Irish gifts are well-stocked but it's also a handy place to pick up an umbrella when it's pouring rain or a baseball cap when the sun comes out.

Dunnes Stores
Henry Street, Dublin 2 (671 4629). All cross city buses. **Open** 9am-6pm Mon-Wed, Fri, Sat; 9am-9pm Thur. **Credit** MC, V.
The mothers' choice for decades, Dunnes has had its share of scandal, but continues to profit from several branches around Dublin and is actually a great place for clothes bargains if you're not expecting to hold on to what you buy for years yet. Mostly gents' and ladies' casuals, Dunnes also caters heavily for children and babies and reflects this in the amount of floor space devoted to them. Some of the larger stores also offer groceries.
Branches are too numerous to list here. Check the telephone directory for your nearest.

Guiney & Co
79 Talbot Street, Dublin 1 (878 8835). All cross city buses. **Open** 9am-6.30pm Mon-Wed, Fri, Sat; 9am-7pm Thur. **Credit** MC, V.
Just off O'Connell Street, Guiney's is the kind of shop where you can pick up a new suit, a duvet, a pair of Hush Puppies and a three-pack of Y-fronts and still have change out of a fiver. Not the most stylish of shops, the advantage to Guiney's is that it's cheap, cheap, cheap. Just don't expect to impress anyone.

Marks & Spencer
15-20 Grafton Street, Dublin 2 (679 7855). All cross city buses. **Open** 9am-7pm Mon-Wed, Fri, Sat; 9am-9pm Thur; noon-6pm Sun. **Credit** MC, V.
Marks & Sparks has brushed up its image in recent years and revamped their shops in Dublin, so that the main city centre stores are now quite plush and elaborate, a fact reflected in the increase in prices and the decrease in the number of bargains.

Harassed staff everywhere. A third branch at Liffey Valley, westwards out of the city on the M50, will open in late 1998. **Branch:** Mary Street, Dublin 1 (872 8833).

Roches Stores

54 Henry Street, Dublin 1 (873 0044). All cross city buses. **Open** 9am-6pm Mon-Wed, Fri, Sat; 9am-9pm Thur. **Credit** MC, V.

A popular department store which has a greater emphasis on home accessories and furnishings, along with the standard clothing departments. It's generally well air-conditioned, unlike a lot of the other city centre stores; vast range of goods with decent prices.

Electronics

Beyond 2000

Clery's, O'Connell Street, Dublin 1 (878 7023). All cross city buses. **Open** 9am-6.30pm Mon-Wed; 9am-8pm Fri; 9am-5.30pm Sat. **Credit** AmEx, DC, MC, V.

Stockists of mainly computers but they also have a range of hi-fi equipment, computer accessories and CD ROMs. Friendly staff who don't try to sell you something that you don't want makes Beyond 2000 – on the top floor of Clery's department store – a good choice.

Dixon's

15 Jervis Centre, Dublin 1 (878 1515). All cross city buses. **Open** 9am-6pm Mon-Wed, Sat; 9am-9pm Thur; 9am-7pm Fri; noon-6pm Sun. **Credit** AmEx, MC, V.

In the Jervis Centre, Dixon's stocks the standard broad range of electrical equipment, televisions and stereos, computers and Walkmans. If you're staying in Dublin, ask about their instalment-paying policies.

Branches: Blanchardstown (820 2333); Tallaght (452 2855).

Hi-fi Corner

14 Aston Quay, Dublin 2 (671 4343). Bus 78A. **Open** 9.30am-6pm Mon-Wed, Fri, Sat; 9.30am-8pm Thur. **Credit** MC, V.

Attached to the Virgin Megastore, Hi-fi Corner can be a bit pricey, attracting the top end of the market in terms of cost and quality. Stockists of a good range of hi-fi equipment and separates, they also sell laser discs and have a home cinema demonstration room.

Branch: Ballsbridge (667 0990).

Peats World of Electronics

197-200 Parnell Street, Dublin 1 (872 7799). Bus 19, 19A, 40, 40A, 134. **Open** 9.30am-6pm Mon-Sat. **Credit** MC, V.

Huge range of electrical goods, this is a well known Dublin store which can be relied upon for quality, cost and after-sales service.

Sony Centre

25 Parnell Street, Dublin 1 (872 1900). Bus 19, 19A, 40A, 134. **Open** 9.30am-6pm Mon-Sat. **Credit** MC, V.

Brand stockists, but they're good at putting together systems out of separates at reasonable enough prices.

Entertaining

Balloon Man Party Shop

5 Upper O'Connell Street, Dublin 1 (874 8575). All cross city buses. **Open** 9.30am-6pm Mon-Sat. **Credit** AmEx, MC, V.

Everything you could want to run a party, from streamers and lights to balloons and banners. Delivery service available and they'll run up quotes for you quickly if you need one. **Branch:** St Stephen's Green Shopping Centre (478 2328).

Dublin Balloon & Party Shop

Balloon Centre, Donnybrook, Dublin 4 (269 3500). Bus 10, 46A. **Open** 9am-6pm Mon-Wed, Fri; 9am-7pm Thur; 10am-6pm Sat. **Credit** MC, V.

The same sort of stuff, reasonable prices; usually able to find the kind of off the wall items you might want to run a successful party.

Food

Bakers & confectioners

Ann's Hot Breadshops

Mary Street, Dublin 1 (872 7759). All cross city buses. **Open** 7.30am-6pm Mon-Wed, Fri, Sat; 7.30am-8pm Thur.

Popular bakery, worth visiting early in the day when the smell of cooking and fresh bread makes you want to eat breakfast all over again. Also serve tea, coffee and cakes. **Branches:** 26 North Earl Street, Dublin 1 (874 5796); Stillorgan Shopping Centre (288 4512).

Bewley's Oriental Café

Grafton Street, Dublin 2 (677 6761). All cross city buses. **Open** 8am-1am Mon-Thur, Sun; 7.30am-5am Fri, Sat. **Credit** AmEx, DC, MC, V.

Dublin's most famous eating place also has a good – if expensive – take-away service, with bread, cakes, scones, and bags of tea and coffee available at a price. Always busy, but always worth waiting for. The Grafton Street in particular has several floors, with self-service or table-service, depending on which you choose, and the prices reflect this. Still, you have to experience a full Irish breakfast there at least once. (*See also chapter* **Bistros, Cafés & Coffee Shops.**) **Branches:** Mary Street (closes 6pm); Westmoreland Street (closes 8pm).

Kylemore

1 O'Connell Street, Dublin 1 (878 0494). All cross city buses. **Open** 8.30am-5.30pm Mon-Sat. **Credit** MC, V.

Almost as famous as Bewley's, the Kylemore runs several small cake shops around the city. Check out the Nassau Street branch in the mornings and enjoy squeezing in between the counter and the huge trays in which the bread arrives.

Branches are too numerous to list here. Check the telephone directory for your nearest.

Teatime Express

Dawson Street, Dublin 2 (671 4899). All cross city buses. **Open** 8.30am-5.30pm Mon-Sat. **Credit** MC, V.

Fresh cakes, bread, scones, rolls and sandwiches, available to eat in or take away.

Branches: Irish Life Mall, Talbot Street (872 9955); Dun Laoghaire Shopping Centre (280 8995).

Delicatessens

Big Cheese Company

14-15 Trinity Street, Dublin 2 (671 1399). All cross city buses. **Open** 10am-6pm Mon-Fri; 9.30am-6pm Sat. **Credit** MC, V.

A great shop (confusingly, located on St Andrew's Lane), with a selection of cheeses from around the world. Also serves bread and other delicatessen supplies.

Jones' Delicatessen

137 Baggott Street Lower, Dublin 2 (661 8137). All cross city buses. **Open** 7am-7.30pm Mon-Sat. **Credit** MC, V.

Standard deli with about eight branches scattered around Dublin. It stocks bread, cheese, cold meats and so on. **Branches** are too numerous to list here. Check the telephone directory for your nearest.

Molly's mussels

'In Dublin's Fair City, where the girls are so pretty,
I first set my eyes on sweet Molly Malone,
As she wheeled her wheelbarrow, through streets broad
and narrow, Crying,
"Cockles and Mussels! alive, alive oh!"
She was a fishmonger, but sure 'twas no wonder,
For so were her father and mother before;
And they each wheel'd their barrow through streets broad
and narrow, Crying,
"Cockles and Mussels! alive, alive oh!"
She died of a fever, and no one could save her,
And that was the end of sweet Molly Malone;
Her ghost wheels her barrow through streets broad and
narrow, Crying
"Cockles and Mussels! alive, alive oh!"'

Everyone knows the song. It has become a kind of unofficial anthem for Dublin's Fair City, just as Molly Malone has become an unofficial symbol. The image of sweet Molly, walking the streets, shouting out her wares, conjures up pictures of Dublin street life that are, in many ways, as familiar today as they were in the eighteenth century when she is thought to have lived and died.

By the turn of the eighteenth century, Dublin city was at the height of its glamour. Much of the unrest that had besieged Ireland in the previous centuries had come to a halt and the country had began to enjoy a new phase of peace and prosperity. Consequently, the population of Dublin soared and high society in the capital soon matched that of any major European city for elegance and sophistication.

Yet amid this brash new elegance, Dublin remained a city of beggars, newspaper sellers, dealers, penny boys, buskers, rapparees and scores of street sellers. The women traders, pushing their wicker baskets through the streets crying 'Cockles and Mussels', were a distinctive feature of this unique Dublin street life.

A fishmonger's trade was passed down through the generations, from mother to daughter. 'Sure 'twas no wonder', what else would they do? It was in their blood. Girls would go to the markets as small children to help their mothers and often begin trading themselves as young as 14. The street traders were almost always women and a woman could shoulder the sole responsibility of raising and supporting a family with as many as 17 children. Their humour kept them going, but life was hard, and death from fever and other ills was always around the corner. The glamour and prosperity of eighteenth-century Dublin left little impression on these women of the streets. Perhaps the price of mussels was raised a penny or two but their life continued as always, a struggle to survive.

Was Molly Malone a real person? Who knows? It is claimed that she lived between 1663-1734. But there is discrepancy over this, and many believe she is a fictitious character. Yet whether she lived or not is irrelevant to her importance as a symbol of Dublin. In 1989, a statue of her, dressed in seventeenth-century style costume, was erected and stands today on the corner of Grafton Street. Many street traders refer to themselves as 'Molly Malones' and Dublin Corporation have even held a competition, the Molly Malone Award, among the vendors on Moore Street.

These days, there are only a few women traders left in Dublin who walk the streets in the style of Molly. But business among the licensed traders of Moore Street is booming and is as significant to the character of the city as ever. Molly Malone may cry 'Cockles and Mussels' no more, but take a walk down today's Dublin streets broad and narrow, particularly that of Moore Street, and the sellers will cry strawberries, grapes, peaches, apples, flowers, old clothes, whatever you will. Some things don't always change that much.

Health food

General Health Food Stores

93 Marlborough Street, Dublin 2 (874 3290).
All cross city buses. **Open** 9am-6pm Mon-Sat.
Credit AmEx, MC, V.
Organic food shop with branches around the city and the
suburbs. Wide range of stock in a long-established store.
Branches are too numerous to list here. Check the
telephone directory for your nearest.

Nature's Way

*Parnell Mall, Ilac Centre, Dublin 1 (872 8391). All cross
city buses.* **Open** 9am-6pm Mon-Wed, Fri, Sat; 8am-8pm
Sat. **Credit** MC, V.
Specialists in health food, vitamin supplements, skin care
products. The best thing about Nature's Way is their
informed staff who can advise on the best natural remedy
for your complaint, assuming your complaint has nothing to
do with their somewhat high prices for some of their prod-
cuts. Mail order (056 65402) service useful for for some of
their exclusive products.
Branches: Blackrock (288 6696); Blanchardstown (822
2560); Donnymead (867 1174); Tallaght (459 6068); St
Stephen's Green (478 0165).

The Nut Keg

*The Square, Tallaght (452 1181). Bus 49, 54A, 56A,
65, 65A, 65B, 77A.* **Open** 9am-6pm Mon, Tue, Sat; 9am-
9pm Wed, Thur. **Credit** MC, V.
Health food specialists, stocking wholefoods, frozen foods,
homeopathic remedies, homebrew equipment, herbs and
spices, vitamin supplements and aromatherapy.
Branches Blanchardstown (822 2036); Bray (286 1793);
Swords (840 4438).

Tony Quinn Health Stores

Eccles Street, Dublin (830 8588). All cross city buses.
Open 8.30am-9.15pm Mon-Fri; 9am-6pm Sat; 12-4pm
Sun. **Credit** MC, V.
Chain of health stores around Dublin with a good range in
spacious, well-laid out stores.
Branches Dun Laoghaire (280 9891); St Stephen's Green
(478 5404); Rathmines (497 4234).

Furniture

The main department stores offer a good range of
furniture, plus there's Capel Street, Dublin 1, which
is filled with furniture stores. Then the following:

Bean Bag Shop

*South Great George's Street, Dublin 2 (088 514739).
All cross city buses.* **Open** 11am-5.30pm Mon-Sat.
No credit cards.
Set in the trendy market space of George's Arcade, the name
gives away what they do and this is a fun shop to visit. Bean
bags also made to order – they say they do them for pets, too.

Bedrooms Elegance

*63 Upper Dorset Street, Dublin 1 (872 8210).
All cross city buses.* **Open** 9.30am-5.30pm Mon-Sat.
No credit cards.
Design bedroom furniture to your own ideas and estimates.

Gardens & flowers

For those simply looking for a bunch of flowers
for the person who's just walked past you on the
street or the significant other sitting seething in a
hotel room after you rolled in drunk at three in the

morning, the simplest way to get some flowers is
from the many street vendors scattered around the
city. On Grafton Street, regular vendors work from
the early hours of the morning and sell from a huge
range of flowers at terrific prices. The more you
buy, the better deals they'll give you.

Baccara Florist

*16 Pembroke Cottages, Dundrum, Dublin 14
(298 9057). Bus 44, 48.* **Open** 9am-6pm Mon-Sat.
Credit AmEx, MC, V.
Will arrange flower baskets with almost anything added –
fruit, chocolate, teddies. Also put together bouquets for
weddings or funeral wreaths. Same day delivery generally
and can also send flowers around the world.

Interflora

(Freephone 1 800 434343). **Credit** AmEx, MC, V.
Reliable, round-the-world florists. Should usually be able to
get flowers from Dublin to Tasmania in the shortest possible time at the best price.

Justyne Flowers

*Irish Life Mall, Talbot Street, Dublin 1 (878 8455). All
cross city buses.* **Open** 8.30am-6pm Mon-Sat. **Credit**
AmEx, MC, V.
Interflora shop with branches around the city.
Branches are too numerous to list here. Check the
telephone directory for your nearest.

Max Florist

*34 Bachelor's Walk, O'Connell Bridge, Dublin 1 (873
1222). All cross city buses.* **Open** 9am-6pm Mon-Fri; 9am-
5pm Sat. **Credit** AmEx, MC, V.
Arrangements, funeral wreaths, bouquets, house or office
plants, baby cradles. Added extras include champagne,
chocolate or a gift of your choice delivered with the flowers.

Rosary Florists

2 Prospect Avenue, Glasnevin (830 6411). Bus 19. **Open**
9am-6pm Mon-Sat. **Credit** AmEx, MC, V.
Open every day of the year with a two hour delivery service,
and branches around the city and rest of the world.
Branches are too numerous to list here. Check the
telephone directory for your nearest.

Health & beauty

Bellaza Beauty Clinic

*27 Ranelagh Road, Dublin 6 (496 3484). Bus 12, 44,
44B, 48, 61, 62.* **Open** 9.30am-8pm Tue-Fri; 9am-5pm
Sat. **No credit cards.**
Aromatherapy and toning tables available, as well as turbo
sunbeds for that ultra-realistic tan which Dublin's climate
can rarely offer. Electrolysis and manicures form part of the
service plus, for the truly desperate, non-surgical face-lifts.

Body Shop

*82 Grafton Street, Dublin 2 (679 4569). All cross city
buses.* **Open** 9am-6pm Mon, Fri; 9am-8pm Thur;
10am-6pm Sat; 2-6pm Sun. **Credit** AmEx, MC, V.
Standard Body Shop fare: gift packs and small bottles of
colourful liquids guaranteed to turn you into Julia Roberts
or Brad Pitt within minutes, depending on your preference.

Hair & Beauty Clinic

31-32 Mary Street, Dublin 1 (872 5544). Bus 24. **Open**
10am-6pm Mon-Wed, Fri, Sat; 9am-8pm Thur. **Credit**
AmEx, MC, V.
Aromatherapy, body wraps, Eurowave slimming, manicures
and pedicures. A couple of branches around the city but it's
still advisable to phone and book ahead.

*Every Sunday **Blackrock Market** tempts the unwary with a vast array of goods and chattels.*

Peter Mark

*Level 2, St Stephen's Green Centre, Dublin 2 (475 1126).
All cross city buses.* **Open** 9.30am-6pm Mon-Wed, Fri,
Sat; 9.30am-8pm Thur; 2-6pm Sun. **Credit** MC, V.
Probably the best known hairstylists in the city, Peter Mark
seems to have branches everywhere you can go. Call in or book
ahead if you want something special, their prices are competitive, but they give a good service as well as offering such
extras as waxing, electrolysis, make-up tips, and manicures.
Branches are too numerous to list here. Check the
telephone directory for your nearest.

Jewellery

Weir's of Grafton Street (No.96; 677 9678) is
Dublin's largest and most prominent jewellery
store, with a particularly strong line in risibly
expensive designer wristwatches from around the
world. Pierre Cardin, Tag Heuer, Cartier, Piguet,
and (real) Rolexes are all here in elegant surroundings. Weir's is also unrivalled as a stockist
of quality silverware and leather goods.

Further south along the same street, **West's**
typifies the numerous jewellers in this area – of
unimpeachable quality, but impeachably conservative graduates of the how-many-diamonds-on-
the-head-of-a-pin school, at the expense of modern
and/or Irish produce. Close by on Anne Street
South, a selection of older, friendlier and more
open-minded stores stocks a broad range of new
and antique jewellery, which makes this is a good
street for the serendipitous silver-lover.

At the back of St Stephen's Green Centre's
ground floor, a stall called **Celtic Spirit** sells
cheap, Celtic-inspired jewellery.

Johnson's Court, a narrow, dark and atmospheric lane that runs down the side of Bewley's on
Grafton Street, is a must if you're serious about
jewellery-hunting in Dublin. The shops here range
from **Appleby's** (5-6 Johnson's Court; 679 9572) –
Dublin's most exclusive jeweller, which stocks an
extensive range of fabulous (though again, very
conservative) silver, gold and gems, and offers
friendly and intelligent advice (as long as you don't
mind being visually frisked at the door) – to the
nameless shop at the very end of the street, which
changes watch batteries cheaper than just about
anywhere else (and does so without regard for
your social standing).

Upstairs in the nearby Powerscourt Townhouse
Centre, the antiques section is worth a visit for its
silver and semi-precious stones; but the main
attraction here must be the **Crafts Council of
Ireland's** fine collection of modern Irish jewellery,
gathered from all corners and counties of the country. The standard is remarkably high, but so, too,
are the prices. Nevertheless, even without the
means or the inclination to purchase, the centre is
worth a visit for a covetous gaze alone.

If your taste in jewellery leans in any way
towards the innovative, then Temple Bar's **Design
Yard** is the ultimate feast. Like the Powerscourt
Centre, it stocks a fascinating range of contemporary Irish jewellery, of a superb artistic and
technical standard. But again one thing is clear, as
much from the methods of display as from the
prices – these pieces are being sold as works of art,
not trinkets or disposable adornments.

*Bodhrán and roll at **Celtic Note**, the Nassau Street store dedicated to Irish music.*

Markets

As Molly Malone would probably testify, Dublin has a long history of lively street-trading. The city's most famous street market, and one of its oldest, is to be found on Moore Street, one of the pedestrianised streets off Henry Street on the Northside of the city. Here, in amongst countless stalls of fruit, vegetables, portable radios, and Christmas cards in June, you can listen for hours to the unconducted orchestra of street-traders. 'Mandarins, eight for feeftee!', or 'Sports socks, last pair, two pairs for a peeownd!'; or again, in the lower but more urgent voices of those selling contraband cigarettes, 'Jimmy! Pigs!'

Across the river on the Temple Bar square, every Saturday a food market draws an altogether different crowd. D4s (as they're called, after Dublin's most desirable postcode), who mysteriously don't eat fruit, vegetables or portable radios and give their favour instead to such staples as olives and fresh south American enchiladas. The cries, too, are different. 'Tristan – Fitzers for an espresso, yaw?'

Of course, there is peaceful middle ground. Being indoors is an immediate advantage for the George's Arcade (between George's Street and Drury Street), undoubtedly Dublin's finest and most varied sheltered market. Mentioned already for its excellent used clothes shops, it also has some fine secondhand book and music stalls, a small print stand with a Republican leaning, a fortune-teller, and (if your future's so bright that you may have to move to D4), an excellent olive stand.

Camden Street also has a sizeable food market, though the heavy traffic of recent years has affected it badly. Some of this traffic is no doubt crawling towards Blackrock, where every Sunday an expansive and varied market – part indoors and part out – opens to the public. The stalls vary with time, but on an average Sunday one could expect to find crafts of all kinds and qualities, cushions, books, music, electrical goods, furniture, beanbags, paintings and clothes. But no olives. Or dodgy cigs.

Music

Megastores

The three bigfellas – **HMV**, **Tower**, and **Virgin** – dominate recorded music sales in Dublin. HMV (65 Grafton Street; 679 5334) is the most reliably stocked, with three large floors catering well for every genre and format. Though it usually has some breed of sale going at all times, it is on the whole the most expensive music shop in the city. The Grafton Street branch also has a good events guide and ticket shop.

Tower Records (16 Wicklow Street; 671 3250) has a terrific range of alternative and world music, as well as good jazz, traditional and country sections. The rear left of the ground floor houses an

Virgin *on Aston Quay, Dublin 2 – the grandest, friendliest and cheapest of the music megastores.*

unequalled selection of music books and magazines. Tower's prices are relatively reasonable.

The **Virgin** building at 14 Aston Quay (not to be confused with several local convent schools of the same name) is the grandest, but also the friendliest and cheapest, of the larger stores. Off the ground floor on the left is a formidable classical room; upstairs is a great selection of videotapes and games. Its telephone number is 677 7361.

Golden Discs (8 North Earl Street; 874 0417) is the largest chain of music-stores in Ireland, with 15 branches throughout Dublin alone. It tends to carry a reliable, mainstream stock, with a definite emphasis on the presently strong Irish music scene. The small size of the average Golden Discs outlet cramps the range, but this is made up for with competitive prices and generous offers.

Smaller stores

A new store dedicated to Irish music is the **Celtic Note** on Nassau Street (at No.12; 670 4157). Five minutes away on Duke Lane, **Borderline** (679 9067) buys, sells and swaps secondhand music. **Phoenix Records**, off the northwest corner of Temple Bar Square, combines a great range of secondhand, underground and indie at reasonable prices with affable and knowledgeable service.

Traditional Irish instruments, from uileann pipes to bodhráns and tin whistles, make excellent gifts. **McCullough Pigott's** is probably Dublin's most popular instrument (and sheet music) retailer, though the Suffolk Street store down-sized drastically five years ago (25 Suffolk Street; 677 3138). **McNeill's** of Capel Street is a small and beautiful store which has been in business for over a 150 years; its selection of and advice on traditional instruments is second to none (140 Capel Street; 872 2159). The curiously titled **Charles Byrne Musik Instrumente** of Stephen Street Lower (No.21; 478 1773) is similarly atmospheric and worth a visit. But for modernists who think that whistles are for wimps and spoons for spanking, **Rock Steady** of Chatham Row may be more supportive (3 Chatham Row; 679 4253).

Newsagents & stationers

Bus Stop
Grafton Street, Dublin 1 (671 4476/677 3661). All cross city buses. **Open** 8am-10pm Mon-Sat; 10am-10pm Sun.
Bus Stop stocks a large range of newspapers and magazines, cards, gifts and confectionery. They often stock a range of specifically 'Irish' gifts, such as leprechaun soft toys.
Branches: Eden Quay, Dublin 1 (874 1772); D'Olier Street, Dublin 2 (677 9142); Nutgrove Shopping Centre, Dublin 14 (493 2515).

Metro
115 Grafton Street, Dublin 2 (670 4512). All cross city buses. **Open** 8am-10pm Mon-Sat; 10am-10pm Sun.
Standard newsagent in the heart of Grafton Street with the full range of papers, mags and snacks.

News Express
46 Upper O'Connell Street, Dublin 1 (873 1028). All cross city buses. **Open** 7.30am-10pm Mon-Sat; 9am-10pm Sun.
Like most of the newsagents in the city, they also stock a range of sandwiches and easy lunchtime fare along with the typical news fodder.

Reid's
Nassau Street, Dublin 2. Bus 10, 11, 13. All cross city buses. **Open** 7.30am-10pm Mon-Sat; 9am-10pm Sun.
An excellent newsagent with one of the widest ranges in the city, Reid's also has a basement floor stocked with every possible stationery item you could need, as well as a full photocopying service (including colour), plus binding and laminating facilities.

Tower Records
16 Wicklow Street, Dublin 2 (671 3250). **Open** 9am-10pm Mon-Sat; noon-7pm Sun. **Credit** AmEx, MC, V.
Actually a record shop, but they stock the best range of foreign papers (including Sunday editions) in Dublin. They're often a couple of days behind, but at least they have them. They'll also order in any paper or magazine you're want.

Off-licences

Lots of pubs do take-outs, and Dunnes Stores in the ILAC Centre and in Stephen's Green have off-licences, as do Mark's & Spencer, Roches Stores, and the Quinnsworth/Tesco in the Jervis Street Shopping Centre. Plus the following:

Cheers
238 Harold's Cross Road, Dublin 6 (497 4239). Bus 65B. **Open** 10.30am-11pm Mon-Sat. **Credit** AmEx, MC, V.
With branches all around the city, Cheers are developing into the place to buy all your party needs, beer, wine, spirits, new release videos, pizzas and snacks. Home delivery also available.
Branches are too numerous to list here. Check the telephone directory for your nearest.

Deveney's
31 Main Street, Dundrum, Dublin 16 (298 4288). Bus 44, 48A. **Open** 10.30am-10pm Mon-Sat; 12.30-2pm, 4-10pm, Sun. **Credit** MC, V.
Several branches offer a sale or return service for large party supplies. Wines, spirits, beers and liqueurs. Will put together supplies for you, if you give them a rough idea of numbers attending a party.
Branches are too numerous to list here. Check the telephone directory for your nearest.

Molloy's
Nutgrove Shopping Centre, Nutgrove Avenue, Rathfarnam, Dublin 14 (493 6077). Bus 16A. **Open** 10am-11pm daily. **Credit** AmEx, MC, V.
The usual range of drinks, and sale or return party drinks, plus glass hire. All at reasonable prices.

Redmond's
25 Ranelagh Village, Dublin 6 (497 1739). **Open** 9am-10.20pm Mon-Sat. **Credit** MC, V.
Good for local delivery or just call in for a few cans at the end of the night.

Outdoor supplies

If a camping trip is on the cards, then a trip to Mary Street and Mary's Lane will almost certainly guarantee a good deal. Simply continue to walk

If you can't find what you're after in any of the shops, maybe it's lurking on **O'Connell Bridge**.

westwards at the end of Henry Street, and on your left you'll find a Rambo's delight of army surplus stores, survival shops, and tent warehouses. *See also below* **Sports equipment**.

Army Bargains

30 Little Mary Street, Dublin 1 (874 4600). **Open** 9am-6pm Mon-Wed, Fri, Sat; 9am-7pm Thur. **Credit** MC, V.
Honest advice and gags of offers too good to refuse.

Beaten Track

16 Exchequer Street, Dublin 2 (671 2477). **Open** 9am-5.30pm Mon-Wed, Fri, Sat. 9am-7pm Thur. **Credit** MC, V.
Promises to help you 'face the elements with confidence', though whether any of the designer-labelled fleeces purveyed therein ever make it beyond the landscaped wildernesses of Killiney or Dublin 4 is up for discussion.

Millets

26 Little Mary Street, Dublin 1 (873 3571). **Open** 9am-6pm Mon-Sat. **Credit** MC, V.
Amazingly low prices on an extensive range of high quality tents and camping/survival equipment.

Pharmacies

Donnybrook Pharmacy

8 The Mall, Donnybrook, Dublin 4 (269 5236). **Open** 9am-10pm daily. **Credit** AmEx, MC, V.
Late night pharmacy, only closed on Christmas Day, for all your pharmaceutical needs.

Hayes Conyngham & Robinson

Unit 319, The Square, Tallaght, Dublin 24 (462 2155). Bus 49, 50, 65, 65B, 77, 77A. **Open** 9am-11pm Mon-Sat; 2-11pm Sun. **Credit** AmEx, MC, V.
With branches spread around the city and a long-established reputation, HC&R have several large stores stocking the full range of goods, from band-aids to hair dyes, barley sugar to condoms. Prescriptions made up on the spot.
Branches are too numerous to list here. Check the telephone directory for your nearest.

O'Connells

Grafton Street (679 0467). All cross city buses. **Open** 8.30am-8.30pm Mon-Sat; 11am-6pm Sun. **Credit** AmEx, MC, V.
Late night pharmacies spread mostly around the city centre with the standard range of goods and prescription facilities.
Branches are too numerous to list here. Check the telephone directory for your nearest.

Photography

Camera Centre

56 Grafton Street, Dublin 2 (677 5594). All cross city buses. **Open** 9am-6pm Mon-Sat. **Credit** AmEx, MC, V.
With several branches around the city, Camera Centre is a reliable choice for anything in this field: cameras, camcorders, binoculars and telescopes. Also has a one-hour film processing/enlargement service. Will do part exchanges.
Branches are too numerous to list here. Check the telephone directory for your nearest.

Camera Exchange

9B Trinity Street, Dublin 2 (679 3410). All cross city buses. **Open** 9am-5pm Mon-Sat. **Credit** AmEx, MC, V.
Stockists of both new and used cameras, this is a good place to go if you're on a budget but still want to get something that isn't going to break down after one roll of film.

Hall Cameras

95 Talbot Street, Dublin 1 (878 8332). All cross city buses. **Open** 9.30am-5pm Mon-Sat. **Credit** AmEx, MC, V.
Film, digital and video cameras available here, as well as a knowledgeable staff who are usually eager to help a novice along with queries, without trying to sell them the latest model.

Slattery's

52 Upper O'Connell Street, Dublin 1 (873 0918). All cross city buses. **Open** 9.30am-5.30pm Mon-Sat. **Credit** AmEx, MC, V.
Mainly stockists of Canon cameras and videos, this is a fairly large store with a good reputation for reasonable prices.

Dun Laoghaire Shopping Centre *early in the morning before the seething crowds descend.*

Shopping centres

Blackrock Shopping Centre
Frascati Road, Blackrock (283 1660). DART Blackrock.
Away from the city centre, Blackrock is convenient for the DART line but, like any suburban centre, can be more expensive than its city counterparts. A relatively small centre, it's nicely designed and a good place to browse for an hour or two. A couple of nice restaurants and coffee shops, too.

Dun Laoghaire Shopping Centre
Marine Road, Dun Laoghaire (280 2981). DART Dun Laoghaire.
Much larger than Blackrock Shopping Centre, and only three DART stops down the line, Dun Laoghaire operates over several floors and is often quite busy, so be prepared to get caught in the rush. Everything from clothes to books, groceries to electrics.

Dundrum Shopping Centre
Dundrum, Dublin 14 (298 4123). Bus 44, 48A.
Another suburban centre, with one large grocery store, Quinnsworth, and two floors of smaller shops, including cafés, restaurants, clothes shops and art suppliers. There's a thriving village around the shopping centre, where more shops and banks are contained together, including a video shop and bargain centre.

Ilac Centre
Henry Street, Dublin 1. All cross city buses.
A large, busy centre in the middle of Dublin city, the Ilac plays host to a huge number of shops, carrying every possible product, but it's so huge and it spreads out in so many different directions that it can be very easy to get lost there, so look out for the maps.

Irish Life Shopping Mall
Talbot Street, Dublin 1 (704 1452). DART Connolly Station/all cross city buses.
Somewhat off the beaten track, the Irish Life suffers from still being relatively unknown, despite having been in existence for some years now. A cluster of shops spread around

a flat complex, it can be a little intimidating at first, but there are some bargains to be found there and shouldn't be just used as a thoroughfare.

Jervis Shopping Centre
Mary Street, Dublin 1. All cross city buses.
Dublin's newest shopping centre extends the city centre a little further down Henry Street. Containing a wide range of shops over several floors, the Jervis Centre is worth visiting for its customer-friendly layout and wide range. Flagship shops include Debenhams, Waterstone's, Argos and Dixon's.

St Stephen's Green Shopping Centre
Dublin 2 (478 0888). All cross city buses.
A huge complex with excellent car parking facilities, the St Stephen's Green Shopping Centre combines pricey, specialist shops with cheaper, bargain shops.

Square Town Centre
Tallaght, Dublin 24. Bus 49, 54A, 56A, 65, 65A, 65B.
A large centre way outside of the city centre with the added attraction of a multiplex UCI cinema. Lots of good shops, all of which try to be as reasonable as possible on prices.

Sports equipment

Champion Sports
49 Lower O'Connell Street, Dublin 1 (872 9500). All cross city buses. **Open** 9am-6.30pm Mon-Wed, Fri, Sat; 9am-8pm Thur; 1-6pm Sun. **Credit** MC, V.
Billed as Ireland's No 1 sports and fitness stores, Champion Sports does stock a wide range of goods and equipment at fairly cheap prices, although sometimes the prices can reflect the quality of the goods. Branches all around the city centre – just watch out for the spotty kids in shiny tracksuits and you'll find one.
Branches are too numerous to list here. Check the telephone directory for your nearest.

Great Outdoors
Chatham Street, Dublin 2 (679 4293). All cross city buses. **Open** 9.30am-5.30pm Mon-Wed, Fri, Sat. 9.30am-8pm Thur. **Credit** AmEx, DC, MC, V.

Quality sports shop, with a lot more to offer than just that. Caters for the more exotic sports, such as scuba diving, canoeing and skiing, but worth checking out.

Lifestyle

O'Connell Street, Dublin 1 (872 9100). DART Connolly Station/all cross city buses. **Open** 9am-6pm Mon-Wed, Fri, Sat; 9am-8pm Thur; noon-6pm Sun. **Credit** MC, V.
Standard range of good and equipment in large stores spread around Dublin. Often quite busy and it's not always easy to catch the eye of an assistant.

Tailors

Dun Laoghaire Express Alteration Tailors

64A Convent Road, Dun Laoghaire (280 2962). DART Dun Laoghaire. **Open** 9.30-5.30pm Mon-Sat. **No credit cards.**
Ladies' and gents' alterations and leather repairs. This is outside of the city centre and handy if you're travelling along the DART line.

Louis Copeland

39-41 Capel Street, Dublin 1 (872 1600). All cross city buses. **Open** 9am-5.45pm Mon-Wed, Fri, Sat; 9am-8pm Thur. **Credit** AmEx, MC, V.
Famous Dublin tailor Louis Copeland offers his own range in his shops as well as making alterations and repairs to what you already own. He may be expensive but he's

worth it, aiming at the business end of the market and displaying a professionalism to match his clients. *See also above* **Fashion: Designer**.

Kennedy & McSharry

39 Nassau Street, Dublin 2 (677 8770). All cross city buses. **Open** 9am-5.30pm Mon-Wed, Fri, Sat; 9am-8pm Thur. **Credit** AmEx, DC, MC, V.
Well-established Dublin tailors, they offer the standard range of services at attractive prices. Can do things in a hurry if that's what you need.

Professional Alterations

South Great George's Street Arcade, Dublin 2 (679 1501). All cross city buses. **Open** 9.30am-6pm Mon-Sat. **No credit cards.**
Dressmaking and alterations to outfits with a good same day service available. Reasonable prices.

Tobacconists

Kapp & Peterson

117 Grafton Street, Dublin 2 (671 4652). All cross city buses. **Open** 9am-5.30pm Mon-Sat. **Credit** MC, V.
These tobacconists make their own pipes in Sallynoggin, and sell them in the city centre, along with everything else even the most demanding tobaccoholic could require – cigarette-cases, Swiss Army knives, little fiddly bits for Swiss Army knives, cigars, Zippos galore… and tobacco. The address is misleading: find them across from the main gates of Trinity College, then a few doors to the left.

Satellites

Dublin has dozens of satellite towns, spread out in every direction from the city centre, as far west as Co Kildare and as far south as Co Wicklow (and as far east, some would say, as Liverpool). Some of the towns, like **Tallaght** in the south and parts of **Ballymun** to the north, have been developed deliberately to accommodate an exploding population; others have been connected and absorbed gradually, first falling within commuting distance, then just falling within. It is a startling measure of this expansion that in seventeenth- and eighteenth-century Dublin, a family who were domiciled on, say, Fitzwilliam Square, might have had a 'country home' in **Ranelagh** or **Rathmines**.

Such city expansion has been a mixed blessing. For some towns, it's been the kiss of life, while for others it's proved as bad as a bad kiss can be. Persistent poverty on the Northside of the city meant that, though they were strong of character, many of its towns have in practical terms not survived. Only in recent years has any effort been made to cure this (and, in many cases, the cure has not been much better than the disease), with the construction of a generic shopping centre bearing the name of the town on which it sits. Southside towns

close to the city centre and attractive coastal towns such as **Blackrock**, **Dun Laoghaire** and **Dalkey** have faired best in the long run. **Blackrock**, with its Sunday market, its two upmarket, bright and bubbly shopping centres (one is even called the Frascati), and its curling main street, is a supremely comfortable town to shop in. Easy access by DART adds to the attraction.

Further out along the coast, the two piers of **Dun Laoghaire** are a favourite Dublin walk (though the jump between them takes years of practice); parallel to the seafront is Dublin's other George's Street, even busier than the first one. A highly publicised new food hall adds to the attractiveness of a street lined with small local shops and businesses of a sort made extinct in the city centre by higher rents and more aggressive competition.

But between the centre and here there are other, similar streets – the main streets of towns such as **Terenure**, **Rathgar**, **Rathmines** and **Ranelagh**. Though they all now are strung together and attached to the city, each of these streets is still very much a town centre in itself – with varieties of small shops providing all of the necessities of suburban living.

Accommodation

Whether it's Georgian grace or just a sleeping bag space you're after, bear in mind that, as Dublin's tourist profile rises, so too does demand for its beds.

Dublin has a wide range of accommodation possibilities, from five-star international hotels through to hostels and camp sites, but finding any kind of room in the summer months can be difficult and if something is not booked in advance you may well find yourself having to pay more than you bargained for – for a night or two, at least.

Try to book as far ahead as you possibly can. You might want to consider using the tourist board booking facility in the city centre, at the airport or by the harbour in Dún Laoghaire. Credit card bookings can be made on a special line (605 7777), or by fax (605 7787), for a bed in a hotel, guest house, private home, self-catering apartment, hostel or campus accommodation.

A booking service is also available on a 24-hour basis from a touchscreen unit outside the Dublin Tourism Centre on Suffolk Street, Dublin 2, at Dublin airport, and at Dún Laoghaire ferry terminal. The service requires a ten per cent deposit which is payable only by credit card then deducted

from your accommodation bill. A reservation service is also available through the Internet at http://www.visit.ie/dublin.

Bord Fáilte updates annually a comprehensive accommodation guide that covers the whole of the country, and, at £5, this is only worth it for visitors who are taking trips out of town. Well worth obtaining is the annual *Dublin Accommodation Guide* which is available from the Dublin tourist office and which may be available through the Bord Fáilte office in your own country.

Top notch

Berkeley Court
Lansdowne Road, Dublin 4 (660 1711/fax 661 7238/ 0800 181 123 toll-free from UK/1 800 223 6800 toll-free from US). DART Lansdowne Road/bus 7, 8. **Rooms** 200. **Rates** *single £165; double £185; executive suite £225-£250; de luxe suite £450-£550; Penthouse suite £1,600 (room rates excl breakfast, £12.50).* **Credit** AmEx, DC, MC, V.
The verdant setting of the Berkeley Court owes a lot to the

*Personalities queuing up to stay at the **Berkeley Court** have included snooker's Steve Davis.*

Enjoy an evening's cabaret at the **Burlington** *and you'll forever be harping on about it.*

fact that the grounds were once home to the Botanical Gardens of University College Dublin. The hotel was built in the 1970s, but the large lobby has recently been renovated to create a lush atmosphere of luxury and indulgence. Reproductions of period furniture in the bedrooms maintain the mood of stated elegance that is equally apparent in the Royal Court bar with its rich gothic panelling. Afternoon tea is served in the Court Lounge and, while the Berkeley Room has all the hallmarks of a distinguished dining room, the Conservatory serves breakfast, lunch and dinner in a more airy and relaxed setting. Check out the 'hall of fame' with photographs of countless famous guests ranging from Steve Davis to Robert Mugabe. The hotel is located in the embassy-land of Dublin 4 and it's a 20-minute walk to the town centre, but only five minutes by DART from nearby Lansdowne Road station. Enquire about the hotel's weekend rates when substantial reductions may be available.
Hotel services *Baby-sitting & cot available. Business centre. Bars. Car parking. Conference facilities. Hotel shop. Lift/elevator. No-smoking bedrooms. Restaurants.* **Room services** *Hair dryer. Room service (24 hours). Telephone. Trouser press. TV.*

Brooks Hotel
59-62 Drury Street, Dublin 2 (670 4000/fax 670 4455). All cross city buses. **Rooms** 75. **Rates** *single* £125-£155; *double* £150-£180. **Credit** AmEx, MC, V.
Brooks Hotel opened in the middle of 1997. A four-star hotel located within a few minutes' walk of Grafton Street, Trinity College and Temple Bar, its management describes Brooks' style as 'cautiously avant garde with an emphasis on quality, personal service and unhurried timelessness'.
Hotel services *Baby-sitting. Brasserie bar. Business services. Car parking (opposite hotel). Conference facilities. Currency exchange. Laundry (same-day service) & dry cleaning. Residents' drawing room. Restaurant.* **Room services** *Air-conditioning. Computer points (with ISDN connections). Hair dryer. Minibar. Personal safe. Radio. Room service (24 hours). Telephone. Trouser press. TV.*

Burlington
Upper Leeson Street, Dublin 4 (660 5222/fax 660 8496). DART Lansdowne Road/bus 10, 11. **Rooms** 451. **Rates** *single* £123; *double* £139; *suite* £349. **Credit** AmEx, DC,
The largest hotel in Ireland with a disappointingly grey, concrete exterior. Its size allows it to be used by a number of tour groups and the bedrooms are a reasonable size but, surprisingly, there is no swimming pool, gym or even tea/coffee-making facilities in the rooms (room service runs from 6.30am to 11.30pm). Positive features include a car park and a nightclub, Annabels, which is open from Wednesday to Saturday and is free to residents. Two restaurants – the formal Sussex Room and the more relaxed Diplomat Restaurant – and the Buck Mulligan Bar (named after a fairly obnoxious character in Joyce's *Ulysses*). From May to October, there is an Irish Cabaret evening, Monday to Saturday, consisting of an Irish dancing show and a ballad group to keep your feet tapping, and an optional meal of Irish cuisine.
Hotel services *Baby-sitting & cot available. Bar. Business centre. Car park. Conference facilities. Gift shop & boutique. Lift/elevator. No-smoking bedrooms. Restaurants.* **Room services** *Hair dryer. Room service. Telephone. Trouser press. TV.*

Conrad International
Earlsfort Terrace, Dublin 2 (676 5555/fax 676 5424). Bus 10, 11, 13, 14, 14A, 15, 15A, 15B, 44, 46A, 46B, 47, 47A, 47B, 48A, 86. **Rooms** 191. **Suites** 9. **Rates** *single* £175; *double* £200; *suites* £410-£700. **Credit** AmEx, DC, MC, V.
The multi-award-winning Conrad opened in 1989, located opposite the National Concert Hall and just a few minutes' walk from St Stephen's Green. The rooms are what one would expect from a top hotel chain: modern décor, colour co-ordinated furnishings, individual temperature controls, executive desk, roomy bathroom with fluffy bathrobes, nightly turndown service. The Plurabelle brasserie-style restaurant is bright and airy and afternoon tea is served in the Lobby Lounge, complete with pianist. The Alexandra is

*Executive desks and fluffy bathrobes at the **Conrad International** – see page 131.*

the Conrad's gourmet restaurant, while downstairs the more democratic Alfie Byrne's pub (named after a famous tee-totaller Lord Mayor of Dublin) serves pub food and on Saturday nights there is live jazz. Jogging maps are available at reception and special rates are available for the use of the K Club golf course (45 minutes by car). Egon Ronay awarded the 'Best Business Hotel in Ireland' (1994) title to the Conrad; its business centre facilities are impressive, including even a translation service. Room rates are as expensive as one would expect, but there is a special weekend deal covering two nights' accommodation for two guests plus champagne and chocolate on arrival.

Hotel services *Baby-sitting & cot available. Bar. Business centre. Car park. Conference facilities. Hotel shop. Lift/elevator. Restaurants. Two non-smoking floors.* **Room services** *Hair dryer. Mini-bar. Newspaper. Overnight shoe-shine. Room service (24 hours). Three telephones. Trouser press. TV with in-house movies.*

The Gresham Hotel

O'Connell Street, Dublin 1 (874 6881/fax 878 7175). All cross city buses. **Rooms** 200 (increasing to 304 by summer 1998). **Suites** 40. **Rates** *single £146-£242; double £170-£258.* **Credit** AmEx, DC, MC, V.

The climax of Joyce's short story 'The Dead' takes place in a bedroom here, but the amenities have improved since the night in the story when the electric lights didn't work. It is also the only place in Ireland where the Beatles ever played (as the story goes, they set up an impromptu session). They did indeed stay here and their taste was impeccable (it must have been John Lennon who chose the place), for this is the most historic hotel in the city. It is also a very Irish hotel, ironically established by an Englishman in 1817, and charging three shillings a night in the 1830s. It was lucky to survive the shelling from British gunboats in the 1916 Rising, which saw most buildings in O'Connell Street reduced to ruins, and its age shows in the generous size of the rooms. Notwithstanding its ancient lineage, the Gresham is wonderfully modern in its amenities (with the highest percentage of porters per room in Ireland) and has a superb 24-hour,

state-of-the-art business centre with credit card access to the Internet, fax machine and telephones, plus use of a computer and printer. Check out the Toddy bar with the largest range of Scotch whisky – 63 brands – in Ireland, including the 200-year-old Hennessy Richard at £85 a measure. The quiet charm of the residents' lounge extends to the adjoining, elegant Aberdeen Restaurant.

Hotel services *Baby-sitting & cot available. Bars. Business centre. Car parking with valet service. Concierge desk (for booking theatre seats, car hire). Conference facilities. Hotel shop. Lift/elevator. No-smoking bedrooms. Restaurant. Travel agency.* **Room services** *Hair dryer. Private safe. Room service (24 hours). Telephone. Trouser press. TV.*

Jurys Hotel

Pembroke Road, Ballsbridge, Dublin 4 (660 5000/fax 660 5540/0500 303030 toll-free from UK/1-800 843 3311 toll-free from US). DART Lansdowne Road/bus 7, 7A, 8. **Rooms** 290. **Rates** *single £129; double £149 (room rates excl breakfast, £9.50).* **Credit** AmEx, DC, MC, V.

This is the older sister of the two adjoining Jurys hotels (*see below* **The Towers**), going back to the early 1960s and revealing its provenance in its concrete-and-glass exterior. The rooms are a decent size, if somewhat lacking in style. The restaurants are shared by both hotels, but they are all located here in the main hotel. Raglan's is the formal dining room while the Coffee Dock, open 22 hours, is the informal restaurant. The Dubliner's Bar, in the style of an Irish country kitchen, is very popular with non-residents as well as guests but there is also a quieter Library Lounge. Between May-October, Jurys' Cabaret – the longest-running show of its kind in Ireland – offers an enjoyable evening of traditional and modern music, song and dance.

Hotel services *Baby-sitting & cot available. Bar. Business centre. Car parking. Conference facilities. Disabled: access. Facilities for guide dogs. Hotel shop. Indoor swimming pool. Lift/elevator. No-smoking bedrooms. Restaurants.* **Room services** *Hair dryer. Room service (24 hours). Telephone. Trouser press. TV.*

The Gresham Hotel – *see p133 – very Irish.*

Jurys Hotel – *see p133 – very popular bar.*

The Shelbourne

27 St Stephen's Green, Dublin 2 (676 6471/fax 661 6006). All cross city buses. **Rooms** 164. **Rates** *single* £170-£220; *double* £208-£263 (rates excl breakfast, £12.50). **Credit** AmEx, DC, MC, V.

First opened in 1824 as a small town hotel, the Shelbourne is a major landmark in Dublin, overlooking St Stephen's Green. Extensively refurbished in the 1980s and '90s and, while only the finest, most expensive, rooms actually overlook the Green (the view from the back rooms is uninspiring), they are all individually furnished to a near-faultless degree of elegance and comfort. One- and two-bedroom suites, a junior suite and presidential suite are also available. The Lord Mayor's Lounge provides the venue for the two venerated traditions of morning coffee and afternoon tea. The Shelbourne bar is all timber floors and has a fine Georgian ceiling.

Hotel services *Baby-sitting & cot available. Barber shop. Bars. Beauty salon. Business centre. Car parking. Conference facilities. Facilities for pets and guide dogs. Hotel shop. Lift/elevator. No-smoking bedrooms. Restaurants.* **Room services** *Hair dryer. Room service (24 hours). Telephone. Trouser press. TV.*

The Towers

Lansdowne Road, Dublin 4 (667 0033/fax 660 5324/ 0500 303030 toll-free from UK/1 800 843 3311 toll-free from US). DART Lansdowne Road/bus 7, 7A, 8. **Rooms** 100. **Rates** *single* £176; *double* £196. **Credit** AmEx, DC, MC, V.

Adjacent to Jurys and providing an upmarket, exclusive extension to the main hotel. Guests have their own entrance and lounge area and enjoy the largest bedrooms of any Dublin hotel, with walk-in dressing rooms, a work area and beautiful marble bathrooms.

Hotel services *Bar. Business centre. Car parking.*

Conference facilities. Hotel shop. Indoor swimming pool. Lift/elevator. No-smoking bedrooms. Restaurants. **Room services** *Hair dryer. Room service (24 hours). Telephone. Trouser press. TV.*

The Westbury

Grafton Street, Dublin 2 (679 1122/fax 679 7078). All cross city buses. **Rooms** 163. **Suites** 40. **Rates** *single* £194-£212; *double* £228-£246. **Credit** AmEx, DC, MC, V.

Situated in cosmopolitan Grafton Street and close to the business, cultural and shopping areas of Dublin. One of the largest hotels in the city with a suitably vast lobby area quite uncharacteristic of Irish hotels. The booking-in area is discreetly tucked away on the first floor. The Russell Room restaurant gleams with silver and crystal, while the wood-panelled Sandbank Seafood bar serves lunch and dinner in a slightly less ostentatious setting. The Terrace Bar, complete with wrought-iron gates, is suitable for cocktails or small business meetings. Rooms are comfortable and luxurious (with a TV cleverly blended into the mirror surrounding the bath) although the colours and fabrics might be a touch too bourgeois for everyone's taste.

Hotel services *Baby-sitting & cot available. Bars. Car park. Conference facilities. Gym. Lift/elevator. No-smoking bedrooms. Restaurants.* **Room services** *Hair dryer. Room service (24 hours). Telephone. Trouser press. TV.*

Elegant & expensive

Buswells Hotel

Molesworth Street, Dublin 2 (614 6500/fax 676 2090). DART Pearse Station/bus 10, 11, 13. **Rooms** 60. **Rates** *single* £92; *double* £146; *triple* £160; *mini-suite* £170; *suite* £225. **Credit** AmEx, DC, MC, V.

This is a superb hotel, with a real sense of class. The building

*Refurbished **Buswells Hotel** – see page 135.*

itself dates back to 1769 and was a privately owned hotel called Gallagher's until in the 1920s, when it became a hotel owned by Buswell – but Buswell himself, assuming he was a man, remains a mystery as nothing is known about him. The hotel reopened in May 1997 after refurbishment, but original Georgian features have been retained, including a superb plaster ceiling in the lobby.
Hotel services *Baby-sitting & cot available. Bar. Conference facilities. Free overnight parking. Lift/elevator. No-smoking bedrooms. Restaurant.* **Room services** *Fax outlet. Hair dryer. Telephone. Trouser press. TV.*
E-mail: quinn-hotels@sqgroup.com

The Clarence

6-8 Wellington Quay, Dublin 2 (670 9000/fax 670 7800). All cross city buses. **Rooms** 50. **Rates** *single* £178-£203; *double* £190-£216; *one/two-bedroomed suites* £400/535; *penthouse suite* £1,450 (room rates excl continental/full breakfast, £11/£13). **Credit** AmEx, DC, MC, V.
This hotel, originally built in 1852, used to have a certain antique charm until U2 took it over. A complete refurbishment took place in 1996 and the result might charitably be described as a 'contemporary' look.The bedrooms are bizarrely furnished in an ultra-modern style using oak, leather and stone (and carpets of vivid hues) and a miscellany of modernist touches; sometimes it works – for example, the sandstone tables and Egyptian cotton sheets – but the overall effect tends to be aesthetically challenging. The lobby and adjoining residents' lounge create a severe atmosphere, quite in keeping with the staff uniform which is disconcertingly clerical in mood. The Octagon bar is... well, octagonal, with wood-panelled walls as in the lobby, but the Tea Room restaurant has some pleasing touches. The Penthouse suite has a terrific view of the river and the hot-tub on the roof is a canny idea – a pity about the £1,450 price tag.

Hotel services *Baby-sitting & cot available. Bar. Business services. Facilities for guide dogs. Function/ meeting room & banqueting facilities for 120 people. Lift/elevator. No-smoking bedrooms. Restaurant. Valet service & valet parking.* **Room services** *Hair dryer. Mini-bar. PC/fax connection. Private safe. Room service (24 hours). Tea/coffee-making facilities. Telephone. TV/VCR.*

Temple Bar Hotel

Fleet Street, Temple Bar, Dublin 2 (677 3333/fax 677 3088). All cross city buses. **Rooms** 108. **Rates** *single* £100; *double* £140; (rates excl breakfast, £6.50).* **Credit** AmEx, MC, V.
A superb city location, at the heart of the entertainment scene with pubs, restaurants and theatres on the doorstep and a five-minute walk to O'Connell Bridge. A pleasant and roomy lobby with an adjoining cocktail bar at the entrance to the airy, glass-roofed Terrace Restaurant. The highly popular Buskers pub is next door (and under the same management). A multi-storey car park opposite offers special rates for overnight parking.
Hotel services *Baby-sitting & cot available. Bars. Conference facilities. Disabled: access. Lift/elevator. No-smoking bedrooms. Restaurants.* **Room services** *Hair dryer. Tea/coffee-making facilities. Telephone. Trouser press. TV.*

Stephen's Hall Hotel

Earlsfort Centre, Lower Leeson Street, Dublin 2 (661 0585/fax 661 0606). Bus 10. **Suites** 37. **Rates** *single studio* £105; *twin & two-bedroom suites* £145-£220. **Credit** AmEx, DC, MC, V. **Closed** 25 Dec-1 Jan.
An all-suite hotel, adjacent to St Stephen's Green, in a fine Georgian building. All the suites, with the exception of the studios, have separate lounges. The penthouse suites on the top floor provide splendid city views, while the townhouse suites on the ground floor have their own private entrances. Fully equipped kitchens and dining area in all the suites and free underground parking. Suitable for families, business or tourist customers.
Hotel services *Baby-sitting & cot available. Bars. Conference facilities. No-smoking bedrooms. Restaurant.* **Room services** *Hair dryer. Room service (24 hours). Tea/coffee-making facilities. Telephone. TV.*

Parliament Hotel

Lord Edward Street, Dublin 2 (670 8777/fax 670 8787). All cross city buses. **Rooms** 63. **Rates** *single* £90/£100; *double* £110/£140 (low/high season); *triple* £120/£150. **Credit** AmEx, MC, V.
A beautiful Edwardian building, opposite Dublin Castle, is home to this essentially business hotel. The fair-sized rooms may be a little functional, but are perfectly adequate and served with a good range of amenities. The Forum bar serves meals and snacks all day while the Senate Restaurant is the main dining area. The room rates are negotiable during midweek and a 30 per cent discount is often attainable.
Hotel services *Bar. Bedrooms for disabled guests (2). Restaurants.* **Room services** *Hair dryer. Room service (24 hours). Tea/coffee-making facilities. Telephone. Trouser press. TV (& satellite).*

Royal Dublin Hotel

O'Connell Street, Dublin 1 (873 3666/fax 873 3120). All cross city buses. **Rooms** 117. **Rates** *1 Jan-30 Apr & 1 Nov-31 Dec* £78/95 *single/double; 1 May-30 Oct single/double* £95/£120. **Credit** AmEx, MC, V.
Situated at the top end of O'Connell Street, opposite the Gresham and not far from the Parnell statue, this offers a relatively quiet location compared to the south side of the Liffey where the majority of Dublin's hotels are located. The Georgian Rooms directly overlook the main thoroughfare of O'Connell Street and provide the venue for morning coffee

and afternoon tea. The Raffles bar is popular mainly for its carvery service each weekday lunchtime. The main restaurant is the Café Royale brasserie. The pastel-coloured bedrooms are comfortable and smartly furnished.
Hotel services *Baby-sitting and cot available. Bar. Car park. Lift/elevator. No-smoking bedrooms. Restaurant.* **Room services** *Hair dryer. Room service. Tea/coffee-making facilities. Telephone. TV.*

Anchor Guest House
49 Lower Gardiner Street, Dublin 1 (878 6913/fax 878 8038). All cross city buses. **Rooms** 11. **Rates** *single* £30-£35; *double* £45-£54. **Credit** MC, V. **Closed** 17-31 Dec.
A smartly refurbished Georgian house close to bus and train stations. All rooms are en suite and a lock up car park is available. One of the more elegant guesthouses on Lower Gardiner Street.
Room services *Telephone. TV.*
E-mail: gtcoyne@gpo.iol.ie

Cassidy's Hotel
7-8 O'Connell Street, Dublin 1 (878 0555/fax 878 0687). All cross city buses. **Rooms** 68. **Rates** *single* £68; *double* £95. **Credit** AmEx, MC, V.
Opened in 1996, this is a modern, family-owned hotel at the top end of O'Connell Street in another one of those superb redbrick Georgian buildings. The comfortable rooms are decorated in warm colours and there is limited free parking for guests. Groomes bar serves food as well as drinks and the Dining Room is the more formal, but still quite relaxed, restaurant. Although the quoted rates might put Cassidy's into the expensive bracket, there are discounts available according to the time of year and availability of rooms.
Hotel services *Bar. Car parking. No-smoking bedrooms. Restaurants.* **Room services** *Fax point. Hair dryer. Tea/coffee-making facilities. Telephone. Trouser press. TV.*

Clifden Court Hotel
11 Eden Quay, O'Connell Bridge, Dublin 1 (874 3535/ fax 874 9869). All cross city buses. **Rooms** 30. **Rates** *single* £27; *double* £54. **Credit** MC, V.
Located right in the centre of the city overlooking the Liffey and within walking distance of places of interest to the north and south of the river. All the rooms are en suite and its very popular bar, Lanigan's, has traditional music and Irish dancing every evening. Enquire about special weekend rates.
Hotel services *Bar. Cot available. Lift/elevator. Restaurant.* **Room services** *Tea/coffee-making facilities. Telephone. Trouser press. TV.*

Hotel Isaacs
Store Street, Dublin 1 (855 0067/fax 836 5390). All cross city buses. **Rooms** 25. **Rates** *single* £46; *double* £60; *triple* £78. **Credit** MC, V.
Isaacs began life as a small hostel (*see below*) but has now expanded with Jacobs Inn (*see below*) and this smart little hotel, housed in what was once a wine warehouse. Much of the original brickwork remains exposed and embellished with new features, as in the elegant Il Vignardo restaurant. The bedrooms are all en suite and furnished in a modern and comfortable manner. There is a nearby car park with reduced overnight rate for hotel guests.
Hotel services *Restaurant.* **Room services** *Tea/coffee-making facilities. Telephone. TV.*
E-mail: isaacs@irelands-web.ie

Jurys Christchurch Inn
Christchurch Place, Dublin 8 (454 0000/fax 454 0012/ 0500 303030 toll-free reservations from UK/1 800 843 3311 toll-free reservations from US). All cross city buses.
Rooms 182. **Rates** *1 Mar-31 Dec* £55; *1 Jan-28 Feb* £51.
Room rates cover accommodation for up to 3 adults or 2 adults and 2 children, excl breakfast, £6.
Modern, attractive, fair-sized bedrooms at a fixed rate with twin or double beds. All rooms have a bath and shower. No room service. Great value for families and good value for couples. The hotel's Inn Pub is open until 1.30am for residents on Friday and Saturday nights with live traditional music. There is an adjoining 24-hour car park which costs £5.80 a day and £4 overnight.
Hotel services *Baby-sitting and cot available. Bar. Facilities for guide dogs. Lift/elevator. No-smoking bedrooms. Restaurant. Rooms for disabled guests.* **Room services** *Hair dryer. Tea/coffee making facilities. Telephone. TV.*

Jurys Custom House Inn
Custom House Quay, Dublin 1 (607 5000/fax 829 0400/0500 303030 toll-free reservations from UK/1 800 843 3311 toll-free reservations from US). All cross city buses. **Rooms** 234. **Rates** *1 Mar-31 Dec* £55; *1 Jan-28 Feb* £51. Room rates cover accommodation for up to 3 adults or 2 adults and 2 children, excl breakfast, £6.
Same concept as Jurys Christchurch Inn (*see above*); same tariff; same amenities, right down to the names of the restaurant and pub. More rooms than the Christchurch clone, but equally well centrally situated.

Leeson Court Hotel
26-27 Lower Leeson Street, Dublin 2 (676 3380/fax 661 8273). Bus 11. **Rooms** 20. **Rates** *single* £50-£56; *double* £70-£78. (rates excl breakfast, £5). **Credit** AmEx, MC, V.
Before Temple Bar emerged as the trendy nightspot area, Lower Leeson Street was uniquely famous for its late-night discos. The hotel itself is a little haven of tranquillity (with the help of triple-glazed windows) and, very unusually for a two-star hotel in the centre of the city, with its own car park (albeit limited in capacity). The Darby O'Gills bar is a traditional-style pub with timber floors, quite lively in the evening, while the Conservatory overlooks peaceful gardens and serves food throughout the day. The Leeson Court has its own disco which closes at 2am, and the rooms at the top of the house are the quietest.
Hotel services *Bar. Cot available. Lift/elevator. Restaurant.* **Room services** *Hair dryer. Tea/coffee-making facilities. Telephone. Trouser press. TV.*

The Townhouse
47-48 Lower Gardiner Street, Dublin 1 (878 8808/fax 878 8787). All cross city buses. **Rooms** 64. **Rates** *single* £47.50; *double* £60-£80; *triple* £65; *triple/quad with kitchenette* £75. **Credit** MC, V.
One of the best guest houses along Lower Gardiner Street. The building was home to the nineteenth-century playwrights Dion Boucicault and Lafcadio Hearn and they seem to have left an artistic legacy, because the décor of the place is exceptional. A wide range of rooms (including a double dubbed the 'honeymoon suite'), each with a literary name, and they are all en suite. Open 24 hours a day, all year. Room rates include continental breakfast.
Room services *Car park. Lift/elevator. Tea/coffee-making facility. TV.*

Abraham House
82-83 Lower Gardiner Street, Dublin 1 (855 0600/fax 855 0598). Bus 41. **Rooms** 28. **Rates** *bed in multi-bedded rooms* £10-£11.50; *single* £18; *double* £27; *double en suite* £30. **Credit** AmEx, MC, V.
Centrally located hostel which has been extended in size more than once since it opened in 1993. A popular hostel with

*Unusual among Irish hotels, **The Westbury** has a generous lobby – with piano. See p135.*

groups, so try to book ahead. The rates include continental breakfast. Reception open 24 hours.
Facilities *Bureau de change. Free car park. International payphone. Launderette. Safety deposit boxes. Self-catering kitchen.*

Avalon House

55 Aungier Street, Dublin 2 (475 0001/fax 475 0303). Bus 16, 16A, 19, 22. **Rooms** 45. **Rates** *dormitory £10.50; per person in 4-bedded room £12-£13; single £18.50; double £28-£30.* **Credit** AmEx, MC, V.
A well-run establishment with friendly and informative staff. Open 24 hours, with no curfew or lock out. The hostel has a central location, to the west of St Stephen's Green, and within easy walking distance of Grafton Street and Temple Bar.
Facilities *Bureau de change. International payphone. Laundry. Luggage storage. Personal security boxes. Restaurant. Self-catering kitchen. Ticket agent for buses. TV room.*

Charles Stewart

5-6 Parnell Square, Dublin 1 (878 0350/fax 836 8178). All cross city buses. **Rooms** 30. **Rates** *dormitory £12; single en suite £35; double en suite £54. Other en suite rooms are available which may be shared or rented for small groups.* **Credit** MC, V.
This is a new hostel located on the north side of the river just across the road from the top end of O'Connell Street, a 15-minute walk from Temple Bar. The building is a noted Georgian house and was the birthplace of the writer Oliver St John Gogarty (the model for Buck Mulligan in *Ulysses*). The room and bed rates include continental breakfast and all private rooms have satellite TV and tea/coffee-making facilities. Parking is free at weekends and overnight parking can be arranged at £3 a night, but on weekdays during the day there is no nearby free parking. Open 24 hours.
Facilities *Bureau de change. Games room. International payphone. Safety deposit boxes. Self-catering kitchen. E-mail: cstuart@iol.ie*

Isaacs Hostel

2-5 Frenchman's Lane, Dublin1 (855 6215/fax 855 6524). All cross city buses. **Rooms** 48. **Rates** *large dormitory £6.25; small dormitory £7.75; single £18.50; twin room £29.*
Lots of facilities, centrally located and very popular, but some travellers feel the place is soulless and run like a boarding school. Between 11am and 5pm guests are not allowed access to dormitories (even the private rooms don't open until 3pm) and there is a £4 fine if anyone leaves their bags in rooms after 11am. Open all year. Rates include breakfast.
Facilities *Bicycle rental. Bureau de change. Disabled: access. Free luggage storage. Restaurant. Security lockers. Self-catering kitchen.*

Jacobs Inn

21-28 Talbot Place, Dublin 1 (855 5660/fax 855 5664). All cross city buses. **Rooms** 37. **Rates** *dormitory £10.25; per person in 4-bedded room £14; per person in triple room £15; single £29; twin £36.*
This is a new hostel under the same ownership as Isaacs Hostel which is very close by. Pine beds and – because it's new? – a smart and clean look about the place. Be careful about leaving a car parked overnight in the adjoining streets.
Facilities *Lift/elevator. Restaurant. Self-catering kitchen.*

Kinlay House

2-12 Lord Edward Street, Dublin 2 (679 6644/fax 679 7439). All cross city buses. **Rooms** 34. **Rates** *multi-bedded room £9.50; 4/6 bedded room £13; single £18; twin £28; twin en suite £32.* **Credit** MC, V.
One of the best hostels in Dublin and the rates include continental breakfast. Open 24 hours, all year.
Facilities *Bureau de change. Laundry facilities. Left luggage. Meeting rooms. Safe facilities. Self-catering kitchen. TV lounge. E-mail: kindub@usit.ie*

Other hostels

Ashfield House *19-20 D'Olier Street, Dublin 2 (679 7734/679 0852 fax).* **Rooms** 25. **Rates** *dormitory £7.50-£10; private room £9-£18.* **Credit** MC, V. **Closed** over Christmas.

Brewery Hostel *22-23 Thomas Street, Dublin 8 (453 8600/453 8616 fax).* **Rooms** 5. **Rates** *dormitory £7.50-£10; private room £14-£19.* **Credit** MC, V.

Dublin International Youth Hostel *61 Mountjoy Street, Dublin 7 (830 1766/830 1600 fax).* **Rooms** 20. **Rates** *dormitory £7.50-£10; private room £8.50-£12.50.* **Credit** MC, V.

Globetrotters *46-48 Lower Gardiner Street, Dublin 1 (873 5893/878 8787 fax).* **Rooms** 38. **Rates** *private room £9-£13; dormitory £10-£14.* **Credit** AmEx, MC, V.

Goin' My Way Hostel *Cardjin House, 15 Talbot Street, Dublin 1 (874 1720/878 8091 fax).* **Rooms** 3. **Rates** *dormitory £7-£8; private room £9-£13.*

Marlborough Hostel *81-82 Marlborough Street, Dublin 1 (874 7629/874 5172 fax).* **Rooms** 6. **Rates** *dormitory £7.50-£10; private room £13.*

Oliver St John Gogarty's *18-21 Anglesea Street, Temple Bar, Dublin 2 (671 1822/671 7637 fax).* **Rates** *dormitory £14; private room £14-£18.*

Self-catering

Molesworth Court Suites

35 Schoolhouse Lane, Dublin 2 (676 4799/fax 676 4982). **Apartments** 12. **Rates** *1-bedroom apartment* (sleeping 2-4) £95 per week; *2-bedroom apartment* (sleeping 2-4) £120-150 per week; *3-bedroom apartment* (sleeping 2-6) £200 per week. **Credit** AmEx, MC, V.
Three- and four-star self-catering apartments in the heart of the city, off Molesworth Street. Children are welcome, bed linen is provided and food and shops are within walking distance. Depending on availability, it is also possible to rent an apartment on a nightly, weekend or three-night midweek basis.
Facilities *Baby-sitting service. Car park. Dishwasher. Lift/elevator. TV. Washing machine.*

Trident Holiday Homes

24 Lansdowne Road, Ballsbridge, Dublin 4 (668 3534/fax 660 6465). **Apartments** 16. **Rates** *2-bedroom apartments* (sleeping 5) £360-£460 per week; *3-bedroom apartments* (sleeping 7) £400-£520 per week. **Credit** MC, V.
Situated in the leafy residential suburb of Ballsbridge about two miles from the city centre, and easily reached on foot or by DART train from nearby Lansdowne Road station. Smart modern apartments with a good range of facilities. Sandymount Strand close by, along with shops selling food.
Facilities *Baby-sitting service. Car park. Gas-fired central heating. TV. Washing machine.*

Camping & caravans

Shankhill Camping & Caravan Park

Shankhill, Co Dublin (282 0011). About 12 miles south of Dublin city, five miles from Dun Laoghaire car ferry terminal. DART Shankhill; buses 45, 84. From Dun Laoghaire bus 45a. **Rates** *1 caravan/tent plus car* and £1 for each adult/50p child, £5-£6; *backpackers* £4-£5; *motor home* £135-£180 per week.
Scenic location with views of the Dublin mountains. Pitches not bookable in advance. Dogs allowed.
Facilities *Electric points for caravans. Food shop. Gas cylinders for sale. Ice pack freezing facility. Telephone. Washing/ironing facilities.*

The Shelbourne – *see p135* – *city landmark.*

Camac Valley Tourist Caravan & Camping Park

Naas Road, Clondalkin, Dublin 22 (464 0644/fax 464 0643). Bus 69; by car, on N7 (heading to Cork, Limerick & Waterford) just after Green Isle Hotel, 35 mins from city. **Rates** *backpackers* £3; *2-person tent* £7-£8; *caravan/tent/motor home* with 2 adults and up to 4 children £9-£10.
The park is protected by 24 hour security.
Facilities *Electric points for caravans. Food shop. Gas cylinders for sale. Ice pack freezing facility. Telephone. TV. Washing/ironing facilities. Washing machines.*

University accommodation

Dublin City University

Glasnevin, Dublin 9 (704 5736/fax 704 5777). **Open** 9 Jun-20 Sept. **Rates** £20 per person. **Credit** MC, V.
Dublin City University has 256 single rooms with each pair of rooms sharing kitchen and bathroom. There are restaurants, lounge bar, sports complex, shops and banks on the campus which is 15 minutes by road from the city centre.

Trinity College

Dublin 2 (608 1177/671 1267). **Open** 1 Jun-3 Oct. **Rates** £20-£38 per person. **Credit** MC, V.
Trinity has 589 bedrooms, 195 of which are en suite, located in the heart of the city with catering, bar, laundry, sporting and car parking facilities. Rates include continental breakfast.

UCD Village

Belfield, Dublin 4 (269 7111/269 7704). **Open** 16 Jun-14 Sept. **Rates** £22 per person, room only; £350 per week for apartment (3-5 people). **Credit** MC, V.
There are 1,200 bedrooms and 350 apartments on the University College Dublin campus north of the city, which is served by regular buses. The campus has a bar, restaurant and coffee shop which are open to guests, and accommodation is available on a nightly or weekly basis.

Home of :

Candy Club   Genius   Blue   Influx   Quadraphonic   Fever

Student conession monday, tuesday & wednesday. e-mail the kitchen@clubi.ie

Arts & Entertainment

FROM THE HOUSE OF POWDERBUBBLE

alternative 'miss' ireland IV
SAINT PATRICK'S WEEKEND 1998

THE MOST HUGEST SIGNIFICANT POST-CULTURALLY KINKY EVENT OF THE YEAR, TAKING YOU AND ALL THE ASPIRING QUEEN COLLEENS ON A HEEL-CLICKING, SNAKE-BANISHING, ROLLER-COASTER DONKEY RIDE THROUGH POISE, PERSONALITY AND ORIGINALITY THROUGH PAGEANT, PERFORMANCE AND DISCOTHÈQUE

'MISS' SHIRLEY TEMPLE BAR WITH HER WINNING GYMNASTICS ROUTINE

Clubs

Late-night Dublin and everything – except late-night booze – is on offer.

*Overall, music and atmosphere make **The Kitchen**, owned by U2, the best club in town.*

Only a few years ago, clubs in Dublin were not something the city's natives could feel particularly proud of. What opportunities there were for debauchery were more likely to be found in one of Leeson Street's late-night wine bars and, while the seedy dives that made up this clubbing hell are still in existence, Dubliners daily thank the stars that a new range of options is, at last, available.

Stars, in fact, such as U2, whose own club, the **Kitchen**, opened in 1994, at a time when a new confidence about the city was developing after the opening of **PoD** (the Place of Dance) and **Ri Ra** (Irish for 'uproar'). These cool new hangouts have brought a much-needed sense of sophisticated modernity to clubbing in the city.

Right now, the Kitchen itself is running two of the most celebrated club nights in Europe. The fortnightly Quadraphonic on Fridays has been an award-winning pioneer in the promotion of drum 'n' bass in Ireland, converting thousands of young Dubliners to its infectious and often inspirational high-speed collision of ragga and hardcore techno. The length of queues at Quadraphonic's Kitchen shindigs has led to a second (and equally splendid) night, Stereophonic, which runs on Saturdays at the Crypt in the **Temple Theatre.**

The Kitchen has also for the past year been home to Influx, a club specialising in a freestyle mix of hip-hop, house or whatever else the DJ feels like. The popularity of this wild style has launched a second weekly outing for Influx – the peerless Sellout at the **Mean Fiddler**. Ri Ra also celebrates the variety of modern dance music with funk, soul, swing, hip-hop and jungle selections throughout the week but most of all on Tuesday's Clubmilk or Wednesday's Tongue 'n' Groove when all these genres are thrown in the mix together.

For those with a taste for big, uplifting house music, Honey at **The System** (and sometimes the Temple Theatre) keeps fresh the spirit of a genre that in some places seems a little stale. Harder-edged versions of the same can be found at the

Temple of Sound or at one of the regular visits from clubs such as London's the End at the state-of-the-art **Redbox.**

If such in-your-face levels of dance music aren't for you, then you'll be delighted to know that there are plenty of other options. If you fancy some cabaret, the Ultra Lounge which runs on alternate Thursdays at the **Da Club** is a fun and funky mix of kitsch and cool. As, indeed, is Velure at the **Gaiety Theatre** which brings together cabaret, movies and the best in Latin sounds. For those unconvinced by the delights of any dance music, plenty of places provide plenty of other tunes – if you like your indie sounds, try **Fibber Magee's** or **The 13th Floor** which mix the likes of Oasis and Blur with some more leftfield offerings. The gay scene in Dublin has tended to revolve around the huge late-night bar at the George on South Great George's Street, but currently there are excellent alternatives in such full-on nights as HAM (Homo Action Movies) on Fridays at PoD, or Powderbubble, an occasional fetish extravaganza at Redbox (*see also* **Gay & Lesbian**).

In many ways, the scene is alive and kicking, although there is one major source of irritation in the licensing laws. Dubliners look towards London with envy in this regard, as, despite the hype about the Fair City's party atmosphere, the opening times do tend to leave clubbers feeling a little disappointed. Alcohol licences last until 2am and so very few places will keep the music going after 3am. There are one or two later options, but most of these are pretty dire. A better bet is probably an early night, allowing you to do it all again the following evening. Otherwise, grab a coffee and listen out for rumours of parties.

Possibly as a result of the limited licensing laws, entry prices have never really reached the supernova level that they have in some cities. Charges will be pretty standard for the bigger clubs at the weekend (around £8) but one-offs, such as a visit from Liverpool's Cream or London's Ministry of Sound, may set you back a little more. Another upside is the fact that almost all the clubs listed here are centrally located with perhaps only a short walk or taxi-trip needed for the ones which are slightly further off the beaten track. Mind you, finding a taxi on a Saturday night (especially after hours) is a different story: horse and carts at St Stephen's Green cost around £25 and, after waiting in the rain for an hour, this might seem like a genuine bargain.

In general, things seem to be looking good for the Dublin clubs at the moment but if the boom-time is to last we'll need one or two more consistently exciting venues. As it stands, there's enough going on to thrill even the most jaded. Dublin has long been famous for its Guinness-guzzling pub culture, but for now anyway, the real fun is in the clubs with the block-rocking beats.

Clubs

Annabelle's
Burlington Hotel, Upper Leeson Street, Dublin 4 (660 5222). Bus 13, 64A. **Open** 11pm-2am Wed-Sat. **Admission** £8; £4 hotel residents before 11.30pm.
Depressingly 1980s style and attitude. Strict door policy seems to conflict with the fact that nothing of interest lies therein.

Boomerang
Temple Bar Hotel, Fleet Street, Temple Bar, Dublin 2. All cross city buses. **Open** 10.30pm-2.30am Thur-Sun. **Admission** £5 Thur, Sun; £6 Fri, Sat.
One of quite a few clubs which have started to appear in Dublin's Temple Bar area, a part of the city which, depending on who you work for, is either the city's cultural quarter or a holiday camp for stag weekenders. Boomerang's clientèle might give ammunition to the latter view, but it is spacious enough to allow you to avoid the beerboys.

Break For the Border
Lower Stephen's Street, Dublin 2 (478 0300). All cross city buses. **Open** 7pm-2am Thur-Sat. **Admission** £5-£8; free before 11pm.
Western-themed bar which in the later evening becomes a late-night beering and leering den. 'Cattle market' springs to mind, but the crowd seems to thoroughly enjoy the unpretentious mix of hits and classics that provides the soundtrack.

Club M
Anglesea Street, Dublin 2 (671 5485). All cross city buses. **Open** 11.30pm-2.30am Tue-Sun. **Admission** £3-£5 Tue-Thur, Sun; £7-£8 Sat.
Another return trip down misery lane to the kind of flashy clubs that blighted the mid-1980s. Many of the crowd seem to have been born in that era, though, and so might be impressed by the idea of a jacuzzi in the VIP room.

Columbia
Sir John Rogerson's Quay, Dublin 2 (677 8466). DART Pearse Station or Tara Street/bus 1, 2, 3. **Open** 11.30pm-2.30am Thur-Sat. **Admission** £5-£7.
A recently renovated venue which was once the home of Dublin's underground techno scene and is now a base for the city's growing breed of fabulous young creative types with disposable income. The clean, minimal design gives a bright and airy feel to the venue – a refreshing change from the claustrophobic mood of many clubs. Columbia is only open three nights a week, but does feature the weirdest option of them all – the Beauty Spot, on Thursday nights, when pretty young things are treated to mid-club makeovers.

Copper Face Jack's
29 Harcourt Street, Dublin 2 (475 8777). All cross city buses. **Open** 7pm-2.30am Mon-Sun. **Admission** £5-£7 Thur-Sat; free Sun-Wed.
Hugely popular with a late-twenties/early thirties crowd, but it lacks style despite the 'neat dress essential' door policy.

The Da Club
2 Johnsons Place, Dublin 2 (670 5116). All cross city buses. **Open** 10.30pm-2am Mon-Sun. **Admission** £4-£5.
Small and imperfectly formed venue (one toilet downstairs) which nonetheless can be extremely good fun. The Da Club's mix of live music, comedy and diverse DJ talent makes it one of the more unusual clubs in the city, but often one of the most rewarding.

Strictly A Go Go at the Place of Dance or PoD, possibly the most beautifully designed of all Dublin's clubs.

Fibber Magee's

80 Parnell Street, Dublin 1 (872 2575). Bus 23, 40, 40A.
Open 7pm-2.30am Fri, Sat. **Admission** £3-£4.
A favourite with students and those with a taste for rock or indie sounds. Fibber's has two dance floors and several hundred bars. Vigorously anti-glamorous.

Gaiety Theatre

South King Street, Dublin 2 (677 1717). All cross city buses. **Open** 11pm-2.30am Fri, Sat. **Admission** £6-£7.
The Gaiety's Friday and Saturday bashes have, for years now, offered perhaps the most reliable alternative to full-on clubbing in Dublin. There are movies shown in the theatre itself while the three bars feature cabaret, jazz and funk bands; elsewhere DJs spin Latin or soul tunes.

Kitchen

East Essex Street, Dublin 2 (677 6635). Bus 12, 16, 16A, 65. **Open** 11.30pm-2.30am daily. **Admission** £4-£8.
U2-owned club which does well to avoid the snobbery that could come from having superstar owners. The music ranges from the rockin' big beats of Thursday's Homebase to Quadraphonic's 'maximum drum'n' bass' sounds. Dress and door policy is fairly relaxed, but large groups of men are likely to be unlucky. There are two beautifully designed crypt-like rooms, the larger with a moat-bordered dance floor with the smaller often doubling as VIP area when U2 are in town. Music and atmosphere make it the best club in the city.

Lillie's Bordello

Adam Court, Grafton Street, Dublin 2 (679 9204). All cross city buses. **Open** 11pm-2.30am daily. **Admission** 99p-£10.
Home of the very beautiful and the truly fabulous – or so regulars like to insist. The Lillie's crowd is a mix of young models and old men, with a door policy which is ludicrously strict. Can be fun when you're there (particularly the cheap and cheerful Sunday and Monday nights at 99p entrance), but for God's sake don't believe the VIP hype.

Mean Fiddler

26 Wexford Street, Dublin 2 (475 8555). Bus 51, 61, 62, 83. **Open** 7.30pm-2am daily. **Admission** £3-£12.50.
The Mean Fiddler's two floors make it one of the bigger venues in the city, but bear in mind that separate events run in each so you pays your money, you makes your choice. Upstairs is mainly a gig venue but it is also home to some of Dublin's best hip-hop and big-beat action – Saturday's Sellout is the best of its kind, with top international talent and homeboys together giving it unrivalled credibility.

The Mission

Eustace Street, Temple Bar, Dublin 2. All cross city buses. **Open** 11pm-2.30am daily. **Admission** £2-£7.
Located beneath Danger Doyle's pub in Temple Bar, this is a small and not particularly attractive club which tries hard. Monday's Freedom has broken through, proving to be a friendly, busy and much enjoyed new gay night.

PoD

Harcourt Street, Dublin 2 (478 0225). All cross city buses. **Open** 11pm-2.30am Wed-Sun. **Admission** £4-£8.
The Place of Dance, better known as PoD, is possibly the most beautifully designed of all Dublin clubs, and although the styles tend towards the glamorous, the often self-indulgent clubbers are rarely as beautifully designed as they'd like to think. PoD is currently suffering from a lack of exciting music – handbag house is the staple PoD punters' diet – but it's always worth a visit.

*The last of the Mohicans gets stuck in at HAM at the **PoD**, where the magnificent men's toilets are worth a look.*

Red Box

Harcourt Street, Dublin 2. Bus 15A, 15B, 15C, 20, 61, 62, 86. **Open** 10pm-2.30am Thur-Sat. **Admission** £4-£10.
Housed above PoD, its younger but bigger brother, the highly impressive Red Box hosts regular visits from British superclubs such as Cream and Renaissance. It is a gig venue, though, so plastic glasses at the bar lose it a little of PoD's class; however, the sound system has no rival in Dublin.

Renards

23-25 South Frederick Street, Dublin 2 (677 5876). All cross city buses. **Open** 11pm-3am daily. **Admission** £5-£7.
Mostly for the over-thirties, this place isn't bad but tries hard to appear exclusive. It does open slightly later than most but they can be very 'selective' at the door. To visit the pleasanter upstairs bar and shoot a few rounds of pool, you'll either have to be with a member or be dating a celebrity.

Ri Ra

Dame Court, Dublin 2 (677 4835). All cross city buses. **Open** 11pm-2.30am daily. **Admission** £4-£7.
Perhaps the most laidback of all the cool clubs, Ri Ra rarely has big-name guest DJs, but boasts a large and faithful clientèle. Downstairs is the main club area but at 12.30am the excellent Globe bar becomes a chill-and-chat zone. Generally, the vibe is fun and funky, with football table and video games available for those with little interest in dancing.

River Club

Merchants' Arch, Dublin 2 (677 2382). All cross city buses. **Open** 11pm-2am daily. **Admission** £6.
Another haunt of the mid-thirties set, the River Club is largely a members' bar but some lucky others will be allowed entry if they look the part. Dress code is strict.

The System

21A South Anne Street, Dublin 2 (677 4402). All cross city buses. **Open** 11.30pm-3.30am Thur-Fri; 11.30pm-4am Sat. **Admission** £5-£10.
Very much a youth club in that you might expect most of the punters to be picked up by their dads afterwards, but the System does have a vitality which some of the more uptight venues could do with.

Temple of Sound

Beside Ormond Hotel, Ormond Quay, Dublin 1. Bus 24. **Open** 11pm-2.30am Wed-Sat. **Admission** £3-£8.
The cry of 'Large!' might suit the often fierce techno in the Temple of Sound, but it cannot be so easily applied to the club itself. This place has built up a reputation for being cutting edge with regard to new music, although it's often the kind of edge which might make your ears bleed.

Temple Theatre

St George's, Temple Street, Dublin 1 (874 5425). All cross city buses. **Open** 9pm-2am Sat. **Admission** £10-£12.
A vast, superbly renovated church which in its short new life has begun to assume the role as the home of house in Dublin. Big-name guests play regularly to a crowd the size of Scotland, the bouncers not being short on stature either.

The 13th Floor

34 O'Connell Street, Dublin 1. All cross city buses. **Open** 10pm-2.30am Wed-Sat. **Admission** £2-£4.
Mostly populated by students and those with an interest in so-called 'alternative' sounds. Dazed on Wednesdays is the cream of its indie crop, and cheap, too, at £2 before 11pm.

The Vatican

Russell Court Hotel, 21 Harcourt Street, Dublin 2 (478 4066). All cross city buses. **Open** 10pm-2am Tue-Sat. **Admission** £4-£6.
The sacrilegious name is the craziest aspect of quite a common-or-garden, nothing-to-write-home-about discotheque.

Children's Dublin

From nappies to nannies – every parent's quick survival guide.

Up until recently, Dublin had not gone out of its way to attract, entertain or cater for children. With the exception of the zoo or the cinema, parents tended to take their children away from the city. Consequently, there are no permanent amusement parks or circuses in the near vicinity. Funderland takes over the RDS arena for the Christmas period and Fossetts Circus sets up here once or twice a year. However, Dublin is undergoing a face-lift; its old slums are gradually being renovated and the city is reinventing itself as a place for families once more. With the opening of numerous summer schools and the Ark – a cultural centre for children – the presence and the importance of children is finally being recognised. However, there's still a long way to go: consider yourself blessed if you find baby-changing facilities, children's menus or child play areas.

For up-to-date details of children's projects check the *Weekend* section of the *Irish Times* on Saturday or consult the children's page on Aertel.

Activities & sports

There are no permanent adventure worlds in the Dublin area. The closest available is Fort Lucan. If the kids are keen to do courses in hill-walking, canoeing, rock-climbing, orienteering, surfing or caving, contact the Association for Adventure Sports, Long Mile Road, Dublin 12 (450 9845) for details of venues in Dublin and around Ireland.

Ark Children's Cultural Centre
11A Eustace Street, Temple Bar, Dublin 2 (670 7788). DART Tara Street/all cross city buses. **Open** 9.30am-4pm Tue-Fri; 10am-4pm Sat.
The Ark is a 16,000-square-foot arts centre with a theatre, gallery and workshop. Currently offering about ten programmes which range across the cultural spectrum, the emphasis is on art and culture by, for and about children (4-14 years). Phone for programmes details and age groups. Booking is essential.

Dublin Bay Sea Thrill
Carlisle Terminal, East Wall, Dun Laoghaire (260 0949). **Cost** £6-12.
A short, pricey thrill for those who don't suffer from sea-sickness. Two high-speed boats will whizz groups of up to ten people around Dublin Bay. A 40-minute trip costs £12 each, a 20-minute trip £6. Children must be over 5 years.

Dublin Ice Rink
Dolphin's Barn, Dublin 8 (453 4153). Bus 19. **Open** 10.30am-1pm, 2.30-5pm, 7.30-10pm daily. **Admission** £3-£4.
There are three ice-skating sessions daily. The Ice Rink has a skate shop, boutique and coffee shop. Group discounts are available.

Fort Lucan
Off Strawberry Beds Road, Westmanstown, Lucan, Co Dublin (628 0166). **Open** 1.30-6pm daily. **Admission** *Mon-Sat* £3 children; adults, under 2s free; *Sun* £3.50 children; adults, under 2s free.
It has an assault course, high-tower walks, 40-foot slides, trampolines, maze, suspension bridges, and a tots' area. Unfortunately, it only opens weather permitting, so call if in doubt. Suitable for 2-14-year olds.

Irish National Sailing School
West Pier, Dun Laoghaire (284 4195). **Cost** £96 per week.
Summer courses are organised from June-early September. Running from 9am-5pm Mon-Fri, they cater for beginners to the advanced. Students aged 8 to 18 years go out in two-person toppers and four-person squibs; the groups are organised according to age, not ability, so the children will be among people their own age.

Premier Indoor Karting
Unit 1A, Kylemore Industrial Estate, Killeen Road, Dublin 10 (626 1444). Bus 18, 79. **Open** 11am-11pm daily.
At 385 metres, Kylemore's indoor race circuit is 25 metres longer than Phibsboro, but apart from that the two branches offer the same facilities. Whether you want an individual practice session or the Full Grand Prix, it's all available here. Adults are catered for, as are the kids: children's cub karts are available for 3-9-year-olds, with sessions costing a hefty £3 for 6 minutes and £5 for 12 minutes. Also hosts birthday parties at £50 for a one-hour session for up to 10 children. The over-12s and over 54-inches can drive (with an adult's permission) in the Championship Race (£22) and in the Full Grand Prix (£25). Helmets and race suits, race briefing and instruction are all supplied. Half the fun is the 'professionalism' of it all: race commentaries, computerised lap times, certificates, trophies and video monitors – it'll feel like the real thing.
Branch: Phibsboro Karting Cross Guns Bridge, Dublin 7 (830 8777).

Animal antics

Dublin Zoo & Zoological Gardens
Phoenix Park, Dublin 7 (677 1425). Bus 10, 25, 26. **Zoo open** *Summer* 9.30am-6pm Mon-Sat; 10.30am-6pm Sun. *Winter* 9.30am-4pm Mon-Fri; 9.30am-5pm Sat; 10.30am-

*Eugene Lambert, director of **Lambert Puppet Theatre**, with daughter Miriam and friends.*

5pm Sun. **Admission** £5.70; £4 students; £3.10 3-16s; free under 3s; £15.50 family (2+2); £17.50 family (2+4). **Gardens open** 9.30am-4pm Mon-Sat, Bank Holiday Mon; 10.30am-4pm Sun. **Admission** £5.70; £3.10 3-16s; free under 3s; £15.50 family (2+2); £17.50 family (2+4). The zoo houses over 700 animals and included among the endangered species are snow leopards, rhinoceroses and golden lion tamarinds. In recent years, Dublin Zoo has focused on developing its role as educator. In addition to its Discovery Centre (where you can see the world's biggest egg), the zoo offers a range of activities and volunteer programmes, organising summer camps and Young Zoologist Days. It's run with children very much in mind, with ample

picnic facilities and play areas (including tree houses, the Hippo Hop and the Giraffe Slide). There's a Meet the Keeper programme, which enables kids to help out feeding the animals (check information panel at Zoo entrance for feeding times) which runs daily during the summer and winter weekends. Should your children get depressed at seeing the rhinos and elephants looking apathetic, quickly run them over to the jackass penguins which are always good for a laugh. The gardens are especially good for very young children. There's a Pets' Corner, a Zoo Train, and pony and trap rides available at a small extra cost. Also a nursery and, available for hire, children's push chairs.
Disabled: access.

National Aquarium
The Esplanade, Bray, Co Wicklow (286 4688).
Admission £2.50; £2 students, children.
Set on the seafront in Bray, County Wicklow, the National Aquarium is committed to conservation through education. With over 10,000 fish on display, this is where you go to see what's flourishing, what's barely hanging on, and what you can do about it.

Newbridge House & Traditional Farm
Newbridge Demesne, Donabate, Co Dublin (843 6534). **DART** *Howth Junction, then train to Donabate.* **Open** 10am-5pm Tue-Fri; 11am-6pm Sat; 2-6pm Sun. **Closed** Mon. **Admission** *House* £2.75 adults; £2.45 students; £1.50 children; £7 family (2+2). *Supplement to tour the farm* £1; 80p students; free children if accompanied by adult. *Combined family ticket* £9 (2+2).
This eighteenth-century house and farm provide an ideal setting in which to see the workings of preservation and conservation. The focus is very much on education: Newbridge offers the opportunity to learn about the ins and outs of daily rural life 200 years ago. From food production to farm machinery, you can witness it all first-hand here, with the added bonus of following the life-cycle of baby chicks in their incubators. A lovely afternoon out.

Child-friendly restaurants

Dublin restaurants are rarely child-orientated; kids are mostly taken out for fast food, where the ketchup fights and ensuing bawling are inconsequential. There's the usual plague of fast-food outlets. McDonald's have two stores on O'Connell Street, one on Grafton Street and one in the Ilac Shopping Centre on Henry Street. Burger King is located on Grafton Street, O'Connell Street and in the Jervis Street Shopping Centre. Supermacs (an Irish-owned chain) is on O'Connell Street, offering a selection of pizzas, burgers, kebabs, chicken and fish, and an ice-cream parlour. The Bewley's chain of coffee houses are good for sausage and chips and do massively squidgy cream cakes. The following are lively, colourful and reasonably priced:
Bad Ass Café *9-11 Crown Alley, Dublin 2 (671 2596). All cross city buses.* **Open** 11.30am-midnight daily.
Captain America's Restaurant *44 Grafton Street, Dublin 2 (671 5266). All cross city buses.* **Open** noon-midnight daily.
Chicago Pizza Pie Factory *St Stephen's Green Shopping Centre, Dublin 2 (478 1233). All cross city buses.* **Open** noon-11.30pm Mon-Wed; noon-1.30am Thur, Fri; noon-midnight Sat; 12.30pm-11.30pm Sun.
Eddie Rocket's City Diner *7 South Anne Street, Dublin 2 (679 7340) & 52 O'Connell Street Lower, Dublin 1 (873 0027). All cross city buses.* **Open** 8am-1am Mon-Wed; 8am-4am Thur-Sat; 8am-1am Sun.

Try the following for the healthier side of things:
Cornucopia Vegetarian Restaurant *19 Wicklow Street, Dublin 2 (677 7583). All cross city buses.*
Chompy's Deli *Unit 22, Powerscourt Townhouse Centre, Dublin 2 (679 4552). All cross city buses.*
101 Talbot *101 Talbot Street, Dublin 1 (874 5011). All cross city buses.*
Well Fed Café *6 Crow Street, Dublin (677 2234). All cross city buses.*

Childminding

Childminders
22 Kildare Street, Dublin 2 (678 9050).

Freedom For You
38B Camden Row, Dublin 2 (478 0088).

Mother Hubbards
35 Blessington Street, Dublin 7 (860 1101).

Cinemas & theatres

Cinemas

Considering the amount of rainfall in the city, Dublin's cinemas are havens of warmth and dryness, packed with munchies. The UCI chain offers the children-friendliest cinemas in Dublin, hosting a Kid's Club with popular films every Saturday morning. The Coolock and Tallaght branches start at 10.30am, and Blanchardstown at 11am. UCI Coolock has a branch of Leisureplex beside it, offering bowling, quasars and kids' play centre. Check papers for details. (*See also chapter* **Film**).

Ambassador *Parnell Square, Dublin 1 (872 7000).*
Santry Omniplex *Old Airport Road, Santry, Dublin 9 (842 8844).*
Savoy *16-17 O'Connell Street Upper, Dublin 1 (information 874 8487/bookings 874 6000).*
UCI Blanchardstown *(bookings & information 1850 52 53 54).*
UCI Coolock *(information 848 5133/bookings 848 5122).*
UCI Tallaght *(information 452 2611/bookings 459 8400).*
Virgin Cinemas *Parnell Centre, Parnell Street, Dublin 1 (information 872 8400/bookings 872 8444).*

Theatres

Unfortunately, the majority of child-orientated theatre is organised by travelling troupes who play primarily to schools, so there is little in the way of permanent kids' theatre in Dublin. Christmas pantomimes have a great following, and the Dublin Theatre Festival tries to cater for children – the Chinese State Circus always plays to capacity crowds. Your best bet is to check local theatre listings to see what shows would be suitable. (*See also chapter* **Theatre & Dance**).

Lambert Puppet Theatre & Museum
Clifton Lane, Monkstown, Co Dublin (280 0974/280 4772 fax). Buses 7, 7A, 8; DART Salthill & Monkstown. **Show** 3.30pm Sat. **Admission** £5-£6.
Only kids' theatre which is open all year round.
Disabled: access. Licensed. Shop (coffee, confectionery, souvenirs).

Horse-riding

There are numerous stables around Dublin, offering treks in Phoenix Park, the Wicklow Mountains or in the safety of an indoor arena. One place which specialises in children riders is Oldtown Riding Stables (Wyestown, Oldtown, Co Dublin; tel 835 4755). They cater for all age groups, have an indoor sand arena and organise outdoor treks on ponies and horses. The emphasis here is very much on fun. During the summer, there's a very flexible kids club, which they can attend and pay for on a daily basis. Oldtown also organises day trips to events such as the Dublin Horse Show.

Check in the Golden Pages for details of riding stables in your area. Some other possibilities are listed below:

Ashtown Riding Stables

Navan Road, Ashtown, Dublin 15 (838 3807). Bus 37, 37A, 38. **Open** 2-5pm Wed; 10am-6pm Sat, Sun. **Charges** £12 per hour; £7 per hour children.

Carrickmines Equestrian Centre

Glenamuck Road, Foxrock, Dublin 18 (295 5990). Bus 44, 63. **Open** 9am-10pm Tue-Thur; 9am-6pm Fri-Sun.

Deerpark Riding Centre

Castleknock Gates, Castleknock Road, Dublin 15 (821 4947).

Museums

Dublin Viking Adventure

Essex Street West, Temple Bar, Dublin 8 (679 6040). DART Tara Street. **Open** 10.30am-4.30pm Mon-Sat; 11.30am-5.30pm Sun, Bank Holidays. **Admission** £4.75; £3.95 12-18s; £2.95 3-11s; £13 family.
An interactive exhibition which recreates the sights, sounds, even smells, of Dublin as it was 1,000 years ago. It's well located: the relaxed, colourful atmosphere of the Temple Bar area makes it a great place to stroll through, and it's very close to Wood Quay, the centre of Viking Dublin. A large collection of artefacts discovered during the excavations of Wood Quay is also on display here, which means you'll get equal measures of education and entertainment.
Disabled: access.

Dublin Writers' Museum

18-19 Parnell Square, Dublin 1 (872 2077). DART Connolly Station. **Open** 10am-5pm Mon-Sat; 11.30am-6pm Sun, Bank Holidays. **Admission** £2.90; £2.40 children; £1.20 under 12s; £7.75 family (2+2).
The Dublin Writers' Museum devotes much of its energy to catering for children. There's Tara's Palace and Doll's House, with 24 rooms filled with miniature furniture drawn from all over the world. In Seomra Na nÓg, the kids can learn all about almost two dozen of Ireland's best-known children's authors. Taped extracts from the books and illustrations of the most famous characters work to bring the texts to life. The museum also runs a Children's Literature Summer School (details 623 4222).

Dublinia

Christchurch, St Michael's Hill, Dublin 8 (679 4611). Buses 49, 50, 54A, 56A, 77. **Open** *Apr-Sept* 10am-5pm daily; *Oct-Mar* 11am-4pm Mon-Sat; 10am-4.30pm Sun. **Admission** £2.90-£3.95; family ticket £10; free under 5s.
(See chapter **Museums.***)*

Malahide Castle & Fry Model Railway Museum

Malahide Castle Demesne, Malahide, Co Dublin (846 2184). Bus 42/rail Malahide. **Castle open** *Apr-Oct* 10am-12.45pm, 2-5pm Mon-Fri; 11am-12.45pm, 2-6pm, Sat, Sun, Bank Holidays; *Nov-Mar* 10am-12.45pm, 2-5pm, Mon-Fri; 2pm-5pm Sat, Sun, Bank Holidays. **Admission** £2.95; £1.60 3-11s; £2.45 12-18s; £7.95 family. **Railway Museum open** *Apr-Oct* 10am-1pm, 2-6pm Mon-Thur; 11am-1pm, 2-6pm, Sat, Sun, Bank Holidays. *Oct-Mar* 2-5pm Sat, Sun, Bank Holidays. **Admission** £2.65; 3-11s £1.50; £2 12-18s; £7.25 family. **Combined Castle & Railway Museum** £4.60; £2.50 3-11s; £3.50 12-18s; £11.75 family.
This is a good place to head for if you want to get out of the city for a day. Malahide Castle is a small medieval fortress set in 250 acres of park and woodland. The tour focuses on the collection of period furniture, antiques and paintings housed in the castle (*see chapter* **Museums & Art Galleries**), so the kids may not be enthralled. However, the grounds have a superb playground (made entirely of wood) which cannot fail to please, football pitches galore, and the Fry Model Railway Museum. This collection of handmade models of Irish trains charts the development of rail travel in Ireland and is a must for any little trainspotters. If it's a fine day, bring a picnic or continue on to the beaches at Malahide and Portmarnock.
Disabled: access (Fry Model Railway Museum only).

Museum of Childhood

20 Palmerston Road, Rathmines, Dublin 6 (497 3223). **Open** 2-5.30pm Sun.
A private collection of antique dolls and toys, this is not open all year, so call for details. Last admission 4.45pm.

National Wax Museum

Granby Row, Parnell Square, Dublin 1 (872 6340). DART Connolly Station; all cross city buses. **Open** 10am-5.30pm Mon-Sat, Bank Holidays; noon-5.30pm Sun. **Admission** £3.50; £2.50 students; £2 children.
This is Ireland's only wax exhibition. In the main hall the historical and cultural development of Ireland is mapped by life-size figures of sporting, political, literary and theatrical personages. The religious VIPs are also present: there's a replica of Leonardo da Vinci's *Last Supper*, and you can see the actual Popemobile used by John Paul II during his visit here in 1979. More interesting for the kids is the Children's World of Fairytale & Fantasy. All the favourite characters from children's stories are brought to life – Snow White and the Seven Dwarves, Sleeping Beauty, Cinderella, Jack and the Beanstalk, and Robin Hood. If they're up to it, they can brave the Chamber of Horrors and explore the adventure tunnels within Granny's Kitchen and Dracula's Castle. However, if they don't like the sounds of the blood-curdling screams, they can bypass the horrors and go straight to the Hall of Megastars. Filled with children's heroes, this exhibition has stars from the worlds of pop, TV and comics. They're all here – Michael Jackson, Madonna, the Simpsons and Batman. And of course, a special display for our own U2. (*See also chapter* **Museums & Art Galleries.***)
Disabled: access by lift to be installed in 1998.

Natural History Museum

Merrion Square West, Dublin 2 (677 7444). DART Pearse Station. **Open** 10am-5pm Tue-Sat; 2-5pm Sun. **Admission** free.
(See chapter **Museums***).*

Shopping

Most shopping needs can be covered between Dunnes Stores, Roches Stores, Penney's and the big family department stores. Dunnes (North Earl Street, Ilac Centre and St Stephen's Green Shopping Centre), Penney's (O'Connell Street) and Roches (Henry Street) are all excellent for cheap clothes of reasonable quality and they also stock the major toy lines. You'll find the chic labels at the children's clothes departments of Clery's (O'Connell Street) and Arnott's (Henry Street), and their toy departments are besieged throughout the year. The following are smaller shops, where it's more difficult to lose the kids.

Clothes

Baby at Blooming
3 Leinster Street South, Dublin 2 (662 1686). All cross city buses. **Open** *9.30am-5.30pm Mon-Sat.*

Baby Bambino
41 Clarendon Street, Dublin 2 (671 1590). All cross city buses. **Open** *10am-6pm Mon-Sat.*

Baby Boutique
Unit 66, Ilac Centre, Parnell Street, Dublin 1 (873 2169). All cross city buses. **Open** *9.30am-6pm Mon-Sat.*

Baby Shop
14 Chatham Street, Dublin 2 (677 2312). All cross city buses. **Open** *9.30am-6pm Mon-Sat.*

Freckles
1 Liffey Street Upper, Dublin 1 (873 1249). All cross city buses. **Open** *9.30am-6pm Mon-Sat.*

Mothercare
St Stephen's Green Shopping Centre, St Stephen's Green, Dublin 2 (478 0951). All cross city buses. **Open** *9.30am-6pm Mon-Wed, Fri; 9.30am-8pm Thur; 9.30am-6.30pm Sat.*

Our Boys House
24 Wicklow Street, Dublin 2 (677 8658). All cross city buses. **Open** *9.15am-5.30pm Mon-Sat.*

Furniture

Bean Bag Shop
Market Arcade, South Great St George's Street, Dublin 2 (851 4739). All cross city buses. **Open** *11am-5.30pm Mon-Sat.*
As the name suggests – beanies in all colours and sizes.

Murphy's
17 High Street, Christchurch, Dublin 8 (677 8942). All cross city buses. **Open** *9.30am-5.30pm Mon-Sat.*
Murphy's stocks a ranges of cots, car seats, playpens and nursery furniture.

O'Connor's Pram Shop
45A Camden Street Lower, Dublin 2 (475 2237). All cross city buses. **Open** *9am-5.30pm Mon-Sat.*
Prams galore.

Toys

Banba Toymaster
48 Mary Street, Dublin 1 (872 7100). All cross city buses. **Open** *9am-6pm Mon-Sat.*
This is one of the essentials for Christmas shopping. Banba offers the big names at keen prices.

Early Learning Centre
3 Henry Street, Dublin 1 (873 1945). All cross city buses. **Open** *9am-5.30pm Mon-Wed, Fri, Sat; 9am-8pm Thur.*
Primary-coloured educational and fun toys.

The Model Shop
13 Capel Street, Dublin 1 (872 8134). All cross city buses.
Planes, trains and automobiles.

Rainbow Crafts
5 Westbury Hotel Mall, Dublin 2 (677 7632). All cross city buses. **Open** *9am-6pm Mon-Wed, Fri, Sat; 9am-7pm Thur.*
An old-fashioned shop, concentrating on wooden toys, rocking horses, doll's houses, traditional teddy bears and spinning tops.

Teddy Bear & Co
Unit 2A, St Stephen's Green Shopping Centre, Dublin 2 (478 1139). All cross city buses. **Open** *9am-6.30pm Mon-Wed; 9am-8pm Thur; 9am-7pm Fri, Sat; 2-6pm Sun.*
A small shop, crammed full with teddies.

Summer schools

Summer schools have become increasingly popular over the last few years. The *Irish Times'* Weekend section lists details of current programmes, but some of the more popular ones include the **Stoker & Dracula Summer School** (at Clontarf; telephone 851 1027), the **James Joyce Summer School** (at Newman House; tel 706 8480), and the **National Gallery's Summer Club** (676 6488).

Dublin is just riddled with music and drama schools, most of which offer summer courses. They all run to a similar format, so figure out your child's requirements and telephone around to see what suits best.

Betty Ann Norton Theatre School
Clonbrock House, 11 Harcourt Street, Dublin 2 (475 1913). All cross city buses.

Children's Theatrical Work Shop
Sandyford Community Centre, Lambs Cross, Dublin 16 (296 0400). Bus 44.
For those staying in Dublin for a longer period, this workshop offers eight-week courses (between Sept-June) in drama and dance, ranging from Strauss to the Spice Girls. Age groups 4-6, 7-11, 12-16. Cost is £3.50 per class, eight classes per course.

Dublin School of Classical & Contemporary Dance
13 Stamer Street, Portobello, Dublin 8 (475 5451).
Ballet and modern theatre dance for boys and girls.

Gaiety School of Acting
Meeting House Square, Temple Bar, Dublin 2 (679 9277). DART Tara Street/all cross city buses.

Leeson Park School of Music
Grove Park, Rathmines, Dublin 6 (496 7890). All cross city buses.
Music kindergarden for ages 1 to 6.

Leinster School of Music
5 Stephen's Street Upper, Dublin 8 (475 1532). All cross city buses.

Parnell School of Music & Performing Arts
14 Sackville Place, Dublin 1 (878 6909). DART Connolly Station/all cross city buses.

Film

Tax breaks and architecture make Ireland a location manager's dream. But Irish film also has a venerable history and a lively future.

Neil Jordan – director of **Angel**, **The Company of Wolves**, **Mona Lisa** *and* **Michael Collins**.

James Joyce opened the first cinema in Dublin, the Volta, on Mary Street in 1909. Since then, Ireland has boasted the highest cinema-going population in Europe and turned out numerous Oscar-meriting versions of its history and culture. Celluloid visions of Irishness were early foisted upon a world already avid for the literature and poetry of the place via classics such as John Ford's *The Quiet Man* and Carol Reed's *Odd Man Out*. These excited American enthusiasm for a land so beautiful, so unspoilt, so nearly home. Yet neither of them was an Irish film – any more than *Casino Royale*, *The Spy Who Came in From the Cold*, or John Boorman's *Excalibur*, all filmed here during the 1960s and '70s.

It was not until the era of Neil Jordan, Jim Sheridan, Gabriel Byrne and Stephen Rea that an Irish film industry really kicked in. In the last four years, thanks to the dedication of arts minister Michael D Higgins, in maintaining the Government's tax incentives, Ireland has become such a popular spot for the on-location shooting of every conceivable genre of movie that the famously insouciant reception accorded to all celebrities has become actively blasé. *Braveheart* blazed a trail thanks to the delicate poaching that saw this tale of Scottish heroism seduced towards Ireland by Michael D's timely offer of the entire territorial army as extras – a coup he recently repeated with Spielberg's *Saving Private Ryan*.

The current vogue of Irish directors, writers, actors and locations means that, to those interested in cinema, much of Dublin will have all the attractive charm of the very familiar. The Pepper Canister church, the Four Courts, the Ringsend Gasworks and particularly Sheriff Street – a body-double for Belfast and popular icon of Dublin's slum years – should all be instantly recognisable. Irish history, life, identity and locality, both modern and historic, have all served as magnets for movie scripts. They have been exploited to great effect in films as diverse as Alan Parker's *The Commitments* and Stanley Kubrick's *Barry Lyndon*.

These appear daily in the *Irish Times* and the *Evening Herald*. The Irish Film Centre publishes its own guide, available from the IFC itself, tourist centres and most city centre cafés and bars. Except for the IFC and the Screen, cinemas show only current mainstream releases. Ticket prices vary very little, with prices ranging between £2-£3 during the afternoon and £4-£5 for evening shows.

Major cinemas

Ambassador

O'Connell Street, Dublin 1 (bookings 872 7000). DART Connolly Station/bus 11, 13. **Credit** MC, V.
Despite its current shabbiness, this is actually Dublin's most elegant cinema. Its single screen is housed in an eighteenth-century building that was originally part of the Rotunda hospital. Wheelchair access to the stalls only, via a short flight of stairs which must be negotiated with the aid of staff.

Classic

Harold's Cross Road, Harold's Cross, Dublin 6 (bookings 492 3699). Bus 16, 18, 47, 49, 65, 83. **No credit cards**.
Nondescript two-screener, famous for a regular late Friday night showing of *The Rocky Horror Picture Show*, now in its sixteenth year. The programme starts at 11.15pm, the film half an hour later. Log on to www.rockyhorror.com for a list of the props and prompts required to take an active part. *Disabled: limited access.*

Irish Film Centre

6 Eustace Street, Dublin 2 (679 3477). DART Tara Street/bus 54. **Membership** £1-£10. **Credit** MC, V.
With entrances on Eustace Street and Meeting House Square, this is an imaginatively converted seventeenth-century Temple Bar building with two screens, refreshments and the country's largest public archive collection. It shows Irish and European independent and arthouse films. Cinema 1 shows commercial arthouse and retrospectives in order to finance Cinema 2, a smaller, amphitheatre-type venue showing non-commercial films and documentaries. It is frequently the setting for public talks and master-classes. Neil Jordan, Dennis Hopper and Harold Pinter have all given lectures here. Throughout 1998, it will devote the first Thursday of every second month to first-time Irish film-makers. Open-air summer screenings are held in Meeting House Square, for which 100 free tickets a day are available from the IFC reception. Several years ago, the IFC put out a national request for archive material – from scraps of old home movies or advertisements to cans of film left by the closing of old cinemas. The response was enthusiastic, with material arriving in old biscuit tins and plastic bags. Archive screenings are every month, but these are usually of recently restored prints. Those interested in disparate images of Ireland's social and geographical past should contact the IFC archives direct. They are open by appointment for a £5 fee. The restaurant/bar (*see picture facing page*) serves snacks and meals during pub hours, and at weekends has jazz until 2pm. Membership is obligatory; weekly membership costs £1 and can be extended to three guests. Yearly membership is £10 and carries with it a discount on the bookshop and film magazines. *Bar. Bookshop. Café. Disabled: access. Library. Public archive.*

Santry Omniplex

Old Airport Road, Santry, Dublin 9 (bookings 842 8844). Bus 16A, 41. **Credit** MC, V.
Lacking charm, but the parking's good. Ten screens. *Disabled: access.*

Savoy

16-17 O'Connell Street Upper, Dublin 1 (information 874 8487/bookings 874 6000). DART Connolly Station/bus 10, 11, 13, 16, 22. **Credit** MC, V.
Five-screen city centre operation, which includes the largest screen in Dublin. *Disabled: access to Screen 1 only.*

Alan Parker's 1991 movie **The Commitments** was a gritty, naturalistic Northside comedy.

Festivals

Dublin Film Festival

1 Suffolk Street, Dublin 2 (679 2937/fax 679 2939).
Dates 3-12 Mar 1998. **Membership** £3.
Admission £3-£5.
A rock-solid selection of big-, low- and no-budget films, shorts, documentaries and animation from around the world. Plus a festival club for late-night drinking and after-hours networking. The films are screened in a selection of city centre cinemas. Admission and season ticket prices, information and booking details are all available nearer the time from the festival's head office. (*See also chapter* **Dublin By Season**).
e-mail: dff@iol.ie
web site: http://www.iol.ie/dff/

Dublin French Film Festival

French Embassy in Ireland, Cultural Department, 1 Kildare Street, Dublin 2 (festival office 676 2197).
Dates 2-12 Nov 1998. **Membership** £2-£3.

Annual festival showing films and documentaries from France, Canada, Belgium, Vietnam, Algeria, Burkina-Faso and more. First-time screenings, first-time directors and Irish premières appear together with the work of household names and many classics of French cinema. The programme is published mid-October and information is available from the Festival office. Admission prices and season ticket prices will be confirmed nearer the time.

Junior Dublin Film Festival

Irish Film Centre, 6 Eustace Street, Dublin 2 (671 4095). **Admission** £1.50 per screening.
Usually held in late November/early December, Ireland's second largest film festival attracts 10,000 people each year. Founded in 1989, it presents new and classic films from around the world, tailored for the nine to 18 age group. Seminars, workshops and presentations on film-related skills and theory add to its popularity. Screenings are at the Irish Film Centre (pictured) and UCI Tallaght.

Screen

D'Olier Street, Dublin 2 (671 4988 after 3pm daily).
DART Tara Street/bus 3, 15A. **Credit** MC, V.
Shows international, commercial and arthouse films. Rather rundown, it's been due a makeover for years, but retains plenty of loyal affection. Three screens.
Disabled: access to Screen 1 only.

Stella Rathmines

Rathmines Road, Dublin 6 (497 1281). Bus 14, 15, 83.
Credit MC, V.
Pleasant, but small. Two screens.
Disabled: access.

UCI Coolock

Malahide Road, Coolock, Dublin 17 (information 848 5133/bookings 848 5122). Bus 27, 42, 43. **Credit** MC, V (50p charge per credit card booking).

Ten-screen giant miles away from the city centre. Low on character and appeal, but good parking.
Disabled: access.

UCI Tallaght

The Square, Tallaght, Dublin 24 (information 452 2611/ bookings 459 8400). Bus 49, 50, 65, 65B, 77, 77A.
Credit MC, V (50p charge per credit card booking).
This 12-screener is Dublin's biggest cinema.
Disabled: access.

Virgin Cinemas

Parnell Centre, Parnell Street, Dublin 1 (information 872 8400/booking 872 8444). DART Connolly Station/bus 10, 11, 13, 16. **Credit** AmEx, DC, MC, V.
A city-centre multiplex, next door to a games emporium. Something to please most people. Nine screens.
Disabled: access.

Gay & Lesbian Dublin

Once home to the divine Oscar, Dublin's recently legalised gay scene is making up for lost time.

Homosexuality was only legalised in the Irish Republic in 1993, as part of the wave of liberalisation which followed on the heels of the election of Mary Robinson as President in 1990 (as in England, lesbianism was never illegal). When legalisation came, however, it was with a whimper rather than a bang – gay rights, unlike divorce or abortion, do not have the power to cause national turmoil and legislation passed through the Dáil with scarcely a word of complaint from conservative elements in society.

Of course, Dublin had a fully functional scene before 1993, but legalisation has brought many benefits. The city has witnessed a substantial increase in the number of gay venues, particularly in the last two years, and the gay and lesbian community has become generally more confident, energetic and high profile. As Dublin has grown in popularity with visitors, so its gay scene has developed a good reputation. This is largely deserved, for although the scene remains comparatively small for a city of this size, it is growing steadily; it caters for most tastes and doesn't take itself too seriously. The lesbian scene is significantly smaller, but is also developing – check for new venues when you arrive.

Information is easy to come by, with *Gay Community News*, Ireland's monthly gay and lesbian newspaper, available free in most of the venues listed below, and in many bookshops. Also check *GCN* for details of events such as **Pride** (at the end of June) and the **Lesbian and Gay Film Festival** (at the end of July in the Irish Film Centre). A new Irish glossy, *Innuendo*, has just hit the newsstands here and British offerings such as *Attitude*, *Diva* and *Gay Times* are widely available.

Unless otherwise stated, all the clubs, bars, cafés and restaurants listed below welcome lesbians and gay men.

Clubs

The Block
The George, 89 South Great George's Street, Dublin 2 (478 2983). Buses 16, 19, 55. **Open** noon-2.30am Wed-Sun. **Admission** £3, £5 after 11pm.

Advertises itself as 'Dublin's Best and Soon to be Europe's No 1 Gay Venue'. This might be overstating it slightly, but this old reliable of the Dublin scene continues to be popular and is set to expand. Check for details. Open to all, but men predominate.

Candy Club
Kitchen, East Essex Street, Temple Bar, Dublin 2 (677 6635). Buses 21, 68, 69. **Open** 11pm-late Mon. **Admission** £3-£4.

A mixed crowd come here for fun and dancing rather than cruising, but, having said that, there are possibilities…

Freedom
The Mission, Eustace Street (opposite Irish Film Centre), Temple Bar, Dublin 2. Bus 54. **Open** 10.30pm-late Mon. **Admission** £3-£5.

And whoever said Monday nights were dead? The Mission on a Monday is an eclectic mix of the young and not so young. The music can be somewhat dated, but they still pack 'em in.

GetOut
The Furnace, 1-2 Aston Place, Dublin 2 (671 0433). Buses 49, 50, 56, 77. **Open** 9pm-1.30am 2nd Sat of month. **Admission** £5; £4 students, unemployed.

Attracts a more sedate and less hedonistic crowd than many venues. But don't worry – we don't mean that sedate.

HAM (Homo Action Movies)
The PoD, Harcourt Street, Dublin 2 (478 0225). Buses 14, 15. **Open** 11pm-late Fri. **Admission** £4-£5.

'With Jellyslut on the door and the Butcher Boys inside, tenderising begins at 11pm.' Totally queer door policy.

Heaven
Mean Fiddler, 26 Wexford Street, Dublin 2 (475 8555). Buses 16, 55. **Open** 10.30pm-late 1st & 3rd Sun of month. **Admission** £4-£5.

A new mixed gay/straight night at this popular venue.

Mambo
Gaiety Theatre, South King Street, Dublin 2. All city centre buses. **Open** 11.15pm-3am Fri. **Admission** £6.

Gay-friendly club with a world music seasoning, mixing salsa and live Latino bands for a spicy Friday night out.

Mildred
The Da Club, 2 Johnson Place, Lower Stephen Street, Dublin 2 (670 5116). All city centre buses. **Open** 11pm-late Tue. **Admission** £4.

A venue full of the queer and gorgeous population. Make sure your self-esteem is in good shape.

The Playground
The Temple of Sound, Ormond Hotel, Ormond Quay, Dublin 1 (872 1811). Buses 23, 24, 90. **Open** 11pm-late Sun. **Admission** £5.

Smiles all round at one of Dublin's busiest gay bars, **The George** – *see page 160.*

Sunday nights on the quays consist of a mixture of high camp and deep house. The Playground caters for a heaving mass of (predominantly young, predominantly male) Sabbath breakers. Check out the 'Mr Gay Ireland' contest, held during the summer months. Full bar, chill-out room.

Powderbubble
POD, Harcourt Street, Dublin 2 (478 0225). Buses 14, 15. **Open** monthly; call for details.**Admission** £7.
Monthly club at the Red Box. Indulge the devilish side of your nature and join about 1,500 other gays and straights in a heady evening of S&M. After all, a little of what you fancy, perhaps?

Stonewallz
Griffith College, South Circular Road, Dublin 8 (454 9427). Bus 19. **Open** 9pm-2am every 2nd Sat. **Admission** £3; £4 after 11.30pm.
Women-only club on Dublin's southside, featuring two DJs and full bar, together with pool, darts and other games.

Strictly Handbag
Ri Ra, Dame Court, Dublin 2 (677 4835). Buses 16, 19, 22. **Open** 11.15pm-late Mon. **Admission** £3-£4.
As camp as they come, and great fun… dance around your handbag to the sounds of the 1970s and '80s.

Velure
Gaiety Theatre, South King Street, Dublin 2 (677 1717). All city centre buses. **Open** 11.15pm-3am Sat. **Admission** £6-£7.
Gay-friendly club a few seconds from Grafton Street, featuring jazz, cabaret and soul on three floors, with a selection of bars and old movies. Well worth a visit.

Wonderbar
Temple Bar Music Centre, Curved Street, Temple Bar, Dublin 2 (670 9202). Bus 54. **Open** 9.30pm-2.45am 1st & 3rd Sat of month. **Admission** £5-£7.
Come here for the 'campest party in town!' Wonderbar is

currently the most popular gay and lesbian club in Dublin and is generally packed to the rafters with a mixed crowd looking for a good time. Lots of beautiful, well-toned bodies, but fear not – the great unwashed still have the edge.

Bars

Front Lounge
34 Parliament Street, Temple Bar, Dublin 2 (670 4112). Buses 54, 65. **Open** 11.30am-11.30pm Mon-Sat; 4-11.30pm Sun.
One for all the well-heeled people. Well, no, not really, but this is one of Dublin's shiny new pubs. Come here for the comfy sofas and handsome clientèle. Sunday is 'officially' gay evening, but the ambience is decidedly relaxed all week long. Well worth dropping in for a happy pint or two.

The George
89 South George's Street, Dublin 2 (478 2983). Buses 16, 19, 55. **Open** noon-11.30pm Mon-Tue; noon-2.30am Wed-Sun.
Downstairs from the Block (*see above*), and continuing, despite all the competition, to draw the crowds.

The Globe
11 South Great George's Street, Dublin 2 (671 1220). Buses 16, 19, 55. **Open** noon-11.30pm daily.
This smart and fashionable bar, catering to a mixed gay/straight crowd, is pleasantly relaxed by day and thronged by night.

Hogan's
35 South Great George's Street, Dublin 2 (677 5904). Buses 16, 19, 55. **Open** 1-11.30pm Mon-Wed; 1pm-1.30am Thur-Fri; noon-midnight Sat; 4-11pm Sun.
Popular and fashionable bar, catering to pretty much the same crowd as the Globe (*see above*), and having the added attraction of downstairs club.

*Indulge your regal fantasies – as well as a few other ones as well – at **Powderbubble**.*

*On a good night, the room seems to be spinning at **The Globe**.*

Irish Film Centre

Eustace Street, Temple Bar, Dublin 2 (677 8788). Bus 54. **Open** *9am-11pm daily.*
Officially a 'cultural institute', but in reality many different things under one (glass) roof – arthouse cinemas, bookshop and restaurant. The IFC bar is attractive and popular with lesbians and gay men.

Out on the Liffey

27 Upper Ormond Quay, Dublin 1 (872 2480). Buses 24, 90. **Open** *noon-11.30pm Sun-Tue; noon-12.30am Wed-Sat.*
This comfortable pub opts out of the trendy and Temple Bar-esque. Come for a relaxed atmosphere, quizzes and a pint around the fire.

Saunas

Boilerhouse

12 Crane Lane (off Eame Street), Dublin 2 (677 3130). Bus 54. **Open** *6pm-5am Mon-Thur; 6pm-9am Fri-Sat; 6pm-4am Sun.* **Admission** *£10.*
Dublin's biggest and newest sauna includes steam room and jacuzzi, as well as café and solarium.

The Dock

21 Upper Ormond Quay (two doors up from Out on the Liffey), Dublin 7 (872 4172). Buses 24, 90. **Open** *1pm-3am Mon-Fri; 2pm-6am Sat; 2pm-4am Sun.* **Admission** *£6, £7 after 7pm.*
Small, cosy and (as it were) intimate.

The Gym

14-15 Dame Lane, Dublin 2 (679 5128). Buses 16, 19, 22. **Open** *1pm-midnight Sun-Thur; 1pm-3am Fri-Sat.* **Admission** *£8.*

The Gym offers happy hunting grounds for all those who love the daylight cruise.

Incognito

1-2 Bow Lane East (off Aungier Street), Dublin 2 (478 3504). Bus 55. **Open** *1pm-5am Mon-Thur, 1pm-9am Fri-Sat; 2-5pm Sun.* **Admission** *£8.*
Men-only sauna with all the usual delights. Go Incognito and check out the new dungeons – you just might want to stay locked up for ever.

Cafés & restaurants

Café Irie

11 Fownes Street, Temple Bar, Dublin 2 (867 4381). Bus 54. **Open** *7.30am-6pm Mon-Sat.* **No credit cards**.
Small, relaxed and gay-friendly first-floor café, serving some of the best and most varied sandwiches and soups in Dublin. The fresh tomato, orange and basil soup is a winner. Check out their breakfast menu also.

Juice

Castle House, South Great George's Street, Dublin 2 (475 7856). Buses 16, 19, 22. **Open** *12.30-11pm Tue-Sat; noon-10pm Sun-Mon.* **Credit** EC, MC, V.
A few doors up from the George (*see above* **Bars**), this is a first rate and reasonably priced restaurant, serving excellent vegetarian food and a wide range of juices, exotic and freshly squeezed. The service can be a little slow, but well worth a visit, nonetheless.

Marks Bros

7 South Great George's Street, Dublin 2 (677 1085). Buses 16, 19, 22. **Open** *11am-10.30pm Mon-Sat.* **Credit** EC, MC, V.
This laid-back café has long been known as a student hang-

out, with great lunchtime sandwiches and soups; now open and serving vegetarian cuisine in the evenings.

The Olde New Orleans
3 Cork Hill (Dame Street), Dublin 2 (670 9785). Buses 54, 65. **Open** 12.30pm-12.30am daily. **Credit** EC, MC, V.
Gay-friendly, cosy and candle-lit restaurant on the edge of Temple Bar, serving creole-cajun cuisine at pretty reasonable prices.

Sinners Restaurant
12 Parliament Street, Temple Bar, Dublin 2 (671 9345). Bus 54. **Open** 5.30pm-midnight Sun-Wed; 5.30pm-1am Thur-Sat. **Credit** AmEx, DC, EC, MC, V.
Reasonably priced, gay-friendly Lebanese cuisine across the road from the Front Lounge. Worth a visit.

Well Fed Café
6 Crow Street, Temple Bar, Dublin 2 (677 2234). Bus 54. **Open** noon-8pm Mon-Sat. **No credit cards.**
Dublin's original vegetarian café comes as a welcome change in the heart of tarted-up Temple Bar – gay-friendly (and friendly), serving large portions of down-to-earth veggie food at down-to-earth prices.

Accommodation

Unless otherwise stated, the places listed below are open to gay men and lesbians.

The Alternative Guest House
61 Amiens Street, Dublin 1 (855 3671). DART Connolly. **Rates** *double* £57 midweek; phone for other rates. **Credit** EC, MC, V.
Centrally located in the northside city centre, close to O'Connell Street, Connolly Station and Busáras, with secure car parking. Evening meals available on request.

Frankie's Guest House
8 Camden Place, Dublin 2 (478 3087). Buses 55, 83. **Rates** (incl full breakfast) *single* £20; *standard* £47; *double en suite* £56. **Credit** EC, MC, V.
In the southside city centre, a short walk from Grafton Street and Temple Bar. All rooms include TV, tea/coffee-making facilities. En suite room available.

The Horse and Carriage Hotel
15 Aungier Street, Dublin 2 (478 3537). Buses 55, 83. **Rates** (incl full breakfast) *single* £30 Sun-Thur; *double* £45 Fri, Sat; *large double* £50. **Credit** EC, MC, V.
In the southside city centre, a short walk from Grafton Street and Temple Bar. Rooms include tea/coffee-making facilities, and rates include free admission (for male guests only) to Incognito sauna (see above **Saunas**).

Inn on the Liffey
21 Upper Ormond Quay, Dublin 1 (677 0828). Buses 24, 90. **Rates** *double en suite* £45; *three people sharing* £60. **Credit** EC, MC, V.
All rooms are en suite, and most have views overlooking the Liffey. Rates include (for male guests) free admission to the Dock sauna (see above). A private apartment is also available at Batchelor's Walk, close to the Ha'penny Bridge (telephone for rates).

Tig na mBan (The Women's House)
Dublin 8 (473 1781). **Rates** *single self-catering* £12.50; *single with self-service breakfast* £14.50; *full B&B* £16.50; *double* as above for each person; *four sharing* £8.50-£11.50; *three sharing* £10.50-£15. **No credit cards.**
The first and only women's guesthouse in Dublin. Rooms include private tea/coffee-making facilities, but the rest of the house (including bathroom) is shared. House accommodates seven women and double room can take up to four women. Children welcome. Call for information pack and address.

Help & health

AIDS Helpline Dublin
(872 4277). **Open** 7-9 pm Mon-Fri; 3-5pm Sat.

Dublin AIDS Alliance
53 Parnell Square, Dublin 1 (873 3799).

Gay Men's Health Project
19 Haddingdon Road, Dublin 4 (660 2189/668 1577 ext 4221). Bus 45. **Open** 8-9.30pm Tue; 6.30-8.30pm Wed.
Drop-in sexual health clinic for gay and bisexual men. Free, friendly and confidential.

Gay Switchboard Dublin
Carmichael House, North Brunswick House, Dublin 7 (872 1055). **Open** 8-10pm Sun-Fri; 3.30-6pm Sat.

Lesbian Line
Carmichael House, North Brunswick House, Dublin 7 (872 9911). 7-9pm Thur.

LOT (Lesbians Organising Together)
5 Capel Street, Dublin 1 (872 7770). Bus 23. **Open** 10-6pm Mon-Thur; 10-4pm Fri.
Drop-in, resource centre and library in the city centre. Call in for tea or coffee and to check on events.

Outhouse
6 South William Street, Dublin 2 (670 6377). **Open** noon-4.30pm Mon-Thur; noon-4pm Fri.
Situated in a comfortable and airy city centre building, Outhouse aims to provide an accessible meeting place for the lesbian and gay community in Dublin. Call in for information and a cuppa.

Bookshops

Books Upstairs
36 College Green (opposite Trinity College), Dublin 2 (679 6687). All city centre buses. **Open** 9.30am-7pm Mon-Fri; 9.30am-6pm Sat, Sun. **Credit** AmEx, DC, MC, V.
Small, friendly store, much frequented by students, with extensive selection of lesbian and gay literature and magazines. (*See also chapter* **Shopping & Services**.)

Garden of Delight
3 Castle Street (beside Dublin Castle), Dublin 2 (no phone). Bus 65.
Friendly bookstore, café and performance space, hosting regular poetry readings and other events.

Waterstone's
7 Dawson Street, Dublin 2 (679 1415). Buses 13, 14, 15. **Open** 9am-8pm Mon-Wed, Fri; 9am-8.30pm Thur; 9am-7pm Sat; 11am-6pm Sun. **Credit** AmEx, DC, MC, V.
The Dublin branch of the UK bookstore chain. (*See also chapter* **Shopping & Services**.)

Winding Stair
40 Lower Ormond Quay (beside Ha'penny Bridge), Dublin 1 (873 3292). Buses 24, 90. **Open** 10am-6pm Mon-Sat. **Credit** EC, MC, V.
Bookstore and café on two floors with wonderful views of the Liffey and central Dublin. While away the afternoon with coffee in a sunny window seat. (*See also chapter* **Shopping & Services**.)

Media

Hot press, not so hot TV.

Newspapers

All but one of the Republic's national newspapers are based in the capital, in spirit as well as in body. The *Irish Times* acts as Ireland's serious-intellectual broadsheet. Offering objective and insightful reporting of city, national and international affairs, as well as deeper analysis and debate of whatever it sees fit, from theocracy to theatre, politics to puppet-shows, the *Times* is a good choice for a half-an-hour's read, but not for a two-minute skim. Its main rival the *Irish Independent* is a more actively national (and nationalist) paper. What the *Indo* lacks in formality and objectivity, it makes up for in its, well… lack of formality and objectivity. It is more readable (except for the regular smatterings of typos), but also more conservative.

The *Star* is Ireland's very own, very popular, very unsubtly named response to Britain's *Sun*, though with a little more conscience and a lot less cleavage. In fact, its thoroughness of breast-coverage is second only to its sports coverage. The *Irish Sun* differs from the British *Sun* in that it has the word 'Irish' inserted before the title, and whenever there is an article published in the motherpaper declaring all Irish people to be dangerous drink-drenched dorks, it is covered over in the Irish version with a glossy of a topless leprechaun. Otherwise, no differences have been spotted.

The *Evening Herald*, peddled on the streets and newsstands from lunchtime onwards is also a tabloid, but if that threatens to put you off, don't let it. While stray *Times* readers might dismiss the *Herald* for concentrating too much on muggings and too little on matters of the mind, it is vital for its up-to-the-minute events, buy-and-sell information and property-listings, as well as the occasional late-breaking headline. Its sports coverage also benefits from its late press-time.

Of the many papers you will find lined up in a Dublin newsagent's on a Sunday morning, few will be Irish, with most of the shelf-space taken up by cheaper British titles (some modified for the Irish market), brimming over with free magazines, supplements, sample shampoos and, for the most part, nothing original. The few indigenous newspapers do dominate sales, however. The *Sunday Tribune* and the *Sunday Independent* both offer good news coverage and comment (with the relaxed benefit of a week's hindsight), and some excellently entertaining regular columnists (with Ardal O'Hanlon

Hot Press, *cool read – listings and reviews.*

and Hugh Leonard as respective examples). The *Sunday Business Post*, like the *Financial Times*, is good for more than just money-talk, and is, at times, the most outspoken of all the papers mentioned on live national issues. The popular *Sunday World* is much like the *Star* on a Sunday; and finally, *The Title* is a respected sports-only publication.

Magazines

Undoubtedly, the most vital publication for the visitor to Dublin, no matter what the nature or length of the stay, is *In Dublin*. Released every second Thursday, it contains two weeks' worth of listings and reviews for theatre, cinema, music, comedy, exhibitions and festivals, as well as guides to pubs, restaurants and city tours aplenty. And for the very bored, *In Dublin* is also the controversial carrier of several pages of ads for the world's oldest professional euphemism, 'escort agencies'. The various features which fill up whatever pages are left after the listings and lustings are, for the main part, of a rather hollow and hackish ilk, but at £1.50 an issue you shouldn't feel too cheated.

For a more intelligent take on all that's happening in the capital, try the coolly titled *Hot Press*, which also appears fortnightly. A broadsheet with social commentaries shrouded in gig-reviews, *Hot Press* has been up and running for over 20 years, with more or less the same hard core of writers (you may see some around town – long hair and bald patches, black sunglasses so big that only a few jowls are visible). The magazine is by far the best guide to the Dublin music scene, with comprehensive listings and reviews of all gigs and releases great and small; but it is also one of the liveliest forums for comment and debate on Larger Issues, particularly Irish politics.

When it comes to glossy feature mags, Dublin shelves are as packed as any. All of the international mainstays are there, some in special Irish editions. Titles unique to the Irish market include *U*, *IT (Irish Tatler)*, *Social & Personal* and *Image*. The latter is worth mention for its *Hello!*-type social pages. If someone you've never met before suddenly gives you the I-am-of-the-glitterati eye, make your excuses, get to the newsagents, and scour the back pages for their picture. If you don't find it, go back and give 'em the no-you-ain't finger.

For well-researched, readable insights into Irish money matters, read *Business and Finance*; but if buying and selling brings to mind clocks and wares more than stocks and shares, try Ireland's *Buy and Sell*. For bright, light gossip and an all-channel TV and radio guide, get the *RTÉ Guide*; for more personal angles on less chirpy social issues, support those in need by getting the *Big Issue*. For satire you might be better off asking the newsagent what he thinks of tax on magazines than actually buying *Phoenix*, though the covers are always worth checking out. Finally for comprehensive, in-depth coverage of what's current in Irish literature and cinema, look no further than *Books Ireland* and *Film Ireland* or *Film West* respectively.

Television

If watching TV is your idea of a good holiday in Dublin, you're not going to find too much indigenous programming to support your heavy cultural habits. The state channel RTÉ (Radio Telefís Éireann) relies on a mixture of safe programming, from homegrown and international comedies, through sport, to a constant stream of three-year-old blockbuster films. A lot of the quality dramas are imports from the US or the UK, although its news and current affairs shows often hit the mark. RTÉ likes to play it safe and in fairness, when 90 per cent of your programming budget goes on

producing the Eurovision Song Contest every year, there's not an awful lot left for anything else.

RTÉ1 There's nothing challenging here, and rarely anything controversial. Daytime is aimed at the under-eights and the over-eighties; *Live At Three* (and dead by ten past) is the staple of afternoon viewing, offering useful tips on what to do with those old pieces of string you find under the sofa, while if you missed *Upstairs Downstairs* or *Dallas* the first (or tenth) time around, now's your chance to catch up. Primetime programming isn't much better; the only worthy mention is *The Late Late Show*, a regular Friday night marathon chatshow, hosted by national institution Gay Byrne, which has been running continuously since three years before the dawn of time. While countless important events and interviews have taken place on *The Late Late* over the years, it's growing as stale as Gay and has, in recent times, unfortunately favoured back-slapping over controversy. Still, it remains compulsive viewing with a lot of people as there's always the chance of someone famous putting their foot in it, or someone you always trusted giving the game away and admitting they've been at the altar wine for years.

Network 2 More of the same, but with repeats and Aussie soaps. The two most popular homegrown shows are soaps: *Glenroe*, a rural village full of half-wits arguing over fields and cows, and *Fair City*, its urban equivalent dealing with even tougher issues, but still diluted for taste. Still, Network 2 did bring in imports such as *The X Files*, *Ellen* and *Friends* which they run one season ahead of Britain's Channel 4, so it's not all bad.

Teilifís na Gaeilge A brand new Irish-language station, operating for a few hours from six until midnight, offers some homegrown programming, plus a few dubs. A good idea, but it's taking some time to find its feet. And as there are no subtitles, only about 1 per cent of the population understand a word of it.

Radio

There are four main radio stations operating in Dublin. RTÉ Radio 1 (FM 88.2-95.2 MHz, MW 567, 729 KHz) works on a mixture of news programming, sport, and phone-in talk shows, while 2FM (FM 90.4-97 MHz, MW 612, 1278 KHz) aims more at young people, with pop/rock programmes during the day, and the ever reliable *Hotline* request show at 7pm. RTÉ FM3 (FM 92.6-102.7 MHz) is for the dads in the audience, with live link-ups to the National Concert Hall and other classical events. The baby of the pack is Radio Ireland (FM 100-102 MHz) which is getting more and more popular, particularly its *Last Word* with the ever-controversial Eamon Dunphy when you're driving home, while Donal Dineen's late-night music show is probably the best around.

Music: Classical & Opera

After the Dublin début of Handel's Messiah, things all got a bit quieter. Until recently, that is.

Let's begin with a few small, innocuous but startling facts. Dublin is among a tiny minority of European cities and the continent's only capital not to possess its own Opera House. Until the early 1980s, the two national orchestras were scandalously forced to camp out in a grossly inadequate ballroom venue until someone belatedly got the bright idea of providing a dedicated concert hall. And indigenous composers, until recently, received treatment that in less enlightened countries would be reserved for enemies of the state. Even now, a music aficionado might survive even the most rigorous dinner party anywhere in the world without being prevailed upon to drop the name of a single Irish composer of any era.

But despite the many obstacles to be overcome – including the Irish nation's perception of itself as an exclusively literary people and the stubborn after-effects of colonialism – there have been a few glimmers of hope. After years of wanton neglect, the Arts Council is now providing financial encouragement to composers. The festival scene is booming throughout the country, with the Wexford Festival Opera, one of the most unique operatic events in the world, leading the way. Sparkling alternatives to the staid national institutions are now being provided by innovative companies such as the **Opera Theatre Company** and **Concorde Ensemble**. Plans are even being touted for an extensive £40 million 'performing arts and music centre' to be built in the Dublin docklands as a millennium project. If it goes ahead, Dublin will finally have an opera house in all but name.

TICKETS

It is infinitely easier to book a ticket through any of Dublin's agencies for London's Covent Garden or the Bastille in Paris than it is for music events taking place locally. Beyond the occasional visit by an international company or star, the city's agencies provide almost nothing at all. One minor exception is the RTÉ Proms, tickets for which can be obtained at the ticket desk at HMV (open daily) on Grafton Street (679 5334/Ticketline 456 9569) or from Ticket Shop (677 9409).

The majority of purchases must be made through the venues themselves. Since concerts rarely sell out, this is a fairly straightforward operation, even on the night of the performance. Prices range from £3 for a lunchtime concert at the National Concert Hall, to a maximum of around £15 for an evening performance of orchestral music. Opera tickets in the city cost between £9 for a perch in the gods and £44 for a prime seat in the stalls.

Principal institutions

National Symphony Orchestra of Ireland

Like the overwhelming majority of Ireland's orchestral groups, the National Symphony Orchestra, which was founded in 1926 to provide music for radio broadcasts, is run by the country's radio and TV station, Radio Telefís Éireann. And while the huge contribution that RTÉ has made to Irish musical life must be acknowledged, it is also obvious that the orchestra has suffered greatly under the ad hoc care of an inflexible, bureaucratic organisation whose primary business is to produce TV and radio programmes. The result has been an orchestra largely made up of world-class musicians but afflicted by erratic management. The repertoire of the NSOI is a curious balance of popularity and perversity, where Rossini overtures are pitted against such unlovely curiosities as Ravel's *Tzigane*. Only under the baton of dynamic Russian conductor Alexander Anissimov does the orchestra realise its full potential. Anissimov has recently been appointed the next principal conductor to succeed the Dutchman Kasper de Roo, whose tenure has been marked by some blistering reviews. This could mark a new beginning for the troubled orchestra. For programme information, contact Eleanor Collier on 208 2773.

Opera Ireland

Founded in 1941 and known until recently as the Dublin Grand Opera Society, this is as close as Ireland gets to a national opera company. For many years, the society served up near-concert performances of nineteenth-century Italian favourites. Astonishingly, the semi-professional chorus were often joined during this 'golden' period by budding superstars such as Placido Domingo, José Carreras, Kiri Te Kanawa and Pavarotti, who made his international debut here in a 1963 Grand Opera Society production of *Rigoletto*. Only in the mid-1980s did the company begin to transform itself into a professional outfit. However, rabid conservatism – on the part of audiences *and* the Opera Ireland personnel – continues to cripple the repertoire, where the inclusion of Verdi's *Macbeth* or Britten's *Peter Grimes* is considered daring. Sets, stars and costumes are a pick 'n' mix affair selected from the supermarket shelves of Europe's opera houses. The company play two pitifully short seasons, each of only nine performances, every autumn and spring, both of which are staged at the Gaiety Theatre (*see below*). For programme information, contact Opera Ireland on 453 5519.

Opera Theatre Company
Founded in 1986, this is one of the few luminaries in Dublin's dull, grey operatic firmament. Under the careful guidance of crusading artistic director James Conway, their scaled down productions (often referred to as semi-stagings and sometimes accompanied only by a piano) have championed contemporary Irish composers through two seasons of specially commissioned new short operas. They have also carefully excavated some lesser-known works of Handel, overwhelming critics worldwide with their lean, imaginative productions of the composer's *Amadigi*, *Flavio* and *Tamberlane*. OTC strive to put on at least two or three new productions in Dublin every year at various venues. For programme details, contact OTC on 679 4962.

RTÉ Concert Orchestra
Though the Concert Orchestra suffers many of the management problems of its big sister, the effects are cushioned by the less ambitious slant of its programming and by its clearly defined role as a broadcasting outfit. Due to Ireland's astonishing (and faintly embarrassing) winning streak in the Eurovision Song Contest, the orchestra has regularly been called upon to play to television audiences of 30 million. The Concert Orchestra can also be regularly heard at the National Concert Hall playing anything from Brahms, Prokofiev and Britten to Andrew Lloyd Webber. For programme information, contact Eleanor Collier on 208 2773.

Principal auditoria

Gaiety Theatre
South King Street, Dublin 2 (677 1717). All cross city buses. **Credit** AmEx, DC, MC, V (60p booking fee).
Opera Ireland's regular venue is a shambling nineteenth-century theatre that is highly unsuitable for the demands of a modern opera company. Apart from the general shabbiness of the auditorium, the stigma attached to a venue which devotes the rest of the year to a mish-mash of musicals, pantomime and stuffy straight theatre may be instrumental in driving away younger audiences.
Disabled: access.

Hugh Lane Gallery
Charlemont House, Parnell Square North, Dublin 1 (874 1903). DART Connolly Station/all cross city buses. **Open** 9.30am-6pm Tue-Thur; 9.30am-5pm Fri, Sat; 11am-5pm Sun. **Closed** Mon. **Admission** free.
This ample hall in the Hugh Lane Municipal Gallery on one of Dublin's most beautiful Georgian squares hosts about 25 contemporary music concerts annually on Sunday afternoons which have the added bonus of being totally free of charge. Concerts held between Sept-June; see local listings for programme details. (*See also chapters* **Art Galleries** and **Museums**.)
Disabled: access.

John Field Room at the National Concert Hall
Earlsfort Terrace, Dublin 2 (475 1572). All cross city buses. **Open** box office 11am-7pm Mon-Sat. **Credit** AmEx, DC, MC, V.
The NCH's annex space has a capacity of 250 and hosts performances of chamber, jazz, traditional and vocal music. A versatile space that is marred only by its proximity to the main hall, meaning that concerts cannot take place in both simultaneously.
Disabled: access.

National Concert Hall
Earlsfort Terrace, Dublin 2 (475 1572). All cross city buses. **Open** box office 11am-7pm Mon-Sat. **Credit** AmEx, DC, MC, V.
Dublin's main venue for classical orchestral music was established in 1981, in the Great Hall of what was then University College Dublin. It still retains the bland flavour of a lecture hall, and reconversion has done very little for the flat, leaden acoustics of the space.
Disabled: access.

RDS Concert Hall
Royal Dublin Society, Ballsbridge, Dublin 4 (contact Sinéad O'Duinnin 668 0866). Buses 46, 57, 84.
Barn-like but fairly serviceable hall located in Ireland's main horse show-jumping arena. In its favour, the venue is large enough to accommodate a modestly sized opera company without soaking up the more intimate sonorities of a chamber music quartet. The concert hall hosts around 20 concerts a year.
Disabled: access.

Minor venues

The **Museum of Modern Art** in Kilmainham (671 8666) organises two concert seasons a year in an impressive annex hall which it also rents out to independent companies and ensembles.

The **Project Arts Centre** (671 2321) is better known as a dramatic venue but it also hosts a lively programme of contemporary music concerts, events which will be able to take full advantage of the theatre's new acoustically enhanced renovation.

The **O'Reilly Hall** (706 1713) at University College Dublin is regularly used for concerts by all the RTÉ orchestras.

Finally there is **St Stephen's Church**, locally known as the Pepper Canister (288 0663), which hosts a healthy programme of orchestral and choral concerts. In addition to this, matins and evensong are performed regularly along with the occasional choral event at both the magnificent Gothic **Christchurch Cathedral** (677 8099) and the equally impressive thirteenth-century **St Patrick's Cathedral** (475 4817), two of the most historic and beautiful venues in the city – the ideal way to combine the serious business of the tourist trail with a little musical pleasure.

Minor organisations

Concorde Ensemble
(information 091 522 867).
One of the most pioneering quartets working in Ireland, now celebrating more than 20 years together, the Concorde Ensemble plays exclusively modern music and particularly concentrates on work by the Irish composers John Kinsella, Seoirse Bodley and Nicola LeFanu. Concorde Ensemble's free concerts at the Hugh Lane Gallery rank among Dublin's classical music highlights.

*Majella Cullagh (soprano) and Harry Nicoll (tenor) of the **Opera Theatre Company** in Haydn's Life on the Moon.*

Irish Chamber Orchestra

(information 061 202620).
Originally, the ICO was the hobby of a number of musicians from the RTÉ SO who wanted to play a little chamber music in their spare time. Now relocated to the University of Limerick, but playing more Dublin concerts than ever before.

Rathmines & Rathgar Musical Society

Gaiety Theatre, South King Street, Dublin 2 (677 1717).
An almost legendary amateur group affectionately known throughout Dublin as the R&R. The society mounts Gilbert & Sullivan as well as popular musicals with a distinctive and endearingly unpolished approach. This is where Terry Wogan began his career, as a gondolier in *The Gondoliers*. Two seasons a year, one in the Gaiety, the other at the National Concert Hall. For further details, call R&R on 497 1577.

Vanbrugh String Quartet

(information from Eleanor Collier 208 2773).
Also run by RTÉ, the Vanbrugh String Quartet combine faultless musicality with a progressive outlook and perform up to 100 concerts per year around the world. Based in Cork, the quartet is the force behind the West Cork Festival of Chamber Music. The musicians are also committed to the work of contemporary Irish composers and play regularly in Dublin.

Choirs

Cór Na nÓg

(information from Eleanor Collier 208 2773).
RTÉ's youth choir Cór Na nÓg ('choir of youth') has been a breeding ground for many of Ireland's current crop of international-standard singers. Ten years in existence, their concerts meander from baroque to pop.

Goethe Institute Choir

(information from the Goethe Institute 661 1155 & chorus-master Cait Cooper 668 9932).
A very respectable choir made up of German-language students and other enthusiasts. Concerts take place two to three times a year and cover the usual choral repertoire of masses and Requiems as well as more offbeat works by the Irish composer Brian Boydell and other Irish contemporaries. Emphasis also on contemporary German composers.

National Chamber Choir

(information from Eleanor Collier 208 2773).
This is Ireland's only fully professional choir, performing numerous concerts throughout the year. Their repertoire extends from Seiber, Thompson and Samuel Barber all the way to Negro spirituals.

RTÉ Philharmonic Choir

(information from Eleanor Collier 208 2773).
The largest choir in Ireland, the Philharmonic is made up of part-time amateur singers and was founded in 1985. It covers the usual choral repertoire and also teams up with the National Concert Orchestra for less frequently performed or contemporary works. Made up of 120 singers.

Festivals & events

Dublin International Organ & Choral Festival

(information on 677 3066).
A biennial event due to be held again in June 1998. Provides lunch-time and evening concerts of organ, chamber and choral music with some master-classes thrown in for good measure. There is also an organ-playing competition.

Mostly Modern

Bank of Ireland Arts Centre, Foster Place, Dublin 2 (information from Brian Farrell 087 616391). DART Pearse Station/all cross city buses. **Admission** free.
A series of free lunchtime concerts at the Bank of Ireland Arts Centre with a particular emphasis on twentieth-century works. The repertoire of each concert usually revolves around a single musical theme, which in the past have included piano music from South America and flute music from Asia. Concerts take place approximately twice a month from November-April every year.

RTÉ Proms

(information from Eleanor Collier 208 2773).
An international feast of music run by RTÉ in mid-May which usually features a selection of local orchestras, leavened by one or two international names such as Lesley Garrett or Nigel Kennedy. Not much musical direction or even thought goes into the whole affair. Mostly an excuse for starved audiences to gorge themselves on a international celebrity. Tickets available from RTÉ and HMV.

Out-of-town festivals

Castleward Opera

An interesting opera festival which has been called by some a 'mini-Glyndbourne', mostly due to the location in an old stately home on the banks of Strangford Lough in Co Down, Northern Ireland, where it takes place in a converted stables. Repertoire includes Carmen and Lucia Di Lammermoor in miniature productions that can sometimes be inventive, vocally competent, but orchestrally challenged. Takes place in May. Details from 01232 661090.

Kilkenny Arts Week

(box office 056 52175).
Traditionally, the Kilkenny Arts Week has been the arts festival with the largest, most consistent and highest-quality classical music content. Recently, due to the careless loss of talented personnel, there has been a precipitative drop in musical standard. The festival, however, promises to reverse this unfortunate trend in the coming years.

Killiloe Festival

The festival takes place in July every year. An excellent chamber music festival in the tiny town of Killaloe in Co Limerick. Set up in 1996 by members of the Irish Chamber Orchestra, many of whom live in the minuscule, otherwise unremarkable town, the festival has quickly established itself as a music-making event with impeccable standards. In the past, the roster has featured international names such as the renowned Italian violinist Franco Gulli and the violist Bruno Guiranna. Tickets from the ICO (061 202620).

Two Cathedrals Festival

A remarkable choral festival which takes place in Londonderry every October, bringing together the Catholic congregation of St Eugene's Cathedral and the Protestant congregation of St Columb's Anglican Cathedral in a cross-community cultural and musical event, uniting choirs from across the religious divide. Details from 01504 377266.

West Cork Chamber Music Festival

This festival, though begun only in 1996, has established itself as one of the more enterprising in Ireland. The international line-up of musicians is invited to rehearse in Cork for one week prior to the event, allowing for relationships to develop between the musicians and to dispel the 'fly-in, fly-out' haste that is evident in most festival appearances. Information and tickets from 027 61105.

Wexford Festival Opera

(See **Wexford Festival Opera** *facing page.)*

Wexford Festival Opera

The Wexford festival was set up in 1951 by a local doctor and avid opera lover named Tom Walsh. Since then, the festival has become a fixture on the international opera calendar and has developed into a forum for rediscovering works that have toppled from the repertoire.

Apart from supplying opera critics with more than the occasional gem, the festival has been credited with helping to open out and diversify the operatic repertoire worldwide and has been instrumental in reviving the fortunes of Donizetti and Rossini. Three works are produced each year with the help of some of the best of Irish young talent, a surprisingly good, local semi-professional chorus and international stars on the beginning of the upward curve of their meteoric careers – Mirella Freni, Mattiwilda Dobbs and Heather Harper all performed here while still relatively unknown. Of the three operas performed, at least two are usually hurled unceremoniously back into the void, leading some playfully to dub Wexford a 'Festival of Failed Opera'.

Almost as important as the music is the spirit of the town itself, legendary for its hospitality and its ability to party around the clock. There is also a little-documented but thriving gay scene at the festival when all of Ireland's opera queens come out to play for the biggest operatic campfest of the year.

The Wexford Opera Festival takes place in the last two weeks of October, running into the beginning of November. Tickets cost £40; £50 on gala nights. Recitals and concerts cost between £5-£12. Telephone the box office on 053 22144. **Credit** MC, V.

Music: Rock, Folk & Jazz

From sean nós to shamrock 'n' roll.

Time was when a teenager could go off to a first gig and, for a quid or so, catch a few local bands, all hopeful youngsters, on a Saturday afternoon and still be home for tea. Things have changed. Dublin's live music circuit remains vibrant, with new generations of hopefuls coming along every few years. But, as a place where music really matters, Dublin has inevitably absorbed the changes brought about by the triumvirate of grunge, dance and, latterly, Brit-pop/rock. It's now possible to have the best of all worlds as musical barriers have shifted. These days, a club night hosted by a recognised local or international DJ is a gig. Musicians of all permutation and definition proliferate. Ticket sales are up and the standard, variety and volume (pun intended) of live music in Dublin has never been better.

Just about every international act from every genre puts Dublin on their touring schedule these days as a matter of course. There's a thriving local scene too, and, between the two, every taste is catered for. Bigger gigs still happen outdoors in the RDS and indoors at the Point, but with the wider variety available, the need for good mid-size venues has increased, so the likes of Whelans and the Olympia are taking an increasing slice of the cake. No doubt their provision of facilities – like relatively clean toilets, bar extensions and a view of the stage – aren't hindering their success, either.

The only 'problems' in putting together listings are the sheer number of pubs and venues that do occasional live music, and the problem of categorisation. Dublin is still quite a small city and Dubliners have increasingly eclectic tastes, so many places quite rightly refuse to be pigeonholed. The best advice is to consult local guides when you get here. *In Dublin* and *Hot Press* are the local bibles, but the *Event Guide*, which is available free in shops and record stores around the city centre, offers an excellent and well-established listings guide which specifies the type of music being played in each venue on a particular night.

There have been some clouds on the horizon in recent times, as, increasingly, large, open-air gigs have been cancelled or scaled down in response to local pressure and ludicrous planning laws. Irish

crowds are generally impeccably behaved, so these restrictions are unprecedented and unreasonable. U2, one of Ireland's biggest exports, are leading the legal challenge, but it looks like the procedure – and a final result – will take some time.

One more thing. The tragic death of a teenager at a Smashing Pumpkins gig at the Point a while back has led to a major tightening of policy regarding behaviour at the big gigs. While in the middle of 40,000 or so people at the RDS, this can be difficult to enforce, at the Point, the 'no moshing or crowd-surfing' signs are not a joke; if you want to see acts in these venues, you'll have to respect the rules, regardless of your opinion of them.

But Dublin's live scene revels in its diversity. Whatever your preferences, you should have no trouble finding what you're looking for.

Major venues

While large sports grounds such as Lansdowne Road and Croke Park are occasionally used for big acts, the following are where you're most likely to see your idols these days. Dublin's quite lucky in that most of the regular big venues aren't actually that big, so atmosphere isn't always a problem. The Point and the Olympia both have box office facilities on site, but for these and the others, you can get tickets at outlets in HMV in Henry Street and Grafton Street, or in Sound Cellar on Nassau Street. The box office number for bookings is 456 9569, but for big events it gets jammed, so call early and keep calling. There's also a ticket shop in the Tourist Office on Suffolk Street (credit cards holders can call 605 7777).

National Stadium
145 South Circular Road, Dublin 8 (453 3371). Bus 19, 22, 22S. **Open** 7-10.30pm, depending on gig.
Admission varies. **Credit** MC, V.
The National Stadium is actually a boxing ring which the Irish Amateur Boxing Association leases occasionally to promoters when a gig will be by anyone who can fill its 2,200 capacity. It's all seated, with the ring converted into the stage (not quite as cool as it sounds), and, because it is not purpose-built, the quality is not exactly perfect. However, there have been some cracking gigs here by everyone from Youssou N'Dour to Buddy Guy. The all-round stage view tends to be pretty good.

Mass appeal

You don't have to spend long in Dublin to realise that the city is triangulated around certain names which appear constantly on the city's landscape. There's Joyce, whose literature mapped the city; Yeats, whose poetry encapsulated the passionate aspect of the nationalist romance; and there's U2, the rock band who have put modern Ireland on the map and have been described, with all due hyperbole, as the 'biggest band in the universe'. Their album sales, including *Boy, The Joshua Tree, Achtung Baby* and *Pop*, reach 17 million worldwide; Pop Mart, U2's current global tour, expects to play to six million before it ends in April 1998. It's also 1997's biggest tour, grossing $141 million in the US alone.

Intergalactic status aside, U2 are unavoidable. They own the city's swankiest hotel, the Clarence, and its best club, the Kitchen. The walls surrounding their studio at Windmill Lane bear the inscriptions of awe-inspired fans. Simply, U2 are to Dublin what the Beatles were to Liverpool and, considering their fans' fervour, Elvis to Memphis. City elders, too, have applauded the way in which U2 have promoted a vision of Ireland as an energetic, liberal nation, also stressing their economic importance. Two 1997 Lansdowne Road gigs raised some £10 million each for the local economy. U2 have come a long way since 1978 when singer Paul Hewson renamed himself Bono Vox after a hearing-aid shop on O'Connell Street and, with guitarist Dave Evans (to become The Edge), drummer Larry Mullen

and bassist Adam Clayton in tow, formed a band which, depending on your predilection, was named after a 1960s spy plane, a submarine or a type of Ever Ready battery.

The Project Arts Centre provided the venue for U2's début, and success was not overnight. But what U2, then a post-punk band influenced by David Bowie's glory years, lacked in style, they made up for in attitude. From the earliest years, U2 – half Catholic, half Protestant with a strong strain of charismatic Christianity present – were characterised by a passion which cut across political and sectarian boundaries.

Given Ireland's climate, this was to prove contentious: songs such as 'Sunday Bloody Sunday' – not a rebel song, Bono would emphasise – antagonised those who wanted the band to nail their colours to the mast. But their influence has been undeniable; a 1997 single, 'Please', has been greeted as a contribution to the peace initiative. Other songs have tackled issues surrounding sexuality and suicide. Detractors suggested that all this had more to do with the same egoism that had helped to play gigs in Sarajevo or raise millions for Band Aid, Amnesty International and, to benefit Irish charities, Self-Aid.

Whatever. U2 are one of the first bands to recognise their own position in the complications of a consumerist process, playing, at times, a mite uneasily with the messianic iconography it produces. A band who retain a capacity to surprise – what happens next is anyone's guess.

The Point – *a bit of a hike, both in terms of bar prices and the walk from the city centre.*

Olympia Theatre

74 Dame Street, Dublin 2 (677 7744/677 7124). DART Tara Street/all cross city buses. **Open** *evening shows 7pm; midnight shows 11pm.* **Admission** £10-£22. **Credit** MC, V.

Someone said recently that if you have to ask who's on at the Olympia's midnight show, you're missing the point. Ever since the late-night gigs began in 1987, they've featured everything from local blues bands to Björn Again to the Afro-Celt Sound System. They now do early-evening gigs, too, and between both time slots play host to an amazingly eclectic mix of acts. The earlier gigs are generally more established acts, but after midnight anything goes and literally every genre is catered for. It's a beautiful theatre with a state-of-the-art sound system and the seats can be removed downstairs for more of a mosh-pit atmosphere, although they're usually back for the midnight shows. There are bars (with a late licence for late gigs) on all three floors, and the views are pretty good, although the top-floor seats aren't very comfy, so they're probably best avoided, as are seats behind pillars, for obvious reasons. This is, without doubt, one of the city's best venues; even the bouncers have mellowed in recent years. Not to be missed.

The Point

East Link Bridge, Dublin 1 (836 3633/group bookings 836 6790). DART Tara Street or Pearse Station. **Open** 5pm-late. **Admission** £18-£30. **Credit** MC, V.

About a 20-minute walk from city centre, but watch out for special buses (or ferries!) for specific shows. Avoid taxis; traffic is usually so heavy, it's quicker to walk. The Point used to be a depot for storing trains and you can tell; the main, downstairs area is particularly barn-like, which can affect the atmosphere, as well as the sound quality. Capacity varies according to the acts, and downstairs seating can be re-arranged or removed altogether so, if possible, check for seating plans when booking. As well as boasting a large variety

of major pop and rock acts, it's also the city's main venue for musicals (*Riverdance* was staged here), but size restricts it from featuring anything too leftfield. Ticket prices on the high side and bar prices likewise, so be prepared. Fast food available on site.

RDS Showgrounds

Ballsbridge, Dublin 4 (668 0866/box office on site except on the day). DART Sandymount/bus 5, 7, 7A, 8, 45. **Open** 5pm-late. **Admission** £20-£30.

The longest-standing open-air venue in Dublin, this is actually a show-jumping arena and occasional football ground, with a capacity of about 30-40,000, depending on seating arrangements. Seats in the stands (which are more expensive) provide a better view than sitting or standing on the grass, but in the great tradition of the open-air gig, many people prefer to be in the thick of it. Video screens are occasionally used, most memorably for U2's Zoo TV tour, but don't count on them. Irish weather being what it is, a rain-coat can be an essential accessory, and expect some delays getting back into the city afterwards.

SFX Hall

23 Upper Sherrard Street, Dublin 1 (874 5227/no box office except on the night). **Open** 7-10.30pm. **Admission** £10-£20.

The St Francis Xavier Hall (to give it its full, and never used, title) is part of Dublin's rock history. U2 shot part of the video for 'Pride (In The Name Of Love)' here, and there have been gigs by both homegrown and foreign talent here for years. As the name suggests, it's an old community hall, has a capacity of about 1,500 and is, at best, a bit on the basic side. There's no bar (just fairly expensive water), toilet facilities are awful, and when it's full the walls sweat. All that said, the atmosphere can be fantastic. Gets a lot of heavy rock acts, as well as recent Britpop idols such as Kula Shaker or the *NME* Brat tour. The location is a bit dodgy, so be careful walking up there, as there are no direct bus links .

Pub & club venues

Eclecticism is the order of the day here, as venues jostle for custom and the best acts. The Mean Fiddler has a box office, and Whelans sometimes sells tickets in advance for high-profile gigs, which are at the usual outlets, but the majority of these are cash-on-the-night venues. There's a lot more on offer here than mere rock, too, so you'll need to keep a close eye on local listings, but these days, there is as much rock 'n' roll as you can get. Pub opening times are a bit odd here. Roughly, it's 11am-11pm Mon-Sat (staying open until 11.30pm during the summer) and either noon- or 4-11pm Sun (11.30pm in summer). Early houses open at 7am, but there are increasing numbers of late licences, so you may be able to drink until 2am.

Bad Bob's Backstage Bar
East Essex Street, Temple Bar, Dublin 2 (679 2992). Bus 12, 16, 16A, 65. **Open** 4pm-2.30am daily. **Admission** varies, usually free early evening.
A mid-capacity venue, features a middle-of-the-road mix of local covers outfits and rock bands. Quality quite good, if rather an acquired taste, but due to late licence and tendency to feature beer promotions and 'ladies free' offers, is usually heaving, so not a place to go for a mellow night out.

Barney Murphy's
40 Wexford Street. Dublin 2 (475 1931). Bus 55, 61, 62, 83. **Open** pub hours downstairs. **Music** 8.30pm.
Admission £3-£6.
This is a pub venue and features mainly Irish rock, blues and some folk acts with a smattering of international performers. Early in the week, it's local young acts, with more established artists taking the stage towards the weekend.

Break for the Border
Grafton Plaza Hotel, Johnson Place, Dublin 2 (478 0300). All cross city buses. **Open** pub hours until late.
Admission free.
Covers bands late nights Thur-Sat and 8.30pm Sat. Similar ambience to Bad Bob's.

Bruxelles
7-8 Harry Street, Dublin 2 (677 5362). All cross city buses. **Open** pub hours. **Music** 9pm. **Admission** free.
Features mainly local rock and blues acts about twice a week. Quality is variable, so at your own risk, but it's a great pub, so worth a visit anyway. Bruxelles keeps some late nights in addition to the standard band slots.

Charlie's Rock Bar
2 Aungier Street, Dublin 2 (475 5895). All cross city buses. **Open** pub hours. **Music** 8.30pm.
Admission £2-£5.
A brisk five-minute walk from Dame Street, Charlie's Rock Bar is one of the city's longest-standing rock venues, and has played host to a variety of local and international acts over the years. The Manic Street Preachers played their first Irish gig here way back in 1991, and the emphasis is still very much on the live-and-loud type of band. Big enough for a good vibe, not so big it cannot accommodate small acts. Occasional afternoon events, also.

The Da Club
3-5 Clarendon Market, Dublin 2. All cross city buses.
Open evenings-late night. **Admission** varies.
Bands, alternative cabaret and whatever else seems like a good idea. A change of management was imminent as we went to press, so check local listings.

Eamon Doran's
3A Crown Alley, Temple Bar, Dublin 2 (679 9114). All cross city buses. **Open** late licence.
Admission £3-£5; free before 9pm downstairs; free upstairs.
Formerly the site of Dublin's Rock Garden, this is now a different kind of franchise. There's Irish traditional music upstairs every night between 8-11pm and 5-7pm Saturday. There's also a strong policy regarding rock acts, both Irish and international. Rock music can be heard downstairs nightly between 9pm-midnight, also noon-6pm Sat and 4-7pm Sun. Saturday afternoon is a sort of open-mike session for young bands, and the third Thursday of the month features bands from Belfast. It's big for a pub venue, and there's music until 2am most nights after the bands have finished, so it's a good place to check for local talent.

Festivals

Cork Jazz Festival
Cork, Co Cork (information 021 270463). **Time** Oct bank holiday weekend.
Multiple venues, brilliant *craic*. Book accommodation early, as the city books out weeks in advance.

Galway Arts Festival
Galway, Co Galway. **Time** mid-July.
Although this is not primarily a music festival, there is usually at least one big gig, as well as other live music in the city over the weekend. Planning problems have meant alterations in venues for rock concerts, so check with the tourist offices in Dublin and Galway for all the up-to-date information.

Howth Jazz Festival
Howth, Co Dublin. DART Howth. **Time** Easter bank holiday. **Open** all day. **Admission** varies; many gigs free.
Every year, around the Easter bank holiday, the beautiful seaside town of Howth hosts one of Ireland's major jazz festivals. Just about every pub and hotel in town features bands from home and abroad, with lunchtime, afternoon and evening gigs taking place every day. The atmosphere is fantastic, and if the weather is good (which it is occasionally), you can sit outside the bars enjoying the drink, the music and the *craic*. One thing though, between bank holiday daytrippers, jazz fans and people just looking for a good night out, the entire town is likely to be thronged for the weekend, so if there's any gig you particularly want to see, make sure you go early. If you're driving, come even earlier, as parking spaces are almost impossible to get. Information on who's playing where is announced nearer the time; check the tourist office. (On the October bank holiday weekend there's also **Howth Live & Unplugged**; call 873 3199 for information.)

Temple Bar Blues Festival
Temple Bar & around. **Time** mid-July.
Admission varies, some free.
This has become a high-profile annual event, although the massive free open-air gigs at College Green, which in the past have featured Buddy Guy and BB King, seem to have been discontinued for now. Most of the pubs and clubs in the area feature acts for the festival. International acts are complemented by the big names in Irish blues and R&B. Always an event with plenty of atmosphere. Check the tourist office for details.

Foggy Dew

1 Fownes Street Upper, Dublin 2 (677 9328). All cross city buses. **Open** pub hours. **Admission** free.
There's rock, jazz and blues in the bar of the Foggy Dew every Sunday from 5.30-7.30pm.

The Funnel

24 City Quay, Dublin 2 (677 5304). DART Pearse Station or Tara Street. **Open** 8.30pm. **Admission** £5-£6; more for high-profile gigs.
Situated beside the City Arts Centre, this is a brand new venue at time of going to press, but initial reports are very good. The management have creative and exciting plans which include rock, salsa, folk, jazz, alternative cabaret and theatre. It's just the right size for an intimate gig and looks as though its star is very much on the bright side.

IFC Bar

6 Eustace Street, Temple Bar, Dublin 2 (677 8788). All cross city buses. **Open** late at weekends. **Admission** £4-£5 after 11pm; £2-£3 before.
High-quality blues and some jazz from midnight Fri, Sat in sophisticated surroundings. Recommended.

International Bar

23 Wicklow Street, Dublin 2 (677 9250). All cross city buses. **Open** pub hours. **Music** 9pm. **Admission** £2-£4.
Music upstairs Tue, Fri-Sun in this small, but very popular central venue situated one minute's walk away from Grafton Street. Music is mainly blues and soul from bands with long-standing residencies, but Tuesday is singer/songwriter night, and there's acoustic blues in the downstairs bar every Sunday lunchtime. Very well patronised, so come early to get a seat, because it should be worth it.

Mean Fiddler

Wexford Street, Dublin 2 (475 8555). Bus 15A, 15B, 15C, 20, 61, 62, 86. **Open** downstairs bar open all day; late until 2am. **Music** 8.30pm daily. **Admission** £3-£7.
The Irish branch of the franchise, this is a spacious venue that hosts an eclectic mix of Irish and foreign talent, including a young bands' night on Wednesdays. Admission to gigs usually incudes entry to whatever late-night club is on, so it's good value and the quality of acts is generally high. There's a bar downstairs with free DJ every night too, so well worth a visit.

Red Box

Old Railway Station, Harcourt Street, Dublin 2 (478 0210). Bus 15A, 15B, 15C, 20, 61, 62, 86. **Open** varies. **Admission** varies.
Relatively new club venue which features a wide range of acts. It seems rather lacking in atmosphere, but if it's where your favourite band is playing, you could do a lot worse.

Slatterys

129 Capel Street, Dublin 2 (872 7971). All cross city buses. **Open** 7pm daily. **Music** 9pm daily. **Admission** £4-£5 upstairs; free downstairs.
Another well-established venue, Slatterys has catered for Dublin's heavy rock fans for well over 20 years. The emphasis has mellowed in recent years from heavy rock to a more eclectic mix, but it's still traditionally perceived as a rock venue. These days, they have trad gigs downstairs most nights of the week, and both floors feature a mix of local and foreign talent, including new young band nights, so the quality is varied. It's an old fashioned, unglamorous type of place, a bit off the beaten track (to find it, turn off O'Connell Street on to Henry Street and walk for about 5-10 minutes), but worth it for the dedicated fan of pub music.

'How'ya?'

The relationships that Irish audiences tend to have with whatever acts they go to see – whether they're a local punk band or Tina Turner at Croke Park – are passionate, loyal and, at their best, unbeatable. Both REM and Radiohead have played their biggest gigs here in recent years; Michael Stipe likes the place so much he brought his parents over for the gig. David Bowie has played almost-legendary low-key gigs in tiny Dublin venues, while Garth Brooks has named a corner of his ranch 'The Point', in memory of the tremendous reception he got here at his first Irish concerts.

Rock stars like the capital so much that an increasing number of them are coming to live here. Joe Elliot of Def Leppard, Morrissey and Lisa Stansfield are just some of the stars occupying the millionaire belts along the coast of the country these days. They come for the relaxed atmosphere of the locals (we're way too self-important to mob people; we prefer to shout 'How'ya?' across the street and walk on), the fab social life and the handy tax-exile status. They are made so welcome that they tend to stay.

Mind you, if you're a hugely famous star, just in for a flying visit, or a rich tourist, you can sample the rock 'n' roll lifestyle by staying at the Clarence Hotel, owned by U2. If you're a mere mortal, there's always the Octagon Bar there for a pint. You'll notice that the Irish seem to make numerous references to U2 and visitors can find locals' attitude to the band a little puzzling. Publicly, the Irish are terrible begrudgers and certain sections of the press tend to give U2 a hard time but, regardless of what we say about them, we all have at least one of their records and their Irish gigs sell out in record time.

A city whose reputation has always been for rock, Dublin has finally produced a world-famous pop group in Boyzone. Aimed squarely at the pubescent female market, Boyzone are as far from U2 as it's possible to be. But despite the usual purists' griping, most of us are glad to see a local act make it as big on the pop scene as our other successes have in folk and rock. There are times when categories matter, and this is one of them; there's only the club music section left to conquer, and that's only a matter of time.

These musicians are getting into it on Grafton Street, but traditional music is played all over.

Temple Bar Music Centre

Curved Street, Temple Bar, Dublin 2 (764 9202). All cross city buses. **Open** varies. **Music** evening & late night. **Admission** £4-£5.

One of the newest venues in town, adaptable for seated and non-seated gigs. Features a very eclectic mix, from traditional Irish to dance and rock, local and international. Extensive recording and TV facilities; the Irish music programme *Sult* has been recorded here and they record every gig for their own DAT archive (as well as for the bands' benefits, too), so you could find that you've been part of a historic live recording. Nice bar off the main auditorium. Easy-going door policy, and both quality and atmosphere are good.

Whelans

25 Wexford Street, Dublin 2 (478 0766). Bus 55, 61, 62, 83. **Open** pub hours daily. **Music** 8.30pm. **Admission** £5-£8, more for high-profile gigs.

Another essential venue for visitor and local alike, Whelans features a highly eclectic mix of rock and roots in extremely congenial surroundings. The building itself dates back to the eighteenth century and, thanks to extensive renovation in 1989 which uncovered many original fittings, it's a good example of an old Irish pub, well worth a visit in itself. The venue is actually a converted warehouse at the back, and while it's relatively new, it's designed to complement the pub, and its own original use. There's a balcony upstairs, and murals from the Book of Kells downstairs, and it's impossible not to be impressed. This is the place to go to hear everything from Russian Gypsy bands, English folk and Irish trad to international rock, jazz and blues in a venue small enough for intimacy. Absolutely essential.

Traditional, folk & jazz

Dublin doesn't have quite the reputation for traditional music as the likes of Doolin in Clare or Gweedore in Donegal (which is where you'll hear Ireland's plaintive unaccompanied *sean nós* singing), but there's more than enough to occupy the folk fan here. The first thing to remember is that whereas 'traditional' (or trad) means Irish traditional music, 'folk' can have several definitions, from acoustic covers bands to the best of the British or American folk scenes.

Irish traditional music is played all over the city, generally for free, in far too many pubs to be listed here. Often the musicians are just in the background, and with such large numbers it's not always easy to predict quality. Keep an eye on local listings or even signs outside pubs. Visiting several can be a good idea, in more ways than one. Many of the venues listed above feature the bigger folk and traditional acts, as does the National Concert Hall (*see chapter* **Music: Classical & Opera**) occasionally, so don't limit yourself to this section for advice.

Dublin's jazz scene is small but well established, high quality and growing in stature. As above, the following venues are those which specialise, but good jazz can also be found in the bigger rock venues and even in the National Concert Hall.

Tivoli

135 Francis Street, Dublin 8 (454 4472/453 5998). Bus 21, 21A, 49, 49A, 54, 54A. **Open** 10.30pm until late daily. **Admission** from £5.

The downstairs section of the Tivoli Theatre complex, this used to be predominantly a rock venue, but latterly has transformed itself into a jazz/easy-listening lounge joint, with the emphasis on relaxing with a drink in cool surroundings. At time of going to press, this is still a new venue, so the jury is out on quality, but worth a look, if it sounds to your taste.

The Fleet
28 Fleet Street, Dublin 2 (679 8392). All cross city buses. **Open** pub hours daily. **Admission** free.
Trad in the bar Thursday night and Sunday morning.

Paddy Hannon's
117 James Street, Dublin 8 (679 8392). Bus 21, 21A, 78, 78A, 78B. **Open** pub hours daily. **Admission** free.
Trad and ballads in the bar Thur, Sat, Sun.

Mother Redcap's Tavern
The Liberties, Back Lane, Dublin 8 (453 8306). Bus 50, 78A. **Open** pub hours daily with late licence at weekends. **Music** evenings, Sun mornings. **Admission** free, except for benefit gigs upstairs.
This is a lovely, modern pub in the Christchurch area. Friday and Saturday evenings are mainly covers acts, while week nights and Sunday mornings are mainly for unplugged trad and folk sessions. Wide age group and room to roam.

Oliver St John Gogarty
58-59 Fleet Street, Dublin 2 (671 1822). All cross city buses. **Open** pub hours daily. **Music** 4.30-6.30pm, 9-11.30pm, Mon-Fri; 4-7pm, 9-11.30pm, Sat; noon-2pm, 4-7pm, 9-11.30pm, Sun. **Admission** free.
Centrally located pub and restaurant. Again, the quality is pretty good, and it's well worth a visit.

O'Shea's Merchant
12 Lower Bridge Street, Dublin 8 (679 6793). Bus 50, 78A. **Admission** free. **Open** 10.30am-12.30am daily. **Music** 9.30pm.
Large pub and restaurant that features live traditional music every night and set-dancing most nights, so worth checking out if you want an authentic trad experience and a meal.

Harcourt Hotel
60-61 Harcourt Street, Dublin 2 (478 3677/gigline 1850 664455). Bus 15A, 15B, 15C, 20, 61, 62, 86. **Open** 10.30am-11.30pm daily. **Music** 9.30pm Mon-Sat; 2pm Sun. **Admission** varies.
This is one of the premier trad venues in the city. The acts featured are well-established, nothing too leftfield, with an audience to match. They also feature jazz and pop/rock acts, so be sure to check listings or call the gigline, but trad is their principal attraction. There's also a nightclub, which follows gigs (closes 2.30am) but, again, view local listings for details.

Gaiety Theatre
South King Street, Dublin 2 (677 1717). All cross city buses. **Open** 11.15pm-3am Fri, Sat. **Admission** £6-£7.
Strictly speaking these are club nights, but they do feature live acts on the night and both are highly recommended. Mambo on Fridays features Latin, salsa and world music, while Saturday's Velure night resounds to jazz and soul.

The Norseman
29 East Essex Street, Dublin 2 (671 5135/679 8372). Bus 12, 16, 16A, 65. **Open** pub hours. **Music** 9pm. **Admission** £4 jazz; free trad.
Along with JJ Smyth's, this is *the* jazz venue in the city at the moment, as it's recently become the home of the Pendulum club on Mon, Tue, Sun. The standard is high, as the best jazz musicians in the country play to a dedicated audience. Also features trad in the bar downstairs on Sundays and upstairs Wed through to Sat. A lovely pub that's well worth a visit.

JJ Smyth's
12 Aungier Street, Dublin 2 (475 2565). Bus 12, 16, 16A, 55. **Open** pub hours. **Music** 8.30pm. **Admission** £3.
JJ Smyth's is one of Dublin's longest-standing jazz and blues venues, home to residencies by homegrown favourites such as Louis Stewart, who has a long-running residency. Also home to the Irish Blues Club on Mon. Small and informal.

Renards
33-35 South Frederick Street, Dublin 2 (677 5876). All cross city buses. **Open** evenings-late Wed-Sat. **Admission** free.
Live music for grown-ups in this piano and jazz bar.

New Orleans Restaurant & Jazz Club
Dame Street, Dublin 2. All cross city buses. **Open** restaurant hours. **Music** 8.30-11.30pm Fri, Sat.
Live jazz for soul food at (and here's a unique twist) a restaurant where you don't even have to eat.

Satchmo's
13 Parliament Street, Dublin 2 (671 3425). All cross city buses. **Open** 5pm-midnight Mon-Wed, Sat; noon-midnight Thur, Fri; noon-11pm Sun. **Music** 8.30pm nightly; 1pm Sun.
Jazz standards and swing music for diners at a restaurant which serves up a Tex/Mex and cajun menu.

Out-of-town venues

Since planning disputes have affected almost all large venues in and outside the city, festivals such as the Feile, Ireland's only serious rival to the likes of Glastonbury or Reading, haven't happened for a couple of years and are unlikely to return any time soon. In response to this, however, the number of one-day events and 'festivals' has increased and the following listings all host occasional gigs which are worth a visit, mainly during the summer months.

Millstreet, Co Cork
This is another show-jumping arena, and has hosted everything from the Eurovision Song Contest to Daniel O'Donnell and Van Morrison in recent years. It's a big venue, so all the usual precautions about arriving early apply.

Pairc ui Chaoimh
A big Gaelic football stadium in Cork; has hosted gigs by Michael Jackson and, more recently, Oasis.

Semple Stadium
At Thurles in Co Tipperary, this was the venue for the Feile festival, but now has to be satisfied with one-day gigs instead. The Semple is a large-capacity Gaelic football ground.

Slane Castle
Every couple of years (until the recent planning permission disputes), the natural amphitheatre in the grounds of Lord Henry Mountcharles' castle in Co Meath is the site for a concert by one of rock's seriously big acts. Neil Young, David Bowie and REM are some of the acts who've played here, to crowds of up to 80,000. The atmosphere is great but there are drawbacks: there's no motorway, and the sheer bulk of the traffic makes Slane Castle a bit of a nightmare to reach, and worse to get home from. Even if you get the special buses, be prepared for a very long day.

Sport & Fitness

Hang on to your front teeth – it's hurling time.

*Kilkenny's Pat Dwyer challenges John Leahy of Tipperary – **hurling** at Croke Park (see p179).*

Irish people are passionate about sport in all its forms and glories, so it comes as no surprise to note the sheer diversity which is available to visitors in the capital city. While some clubs are run on a strict membership-only basis, publicly owned facilities offer access to most sports at a reasonable rate. These facilities are provided for everyone's use, and cater for both the spectator and the participant. All you have to do is ask in order to enjoy the best of Irish sport.

Basketball

Basketball has become increasingly popular in recent years, particularly among Dublin's youth. As a result, outdoor courts can be found in most parks and these are available, free of charge, for public use. Just bring a ball and find yourself an empty court.

Bowling

Ten-pin bowling

A number of bowling alleys in Dublin are open to the public. Admission costs generally depend on the day and time requested: it's usually cheaper to bowl before 6pm on weekdays. Most of the alleys are part of the Leisureplex group and can be found spread across Dublin's suburbs.

The alley at Stillorgan is the oldest in Ireland and the venue for all the major competitions, including the Irish Open.

The following alleys are open 24 hours a day:

Leisureplex *Malahide Road, Coolock, Dublin 17 (848 5722). Bus 42, 43.*
Leisureplex *Village Green Centre, Tallaght, Dublin 24 (459 9411). Bus 49, 65, 65B, 77A.*
Leisureplex *Stillorgan, Co Dublin (288 1656). Bus 46A, 46B, 63, 84, 86.*

Outdoor bowls

Two outdoor bowling greens – **Moran Park** in Dun Laoghaire and **Herbert Park** in Ballsbridge – are reserved for public use on the southside of the Liffey and are maintained by the Corporation. **Kenilworth Bowling Club** (497 2305) is perhaps the most illustrious club in Dublin. Strictly members only, its grounds include two championship greens and a number of practice pitches.

Cycling

Cycling's enormous popularity in Ireland owes much to the international success of Sean Kelly and Stephen Roche. Domestically, the premier event is the **FBD Milk Race** which runs during the third and fourth weeks of May. This tour of Ireland traditionally begins in Dublin and ends with a criterium in the suburbs. Further information can be got from the Federation of Irish Cyclists (855 1522).

There are no indoor cycling arenas in Dublin, but the **Eamonn Ceannt Park** (679 6111) in Crumlin has an outdoor track run by the local corporation. Facilities are open to the public and are used by cycling clubs at certain hours, so it is worth phoning in advance to check availability.

For those interested in outdoor and rough-terrain cycling, the paths along Dublin Bay and tracks across the Wicklow Mountains provide pleasurable – although sometimes demanding – rides. Touring and mountain bikes can be rented from a number of locations at special one-day and weekly rates; prices range from about a daily £7 to a weekly £30. For a full list, check the *Golden Pages* under the heading 'Bicycle Hire'. However, if you're intending to cycle the historic streets of Dublin's city centre, take care. Some roads should be of a better quality and there are few cycle lanes.

Gaelic football & hurling

The Gaelic Athletic Association (836 3222) was founded in 1884, during the early years of the Irish cultural renaissance, with the intention of promoting indigenous games and so help to fashion a distinctive 'Irish' identity. In this regard, it shared much with the contemporary Gaelic League, which hoped to resuscitate the dying Irish language and celebrate native writing, music and dance (*see chapter* **History**). However, the GAA differed from the Gaelic League by concentrating on the traditions of Irish sport. It aimed to revive and modernise the ancient games of hurling, Gaelic football and handball by employing an agreed code of rules and electing a central governing body. Its success was instant and today the GAA is Ireland's largest amateur sports organisation, with over 2,000 clubs nationwide.

Games are played at club and inter-county level throughout the 32 counties, with the highlights including the **Railway Cup Final**, traditionally played on St Patrick's Day, and the **All-Ireland Hurling** and **Football Finals**, decided annually in the month of September (*see chapter* **Dublin By Season**). Principal games, semifinals and finals at all levels are played in the historic grounds of **Croke Park** – named in honour of Archbishop Thomas Croke, one of its first patrons. Croke Park also provides the headquarters for the modern GAA, from whom a full list of Dublin clubs, grounds and fixtures can be obtained.

At at least 2,000 years old, hurling (or hurly) claims to be Europe's oldest field game and it's possibly the fastest land sport in the world. It is played with a curved stick made of ash, called a camán, and a small, hard ball, called a sliotar. The sliotar is juggled on the blade of the camán, then struck, either on or along the ground or through the air, towards the opposing goal.

The ball used in Gaelic football is roughly the same shape and size as a soccer ball. However, one of the fundamental differences between the games is that Gaelic football permits players to use their hands. Players are not allowed to throw the ball, but must use their hands and feet to dribble, punch and kick the ball towards the opposing team's goal. As in hurling, the football team is made up of 15 players and matches last for two 35-minute periods. Points are scored by driving the ball between two posts: either under the crossbar for one goal (equal to three points) or over the crossbar for a single point. Minor hurling and football matches are played in most public parks from August to May, generally on Saturday afternoons. Those who hanker after the big game experience should try any of the following major grounds and senior GAA clubs.

Ballyboden St Enda's *Firhouse Road, Dublin 16 (494 7950).*
Croke Park *Jones Road, Dublin 3 (836 3222).*
Kilmacud Crokes *Stillorgan, Co Dublin (288 0857).*
Na Fianna *Mobhi Road, Dublin 9 (837 2010).*
Parnell Park *off Malahide Road, Dublin 5 (851 0650).*
St Sylvester's *Malahide, Co Dublin (845 0784).*
St Vincent's *Malahide Road, Dublin 9 (833 5722).*

Golf

Golf can sometimes appear to be an exclusive game in Ireland. Most courses are privately owned, and to play you need to be a member of a recognised golfing union and most have a handicap. Green fees vary substantially from course to course, but reservations and corporate bookings can be made. Further information, including a list of private golf courses, can be obtained from the Golfing Union of Ireland (269 4111).

There are a number of courses in the Dublin area which are owned by the local corporation, and which welcome visitors. They include **Sillogue**, **Elm Green** and **Stepaside**. Dublin Corporation also owns several pitch and putt courses in the suburbs (including **St Anne's** in Raheny), which are open to the public. Further information, including a full list of facilities, hours and rates on all municipal courses, can be obtained from the Corporation itself (834 7208).

The highlight in the annual golf calender is the **Murphy's Irish Open**. This four-day event, traditionally held in early July, attracts top professionals from all over the world.

Greyhound racing

Going to the dogs in Dublin is an all-year-round activity, with races held in two alternating venues. Further information can be obtained from Bord na gCon or Greyhound Board; this is the Shelbourne Park-based governing body which organises all the meetings. At both venues, the admission price includes a race programme.

Harold's Cross

151 Harold's Cross Road, Dublin 6 (497 1081). Bus 16, 16A. **Open** 8pm Mon, Tue, Fri. **Admission** £3; £2 students; 50p accompanied children. **No credit cards**.

Shelbourne Park

Lotts Road, Ringsend, Dublin 4 (668 3502). Bus 3, 7, 7A, 8, 45, 84. **Open** 8pm Wed, Thur, Sat. **Admission** £4 adult; £2 students; 50p accompanied children. **No credit cards**.

Gyms

Most gyms are privately run and require a year's membership for use of equipment. Spread across the city and throughout the suburbs, facilities typically include weights, exercise bikes, treadmills, steps and aerobic classes, plus saunas and sunbeds. Many hotels arrange deals with local fitness centres, and it is usually possible for their guests to negotiate a flat rate for work outs. Details can be obtained from your hotel, but it is advisable to enquire in advance of your stay.

Horse racing

Considering Ireland's fame the world over for the breeding and training of horses, it is scarcely a surprise that racing is so popular here. In Dublin, the thirst for the track has traditionally been slaked in a number of venues, of which perhaps the most beloved is Leopardstown. In addition, there are a number of other racecourses within easy reach of the capital.

The Curragh, Naas and Punchestown are three other famous racecourses situated south-east of Dublin, in neighbouring County Kildare. Easily accessible by road (N7) or rail, they provide the venues for both National Hunt and flat racing.

Leopardstown

Foxrock, Dublin 18 (289 3607). Bus 86; also a special bus on race days from Busaras. **Admission** £7-£13; free accompanied under-14s. **Credit** AmEx, MC, V (advance bookings).

When, on August 27, 1888, the first race meeting was held in Leopardstown (a town at the foot of the Dublin mountains whose original – and distinctly unexotic – name was Leperstown), a crowd of 50,000 Dubliners attended. Since then, it has occupied a special place in the hearts of Dublin race-goers. Situated just six miles south of the city centre, Leopardstown holds top flat and National Hunt races (a total of 23 meetings) all year round, including the Hennessy Cognac Gold Cup in February and the four days of racing of the annual Christmas festival which begins on December 26.

Fairyhouse

Fairyhouse Road, Ratoath, Co Meath (825 6167). Bus from Busaras on race days. **Admission** £6-£10. **No credit cards**.

Located just 12 miles north-east of County Dublin in the Royal County of Meath, Fairyhouse is home to an average of 15 days of racing each year. Of particular interest to race-goers is its annual Easter festival meeting – a three-day event which culminates in Ireland's premier steeple chase, the Jameson Irish Grand National and the Power Gold Cup on Easter Monday and Tuesday respectively.

The Curragh

The Curragh, Co Kildare (045 441 205). Train from Heuston Station. **Admission** £7-£10. **Credit** AmEx, MC, V.

The headquarters of Irish flat-racing, the Curragh hosts all five Classics (including the Airlie Coolmore Irish 1,000 Guineas, the Lexus Irish 2,000 Guineas and the Budweiser Irish Derby) and provides the venue with a further 13 days of racing.

Naas

Pipper Road, Naas, Co Kildare (045 897 391). Special bus from Busaras or train from Heuston to Sallins station then take a feeder bus. **Admission** £6, £7 (Sun); half price OAPs, students with ID. **No credit cards**.

This race-course in Kildare's county town provides a track for both flat and National Hunt racing from October to July. Naas enjoys a unique atmosphere in racing circles on account of the proximity of its crowd to the race and the parade ring: there is no reserved enclosure here.

Punchestown

Naas, Co Kildare (045 897 704). Special bus from Busaras. **Admission** phone ahead for prices. **Credit** MC, V.

The home of National Hunt racing in Ireland, Punchestown is the venue for the three-day National Hunt Festival meeting in the third week of April. The Festival includes the Grade 1 Heineken Gold Cup. Its 13-day calender also features a number of other Grade 1 meetings, including the MMI Stockbrokers Steeplechase in December.

Horse riding & show jumping

All riding schools near Dublin are open six days a week (closed Mondays), from about 9am to 6pm, and most also stay open late on two evenings through the week. Situated outside the capital in the suburbs and neighbouring counties, they all offer the ideal setting for relaxation and instruction, while remaining within easy reach of the city. The premier event in the Irish show jumping calender is, without doubt, the **Kerrygold Horse Show**. For further information, contact the Royal Dublin Society, or RDS, on 668 0866. (*See also chapter* **Dublin By Season**.)

Brennanstown Riding School
Kilmacanogue, Bray (286 3778). **Rates** £15; £13 children.

Cooladoyle Riding School
Newtownmountkennedy (281 9906). **Rates** £13; £10 children.

Cosgrove Shona
Skreen Road, Dunshaughlin (825 9842). **Rates** £10; £7 children.

Ice skating & inline skating

Dublin Ice Rink
Dolphin's Barn, South Circular Road, Dublin 8 (453 4153). **Open** 10.30am-1pm, 2.30-5pm, 7.30-10pm, daily. **Admission** £2.50-£4.
Open daily for sessions.

Silver Skate Ice Rink
North Circular Road, Dublin 7 (830 4405). **Open** 10.30am-1pm, 2.30-5pm, 7.30-10pm, daily. **Admission** £2.50-£4.
Admission charges vary (it's cheaper to skate in the mornings), but cover skate hire costs.

Rollerdome
Ballinteer Road, Dundrum, Dublin 16 (296 1199). **Open** 10am-11pm daily. **Admission** £3.
South of Dublin, the Rollerdome offers indoor facilities (including ramps) for those interested in inline skating and roller hockey. Blades, sticks and other equipment available for hire.

Jogging

With air pollution levels having decreased substantially in recent years, the streets of Dublin are once again a fine place for joggers. But, although the air might be better, the crowds and congestion often prove frustrating, and it's advisable for runners to head out of the city centre to calmer places. A number of parks in the greater Dublin area provide the space for a pleasant and, if required, arduous stretch. **St Anne's Park**, **Malahide Castle** grounds, **Phoenix Park**, **Herbert Park** in Ballsbridge, **Bushy Park** near Terenure, **Marlay Park** in Rathfarnham and **Tymon Park** in Tallaght are all attractive settings. Some have work-out stations along their trails. Furthermore, the beaches and coastal paths of Dublin Bay, together with the hill paths in the nearby Wicklow Mountains, offer scenic routes for the aerobically inclined.

The **National Athletics Stadium** (837 0278), just off the Old Airport Road in Santry, offers both indoor facilities and an outdoor all-weather championship track, and it is open to the public at certain hours during the day. Details can be obtained from the Stadium's office.

For information on the **Dublin City Marathon** and the **Women's Mini-Marathon**, two of the main events in the joggers' calender, *see chapter* **Dublin By Season**. A useful contact for joggers and athletes is Bord Luthchleas na hEireann or BLE (830 8925), which is the governing body for athletics in Ireland.

Karting

The thrill of racing can be experienced in a number of venues in Dublin. Specifically designed indoor circuits are run to the highest of safety standards and can be found at the following locations:

Kart City
Old Airport Road, Dublin 9 (842 6322). **Open** 11am-late daily. **Cost** £6-£30. **Credit** AmEx, V.
In all cases, race and practice sessions are charged by the time spent on the circuit; special Grand Prix and Championship meetings can be arranged for large groups. Children's karting is carefully supervised. It is advisable to book in advance, as corporate outings can sometimes book up an entire circuit. Kart City also offers an outdoor circuit, rough terrain karting and stock car racing.

Kylemore Karting Centre
off Naas Road, Dublin 10 (626 1444). **Open** 11am-late daily. **Cost** £6-£25.
(*See chapter* **Children's Dublin**.)

Phibsboro Karting Centre
Cross Guns Bridge, Dublin 7 (830 8777). **Open** 11am-late daily. **Cost** £6-£25.
(*See chapter* **Children's Dublin**.)

Rugby

Rugby has a historic pedigree in Ireland and some of the Dublin clubs are more than 150 years old. Unfortunately, because the game is concentrated in certain areas, it has gained some regrettable class connotations and, as a result, it can appear exclusive in manner. In Ireland, the rugby season runs between August and May, and is governed by the Irish Rugby Football Union (IRFU). The international game culminates in the **Five Nations Cup** tournament, with two matches being played at Lansdowne Road, the oldest international rugby ground in the world. Domestically, 14 senior clubs from Dublin compete annually – together with several other clubs from neighbouring counties – for the Leinster Senior Club. For a full list of fixtures and senior clubs, contact the IRFU (668 4601). Principal clubs and grounds in the Dublin area include:
Bective Rangers *Donnybrook, Dublin 4 (283 8254).*
Blackrock College *Stradbrook Road, Co Dublin (280 0151).*
Lansdowne *Lansdowne Road, Dublin 4 (668 9300).*
Old Belvedere *Anglesea Road, Dublin 4 (660 3378).*
Old Wesley *Donnybrook, Dublin 4 (660 9893).*
Wanderers *Lansdowne Road, Dublin 4 (668 9277).*

Skiing

Although Dublin might not be especially renowned on the international circuit for its winter sports, an artificial ski slope in Kilternan is the popular home of the **Ski Club of Ireland** (295 5658). This slope is open to the public during the skiing season (September-March) and all appropriate equipment can be hired on site. Further details available from the Ski Club.

Snooker & pool

Snooker and pool are played throughout the city in a number of clubs, halls and leisure centres. Of all these venues, the most famous is Jason's of Ranelagh, home to the 1997 world champion Ken Doherty. Many of these clubs are members only, while many more are always heavily booked, so it is worthwhile phoning in advance to check on the availability of tables. A full list of snooker clubs and pool halls can be found in the *Golden Pages*. Games generally cost between £2-£3.

Competitive snooker in Ireland is governed by the Republic of Ireland Billiards & Snooker Association (450 9850) and its top professional tournament is the annual Benson & Hedges **Irish Masters**, held at Goff's in County Kildare.

Soccer

Soccer is the most popular team sport in Ireland and recent years have seen appropriate developments in both the international and the domestic game. Qualification for consecutive World Cup Finals in 1990 and 1994, preceded by Ireland's historic qualification for the European Championships in Germany in 1988 (the first time the Republic had ever been represented at a major soccer tournament), has done much to enhance the country's reputation as a significant player in international soccer. It has also been responsible for providing unofficial national holidays and producing unprecedented states of hysteria and inactivity throughout the country.

During both World Cups, shops, businesses and transport services were abandoned throughout Dublin while the national team played. Through agreement between the Irish Rugby Football Union (IRFU) and the Football Association of Ireland (FAI), Lansdowne Road functions as the home ground for the Republic of Ireland's international soccer team.

On the domestic front, the game has always been in the shadow of the larger British clubs and many of the great Irish legends have all sought their fame across the water. Inevitably, the local game has suffered as a result. However, recent developments instigated by the FAI have done much to improve the quality of the domestic game,

its season running from August to May. During the summer months, most clubs also host friendly tournaments and entertain some of the bigger clubs from Britain and Europe.

For a full list of fixtures and clubs, contact the FAI on 676 6864. The Premier Division of the National League is represented in Dublin by the teams listed below. If you only have time to take in a single game, Shamrock Rovers are usually a good bet.

Bohemians FC *Dalymount Park, Dublin 7 (868 0923).*
St Patrick's FC *Richmond Park, Dublin 8 (454 6332).*
Shamrock Rovers FC *Spawell Leisure Complex, Dublin 6 West (492 5660).*
Shelbourne FC *Tolka Park, Dublin 3 (837 5536).*
UCD FC *Belfield Park, Co Dublin.*

Sports facilities for the disabled

Almost all of the venues and centres listed in this chapter have the appropriate facilities for disabled participants. However, it would be wise to call your chosen venue in advance to confirm its suitability. The following contacts may be of use:
Cerebral Palsy Sport Ireland *(269 5355).*
Irish Blindsports *(843 6501).*
Irish Deaf Sports Association *(495 6030).*
Irish Wheelchair Association *(833 8241).*
Special Olympics of Ireland *(450 1633).*

Swimming pools

At present, all of the swimming pools in Dublin are 25 metres or less in length, although this may soon change. Thanks to the success of Michelle Smith in the 1996 Olympic Games, the campaign for a full 50-metre pool has gained considerable momentum and plans are currently underway for providing such a facility in Dublin.

Most of the public pools are located in Dublin's suburbs, and are open daily for morning, afternoon and evening sessions. Admission generally costs between £2-£2.50 for adults and £1-£1.70 for accompanying children. In many pools, wearing a swimming hat is compulsory, and these are normally on sale at the ticket offices. As public hours vary from pool to pool, as well as from day to day, it is advisable to phone in advance for a full timetable. A list of pools can be obtained from the *Golden Pages*. The following pools are among the most popular:
Clondalkin Sports Centre *Nangor Road, Dublin 22 (457 4858).*
Glenalbyn Swimming Pool *Stillorgan, Co Dublin (288 1502).*
St Paul's College Swimming Pool *Raheny, Dublin 5 (831 6283).*
St Vincent's CBS Swimming Pool *Glasnevin, Dublin 9 (830 6716).*
Templeogue Swimming Pool *Templeville Road, Dublin 6 West (490 1711).*
Terenure College Swimming Pool *Templeogue Road, Dublin 6 West (490 7071).*

Sheltered from prevailing winds, Dublin Bay offers opportunities aplenty for the watersporty.

Tennis & squash

Most clubs are privately owned and you need either to be a member or to accompany a member to gain access. **Tennis Ireland** (668 1841) and **Irish Squash** (450 1564) can provide further information. A number of Dublin parks have courts which are open to the public. These include:
Albert College Park *Glasnevin, Dublin 9 (837 3891).*
Bushy Park *Terenure, Dublin 6 West (490 0320).*
Eamonn Ceannt Park *Crumlin, Dublin 12 (454 0799).*
Herbert Park *Ballsbridge, Dublin 4 (668 4364).*
St Anne's Park *Raheny, Dublin 5 (833 1859).*
Courts are open daily from 9.30am-8pm (closing earlier in winter) and can be rented by the hour.

Water sports

Sailing

The large harbour of Dun Laoghaire and the attractive peninsula of Howth are both serviced by major yacht clubs with very strong traditions. Unfortunately, most sailing in these clubs is strictly for members only and it is impossible for a member of the public to charter a yacht. However, a number of sailing schools offer courses at beginner, intermediate and advanced level; these are open to all. These include:

Dolphin Offshore Sailing Group
Malahide Marina (832 3938).

Fingall Sailing School
Upper Strand, Malahide (845 1979).

Irish National Sailing School
West Pier, Dun Laoghaire Harbour (284 4195).
The Irish National Sailing School provides intensive training courses in sailing for adults (£110) and children (£96). These courses are run throughout the year to the highest levels of international seamanship standards and include ample time on the water.

Irish Sailing Association
3 Park Road, Dun Laoghaire (280 0239).

Water skiing

Irish Water Ski Federation
(285 5205).
Although the IWSF recommend that all who ski should join an affiliated club, thereby sustaining safety and training levels, visitors are welcome to many clubs in Ireland. Life-jackets, wet-suits and other equipment can all be hired and challenging courses are frequently available for the more advanced skier.

Windsurfing & canoeing

From May to September, courses are available in windsurfing across Dublin Bay. A six-hour intensive course, spread over three two-hour sessions, generally costs about £59, with a further £10 covering rental of equipment.

Although the east coast is not renowned for canoeing (enthusiasts generally prefer the rivers Shannon and Barrow), both Surfdock and Wind & Wave offer courses by agreement in canoeing throughout the summer months.
Fingall Windsurfing *Malahide (845 1979).*
Surfdock Windsurfing *South Docks (668 3945).*
Wind & Wave Watersports *Monkstown (284 4177).*

Theatre, Dance & Comedy

Bards and the boards. The city of Synge, Shaw, Beckett... and Riverdance and Ardal O'Hanlon.

The best way to discover what's on and what's good is always to check the *Dublin Event Guide*, free and available from most cafés and bars around the city centre. *In Dublin* and the *Irish Times* are also reliable. Most of the theatres and companies are very good about producing clear publicity leaflets, which can be found in tourist centres, hotels, bars and cafés. The *Golden Pages* directory has a useful theatre information section, complete with diagrams of seating arrangements. Unless otherwise stated, all theatres accept major credit cards and have wheelchair access.

Theatre

Dublin has long been a city of playwrights and, accordingly, theatre has a high profile here. Aside from the established, full-time theatres, there exist a host of occasional and shifting venues which regularly double as stages. Everywhere you look there are performances; one can see street plays at lunch-time with soup and sandwiches, on bus tours of the city, or over a quiet pint in the evening. Since the early days of the Abbey, Ireland's National Theatre, the stage has been an obvious testing-ground for any change or distortion in Irish life. It is an immediate and public baptism for any confrontational or unconventional ideas or images, and reactions to what appears on it have traditionally been vociferous.

In the last few years, writers such as Frank McGuinness (who won three Tony Awards for his version of *The Doll's House*), Sebastian Barry and Martin McDonagh, the incredibly prolific young author of *The Cripple of Innishman* and *The Leenan Trilogy*, have ensured that Irish theatre continues to sustain and deserve the attention it receives, while upholding its honourable tradition of confrontation.

Dublin stages offer a dynamic and competitive blend of established and new material. It is possible, particularly during the summer months, to catch expensive productions of the milestones of Irish theatre in many of the mainstream theatres,

such as the Gate, the Gaiety, or the Abbey. The plays which established the good name of Irish drama and on which these theatres have built their own reputations are still performed, and are frequently flattered with new, attention-grabbing interpretations.

Alongside this constantly visible canon of Irish classics, there is also a reliable supply of highly energetic and entertaining work from a handful of ambitious young theatre companies who have proved themselves while performing both new and existing work.

Major venues

The Abbey

26 Lower Abbey Street, Dublin 1 (456 9569 ticket shop/878 7222 box office). All cross city buses. **Ticket shop open** 24 hours daily. **Admission** £8-£15; £6 concs Mon-Thur only; £8 previews. **Credit** MC, V (advance bookings).

Ireland's National Theatre, set up in 1904 by WB Yeats and Lady Gregory in order to produce plays for, about and by Irish people. Throughout the golden age of Ireland's literary autonomy, the Abbey was its brightest star. Under Yeats' direction, it showed unexpected and unusual visions of Irishness as they appeared in the newest work of frequently unpopular playwrights such as JM Synge, whose *The Playboy Of The Western World* caused riots among audiences unable to stomach its depiction of brutal and licentious Irish men and women. Sean O'Casey's *The Plough And The Stars* got a reception which caused Yeats personally to berate the audience, who were loudly objecting to this version of 1916 – the heroic, though doomed, struggle for independence from Britain – shown as the idiotic work of drunkards and bully-boys, against the backdrop of a callously looting Irish public. The Abbey is still a very reliable source of Irish drama; production values are always high and it frequently both launches and plays host to the country's most famous actors. There is a good policy of using the space to its fullest advantage, staging lunchtime seasons showcasing new writers, one-act plays (tickets £3-£4) and lectures by writers. The only drawback is the acoustics, which remain poor, despite the rebuilding of the theatre in the 1960s. Shows run for six to seven weeks.

Andrew's Lane Theatre

9-13 Andrew's Lane, Dublin 2 (679 5720). All cross city buses. **Admission** £10-£12; £6-£7 previews. **Credit** MC, V.

One of few specifically commercial theatres in Dublin, Andrew's Lane is a seasoned venue for provincial-based

Theatre Festivals

Children's Season

Children's Cultural Centre, The Ark, 11A Eustace Street, Temple Bar, Dublin 2 (670 7788). All cross city buses. **Admission** £2-6; group booking discounts. **Credit** AmEx, DC, MC, V.

Running alongside the Dublin Theatre Festival, the Children's Season provides child-orientated performances from international and domestic companies who use tumbling, mime, animation, dance, music and puppets to hold the interest of their audience while they tell their stories. Adults forced to accompany a child will find it no hardship. The programme is issued in September and a copy of this can be sent anywhere in the world, free of charge. Showtime is virtually all the time: performances are given during schooltime, evenings and weekends. For information contact the Dublin Theatre Festival box office (677 8439) or the Ark itself.

Dublin Theatre Festival

47 Nassau Street, Dublin 2 (677 8439/fax 679 7709). **Admission** £8-£16; previews less 20%. **Credit** AmEx, DC, MC, V.

Having celebrated its fortieth anniversary in 1997, Dublin's annual theatre festival – held in mid-October across a variety of city venues – has become Europe's biggest theatre-dedicated showcase and, founded just before Edinburgh's Festival, is the elder of the two. And, flushed with the success of 1997's festival (which presented, among others, works by Robert Lepage, Cirque Plumes and Spalding Gray), it's getting bigger. Foreign companies comprise some 40 per cent of Dublin's festival, and recent visitors include the Moscow Art Theatre, the Tokyo Globe and, from Britain, the Royal Shakespeare Company and Royal National Theatre. Always a champion of new Irish writing, it also showcases a wide variety of of large-scale, international acts. But it's the Irish content that's the highlight. In previous years, many productions have been snapped up by international festival directors (who attend expressly for this purpose), so this is an excellent opportunity to see the cream of the crop at its freshest. The festival programme is available from late August and arrangements can be made to have one posted to anywhere in the world by contacting the festival office. Booking begins three weeks before the festival's opening and this can be done by phone or by dropping into the office. Nearly all shows can be booked just days in advance. The venues are all major Dublin theatres, although occasionally special arrangements will be made for particularly large shows or those with unusual requirements.

E-mail: dubfest@iol.ie
Web site: http://www.iftn.ie/dublinfestival

Fringe Festival

Halfpenny Court, 36-37 Lower Ormond Quay, Dublin 1 (872 9016/872 9138). **Admission** £4-£8. **No credit cards**.

Expanding as rapidly as Dublin's main theatre festival, this one is dedicated to providing a focus on the new companies, doing new material or new interpretations. The emphasis is on the unusual, innovative, avant-garde and, most of all, fun. It is frequently a forum for established companies who wish to break out into something more outrageous than their usual wont. Shows are chosen for inclusion on the bases of their production and entertainment values, then performed in a variety of off-beat venues: galleries, cafés, pubs and clubs are all roped in. The festival includes dance, comedy, cabaret and music but concentrates on (mainly Irish) theatre, although a few international shows always find their way in. The festival runs for three weeks, the last two of which coincide with the Dublin Theatre Festival and an information office opens for its duration. The location of this office is confirmed and the programme made available at the beginning of September. The festival has a low ticket-price policy, shows usually run for one week and tickets are usually only obtainable 30 minutes before the show. Anyone wanting more information (or even wishing to submit a proposal and pitch an idea), should contact the Dublin Fringe Festival directly.

Web site: http://indigo.ie/~fmk/fringe/

Guinness Festival Club

Open 11pm-2am every night of theatre festival. **Club membership** £20.

Really an excuse for a late-night drink up, the Guinness Club runs, as its name suggests, as a post-performance event during the theatre festival. Venues are announced soon after the theatre festival itself publishes its programme, and club membership is available from the festival box office. An opportunity to rub shoulders with the festival's movers and shakers, but the entertainment is what you yourselves make.

---

companies touring nationally, and international acts, both dramatic and musical. The building itself may be unattractive, but the shows are well-established and entertaining. Runs of variable length.

The Samuel Beckett Centre

Trinity College, Dublin 2 (608 2266). All cross city buses. **No credit cards**.

Newly added and boasting the most beautiful setting in Dublin, this theatre caters for drama students but also manages to attract many of the most interesting shows around, both theatre and dance. Ticket prices are very variable.

Crypt Arts Centre

Dublin Castle, Dame Street, Dublin 2 (671 3387). All cross city buses. **Admission** £5-£7. **No credit cards**.

Worth a visit for its location alone in Dublin Castle, former centre of the British colonial administration. The theatre is in the old church crypt and has all the atmosphere one would expect. Used by many of Dublin's younger companies and well-liked for its intimate size and elegant appearance.

Focus 6

6 Pembroke Place, off Upper Pembroke Street, Dublin 2 (660 7109/676 3071 bookings). All cross city buses. **Bookings** 9am-noon Mon-Fri; 10am-7.30pm Mon-Sat. **Admission** £6-£8; £5 previews. **No credit cards**.

An institution in Irish theatre life. Small but serious; non-commercially minded, high-profile and unchanged. It has been run for the past 30 years by Deirdre O'Connell, whose actors' studio, based on the Stanislavsky method, turned out Gabriel Byrne, Jayne Snow and Tom Hickey. The theatre's hallmark lies in unearthing strong, usually modern, plays from Europe and America, often never before seen in Ireland and usually directed by O'Connell herself. Shows last four to six weeks.

Gaiety

South King Street, Dublin 2 (677 1717). All cross city buses. **Bookings** 11am-7pm. **Admission** £7-£17.50; £7-£12 previews. **Credit** MC, V.

With its lusciously designed auditorium and foyer, the Gaiety is a receiving-house for tried and tested entertainment of every sort – from classic Irish plays to West End shows, operas, pantomimes, concerts and all traditional variety acts. An excellent place to catch some of the more alternative international touring acts, although it steers clear of experimental Irish theatre. Shows run for two to three weeks and ticket prices can vary considerably.

The Gate

1 Cavendish Row, Dublin 2 (874 4045 & 874 6042 box office/874 4368 group bookings). All cross city buses. **Admission** £12-£14; £9 previews. **Credit** MC, V.

Founded by Micheál MacLiammóir and Hilton Edwards, who together formed a dazzling creative partnership which substantially enriched the stock and quality of Irish drama, and whose flamboyant personal relationship blatantly mocked the homosexuality laws of the time. Their legacy is the Gate, housed in an opulent eighteenth-century building leased from the Rotunda Hospital, with an intimate stage and a democratic auditorium (no pillars, no balcony, no boxes) that is beloved of actors and audience alike. The Gate forged itself a reputation for great daring early in its career – one of the first plays performed there was Oscar Wilde's *Salome*, banned in England at the time. Since its conception, it has been highly cosmopolitan. Both Orson Welles and James Mason made their acting débuts here; it has traditionally shown predominantly European and American dramas (Frances McDormand is appearing in *A Streetcar Named Desire* in Spring 1998), and its Irish content is distinctly Anglo. It has become rather more conservative in recent years, but production values are very solid and performances reliable. Shows run for about eight weeks.

The Lambert Puppet Theatre

5 Clifton Lane, Monkstown, Co Dublin (280 0974/280 1863). DART Monkstown or Salthill/bus 7A, 8. **Open** Sat only. **Admission** £4. **No credit cards.**

Jolly, imaginative retellings of all the traditional fairytales – for children of all ages.

The New Theatre

43 East Essex Street, Temple Bar, Dublin 2 (670 3361). All cross city buses. **Admission** £5-£7. **No credit cards.**

Home to the Sionnach Theatre Company, who have converted the space for use as a stage from which to attack contemporary issues, particularly those affecting young people, through the work of Irish playwrights. Production values are minimalistic, the setting stark, their dedication ferocious.

Olympia

72 Dame Street, Dublin 2 (677 7744). All cross city buses. **Admission** £7.50-£25.50; previews 10 per cent less. **Credit** MC, V.

An old-style variety theatre that was Dublin's first music hall. It is similar in range and genre to the Gaiety, although considerably more hit-or-miss in terms of quality. The on-going highlight is Midnight at the Olympia, which offers late-night concerts and drinking in the recently refurbished bar. Runs of variable length.

The Peacock

26 Lower Abbey Street, Dublin 1 (456 9569 ticket shop/878 7222 box office). All cross city buses. **Ticket shop open 24 hours. Admission** £9-10; £6 concs Mon-Thur only. **Credit** MC, V (advance bookings).

The Peacock is the Abbey's contemporary, experimental second stage. It was set up to give new, young writers an opportunity to show their work and has broken in some of the most electric new talent. Frank McGuinness's *Observe the Sons of Ulster Marching Towards the Somme* started here in 1986.

Project @ the Mint

Henry Place, off Henry Street, Dublin 1 (671 2321). All cross city buses. **Admission** £5-£8; £4-£6 preview; groups of ten or more less 10%. **Credit** MC, V.

Temporary premises for the Project Arts Centre while the original building, in use for 26 years, is being torn down and rebuilt by Shay Cleary (architect of Temple Bar's Arthouse).

The Gate, *housed in an eighteenth-century building leased from the Rotunda Hospital.*

Barabbas the Company – *clowning around and having a ball. See page 188.*

The Project – now a centre for dance, drama, poetry-readings and all other performing arts – began life 31 years ago as a visual arts project in the foyer of the Gate Theatre. It is a regular venue for Dublin's most energetic, exuberant and likeable young companies and individuals, and you're assured of a quality performance. Companies will usually do one signed performance for the deaf; the box office will provide details. Shows run for two weeks.

Tivoli

135-138 Francis Street, Dublin 1 (454 4472). Bus 50, 78A. **Admission** £10-£18; previews less 10%. **Credit** MC, V.

The gamut of live entertainment, from serious theatre to light-hearted musicals. Irish and international shows are favoured equally.

Minor venues

Bewley's

78 Grafton Street, Dublin 2 (677 6761). All cross city buses. **Open** 12.45pm Mon-Sat. **Admission** £6. **No credit cards.**

A treat for all the senses – soup, sandwiches and scene studies or short plays by Irish writers, and all for a few quid. Plays tend to run for one or two weeks.

City Arts Centre

23-25 Moss Street, Dublin 2 (667 0643) Bus 3. **Admission** £4-£5. **No credit cards.**

Until recently, the City Arts Centre ran late-night comedy evenings. These were discontinued just before we went to press, but watch this space.

The Ha'penny Bridge Inn

42 Wellington Quay, Dublin 2 (677 0616). All cross city buses. **Opens** 9pm-late Tue, Thur. **Admission** £2-£4. **No credit cards.**

The Ha'penny Bridge Inn offers evening slots for stand-up comedy and short drama pieces. Informal and hilarious. (*See* **Comedy** *below*.)

The International Bar

23 Wicklow Street, Dublin 2 (677 9250). All cross city buses. **Open** 9pm Mon, Wed, Thur. **Admission** £2-£4. **No credit cards.**

(*See* **Comedy** *below*.)

For those interested in modern Irish theatre, finding a good production can be a touch and go affair. As there isn't a consistent stream of productions, the younger, more innovative companies tend to be unattached to any particular venue. And this means that they float through a variety of theatres and do not perform to regular schedules. It is therefore necessary to keep an eye out for the more unusual or peripatetic companies. Luckily, most of them make a great effort to keep themselves visible. The most exciting, high profile, popular and prolific of these are a virtual guarantee of quality.

Barabbas the Company
7 South Great George's Street, Dublin 2 (671 2013).
Often at the Project Arts Centre and other venues besides, so keep an eye on the local listings for locations where you may find this three-person company. They began life as a simple clown act, and now undertake bright, bubbly and colourful interpretations of new and devised works – mostly done through physical theatre – and are incredibly popular with critics and children alike. They specialise in 'pay what you can' matinée performances. Advance information is available from their office at the above address.

Bedrock Halfpenny Court
36-37 Lower Ormond Quay, Dublin 1 (872 9300).
The creators of the Fringe Theatre Festival three years ago, Bedrock Halfpenny Court perform modern British, European or American plays which haven't been produced before in Ireland. A recent addition to the company has been writer

Alex Johnston, so expect some original work in the near future shortly to be joining its repertoire of existing international dramas.

Fishamble (formerly Pigsback) Theatre Company Ltd
Shamrock Chambers, 1-2 Eustace Street, Dublin 2 (670 4018).
Fishamble have performed many times at the Dublin Theatre Festival, as well as in Galway, Belfast, London, Glasgow and Edinburgh. They produce sturdy new plays by Irish writers with strong, contemporary themes which are buoyed up by lively acting and directing with colourful sets.

Loose Cannon
43 Morehampton Road, Dublin 4.
They stage Elizabethan, Jacobean and Shakespearean classics to very funky effect. Themes of betrayal, revenge, lust and incest are given a modern twist and a breakneck interpretation; the results are fun for both actors and audience.

Dance

Dance in Dublin makes no secret of the hardships it faces. It is rare to come across companies which limit themselves to an exclusive form of theatre art: dancers here are well aware of the difficulties attached to a medium which is still finding its feet in this city, tending to incorporate poetry, drama, design, sculpture, live music, literature and mythology into their shows. As a result, shows tend to become many-layered and highly dramatic, with

Watch out for dance companies **Tapestry...**   *... and* **Irish Modern Dance Theatre.**

a strong emphasis on story lines. As a strategy designed to attract audiences who know little about contemporary dance itself, it's been a successful one, with the knock-on effect of increasing their entertainment value. Accessibility, humour and narrative content are very important and are achieved by any means possible.

The most interesting companies work constantly with many of the country's finest visual artists, writers and musicians in order to present something readily comprehensible and highly charged. They also have deliberately strong European and international links, both in terms of influence and collaboration. Keep an eye out for **Rubato Ballet**, **CoisCéim Dance Theatre** and **Irish Modern Dance Theatre**; also **Tapestry**, the **Dance Theatre of Ireland** and **Metropolis Dance Company**. Although none of these companies has a venue of their own, they can be seen often at many of the theatres listed above; Rubato Ballet appear regularly at the National Gallery. For information about up-coming shows and ongoing classes get in touch with the Association of Professional Dancers.

RIVERDANCE

Riverdance exists in a category all of its own; there are no clear plans for a performance of this extravagant and emotionally charged show in Dublin in the foreseeable future, but for Internet users, its website (http://www.@riverdance.com) offers up-to-date information that'll keep confusion at bay.

Traditional Irish dancing

This has remained wonderfully informal, almost impromptu, and even the regular nights seem largely improvised. If you've never tried it before, don't worry. You'll soon pick it up once you find yourself thrown in at the deep end.

Cultúrlann na hÉireann

Belgrave Square, Monkstown (280 0295). **Dancing** 9pm Fri. **Admission** £5.
Large céilis or communal dances, which prove great fun for all concerned.

The Merchant Pub

12 Lower Bridge Street, Dublin 8 (679 3797). **Set dancing** 9.30pm Mon-Thur; *Summer* 9-10.45pm Fri.
Traditional music, song and set-dancing.

Searson's

42 Upper Baggot Street, Dublin 4 (660 0330). **Set dancing** 9pm Thur.
Traditional music and dance which draws in many dedicated regulars.

Dance classes

Association of Professional Dancers *31 Lower Churchtown Road, Dublin 14 (475 4790/298 1461).*
For details of forthcoming shows, ongoing dance classes and Dance Fest 98, a festival which will be held sometime in

November or December, featuring a much expanded niche for folk, ethnic and street dance.
The College of Dance *De Valoif House, 5 Meeting House Lane, off Mary's Abbey, Dublin 1 (873 5536).*
Holds classes in most forms of dance.
Litton Lane Dance Studios *Litton Lane, Dublin 2 (872 8044).*
Both studios also give classes, though these tend towards the eastern and south American style dances. They can usually be joined at any stage. If you are looking for something specific, try ringing the Association of Professional Dancers (475 4790/298 1461) who will help all they can.
Jackie Skelly's Studios *41 Clarendon Street, Dublin 2 (677 0040).*

Comedy

While Ireland has, in recent times, produced some of the best and most successful comics on the international circuit – Ardal O'Hanlon, Sean Hughes and Dylan Moran are names which immediately spring to mind – the comedy scene in Dublin is, in general, less than thriving. There are only a small number of clubs operating comedy shows at the moment, and they all tend to have the same performers working around them as some kind of mini-circuit. Most of the big exports named above started off working these clubs with a lot of the people who are still there now. The **International Bar** is probably the best known venue for laughs,

Not forgetting **CoisCéim Dance Theatre**.

but some of the smaller clubs and pubs also put on special comedy evenings.

If you're inclined towards performing yourself, it's worth mentioning the Norseman pub (*see* chapter **Pubs & Bars**) in Temple Bar which hosts open-mike evenings from time to time. Make sure you're prepared, as the crowds take no prisoners.

Venues

Comedy Cellar at the International Bar

23 Wicklow Street, Dublin 2 (677 9250). All cross city buses. **Open** doors 8.45pm; show 9.15-11pm Mon. **Admission** £3.50; £2.50 unwaged, students.

A regular Monday night upstairs at the International Bar, this is basically a live-action version of British TV's *Whose Line Is It Anyway?* Four or five local comics take suggestions from the audience for spoofs and skits and, while it depends on the talent available on the night, more often than not it's hilarious. There's the odd dud, of course, and the performances could often do with the kind of editing made possible only by the magic of television, but that's partly the point; the rapid changes and movements and steady stream of one-liners delivered by the cast hit their mark more often than not and the audience greets the gaffes with as much enthusiasm as they do the giggles. Usually by the end of the night, everyone's a comedian.

Olympia Theatre

72 Dame Street, Dublin 2 (677 7744). DART Pearse Street/all cross city buses. **Open** varies. **Admission** varies.

Probably better known as a theatre or musical venue, the Olympia does have a track record of playing host to international comedians working the European circuit. They generally play several nights in a row, so ask about alternative evenings if it's booked out. Irish comics who have made their name abroad often see playing the Olympia as something of a homecoming, although it's a lot more upmarket and refined than most comedy venues they would have been used to. Still, these shows are few and far between so it's best to phone in advance for such details of bills, opening times and admission prices.

Ha'penny Bridge Inn

42 Wellington Quay, Dublin 2 (677 0616). All cross city buses.

A small pub on the quays, this is another venue that the local circuit has used from time to time and which hosts some of the more down and dirty comics based in Dublin. When (and we mean when) they do have shows on, they tend to run them every week for a couple of months and then forget about them for a while, which makes it a little unreliable. Still, it's a good venue, a great place for a pint, and if the comics don't show up, you're sure to find something else to distract you. There are also some Thursday shows, but once again, dates are irregular: it's wise to phone for details.

Stand up Ardal O'Hanlon

Best-known these days for the singularly vacant expression which he perfected as Father Dougal Maguire in the award-winning comedy show *Father Ted*, Ardal O'Hanlon's auspicious comic beginnings stretch back as far as 1988 to a small, cavern-like upstairs room at the International Bar on Wicklow Street in Dublin.

This tiny room, until then a venue for fringe theatre and folk bands, became the showplace for Mr Trellis, a comic act consisting of Ardal and three of his fellow Dublin City University graduates, who began to perform a series of songs, monologues and comic sketches there on a regular basis. The sketches, which ranged from the ridiculous to the even more ridiculous, revolved around Mr Trellis, a Mormon, and the various difficulties he managed to get into, not least among them having his son kidnapped by a half-crazed car wash (Ardal), in the now historic sketch 'Mr Trellis and the Car Wash'.

After a slightly dubious start that often saw the boys performing only for a few loyal friends and the odd bemused Icelandic tourist, the act began to attract the attention of other comedians

in Dublin. Encouraged by this interest, the performers moved the show from a Tuesday to a Wednesday night and changed the name of the room to the Comedy Cellar.

Hard to imagine that a city such as Dublin, famed for the humour and quick wit of its populace, had no fixed venue for comedy until then. Nine years on, other comedy clubs have sprung up, although the Cellar remains regularly open and is acknowledged as a vital platform for comedy talent in Dublin.

Trellis has now ceased to exist but Ardal can still be seen in the International Bar. However, these days it is more in the role of punter than performer. Since 1994, when he won the Hackney Empire New Act of the Year award after taking the UK stand-up circuit by storm, his star has continued to rise. Apart from *Ted*, his recent successes include sell-out gigs at the Gaiety Theatre in Dublin, film roles in *Moll Flanders* and Neil Jordan's *The Butcher Boy* and a season hosting the BBC's *Stand Up Show*, which continues next year. He is even currently working on his first novel.

Trips Out of Town

Trips Out of Town

Away from the city, Ireland presents itself in astounding contrasts: wild seas and 'soft days', lush fields and rocky islands.

'And far from cities, and the sights of men,
Lived with the sunshine, and the moon's delight.'
A hundred years ago, the Irish playwright John Millington Synge left Dublin looking for an older, wilder Ireland. Anyone wanting to do the same today is overwhelmed by choice: Ireland is a small country and easy trips out of Dublin can lead to the shores of the Atlantic Ocean, the rugged wilderness of Donegal or the city of Belfast in the north.

To maximise the chance of finding the sunshine that Synge enjoyed, consider the 'Sunny Southeast' – the sobriquet given by the tourist industry to the county of Wexford on the grounds that it's marginally less wet than any of the other 31 counties. The neighbouring county of Waterford is not climatically very different, but the rich colours of its landscape prepares for what lies further to the west in Cork and Kerry. These two counties open up some of the most dramatic seascapes in the country and, although there is always the possibility of days of misty rain and cloudy skies, the risk is well worth taking: the delights of West Cork and the Kerry peninsulas are immense.

There are further attractions in the county of Galway. A straight line running west of Dublin leads to Galway city on the other side of the country. Here is a city that confidently rivals Dublin for an exuberant nightlife based around lively pubs, live music and fine restaurants. To the northwest of Galway, easily reached by car or public transport, lies the sublime Connemara and, off the coast, the three Aran Islands – home to the sweater – are reached by boat or plane. Spend a blissful day walking the lanes between stone walls patiently built up over the centuries. Geolog-

ically, the Aran Islands are a continuation of the strange limestone moonscape that characterises the Burren region of County Clare and here too it's possible to wander for hours along quiet country lanes before dropping in at the village of Doolin to hear some of the country's finest Irish music.

But even just outside Dublin, the county of Wicklow has its own wild landscape, lonely walks and splendidly preserved early Christian remains at Glendalough.

County Wicklow

Easily accessible from central Dublin by public transport or car, the Wicklow Mountains offer the ideal short trip out of town. The combination of spectacular scenery and major cultural attractions appeals to a wide range of people and, not surprisingly, thousands of Dubliners take advantage of their proximity to the county of Wicklow. Even so, it's still easy to find peace and solitude. At the height of summer you should leave as early as possible in order to enjoy a visit to the monastic site of Glendalough, but the surrounding countryside can accommodate walkers who like to head off on their own. The popularity of the Wicklow Mountains ensures a generous supply of places to stay and, although it is possible to do a whistle-stop tour in one day, it pays to slow down the pace and spend at least one night in the countryside.

Getting there
By car Take the N11 that connects Dublin with Wexford, and Enniskerry is signposted off it. From Enniskerry travel on to Glencree and head south through the Sally Gap as the road winds its way into the Wicklow Mountains. At Laragh turn west for Glendalough; from Glendalough the road continues on to Hollywood and meets the N81. Turn right here and head north back to Dublin, taking in Blessington and Russborough House.
By bus *To Enniskerry* Dublin bus 44 goes to Enniskerry from Hawkins Street in Dublin or Bus Eireann (836 6111) express buses to Wicklow town or Wexford will drop passengers off at the turn-off for Enniskerry, from where it's just over a mile to walk to Enniskerry.
To Glendalough St Kevin's Bus Service (281 8119) runs a twice-daily service to Glendalough via Roundwood. Buses depart from outside the College of Surgeons off St Stephen's Green in Dublin at 11.30am and 6pm. A return bus to Dublin departs at 4.15pm Mon-Sat and 5.30pm Sun.
To Blessington From Eden Quay in Dublin take bus 65 to Blessington.
By train *To Enniskerry* Take the DART train to Bray and catch bus 85 from there to Enniskerry.

Sugarloaf Mountain, *County Wicklow.*

Lough Tay, *County Wicklow – an atmospheric location for John Boorman's film* Excalibur.

The Wicklow Mountains

When the British were establishing themselves in Dublin, they faced the threat of Gaelic resistance from native settlements in the then inaccessible valleys of the Wicklow Mountains. The fortified road built by the British through the Wicklow Mountains after the 1798 Rising – suitably named the Military Road – now serves a different purpose. It allows visitors to travel south from the Dublin suburbs through increasingly wild scenery to the remote heart of the mountains and the dramatic surprise of clean air, gorse and heather, lonely stretches of bogland and rounded smooth mountains dominated by the granite peak of Lugnaquillia at just over 3,000 ft.

One route that takes in many of the places of interest begins in the postcard-pretty village of Enniskerry just south of Dublin on the R117. Quaint cottages and idyllic teahouses make Enniskerry the perfect rest stop. The Anglo-Irish felt relatively secure in this part of northern Wicklow and the village was created to complement and serve the imposing Powerscourt House (see below) that was built just over a mile to the west. The house was burnt out in 1974 just after extensive renovation and refurbishment, but the shell of the building that remains intact still manages to envoke the Anglo-Irish Ascendancy. The Victorian gardens are well worth visiting; not least because of the spectacular backdrop of the Great Sugar loaf Mountain(1,650 feet), best admired from the terrace of the big house. A signposted four-mile walk through the gardens leads to a photogenic waterfall where the river Dargle cascades nearly 300 feet into a glen. There is an admission charge to view the waterfall.

From Powerscourt the village of Glencree – bereft of a pub, extraordinarily – is only five miles away to the west. The village has a cemetery dedicated to German lives lost in Ireland during the two world wars in shipwrecks and plane crashes. From Glencree, the Military Road can be met on its journey south to Sally Gap. From Sally Gap, there are two nearby attractions, quite different in their appeal. Lough Tay, whose atmospheric quality provided John Boorman with a suitable location for his film *Excalibur* (and Laurence Olivier's *Henry V* used part of the Powerscourt estate), is about three miles away; and although the lake forms part of a private estate there are good walking routes in the vicinity that are accessible to the public. The other attraction is Roundwood (the highest village in Ireland at 780 feet above sea level), a small village where food, drink and accommodation may be found and from where the Wicklow Way may be joined.

The popular Wicklow Way trail stretches for over 80 miles from the suburbs of south Dublin, through Glencree to Glendalough and further south into County Carlow. At least eight days are required to complete the walk but with the necessary maps and literature from the tourist office in Dublin, it is easy to choose a section that suits your needs.

*A tenth-century round tower at **Glendalough** – 'valley of the two lakes' – County Wicklow.*

From Roundwood, the road heads south to the primary attraction in this part of the country: the monastic site of Glendalough (*see below*). Translated from the Gaelic as 'valley of the two lakes', Glendalough is beautifully located between two lakes and surrounded by ancient mountains. Despite the number of daily visitors, the place still manages to convey an air of spirituality – although it helps to be there early in the morning or late in the evening when fewer people are about. Founded as a solitary hermitage in the sixth century by St Kevin, and withstanding repeated Viking raids, Glendalough developed into a major centre of Christian learning. The English burned the place down in 1398, but it was salvaged by the monks until Henry VIII closed it down for good in the sixteenth century.

The present stone buildings are spread out across a valley and it pays to call in at the visitor centre, collect a map and ask about guided walks. From the centre it is a short walk to the crumbling gatehouse of the monastery – the last of its kind anywhere in Ireland – and on the other side is a graveyard and a tenth-century round tower, the roof and upper parts of which were restored in 1876. In the vicinity there are the remains of a number of churches, including the enchanting St

Kevin's Kitchen. This barrel-vaulted church with a round belfry – why it should be called a kitchen remains a mystery – dates back 1,000 years and was used for services up until the mid-nineteenth century. Up by the Upper Lake, the site of St Kevin's first hermitage is thought to have been located and it was here, legend has it, that the virtuous saint was forced to repulse the passionate advances of a woman and dampen her ardour by dumping her in the lake.

One of the best walks in the Glendalough area is a half-hour stroll along the northern shore of the Upper Lake to the remains of nineteenth-century lead and zinc mines. Information on a variety of local walks is available from the Wicklow Mountains National Park information centre, located by the Upper Lake.

From Glendalough the road travels across the Wicklow Gap to the west of the county. The journey there is a picturesque one although the actual scenery of west Wicklow is not as dramatic as what has already been experienced. The best reason for travelling in this direction is to visit the superb Russborough House (*see below*), close to the village of Blessington. The house, one of the very finest in the country, was built in the mid-eighteenth century to a design by the German Richard Castle (who also designed Powerscourt). Its Palladian opulence reflected the tremendous wealth of Joseph Leeson, a magnate in Ireland's brewing industry, who later became Lord Russborough in 1756 when Ireland still had its own parliament. Even more astonishing than the architecture is the amazing collection of paintings by Rubens, Hals, Velazquez, Goya and others. They were purchased by a co-founder of the De Beer Diamond Mining Company whose nephew purchased Russborough in 1952 and filled the stately interior with the priceless collection he inherited. Security was more relaxed in the past, and in 1974, 16 of the paintings, all later recovered, were stolen in an attempt to raise funds for the IRA. Twelve years later, there was another major theft of paintings, albeit it non-political, and nowadays security is very tight.

Blessington is on the main N81 road that heads back to Dublin and stagecoaches used to stop here on their journey between the capital and Waterford. With your own transport, consider a short excursion south to the other side of Hollywood village and take a left turn onto a small road signposted for Donard. Here are the Athgreany Piper's Stones, a stone circle with one separate stone outside the circle. The boulders are said to be people turned to stone, the separate stone being the piper himself.

COASTAL TOWNS

There is little to be gained by continuing south on the N11 from Dublin after the turn-off for Enniskerry, notwithstanding the publicity attached to the coastal towns south of Dublin. The N11 passes the too-popular coastal town of Bray, which resembles an English south coast resort town but has little more to offer than that (though Joyce did live here for two years). The best reason for a trip to Bray (which may be easily reached on a DART train from Pearse, Tara or Connolly stations in Dublin) is the bracing five-mile cliff walk around Bray Head to Greystones. Wicklow Town is 16 miles further south but, again, there is little to detain one here. As with Bray, the best option is the pleasant walk to Wicklow Head along the cliffs. However – continuing south from Wicklow town – there are some superb beaches further along the coast. Brittas Bay is especially wonderful and even though it is popular with jaded Dubliners it rarely feels crowded.

Attractions

Glendalough

Glendalough (0404 45325/45425) is off the R756 between Laragh and Hollywood. **Open** 9.30am-6pm daily. **Admission** £2 adults; £1 children.
The modern visitor centre has a first-class exhibition and 20-minute audio-visual show. Guided tours available.

Powerscourt Estate

Entrance is 500m south of Enniskerry (286 7676). **Open** *Mar-Oct* 9.30am-5.30pm daily. **Admission** £2.80 adults; £1.70 children; £2 students.
There are plans to restore the interior of Powerscourt House. Guided tours available.

Russborough House

Three miles south-west of Blessington which is on the N81 (045 65239). **Open** *June-Aug* 10.30am-5.30pm daily; *Apr-May, Sept-Oct* 10.30am-5.30pm Sun, Bank Holidays. **Admission** £3 adults; £2 students; £1 children.
Admission to Russborough House includes a 45-minute tour of the main rooms and paintings. A tour of the bedrooms costs £1.50, children free.

Tourist information

Consider calling in at Dublin tourist office for general literature, and perhaps the booking of accommodation, before heading off to Wicklow. There are no tourist offices in the Wicklow Mountains area. From early June to the end of August, there is a tourist office in Blessington (045 865850), another seasonal office in Bray (286 7128) and an all-year facility in Wicklow town (0404 69117). For walking the Wicklow Way, there is a Bord Fáilte Information Sheet (no 26B) and for short walks in the Glendalough area the national park information office at the Upper Lake (0404 45581) may be of some help. For longer walks along the Wicklow Way, consider purchasing one of the specialist guides by Michael Fewer, available in the Dublin tourist office or any of the city's bookshops.

Where to stay

During the summer months, it is not advisable to tour Wicklow without booking accommodation in advance (unless you're starting off very early and planning to return to Dublin late the same day). Glendalough is your best bet.

Blessington

The Heathers *Poulaphouca, Ballymore-Eustace, Blessington, Co Wicklow (045 867044/088 673112).* **Rates** single £28-£32; double £38-£42. **Credit** MC, V.
Views of Poulaphouca reservoir from this B&B situated on the Baltinglass road and within walking distance of Russborough House.

Enniskerry

Enniscree Lodge Hotel *Cloon, Enniskerry, Co Wicklow (286 3542/fax 286 6037).* **Rates** single £51-£59; double £75-£80. **Credit** AmEx, DC, MC, V. Ten beds in this cosy two-star establishment. Terrific location, just out of town on the road to Glencree.
Summerhill House Hotel *Enniskerry, Co Wicklow (2867928/fax 286 7929).* **Rates** double single £40-£50; £60-£80. **Credit** MC, V. Reasonably comfortable one-star hotel, smack in the middle of the village.

Glendalough

Mrs Valerie Merrigan *Glendale, Glendalough, Co Wicklow (0404 45410).* **Rates** single £21-£28; double £28-£32. Less than a mile from Glendalough and open all year. No-smoking bedrooms.

Roundwood

Woodside *Roundwood, Co Wicklow (281 8195).* **Rates** single £22-£26; double £28-£32. Three rooms, two en suite, in Mrs Nancy O'Brien's pleasant no-smoking B&B, open from 1 April to the end of September.

Wexford *town and harbour – renamed Waesfjord, 'harbour of the muddy flats', by the Vikings.*

Where to eat

Bray

Avoca Handweavers *Kilmacanogue, Bray, Co Wicklow (286 7466)*. The long queues at lunchtime are a demonstration of the affection and respect with which Avoca is regarded by the folk from south County Dublin. Joanna Hill's cooking in the self-service restaurant is the draw: tomato and red pepper soup, piperade tart, sesame chicken with cauliflower, broccoli and peanut salad. There is a section of the shop which sells stylish food products and a café area out in the front gardens.

The Tree of Idleness *Sea Front, Bray (286 3498)*. A unique outpost of Greek-Cypriot cooking for almost 15 years, the Tree's classic dishes, such as suckling pig stuffed with fruits, saddle of lamb with feta cheese, perfect taramasalata and moussaka, amount to a definition of noble cuisine. A homey room, with great service and one of the country's most interesting wine lists.

Enniskerry

Gallery Restaurant *Powerscourt, Enniskerry (654 0993)*. Beautifully restored after almost a quarter of a century as a ruin, Powerscourt House is newly home to all manner of craft shops, nurseries, golf courses, and the newest venture by the Pratt family of Avoca Handweavers (*see above*). Leylie Hayes has charge of the kitchens, and the food is as fine as that found in Avoca: oriental beef with peppers, chicken in a pistachio and pepper marinade, spinach, pine-nut and Emmenthal tart. A seat out on the terrace on a sunny day is hard to leave.

Roundwood

Roundwood Inn *Main Street, Roundwood, Co Wicklow (281 8107)*. Jurgen Schwalm's pub and restaurant is reliable and full of character, the food enjoying a Teutonic forcefulness of flavour in schnitzels and goulash, with good local smoked trout and creamy desserts among the best choices. There are some fine, rare German wines on the list.

County Wexford

The flat and tame landscape and the peaceful lifestyle of contemporary Wexford seems almost at odds with its troubled and turbulent history. In the distant past, it was the domain of the MacMurrough clan whose Gaelic chiefs were well aware of their English peers across the water. In the eleventh century, the MacMurroughs crossed the sea and laid siege to Bristol but a century later King Dermot MacMurrough was seeking the allegiance of the Norman Earl of Pembroke, better known as Strongbow, to help him in a local power struggle. Strongbow duly arrived and land was granted as a reward for his support, setting in train 800 years of British involvement that continues in the north of the island.

The bitter fruit of the deal between MacMurrough and Strongbow was felt in 1649, when Oliver Cromwell slaughtered three-quarters of the town's population after its refusal to surrender. Irish rebels made another defiant stand during the 1798 Rising in Wexford town.

Apart from the odd monument or two, there is little to remind today's visitors of the past. Wexford town is a prosperous centre with good restaurants and cultural attractions and the surrounding countryside offers comfortable terrain that invites a relaxing meander. This is the place to unwind and enjoy good food, drink and traditional Irish music.

Getting there

By car The N11 connects Dublin with Wexford town. If arriving from Wales or France by car off the ferry at Rosslare, the N25 connects Wexford town with Rosslare Harbour. Parking discs are required for parking almost anywhere in Wexford town and tickets may be purchased from many newsagents, small stores and the tourist office.

By bus There are up to five Bus Éireann trips daily between Dublin and Wexford town and six daily buses between town and Rosslare Harbour. The Wexford bus station (053 22522) is situated at the railway station. There is also a private bus company, Ardcavan Coach (053 22561), that runs a daily service between Dublin and Rosslare Harbour.

By train The thrice-daily train service between Dublin and Rosslare Harbour stops in Wexford town at the O'Hanrahan railway station (053 22522). There is also a local train service between the harbour and town.

By boat/ferry Irish Ferries (from UK 0171 491 8682) run a ferry service from Pembroke to Rosslare and Stena Sealink (from UK 01233 647047) handles the Fishguard-to-Rosslare route. Irish Ferries also handle the Le Harve-to-Rosslare route (20 hours) and the slightly faster Cherbourg-to-Rosslare route. In France, contact Transport et Voyages (1 42 669090) in Paris.

Wexford town

On Ptolemy's map of the second century, the location of Wexford town is marked as Menapia, so when the Vikings arrived in the middle of the ninth century there was probably a sizeable settlement fronting the natural harbour at the mouth of the river Slaney. The Vikings appreciated the ease with which they could draw up their ships and they renamed the settlement Waesfjord, 'harbour of the muddy flats'. The mouth of the harbour has now silted up and is hardly used; the extensive quays serve as a reminder of its maritime past.

The Bull Ring, where the long North Main Street forms a junction with Cornmarket, is the historical heart of the city. It was the entertainment centre of medieval Wexford and the site of Cromwell's massacre. The Lone Pikeman statue in the middle of the junction commemorates the 1798 Rising. The clothing store in the north-east corner of the Bull Ring, near North Main Street, was the birthplace of Speranza, Jane Francesca Elgee, the mother of Oscar Wilde.

If you walk up Cornmarket and turn right into Abbey Street it is possible to view the remnants of the town walls, and following the street up past Selskar Abbey leads to Westgate, the only surviving towngate which dates back to the beginning of the fourteenth century.

The decrepit state of Selskar Abbey bears testimony to Cromwell's visit in 1649 and there is an unlikely legend that in 1172, Henry II spent the 40 days of Lent inside the church as an act of repentance for the murder of Thomas à Becket.

Back down at the other end of North Main Street, Henrietta Street leads to the Crescent where

*Wexford seaman **John Barry**.*

the tourist office looks out at a United States-sponsored statue of John Barry, a Wexford seaman who emigrated to America and, in the course of the American Revolution, founded the US navy.

Wexford town's major cultural draw is the annual October Opera Festival. Established in 1951, the festival has a secure world-wide reputation and wins particular acclaim for its policy of mounting productions of lesser-known operas. Seats are always completely booked out months ahead (*see chapter* **Music: Classical & Opera**). Opera apart, there are a number of theatres in Wexford and there is usually something interesting at the Theatre Royal (053 22144) in High Street or the Wexford Arts Centre (053 23764) in the Cornmarket. There are plenty of hospitable pubs – many are strung out along North and South Main Streets – with regular musical evenings.

Attractions

Historical walk

From outside the Talbot Hotel in Trinity Street and White's Hotel in George Street. Free.

The walks – which are free of charge – are organised by the Wexford Historical Society and depart daily at 11am and 2.30pm. Confirm with the tourist office.

Westgate Centre

Corner of Westgate & Slaney Street. **Open** *July, Aug* 9am-1pm, 2-5pm; *May, June, Sept* 11am-1pm, 2-5pm ?? days??. **Admission** £1.50; £1 children.

An audio-visual presentation on the history of Wexford.

Rosslare Harbour – *point of entry into Ireland for ferry passengers from Wales and France.*

Tourist Information

Crescent Quay, Wexford, Co Wexford (053 23111/fax 053 41743). **Open** *May, June, Sept* 9am-6pm Mon-Sat; *July, Aug* 11am-5pm Sun; *rest of year* 9am-5.15pm Mon-Fri.
The tourist office is on the waterfront.

Festivals

Wexford Opera Festival

Wexford Opera Festival, Theatre Royal, High Street, Wexford (053 22240/22144).
Write as early as possible for the programme and plan to book by July to secure a seat in October. *See chapter* **Music: Classical & Opera.**

Where to stay

Wexford town

Saint George Guesthouse *George Street, Wexford, Co Wexford (053 43474/fax 053 24814/e-mail stgeorge@indigo.ie).* **Rates** *single* £20 single; *double* £40. **Credit** MC, V. A two-star, family-run, guesthouse with nine beds. Centrally located and comfortable, with tea/coffee making facilities and private car park. Mid-week specials available.
Westgate House *Westgate, Wexford, Co Wexford (053 22167/fax 053 24814).* **Rates** £30-£38 double; £18-£30 single. **Credit** MC, V. A hotel built in 1812, refurbished in period style. Within walking distance of the bus and railway station, and a lock-up car park is provided.
White's Hotel *George Street, Wexford, Co Wexford (053 22311/fax 053 45000).* **Rates** *double* £75-£138. **Credit** AmEx, DC, MC, V. One of the best town hotels, busy, but well-managed and comfortable; 82 en suite rooms with tea/coffee making facilities, a health and fitness club with sauna, solarium and gym.

Where to eat

Wexford town

The Granary *Westgate, Wexford (053 23935).* Paddy and Mary Hatton's restaurant is the best known in Wexford town, a cosy space with undemanding but nevertheless enjoyable cooking, using local ingredients such as Kilmore crab and scallops. An early opening time suits Opera Festival-goers.
White's Hotel *George Street, Wexford (053 22311).* White's forms the annual social centrepiece of the Opera Festival, with everyone in a bow tie and a long dress hanging out here. In recent years, some folk have tended to head out of town to the Ferrycarrig Hotel for drinks before and after performances.

Around Wexford town

Places of interest close to Wexford town include cultural attractions as well as natural ones, such as some fine beaches. The Irish National Heritage Park (*see below*), less than three miles north of town off the N11 road to Dublin, is the chief cultural draw. The guided tour and the life-sized models provide visitors with a good overview of Ireland's ancient past, from prehistoric times through to the Norman era. This is the place to sort out the difference between a ring fort and a crannóg (lake settlement), or the Mesolithic and Neolithic periods in Irish history.

On the other side of Wexford town, off the road to Rosslare, the gardens of Johnstown Castle (*see below*) are open to the public. The castle itself is a mock-Gothic edifice from the nineteenth century and is not open to the public, but an agricultural museum is situated in the grounds of the gardens. Original farm equipment is on display along with model workshops relating to rural crafts.

The splendid Curracloe beach is reached by taking the R742 out of Wexford town for about five miles. There are a number of busy villages in the area providing pub lunches, but it is easy to find space along the seven-mile stretch of beach that's ideal for a picnic. Another dazzling stretch of golden beach is Rosslare Strand, stretching north of Rosslare Harbour; it attracts more visitors than Curracloe, one reason being its suitability for windsurfing. Equipment may be hired from the Rosslare Windsurfing Centre (053 32566).

The two Saltee Islands (*see below*) are uninhabited and make up one of the country's most important bird sanctuaries. Countless numbers of puffins, shearwaters, auks, razorbills, gannets, cormorants and other species nest here each year between spring and early summer. By July, most of the young birds have learnt to fly and by the end of the month there is little to see. Before then, anyone with an interest in birds will enjoy a visit to the islands (*see below*).

The Saltees provided the last refuge for two local rebel leaders of the 1798 Rising who were captured on the Saltees and taken to Wexford for execution. In 1943, they were bought by a man who anointed himself Michael I; he is said to have carved a throne out of the limestone for his royal line.

Boat trips to the Saltee Islands depart from the small fishing village of Kilmore Quay and a visit here for lunch or an evening's entertainment in one of the bars is well worth considering, even if the closest you get to the islands is gazing at them from the quayside. There is a small maritime museum and in the first half of July there is usually a seafood festival.

Getting around

Places of interest close to Wexford town may be visited by car, bicycle or public transport. The Bike Shop, 9 Selskar Street (053 22514), and Hayes, 108 South Main Street (053 22462), both hire bicycles by the day or week. Murrays Rent-a-Car (053 22122) have an office near the bus and railway station on Redmond Place. Some places, like the Irish National Heritage Park and Curracloe beach for example, may be reached by a bus from town; ask at the tourist office and check the times of the return buses to Wexford town. Public transport to Kilmore Quay is not so regular and there are only buses each Wednesday and Saturday, returning the same day.

Attractions

Irish National Heritage Park

Ferrycarrig, Co Wexford (053 20733). **Open** *Apr-Sept* 10am-7pm; last admission 5.30pm. **Rates** £3.50; £3 students; £2.50 children; family ticket (2 adults, 3 children) £9.50; free under-6s. **Credit** MC, V.
Enquire at the tourist offices about possible tours of the park from Wexford town.

Johnstown Castle & Gardens

About four miles south-west of Wexford (053 42888). **Open** *garden* 9am-5pm daily. **Open** *museum* 9am-5pm Mon-Fri; 2-5pm Sat, Sun. Opening hours restricted during winter. **Admission** £1.50; 50p children.
Enquire at the tourist offices about possible tours of the Garden and Museum from Wexford town.

Maritime Museum

Open *June-Sept* noon-6pm daily. **Admission** £1; 50p children.
Housed in a lightship in the harbour at Kilmore Quay, this is a small unpretentious museum with local exhibits.

Saltee Islands

About two miles from Kilmore Quay, where boats may be hired for the return journey to the islands.
Enquire at the tourist office in Wexford about booking a boat trip or try locals such as Declan Bates (053 29684) or Tom O'Brien (053 29684). The cost will depend on the number of passengers but you should expect to pay around £15 for the return trip.

Tourist information

There is a tourist office at Rosslare Harbour (053 33622) which opens to meet incoming ferries.

Where to stay

There are plenty of small B&Bs and guest houses, and four three-star hotels at Rosslare Harbour for anyone using the car ferries. Kilmore Quay has half a dozen accommodation possibilities and there are a couple of places at Curracloe.

Kilmore Quay

Hotel Saltees *Kilmore Quay, Co Wexford (053 296020).* **Rates** single £16-£31; double £26-£52. **Credit** AmEx, DC, MC, V.

Rosslare Harbour

Aisla *Rosslare Harbour, Co Wexford (053 33230; fax 053 33581).* **Rates** single £30; double £40. **Credit** MC, V. This is the largest guest house in Rosslare Harbour, with ten bedrooms, and a five-minute walk to the bus/train/ferry terminal.

Where to eat

Carne

The Lobster Pot *Ballyfane, Carne, Co Wexford (053 31110).* There is both bar food and a restaurant menu offered in Anne and Ciaran Hearne's popular Lobster Pot, which has been successfully attracting folk for more than two decades. Wexford mussels, crab claws in garlic, Bannow Bay oysters and grilled Dover sole feature on a menu which also includes steaks, duck and other classics.

Rosslare

La Marine Restaurant *Kelly's Hotel, Rosslare (053 32114).* Eugene Callaghan heads up the kitchen in Bill Kelly's newest venture, and, in combination with Kelly's brilliant design, he has pushed La Marine to the forefront of Wexford cooking. Gratin of cod with leeks and mushrooms, seared rib steak with crispy onions and gratin dauphinoise, spiced lamb casserole with Basmati rice, grilled chicken salad with red onions and green beans are just some of Mr Callaghan's bistro signatures, executed with great aplomb.

The Hook Head peninsula

Travelling west from Kilmore Quay on the R736/733 brings you to the eastern side of Waterford Harbour and the Hook Head peninsula. There are various minor sites of interest along the way but the chief pleasure consists in simply travelling around the area, taking in the fine scenery.

Oliver Cromwell did something similar when considering his options for an assault on Waterford town. He saw two possible places to land his troops, either at Crooke in the county of Waterford, or here on the peninsula: hence his saying, 'by Hook or by Crooke'. Today, there is a car ferry that links Ballyhack on the west side of the peninsula with Passage East in County Waterford, but the area is far more than a convenient transit point and you could easily while away a day and a night here just enjoying the countryside.

The peninsula is soaked in history: it was at Baginbun Head that the Anglo-Normans disembarked in 1169, and in the following year more soldiers arrived. Irish troops unsuccessfully attacked Baginbun from Waterford, and the 70 Irishmen who were captured had their bones broken before being tipped over the cliffs.

At the peninsula's tip of Hook Head, there is an ancient lighthouse that is very likely the oldest in Europe. This is also a beautiful spot to head for, as there are fine country walks to be enjoyed, limestone-encased fossils to be found, magnificent views out to sea and a rich variety of seabirds to try to identify.

Food and accoommodation can be found in the villages of Arthurstown and Duncannon. The latter has a decent beach, but the village of Slade is much more secluded, signposted just under a mile before reaching Hook Head. There is little here apart from an old ruined castle and a few fishing boats, but it's a great place for a picnic.

Attractions

Ballyhack Castle

Ballyhack, Co Wexford. **Open** *July, Aug* 10am-6pm daily. *Apr-June, Sept* noon-6pm Wed-Sun. **Admission** £1.
A recently restored sixteenth-century tower house.

Dunbrody Abbey

Close to the village of Campile, north of Ballyhack off the R733. **Open** *Apr-June, Sept* 10am-6pm daily; *July, Aug* 10am-7pm daily. **Admission** £1.50; 50p children.
Built around 1200 by Cistercian monks from England and modified in the sixteenth century. There is little to see inside the abbey but its grand setting is worthy of a visit in its own right.

Tintern Abbey

Saltmills, about five miles east of Arthurstown, on the R733, Co Wexford. **Open** free access at any time.
A twelfth-century Cistercian abbey, which was founded by an earl of Pembroke after he survived being caught in a storm off shore.

Passage East, *County Waterford.*

Places to stay

Arthurstown

Arthur's Rest *Arthurstown, Co Wexford (051 389192; fax 051 389192).* **Rates** *double* £32. **Credit** MC, V. A comfortable and pleasant B&B in Arthurstown, which makes a good base for exploring the peninsula.

Places to eat

Ballyhack

Neptune Restaurant *Ballyhack, Co Wexford (051 39284).* Pierce and Valerie McAuliffe's restaurant is a fixture of the Hook Head. Situated at the car ferry just across from Passage East, it's a popular lunchtime venue for opera buffs who like to tour the Head during the Wexford Festival. The lively mix of local fish and seafood, with specialities such as Wexford lamb, amount to an enduring mix.

County Waterford

Waterford city °

The ancient city of Waterford still retains a flavour of the past, its modern shopping centres standing on medieval streets across from Norman and Viking buildings. But even without its heritage and tourism industry, the place is thriving, and Waterford is a city where visitors may begin to shake off some of their own cultural baggage and enjoy the experience of an Irish city in the throes of discovering itself.

The Vikings founded a settlement here in AD 850, attracted by the safe harbour and the three rivers that provided easy access to the interior. Vadrefjord, as they christened it, developed into the most important Viking town in Ireland. Archeological evidence suggests that the foundations for their permanent fortified town were laid around 915 and the narrow thoroughfares leading to long quays, still a distinguishing feature of Waterford, are a direct inheritance from Viking times. City walls were first built by the Vikings, and added to by the English in the thirteenth century, and remnants may still be seen in the vicinity of the Theatre Royal. In 1170, the Anglo-Norman Strongbow besieged the city and the following year Henry II of England sailed into Waterford with a fleet of about 400 ships. The English king wanted to remind Strongbow who was really in charge and Waterford was declared a royal city.

The most impressive reminder of the Norman presence is Reginald's Tower (*see below*), a fortified tower on the city walls that was built over an earlier wooden fort established by the Vikings. The wooden fort had been the most stoutly defended part of the town against Strongbow's attack and the Normans duly made their replacement tower the cornerstone of their defence of the town. The tower has now been thoroughly restored and is open to the public. Directly behind the tower, a section of the city walls has been retained inside Reginald's Restaurant and Bar, and drink may be taken here in the scholarly pursuit of history.

The Waterford Heritage Centre (*see below*), in Greyfriars Street, is recommended for anyone wishing to learn more about the city's Viking and Norman past, as recent excavations have unearthed some precious artefacts from this era.

By the fourteenth century, Waterford had become the most powerful city in Ireland, based upon its prosperity as a trading centre and reinforced by an English military presence. In the following centuries, trade became international and Waterford's well-being lasted well into the eighteenth century. Ships of 300 tons were not an uncommon sight at the city's quays. The famous Waterford crystal was first produced around this time and the factory remained in operation for 68 years until it closed in 1851, as a result of punitive taxes imposed by the British. One hundred years later, the factory reopened and is still going strong; visitors can join the daily 40-minute tours of the glass factory and see the glass-cutting and glass-blowing in operation. During the summer, it is best to book a place through the tourist office or contact the factory direct (051 73311).

Christ Church Cathedral is one of the city's best-preserved buildings from the Regency period and, like many other notable buildings from this era in Waterford, it was designed by talented local architect John Roberts. This handsome and well-proportioned Protestant church was rebuilt in the 1770s following a design by Roberts based upon ideas of Sir Christopher Wren. The exterior is exquisite, although it is the ghastly tomb of James Rice inside the church that unfairly draws more attention: the effigy of the fifteenth-century Lord Mayor portrays a rotting corpse being fed upon by various nasty crawling creatures.

The work of John Roberts also lends grace to the Mall where two of his buildings, the City Hall and the Theatre Royal, show him to have been a remarkable architect. In one of the meeting rooms in the City Hall, there is a resplendent chandelier

Norman **Reginald's Tower**, Waterford city.

made from Waterford glass, a copy of which hangs in Independence Hall in Philadelphia. Ask at reception and, if the room is not in use, visitors are welcome to take a look.

Perhaps the single best example of Roberts' talent is to be found inside the Chamber of Commerce in George Street where the cantilevered oval staircase is eloquent testimony to his skill. Roberts also designed the Catholic Holy Trinity Cathedral on Barronstrand Street which looks rather modest on the outside, until the opulent interior betrays the decorative remodelling that took place in the nineteenth century.

One other fine church worth viewing, albeit roofless, is the French Church tucked away behind Reginald's Tower. It was founded by Franciscans in 1240 and, from 1693 to 1815, it was used by French Huguenot refugees fleeing religious persecution. The house directly opposite holds the key to the building and visitors can enter the church to admire the triple-lancet windows and search out the memorial stone to the industrious John Roberts.

Quite misleadingly, the above may give the impression that Waterford is only of historical interest. Not so, for the city has a lively entertainment scene and there are plenty of good pubs with live music. Ones to check out include T & H Doolan, on Great George's Street, and Geoff's and the Pulpit, where John Street becomes Michael

*Six miles south of Waterford, **Tramore** boasts a lovely three-mile stretch of sandy beach.*

Street. Clubs include Snag, on Barronstrand Street, and the Roxy Theatre Club on O'Connell Street. At 5 and 22 O'Connell Street there are two venues for the Garter Lane Arts Centre (051 855038) where a mixture of theatre, exhibitions, poetry readings and films take place. It is also worth asking at the tourist office for details of the Waterford Show, a mix of music, dance, song and wine that accompanies a programme on the history of the city.

Getting there

By car The most enjoyable road journey to Waterford from Dublin is via County Wicklow and Wexford town. From Wexford town, head to Ballyhack on the Hook peninsula, from where a ferry crosses Waterford Harbour to Passage East. The main roads from Dublin and Wexford enter Waterford from north of the river before crossing the only bridge to the city centre. The road from Passage East enters the city from the east side on the south side of the river.

By bus The bus station (051 879000) is on the north side of the river and there are regular daily services to Dublin (3 hours) and Wexford. Two private companies, Funtrek (873 0852) and Rapid Express Club Travel (01 679 1549/051 872149), also run bus services between Dublin and Waterford.

By train The train station (051 873401) is also on the north side of the river, next to the bus station and there are daily trains to Dublin (2 hours) and Rosslare (80 minutes).

By air Suckling Airways, based in the UK (01223 293393), runs a service between Cambridge and Luton and Waterford. British Airways Express (UK 0345 256256) connects Waterford airport (051 75589) with London's Stansted Airport and Manchester.

Attractions

Reginald's Tower

Parade Quay, Waterford, Co Waterford (051 73501).
Open *Apr-June, Sept, Oct* 10am-5pm Mon-Fri; *July-Aug* 10am-8pm Mon-Fri; 10am-5pm Sat, Sun. *Nov-Mar* 10am-5pm Mon-Sat. **Admission** £1.50; 75p children. Joint ticket for Reginald's Tower and Heritage Museum £2; £1 children.

Waterford Heritage Museum

Greyfriars, Waterford, Co Waterford (051 871227).
Open *Apr-Oct* 10am-5pm daily; *Nov-Mar* 10am-5pm Mon-Fri. **Admission** £1.50; 75p children. Joint ticket for Reginald's Tower and Heritage Museum £2; £1 children.

Tourist information

Tourist Office, 41 Merchant's Quay (051 875823).
Open *Sept-June* 9am-6pm Mon-Fri; *July-Aug* daily.
Walking tours of the city, focusing on history, leave twice daily from the Granville Hotel, at noon and 2pm. Confirm with the hotel (051 855111) or the tourist office. Each September, the Waterford Light Opera Festival extends the summer season with a programme of operas and associated events around the city. Tickets are less expensive than Wexford's Opera Festival, but booking ahead is still advisable. Contact the Theatre Royal, The Mall, Waterford (051 874402), or the Waterford Opera Festival (051 32001).

Where to stay

Waterford is a popular holiday destination and visitors arriving in the city may find it difficult to find less expensive accommodation. Try to book ahead by yourself or through the tourist office in whatever town you are leaving before coming to Waterford.

Waterford city

Granville Hotel *Meagher Quay, Waterford, Co Waterford (051 855111/fax 051 870307).* **Rates** *single* £52.50; *double* £80. **Credit** AmEx, DC, MC, V. A family-run three-star hotel, centrally located overlooking the river Suir, with 74 beds. An olde-worlde Georgian character and two good restaurants. Golf and fishing trips arranged.
Portree Guesthouse *Mary Street, Waterford, Co Waterford (051 74574).* **Rates** *single* £18-£22; *double* £27-£36. Centrally located, most rooms have their own showers, tea/coffee-making facilities, car parking.
Viking House *Coffee House Lane, Greyfriars, Waterford, Co Waterford (051 853827/fax 051 871730).* **Rates** £16. An excellent hostel in the heart of the city, with first-class facilities. Single beds and private family rooms are available. Recommended, but book ahead as £16 represents the maximum bed price. Wheelchair-friendly.

Where to eat

Waterford city

McCluskey's *High Street, Waterford, Co Waterford (051 57766).* Paul McCluskey has been working in various kitchens for decades, but retains a youthfulness and spirit in his cooking more appropriate to a much younger man. The simple room of his restaurant suits the food's casual style: Dunmore plaice with a pecan and red pepper pesto, Moroccan braised beef with couscous, tagliatelle with salmon. Keen value for money.
The Wine Vault *High Street, Waterford, Co Waterford (051 53444).* David Dennison's restaurant and wine shop is the most happening place in town, powered by the proprietor's sheer love of food and wine. The wine list has won many awards, and the matching of food and wine is a major ambition, so there are special dinner and tasting menus, where all the wines are chosen to match the food. Good, simple cooking and excellent value for money.

Waterford to Cork

Only six miles south of Waterford, the seaside resort of Tramore has developed around a superb three-mile stretch of sandy beach, although many find the atmosphere too brash. There is the usual array of amusement arcades, bumper cars and fast-food outlets, also a mildly entertaining diversion in the multi-media Celtworld (051 386166) which aims to transport visitors 'back through centuries to the arrival of ancient tribes to Ireland'.

The road west from Tramore to Dungarvan hugs the coast for most of the way and there are a number of villages along the way offering pub food in beautiful settings. There are safe sandy beaches at Annestown and Bunmahon and a few miles west of Stradbally at Clonea, there is another fine beach and excellent sport facilities at the Clonea Strand Hotel (058 42416). Clonea is on the doorstep of Dungarvan town, cradled at the foot of a pine tree-clad hill and looking out at a wide expanse of sea. It's a good base from which to explore the area.

Those seeking peace and quiet, rather than sea and sand, should head north-west from Dungarvan to the beautifully situated Lismore, a centre of

Lismore, *County Waterford – bucolic peace.*

learning founded by St Carthage (or Carthach) in 636, which developed into an important monastic university in the eighth century under St Colman. It was repeatedly looted by the Vikings before the Normans finished the place off in 1173. Little remains from that period and the only ecclesiastical building of note is the attractive Protestant St Carthage's Cathedral, built on the site of a medieval cathedral destroyed by Elizabeth I's army in the late sixteenth century. Look for the statue of a book-holding bishop which may date back to the ninth century and the attractively carved McGrath family crypt. Lismore Castle, best viewed from the Cappoquin road, has been home to the Anglo-Irish since 1185, when a home for the local bishop was built here. It passed into the hands of Walter Raleigh and, in the sixteenth century, Robert Boyle, of Boyle's Law fame, was born here. Today, the castle is basically Victorian mock-Tudor and inhabited by descendants of the Duke of Devonshire. The gardens, but not the castle, are open to the public.

To the south-west of Dungarvan lies the seaside resort of Ardmore. It is a deservedly popular place with a delightful beach and the ruins of St Declan's Oratory (*see below*), complete with a fine round tower from the twelfth century.

Getting there

By bus Over a dozen Bus Éireann buses run daily between Waterford city and Tramore. Bus Éireann also run services connecting Dungarvan with Dublin,

Waterford, Killarney and Cork. Ardmore is linked by Bus Éireann to Dungarvan, Waterford and Dublin.
By road The N25 is the main road between Waterford and Cork but the coastal road (R675) between Tramore and Dungarvan is more interesting. The N72 links Lismore with Dungarvan.

Attractions

Lismore Castle Gardens
Lismore, Co Waterford (058 54424). **Open** *May-Sept* 1.45-4.45pm daily. **Admission** £2.50; £1.50 children.
The Anglo-Irish were more Anglo than Irish when it came to landscape gardening, and this is apparent not only in these gardens, but also in the surrounding countryside – designed and altered to suit English fashion.

Lismore Heritage Centre
Old Courthouse, Lismore, Co Waterford (058 54975). **Open** *Apr, May, Sept, Oct* 9.30am-5.30pm Mon-Sat; *June-Aug* 9.30am-6pm Mon-Fri; noon-5.30pm Sun. **Admission** £2.50.
Situated in the centre of town, a 30-minute audio-visual show focusing on the historical and natural attractions of the area.

Mt Melleray Cistercian Abbey
Four miles north of Cappoquin, which is 11 miles north-west of Dungarvan, Co Waterford (058 54404). **Open** daily. **Admission** by donation.
A functioning monastery that welcomes visitors who would like to look around.

St Declan's Church, Oratory & Round Tower
Above the town of Ardmore, Co Waterford. **Open** daily. **Admission** free.
Easily reached on foot from the town, these are the ruins of a thirteenth-century church with stone carvings from the earlier ninth-century church and Ogham stones. The oratory was restored in the eighteenth century, but it predates the 30-metre, twelfth-century round tower.

St Declan's Well & Stone
Reached by a path from the Cliff House Hotel, Ardmore, Co Waterford. **Open** daily. **Admission** free.
Fresh water still springs from the holy well where pilgrims washed and, at the south end of the beach, there is the stone that is said to cure both bodily and spiritual distress. The cliff walk from the holy well – overlooking sea and beach – is recommended.

Tourist information
There are tourist offices in Dungarvan (058 41741) and Ardmore (024 94444) that open in the summer.

Where to stay

Ardmore
Byron Lodge *Ardmore, Co Waterford (024 94157).* **Rates** £14-£19 per person. Six rooms, three en suite, in a Georgian town house overlooking the beach.

Dungarvan
Dungarvan Holiday Hostel *Youghal Road, Dungarvan, Co Waterford (058 44340/fax 052 36141).* **Rates** £8 per person. A tourist-board approved hostel with eight rooms, two of which can be booked as private rooms.
Park Hotel *Shandon, Dungarvan, Co Waterford (058 42899/fax 058 42969).* **Rates** single £45-£52; double £70-£84. **Credit** AmEx, DC, MC, V. Overlooking an estuary of the River Colligan. Comfortable rooms with telephone, private bathroom and satellite television. A 20-metre pool in the leisure centre; sauna, steam room and gym also.

Lismore
Buggy's Glencairn Inn *Glencairn, Lismore, Co Waterford (058 56232).* **Rates** £22 per person sharing. **Credit** MC, V. *See below* **Where to eat**.
Lismore Hotel *Main Street, Lismore, Co Waterford (058 54304/fax 054 54068).* **Rates** £25-£30 per person. **Credit** AmEx, DC, MC, V. Centrally located in the town, overlooking the river Blackwater. Ask about weekend specials.

Where to eat

Cheekpoint
McAlpin's Suir Inn *Cheekpoint, Co Waterford (051 82182).* A handsome pub down on the water just a few miles out of Waterford, McAlpin's is a staple of the area, much loved by locals who enjoy the speedy service and the tasty cooking which is always impressive: cod in Dijon mustard and dill, fillet of beef with pepper and mushrooms, the popular crab bake. There is a courtyard out by the water's edge for when the sun appears.

Dungarvan
The Tannery *Quay Street, Dungarvan, Co Waterford (058 45420).* Paul Flynn is a local lad who cut his teeth with Nico Ladenis for almost a decade before returning home (via a spell in Dublin's La Stampa) to this modernist room which is unlike anything else in the county. His skills are resplendently demonstrated in his modernised classical cooking: crispy duck confit with creamed peas and bacon and fondant potato; baked cod Niçoise with garlic and lemon; saffron risotto with aubergine and chorizo; crab linguini with tomato, garlic and ginger; spiffing strawberry crème brûlée, and the local Waterford cheeses – Ring, Knockanore and Ardsallagh – in tip-top condition.

Lismore
Buggy's Glencairn Inn *Glencairn, Lismore, Co Waterford (058 56232).* A tiny village just a few minutes' drive from Lismore, Glencairn now plays host to one of Ireland's most celebrated B&B keepers, publicans and cooks. Ken Buggy, with his wife Cathleen, has an inimitable eye for designing the places he runs, and Buggy's Glencairn Inn is no exception. The bar is a delight, the three guest rooms splendid, and the cooking mighty: fresh fish, good entrecôtes, lovely puddings. Unique.

County Cork

The largest county in Ireland, County Cork is a place of extremes: a wild coastline, small villages steeped in peat smoke, busy market towns with trifling traffic jams and fervent cattle marts and – best of all – Cork city with its delicious combination of flourishing commerce, ironic self-deprecation and good, clean 'craic'. Coming to Cork as your first trip out of Dublin, you will sense a definite change in pace which, for the habitual city dweller, may come as a shock. This is a county and a city which lives life to a slower rhythm. You should also be prepared to take whatever the weather throws at you. Blessed in recent years with almost continental summers, Cork can also experience days on end of the light misty rain which local people call 'soft days'.

Besides the small, vibrant city there are many places in West Cork which could prolong your stay. The Mizen Head and Beara peninsulas are littered with ancient sites, tiny villages, pretty beaches, stunningly bleak countryside, and innumerable historical, ecological and cultural attractions. Your nights will never be dull, especially in the summer when the packed pubs resound to authentic traditional music.

Getting there

By bus Bus Éireann services connect Cork with Dublin (4 hours) and all other major towns across Ireland. The bus station (021 508188) is at the junction of Parnell Place and Merchant's Quay in the centre of the city.
By train It takes 2 hours to reach Cork from Dublin by train. The train station (021 506766) is on Lower Glanmire Road and there are also connections from Cork to Killarney and Waterford.
By air There are direct flights to Dublin on Aer Lingus. The national airline also connects Cork with London Heathrow while Ryanair flies to Cork from London Stansted. There are also direct flights to Manchester, Paris, Amsterdam and other European cities. The airport (021 313131) is about five miles south of the city and there is a bus service to and from the city centre.
By ferry There are ferry connections with Swansea in the UK and the company has an office at 52 South Mall (021 271166) as well as at the Ringaskiddy ferry terminal (021 378036), which takes about 20 minutes to reach from the city centre. For foot passengers, there is a bus service to and from the city. Ferry connections to Roscoff and St Malo in France are handled by Brittany Ferries (021 277801) whose office is next to the tourist office. Irish Ferries handles the service to Le Harve, Cherbourg and Roscoff and their office is at 9 Bridge Street (021 504333).

Cork city

The second largest city in Ireland, Cork is compact and accessible, built around an island in the river Lee and overlooked by nineteenth-century suburbs which spread across the surrounding hills. It was founded in the seventh century by a monk, St Finbarr, who built a school and monastery on the site of the present St Finbarr's Cathedral. The area around the new settlement was river and marsh, hence the name Corchai – 'a marshy place'. Two centuries later, the Vikings arrived, pillaging and burning as they went, destroying the abbey and settlement and rebuilding on the island in the middle of the river. The settlement thrived on trade and shipping, accommodated the Anglo-Normans in the twelfth century, adding fortified walls which kept Cromwell out in the mid-seventeenth century, but fell to William of Orange in 1690.

Under new management, the city continued to thrive, its new masters draining the marshes around the settlement and building canals to bring boats further into the city. The remains of these can still be seen in Grand Parade, where the mooring posts are still at the kerbside of what was once a waterway. In the eighteenth and nineteenth centuries, the characteristic style of modern Cork was established with grand bow-fronted mansions and

great gothic monstrosities of churches and public buildings built in limestone and sandstone.

During the Troubles of the early twentieth century, Cork was strongly Republican and suffered under the Black and Tans. In 1920, the mayor of Cork was shot by the Black and Tans, and his successor died in jail on hunger strike.

In the economic malaise which struck Ireland after independence, Cork gradually declined as a trading centre. Its stagnation over those years meant that few of the horrific building projects of the 1960s and '70s damaged its austere nineteenth-century buildings. What you see when you visit is how parts of Britain might have looked without the ugly developments of the post-war years. Cork, like the rest of Ireland, is currently booming, giving rise to the wonderful irony of Englishmen being recruited to work on Irish building sites.

There is a lively entertainment scene in the city. The Triskel Arts Centre, the Firkin Crane Theatre, Opera House, Cork Arts Theatre and City Hall have lots of theatre and performances to offer, while there are many pubs catering to various types of music. On Union Quay are three pubs – the Donkey's Ears, the Phoenix and the Lobby – where you can choose between traditional music, reggae, blues, folk, bluegrass and hip-hop. Music and comedy clubs are also very popular. Try City Limits at Coburg Street.

St Finbarr's Cathedral, *Cork city – see p207.*

*City Hall, **Cork city**, where the local accent is one of the loveliest but most impenetrable.*

The best way to discover the mood and sights of the city is a leisurely stroll around its centre. The heart of the city is Patrick Street, its curved lines marking what was once a waterway. As you walk towards the river, the essential nature of the city centre lies before you. Mothercare, Waterstone's and Burger King sit beside much older local establishments such as gentlemen's outfitters and coal-merchants, while local chainstores mimic their British counterparts. All along the road, medieval side alleys lead off to fascinating little shops, restaurants and, of course, pubs. The streets are filled with buskers, pavement artists and wide boys with fake perfume and posters spread out on the street: the likelihood of there not being a gaggle of young girls collecting for one of Ireland's hundreds of charities is remote.

At the top of St Patrick's Street, past the statue of Father Theobald Matthew, one of the leading lights of the temperance movement, is St Patrick's Bridge. The bridge once looked over a busy waterfront with huge merchant ships docked below it. Nowadays, the occasional freighter can be seen but the river banks are largely empty. Across the bridge and left along the riverfront is Camden Place with its eighteenth-century Georgian houses. A right turn up John's Street and then a left into Dominick Street brings you to the Shandon area, and what was once an important butter market. People from all over Cork and Kerry once spent days journeying here along the 'butter roads' bringing their firkins of butter for sale to the Butter

Exchange, where it was tested, weighed and probably shipped abroad. The building and its surroundings have been renovated and turned into bijou craft shops and an arts centre.

Close by, recognisable by the 11-foot-long salmon weather vane on the top, is St Ann's Church, Shandon, built in the eighteenth century. You can climb to the top of the pink and white tower and ring the bells for a small fee, or just look at the views from the top. The giant salmon is accounted for by the fact that the monks of Cork were the only people allowed to fish for salmon in the area.

Heading back down to the river and across the Opera House bridge to Emmet Place brings you to the Opera House and, beside it, the Crawford Municipal Art Gallery, a distinctive red brick building. Inside you'll find sculptures by Seamus Murphy and paintings by Harry Clarke and James Barry. Along the adjoining Paul Street with its trendy shops, is Corn Market Street where the Coal Quay Market is held. This flea market has been held here for at least a century and all manner old clothes and otherwise unsaleable stuff exchanges hands.

Heading out west, first along Liberty Street, then Sheares Street into Mardyke Street, you come to the Public Museum and Fitzgerald Park. The museum has exhibits on Republican history as well as archeological material. More to the point, if you are still on this walk, it has a café where you can rest before the next part of the journey.

The walk could continue south over towards the river and into the University campus where there is a collection of Ogham stones (in the quadrangle building that faces Western Road), the Honan Chapel just behind it, built in 1915 with some beautiful modern stained glass, and some life-size bronzes by Seamus Murphy in the campus grounds. Walking through the campus grounds to College Road and heading east back into town, you come to St Finbarr's Cathedral, the site of the first settlement of Cork. The present building is late nineteenth-century gothic, built by William Burgess. An earlier cathedral stood here until 1690 and the Siege of Cork. Some remains of an Elizabethan fort have been recovered nearby.

From the cathedral you can make your way back into town along Bishop Street and Proby's Quay to South Bridge Street, the site of the medieval entrance to the city. From there, you can walk along Grand Parade, stopping in the covered English Market to admire the goods for sale and then back to Patrick Street.

There are many other walks possible around this compact city. A walk along the river banks reveals more of Cork's history, while the many side streets reveal excellent craft and clothing shops, antiquarian bookshops, and elderly haberdasheries, bootmenders, and many other stores long since gone from the rest of the British Isles.

Attractions

View from Patrick's Hill, **Cork city**.

Cork City Gaol

Sunday's Well, Cork, Co Cork (021 305022). **Open** 9.30am-5pm daily. **Closed** 24-26 Dec. **Admission** £3.
West of the city along Sunday's Well Road, the prison was built in the nineteenth century and turned over to tourism quite recently. The tour of the prison shows the cells themselves with a few models of inmates having a miserable time. The prison is remarkably untouched and gives a genuine feel of what life in this place must have been like. You can collect a sound tape and go around on your own or join a guided tour. At the end is a watchable audio-visual show. It's a good half hour's walk out of town but a bus goes from the tourist office in Grand Parade. Last admission 5pm.

Cork Public Museum

Fitzgerald Park, Western Road, Cork, Co Cork (021 270679). Bus 8. **Open** 11am-1pm, 2.15-5pm (6pm in summer), Mon-Fri; 3-5pm Sun. **Admission** free.

Crawford Municipal Art Gallery

Emmet Place, Cork, Co Cork (021 273377). **Open** 9.30am-5pm Mon-Sat. **Admission** free.
A delightful gallery that doesn't exhaust and with a pleasant restaurant.

Firkin Crane Centre

Dominick Street, Cork, Co Cork.
Once the weighing station for the butter exchange, now a theatre with occasional dance and music performances. Check with the tourist offices regarding times and prices.

St Anne's Church, Shandon

Corner of Church Street and Eason Hill, Cork, Co Cork. **Open** 10am-5pm daily. **Admission** £1.50.
The charge covers viewing the church, climbing the tower and ringing the bells. The church also has a collection of antique books.

St Finbarr's Cathedral

Bishop Street, Cork, Co Cork. **Open** 10am-5pm Mon-Sat; open for services, Sun. **Admission** £1 donation requested.
Highly ornamental mosaic work, carvings and stained glass are the principal attractions. Guided tours available.

Tourist information

Grand Parade, Cork, Co Cork (021 273251). **Open** *July, Aug* 9am-7pm Mon-Sat, 2-5pm Sun; *Sept-May* 9am-5.30pm Mon-Sat. **Closed** 1-2pm.

Festivals & events

The Cork Jazz Festival is held in late October. The major events sell out quickly but advance booking is possible through the Opera House (021 270022). You should also book your hotel room a long time ahead. Earlier in the month is the Film Festival, less well attended but tickets can be difficult to get on the day. Programme and tickets can be obtained at the Opera House. At the end of May, there is a choral festival and in June there is the Cork Youth Arts festival, programmes for which can be obtained from the Triskel Arts Centre in Main Street (021 507487).

Tours & cruises

The tourist office in Grand Parade organises evening walking tours of the city on Tuesdays and Thursdays. There is also an organised tour of the University, at 2.30pm Monday to Friday, starting

River Lee and Fr Matthew Church, **Cork city.**

from the main gate in Western Road, costing £2.
Cycle tours around the city and the surrounding
area are organised by Rothar (021 274143).

Where to stay

Cork city

Kinlay House Budget Accommodation Centre *Bob
and Joan Walk, Shandon, Cork, Co Cork (021 508966;
fax 021 506927; e-mail kincork@usit.ie).* **Rates** B&B
from £7.50 per person. Four-bedded and two-bedded
rooms, self-catering kitchen, open 24-hours, launderette.
Metropole Hotel *Maccurtain Street, Cork, Co Cork
(021 508112/fax 021 506450).* **Rates** single £85; double
£130. **Credit** AmEx, DC, MC, V. A genteel Victorian ex-
temperance hotel with lots of luxuries and a fully
equipped leisure centre with three pools, jacuzzi, steam
room, massage and gymnasium. Central, close to station.
Seven, North Mall *North Mall, Cork, Co Cork (021
397191/fax 021 300811).* **Rates** single £35; double £50.
Credit DC, MC, V. Centrally located, gardens, 250-year-
old listed building, private car park.
Shandon Bells B&B *Western Road, Cork, Co Cork
(021 276242).* **Rates** single £15; double £30. **Credit** MC,
V. Small guest house close to town; parking.
Victoria Inn *Patrick Street, Cork, Co Cork (021
278788/fax 021 278790).* **Rates** single £35; double £70.
Credit AmEx, MC, V. Georgian building, very central,
full of history, bar, music, family suites.

Where to eat

Cork city

Café Paradiso *Lancaster Quay, Western Road, Cork,
Co Cork (021 277939).* Denis Cotter is the most creative
vegetarian cook in Ireland, his style enjoying a lushness

and spontaneity which perfectly suits the ambience of
the small room where Bridget Healy masterminds
service. Courgette and sweet potato tortilla with
avocado salsa, potato and rocket cakes with a stew of
butterbeans and vegetables, roasted sweet peppers
stuffed with pine nuts and capers on wilted chard with a
mushroom cream. The food is rich, yet light, and
confidently improving all the time.
Isaac's Brasserie *MacCurtain Street, Cork, Co Cork
(021 503805).* The elegant brasserie-style room of
Isaac's, spacious and airy, is one of the reasons for its
success, while Canice Sharkey's cooking supplies the
culinary backbone of an efficient organisation.
Provençale bean stew with Clonakilty black pudding,
haricot and lamb stew with a Parmesan crust, pheasant
with potato and a light butter sauce, classics such as
sirloin with a bearnaise. Keen prices; excellent staff.
The Ivory Tower Restaurant *35 Princes Street,
Cork, Co Cork (021 274665).* Seamus O'Connell's
culinary style is as iconoclastic as you can get in Ireland.
He may run his first-floor restaurant in a laid-back style,
but his cooking has all the fizz and urgency of an
instinctive improviser at work. Dishes are rarely the
same twice, and his fluency means he makes the best
sushi in the country, the best chicken chimichanga, the
best blackened grey mullet, the best mackerel teriyaki,
the best warm duck confit with shiitake. The music is as
urgently up-to-the-minute as the food, while service
operates at its own pace.
The Long Valley *Winthrop Street, Cork, Co Cork.*
Surreal is the only word for it. Ladies wearing operating
theatre gowns and dead-pan expressions pull pints and
make bumper sandwiches behind the bar of this great
Cork institution, whilst the weirdest music you have
never heard before wafts around the bar and the snugs.
This is the pub from another planet.

Around Cork city

Several places of interest around Cork can be
reached by bus, car or bicycle. Cycle Scene at 396
Blarney Street (021 301183) and the Cycle Repair
Centre in Kyle Street (021 276255) hire bikes out
through the Raleigh rent-a bike scheme. There are
several car hire places around Cork. The most centrally located is Great Island Car Rentals, at 47
MacCurtain Street (021 503536). Cobh and Fota
Wildlife park are accessible by train while other
places are on bus routes. You should check with
the tourist office or bus station.

Six miles west of Cork, Blarney is a major
tourist centre with tour buses lining up to spill
out their passengers all intent on kissing the
Blarney Stone. Beside this, the castle is a fine
place to visit, built in 1446 by Dermot McCarthy.
The Stone itself is a limestone block set high in
the battlements and to kiss it involves being dan-
gled by the legs and leaning over backwards.
Apart from a brush with death, the encounter is
said to turn the kisser into a mellifluous and
loquacious speaker.

In the grounds of Blarney Castle there lies an
ancient site with wizened holly and yew trees
called Rock Close, which is thought to be a
pre-Christian place of worship. Also part of the
attraction is Blarney House and gardens, a

nineteenth-century building with lashings of over-the-top Victoriana and earlier furnishings, as well as Waterford crystal chandeliers. The Blarney Woollen Mills are also here and do a roaring trade with the tourists.

Formerly known as Queenstown, Cobh is a pretty little village set on a hillside overlooking the sea. The extravagant gothic cathedral, designed by Pugin, is way up the hill and has great views over the village and the sea.

It was from Cobh that thousands of Irish people left in a desperate attempt to find a better life. Convicts were also brought here from Cork gaol to the prison ships bound for Australia. In 1838, the first transatlantic steamer left this port with New York as its next port of call and, with a little less luck, the *Titanic* also berthed here before her doomed voyage. The *Lusitania*, sunk by the Germans during World War I, was on her way to Liverpool and passing this part of the coast when she was torpedoed: the survivors and many of the 1,198 dead were brought here. A very good heritage centre, the Queenstown Story tells Cobh's long history as a fishing port and maritime centre. Cobh has a stony beach and sailboats can be hired locally while harbour trips (021 811485) go out regularly.

Nearby Fota Wildlife Park is a great day out, especially for children. The wildlife really does wander around the place – except, mercifully, for the cheetahs, which are currently conducting a highly successful breeding programme behind bars. You can watch ostrich eggs being hatched in the hatchery and may even come across a stray egg lying about the park. Nearby Fota House is not open to the public, but its exterior is magnificent and there is an arboretum with a collection of rare and exotic plants. If you stop for a break in the coffee shop keep a wary eye out for the sweet-toothed lemurs. There is also a tour train carrying visitors who prefer not to walk around the park and a games park for children.

The Jameson Heritage Centre in Midleton, about ten miles east of Cork, is also worth a visit. The hour-or-so-long tour is excellent, taking you through the process of whiskey distilling and the daily work of the employees. Among other things, you will see the world's largest whiskey still. The tour ends with a drop of the hard stuff.

The Royal Gunpowder Mills is another newish, tourist-oriented heritage site, although the mills themselves date back to the nineteenth century and were one of the largest gunpowder factories in Europe. There is a guided tour of the factory, an audio-visual show, extensive grounds and a coffee and craft shop.

Youghal is an interesting little town to the east of Cork city, close to the county of Waterford. There is the inevitable heritage centre, from which you'll be directed to Cromwell's Arch, a thirteenth-

Tourists can enjoy touring **Blarney Castle**...

century water gate in the fifteenth-century town walls, through which Cromwell is said to have departed from Ireland. There are some seventeenth-century alms houses, a fifteenth-century castle and the alleged home of Sir Walter Raleigh, who was mayor of the place in 1588 and is said to have introduced the potato to Ireland via his estates here. There's also a rather lovely thirteenth-century Church of Ireland church.

Away from the history, both Blarney and Youghal have pubs with live music at night. Blarney caters to the shillelagh-waving tourist crowd, but Youghal has a more vibrant nightlife, including discos, traditional music, jazz and Irish ballads.

... and kissing the **Blarney Stone**.

*Clock Gate, Main Street, **Youghal**, Co Cork.*

*Picture-postcard **Kinsale**, County Cork.*

Attractions

Blarney Castle & Blarney House
Blarney, Co Cork (021 385252). **Open** Castle 9am-sundown Mon-Sat. House *June-Sept* noon-6pm Mon-Sat. **Admission** *combined ticket to both sites* £5; £3 children.

Clock Gate Heritage Centre
Main Street, Youghal (024 92390). **Open** *Apr-Sept* 9.30am-5.30pm daily. *Oct-Mar* shorter hours. **Admission** £1.
Walking tours of the town can be arranged from May to September, at 11am and 3pm Monday to Saturday, through the tourist office in this building. Enquire there also about harbour cruises.

Fota Wildlife Park
Fota Island, Co Cork (021 12678). **Open** *Apr-Oct* 10am-5pm Mon-Sat; 11am-5pm Sun. **Admission** £3.50; £2 children. **Parking** £1.

Gunpowder Mills, Ballincollig
Ballincollig, eight miles west of Cork on the main road to Killarney. **Open** *Apr-Sept* 10am-6pm daily. **Admission** £2.50, £1.50 children.

Jameson's Heritage Centre
Midleton, Co Cork (021 613594). **Open** *Mar-mid Nov* daily. **Admission** £3.50; £1.50 children.

The Queenstown Story Heritage Centre
Cobh Railway Station, Cobh, Co Cork (021 813595). **Open** *Mar-Oct* 10am-6pm Mon-Sat. **Admission** £3.50; £2 children.

Festivals & events

Cobh has a regatta weekend in mid-August and the Ford Yacht Week is across the bay in Crosshaven in the third week in July on alternate summers (next Yacht Week in July 1998).

Where to stay

All these places are easily day trips out of Cork, but could instead form part of a journey around the county, in which case staying at Youghal, Cobh or Blarney might prove useful.

Blarney
Blarney Castle Hotel *Blarney, Co Cork (021 385116/ fax 021 385542).* **Rates** *single* £32; *double* £54. **Credit** AmEx, MC, V.

Cobh
Rinn-Ronain Hotel *Rushbrooke, Cobh, Co Cork (021 811407; fax 021 812042).* **Rates** *single* £25; *double* £34. **Credit** MC, V.

Youghal
Aherne's *163, North Main Street, Youghal, Co Cork (024 92424/fax 024 93633).* **Rates** *single* £70; *double* £100. **Credit** AmEx DC, MC, V. **Closed** 24-28 Dec. Small classy guest house with noted restaurant.

Where to eat

Midleton
The Farm Gate *Midleton, Co Cork (021 632771).* Marog O'Brien keeps things simple at this buzzing shop

and restaurant – the elder sister to Cork city's Farm Gate Café – just off the main street. Lunchtime food – pasta dishes, open sandwiches, pancakes, creamy desserts – is well judged, while for Friday and Saturday dinners, Marog waits to see what fish and shellfish arrives, and treats her lamb and free range ducks as simply as you could hope for.

Youghal

The Earl of Orrery *North Main Street, Youghal (024 93208).* Youghal is celebrated for the institution which is Aherne's (*see above* **Where to stay**) seafood restaurant – where the pub lunches are also excellent – but don't overlook the simple space which is Colm Falvey's Earl of Orrery restaurant. A single room put together on a shoestring, the cooking is spirited and well-realised, and very good value. Wild salmon with tomato and fresh herb salsa, deep-fried squid with a provençale sauce, duck confit with lentils and pork with fresh herbs, all show the care and ambition of an unpretentious young man.

Kinsale

This once-flourishing port town marks the beginning of a meandering coastal route west. It is picture postcard pretty and, apart from the serious traffic congestion in summer (well, serious by Irish standards at least), an idyllic place to stay – especially if you enjoy good food, for Kinsale is justly called the gourmet capital of Ireland.

Like Cork and the other sheltered harbours around the area, it was settled in very early times, before succumbing to the Anglo-Norman invasion in the fourteenth century. Trade with Europe flourished until 1601, when a Spanish fleet landed here. Spain was at war with England and offered the rebel forces of Ulster support. They landed at Kinsale and the English fleet began a blockade of the Spanish, forcing the Irish land army to march through frozen countryside from Ulster to Kinsale. English and Irish forces met at Kinsale on Christmas Eve and the Irish were defeated. The battle was a decisive moment in the demise of Gaelic Ireland. Catholics, that is the Irish, were barred from the town completely. By the end of the century, Kinsale had given way to other ports, and trade with Europe in general had declined in favour of trade with Britain.

Nowadays, Kinsale has much to offer. It has abundant bird life, there are several signposted walks in the area, and the evenings are good for tasting the local food and enjoying some good music. It isn't hard to find the music in Kinsale – just stand and listen. Particularly good are the 1601 pub and the Lord Kinsale on Main Street. Music sessions are usually advertised in advance on little hand-written notices in windows. There is a tiny museum (*see below*) in what used to be the courthouse; it contains memorabilia from the sinking of the *Lusitania* in 1915. A little east of town are the ruins of Charles Fort (*see below*), built to protect the town after the siege of 1601, and in use until it was destroyed by the IRA in 1922.

Getting there

By bus Buses depart regularly from Cork to Kinsale three or four times a day. If you aren't sure of your next destination, check the price of a return ticket which is often the same as a single.

Attractions

Charles Fort

2 miles east of town, follow the signposts from the centre of Kinsale. **Open** *summer* 9am-6pm Mon-Sat. **Admission** £2. Excellent guided tours.

Desmond Castle

Cork Street, Kinsale, Co Cork. **Open** *spring-autumn* 9am-6pm Tue-Sun. **Admission** £1 (incl guided tour).

Kinsale Museum

Market Square, Kinsale, Co Cork. **Open** check with tourist office. **Admission** £1.
The old courthouse where the enquiry into the sinking of the *Lusitania* was held.

Festivals & events

The gourmet festival is held in early October, usually for four days. Four-day membership costs £70 and includes entrance to the events and a discount at the restaurants. You can also buy a day ticket. To book a place contact Peter Barry, Scilly, Kinsale, Co Cork (021 774026).

Tours & cruises

The tourist office (021 772234) in the centre of town organises walking tours of the town in several languages or you can hire a horse and carriage. Otherwise, try a pony trekking tour organised by Ballinadee Stables (021 778152).

Where to stay

Kinsale

Kilcaw Guest House *Kilcaw, Kinsale, Co Cork (021 774155/fax 021 774755).* **Rates** £20 per person sharing (£10 supplement for single occupancy). **Credit** DC, MC, V. Ten-minute walk from centre of Kinsale. Plenty of parking; private gardens.
Tierney's Guesthouse *Main Street, Kinsale, Co Cork (012 772205/fax 021 774363).* **Rates** *single* £25; *double* £35. **Credit** AmEx, DC, MC, V. In town centre, lots of amenities; wheelchair-friendly.
Trident Hotel *World's End, Kinsale, Co Cork (021 772301/fax 021 774173).* **Rates** *single* £77; *double* £124. **Credit** AmEx, DC, MC, V. **Closed** 25-26 Dec. Views of the harbour, good restaurant, leisure facilities.

Where to eat

Kinsale

Man Friday *Scilly, Kinsale, Co Cork (021 772260).* The style of Man Friday, and Philip Horgan's casual, full-flavoured food, suits the spirit of the popular, raucous town of Kinsale. The room is noisy, service speedy and the food simple – deep-fried Brie with a plum sauce, rack of lamb with rosemary, chocolate terrine – and everyone piles out afterwards into one of the many pubs in the village.

The largest county in Ireland, Cork has room for variety, from bustling city to rolling countryside.

The Oystercatcher *Oysterhaven, near Kinsale, Co Cork (021 770822).* A few miles out of Kinsale, Oysterhaven is the perfect quiet setting for the low-slung, white-washed cottage where Bill and Sylvia Patterson combine their talents in and out of the kitchen to create the best food for miles around. Enjoy rock oysters with angel hair pasta, fresh tuna with pickled lemons and sorrel, squab with Pineau de Charentes, their near-legendary oyster sausage, even savoury desserts such as angels and devils on horseback. The accomplishment is memorable.

Clonakilty & around

The coastline west from Kinsale is a pleasant muddle of villages and coves which warrant much more than a cursory glance through the windscreen as you drive past. Ballinspittle is the putative home to a weeping Virgin Mary statue. It is a pleasant, usually quiet little village, which did a roaring trade for a few months until the coachloads of miracle hunters went off to County Mayo in pursuit of new revelations. Ballinspittle is also the closest village to the Old Head of Kinsale, a promontory to the south with the remains of a fifteenth-century castle.

Further west you come to Timoleague, with its Franciscan friary established in the thirteenth century and damaged by the British in 1642. The ruins are definitely worth a visit. Also in Timoleague are the castle gardens (*see below*) which are open to the public and contain the scanty remains of the thirteenth-century castle.

The gardens are sheltered and the plants are typical of a more Mediterranean climate. From Timoleague, there is a pleasant coastal road through Courtmacsherry, a quiet holiday spot, and Butlerstown to Clonakilty.

Clonakilty is a pretty, bustling, touristy sort of town, with good night life and traditional music, even out of the summer season. It began life as a Protestant settlement in the seventeenth century and became a linen production centre, until the bottom fell out of that market. Its town planners have made good use of its ancient buildings, the original Presbyterian church now home to the post office, while the library is housed in an old mill. A good hour or so can be spent in the local museum, which is well laid out and contains interesting material on schools, local cottage industries and memorabilia of the struggle for independence and the civil war. East of town is the Lisnagun Ring Fort (*see below*), a reconstructed tenth-century fortified farmhouse complete with protective ditch, thatched daub and wattle buildings and souterrains.

South of Clonakilty, beyond the huge sandy expanse of Inchydoney beach, is Castlefreke, an eighteenth-century castle which now stands in glorious ruin with notices warning of the falling masonry. Also nearby is the Drombeg Stone Circle (*see below*), a particularly well-preserved pre-Christian site aligned to the midwinter sunset with what is thought to be a cooking place. West of town is the Michael Collins Memorial Centre (*see below*) where he was born and lived until 1906.

Moving west away from Clonakilty towards Rosscarbery is Castle Salem, a quite extraordinary seventeenth-century farmhouse built on to the side of a fifteenth-century castle complete with roof: worth a visit for the eccentricity value. Next along the N71 is Rosscarbery, with its narrow inlet from the sea, full of interesting birdlife. The village has a twelfth-century church. More tiny villages along the route to Skibbereen are Glandore and Union Hall. Glandore was the home of William Thompson, a noted communist who established a model community here in the nineteenth century and was mentioned in Marx's *Das Kapital*. At Union Hall, named after the Act of Union, is the tiny Ceim Hill Museum, full of bits and pieces unearthed by a local farmer.

Getting there

By bus There is one bus a day from Cork to Timoleague, leaving Cork at 5.45pm and starting its return journey from Timoleague at 8am. There is a daily bus to Clonakilty leaving Cork at 10.25am. Two buses travel from Clonakilty to Cork leaving from the Pearse Street bus stop at 7.10am and 7.20pm.
Bike hire is possible in Clonakilty from MTM cycles in Ashe Street (023 33584).

Attractions

Drombeg Stone Circle
Signposted off N71 west of Rosscarbery. **Admission** free.
West Cork has a significant smattering of New Age folk who value the site highly.

Lisnagun Ring Fort
Lisnagun, Clonakilty, Co Cork. **Open** 1-6pm. **Admission** £1.50.

Michael Collins Memorial Centre
Signposted on N71, three miles west of Clonakilty, Co Cork. **Admission** free.
You've seen the film, now see his home which was burnt by the British.

Timoleague Castle Gardens
Timoleague, Co Cork. **Open** 11am-5.30pm Mon-Sat. **Admission** £1.50.

West Cork Regional Museum
Oliver Plunket Street, Clonakilty, Co Cork. **Open** *May-Oct* 10.30am-5.30pm Mon-Sat. **Admission** £1.

Tourist information
Asna Street, Clonakilty (023 33226). **Open** *July-Aug* 10am-6pm Mon-Sat.

Festivals & events

The Clonakilty Festival is in late June or early July and is well worth attending. Lots of music, street theatre, jugglers, a carnival and other events. In the last weekend in August, there is a country and western festival.

At Courtmacsherry, there is a harbour festival in late July/early August. Music, storytelling, football matches and teddy bear competitions make for good family fun.

Where to stay

Clonakilty
Inchydoney Hotel *Clonakilty, Co Cork (023 33143).* **Rates** *single* £20; *double* £40. **Credit** MC, V. Overlooks two excellent sandy beaches, playgrounds and tennis courts.
O'Donovan's Hotel *Pearse Street, Clonakilty, Co Cork (023 33250/fax 023 33250).* **Rates** *single* £23; *double* £46. **Credit** AmEx, DC, MC, V. Historic local inn where both Parnell and Michael Collins stayed.

Where to eat

Butlerstown
Dunworley Cottage Restaurant *Butlerstown, Co Cork (023 40314).* A Swedish cook works with Irish ingredients, and creates the unique synthesis which is Dunworley Cottage. Katherine Noren's appreciation of the local foods marries perfectly with her native dishes – steamed bread, cured fish salad, nettle soup, mussel soup, smoked veal loin – and in the almost stoic simplicity of the pair of rooms a dinner can yield tastes and textures which are mesmeric.

Clonakilty
Fionnuala's *Ashe Street, Clonakilty, Co Cork (023 34355).* A quaint little room with a jumble of furniture and personal effects, Fionnuala's offers an Irish spin on Italian dishes of pizza and pasta, all served with a fizzy energy and charm. Dinners by candlelight may offer scrummy classics such as chicken cacciatore.

Timoleague
Lettercollum House *Timoleague (023 46251).* An old convent, transformed into a lively restaurant and a comfortable place to stay, is where Con McLoughlin and Karen Austin demonstrate that their experimentalism and multi-cultural influences are exactly understood. Grilled polenta with Cashel Blue and walnut vinaigrette, rack of lamb with roasted Mediterranean vegetables and radish tzatziki, farmyard duck with Chinese five spice and ginger and honey glaze, charlotte of sweet red peppers, courgette and brown lentils with tomato butter sauce. Great value, great vegetarian dishes, and Sunday lunch is one of the treats of the county.

Skibbereen & around

Once past Clonakilty, you are in deepest West Cork and a whole new way of life. The area has been extensively settled by blow-ins from Europe and beyond. Besides affluent Germans and Swiss, there are whole tribes of New Age travellers who liven up the area. Newcomers and local country people mix with those relics of a bygone age – the Anglo-Irish – to make a heady mix of ideas and cultures which can be seen in the little hostels, cafés and country houses, especially on fair days and festivals.

The countryside is beautiful, with little coves, nineteenth-century architecture and ancient sites which appear suddenly before you. Skibbereen is a remarkable little town with ancient shops sitting beside bijou coffee shops, a department store/supermarket/electrical shop and a lively cattle mart: on fair days, horses and carts are a common sight.

Skibbereen began life after a raid – by Algerians, of all people – on nearby Baltimore in 1631 led people to move inland for security. Like many other market towns, Skibbereen was largely dominated by Protestants, although during the Famine many thousands of Catholic peasants in the area died or emigrated. The town lost half its population either from the Famine itself or through emigration over the next hundred years. It thrives nowadays on the Wednesday mart and on the tourist trade.

There's plenty to see in and around Skibbereen. In town is an arts centre, exhibiting and selling the work of local artists. Just outside town is the ecological anomaly that is Lough Hyne (*see below*), a saltwater lake fed by the sea at high tide and by a stream at low tide. Its peculiar nature means that the sea water in it is much warmer than the sea around these shores and several species of fish and plants more common to warmer climates thrive here. There are some lovely walks in the wildlife-rich Knockomagh Woods behind the lake.

Further south-west along the coast is Baltimore, scene of the Algerian raid and now a pleasant little fishing village full of pretty pubs and restaurants and deck-shoed nautical types. From Baltimore, ferries can be taken out to Clear Island (*see below*) which has sandy beaches and scenic walks and, for bird lovers, vast numbers of migrating seabirds. Also accessible from Baltimore is Sherkin Island (*see below*), with its three silver-sand beaches and lively pubs. For those who like the wild life, sandy beaches and flexible pub opening hours in a place where the Garda rarely bother to visit, there are camp sites, hostels and B&B places on both islands.

West of Skibbereen, the road meanders along to Ballydehob, a place almost too pretty to be true. The entrance to the village from the east is particularly pleasant, passing the old five-arched railway viaduct. West again from Ballydehob, is Schull with the peak of Mount Gabriel towering over it. The strange-looking globes on the top are tracking stations but what they track, and for whom, isn't clear. It is possible to drive up Mount Gabriel from where you can see, among other things, the Fastnet Rock. Schull has a planetarium (*see below*), the only one in the Republic, shops to interest tourists and a well-appointed harbour.

Carrying on west, you pass through the village of Goleen to Crookhaven and Barleycove where the beach is excellent and never crowded. From Barleycove, an excellent walk can be taken to Three Castles Head, the site of a thirteenth-century castle. The remains stand eerily by a silent lake amid surrounding hills, with steep cliffs to the rear. Also nearby is the Mizen Head Lighthouse (*see below*), now open to the public with displays about the lives of the men who once manned the lighthouse and some facts about local wildlife.

Getting there

By bus A bus travels twice a day between Clonakilty, Skibbereen, Ballydehob and Schull. Buses go to Skibbereen from Cork city and Killarney daily. Buses to Baltimore travel daily from Skibbereen. There is no bus service to Crookhaven or Barleycove.

By ferry There is a daily ferry from Baltimore to Schull each day except Tuesday and Sunday in summer (028 39153). Boats for Clear Island leave Baltimore at 10am, 2.30pm and 4.30pm daily in July and August. There is also a ferry to Clear Island from Schull. To Sherkin, there are seven boats a day from Baltimore (028 20125), the last boat leaving Sherkin at 8.45pm.

Bikes can be hired from Roycrofts (028 21235) in Ilen Street in Skibbereen, Cotter's Yard (028 28165) in Main Street, Schull, or the Barleycove Caravanning and Camping Park at Barleycove.

Attractions

Clear Island
45 minutes by ferry from Baltimore, Co Cork.
Bird Observatory, stunning walks, mini museum, shops. Clear island is part of the Gaeltacht, where you will hear Gaelic spoken.

Lough Hyne
Four miles south of Skibbereen, Co Cork.
Set in a peaceful nature reserve.

Mizen Vision
Mizen Head, Co Cork (028 35225). **Open** *June-Sept* 11am-5.30pm daily. **Admission** £2.
Views, the Keeper's House and the engine room.

Planetarium
Schull, Co Cork (028 28552). **Open** *July-Aug* 2-5pm, 7-9pm, Tue-Sat. **Admission** £2.
Includes a star show in the eight-metre dome, video and slide shows. Opening times for rest of the year vary, so check local listings.

Sherkin Island
Ten minutes by ferry from Baltimore, Co Cork. Boats go regularly throughout the day.
Three sandy beaches, two pubs selling bar food.

West Cork Arts Centre
North Road, Skibbereen, Co Cork. **Open** from 12.30pm daily. **Admission** free.
Temporary exhibitions and small craft shop.

Festivals & events

Skibbereen Welcome Home Week is an annual event taking place in late July/early August. With excellent music performances, street entertainment and football, it also offers such dubious treats as the Homemaker of the Year competition (festival office 028 22070).

Baltimore Regatta Weekend is usually just after the August Bank Holiday. It is a one-day event of yacht races, treasure hunts (028 39119). Courtmacsherry Harbour Festival is a ten-day festival from late July to early August.

Cape Clear Storytelling Festival is a three-day event on the island in late August. Stories told around the fires in local homes, seminars for storytellers, boat trips, nature walks (028 39157).

Where to stay

Schull

East End Hotel *Main Street, Schull, Co Cork (028 2810/fax 028 28012)*. **Rates** *single* £35; *double* £50; lower rates for rooms without en suite bathroom. **Credit** AmEx, MC, V.

Skibbereen

West Cork Hotel *Glen Street, Skibbereen, Co Cork (028 21277/fax 028 22333)*. **Rates** *single* £35; *double* £70. **Credit** AmEx, DC, MC, V. Three-star hotel in quiet end of town, gardens, pleasant location. Closed 23-28 December.

Windmill Guesthouse *46 North Street, Skibbereen, Co Cork (028 21606)*. **Rates** *single* £30; *double* £52. **Credit** MC, V.

Tourist information

The tourist office in Skibbereen is in North Street (028 21766), open 9.15am-5.15pm Monday to Saturday all year. There is a tiny tourist information office at Baltimore harbour (028 20441), open 9.30am-5.30pm Monday to Saturday in summer. In Schull, a free tourist information leaflet including walks can be obtained from the Courtyard and several shops and pubs.

Where to eat

Ballydehob

Levis' Pub *Main Street, Ballydehob, Co Cork*. Cared for by the Misses Levis, this is a lovely little pub, which exists in a perfect time warp, and which acts as a waiting area for the diners from Annie's Restaurant, just across the road.

Baltimore

Chez Youen *The Pier, Baltimore, Co Cork (028 20136)*. Youen Jacob has been cooking in the traditional French style for decades now, and his staples – the bumper shellfish platter, sweet local lamb – are as good as ever.

Durrus

Blair's Cove *Durrus, Co Cork (027 61127)*. A gorgeous, high-vaulted room, centred around a huge hors d'oeuvre table with a wood-burning fire at the end for grilling meats, Blair's Cove is a favourite restaurant for many people, and can produce sublime food. In Durrus village itself, there is good food to be enjoyed in three of the pubs– Suzanne's, Ivo's and the Long Boat.

Schull

Adele's *Main Street, Schull, Co Cork (028 28459)*. This bakery-cum-café is one of the best west Cork classics, with superb breads and bakes, and smashing lunchtime food. The height of the season can see the restaurant open also in the evening when the pasta cooking is hugely enjoyable.

The Courtyard *Main Street, Schull, Co Cork (028 28390)*. A shop, pub and restaurant all rolled into one, and each element is as good as the other. Bar food is superb, especially the Courtyard Special, which unites slurpy soups with two local cheeses – Gubbeen and Gabriel – and the Courtyard's own bread.

Skibbereen

Island Cottage Restaurant *Hare Island, near Skibbereen, Co Cork*. You have to take a boat across to John Desmond and Ellmary Fenton's Island Cottage restaurant, then walk across the little island to the single room and when you get there you have no choice of what you will eat. But droves of folk make the trip every year, to enjoy one of the unique dining experiences, and to savour Mr Desmond's precise, logical food.

Bantry Bay, *County Cork – cliff-edge drives.*

Liss Ard Lake Lodge *Skibbereen, Co Cork (282 2365)*. Minimalist and modernist in style, the restaurant and country house of the Liss Ard Foundation offers Claudia Meister's rigorously conceived cooking in sublimely comfortable rooms. Vegetarian cooking is especially creative, and whilst prices are high, the style is unique.

West Cork Hotel *Ilen Street, Skibbereen, Co Cork (282 1277)*. The Murphy family's great old railway hotel is as vibrant and welcoming as ever, with cooking that is much, much better than hotel food elsewhere in the country. John Murphy is an inimitable host, and the atmosphere of the dining room is cosy and serene.

Bantry, Glengarriff & the Beara

Bantry is famous for what nearly happened there in 1796 when a French fleet, coming to the aid of the Irish rebels, was forced out to sea by storms and broken up. Bantry's second disaster came in 1979, when an oil terminal on Whiddy Island out in the bay caught fire, killing 51 workers.

Bantry's major attraction is Bantry House (*see below*), built by the White family, one of whom loyally attempted to warn the army in Cork that the French were approaching and got a peerage for his troubles. The house is beautifully renovated after years in the doldrums and has an amazing collection of art work and artefacts collected by various earls. The gardens are free to the public. In an old stable is an exhibition dedicated to the failed French invasion.

Castletownbere, *Beara peninsula, Co Cork.*

Inland from Bantry is Gougane Barra Forest Park
(*see below*), which has a number of well-marked
walks. On an island in the lake is a hermitage
where St Finbarr, the founder of Cork, once lived.
West of Bantry is the Sheep's Head peninsula
which, thankfully for those who live there, is often
missed by tourists, since it has no major sites
or beaches. But it is a beautiful, unspoiled little
peninsula, full of stone-walled fields, tiny cottages
and a glorious cliff-edge drive around Bantry Bay.
A walk has been marked out around the peninsula, and, as the land draws to its narrowest and
highest point at its end, wild flowers and cultivated
fields give way to rocks and sea views. Eileen's
pub in the village of Kilcrohane is recommended for
its friendliness.

To the north and west of Bantry lie Glengarriff
and the Beara peninsula. Glengarriff was once a
major tourist location when a popular holiday trip
was London to Ireland by boat and then train to
Bantry and another boat to Glengarriff. Nowadays, it is still popular for the many forest walks
in the area and as a stopping-off point for Garinish
Island (*see below*), which has an Italianate garden
built out of bare rock by Harold Peto, who shipped
everything, soil and all, out to the island.

Beyond Glengarriff is Castletownbere, the largest
town on the Beara peninsula. It is a very basic place,
little changed in the last hundred years. From
Castletownbere, trips are possible out to Bere Island.
West of Castletownbere are the ruins of Dunboy
Castle and Puxley Castle (*see below*); the first being
the fortress of the O'Sullivan clan, destroyed by the
English in 1602, and the second much grander but
much more recent set of ruins being the grand house
built by the Puxley family who mined copper in the
area and whose house was burned by the IRA during the War of Independence. Daphne Du Maurier's
novel *Hungry Hill* is based on this family.

At the end of the peninsula is Allihies, a pretty
little village with a single sandy beach, created, it
is said, by the outflow of the old copper mines which
stand above it. There are good walks around the
old mineworks and into the hills above. At the very
tip of the peninsula is a cable car, connecting the

mainland to Dursey Island. It is well worth risk-
ing the rather shabby cable car ride, even though
there isn't much to see on the island, but the walk
across it is pleasant. Bikes are not allowed on the
cable car and if there are cattle waiting to cross,
you will have to wait your turn. Turning back
inland there are two good hill climbs to consider –
Hungry Hill and Sugarloaf Mountain, a morning's
and a day's climb respectively.

Getting there
By bus There are three buses a day between Cork and
Bantry. In summer, there are also buses from Cork to
Killarney via Clonakilty, Skibbereen, Bantry, Glengarriff
and Kenmare.
Bikes can be hired in Bantry from Carrowell's (027
50278), in Castletownbere from Dudley Cycles (027
70293), r the Bonnie Brae's hostel in Allihies.

Attractions

Bantry House
Bantry, Co Cork (027 50047). **Open** 9am-6pm daily.
Admission *house £3; French Armada exhibition £3.*
The house contains tapestries, marbles and other works collected over the last century, while the Armada exhibition is
centred around the French ship La Surveillante which was
scuttled in Bantry Bay as the French fleet retreated and were
blown out to sea.

Bantry Museum
Behind the fire station, Bantry, Co Cork. **Open**
July-Sept 10.30am-1pm Tue, Thur; 3-5.30pm Wed-Fri.
Admission £1.
The usual tumble of local-interest items.

Dunboy & Puxley Castles
*Signposted from the road west of Castletownbere, Co
Cork.* **Open** daily. **Admission** free.

Garinish Island
*Boats leave from the Blue Pool at Glengarriff and various
spots along the main road in Glengarriff (027 63170).*
Boat fare around £5. **Admission** *to the gardens £2*
(027 63040).

Glengarriff Woods
*On the road out of Glengarriff to Kenmare, entrance is
about 1km on left.*

Gougane Barra Forest Park
*5km out of Bantry on the road to Glengarriff take the
road signposted to Macroom. Gougane Barra is
signposted to the left off this road.*

Festivals & events

Bantry Mussel Fair is usually held early in May.
There are the usual music nights, often a couple of
big names in a concert in the square, and lots of
free mussels with your pint in the pub. In the tiny
village of Kilcrohane, usually over the Easter
weekend, is the Craic on the Coast Festival when
the three pubs strain at the seams and there's
music in every bar and shed, as well as street performances. Castletownbere has a Festival of the
Sea in early August – a regatta with fishy competitions including filleting, net-mending and cooking, with lots of traditional music as well as jazz,

set-dancing and much more. On more classical lines, Bantry has a Festival of Chamber Music held in Bantry House in late June/early July (027 61105).

Where to stay

Ballylickey
Dromkeal Lodge Hotel *Ballylickey, Co Cork (027 51519/fax 027 51519)*. **Rates** *single* £30; *double* £72. **Credit** AmEx, DC, MC, V. Outside of town on the road to Glengarriff, set in pretty gardens with sea views.

Bantry
Vickery's Inn *New Street, Bantry, Co Cork (027 50006/fax 027 50006)*. **Rates** *single* £25; *double* £40. **Credit** MC, V. An old coaching inn in the centre of town.

Glengarriff
Eccles Hotel *Glengarriff, Co Cork (027 63003/fax 027 63319)*. **Rates** *single* £40; *double* £60. **Credit** AmEx, DC, MC, V. Historic old hotel, set in elegant gardens with beautiful sea views. Can be noisy at weekends.

Tourist information

The tourist office (027 50229; open May-Sept) in Bantry is in the square close to the two banks. The first Friday of each month is Fair Day, when travelling stalls come to town, as well as people selling horses and other livestock. There are also tourist offices in Castletownbere and Glengarriff in temporary buildings, open 9.30am-5pm, but closed for lunch.

Where to eat

Ahakista
Shiro Japanese Dinner House *Ahakista, Co Cork (027 67030)*. Kei and Werner Pilz's restaurant doubled in size a few years back, when its two tables multiplied to four. The extra pressure has reduced the intricate elaboration of Mrs Pilz's Japanese cookery somewhat, but the Shiro, and Old Bishop's Palace, remains one of the most singular dining experiences.

Ballylickey
Sea View House Hotel *Ballylickey, Co Cork (027 50073)*. Kathleen O'Sullivan's grand hotel sails serenely along on guileless charm and rich cooking; the food is buttery and creamy right from breakfast to dinner.

Bantry
Clarets *Barrack Street, Bantry, Co Cork (027 52187)*. Shirley Hurley's little restaurant is tucked away off the main square in Bantry, but good comfort food and friendly service make it a fine choice for lunch and dinner. In the square itself, O'Connor's Seafood Restaurant (027 50221) is perennially popular.

County Kerry

From one extreme to another, this county is home to some of the more tasteless tourist developments that Ireland has to offer, while also offering some of the most unspoiled scenery and authentically Irish villages in the country.

At one extreme is Killarney with its two-wheel horse-drawn jaunting cars, tour buses and leprechaun shops, while at the other is Dingle, where you will hear Gaelic spoken, and where the twentieth century has had the least effect on the lives of the local people.

*Lough Leane, glittering jewel in the crown of the **Killarney National Park**, County Kerry.*

Take a jaunting car, a bicycle or just a pair of shoes to explore the **Gap of Dunloe**, Co Kerry.

Getting there

By bus There are Bus Éireann services to most major towns including Tralee, Cork, Limerick, Galway, Waterford and Rosslare.
By train Trains go daily to Cork and Dublin via Mallow and Limerick (064 31067).

Killarney & around

Unlike many other Irish towns with their long histories of invasion, massacre and emigration, Killarney is a complete fabrication. It was created solely for the eighteenth-century upper-class tourist trade. Lord Kenmare, who owned all the land around, spotted a niche in the market and built the entire centre of Killarney, leased out land for inns and coaching houses and constructed roads into the area. Killarney's role as a tourist destination reached its peak in 1861, when Queen Victoria visited and an entire cottage was built in the woods for her to have tea one particular afternoon. If Lord Kenmare could see Killarney now, he might feel quite proud.

Killarney is quite a pretty little town, except for the traffic, coach tours and shops selling tourist junk. Outside of the short tourist season, it is quiet and, even during the season, outside the centre of town is as pleasant as anywhere in Ireland. For locals, it is a place to go shopping, second only to Cork city, and even the tourist shops can have excellent bargains in woollens, linen or pottery.

Around the town there's plenty for the dedicated consumer of tourist venues. The cathedral, built by Pugin in the middle years of the nineteenth century, is worth a short visit, as is St Mary's Cathedral (*see below*) in Main Street. A church has stood here for centuries, and it is thought there may have once been a pagan temple on this spot. The current church is nineteenth century and has some lovely stained glass and a splendid organ. Also in town is the National Museum of Irish Transport (*see below*), a good visit for children or motoring fanatics. The highlight of the exhibition is a 1910 Wolsely owned by the Gore-Booth family and driven, with WB Yeats in the passenger seat, by Countess Markievicz, the first woman to be elected to the British parliament.

Outside of Killarney, the Gap of Dunloe is essential viewing. It was carved several million years ago by a huge glacier. Six miles in length, it is a narrow pathway with mountains towering on either side. Do not be put off by the tour groups, jaunting car drivers and gift shops. Once you're inside the Gap, the crowds disappear and you can spend a day walking, cycling – or even riding in a jaunting car.

Ross Castle (*see below*), on the shores of Lough Leane, was built in the fifteenth century and was one of the last strongholds to hold out against Oliver Cromwell's forces in the seventeenth century. Cromwell handed it and its land over to a loyal Protestant family. From the castle you can see Innisfallen Island (*see below*), where a monastery was built in the seventh century. The *Annals of Innisfallen*, looted and now in the Bodleian library in Oxford, were written here. South of town is the Muckross Estate (*see below*), a good day's wander. Inside is the wonderfully preserved Muckross House, three excellently laid-out and illustrated nature trails around Muckross Lake, a model farm, and the ancient ruins of the Muckross Friary founded in 1448 by the McCarthy clan. The model farm in particular is very good. Several farmhouses from various periods of history have been brought here and reconstructed to show what rural Irish life was like over the centuries.

Four miles out of Killarney to the south is the Torc Waterfall (*see below*), another widely visited spot in the tourist season but well worth visiting early or late in the day. It is a pleasant scramble along signposted paths to the waterfall and you can carry on from there along part of the Kerry Way which begins in Killarney. The Kerry Way is a demanding, but remarkable, long-distance walk. It travels close to roads for much of its route and is perfectly easy to join or leave at points convenient to you.

North of Killarney are the Kerry Woollen Mills, renovated and open to the public with guided tours around the factory. Some of the buildings date back to the seventeenth century and there is a shop selling woollen products and a tea shop. Some distance east of Killarney, near Castleisland, are the Crag Caves (*see below*), explored for the first time in 1985 and now opened to the public.

Getting around

A bicycle is the most convenient way of getting around town. They can be hired from several places: O'Sullivan's in Pawn Office Lane (064 31282), the Laurels pub in Old Market Lane (064 31970), and O'Neill's in Plunkett Street (064 31970). Cost is around £7 a day. Several of the hostels hire out bicycles to their guests as well. Jaunting cars are another, rather silly way of getting about. They wait for customers around East Avenue Road or outside Muckross House.

Attractions

Crag Caves
15 miles from Killarney on the N21 near Castleisland. Signposted to the right (066 41244/fax 066 42352). **Open** *Mar-Nov* 10am-6pm daily. Last tour 30 mins before closing. **Admission** £3; £1.75 children.
A perfect destination for a wet afternoon. Craft shop and restaurant.

Innisfallen Island
Rowing boats can be hired from alongside Ross Castle. **Rates** £3 per hour.
Rowing time to the island is about 20 minutes. On the island are the ruins of a twelfth-century oratory.

Muckross House & Estate
Kenmare Road, Killarney, Co Kerry (064 31440). **Open** *summer* 9am-7pm daily; *winter* 9am-5.30pm daily. **Admission** *House* £3.
A whole day's outing, looking at the model village, the craft workshops in the basement of the building and around the paraphernalia of what life in a grand old house must have been like. The walks are excellent and the walk leaflets are very informative about the unusual flora and fauna of the area. Around the lake you can see the weathered limestone

National Museum of Irish Transport, *Killarney.*

rocks that have given Muckross Lake its particular ecology. Cars are not allowed inside, but there are car parks outside the estate and you can walk or cycle inside.

National Museum of Irish Transport
Scott's Garden, East Avenue, Killarney, Co Kerry (064 346 77). **Open** 10am-6pm daily. **Admission** £3.

Ross Castle
Take the road to Kenmare, turn right by the Esso garage. **Open** 9am-5pm daily. **Admission** £2.50.

St Mary's Cathedral
Cathedral Place, New Street, Killarney, Co Kerry.
Built in the nineteenth century over a period of decades, the half-built church was used as a hospice for the dying Famine victims. Consecrated in 1855, the building wasn't completed until 1912 when the 285-foot spire was added.

Torc Waterfall
4.5 miles out of town on the N71 between Killarney and Kenmare.
Well sign-posted; car park.

Tourist information
The tourist office is in the main street beside the town hall (064 31633) and is open from 9.15am-5.30pm Monday to Saturday.

Festivals

The Pan-Celtic Week is held in spring when artists with Celtic connections arrive from Scotland, the Isle of Man, Cornwall, Wales and Brittany. In May, July and October, Killarney hosts race meetings which are a great excuse for gambling, drinking and trading horse-flesh.

Where to stay

Killarney has the highest number of registered places to stay in Ireland outside of Dublin. Even so, it is best to book in advance or rely on the tourist office to find a place for you during the height of a good summer.

Killarney
Killarney Great Southern Hotel *Killarney, Co Kerry (064 31262/fax 064 31642).* **Rates** *single* £120; *double* £120. **Credit** AmEx, MC, V. Four-star hotel with long history, lots of facilities including pool and leisure centre.

The **Ring of Kerry** *is one of the most beautiful – and most heavily visited – parts of Ireland.*

Muckross Park Hotel *Muckross Village, Killarney, Co Kerry (064 31938/fax 064 31965).* **Rates** *single* £60-£80 single; *double* £80-£120. **Credit** AmEx, DC, MC, V. Four-star hotel set in parkland outside town near to Muckross House. Quiet atmosphere, award-winning restaurant.

McCarthy's Town House *19 High Street, Killarney, Co Kerry (064 32432/fax 064 35745).* **Rates** *single* £30; *double* £50. **Credit** AmEx, DC, MC, V. Centrally located guest house above a pub. Car park.

Ross Hotel *Kenmare Place, Killarney, Co Kerry (064 31855/fax 064 31139).* **Rates** *single* £65; *double* £90. **Credit** AmEx, DC, MC, V. Family-owned hotel, with access to leisure facilities, private car park.

Killarney hostels

Bunrower House Hostel *near Ross Castle, Co Kerry (064 33914).*

Four Winds Hostel *43 New Street, Killarney, Co Kerry (064 33094).*

Neptune's Killarney Town Hostel *off New Street, Killarney, Co Kerry (064 35255).*

Railway Hostel *off Park Road, Killarney, Co Kerry (064 35299).*

Sugan Kitchen Hostel *Lewis Road, Killarney, Co Kerry (064 33104).*

All the hostels do dormitory rooms at around £7, and most have double rooms available for £20 or more. They have cooking facilities, often have small libraries, common rooms and good notice boards.

Where to eat

Killarney

Gaby's *High Street, Killarney, Co Kerry (064 32519).* The formula of Gaby's remains unchanged and unchangingly successful, the lunchtime cooking simple and appropriate – seafood salads, quiches – the dinnertime cooking more expansive and luxurious, and centred firmly around their expert fish and shellfish cookery.

The Strawberry Tree *Plunkett Street, Killarney, Co Kerry (064 32688).* Evan Doyle expertly directs both the Strawberry Tree restaurant and its downstairs partner, Yer Man's pub. The restaurant offers clever and wholly unclichéd versions of Irish staples such as bacon and cabbage, Irish stew and wild salmon with sorrel, and almost all of the food used is both local and organic.

Yer Man's Pub *Plunkett Street, Killarney, Co Kerry.* Underneath the Strawberry Tree restaurant, Yer Man's is a lovely old-style pub, with good simple bar food delivered with care – soups, sandwiches, pies, ice creams. Turf fires and music may spontaneously erupt at any time when a few musos collect together.

The Ring of Kerry

Thousands of people come each year to this part of Ireland and with good reason. The Ring of Kerry has some beautiful scenery and, once off the main tour-bus trail, all the stresses of driving the narrow roads behind huge vehicles dissipate and you are on your own in stunning countryside. The best way to see it is by getting out of the car as much as possible and exploring on foot or bike.

A good place to start a tour of the Iveragh peninsula is at its head in Kenmare, which makes a good alternative base to Killarney. The town is seriously dedicated to the tourist trade, with lots of restaurants and pubs, although smaller and quieter than Killarney. It was a Planter settlement, laid out in

1670 in two intersecting lines by the Marquis of Lansdown. There's a good tourist information office and a new heritage centre (*see below*) giving the history of the area.

From Kenmare the road takes you across sheep-farming land with low, white, stone walls, across the river Blackwater to Sneem, another tourist-conscious village with woollen shops and pub-restaurants. It has an unusual sculpture park (*see below*) and a museum (*see below*), still thankfully unre-constructed into a heritage centre. By now the lush fields have given way to barer land, with trees showing the effect of the biting salt winds of winter. Beyond Sneem is Caherdaniel, which is an important base for diving, with long stretches of sandy beach. You can take in the home of Daniel O'Connell while you're here.

Nearby is Staigue Fort (*see below*), two thousand years old and still as sturdy as ever. Further on again, Waterville is a popular seaside spot with more silver-sand beaches and crystal-clear waters. Pop into the Butler's Arms pub for photos of Waterville's most famous temporary resident, Charlie Chaplin. From Waterville, a sidetrack from the main Ring of Kerry circuit is the Skellig Ring, where tiny winding roads lead to tinier villages. On a misty day, this landscape seems other-worldly, and, even in hot weather, its bleak beauty is exceptional. Ballinskelligs Bay is a Blue Flag beach overlooked by the ruins of an ancient castle.

From Portmagee, you can drive over to Valentia Island. The first transatlantic cables were laid from this island and, for a few days, it was possible to telegraph New York from here, but not Dublin. The old houses of the telegraph station are now decaying, as is the slate quarry (*see below*) which once supplied the roofs for some of London's finest buildings. A visit to the quarry is an eerie experience.

The off-shore island of Skellig Michael (*see below*) harboured a religious community from the seventh century to the thirteenth century and several of their small beehive buildings are intact. After 1582, Skellig Michael was a popular spot for marriages. Weddings were forbidden during the 40 days of Lent but on Skellig Michael, Lent started later than in the rest of Ireland since it had not adopted the Gregorian calendar. Those who needed to marry but couldn't wait until Easter took their whole wedding party out to the island, booze and all. Songs were invented called the Skellig Lists, which jokingly matched up eligible partners for the trip to Skellig.

Back on the Ring of Kerry, the next town is Caherciveen, the birthplace of Daniel O'Connell. The ruins of his home are still here, as is an old police barracks, now yet another heritage centre (*see below*), albeit an interesting one. Glenbeigh is the next village of any size. Seefin, the seat of the legendary giant Fin, looms over the place and the long Blue Flag beach attracts many visitors.

Further east is Killorglin, the last town on the Ring of Kerry, and the home of the infamous, probably pagan, Puck Fair. Held every August, the pubs are flung open all night and much energy is expended capturing and tethering a wild goat. Once caught, the hapless beast is named king of the fair, festooned in ribbons and tethered in the middle of the town for the duration of the festivities.

Getting around

It is possible to get to most places on the Ring of Kerry by public transport. There are two buses a day leaving Killarney at 8.45am and 1.25pm, stopping at Caherciveen, Waterville, Caherdaniel and Sneem. There are other local buses. For details ring 064 34777. Cycles can be hired from O'Shea's in Lower Bridge Street in Killorglin (066 61919), Casey's in the main street in Caherciveen (066 72474), Curran's at Chapeltown in Valentia (066 76297), Burn's Bike Hire in Sneem (064 45140), and Finnigan's in Kenmare (064 41083).

Attractions

Caherciveen Heritage Centre

Main Street, Caherciveen, Co Kerry (066 72955).
Open *June-Sept* 10am-6pm Mon-Sat; 1-6pm Sun.
Admission £2.50.
A display of local history and art work by local artists in the former police barracks.

Derrynane House & Park

Signposted from the Ring of Kerry at Caherdaniel, Co Kerry. **Open** *May-Sept* 9am-6pm Mon-Sat. **Admission** £2; £1 children.
The house is full of artefacts from the life of the famous campaigner for Catholic emancipation, Daniel O'Connell. The dining room is the highlight, full of gifts of silverware given

Caherciveen, *on the Ring of Kerry, Co Kerry.*

*The Puck Festival at **Killorglin**, County Kerry.*

by grateful Catholics and a grand table which reputedly took two years to carve. The park sits behind an excellent beach, an Ogham stone stands in the grounds.

Kenmare Heritage Centre
Town Square, Kenmare, Co Kerry (064 41233). **Open** 9.30am-7pm Mon-Sat; *July-Aug* Sun only. **Admission** £2 adults; £1 children.
In a very pretty renovated building, the heritage centre focuses on the history of the town. Notable figures from the region are featured, including the nun of Kenmare and Sir William Petty.

Kerry Bog Village
On the Killorglin-Glenbeigh Road, beside the Red Fox pub (066 69184). **Open** 8.30am-7pm. **Admission** £2.50.
A recreation of a nineteenth century Kerry village complete with equipment and furniture.

Skellig Michael
Accessible by boat from Ballinskelligs, Portmagee & Valentia. **Open** summer months and good weather only. **Fare** negotiate with skippers, expect to pay around £20 a head.
A highlight of any trip to Ireland, this needs a whole day and a picnic lunch. Skellig Michael is a 712-foot jagged piece of rock with patches of life clinging to its nooks and crannies. The monastic buildings are still in excellent condition, and there are rare birds to spot, particularly the puffins which make their nests in burrows in the ground all over the island. Guides, who live out on the island, will take you around the ruins explaining them. On Valentia, there is the Skellig experience for those who can't make the strenuous trip out to the island or who want to know more about the place before they go. Admission to the centre, just over the bridge from Portmagee, is £3 but you can do a combined visit and trip around the island, without landing, for £15.

Sneem Museum
The Old Courthouse, Main Street, Sneem, Co Kerry. **Open** 10am-1pm; 2pm-5.30pm Mon-Sun. **Admission** £1.
A lively, cluttered little museum, one of the few left in the area not to have suffered the heritage centre makeover.

Sneem Sculpture Park
Sneem, Co Kerry. **Open** daily. **Admission** free.
A motley collection of sculptures from various donors, including a marble panda donated by the Chinese government and an abstract pyramid in honour of an ex-President of Ireland.

Staigue Fort
Signposted off the Ring of Kerry near Castlecove, Co Kerry. **Open** daily. **Admission** 50p in the honesty box.
A 2,000-year-old, 18-foot-high circular dry stone wall, 13 feet

thick. No one is entirely sure of the function of this structure besides the obvious one of defence. It has never been excavated, so there is no indication of any buildings inside. Travelling by car, be prepared for traffic jams on the tiny road leading to the fort.

Valentia Museum
On the quarry road, outside Knightstown, Valentia Island, Co Kerry. **Open** May-Sept 11am-6pm Mon-Sat. **Admission** free.
An excellent little museum with an intact schoolroom, lots of pictures of the island's role as a telegraph station and some excellent information on the local linen-making and dyeing crafts.

Valentia Slate Quarry
Signposted from Knightstown, Valentia Island, Co Kerry. **Open** daily. **Admission** free.
Begun in 1816, this quarry provided slate for building as far apart as London and San Salvador. In its heyday, the quarry employed 400 men, providing an income for the area even during the Famine. It closed in 1884 when it became unprofitable. The slate was made into roof tiles, furniture, headstones and billiard tables. A visit there takes you through the vast heaps of broken material where early buildings were buried in the spoil heaps and new ones built over the top. Single pieces of slate 14 feet long were typical of one of the slate beds.

Tourist information
There are tourist offices in the Caherciveen and Kenmare heritage centres (*see above*).

Festivals

The big festival on the Ivearagh peninsula is the Puck Fair in Killorglin. It is held over three days usually in the second weekend in August. Lots of music, drinking and other activities. It is is a very popular local event and most places to stay get booked up well in advance.

Where to stay

Caherciveen
Sive Hostel *Caherciveen, Co Kerry (066 72717).*

Caherdaniel
Carrigbeg Hostel *Caherdaniel, Co Kerry (066 75229).*

Glenbeigh
Hillside House Hostel *Glenbeigh, Co Kerry (066 68228).*
Towers Hotel *Glenbeigh, Co Kerry (066 68212/fax 066 68404).* **Rates** *single* £47-£55; *double* £64-£80. **Credit** MC, V. Built in 1792, this is a quiet and historic little hotel.

Kenmare
Failte Hostel *Henry Street & Shelbourne Street, Kenmare, Co Kerry (064 41083).*
Foley's Shamrock *Henry Street, Kenmare, Co Kerry (064 41361).* **Rates** *single* £25; *double* £37. **Credit** MC, V. In the centre of town with a good restaurant and open fires. Owner-manager.
Sheen Falls Lodge *Kenmare, Co Kerry (064 41600/fax 064 41386).* **Rates** *single* £135-£185; *double* £160-£240. **Credit** AmEx, DC, MC, V. Set in 300 acres and including country pursuits such as clay pigeon shooting, horse riding and fishing for salmon in the estates rivers. This is a place to revel in luxury. Fitness centre, billiard room, and an award-winning restaurant.

*You'll go a long way to find better sunsets than those enjoyed on the **Dingle peninsula**.*

Killorglin

Bianconi *Killorglin, Ring of Kerry, Co Kerry (066 61146/fax 066 61950).* **Rates** *single* £30; *double* £54. **Credit** AmEx, DC, MC, V.

Laune Valley Farm Hostel *Killorglin, Co Kerry (066 61488).*

Valentia Island

An Oige Valentia *Knightstown, Valentia Island, Co Kerry (066 76141).*

Ring Lyne Hostel *Chapeltown, Valentia Island, Co Kerry (066 76103).*

Where to eat

Kenmare

An Leith Phingin *Main Street, Kenmare, Co Kerry (064 41559).* Con Guerin's restaurant is one of the staples of a town where it is hard to eat badly, and his refined Italianate cooking – ravioli with aubergine and courgette, braised beef with risotto alla Milanese – is as charming as the room and the service.

Packie's *Henry Street, Kenmare, Co Kerry (064 41508).* Maura Foley may well have been cooking for 30 years, but there is a youthful sense of enquiry about her work which means her cooking is as up-to-the-minute as any Irish restaurateur. The fish cooking is second to none, its simplicity perfectly expressive and delicious – cod in a cheese bechamel, Moroccan-style brill with chermoula – and classics such as traditional lamb stew with thyme seem born anew. Excellent value, and a lively room.

Caherciveen

Brennan's Restaurant *Main Street, Caherciveen, Co Kerry (066 72021).* One of the best kept secrets on the Ring, Conor and Teresa Brennan's restaurant is a valuable respite from the tourist trail of the area, with highly considered cooking that utilises to the full local Kerry ingredients – spring lamb with a julienne of garlic and garden rosemary, Atlantic salmon with Valentia scallops and a dill beurre blanc, brill with a warm raw tomato sauce – and does so with panache and care.

The Old School House *Knockeens, near Caherciveen, Co Kerry (066 72426).* Simple cooking and a warm welcome, along with a willingness to cope with the demands of families and groups, have made Ann O'Kane's restaurant a fixture of the Ring of Kerry.

Killorglin

The Bianconi *Annadale Road, Killorglin, Co Kerry (066 61146).* A rather nice bar features reliable pub food during the day, but the brothers Sheedy show their ambitions more at dinnertime, when the cooking is imaginative and the atmosphere lively.

Nick's Restaurant *Lower Bridge Street, Killorglin, Co Kerry (066 61219).* Nick Foley's restaurant is a near-legend in the area, renowned for bumper helpings of simple food, maternal service and an atmosphere as raucous as a sports stadium following a goal.

The Dingle peninsula

The most inaccessible and wildly romantic area of Kerry, the Dingle peninsula rarely feels crowded even in its busiest villages. At the head of the peninsula is the town of Tralee, with its industry and its tourism, while at the other end is Dunquin, with its beehive huts that have sat on the hillsides here for centuries. If you have time for only one trip to the south-west, make it Dingle, the strangest and most fascinating part of the west of Ireland.

Even driving, a mundane activity at the best of times, is rewarding on this peninsula as you cross the Connor Pass or wind your way around narrow coast roads with ancient hillsides looming above

Tralee Bay, *north side of Dingle peninsula.*

you. If you have longer, there is the Dingle Way to consider, a long-distance pathway around the peninsula taking in the best of the sights and some beautiful, unspoilt countryside. If you are a sandy beach fan, the peninsula's long stretches of silver sand and good surf will seem like heaven.

You won't want to linger too long in Tralee, although those with children in tow could spend an amusing half-day in the Kerry the Kingdom heritage centre (*see below*) and the Blennerville Windmill (*see below*). A steam railway goes out to the windmill from Tralee.

Around the peninsula itself, the north shores have miles of glorious sandy beaches which can get crowded the nearer they are to Tralee. Castlegregory is a little spit of land jutting out and dividing Tralee Bay from Brandon Bay. Its beaches are rarely full and are fine for all manner of beach activities. Further west, the Connor Pass carries the main road across the peninsula to Dingle through a flat U-shaped valley. To the north-west is Brandon Peak at 1,000 metres. The route across the mountains is quite stark in its beauty, like a demonstration of the powers of the huge glaciers of the last ice age. It is possible to work out the movements of the ice from the features of the pass.

Dingle itself is a busy and historic town. There are a number of little shops and craft centres, as well as a good library, boating and scuba diving and some fine restaurants. If he is still around, there's also Fungie, a solitary dolphin who lives in the harbour, although it's slightly more fun to watch the dolphin watchers than the dolphin.

Dingle was settled and developed by the Anglo-Normans and there is much evidence of a Spanish community living here – it is thought that trade between this tiny town and Spanish towns was common. In the sixteenth century, Dingle took part in the rebellions against the crown, but in 1585 it received a charter and a grant from Elizabeth I allowing it to rebuild its walls.

Beyond Dingle, the road narrows and the rocks proliferate. This part of the peninsula has an amazing number of ancient sites. Offshore are the

Blasket Islands, inhabited until 1953 and currently in danger of becoming yet another heritage item. The little towns of Ballyferriter and Dunquin are good places to stay – there's no shortage of holiday cottages. From here you can make the strenuous, five-hour ascent of Mount Brandon to see the remains of St Brendan's Oratory at the summit. Louis Mulcahy's pottery at Clogher has some lovely work.

Getting around
There are several ways to get about the peninsula. Buses travel from Tralee and Killarney daily to Dingle, while there is a ferry from Valentia Island and Caherciveen twice daily. A further bus runs daily from Dingle to Dunquin, passing the villages in between. The earliest connects with the ferries leaving Dunquin for the Blasket Islands. Bikes can be hired from Lynch's in Castlegregory, Moriarty in Main Street, Dingle (066 51316), and from Tralee Gas and Bicycle Supplies in Strand Street in Tralee (066 22231).

Attractions

Ballyferriter Heritage Centre
Ballyferriter, Co Kerry. **Admission** free.
Another heritage centre, but not, for once, a heart-sinking experience. The town is named after Piaras Ferriter, a poet and soldier who led an army during a rebellion in 1641 and was executed in Killarney in 1653. The parish includes the Blasket Islands and is significant in that members of the parish have published 50 books in the last 50 years: quite amazing, when you see the size of the village.

Blasket Islands
Boats leave Dunquin harbour daily in good weather (066 56188). **Fare** boat ride costs around £10 per head.
A good whole-day trip with picnic food is possible on Great Blasket, the bigger of the islands. There isn't much there at the moment in the way of facilities, but during the summer there is a restaurant. There is one beautiful, sheltered beach and lots of walks around the bare grassland. The people who lived here until the last few diehards left in 1953 were non-English speakers and several of them wrote stories about the island's life. These can be bought in translation in the bookshops of Dingle. A community lived here in the eighteenth century and when parish records began in 1808, there were 128 residents. They survived the famine better than their peers on the mainland. The islanders were never buried on the island; only unbaptised babies and shipwrecked foreigners were buried here. In the early years of this century, all newly married islanders left for the mainland and the four last families left in a violent storm in 1953.

Blasket Islands Interpretive Centre
Dunquin, Co Kerry. **Open** *Easter-Sept* 10am-6pm daily. **Admission** £2; £1 children.
The history and heritage of the amazing island community, focusing in particular on the lives and writing of the local people.

Blennerville Windmill
Blennerville, Co Kerry. **Open** 10am-6pm daily. **Admission** £2.50; £1.50 children.
A working windmill, built around 1800 and functioning for about 80 years before falling into ruin. Now back in full working order, it comes complete with a video on how to mill flour and an exhibition about the many people who emigrated from this part of Ireland. Also craft shops where you can buy milled flour as well as the usual junk, and a café. A good way to get to the windmill is to take the reopened steam railway which leaves every hour from Ballyard between 11am-5pm.

Dingle Aquarium

Near Dingle harbour, Dingle, Co Kerry (066 5211).
Open *July, Aug* 10am-5pm daily. **Admission** £4;
£2.25 children.
Large fishtank with sea creatures, touchy-feely exhibitions
and an imaginative exhibition of St Brendan's journey across
the Atlantic.

Dingle Heritage Centre

*Junction of Main Street and Green Street, Dingle, Co
Kerry.* **Open** 10.30am-5pm Tue-Sat. **Admission** free.
Exhibitions of local history, flora and fauna, as well as the
Dingle railway.

Dun An Oir Promontory Fort

3.5 miles north of Ballyferriter, Co Kerry. **Open** daily.
Admission free.
Although there is little to see of the sixteenth-century promontory fort, it is well worth seeking out for the events that took
place there in 1580. It is named after a ship laden with iron
pyrites which sank there, scattering the golden rock over the
beach below. In 1580, an invading force of Spanish and Italian
mercenaries arrived at the promontory fort with weapons
ready to take on the English. The English, led by Lord Grey
and including Sir Walter Raleigh and poet Edmund Spencer,
laid siege to the tiny fort which had no supplies of fresh water
or food. After three days the troops surrendered and 600 men
and women, foreigners and Irish, were massacred.

Gallarus Oratory

*From Dingle take the road to Ballyferriter, 2.5 miles out
of Dingle take the left fork at the Y junction, then bear
right. The oratory is signposted half a mile along this
road.* **Open** daily. **Admission** free.
Twelve centuries old, this beehive hut stands in near perfect
condition, every slate intact. Unlike other such huts, it is
boat-shaped. The overlapping wall stones run seamlessly
into the roof in a method known as corbelling. It was once a
small private hut where a monk could go to pray and must
have inspired some beautiful prayers with the serenity of its
lines and surroundings. Don't miss it.

Kerry the Kingdom

Ashe Memorial Hall, Denny Street, Tralee, Co Kerry.
Open *July, Aug* 9.30am-6pm daily; *Sept-June* 3pm-5pm
daily. **Admission** £4; £2.50 children.
Upstairs is a good museum with a wordy history of Kerry,
while downstairs there's a fairly silly ride around an imagi-
nary fifteenth-century Tralee.

Kilmalkedar Church

Kilmalkedar, near Ballyferriter, Co Kerry. **Open** daily.
Admission free.
If you are visiting the beehive huts of the area, this twelfth-
century Romanesque church is fascinating because it shows
the development in architectural styles from the Gallarus
Oratory to tiled roofs. The church is part of a complex of
buildings all thought to be part of a sophisticated religious
community that once lived here in two-storey stone houses.
Between the church and the ruin known as Brendan's House
begins the Pilgrim's Way, the traditional path up the slopes
of Mount Brandon.

Reasc Pillar Stones

1.25 miles north east of Ballyferriter, Co Kerry. **Open**
daily. **Admission** free.
This site was excavated in the 1980s and, beside the pillar
stone, the ruins of an entire monastic settlement have been
found, including beehive huts, crosses and an oratory. The
biggest stone is inscribed with a curling pattern and is interesting for the fact that a pre-Christian style has been used to
illustrate a Christian artefact, suggesting that this is a very
early piece of Christian art indeed. The monks who lived here
probably smelted iron and lived in large thatched buildings.

Tourist information

There are tourist offices in Tralee, in the Ashe Memorial Hall
(066 21288), and in Dingle in the town centre (066 51188). The
Tralee office is open daily during the summer from 9am-7pm,
while the Dingle office is open from April to October.

Where to stay

Ballyferriter

An Cat Dubh *Ballyferriter, Co Kerry (066 56286).* Hostel.
Carraig An Fhiona *Gallarus Cross, Ballyferriter, Dingle,
Co Kerry (066 56470/fax 066 56399).* **Rates** *single* £25-
£28; *double* £36-£40. **Credit** MC, V. Out of town and close
to the Gallarus Oratory, this is a comfortable guest house
with its own restaurant and gardens.

Castlegregory

Connor Pass Hostel Stradbally *near Castlegregory,
Co Kerry (066 39179).*
Euro-Hostel *Fitzgerald's Bar, Castlegregory, Co Kerry
(066 39133).*

Castlemaine

Inch Hostel *Inch, near Castlemaine, Co Kerry
(066 58181).*

Dingle

Alpine House *Mail Road, Dingle, Co Kerry (066
51250/fax 066 51966).* **Rates** *single* £30-£35; *double*
£36-£42. Set in quiet area on the outskirts of town.
Dingle Skellig Hotel *Dingle, Co Kerry (066 51144/fax
066 51501).* **Rates** *single* £71; *double* £112. **Credit**
AmEx, DC, MC, V. A three-star hotel set in the harbour at
Dingle with a leisure centre and pretty gardens.
Grapevine Hostel *Dykegate Street, Dingle, Co Kerry
(066 51434).*
Marina Hostel *Dingle, Co Kerry (066 51065).*

Dunquin

An Oige Dunquin Hostel *Dunquin, Co Kerry
(066 56145).*

Where to eat

Dingle

Beginish Restaurant *Green Street, Dingle, Co Kerry
(066 51588).* Pat Moore's cooking enjoys all the
smartness of a woman who adores the business of
cooking and who never allows any egotism to intrude
upon the necessity for the food to be delicious. Roasted
john dory with a dijon mustard sauce, fillet of beef with
rosti, smoked haddock with a parsley sauce, the amazing
rhubarb soufflé tart with a crème anglaise.
The Chart House Restaurant *Dingle, Co Kerry (066
52255).* Jim McCarthy was one of the most respected
wine waiters in Ireland before opening up the Chart
House with head chef Paul Cosgrove, and his meticulous
application has seen the restaurant achieve speedy
success. Lunch food is simple and concentrates on
imaginative open sandwiches; at dinner, dishes such as
cassoulet of monkfish and mussels with a tarragon
cream, cod with a peanut and breadcrumb crust with
soya or fillet of beef with a ragout of wild mushrooms
show an attentive sureness. Short, but splendid, wine list.

Tralee

Aisling Ghael *Ivy Terrace, Tralee, Co Kerry (066
29292).* Ann and Tom Galvin's restaurant is the smart
choice in town, with good food and a genial atmosphere.
Oysters with a hot tomato sauce, Cromane mussels in
garlic butter, aubergine mille feuille, Thai beef salad,
chocolate and orange truffle cake are some signature
dishes, and prices are keen.

Listowel

Allo's Bar & Bistro *Listowel, Co Kerry (068 22880).*
Listowel has many famous pubs, but Allo's is the jewel in
the crown, not merely because it is such a splendid bar,
but because Armel Whyte's cooking is so creative.
Panfried scallops with a lime beurre blanc, Limerick ham
with colcannon, local ducks which are roasted and served
with a tart berry sauce. Helen Mullane takes care of the
front of house with instinctive command.

County Clare

A trip to Clare is indeed a trip out of town and,
because it lacks the high-profile publicity of neighbouring Galway and Kerry, the county is frequently skipped by travellers. In the north, the
barren, limestone face of the Burren attracts geol-
ogists and botanists, but the landscape and ancient
monuments are universally appealing.

On the Atlantic coast, the tiny village of Doolin
(*see below*) functions unofficially as the fringe capital of traditional Irish music, and every year
young people make their way here from all over
the world, clutching their tin whistles and violins.
A short distance to the south of Doolin, the astonishing finality of the Cliffs of Moher are guaranteed to stir your heart, as well as test your nerves.
There are no major towns apart from the county
capital, Ennis, with a rich nationalist history that
serves as a reminder that Britain's colonial authority over the country was never complete.

The town of **Ennis** – *capital of County Clare.*

Getting there

By bus Bus Éireann services link Ennis with Dublin,
Cork and Galway. There is also a direct service between
Doolin and Dublin and, during the summer, between
Doolin and Galway. The bus station (065 24177) is a ten-
minute walk from the centre of Ennis.
By train There is a daily train service between
Ennis and Dublin, taking just over 3 hours. The train
station (065 40444) is next to the bus station, close to the
town centre.
By air There are flights to Shannon Airport in County
Limerick from London Heathrow on Aer Lingus and from
Manchester on British Airways Express. Air Lingus
connects Shannon with Dublin. A bus from Shannon
airport to Limerick city takes 45 minutes and it's another
hour from Limerick city to Ennis.
By ferry *See* **Doolin** *and* **Cliffs of Moher** *section
below* for details of ferries between the Aran Islands
and Doolin.

Ennis & around

County Clare's capital is the town of Ennis and,
although there is not a tremendous lot to see, this
is a part of Ireland that has not succumbed to the
deadening spread of mass tourism. A good place
to start a tour of the town is at the Daniel O'Connell
statue at the juncture of several characteristically
narrow and antique-looking streets (O'Connell,
Abbey and Parnell Streets).

Daniel O'Connell (1775-1847), 'The Liberator', led
a successful fight for the rights of Catholics to
sit in the British House of Commons, after being
returned as MP for County Clare with an overwhelming constitutional and moral majority. The
county's reputation as a hotbed of nationalism goes
back to the days when the Irish were expelled by
the British to Clare and other parts of the far west
of Ireland. It was also in Ennis that Parnell
launched his boycotting campaign against landlords. De Valera was elected to represent Clare
between 1917-59.

From the O'Connell Statue, a short walk up
Abbey Street leads to Ennis Friary on the right,
just before the street turns to cross the river
Fergus. It was founded around 1250 as a Franciscan friary, although it is the additions that
were mostly made in the following century that
attract the modern eye. The lancet east windows
still stand as a statement of elegance and there
are many fine stone sculptures whose details
will reveal themselves to patient scrutiny. The
McMahon tomb from the mid-fifteenth century has
grand alabaster panels showing scenes from the
Passion of Christ.

The Cloister's Pub and Restaurant next to the
friary is one of the better places in Ennis, but
there are many snug pubs where traditional music
is played at night. Brogan's and Brandon's, both
on O'Connell Street, are worth checking out and,
just under a mile out of town, on the Gort road, Cois
Na hAbhna (065 20996) holds traditional music
and dancing sessions.

Some six miles to the north of Ennis, on the road to Corofin (R476), the early Christian site of Dyseart O'Dea reveals the remains of a church and round tower and a High Cross, known as the White Cross, with Celtic patterning and a depiction of Daniel in the Lions' Den. There is a small museum nearby.

Following Station Road out of Ennis leads to the R469 and the elegant, peaceful Quin Abbey, a well-preserved friary run by Franciscans from its foundation in 1433 right up until the nineteenth century. A spiral staircase takes you up to the first floor, providing a bird's eye view of the abbey's cloister.

Nearby Knappogue Castle (*see below*), by comparison, offers a more macho architecture, as befits one of the homes and headquarters of the McNamaras who once ruled a substantial part of the county. It survived the usual fate of the McNamara castles under the English because Cromwell chose to make it his own headquarters when 'subduing' the Irish in 1649.

The main rooms of the castle are used for medieval banquets and many features, including the oak fireplaces, have been carefully restored and period furniture added to create ambience. The medieval banquets are held twice-nightly at the height of summer (061 360788) and can be booked through the tourist office in Ennis.

Head south out of Knappogue Castle for two miles and the second turning on the left will be signposted for the Craggaunowen Project (*see below*). A complex of structures – a ring fort, a crannóg and an original Iron Age road – have been reconstructed around a McNamara fortified tower house.

The idea is to introduce aspects of ancient Irish culture, complemented by displays of arts and crafts using traditional tools and methods. A famous exhibit here is the Brendan, a leather boat made by Tim Severin and used by a crew of five to cross the Atlantic in 1976, thereby proving that St Brendan could indeed have been the first European to sail to America – as recorded in a ninth-century text.

Attractions

Bunratty Castle & Folk Park
On the N18 between Limerick and Ennis (061 361511).
Open Castle is open daily; *June-Aug* Park. **Admission** £5.
The very touristy medieval banquets held in Bunratty (061 360788) should not detract from the value of visiting the castle and Folk Park. The fifteenth-century castle is superb and the range of furniture and artefacts inside is very impressive. The Folk Park is a reconstruction of a nineteenth-century village and, despite the coach tours and boisterous children, there is plenty to see and learn.

Craggaunowen Project
Two miles south of Knappogue Castle, reached by taking Station Road out of Ennis. **Open** *May-Sept* 10am-5pm daily. **Admission** £4.
An educational introduction to ancient Irish culture with the aid of reconstructed dwellings, displays of craftwork and exhibits.

De Valera Library Museum
Harmony Row, Ennis, Co Clare. **Open** 11am-5.30pm Mon-Fri. **Admission** free.
A small, but quite fascinating, little museum, with exhibits relating to the struggles of O'Connell and De Valera.

Knappogue Castle
Two miles south of Quin Abbey, reached by taking Station Road out of Ennis. **Open** *Easter-Oct* 9.30am-5.30pm daily. **Admission** £3.
Skillfully restored interior with superb furniture and decorations and medieval banquets to boot.

O'Dea Castle Museum
Dysert O'Dea, six miles north of Ennis, on the road to Corofin. **Open** *May-Sept* 10am-6pm daily. **Admission** £2.
A small museum next to the Dysert O'Dea monastic settlement, devoted to local archaeology and history.

Tourist information
For anyone without their own transport, the tourist office (065 28366) is inconveniently located two miles outside of town on the Limerick Road. The gift shop on the corner at O'Connell Square, Upstairs, Downstairs, is happy to dispense local tourist information, but cannot book accommodation.

Festivals

Two music festivals are held in Ennis each year: the Fleadh Nua in late May and the Guinness Traditional Music Festival in November. Information is available from the tourist office.

*Fifteenth-century **Bunratty Castle** – outside...*

... and in – between Limerick and Ennis.

and restaurant. All ten bedrooms have direct-dial telephone and there's a pleasant residents' lounge. **Queens Hotel** *Abbey Street, Ennis, Co Clare (065 28963/fax 065 28628)*. **Rates** £30 per person. **Credit** AmEx, DC, MC, V. Overlooking the thirteenth-century Franciscan Abbey; all rooms are en suite with satellite TV, radio, telephone, hair-dryer, tea/coffee.

The Burren

The Burren's name in Irish – Boireann or 'rocky land' – points to the elemental nature of this immense plateau of limestone (the largest in Ireland or Britain) formed some 350 million years ago at the bottom of what was then a sea. About one hundred million years later, convulsive earth movements thrust the seabed to the surface, cracking the stone and allowing rainwater to deepen the fissures and feed subterranean channels and rivers. The result today is an astonishingly grey landscape of rock, punctuated by pockets of green and set against a magnificent backdrop of ocean and sky.

One of Cromwell's men only saw the negative aspects of this karst landscape, railing against a land that lacked 'water enough to drown a man, nor a tree to hang him, nor soil enough to bury'. However, most visitors are gradually drawn into its unique and strange beauty. Part of the attraction is the wonder that such an apparently austere landscape still manages to conjure up a heaven of wild flowers. Try to be here in early summer or late spring, when pockets of well-drained limey soil, helped by a benign Atlantic climate, nurture an extraordinary collection of Alpine and Mediterranean flora (saxifrages, cranesbills, gentians, maidenhead ferns…). Later in the summer, it's the turn of numerous different varieties of orchid: bring a wild flower guide.

The Burren is also rich in ancient monuments. Around 4,000 BC, when the soil was not so sparse and woodland common, the land was settled by farmers who constructed fine megalithic tombs for their dead. The best example is the photogenic Poulnabrone Dolmen, in a field off the road between Ballyvaughan and Corofin, best seen at an irregular hour when there is a good chance of no one else being around. It is over 5,000 years old and would originally have been submerged beneath an artificial hill. About one mile to the north-west of Poulnabrone there rests the Gleninsheen Wedge Tomb, noted for the priceless gold collar found nearby by a boy in 1930 and now on display in the National Museum in Dublin.

The best way to explore and appreciate the Burren is on foot or with the help of a bicycle. Bikes can be hired from Burkes Garage in Lisdoonvarna (065 74022) or from one of the hostels in Doolin (*see below*). The Burren Way is a 28-mile walk that stretches from Ballyvaughan in the north to Liscannor in the south, taking in the village of

The Burren – *extraordinary rocky landscape.*

Where to stay

Ennis

Auburn Lodge Hotel *Galway Road, Ennis, Co Clare (065 21247/fax 065 21202)*. **Rates** *single* £40-£45; *double* £70-£80. **Credit** AmEx, DC, MC, V. Conveniently located, if you have your own transport, with its 100 rooms unlikely to be booked out. Ask about weekend specials.

The Clare Hostel *Cornmarket, Summerhill, Ennis, Co Clare (065 29370/fax 065 41225)*. **Rates** £10 for bed in multi-bedded rooms; *double* £25-50. **Credit** AmEx, MC, V. New 16-roomed hostel which has opened in the centre of Ennis, open from 7am to 10.30pm. The rates include a continental restaurant, and a card-key system for all the rooms provides a degree of security not always found in hostels.

Mungovans *78 Parnell Street, Ennis, Co Clare (065 24608/fax 065 20982)*. **Rates** £17 per person. **Credit** MC. Plum in the centre of town with rooms above a bar

Doolin and some spectacular cliff walks. The Ordnance Survey of Ireland map No 51 in the 1:50,000 series is the best single map showing the route. Burren Hill Walks Ltd (065 77168), based in Ballyvaughan, conduct guided walks.

Possible bases for a stay in the Burren include Ballyvaughan, if coming down from Galway, Doolin on the Atlantic coast for the added bonus of live music and lively pubs, or a quiet village such as Kilfenora or Lisdoonvarna.

Getting there

By bus Bus Éireann runs a local service between Ennis, Ennistymon, Lisdoonvarna and Doolin. From Galway there are services to Ballyvaughan, Lisdoonvarna and Doolin.
By car From Ennis head to Corofin on the R476 and from Galway head for Ballyvaughan on the N67.
By ferry *See below* for details of ferries between the Aran Islands and Doolin.

Attractions

Burren Display Centre
Kilfenora, Co Clare (065 88030). Open Easter-Oct 10am-5pm daily. Admission £2.
A good place to visit for maps and literature on the Burren and there are good displays on the geology and history of the region as well as a video presentation. Café serving decent food.

Doorty High Cross
Kilfenora Cathedral, Kilfenora, Co Clare.
Standing near the door of the church, the 800-year-old Doorty Cross is atypical, having no wheel on the top, but the Celtic patterning is superbly rendered. There are other High Crosses in the churchyard and in an adjoining field to the west.

Killinaboy's Sheila na gig
Killanboy, Co Clare, on the R476 north from Corofin.
The ruined church in the village of Killanboy is worth visiting if you haven't yet met a Sheila na gig – a carved figure depicting a woman with very pronounced and exaggerated genitalia. The impressive example here is located over the doorway.

Leamenah Castle
About two miles east of Kilfenora, five miles north of Corofin. Open daily. Admission free.
Two buildings: a late fifteenth-century tower house with five storeys and a mid-seventeenth-century house with four storeys built by Conor O'Brien, who later died fighting Cromwell.

Ailwee Caves
South of Ballyvaughan, reached by turning left off the N67 heading south from Ballyvaughan. Well signposted. (065 77036). Open Apr-Sept 10am-6pm daily. Admission £3.85.
Recommended for anyone new to the delights of subterranean nature, the Ailwee Caves were discovered accidentally by a man out walking his dog. The dog disappeared from view and when the man went to investigate, he found an old hibernation site for bears and three bear pits. Now, it's the only Burren cavern open to tourists, there's a café and a mini-market of souvenirs.

Tourist information
The nearest tourist information office is at the Cliffs of Moher visitors' centre (065 81171) and there may also be a summer tourist information office in Ballyvaughan. Local information is also available at the Burren Display Centre

Ballyvaughan – *start of the Burren Way.*

in Kilfenora (*see above*) and useful literature is also available at the Ennis tourist office. All these places sell Tim Robertson's exemplary map of the Burren.

Where to stay

Ballyvaughan
Cregans Castle Hotel *Ballyvaughan, Co Clare (065 77005/fax 065 77111/e-mail: gregans@iol.ie).* **Rates** *single £78-£90; double £96-£120.* **Credit** AmEx, DC, MC, V. Four-star, country-house luxury amid the Burren landscape. Large rooms with no TV, award-winning garden.

Corofin
Burren House *Kilnaboy, Corofin, Co Clare (065 37143).* **Rates** *single £19-£22; double £28-£32.* Three rooms, two en suite, in a typical Irish bungalow. Well-located for exploratory trips in the Burren.

Kilfenora
Carraig Liath *Kilfenora, Co Clare (065 88075).* **Rates** *single £19-£21; double £29-£32.* Bungalow with five rooms, three en suite, ideal for Burren trips and the village has restaurants and bars with traditional music. No smoking in bedrooms.

Doolin & Cliffs of Moher

Doolin is the traditional music capital of Ireland – and a less attractive village could hardly have been found to shoulder the responsibility. The village is strung out ungraciously along a road that leads to the harbour, where a service to the Aran Islands operates. Should you arrive during the day, do not let appearances dampen your spirits, for at night

*The breathtaking **Cliffs of Moher** – next stop North America, or indeed the Aran Islands.*

the pubs are packed and buzzing to the sound of lightning-fast gigs and reels played on an assortment of instruments. Check out both O'Connor's and McGann's and look for notices advertising any special musical events in the area.

The coast road south from Doolin leads to the renowned Cliffs of Moher which stretch for five miles around Hag's Head, almost to Liscannor. The highest point – well over 200 metres/660 feet – is just north of O'Brien's Tower and on a good day there are clear views of the Aran Islands and Connemara. It is easy to escape the crowds by setting out along the five-mile walk along the cliff edge.

Getting there

By bus *To Doolin* Bus Éireann services connect Doolin with Ennis, Galway and Dublin.

Lisdoonvarna *– bike hire and operating spa.*

By ferry *To Doolin* A ferry runs between Doolin Harbour and Inis Oirr (the smallest of the three Aran Islands) and in the summer months there is also a service to Inis Mór (the largest island). There are two companies: Doolin Ferries (065 74189/77086) and Inis Thiar Ferries (065 74500).

Attractions

Ballinalacken Castle

Just over two miles north of Doolin on the road to Fanore, Co Clare. **Open** daily. **Admission** free.
A well-preserved fifteenth-century tower house, the staircase of which may be climbed for fine views of the enigmatic Burren landscape.

The Spa Wells Centre

Lisdoonvarna, Co Clare (065 74023).
The only operating spa in Ireland, complete with sulphur spring, massage room, sauna and mineral baths.

Tourist information

The Cliffs of Moher visitors' centre, where the main car park is, has a tourist information office (065 81171).

Festivals

Tradition has it that, once the hay and corn was harvested, eligible men and women would try their luck in Lisdoonvarna, tempted by the fame of the professional matchmakers who lived there. Nowadays, the Matchmaking Festival each September is a good excuse for late-night drinking and general carousing. No computerised forms to fill out, but who knows…?

County Galway – *highlights include Galway city, rugged Connemara and the Aran Islands.*

Where to stay

Doolin

Aille River Hostel *Doolin, Co Clare (065 74260).*
Aran View House *Coast Road, Doolin, Co Clare (065 74061/fax 065 74540).* **Rates** *single* £35-£45; *double* £54-£70. Located at the quiet end of the village, away from the harbour, but within staggering distance of the pubs. A quiet and restful place with a good restaurant.
Churchfield *Doolin, Co Clare (065 74209/fax 065 74622).* **Rates** *ingle* £19-£21; *double* £28-£32. The house attached to the village's post office, with views of the Cliffs of Moher; six rooms, nearly all en suite.
Fisherstreet House & Paddy's Doolin Hostel *Doolin, Co Clare (065 74006/fax 065 74421).*
Flanagan's Village Hostel *Doolin, Co Clare (065 74564).*
Rainbow Hostel *Doolin, Co Clare (065 74415).*

Where to eat

Doolin

Bruch na hAille *Broadford, Doolin, Co Clare (065 74120).* One of Doolin's most easy-going restaurants, with easy-going food such as sole cooked in cider and gratin of crab. John and Helen Browne have almost two decades' worth of experience of coping with the summertime invasion of the village.

Liscannor

Egan's *Liscannor, Co Clare (065 81430).* Patrick Egan's pub is a wine-drinker's dream, with shelves groaning with choice clarets and bosomy Burgundies.

Tulla

Flapper's Restaurant *Main Street, Tulla, Co Clare (065 35711).* A few miles from Ennis, in a village famed for its ceilidh bands, Patricia Cahill's restaurant

is effortlessly the best in the area, with sassy cooking in a simple, relaxed way. Spicy crab cakes with chilli mayonnaise, rack of lamb with flageolet beans and curried monkfish with an apple and date compôte are all expertly delivered. Cooking at lunchtime is simpler, and the value for money is exceptional.

County Galway

There are three major attractions in the county of Galway: the city of Galway, the untamed terrain of Connemara to the west of the city and the three Aran Islands off the coast.

Together, they serve as the ideal introduction to the west of Ireland and should whet the appetite for future trips into the bordering county of wild Mayo to the north.

Getting there

By bus Bus Éireann services connect the city of Galway with Dublin, Doolin in County Clare (1 hour) and Cork (4 hours). There is also a private bus company, North Galway Club (093 55492), with a daily Dublin-Galway service, and another company, Feda O'Donnell Coaches (075 761655), runs from Galway to Donegal and Letterkenny. Nestor's (091 797144/01 832 0049) run a daily bus between Galway and Dublin airport.
See below for details of bus transport from Galway to Connemara and boats to the Aran Islands.
By train Trains run daily between Dublin and Galway.
By air From Galway Airport (091 755569), lying six miles east of the city, Aer Lingus have daily flights to Dublin.

Galway city

The city of Galway is a heady and energetic place, dedicated to the art of enjoyment. It's a university city – very European and very un-English – which draws enervated Dubliners, who have long known about its recuperative qualities.

Galway could make a convincing case for being the most culturally Irish city in the country. The busiest time is during the Galway Arts Festival in the last two weeks of July, which has an international mix of the performing and visual arts. Book your accommodation a long way in advance. But throughout the summer Galway has a lively roster of cultural events and it's always worth checking what's showing at the Druid Theatre Company (091 568617) in Chapel Lane, off Quay Street, or the Punchbag Theatre Company (091 565422), opposite Jurys Galway Inn down by the quayside. The Galway Arts Centre (091 565886), Nun's Island, off Mill Street, has a good noticeboard, and touring groups often show up here.

Galway is something of a haven for media darlings: the Irish-speaking TV station Teilifis na Gaelige is based here, and Roger Corman, king of the B-movies, set up a film studio 16 miles west of Galway city in the small town of Inverin, in 1994.

Eyre Square, in the heart of the city, serves as a general reference point and a natural meeting place

Eyre Square – *Galway's natural meeting place.*

where time can be pleasantly passed observing people and the anarchic mix of surrounding architecture. Slabs of limestone in the form of the Great Southern Hotel dominate one side of the square, and behind the hotel lie the bus and train stations. The shops in the adjacent Eyre Square Centre are nothing special, but the mall incorporates sections of the medieval city walls.

Follow William Street out of the square as it leads to Shop Street, a main pedestrian street in the city: halfway down on the right side, on the corner with Upper Abbeygate Street, stands the most significant branch of the Allied Irish Bank in Ireland. The bank building, known as Lynch's Castle, is a splendid example of medieval town architecture and it once belonged to the important Galway family, the Lynchs.

The grim story is that in 1493, the town mayor, James Lynch Fitzstephen, personally hanged his own son for an act of murder because the young man's popularity ensured no one else would act as executioner. Many of the building's architectural details, including the gargoyles, are worth admiring, and inside there is a display on the history of the building.

A short walk away on Market Street, there are more finely wrought gargoyles decorating the Collegiate Church of St Nicholas, where legend decrees Christopher Columbus sent a prayer to heaven before sailing west with a Galwayman, Rice de Culvery, on board. The interior boasts a lepers gallery, while outside the church, the Lynch Memorial marks the spot where James Lynch carried out the execution of his son.

It helps to have an inkling of Galway's history because the present mood of prosperity and self-esteem – and its decidedly continental flavour – is a resurgence of the spirit that characterised its past. In the centuries that followed the arrival of Anglo-Normans in 1234, Galway developed into the major port on the Atlantic seaboard, and was built upon close trading links with Spain and Portugal. It rivalled Bristol, and even London, in the volume of its trade and a cosmopolitan sense of its own importance developed. Its ruling merchants only came to grief when Cromwell besieged the city in 1651, slaughtered the citizens and destroyed the economy. Galway fell into near-terminal decline and in the nineteenth century, the city was subsumed by the horrific poverty that was so typical of the west of Ireland.

Until its recent dramatic resurgence, the only hope for young people was to leave home and head for Dublin or England. This is what Nora Barnacle did at the turn of this century, heading for Dublin and a job in a hotel. One day she was chatted up on the street by the young James Joyce and before long they left Ireland together to spend the rest of their lives overseas. Nora Barnacle's home, at 8 Bowling Green, is now a small museum (*see below*).

A faint reminder of the era when Gaelic and Spanish were as commonly spoken on the quayside as English may be found at the Spanish Arch, down by the River Corrib on Spanish Parade. It requires a little imagination to conjure the scene, but the stone arches were probably incorporated into the city walls, allowing ships to pass through and unload cargoes of wine and spices from Iberia.

The narrow streets between the river and Eyre Square are the food and entertainment heart of the city. Pubs and restaurants are easy to find here, but is also worth venturing across the Wolfe Tone Bridge to Upper Dominick Street and Sea Road where there are more pubs moving to the rhythms of Irish music. This area is known as the Claddagh, home to the famous Claddagh ring, depicting two hands encircling a heart.

Festivals

A jazz festival in February kicks off the year, followed in early May by a rhythm 'n' roots festival. Around Easter, the Cúirt Festival of Literature springs into action. The Galway Arts Festival takes place during the last two weeks of July, followed by the Galway Races in the first week of August. The races take place at Ballybrit, about four miles from the city centre, and their terrific popularity puts a premium on any kind of accommodation. The Galway Oyster Festival at the end of September rounds off the year. Information on all festivals is available from the tourist office.

Attractions

Galway City Museum
Entrance by the Spanish Arch, Spanish Parade, Galway, Co Galway (091 567641). **Open** 10am-1pm, 2.15-5pm, Mon-Sat. **Closed** 1-2.15pm. **Admission** £2.50.
A local history museum, unspectacular but worth considering on a wet afternoon.

Galway Irish Crystal Heritage Centre
Merlin Park, Dublin Road, Galway, Co Galway (091 757311). **Open** daily.
A new attraction focusing on the craftsmanship of crystal. A video theatre, exhibits and restaurant and, of course, showrooms.

Nora Barnacle's House
8 Bowling Green, Galway, Co Galway (091 64743). **Open** 10am-1pm, 2.15-5pm, Mon-Sat. **Admission** £1.
This small terraced house will be of great interest to readers of Joyce, but remarkably uninteresting to most other visitors. Joyce rarely travelled outside of Dublin and his two visits to this house were his introduction to Ireland's wild west.

Tourist information
The tourist office (091 563081) is close to Eyre Square at the corner of Victoria Place and Merchant's Road. Expect long queues for accommodation and information at the height of summer. Enquire here about guided walking tours of the city, rowing boats on River Corrib and the twice-daily Lough Corrib river cruise.

Where to stay

Galway
Ashford Manor *7 College Road, Galway, Co Galway (091 563941/fax 091 563941).* **Rates** single £20-£35; double £36-£50. **Credit** MC, V. A large town home, a five-minute walk to the city centre, with en suite bedrooms and tea/coffee making facilities.
Corrib Villa Hostel *4 Waterside, Galway, Co Galway (091 562892).*
Great Western House *Eyre Square, Galway, Co Galway (091 561139/1-800 425929/fax 091 561196).*
Imperial Hotel *Eyre Square, Galway, Co Galway (091 563033/fax 091 568410).* **Rates** single or double £65-£100. **Credit** AmEx, DC, MC, V. A bustling hotel in the heart of the city and within walking distance of bus and train stations; 84 en suite rooms in a three-star hotel.
Jurys Galway Inn *Quay Street, Galway, Co Galway (091 566444/fax 091 568415).* **Rates** £70-£85 per room. **Credit** AmEx, DC, MC, V. The room rate is for an en suite room with up to three adults or two adults and two children, breakfast not included. Weekend specials make a better deal.
Kinlay House *Galway, Eyre Square, Galway, Co Galway (091 565244/fax 091 565245/e-mail kingal@usit.ie).*
Quay Street House Hostel *10 Quay Street, Galway, Co Galway (tel/fax 091 568644).*
Stella Maris *151 Upper Salthill, Galway, Co Galway (tel/fax 091 521950).*

Where to eat

Galway
Kirwan's Lane Creative Cuisine *Kirwan's Lane, Galway (091 568266).* Michael O'Grady's title suggests more thrills than you will actually find in Kirwan's Lane. The cooking is actually at its best when least experimental – lamb's liver with onion confit, homemade sausages with sauerkraut and mash – and when they do get creative with things, like experimenting with Caesar salad, the results can be indulgent. A simple room, full of life and that inimitable Galway bonhomie.
Neachtain's *17 Cross Street, Galway (091 566172).* Galway has more classic pubs than anywhere else, but Neachtain's (pronounced Nockton's) is a definition of an unselfconscious, classic pub. There is bar food available, of a decent standard, but the pints and the craic are the eternal draw.
Da Tang Noodle House *Middle Street, Galway (091 561443).* The first Chinese noodle house in Ireland is an enjoyable space, the fresh noodle dishes forming the centrepiece of the cooking – served with lamb in a black bean sauce, with pork in yellow bean sauce or with mixed vegetables and tofu.

No shortage of decent pubs in **Galway city**.

Kinvarra

Merrimann Inn *Kinvarra,Co Galway.* A new hotel, with the largest thatched roof in Ireland, has the great attraction of having Michael Clifford, one of Ireland's most original and exacting chefs, at work in the kitchen. Claire Walsh, one of the best hostesses in the country, matches Mr Clifford's skills out front, and the location of the Merrimann, in the sedate village of Kinvarra, is perfect respite from the feverishness of Galway city.

Moycullen

Drimcong House *Moycullen, Co Galway (091 555115).* Gerry Galvin is the philosopher of Irish cookery, and each day he puts his considered philosophy to work in Drimcong House, one of the glories of Irish cooking. Slow cooked ox cheek with oysters, bacon and lovage, eel and pike mousse with horseradish, pork steak with crispy risotto a la crème, fillet of lamb with a summer salad. Everything about Drimcong radiates care, the service is outstanding, children are welcome, and a meal here is a chance to see a restaurant which is in love with the whole business of cooking and serving Irish food.

Connemara

The wild and inhospitable landscape west of Galway city remains a hard place to earn a living as a farmer, but its romantic scenery of mountains and peat bogs continues to exert a strong pull over travellers in search of the 'real' Ireland. If the days are wet, then Connemara is really very Irish indeed – damp and depressing days in the country are as Celtic as megalithic tombs and High Crosses – but when the sun shines, the place suggests one of the world's best-kept travel secrets. Parts of Connemara are Gaeltacht areas where the Irish language is still in use and visitors may occasionally be banjaxed by road signs that don't use English.

The small town of Oughterard is the first port of call in Connemara. The landscape is relatively tame compared to what lies further west, but it's still worth a short visit. Boats can be hired to tour Lough Corrib and the uninhabited island of Inchagoill, with atmospheric ecclesiastical ruins carrying Latin inscriptions claimed to be the oldest example of Latin as used by Christians outside of Rome. Cinéastes may not be able to resist catching a ferry across the lough to Cong in Mayo, where Maureen O'Hara and John Wayne starred in the

Scenery around **Leenane**, *County Galway.*

faintly preposterous 1956 film *The Quiet Man*. The film locations are all lovingly recorded for posterity and guided walks based around the film are popular. The proximity of Lough Corrib – home to salmon and trout – has also turned Oughterard into a popular base for anglers; the tourist office has information on where to hire boats and gear.

From Oughterard, head due west for Maam Cross, and then drive north to Leenane, which takes in some staggering scenery. Otherwise, stay on the main road west as far as Recess where another, even more attractive option is to turn north and follow the road through the ravishingly beautiful Lough Inagh valley. The road leads past Kylemore Abbey (*see below*) and continues west to Letterfrack and Clifden.

Another possibility is to go south from Oughterard, heading for the fishing village of Roundstone on the western coast. From the village, it takes an undemanding two hours to walk to the summit of Mt Errisbeg and glory in the stupendous view of the Connemara mountains and the surrounding bogland. There is also an extraordinary white sand beach at Gurteen Bay, just over a mile to the west of Roundstone, which would probably be spoilt by tourist developments were it not for the unpredictable climate.

The nearby town of Clifden – where Alcock and Brown landed after the first non-stop transatlantic flight in 1919 – has successfully established itself as the visitors' capital of Connemara, and some would say wrecked itself in the process. Nevertheless, it does possess a good range of accommodation and restaurants, and it makes a decent base for a stay in Connemara. Bikes can be hired, walking and hiking trips organised, or guided tours booked through the Island House in Market Street (095 21379). There are also opportunities for pony trekking, dinghy sailing and windsurfing in the area.

Best of all, Clifden is perfectly placed for quick access to inspiring scenery, and a favourite local walk is the coast road that passes Leo's Hostel (*see below*). A longer walk is the sky road that leads to the tiny village of Claddaghaduff, where there are fine beaches. To the south of Clifden, the Ballyconneely Road leads to the dramatic memorial to Alcock and Brown who landed here in 1919 after the first non-stop flight across the Atlantic. The nearby beach at Mannin Bay is safe for swimming.

For more rugged walks, it is best to head for the Connemara National Park, which includes part of the Twelve Bens mountain range and is home to a 4,000-year-old Megalithic Court Tomb. The park's visitor centre (095 41054) is close to the town of Letterfrack, easily reached on the road north from Clifden. Drop in for literature and advice on hikes, as well as information about their guided nature walks.

One good day trip from Clifden is to the island of Inishbofin, which is every bit as Irish as it sounds.

*The Twelve Bens mountain range and the town of Clifden in **Connemara**, County Galway.*

Clifden Castle – *another of the many attractions Connemara has to offer the visitor.*

Take a day trip to the island of Inishbofin.

Come to enjoy nature and laze on the sandy beaches, while spotting seals in the water. There is mercifully little to see except for the ruins of a thirteenth-century church and the remains of a Grace O'Malley castle. Grace O'Malley was a shrewd 'pirate queen', whose visit to the court of Elizabeth I did little to diminish her authority over parts of west Mayo. She used Inishbofin for her fleet, and the castle was built to protect them. Tickets and timetables are available at the tourist office in Clifden.

Getting there

By bus Roundstone and Clifden may be reached by Bus Éireann services from Galway bus station (091 562000).
By road A suggested tour of Connemara by car or bicycle route is to head north-west out of Galway city to Oughterard on the N59, with views of Lough Corrib, before continuing on through the rugged countryside to Clifden. The alternative coastal route via Spiddal is spoilt in places by bungalow developments along the road.

Attractions

Aughnanure Castle

Two miles south of Oughterard, Co Galway. **Open** *May-Sept* 9.30am-6.30pm daily. **Admission** £2.50.
A six-storey tower house that was home to the bellicose O'Flaherty clan.

Kylemore Abbey

Two miles east of Letterfrack, Co Galway. **Open** *Easter-Oct* daily. **Admission** £2.
A nineteenth-century edifice built by a millionaire Englishman, which was later adopted by Benedictine nuns and is now a private boarding school run by nuns.

Leenane Cultural Centre

Leenane, Co Galway. **Open** *April-Sept* daily.
Admission £2.
Dedicated to the history of spinning and weaving wool and – thanks to the live sheep – more interesting than people might imagine.

Pearse's Cottage

To the west of Screeb (between Maam Cross and Rossaveel) but may also be reached from Cashel, Co Galway. **Open** *mid-June-mid-Sept* 9.30am-6.30pm daily. **Admission** £1.
Padraic Pearse (1879-1916) was one of the leading lights in the Gaelic revival and it was partly his mystical sense of the need for a blood sacrifice that led to his involvement in the 1916 Rising and subsequent execution by the British. He lived in this cottage for a while. For details of Dublin's Pearse Museum, *see* **Museums**.

Tourist information

There is a small tourist office open in Oughterard in the summer but the main office is in Clifden, Market Street (095 21163).

Festivals

Around the third week in August, Clifden hosts the Connemara Pony Show and, in early September, the town is the venue for a country blues festival.

Where to stay

Clifden

Brookside Hostel *Hulk Street, Clifden, Co Galway (095 21812).*
Clifden Town Hostel *Market Street, Clifden, Co Galway (095 21076/fax 095 21701).*
Kingstown House *Bridge Street, Clifden, Co Galway (095 21470/fax 095 21530).* **Rates** £28-£36 double. A family-run house in the town, two minutes from the Bus Éireann stop and close to amenities. Eight rooms, six en suite.
Leo's Hostel *Sea View, Clifden, Co Galway (095 21429).*

Letterfrack

Old Monastery *Letterfrack, Co Galway (tel/fax 095 41132).*

Oughterard

Canrawer House *Station Road, Oughterard, Co Galway (tel/fax 091 552388).*
Lough Corrib Hostel *Camp Street, Oughterard, Co Galway (091 552866/fax 091 550279).*
Waterfall Lodge *Oughterard, Co Galway (091 552168).* **Rates** *single* £23; *double* £36. Graceful period house with antique furnishings, private game fishing, and en suite rooms. A cut above the average B&B.

Roundstone

Heatherglen House *Roundstone, Co Galway (095 35837).* **Rates** *single* £19-£30; *double* £32-£36. A typical Irish bungalow in a wild setting overlooking Roundstone Bay, with a bleak hill outside the back door for a morning constitutional.

Where to eat

Ballyconneely

Erriseaske House Hotel *Ballyconneely, Co Galway (095 23553).* The lovely, lonely location of Erriseaske is the perfect place in which to encounter Stefan Matz's rigorous cooking. Bristling with skillfulness and exactitude, he conjures ethereal flavours from his ingredients: lobster salad with chervil vinegar, watercress soup with a fish julienne, a quartet of raviolis, fresh tomato consommé, Connemara lamb with a jus of fresh thyme, wispy lemon tart.

Clifden

Destry's *Clifden, Co Galway (095 21722).* This sparky restaurant is a tribute to Marlene Dietrich (its full title is *Destry Rides Again*, after Marlene's classic western with Jimmy Stewart), but irrespective of its design, Marlene has to play a supporting role to Dermot Gannon's food, which is the real star. Timbale of smoked lamb with quail eggs and Parmesan and a garlic and horseradish cream, venison with cabbage stewed with garlic and smoked bacon, field mushrooms stuffed with ricotta and herbs with a couscous and sesame crust are just some of his thrilling inventions, and, at weekends, the raucous fun of the room matches the fireworks in the kitchen.

Visit **Inis Mór**, the largest of the three Aran Islands, for jaw-dropping scenery such as this.

Roundstone

O'Dowd's *Roundstone, Co Galway (095 35809).* A smashing old pub on the main street, with good pub food – shark and chips, proper soups and sandwiches – and a timeless atmosphere.

The Aran Islands

The Irish Nobel prize winner for literature, Seamus Heaney, described the three Aran islands – Inis Mór, Inis Meáin and Inis Oirr – as 'stepping stones out of Europe'. They are placed some 30 miles off the Galway coast and are undoubtedly the most famous of the many islands dotted around the coasts of Ireland. They first became known outside Galway when the cultural wing of the nationalist renaissance, emerging around the turn of this century, realised that its Gaelic identity was endangered. Nationalists looked to the west of Ireland for their cultural roots and little-visited places such as the Aran Islands were sought out for their Gaelic integrity, most manifest in their inhabitants' inability to speak English.

The first influential visitor to Aran was the playwright JM Synge who came to Aran on the advice of his friend WB Yeats – 'Live there as if you were one of the people themselves; express a life that has never found expression.' – followed in the 1930s by the documentary filmmaker Robert Flaherty, whose *Man of Aran* is still regularly shown on Inis Mór. Irish people still come to the Aran islands to practise their Gaelic, possibly spending much of the time discussing the consequences of the islands' growing dependence on tourism.

It is possible to spend just a day on the islands and feel you've absorbed some of their unique atmosphere. Inis Mór is too large to explore just on foot, but there are bicycles for hire and minibuses and pony and traps plying the island. Accommodation is available on all three islands. Apart from the astonishing archeological sites on the islands, especially those of Inis Mór, the best reason for visiting is the jaw-dropping scenery. You can spend your day studying the effects of light on the dry stone walls, which often run down to the end of the land, then just seem to disappear over the edge into the swirling ocean that encircles the islands.

Inis Mór is the largest of the three islands and receives a flood of visitors, but the massed ranks of bicycles for hire, seen immediately after disembarking at Kilronan, let you escape quickly. The single most important archeological site is the dramatically situated Dún Aengus, reached by taking the main road west from Kilronan, then turning left at the signpost after about four miles. It is a huge semicircular ring fort perched on the edge of a cliff about 300 feet above the Atlantic. The defensive stone walls blend perfectly with the landscape and the whole construction is a wonderful testimony to the Iron Age people who built it some 2,000 years ago. Equally impressive, but far less visited, is Dún Dúchathair – surrounded on three sides by cliffs – which is within walking distance of Kilronan. A third prehistoric site worth visiting

*Home of **WB Yeats** in Gort, County Galway.*

*Part of **County Donegal**'s 200-mile coastline.*

is Dún Eoghanachta, reached by staying on the main road that turns off to reach Dún Aengus. A turning to the left is signposted about a mile after the Dún Aengus turning.

Inis Meáin receives far less visitors than Inis Mór and is more suitable for those who like to wander along country lanes and soak up the atmosphere. Dún Chonchúir is the one archeological site of note and its strategic position provides an excellent viewing point for today's visitors.

Inis Oírr is the smallest of the three islands and its proximity to the coast of Clare makes a day trip from Doolin very possible (*see below*). There is little to see, apart from an old castle set inside a ring fort, but you can spend a fine day meandering along the narrow lanes.

Getting there

The details below only give the essential details and as there are many options to consider – intra-island tickets, fly/ferry combinations and various package deals – it is advisable to pay a visit to the Galway city tourist office and consider the various possibilities. Most boats depart from Rossaveel, west of Galway city, but although car parking is possible at Rossaveel, the charges for this are steep, and little is gained by not taking the company bus from Galway city.

By sea There is more than one ferry company competing for passengers, so check timetables carefully if purchasing a return ticket. Aran Island Ferries/Island Ferries (091 561767), Victoria Place, Eyre Square, Galway, service all three islands and also offer packages that include hostel accommodation. Boats depart from Rossaveel, with a bus connection from Galway city. Aran Ferries (091 568903), based within the Galway tourist office, have a similar schedule and also run a bus to Rossaveel and offer package deals including accommodation. O'Brien Shipping (091 567283), also within the tourist office, run a service direct from Galway. Doolin Ferry Co (065 74455/74189) has a summer service between Doolin in Clare (*see above*) and Inis Oírr and Inis Mór.

By air Aer Arann (091 593034) fly from Inverin, near Spiddal to the west of Galway city, to all three islands with a bus connection to the Galway airport that takes longer than the actual flight itself (less than ten minutes).

Tourist information

There is a small summer-only tourist office (099 61263) in Kilronan on Inis Mór. There is no tourist office on Inis Meáin, but Inis Oírr has a seasonal office at the harbour where maps of the island are available.

Where to stay

Inis Meáin

Angela Faherty *Creigmor, Inis Meáin, Aran Islands, Co Galway (099 73012/fax 099 73052)*. **Rates** *double* £25. Five non-smoking bedrooms and an evening meal for £10.

Inis Mór

Aran Islands Hostel *Inis Mór, Aran Islands, Co Galway (099 61255)*. Within walking distance of the harbour.
Cregmount House *Creig-An-Cheirin, Kilronan, Inis Mór, Aran Islands, Co Galway (099 61139)*. **Rates** £14 per person. Modern bungalow with three non-smoking bedrooms with shared bathroom facilities and spectacular views of the sea.
Dún Aengus Hostel *Inis Mór, Aran Islands, Co Galway (099 61318)*. Seven miles west of Kilronan at Kilmurvey Bay.
Kelly House *St Ronan's Road, Kilronan, Inis Mór, Aran Islands, Co Galway (099 61259)*. **Rates** *single* £15.50-£18; *double* £24-£30. Conveniently close to the harbour for an early return to the mainland but only two bedrooms.
Mainistir House Hostel *Inis Mór, Aran Islands, Co Galway (099 61199)*. Just north of Kilronan and a hostel bus meets passengers at the harbour.

Inis Oírr

Bru Radharc Na Mara Hostel *Inis Oírr, Aran Islands, Co Galway (099 75087)*. Within walking distance of the harbour.
Inishere Hotel *Lurgan Village, Inis Oírr, Aran Islands, Co Galway (099 75020; fax 099 75099)*. **Rates** *single* £19-£23; *double* £34-£46. Fifteen bedrooms, open from April to the end of September.

Where to eat

Inis Mór

An T-Sean Cheibh *Kilronan, Inis Mór (099 61228)*. There is fast food in the café part of this roadside restaurant, and more formal and enjoyable cooking in the restaurant. There is also a verandah for those sunny days.
Joe Watty's Pub *Kilronan, Inis Mór (099 61155)*. Lovely chowders and unexpectedly well executed pastas and chilli dishes are the things to go for in Rhoda Twombly's cosy little bar, just up the hill out of Kilronan.

Inis Oírr

Fisherman's Cottage *Inis Oírr (099 75073)*. A popular and friendly little cottage which produces enjoyable seafood to accompany some cool chardonnay.

The beautiful coastal scenery of Glencolumbcille is just one reason to visit **County Donegal**.

County Donegal

Dramatic seascapes and exhilarating cliffs along Donegal's 200-mile coastline are matched inland by a rugged landscape of glens, peat bogs and rushing rivers. The county of Donegal stretches further north than any point in Northern Ireland and at times it can also seem more remote from cosmopolitan Dublin than anywhere else in the Republic. The journey by bus from Dublin takes four hours, a lot less by car. Having arrived in the county, it is best to make a base in one or two places and resist the temptation to make too many further excursions; Donegal is so large, with so many peninsulae and promontories to explore, that too much time can be spent just travelling on a first visit. And the pleasure of being in County Donegal only comes when there is the time to slow down and gradually absorb the splendid landscape and rural lifestyle which unfold around you. Donegal is Ireland without the painted leprechauns, the tacky Celtic souvenirs and coach tours – the 'real' Ireland?

County Donegal has the country's largest concentration of Gaelic speakers and there is no more robust Gaeltacht (Irish-speaking area) in Ireland. Culturally and historically – until 1922 at least – the county has been part of the ancient province of Ulster, but its strong Irish identity was anathema to the Unionists of Ulster who wanted to ensure that their protected new state would retain a majority of loyal Protestants. Consequently,

when Partition split the land in 1922, Donegal was allowed to remain part of the Republic.

If you're travelling from Dublin, it can be best to base yourself in Donegal town and explore the south-western corner of the county as far as lovely Glencolumbcille. Otherwise, particularly if you're travelling from Belfast, head for Letterkenny and then perhaps to Dunfanaghy on the northern coast, taking in Glenveagh National Park along the way. Either of these will provide a manageable introduction to what many travellers consider to be the most untouristy region of the country.

Getting there

By bus Bus Éireann services link Dublin with Donegal town, Letterkenny and Belfast. There are also a number of private bus companies, one of the largest being Feda O'Donnel buses (075 48114) which operates a regular service between Galway city and Donegal town. Funtrek (01 873 0852) runs a daily service between Dublin and Letterkenny, and McGeehan's (075 46101) runs a service between Dublin and Glencolumbcille. *See below* for details of bus services within Donegal.

By road *From Dublin* take the N3 through Navan, Cavan and Enniskillen and on to Ballyshannon and then Donegal town. Letterkenny is north-east of Donegal town on the N16.

From Belfast take the road to Londonderry and then the N3 to Letterkenny.

Donegal to Glencolumbcille

Donegal town is a small and compact place with a road junction at its centre known as the Diamond. Buses arrive and depart here, the tourist

Book a sea-angling trip out of **Killybegs** *– on the road from Donegal town to Glencolumbcille.*

office is only a short walk away and one of the best shops in the county, Magee's, overlooks the Diamond. Magee's is delightfully unmodernised, with its own garment factory and quite superb selection of tweeds. The Four Masters store next door also has a good selection of garments and gift items.

Another shop worth visiting is the Donegal Craft Centre, about a mile out of town along the road to Bundoran. Crystal, pottery, clothes and gifts are made in a series of workshops and there is a small café on the site. If you are on your way to Glencolumbcille, there are also a number of small factory shops along the way, and then in Glencolumbcille itself.

There are few places of interest in the town itself apart from Donegal Castle. It dates back to the fifteenth century but its Jacobean features derive from the extensive rebuilding that took place when an Englishman, Sir Basil Brooke, became the new owner at the end of the sixteenth century. Apparently, Hugh Roe O'Donnell, whose family first built the castle, burnt it down when it became obvious it would be confiscated by the English. There are many fine architectural features, particularly the grand fireplaces and their ornate decorations.

In the centre of the Diamond stands an obelisk commemorating those who researched and wrote the *Annals of the Four Masters*. The *Annals* are an extraordinary work of scholarship compiled by monks in Donegal Abbey (which no longer stands),

recording the history of Celtic Ireland from before the Flood to 1618. The four friars, realising that the arrival of the English presaged the end of Celtic culture, wrote the history before it was too late.

There's a good cycle ride leaving town on the N56 to Killybegs and turning right shortly after the bridge, following the sign for Harvey's Point hotel and restaurant. The road eventually rejoins the N15 road out of Donegal town, but not before passing through some balmy scenery around Lough Eske and the ruins of a tower house built by the Brooke family in the seventeenth century.

Enjoyment is not on the agenda at Lough Derg, further inland from Donegal town. Pilgrims to this retreat spend three days living on a diet of black tea and one basic meal each day, while completing the Stations of the Cross on bare feet and reciting 1,449 prayers. Appararently, St Patrick spent some days on an island in the lake, fasting and hallucinating. The ten-week pilgrim season lasts from June to mid-August and there is a visitor centre (072 61546) in Main Street, in the border town of Pettigo, dealing with the history of the lake and St Patrick's times here.

A longer jaunt from Donegal town begins by taking the N56 to Killybegs. On the way is the small village of Inver, which has a tiny beach and a pleasant old pub. From the promontory of St John's Point at Dunkineely there are great views of Donegal Bay. But it's best to push on to Killybegs, which was once a minor fishing village and is now home to a very successful fish processing plant. It marks the end of relatively drab scenery and the start of something more spectacular. Sea angling trips can be arranged here.

When in the town visit the McSweeney tombstone in St Catherine's church at the top of the hill. The tomb is easily found, distinguished by its Celtic-inspired carving of gallowglasses (mercenaries from Scotland who settled and earned their livings as minders and policemen).

West of Killybegs is Gaeltacht territory, so you may hear Gaelic spoken. The landscape becomes more rugged and the thatched cottages are not the tourist tea-shop variety from Killarney. The N56 turns north to Ardara, but stay on the coast road for Kilcar, Carrick and Glencolumbcille. From the village of Carrick, a road follows the river Owene to the smaller village of Teelin from where signs point the way to Bunglass. In Irish 'bunglas' means 'end of cliff' and the road leads to just this, a vantage point for Slieve League, when the road stops nearly 2,000 feet above the ocean. To say the view is spectacular – 'a Wagnerian overture made gloriously visible' is how one writer described its impact – is an understatement, as there are few finer sights in the country. During the summer, there are boat trips from the pier in Teelin (073 39079) so you can experience the awesome sight from sea level.

Experienced walkers will warm to the challenge of a trek along Slieve League, following the somewhat daunting One Man's Path, but it is best to use one of the walking guides available in the Donegal bookshops and let someone know where you are going.

The village of Glencolumbcille (literally 'the glen of St Colmcille') is named after St Colmcille (Columba) who lived in the valley after founding a monastery here in the sixth century. He is more famous for his evangelical work in Scotland which came about as a result of his exile from Ireland, following accusations of involvement in the bloody battle of Cuildreimhne in 561. He set out with a dozen disciples and founded a monastery on the island of Iona, spending the last 34 years of his life in Scotland.

The present Folk Village heritage centre in Glencolumbcille (*see below*) owes a great deal to another man of the cloth, a parish priest named James McDyer who galvanised the local population with community schemes to halt emigration from the area in the 1950s. It's easy to suffer an attack of heritage centre-fatigue in Ireland, but at least the one in Glencolumbcille was one of the first of its kind. It is made up of three model buildings illustrating aspects of rural life in Donegal from the eighteenth and nineteenth centuries; the shebeen house retails local wines and food produce.

The beach next to the folk village is not the safest for swimming, but at Doonait, to the west

Slieve League – *pack your head for heights.*

of the village and within walking distance, there are two sandy beaches. A wide range of adventure sports – scuba diving, snorkelling and fishing – can be arranged through the nearby Malinmore Adventure Centre (073 30123). And if you're toying with the idea of learning some Irish, the village of Glencolumbcille hosts language schools throughout the summer. Telephone (073 30248) or write to Oideas Gael, Gleann Cholm Cille, County Dhún na nGall for details. There are also courses teaching traditional skills such as set dancing and weaving.

The Donegal Woollen Centre in the village has a selection of Donegal tweed jackets, Aran jumpers and other less expensive clothing and accessories. The Lace House Centre in the village sells a similar range of clothes, including some rugs, and the workshop area is open to the public. There are more shops selling locally made knitware in the town of Ardara, reached via a lovely road through the Glengesh Pass.

Getting there

By bus There are daily buses between Donegal and Glencolumbcille, stopping at Killybegs and Carrick. Bus Éireann's regular Galway-Derry service stops in Donegal town and Letterkenny.
By road From the Diamond in Donegal town take the N56 road across the bridge. This leads to Killybegs, via Mountcharles and Bruckless, before turning north to Ardara. The route suggested here involves staying on the coastal road after Killybegs and reaching Glencolumbcille via Carrick.

Attractions

Ardara Heritage Centre

Ardara, Co Donegal. **Open** *Easter-Oct* 10am-6pm Mon-Sat; 2-6pm Sun. **Admission** free.

Focusing on the history of tweed-weaving in Donegal through practical demonstrations and video show. A tea-shop is attached.

Donegal Railway Heritage Centre

Old Station House, Donegal, Co Donegal. **Open** *June-Sept* daily. **Admission** £2.

Railway enthusiasts will drool over the restored old steam engines and their carriages.

Glencolumbcille Folk Village

Glencolumbcille, Co Donegal. **Open** *Apr-Sept* daily. **Admission** £2.

The admission charge covers a guided tour of the recon-structed buildings and entry to a small museum.

St Connell's Museum & Heritage Centre

Glenties, Co Donegal. **Open** *mid-May-Sept* 10am-12.30pm, 2-4.30pm, Mon-Fri; 10.30am-noon Sat. **Admission** £1.

A local-history museum, distinguished by its strange col-lection of bathroom furniture.

Tourist information

The tourist office in Donegal town (073 21148) is on Bally-shannon Road. It is well stocked with literature and infor-mation on the county as a whole. Ask about the guided historical tours of the town that take place in the summer months. Bicycles and fishing gear may be hired from O'Doherty's on Main Street (073 21119), and the helpful pro-prietor will suggest cycling routes and places to fish. In the summer there is a tourist information point in Killybegs and in Glencolumbcille the Lace House Centre (073 30116) is a good source of tourist information.

Festivals

Killybegs has a popular sea angling festival in mid-July and local festivities at the beginning of August. Ardara has a Weavers' Fair in early June. At the beginning of August, a highly regarded folk and traditional music festival brings Ballyshannon to life.

Where to stay

Bruckless

Gallagher's Farm Hostel *Darney, Bruckless, Co Donegal (073 37057).*

Derrylahan

Derrylahan Independent Hostel *Derrylahan, Co Donegal (073 38079/fax 073 38447).*

Donegal

Abbey Hotel *The Diamond, Donegal, Co Donegal (073 21014/fax 073 21014).* **Rates** *single* £41; *double* £80. **Credit** AmEx, DC, MC, V. A family-run, three-star hotel in the centre of Donegal town, close to various amenities. All rooms are en suite. Enquire about the availability of those overlooking Donegal Bay.
Atlantic Guesthouse *Main Street, Donegal, Co Donegal (073 211870).* **Rates** *single* £18-£22; *double* £28-£35. Comfortable, centrally located, two-star guesthouse with 17 bedrooms.
Donegal Town Independent Hostel *Doonan, Donegal, Co Donegal (073 22805).*

Glencolumbcille

Corner House *Cashel, Glencolumbcille, Co Donegal (073 30021).* **Rates** *single* £19-£21; *double* £28-£32. Yellow-painted house five minutes from the Glencolumbcille Folk Village. Four rooms, three en suite.
Sunset Heights *Doonait, Glencolumbcille, Co Donegal (073 30048/fax 073 30048).* **Rates** *single* £15; *double* £26. The best aspect is the delightful beach nearby, one that you may often have completely to yourself. Three bedrooms, open from Easter to end of September.

Glenties

Campbell's Holiday Hostel *Glenties, Co Donegal (075 51491).*

Killybegs

Bay View Hotel & Leisure Centre *Main Street, Killybegs, Co Donegal (073 31950/fax 073 31856).* **Rates** *single* £50-£60; *double* £80-£100. **Credit** AmEx, MC, V. A fairly new hotel overlooking Donegal Bay and boasting a leisure centre and indoor swimming pool. All 40 rooms are en suite, equipped with satellite television, hair-dryer, trouser press and tea/coffee making facility. Weekend specials usually available.
Lyndale *Doonan, Donegal, Co Donegal (073 21873).* **Rates** *single* £19; *double* £28-£32. Under a mile from the town centre, 200 metres off the N56 coast road. Four rooms, three en suite, open from April to the end of October.

Where to eat

Bruckless

Castlemurray House *Bruckless, Co Galway (073 37022).* Thierry Delcros produces the best food in the county, his French métier marrying perfectly with Irish ingredients and an understated dining room which enjoys utterly gorgeous views across the bay. Onion soup, duck paté, fillet of beef with wild mushrooms, crispy lobster – all are cooked with enjoyment. The rooms are simple and excellent value, and breakfasts are terrific.

Donegal

McGroarty's Pub *The Diamond, Donegal, Co Donegal (073 21049).* Stella's Salad Bar is the attraction in McGroarty's pub, a big favourite with locals thanks to simple, tasty food – good stir-fries, good salads – in a town which has a high, and baseless, opinion of its food.

Rossnowlagh

Smugglers Creek *Rossnowlagh, Co Donegal (072 52366).* The views out across Donegal Bay are mesmerising, as you sit and enjoy a pint in this restored pub, close to the main road. The bar food is simple and enjoyable, the restaurant concentrates on fish cookery in the evening, and there are five rooms for those who want to peer out at the Atlantic some more.

Letterkenny to Dunfanaghy

Letterkenny is the largest and liveliest town in Donegal. Like Donegal town, it takes about four hours to reach from Dublin by bus and it makes a good base for exploring this side of the county.

Unusually for Irish towns, Letterkenny has few sites of historical interest, but it does have an animated entertainment scene with an array of decent pubs with Irish music along Lower Main Street (McGinley's, Cottage Bar and Downtown are all worth checking out) and nightclubs that at weekends attract a wide following from all corners of Donegal's north-west.

Letterkenny also has a number of shopping malls which, as well as the usual consumer goodies, harbour a few art and craft shops. With the town's Main Street claiming to be – and certainly seeming to be – the longest high street in Ireland, it is easy to spend a long time in Letterkenny just looking around. This is not an unpleasant experience, because the town does exert a strong appeal. Its air of modernity and quiet self-esteem is rare in Irish towns.

Letterkenny makes a good base from which to explore the county. It is the main transport interchange for the north-west and there are buses to most corners of the county (and the country). The tourist office, inconveniently situated for the pedestrian outside of town on the main Londonderry road, has information and literature on all the main attractions of the north-west. For information about fishing in the area – there are fine salmon and trout rivers in the area – ask at one of the tackle shops along Main Street.

Opposite the Manse Hostel, on High Road at the top of Main Street, is the Letterkenny Leisure Centre (074 25251) which has a swimming pool and sauna room open to the public. For adventure sports, ask at the Gartan Outdoor Education Centre (074 37032), in the nearby village of Churchill. They conduct courses throughout the summer on rock climbing, sea canoeing, hill climbing and windsurfing; residential courses with hostel accommodation are available.

There are two places of interest close enough to Letterkenny to make a pleasant day trip. The major attraction is Glebe House and Gallery (*see below*), a splendid Regency building. It was originally a rectory but was bought in the 1950s by the artist Derek Hill and decorated in a highly individual style. Hill had travelled extensively, absorbing a variety of art forms and his particular interest in Islamic art becomes evident in the fascinating 40-minute tour of the house.

The kitchen is packed with paintings by artists from the Tory Islands (off the north-west coast of Donegal), one of whom, James Dixon, was inspired to paint in his sixties after Hill visited the island in the mid-1950s. But this is only a taster, as Glebe House also has paintings by Picasso, Pasmore, Landseer, Kokoschka, Hokusai, Jack B Yeats (brother of the poet) and others. On top of all this there are rooms with original William Morris wallpaper and a decorated bathroom that could change

A short drive from Letterkenny are the loughs and mountains of **Glenveagh National Park**.

Glenveagh Castle – *the large drawing room.*

all your notions of interior design. There is also a delightful garden.

Close to Glebe House is the Colmcille Heritage Centre (*see below*), dedicated to the life and times of St Columba who was born nearby. The centre has an exhausting amount of information on the saint, but the displays on illuminated manuscripts offer light relief.

Two miles south of Raphoe, a small town just outside Letterkenny, is one of the largest stone circles in Ireland. Comprising 60 stones, it measures 44.2 metres in diameter. In Pagan times it was the venue for the annual Beltane celebrations.

Glenveagh National Park (*see below*) is another fine day out from Letterkenny. The park's existence has an unfortunate provenance: in 1861 the landowner, the egregious John George Adair, evicted 250 tenants from his land to make way for his new stately home, the present Glenveagh Castle (*see below*). Eventually the estate passed to an American, who later donated the castle to the state. The park, between the Derryveagh and Glendowan mountains, has a nature trail and during the summer there are guided walks. There are also guided tours of Glenveagh Castle which take in some of the rooms as decorated by Henry McIlhenny, the American owner. The gardens are beautiful and well worth a visit.

To experience a sense of having severed all links with urban civilisation, travel north from Letterkenny to the village of Dunfanaghy on the northern coast. This is a quietly popular holiday resort for people from both the Republic and Northern Ireland, but no one makes too much fuss in case the word gets out. There are vast sandy beaches, a fair range of accommodation to suit most budgets, some extraordinary coastal scenery around Horn Head, healthy walks and a couple of interesting places of historical note.

A walk that requires only stamina and a lust for fresh air begins by heading west out of the village and taking the first turning on the right after Corcreggan Mill Hostel. Follow the track down to the sand dunes, and the expansive Tramore Beach is waiting on the other side. The

walk may be extended by walking east to the end of the beach and following a path that leads on to Pollaguill Bay.

If you're travelling by car or bike, pack a picnic and follow the circular road that winds its way around Horn Head from the west end of Dunfanaghy. On a clear day, Scotland comes into view beyond Malin Head to the north-east and the views are always spectacular.

Dunfanaghy guided walks are organised by Donegal Walking Holidays (074 36376), Sessiagh Cottage, Woodhill, Dunfanaghy, Co Donegal. The largest hotel in the area, Arnold's (074 36208) in Dunfanaghy village, organises horse riding and runs various arts and crafts programmes.

Getting there

By bus Bus Éireann (074 21309) run buses between Dublin and Letterkenny and the useful Cork-Londonderry service connects Letterkenny with Galway and Cork. There is also a Galway-Londonderry service that stops in Letterkenny as well as Donegal town.
Private bus companies provide the best services for travel from Letterkenny to Dunfanaghy and other local towns. Lough Swilly (074 22400) do a regular run to Dunfanaghy and Londonderry, and McGeehan (075 461010) connect Letterkenny with Glencolumbcille. All buses depart from the large bus station (074 22863) at the beginning of the road to Londonderry.
By road To reach Letterkenny from Dublin, take the N2 heading north to Monaghan and then the A5 to Omagh and Strabane and then the N14 on to Letterkenny.
By air The nearest airport is in Londonderry, which is a short distance from Letterkenny on the N13.

Attractions

Colmcille Heritage Centre

Churchill, Letterkenny, Co Donegal (074 37306). **Open** Easter weekend, mid-May-Sept 10.30am-6.30pm Mon-Sat; 1-6.30pm Sun. **Admission** £2.
The Heritage Centre is within walking distance of Glebe House on the shores of Lough Gartan.

County Museum

High Road, Letterkenny, Co Donegal. **Open** 10am-12.30pm, 1-4.30pm, Mon-Fri; 1-4.30pm Sat. **Admission** free.
A very modern-looking museum devoted to local history and with space for temporary exhibitions downstairs. Worth seeing the collection of nineteenth-century photographs.

Doe Castle

Just over two miles from Cresslough, on the N56 between Letterkenny and Dunfanaghy, and well sign-posted. **Open** daily. **Admission** free.
Built in the early sixteenth century, this fine fortress passed into the hands of the expatriate MacSweeny clan, gallowglasses from Scotland. In 1650, it succumbed to English firepower and was lived in until the nineteenth century. The setting is striking, perched on a spit of land with a rock-hewn moat, and ideal for a picnic.

Dunfanaghy Workhouse

Dunfanaghy, Co Donegal (074 36540). **Open** Easter-Sept 9am-6pm daily. **Admission** £1.
This workhouse was built in 1845 and accommodated over 600 people at the height of the famine that began shortly after it opened. It now houses a small local history museum. Suitable for a wet afternoon.

Glebe House & Gallery

Churchill, Letterkenny, Co Donegal. **Open** *Easter weekend, mid-May-Sept* 11am-6pm daily. **Closed** Fri. **Admission** £2.

To reach Glebe House from Letterkenny, take the R250 to Glenties but turn right after a couple of miles on to the R251 to the village of Churchill.

Glenveagh Castle

Glenveagh National Park, Co Donegal. **Open** *Easter-Oct* 10am-6.30pm daily. **Admission** £2.

Tastefully decorated rooms and carefully nurtured gardens. There are daily guided tours around the house and in the summer months there are also occasional tours of the gardens. A free shuttle bus runs between the park's visitor centre and the castle.

Glenveagh National Park

Glenveagh National Park, Co Donegal. **Open** daily; *visitor centre Easter-Oct* 10am-6.30pm daily. **Admission** £2.

Some 4,000 acres of forest and parkland, with herds of red deer. Excellent visitor centre which includes a restaurant.

Festivals

Letterkenny holds a four-day festival of music and dance at the end of August. Ask at the tourist office for programme information.

Where to stay

Dunfanaghy

Carrig-Rua Hotel *Dunfanaghy, Co Donegal (074 36133/fax 074 36277).* **Rates** *single* £45-£50; *double* £70-£80. **Credit** AmEx, MC, V. Originally a coaching inn, now a snug hotel with a decent seafood restaurant and a convivial bar. All 22 rooms are en suite.

Corcreggan Mill Hostel *Just west of Dunfanaghy, Co Donegal (074 36409/3650).* **Rates** *single* £6-£8; £9 per person in private room. Good facilities that include laundry, bike hire, cooked meals. and camping space outside that allows for use of hostel facilities.

Rosman House *Dunfanaghy, Co Donegal (074 36273/36393).* **Rates** *single* £21; *double* £32. **Credit** MC, V. A modern bungalow with excellent views and all rooms have radio, television and tea/coffee-making facility. Breakfast menu.

Falcarragh

Shamrock Lodge *Main Street, Falcarragh, Co Donegal (074 35859/fax 074 35192).* **Rates** *single* £6; £8 per person in private room. Few amenities beyond use of the kitchen, but this hostel in Falcarragh, eight miles west of Dunfanaghy, is worth considering for an inexpensive night's accommodation in the area.

Letterkenny

Gallaghers Hotel *100 Main Street, Letterkenny, Co Donegal (074 22066/fax 074 21016).* **Rates** *single* £30; *double* £100. **Credit** AmEx, DC, MC, V. This comfortable old hotel in the town centre makes a pleasant base for exploring this corner of Donegal. Open all year, all 27 rooms en suite.

The Manse Hostel *High Road, Letterkenny, Co Donegal (074 252238).* **Rates** *single* £6; £7 per person in private room. Open all year with 24 beds, including six private rooms.

Town View *Leck Road, Letterkenny, Co Donegal (074 21570/25138).* **Rates** *single* £21; *double* £32. **Credit** MC, V. Six rooms, all en suite, with tea/coffee-making facility, hair-dryers and television. The

breakfasts are a cut above the average. Located over the bridge at Dunnes department store at the top of Main Street and under a mile from there. Open all year.

Where to eat

Carndonagh

The Corncrake *Malin Street, Carndonagh, Co Donegal (077 74534).* Brid and Noreen's little restaurant, right at the tip top of the country, has a clever little menu of local foods – grilled lamb cutlets with rosemary, mussel and crab chowder, chicken with garlic and fresh tarragon.

Greencastle

Kealy's Seafood Bar *Greencastle, Co Donegal (077 81010).* Sited just across from the pier in Greencastle, the fish cooking in James and Tricia Kealy's restaurant is every bit as distinguished as you might hope, given such a location. Grilled fillet of wild salmon with a lime butter, superb Greencastle chowder, poached fillet of cod with Stilton, hake with a saffron butter sauce. Lunchtime food is just as good as the more complex dinner dishes, and the bar itself is lovely for a drink – check out the fine bar counter itself. They frequently exhibit and sell works by local painters.

Letterkenny

Carolina House *Letterkenny, Co Donegal (074 22480).* Mary Prendergast's purpose-built restaurant, just beside the road to Ramelton, looks somewhat like a domestic bungalow, but the food is confident and classical – smoked salmon with a herb and cheese paté, confit of duck, spiced beef with a tomato sauce.

Belfast

The announcement of the second IRA ceasefire in July 1997 provided Belfast with another opportunity finally to shrug off the curse of being labelled a war zone. The truth is that, even before the first ceasefire in 1994, first-time visitors were invariably surprised by the air of normality that characterised life in the city and the attractiveness of Belfast as a place to stay in and explore. That said, it's essential to have at least some understanding of the city's turbulent history if you're going to get the most out of your visit. (*See also chapter* **History**.)

The story begins in 1604 when Sir Arthur Chichester, a Protestant knight from the south-west of England, was 'planted' here by James I. Chichester's first settlement was slow to develop, and even by the middle of the seventeenth century, only a few hundred people could call it their home. The arrival of Huguenots from France strengthened the small linen industry and the eighteenth century witnessed an economic boom as the trade in cloth was accompanied by the successful birth of a shipbuilding industry.

Many more settlers arrived from Scotland and England, reinforcing the Protestant grip on economic power. In the nineteenth century, the fruits of this commercial and industrial success began to manifest themselves in architecture, and the

Belfast *city centre – in Northern Ireland – is far from the war zone some visitors expect.*

Victorian city centre still stands as one of the chief delights of any visit to the city. As well as the usual civic buildings, Belfast is blessed with some splendidly ornate Victorian pubs.

There is also west Belfast, the working-class heart of the city without whose people there would be no Victorian architecture. The bitter sectarian divisions of west Belfast, that we are now so familiar with, did not always exist.

In the eighteenth century, the nationalist society of United Irishmen did indeed unite Catholics and Protestants in a common cause and it was only in the following century that evangelising Presbyterians began to foster apartheid-like attitudes. In the early years of the twentieth century, as the possibility of an independent Ireland began to emerge, the Protestant ruling class made it clear that they would use violence to resist an independent Irish state in which their grip on economic and political power would inevitably weaken. The British government accepted the idea of retaining a part of Ireland, as (eventually) did Michael Collins and his team of nationalists who came to London to negotiate with Lloyd George in 1921.

Collins, who knew that his guerrilla army back in Ireland might not be able to sustain what until then had been a reasonably successful war of attrition against the British, accepted the deal partly because of the promise of a Boundary Commission. Collins was led to believe that the

Commission would in time be able to change the nature of the border between Northern Ireland and the rest of the country; this never happened. These dramatic events, and the tragic civil war that followed, are well covered in Neil Jordan's 1996 film, *Michael Collins*.

Between the 1920s and '60s, the Protestants were left alone to govern their mini-state with minimal interference from British governments. The Northern Ireland government eventually established itself at Stormont, a palatial building close to Belfast, until the Troubles that followed the civil rights movement led to the British imposing direct rule and abolishing the Protestant-controlled government.

There is more to Belfast, though, than Victorian architecture, partisan murals and a terrible legacy of bloodletting. As if to compensate for the Troubles, the city has developed a remarkable entertainment scene with very lively pubs, clubs and superb restaurants. The area to head for is south of the city centre along Great Victoria Street and around Queen's University. Some excellent pubs are clustered around Blackstaff Square, behind the Crown Liquor Saloon in Great Victoria Street.

There are also good cinemas and a host of theatres and concert halls. In case readers are in any doubt, be assured that visitors to Belfast – and this includes English people visiting nationalist areas of Belfast – need not be overly concerned for their safety. In the 30 years of bloody conflict, not one single tourist, in Belfast or indeed in any other part of Northern Ireland, has fallen victim to the violence that has taken so many lives and shattered so many families. And it has always been true over this period that the average citizen's life in the North is more endangered by the motor car than Semtex or the sniper's bullet. If the second ceasefire does hold and a political solution is found, then there is even less reason to worry and more reason than ever to visit and enjoy the city of Belfast.

Getting there

By bus There are four daily buses connecting Belfast with Dublin, journey time about 3 hours, run by Ulsterbus (01232 320011). Lough Swilly Bus Company (01504 262017) connect with Londonderry and Donegal. The main Belfast station is in Glengall Street, behind the Europe hotel.
By train There are regular train services to Dublin and Londonderry and the train ride to or from Dublin takes about two hours.
By air There are two airports, Belfast City Airport (01232 457745) and Belfast International Airport (01849 422888), but nearly all mainstream airlines use Belfast International Airport. The City airport is used for flights from smaller airports in Britain. Belfast International Airport is just under 20 miles from the city centre and there is a regular bus service to the city. A taxi costs around £20. The City airport is only a couple of miles from the city centre and, as well as a regular bus service (No 21) with the city centre, a train can be boarded at Sydenham Halt station just across the road from the terminal. A taxi costs about £5.
By ferry The catamaran route between Belfast and Stranraer uses Belfast Harbour on Donegall Quay which is easily reached by bus or taxi from the city centre. The regular ferries from Scotland use Larne, 20 miles to the north of Belfast, but well connected by bus and train. There are also ferry connections with Liverpool with Norse Irish Ferries (01574 779090), and with the Isle of Man through the Isle of Man Steam Packet Company (01574 351009).

Getting around

By bus The city has a comprehensive bus system and there are day and weekly tickets that offer savings. Buses depart from Donegall Square, in the city centre, and timetables and bus route maps are available from the kiosks on Donegall Square West (or call 01232 24685).
By taxi Notwithstanding the ceasefire, it will be some time before hailing regular taxis on the street becomes commonplace. They are easily picked up at the main taxi rank in Donegall Square East or call one of the well-established taxi/minicab companies (01232 233333 or 01232 323278). Black taxis operate like buses along Falls Road and Shankill Road and are almost as inexpensive.
By car People 'borrowing' cars for joyrides pose the biggest problem when considering where to park. There are clearly marked control zones where no parking is allowed, but there are plenty of pay-and-display areas as well as multi-storey car parks. The tourist office provides a sheet detailing all the secure car parks. The AA office is at 108 Great Victoria Street (0345 500600; breakdowns 0800 887766) and the RAC is at 14 Wellington Place (01232 232640; breakdowns 0800 828282).
There are car rental companies at both the airports and Avis have an office at 69 Great Victoria Street.

Central Belfast

Belfast City Hall is a building of intrinsic interest and its location in Donegall Square makes a handy reference point as the centre of the city and the starting point for a walking tour. The building was completed in 1906 as a self-conscious celebration of the city's prosperity, and the first meeting of the Northern Ireland Parliament took place here in 1921.

When the Anglo-Irish Agreement was signed in 1985 – acknowledging for the first time that the Republic had a legitimate interest in this corner of the country – the response was to display a huge 'Belfast Says No' banner across the exterior of the building. It remained there for a number of years, but was taken down well before Unionists lost their overall majority of council seats in the 1997 elections. The exterior of the building is worth appreciating for its classical proportions, although the real pleasure comes from joining one of the tours that guide visitors around the interior (*see below*). The building's entrance hall, dome and robing room can all be visited, but it's the council chamber itself that competes with Westminster in stately ambience.

The Linen Hall Library is the other main building of note in the north-west corner at 17 Donegall Square. It dates back to 1788 and houses an unrivalled collection of nineteenth-century Belfast publications and Northern Ireland political literature of the last 30 years. The library is open to members, but non-members may ask to be allowed to browse. Other buildings worth singling out in the square include the baroque Scottish Provident Building in Donegall Square West, now a gift store, and the Robinson & Cleaver Building.

The main shopping district lies immediately to the north of Donegall Square North along Donegall Place and Castle Lane that runs off on the right a short way up Donegall Place. The names of the stores are familiar enough from any high street in Britain, but the buildings are classic Victorian and spotting the original features can be fun. Walk down Castle Lane and cross Cornmarket to reach Ann Street. The alleyways that run off Ann Street on the left, leading through to High Street, are known as the Entries and are worth exploring for the marvellous old Belfast saloon bars that are tucked away here. The Morning Star in Pottinger's Entry is one of the best and the Crown Entry was where the Society of United Irishmen was founded in 1791. Off High Street, White's Tavern in Wine Cellar Entry is the oldest pub in the city.

Where High Street meets Victoria Street, the Pisa-like Albert Memorial serves as a useful landmark. It is close to the River Lagan and in the surrounding streets, there are fine examples of the work of Charles Lanyon (1813-89), the architect of some of the city's principal buildings that were completed in the 1850s and '60s. The restored Custom House on the north end of Donegall Quay is probably his finest achievement. Opposite the Custom House, by the riverside, is the Lagan Lookout – a modern visitors' centre explaining the technology of the nearby weir and the role of the river in Belfast's history – from where there are good views of the Harland & Wolff shipyards and their alien-looking cranes dominating east Belfast. This is where the Titanic was built and there is a memorial to the ship's fate on the east side of City Hall.

Two other places of interest that no first-time visitor to the city should miss are both on Great Victoria Street, close to the Europa Hotel and bus station. The Crown Liquor Saloon, opposite the Europa Hotel, is now a National Trust property and the supreme expression of Victorian pub architecture (*see below* **Where to eat**). The Grand Opera House (01232 241919) is on the other side of the road, just north of the Europa Hotel, and like the hotel, it has survived more than one bombing. There is always some event being performed here and the ornate Victorian interior has been exceptionally well restored.

Great Victoria Street, the Golden Mile, leads to the university area and a surfeit of pubs, clubs, restaurants and places to stay. There are a few secondhand bookshops, including the seriously expensive Books & Prints, and the architectural magnificence of Queen's University in University Road, a continuation of Great Victoria Street. The college building, modelled on Magdalen College, Oxford, was designed by Lanyon and completed in 1849. There are a number of places of interest in the vicinity: University Square, to the north of the college, has pristine Georgian buildings, and nearby are the Botanic Gardens and the Ulster Museum.

West Belfast

Belfast is the only city in Ireland to have experienced the Industrial Revolution and West Belfast was the result, responding to the need for human fodder to fuel the flax and linen mills and, later, the shipyards.

The sectarianism that has literally divided the area into sharply demarcated Catholic and Protestant zones first developed in the nineteenth century and exploded in 1968, when West Belfast came perilously close to tearing at the seams. Many hundreds of Catholic families had to leave their homes for fear of being burnt alive by rampaging mobs or shot by snipers.

It's true that West Belfast is where the sectarian divide is sharply illustrated by one of only two walls left in Europe since the Berlin Wall fell (the other's in Cyprus). The long barrier of iron sheeting separating the one Protestant neighbourhood

in the west of the city from the Catholic areas that surround it was initially welcomed by both sides as a way of stemming the on-going tit-for-tat battles between two antagonistic communities. It's known as the 'peace line'.

Now, with the tentative resumption of what all sides hope may be some kind of settlement to the province's troubles, there is no reason not to visit West Belfast. This can be done by foot or by taking a black taxi. The black taxi rank is at the western end of Castle Street and for about £10, a tour of the area could be arranged, although it is just as easy to set off down Castle Road and into Catholic Falls Road on foot. This was once one of the most desirable areas in the city, and still reveals an area proudly self sufficient and resilient, with a vibrant cultural life quite unique in the British Isles.

The people are friendly, but one look at the astonishing street murals that cover the sides of many buildings supporting the 'liberation struggle' led by the IRA and Sinn Fein (with references to fellow struggles in South Africa and Palestine) suggest that a low key, understanding and polite approach is advisable. This is not the place to be an ugly tourist.

The Protestant equivalent to Falls Road is Shankill Road, which may be reached by continuing up North Street, past the tourist office, into Peter's Hill where the black taxi rank is situated. Perhaps surprisingly, the area is even more run down than the Falls. In recent years the Protestant mural painters have begun to catch up with those in the Catholic areas in terms of scale and ambition, and possibly self delusion. It helps to have a nodding acquaintance with seventeenth-century Irish history to make sense of the references to King Billy and the apprentice boys slamming shut the gates of Londonderry in 1689.

Again, being a British tourist is not necessarily a recipe for instant popularity, as many loyalist Protestants feel abandoned, by the English in particular. But what is tragically obvious from a visit to both Falls Road and Shankill Road is that the inhabitants have so much in common in terms of social class and lost opportunities.

Also worth a visit is the Milltown Cemetery situated at the top of the Falls Road where it meets the strongly Republican Andersonstown area. Flanked by the forbidding fortress of the Andersonstown RUC police station (all watchtowers, barbed wire, and wary guards) this is the place where hunger striker Bobby Sands was buried and you may recognise it from the TV coverage. Much more than a civic burial site, it is a fascinating shrine to Republican history resplendent with Celtic imagery and the grave stones of numerous IRA and Republican dead. Look out for an enormous memorial tablet commemorating 'martyrs' from as far back as 1798 up to the present day.

West Belfast *– divided into Catholic and Protestant zones by sectarianism.*

Try not to look like you are a British MI5 spook on a surveillance mission by filming anyone alive in this hot spot. That said, anyone visiting West Befast will gain a more informed view of what it's all about than by simply sampling Belfast city centre, which is rather like an upmarket version of Glasgow.

Attractions

Arts Council Gallery

Ormeau Avenue, Belfast (01232 321402). **Open** 10am-5pm Mon-Fri. **Admission** free.
A gallery of modern art that complements the smaller collection in the Ulster Museum.

Belfast Castle

Bellevue, Belfast. **Open** *Apr-Sept* 9am-9pm daily; *Oct-Mar* 9am-6pm daily.
A nineteenth-century edifice with a small heritage centre, as well as being home to an expensive bar and café, the Belfast Castle Restaurant (01232 776925).

Belfast Zoo

Bellevue, Belfast (01232 776277). Bus 2, 3, 4, 5, 6, 45. **Open** *Apr-Sept* 10am-6pm daily. **Admission** £4.20.
Not the usual, oppressive place of incarceration for unfortunate animals. An excellent location but way out of town to the north, reached by bus from Donegall Square West.

Botanic Gardens

Next to Queen's University, Belfast. **Open** daily. **Open** Palm House *Apr-Sept* 10am-noon, 1-5pm, Mon-Fri; 2-5pm Sat-Sun. **Admission** free.
People have been enjoying this oasis of peace in the metropolis since 1827. The highlight is the white-painted, iron-and-glass hot-house known as the Palm House.

Cave Hill Country Park

Bellevue, Belfast (01232 776925). **Open** daily. **Admission** free.
Some 750 acres spread out between Belfast Zoo and Belfast Castle in the north of the city.

City Hall

Donegall Square, Belfast (01232 320202 ext 2227). **Tours** *July-Aug* 10.30am, 2.30pm, daily; *other months* 10.30pm Wed. **Admission** free.

Lagan Lookout

Waterfront by Donegall Quay, opposite the Custom House, Belfast. **Open** *Mar-Sept* Mon-Fri 11am-5pm; noon-5pm Sat; 2-5pm Sun. **Admission** £1.50.

Stormont

Four miles to the east of Belfast (01232 520600). Bus 22, 23.
The former home of the Northern Ireland government is a very grand building set in its own extensive grounds which may be freely visited. Enquire at the tourist office or call Stormont (the building is currently occupied by civil servants) about possible visits. At some time in the future, the building may perhaps be home to a new power-sharing government of Northern Ireland.

Ulster Museum

Stranmillis Road, Belfast (01232 381251). Bus 69, 70, 71. **Open** 10am-5pm Mon-Fri; 1-5pm Sat; 2-5pm Sun. **Admission** free.
Situated next to the Botanic Gardens (*see above*) and close to Queen's University, the Ulster Museum houses a vast collection – far too much to absorb in one visit – covering history, ecology, art, technology and a whole lot more. Highlights include the wreck of the *Girona* (from the 1588 Spanish Armada and salvaged in the 1960s off the coast) and an art gallery containing works by Francis Bacon and Henry Moore among others.

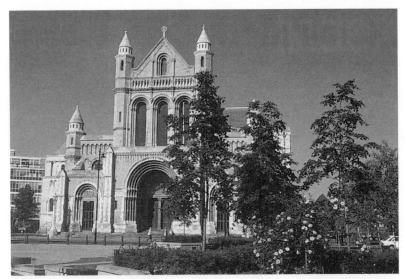

St Anne's Anglican Cathedral – *worth a visit for its most unusual Book of Common Prayer.*

Tourist information

The well-provided tourist office is at St Anne's Court, 59 North Street (01232 246609). As well as loads of information on Belfast (including the free *That's Entertainment*) and the rest of Northern Ireland, there is also an accommodation service, bureau de change and shop. There are also tourist information offices at both airports. Bord Fáilte, the Republic of Ireland's tourist board, have an office at 53 Castle Street (01232 327888).

Churches

Most of the churches in Belfast are of little architectural or historical interest, but one or two are worth visiting.

St Anne's Anglican Cathedral

At the corner of Donegall Street & Talbot Street.
Architecturally insignificant, but distinguished by the fact that the only tomb to be found inside is that of Edward Carson, a politician whose virulent championing of the Protestant cause played no mean part in the creation of Northern Ireland. What does stir the emotions is the church's Book of Common Prayer written on cigarette papers in a Japanese prisoner-of-war camp.

St Malachy's

Alfred Street, Belfast.
This is probably the most interesting church in the city. It was completed in 1844 and its gratifying features include a fan-vaulted ceiling, a captivating pulpit, a sculptured marble altar and the relics of a Trappist monk who died in the eighteenth century.

Sinclair Seamen's Church

Corporation Square (just north of the Custom Office and close to the SeaCat ferry terminal).
Designed by the prolific Charles Lanyon, but chiefly of interest to those of a nautical persuasion. Check out the shape of the pulpit and the amazing collection of maritime material.

Theatres & music venues

For the latest news about what's on and where consult the free *That's Entertainment* available from the tourist office and some hotel lobbies. The Grand Opera House (01232 241919/249129) on Great Victoria Street has a busy programme of events, as does the Belfast Civic Arts Theatre (01232 324936) in the university area. A major venue for concerts of classical and rock music is the Ulster Hall (01232 323900) on Bedford Street. The Empire Laughs Back (01232 228110), in the university area at 42 Botanic Avenue, is a good stand-up comedy venue on Tuesday nights.

Nightlife

Check *That's Entertainment* for the latest information, but pubs with music and/or discos include Bob Cratchit's (01232 332526), the Elms (01232 322106), the Botanic (01232 660460) and the Eglantine Inn (011232 381994). Popular clubs/discos include the Limelight (01232 325968) in Ormeau Avenue and the Manhattan (01232 233131) in Bradbury Place. The Parliament Bar in Dunbar Street and the Crow's Nest in Skipper Street are currently popular with gay men.

Where to stay

Soon after the first ceasefire in 1994, the number of visitors seeking hotel beds increased by almost 100 per cent, so it is not advisable to turn up in Belfast late at night without accommodation.

The tourist office operates a very useful booking service for anyone arriving during the day and credit card bookings may be made on freephone number 0800 317153; many of the B&Bs are located in the university area.

Belfast

Belfast International Youth Hostel *22-32 Donegall Road, Belfast (01232 315435). Buses 69, 70, 71, 89, 90.* **Rates** *single* £11; *double* £24 (incl continental breakfast). **Credit** DC, MC, V. Another oversubscribed hostel which usually needs advance booking. No kitchen, but laundry facility.

Botanic Lodge Guesthouse *87 Botanic Avenue, Belfast (tel/fax 01232 327682). Buses 83, 85, 86.* **Rates** *single* £20; *double* £36. **Credit** V. A smart and clean place, close to restaurants, pubs and clubs.

Eglantine Guest House *21 Eglantine Avenue, Belfast (01232 667585).* **Rates** *single* £19; *double* £36. Located in a pleasant, quiet area close to the university.

Europa Hotel *Great Victoria Street, Belfast (01232 327000/fax 01232 327800).* **Rates** *single* £80; *double* £145 (£60/£105 for doubles/singles on Fri, Sat). **Credit** AmEx, DC, MC, V. Belfast's much-loved and much-bombed landmark hotel. Even if not staying here, visit the bar for the views. The weekend rates, unlike the weekday ones, include breakfast.

The George *9 Eglantine Avenue, Belfast (01232 683212).* **Rates** *single* £19; *double* £36. Another standard B&B in Eglantine Avenue.

Where to eat

Belfast

Crown Liquor Saloon *46 Great Victoria Street, Belfast (01232 249476).* The fact that it is now owned by the National Trust hasn't dented the wild character of this Belfast institution a jot, and the Crown remains a pell-mell pub, its grievously hallucinogenic styling likely to convince you that you have had one too many even before you have had one at all. There is decent pub food served – stews, oysters, sandwiches – but simply mulling over a drink and marvelling at the style is what it is all about.

Deane's *38-40 Howard Street, Belfast (01232 560000).* Michael Deane's new restaurant allows this formidably gifted cook more room to express the duality of his style: informal in the brasserie downstairs, more involved and considered in the restaurant upstairs. Raymond McArdle controls the brasserie, coping easily with prodigious numbers, whilst upstairs his boss cuts the mustard with dishes such as canon of lamb with Asian ratatouille or pigeon with pearl barley and foie gras. Deane fuses the flavours of east and west better than almost anyone, and his cooking is truly exciting.

Equinox Café *32 Howard Street, Belfast (01232 230089).* Kay Gilbert's ultra-modish gift shop conceals a small café-restaurant at the back, where the coffee (served in tiny Rosenthal cups) is superlative, and the lunchtime cooking is imaginative, while firmly centred around the vogue for Italian tastes.

Nick's Warehouse *35-39 Hill Street, Belfast (01232 439690).* A man of great good humour, Nick Price will say that the business of being a restaurateur is the business of inflicting your tastes on others. Just as well, then, that Mr Price and his wife Kathy have such good taste, in everything from ambience and cooking, right through to the wittily presented wine lists. Marinated brie and oven-dried tomato salad, black pudding with red wine lentils, casserole of barley and haricot beans, lamb chops with garlic and rocket are just some of his

vividly flavoured dishes. Atmosphere, especially downstairs in the wine bar, is thunderous.

Roscoff *Shaftesbury Square, Belfast (01232 331532).* Paul Rankin's superstar status means that he spends a fair amount of time out of the kitchen at Roscoff, but, even in his absence, the cooking in this stylishly minimal restaurant is formidable. With him at the stove, it can be the greatest in the country: squab on mustard greens with shallots and chives, wild trout with dill hollandaise, chicken with a saffron mash, fillets of sole with creamed lentils and coriander, caramel crème brûlée with rhubarb compôte. Service is brilliant and value for money is exceptional. An offshoot of the restaurant, Roscoff Café, on Fountain Street in the city centre, run by Gillian Hayes, has excellent breads and sandwiches and good lunchtime specials.

The Sun Kee *38 Donegall Pass, Belfast (01232 312016).* A single room, where a television bleats constantly in the corner and every customer may be a member of Belfast's Chinese community, the Sun Kee is home to the best Chinese cooking in Ireland. Edmund Lau and his team make no compromises for western sensibilities, serving rustic hot-pots of beef flank with potatoes and turnips, char siu with monkfish or lovely, slithery things like duck stuffed with prawns. You bring your own wine, and the prices are as close to give-away as you get anywhere. The waiters even kiss your babies.

Tours

Citybus (01232 458484) has a city tour every Wednesday during the summer. They also conduct a 'Living History' tour that takes in the political hot spots every Tuesday, Thursday and Saturday. At weekends, a pub tour (01232 658337) crawls its way around the more notable pubs.

Festivals

An annual Civic Festival takes place each May and the tourist board issues a useful programme giving details of the diverse activities and events. There is also a folk festival in mid-June.

Further information

Bookshops
Waterstone's *8 Royal Avenue.*
Dillon's *42 Fountain Street.*
Eason *16 St Ann Street.*
University Bookshop *Queen's University, Green Cross, 51 Falls Road.*

Bureaux de change
Exchanging Irish punts for British pounds and vice versa may be conducted at any of the banks, the tourist office and most Thomas Cook offices (there's a large branch in Donegall Place). Most of the major banks have cash dispensing machines for Visa and MasterCard card-holders.

Emergency services
Telephone 999.

Hospitals
Royal Victoria Hospital *Falls Road (01232 240503). Buses 12, 13, 14, 15.*
Belfast City Hospital *Lisburn Road (01232 329241). Bus 58.*

Post offices
Main office Castle Place, where Royal Avenue meets Donegall Place; **branch** Shaftesbury Square.

Directory

Directory

Essential information

• Holders of passports from the following countries will not need visas to enter Ireland: Andorra, Argentina, Australia, Austria, Bahamas, Barbados, Belgium, Botswana, Brazil, Canada, Chile, Czech Republic, Costa Rica, Cyprus, Denmark, Ecuador, El Salvador, Estonia, Finland, France, Germany, Greece, Grenada, Guatemala, Honduras, Hungary, Iceland, Israel, Italy, Jamaica, Japan, Korea (North or South), Latvia, Lesotho, Liechtenstein, Lithuania, Luxembourg, Malawi, Malaysia, Malta, Mexico, Monaco, Mauritius, Netherlands, New Zealand, Nicaragua, Norway, Panama, Paraguay, Poland, Portugal, San Marino, Singapore, Slovakia, Slovenia, South Africa, Spain, Swaziland, Sweden, Switzerland, Trinidad & Tobago, Tonga, UK & colonies, Uruguay, USA, Vatican City, Venezuela, Western Samoa, Zimbabwe.
• Transit visas are required by nationals of Albania, Bulgaria, Cuba, Iran, Romania, Lebanon, Moldova, Montenegro, Serbia, Somalia, Sri Lanka.
• Those with a Hong Kong Certificate of Identity will need an entry visa for Ireland.
• Applications for visas should be made through your country's Irish Embassy or Consulate. You'll probably need to attend an interview. If there is no Irish representative in your country, direct applications may be made to: **Consular Section, Department of Foreign Affairs**, *72-6 St Stephen's Green, Dublin 2 (478 0822/fax 668 6518)*.

Customs

There are plans being made to abolish the EU duty-free allowance in 1999, so you'd better take advantage of it while you still can. The following allowances apply for non-EU citizens and for those purchasing duty-free goods:
• 200 cigarettes or 100 cigarillos or 50 cigars or 250g tobacco;
• 2 litres port, sherries, sparkling wines or 1 litre spirits or strong liqueurs (over 22% alcohol);
• 60 ml perfume;
• 250 ml toilet water.
• There are restrictions on importing meat or meat products.
• Importing and exporting currency is not restricted.

EU citizens 18 years and over are not required to make customs declarations, which means that you can bring in as much drink as you like, once you've paid tax on it.

Non-EU citizens aged 16 or over may bring in goods (for non-commercial use) on which tax has been paid up to the value of £142. Those aged 15 have an allowance of £73.

If you have queries, contact **Customs & Excise**, *Custom House, Dublin 1 (873 4555)*.

Insurance

If you're an EU citizen, the form you need is an E111, which will cover you for most medical (but not dental) emergencies. However, if you can afford to take out private medical insurance then it's well worth doing; it'll save you the effort and stress of trying to wade

through the red tape of EU reciprocal health agreements. It's also advisable to take out baggage insurance. Read the fine print: there's sometimes a limit of value per item, so things like portable CD players or cameras may not be covered. Whatever kind of insurance you're going to organise, do it before you set foot in Ireland, because it's impossible to sort out once you're there.

Money matters

The unit of Ireland's currency is the punt, or the Irish pound (IR£). 1p and 2p coins are copper; 5p, 10p, 50p and £1 coins are all silver; and 20p coins are gold-coloured. Notes start with £5 (yellow/brown, picture of a nun), £10 (green, James Joyce), £20 (purple, Daniel O'Connell) and £50 (blue, Douglas Hyde).

Ireland is still a cash culture, but most places accept American Express, Diners' Club, MasterCard and Visa (abbreviated in the guide to AmEx, DC, MC and V respectively). If you're staying in Ireland for some time, the safest thing is to take travellers' cheques and open a bank account (for which you'll need identification). Make sure your bank gives you IR£ travellers' cheques and not sterling – this is a common mistake. As always, bring your passport when cashing cheques.

Banks

In general, banking hours are 10am-4pm Mon-Wed, Fri; 10am-5pm Thur. The banks' automatic cash machines are all

linked up, so if you have an account with an Irish bank then you can probably withdraw money from any machine. The building societies' machines are similarly connected, and most of these also accommodate withdrawals from banks, so you'll have easy access to your money. Nearly all banks, building societies and post offices do foreign exchange, so there's no trouble changing currencies. The major bus depot **Busáras** (Dublin 1; 661 4337) and **Connolly Station** (Dublin 1; 661 4334) can stock you up with punts as soon as you arrive in the city. If you're in mid-shopping spree then bear in mind that the department stores **Arnotts** (Henry Street, Dublin 1; 872 1663) and **Clery's** (O'Connell Street, Dublin 1; 878 8291) both offer bureaux de change facilities. Other useful addresses are:
American Express Travel Service *116 Grafton Street, Dublin 2 (677 2874). Particularly good deals for cashing AmEx cheques.*
First Rate Bureau de Change *88 Camden Street Lower, Dublin 2 (478 3155).*
Foreign Exchange Company of Ireland *12 Ely Place, Dublin 2 (661 1800).*
Joe Walsh Tours ForEx *69 Upper O'Connell Street, Dublin 1 (872 5536) & 34 Grafton Street, Dublin 2 (677 9836).*
Thomas Cook *118 Grafton Street, Dublin 2 (677 1307).*

Bank Holidays

Bank Holidays or public holidays are as follows: 1 January (New Year's Day), 17 March (St Patrick's Day), Good Friday, Easter Monday, first Monday in May, June and August, the Monday closest to Hallowe'en (31 October), 25 December (Christmas Day), 26 December (Boxing Day), 29 December.

Crime & safety

Levels of street crime have risen dramatically in the last decade. Pickpockets and bag-snatchers have always been

there, but in recent years assailants have taken to using syringes as weapons. They have even been known to operate on city buses, walking the victim off at needle-point to get to a cash machine.

The majority of safety hints amount to common sense. If you're worried about travelling on buses, then sit downstairs in plain sight of the driver. When you're wandering around town, avoid jewellery that says 'Rob me' and strap your bag across your chest with the opening facing inwards. When withdrawing money from cash machines, don't stand counting wads of £20 notes; put your money away quickly, and, if there's a machine inside the bank, use that instead. Don't leave your wallet on a pub table when you're drinking, and unless your bag is really bulky, keep it on your lap when you stop for coffee.

Most of all, safety is about being aware: if you don't like the look of the area you're in, then walk out confidently. This is especially important during the evening: if you're on your own you need to stay to well-lit, populated areas. Arrange to meet people inside a pub or restaurant rather then waiting outside on your own.

Police

The emergency telephone number for police (called Garda), fire and ambulance is **999** or **112**. City centre Garda stations are located at:
Store Street, Dublin 1 (855 7761).
Pearse Street, Dublin 1 (677 8141).
Fitzgibbon Street, Dublin 1 (836 3113).
Garda Síochána Dublin Metropolitan HQ, Harcourt Square, Dublin 2 (475 5555).

Time & weather

Ireland is in the same time zone as Britain, and so runs according to Greenwich Mean Time. In spring (normally at

the end of March), the clocks go forward one hour for Summer Time, and they return to normal at the end of October. For the speaking clock, telephone **1191**.

Irish weather is notoriously unpredictable. There's little point in trying to summarise seasonal trends: just know that whatever time of year you visit, make sure to pack a warm sweater and a raincoat in addition to fine-weather gear.

For an up-to-date weather forecast for Dublin, telephone **1550 123 854** (calls cost 58p per minute).

Tipping

In restaurants you should tip around 12-15 per cent. If service charge is included on your bill, ask the staff if they actually receive it – you can refuse to pay it if they don't. It's generally accepted that hairdressers and lounge staff receive tips of around 10 per cent; so do taxi drivers for longer journeys.

Tourist information

Ring **1550 112 233** for 24-hour visitor information (calls cost 58p per minute). The general administration number is 605 7700. Reservations can be made on 605 7777. Tourist Information Offices can be found at the addresses below.
Dublin Tourism Centre *Suffolk Street, Dublin 2 (information 605 7799).* **Open** 9am-5.30pm Mon, Wed-Sat; 9.30am-5.30pm Tue. Located in a renovated church, the centre offers numerous services, including a bureau de change, car rental, café, shop and an accommodation and ticket reservation facility. Open all Bank Holidays except 25 & 26 Dec, 1 Jan.
Dublin Airport. Open 8am-10pm daily. **Closed** 25 & 26 Dec, 1 Jan.
Dun Laoghaire Ferry Terminal. Open 8am-8pm daily. **Closed** 25 & 26 Dec, 1 Jan.
The Square, Town Centre, Tallaght. **Open** 8am-1pm daily. **Closed** Bank Holidays.

Baggot Street Bridge. Open 9.30am-5.15pm Mon-Fri. **Closed** Bank Holidays.
Exclusively Irish *O'Connell Street, Dublin 2.* **Open** 10am-5.30pm daily. **Closed** 1.30-2pm & Bank Holidays.

Emergencies

Telephone **999** or **112** and ask for the emergency service you need – Fire, Garda (police), Ambulance, Irish Marine Emergency Service, Mountain & Cave Rescue.
Garda confidential line *(1800 666 111).*
Electricity Supply Board (ESB) *(604 0900 north Dublin/604 0910 central/604 0920 south).*
Gas emergency *(1850 205 050).*

Helplines & agencies

Samaritans *(872 7700).* **Open** 24 hours daily.
Childline *(1800 666 666).*
Parentline *(873 3500).*
Missing Persons Helpline *(1800 616 617).*
Poisons Information Service *(837 9964).*
Alcoholics Anonymous *(453 8998/after office hours 679 5967/679 6555).*
Alcoholics Anonymous Information Centre *5 Capel Street, Dublin 1 (873 2699).*
Drug Advisory & Treatment Centre *(677 1122).*
Narcotics Anonymous *(830 0944).*
Gamblers Anonymous *(872 1133).*
Asthma Line *(1850 445 464).*
Dublin Aids Alliance *53 Parnell Square, Dublin 1 (873 3799).*
Victim Support *29 Dame Street, Dublin 2 (679 8673).*
24-Hour National Helpline *(054 76222).*
For women's support, *see below* **Women's Dublin**.
For gay and lesbian helplines, *see chapter* **Gay & Lesbian**.

Accommodation

Dial **1800 724 724** for help with out-of-hours emergency accommodation for adults. Otherwise, the following contacts are useful.
Focus Point *14 Austace Street, Dublin 2 (671 2555).*
Cross Care Hostel *64 Eccles Street, Dublin 7 (830 4353).*
Salvation Army Men's Hostel *York Street, Dublin 2 (475 4039).*
Homeless Girls Society *(874 3742).*

Communications

Post offices are generally open 9am-5.30pm Mon-Fri; 9am-1pm Sat. Some will close for lunch, but the larger offices in Dublin (for example GPO, South Anne Street) remain open.

Post boxes are green and many have two slots: one for *Dublin Only* and one for *All Other Places.* It costs 32p to post a letter (weighing up to 20g) to anywhere in the EU; Europe (excluding EU) costs 44p; anywhere else costs 52p. Postcards and unsealed greeting cards cost 28p (EU), 37p (Europe), and 38p (all other countries). All airmail letters (including UK) should have a priority airmail (*Aerphost*) label affixed – these are free at all post offices. If you want to have mail retained in a post office for collection, address the envelope *Post Restante, GPO, O'Connell Street, Dublin 1* and print the addressee's name clearly.

Telephones

Public phones take any silver coins. The dialling code for Dublin is 01 – you don't need to use the prefix within the county of Dublin itself. 1800 numbers are free. Local phone numbers are 7 digits long, but outside of Dublin they may be shorter.

It's normally 20p for a three-minute local call, but phoning from a pub may cost you 30p. If you have access to a private phone, the costs will be much cheaper (11.5p for a three-minute local call, or 11.5p for a 15-minute local call during economy hours).

Reduced rates are charged 6pm-8am Mon-Fri, and all day Sat, Sun and Bank Holidays. International calls are much better value this way, and for an extra charge of 36p the operator will tell you the exact cost of the call.

If you can't use a private phone, the next easiest way to make long-distance calls is to buy a call card, available from most newsagents and post offices. They are especially useful out of town. Make sure to keep them afterwards, because they're fast becoming collector's items.

International dialling codes

Dial 00 and the appropriate country code. Here are a few commonly used international codes: **Australia** 61; **Belgium** 32; **Denmark** 45; **France** 33; **Germany** 49; **Great Britain** 44; **Greece** 30; **Italy** 39; **Japan** 81; **Netherlands** 31; **Norway** 47; **South Africa** 27; **Spain** 34; **Sweden** 46; **Switzerland** 41; **USA** 971. To telephone Dublin from abroad dial the international access code then 353 for Ireland and 1 for Dublin.

Operator assistance

Call **10** for Ireland and the UK, and **114** for international help.

Alarm & reverse charge calls

Alarm calls are available from the operator, costing 91p. Reverse charge calls cost 61p.

Directory enquiries

Dial **1190** for Ireland and Northern Ireland; **1197** for the UK; **1198** for international enquiries.

Telegrams

Or telemessages as they're now called. Call **196** for full details. Messages can also be sent from post offices during opening hours. A 12-word telemessage to the UK costs just over £4 (incl VAT).

Motoring

For Brits, the advantages of taking one's car to another country where they drive on the left are quickly outweighed by Dublin's driving conditions, cheerfully described by Dubliners themselves as hellish. Like London, there are too many cars and not enough parking spaces. You have been warned. Check beforehand to see whether your hotel or guest house has its own parking.

When touring, you will find the driving conditions much more pleasant. Country roads may not always be of the highest standard, but they are rarely choked with traffic. Do take care, however: distances on road signs are given sometimes in miles, sometimes in kilometres. Just relax and enjoy the scenery.

The following operate 24-hour services:
Automobile Association *23 Suffolk Street, Dublin 2 (677 9481/breakdown 1800 677 788).*
RAC *(breakdown 1800 535005).*
Aidan Flynn Motor Services *(843 3419).*
Alert Towing & Breakdown *(855 5220/088 595 755).*
Auto Centre *(490 1600/088 582 534).*
Glenalbyn Motors *(288 4367).*
Rainbow Recovery *(088 640 806).*
Tom Kane Motors *(833 8143/ after 6pm 831 5983).*

Health

If you need an ambulance telephone **999** or **112**. The following hospitals have 24-hour accident and emergency departments:

Accident & emergency
Adelaide & Meath Hospital *Tallaght, Dublin 2 (414 3500). Bus 16, 19, 22.*
Beaumont Hospital *Beaumont Road, Dublin 9 (809 2714). Bus 27B, 51A.*
If a baby is imminent, then head for the **Rotunda Hospital** *Parnell Street, Dublin 1 (873 0700). All Cross City buses;* or **The Coombe**, *Dolphin's Barn Street, Dublin 8 (453 7561). Bus 50, 56A, 77, 77A, 150.*

Children's hospitals
Temple Street Hospital *Dublin 1 (874 8763). Bus 3, 11, 11A.*
National Children's Hospital *Harcourt Street, Dublin 2 (475 2355). Bus 14, 14A, 15A, 15B, 48A.*
Our Lady's Hospital for Sick Children *(455 8111). Bus 50, 56A, 77, 77A, 150.*

General medical care
Mercer's Medical Centre *Stephen Street Lower (off St Stephen's Green), Dublin 2 (402 2300).*
Grafton Street Medical Centre *Dublin 2 (671 2122).*

Alternative medicine
Holistic Healing Centre *38 Dame Street, Dublin 2 (671 0813).*
Holistic Sourcing Centre *67 Camden Street Lower, Dublin 2 (478 5022).*
Pu-Shan Chinese Medicine Centre *Suite 14, 24-26 Dame Street, Dublin 2 (679 9753).*

Contraception
Condoms are available in pharmacies, many newsagents, and in vending machines in some pubs (this raised absolute hell, so appreciate the privilege). For those who want to stock up, or indulge in something a little different, try Condom Power, *57 Dame Street, Dublin 2 (677 8963). Also see below* **Women's Dublin.**

Dentists
Grafton Street Dental Practice *Grafton Street Medical Centre, Dublin 2 (671 9200).*
Molesworth Clinic *2 Molesworth Place, Dublin 2 (661 5544).*

Pharmacies
The following are late-night pharmacies:
Corrigans *80 Malahide Road, Dublin 3 (833 8803).* **Open** 9am-10pm Mon-Sat; 10.30am-7pm Sun; 10am-7pm Bank Holidays.
O'Connell's Late Night Pharmacies *Grafton Street, Dublin 2 (679 0467).* **Open** 8.30am-8.30pm Mon-Sat; 11am-6pm Sun. *Westmoreland Street, Dublin 2 (677 8440).* **Open** 8.30am-7pm Mon-Sat. *Henry Street, Dublin 1 (873 1077).* **Open** 8.30am-6.30pm Mon-Wed, Fri, Sat; 8.30am-6.30pm Thur. *O'Connell Street, Dublin 1 (873 0427).* **Open** 8.30am-10pm Mon-Sat; 10am-10pm Sun.
To get homeopathic prescriptions dispensed go to **Nelson's Homoeopathic Pharmacy** *15 Duke Street, Dublin 2 (679 0451).*

Legal

Legal Aid Board Law Centres are located at the following addresses:
Head Office *St Stephen's Green House, Dublin 2 (661 5811).*
Law Centre *45 Gardiner Street Lower, Dublin 1 (874 5440).*
Law Centre *9 Ormond Quay Lower, Dublin 1 (872 4133).*

Other useful contacts include:
AIM Family Services *6 D'Olier Street, Dublin 2 (670 8363).*
Employment Equality Agency *36 Mount Street, Upper, Dublin 2 (662 4577).*

Lost property

Make sure you always notify the police in the unhappy event of losing anything of value (you'll need their reference number to validate any subsequent insurance claims).
Airport *(704 4481).*
Bus Éireann *coaches (703 2489).*
Dublin Bus *(703 3055).*
Irish Rail (Iarnród Éireann) *Connolly Station (703 2587); Heuston Station (703 2102).*
Taxis *Carriage Office, Lower Yard, Dublin Castle (475 5888).*

Credit cards
Report lost or stolen credit cards to both the police and the 24-hour numbers listed below. Inform your bank by phone.
AmEx Customer Services *(1800 709 907/24-hour authorisation service 1800 626 500).*
AmEx Travellers' Cheques *(1800 626 000).*
Diners' Club Customer Service *(1800 409 204/24-hour authorisation service 1800 709 944).*
Visa *(1800 558 002).*
MasterCard Emergency Assistance *(1800 557 378).*

Religion

Church of Ireland
Christchurch Cathedral *Dublin 8 (677 8099).*
St Patrick's Cathedral *Dublin 8 (475 4817).*
St Ann's Church *Dawson Street, Dublin 2 (288 0633).*

Roman Catholic
Pro-Cathedral *Marlborough Street, Dublin 1.*
Church of St Francis *Gardiner Street, Dublin 1 (836 3411).*
Church of St Laurence O'Toole *Seville Place, Dublin 1 (874 0796).*
St Agatha's *North William Street, Dublin 1 (855 6474).*

Methodist
Abbey Street, Dublin 1 (874 2123). Clontarf, Dublin 3 (832 3143).

Presbyterian
Abbey Church, Dublin 1 (874 2810).

Lutheran
Adelaide Road, Dublin 2 (676 6548).

Greek Orthodox
46 Arbour Hill, Dublin 7 (677 9020).

Baptist
Grace Baptist Church *28A Pearse Street, Dublin 2 (677 3170).*

Devines Locksmiths *(298 9614).*
JC Locksmiths *(086 588 476).*
Peden Security Ltd *(088 524 431/evenings 493 7281).*

Embassies

It's advisable to telephone embassies first to check opening hours. For embassies and consulates not listed below, consult the telephone directories.
American Embassy *(668 8777).*
Australian Embassy *(676 1517).*
Belgian Embassy *(269 2082).*
British Embassy *(475 6000).*
Canadian Embassy *(478 1988).*
French Embassy *(260 1666).*

German Embassy *(269 3011).*
Israeli Embassy *(668 0303).*
Italian Embassy *(660 1744).*
Japanese Embassy *(269 4244).*
South African *(661 5553).*
Spanish Embassy *(269 1640).*
Swiss Embassy *(269 2515).*
New Zealand Consulate *(676 2464).*

Photography

One Hour Photo *110 Grafton Street (677 4472); 5 St Stephen's Green (671 8578); Ilac Centre, Henry Street (872 8824).*
Camera Centre *56 Grafton Street, Dublin 2 (677 5594).*
Conns 1 Hour Photo *Royal Hibernian Way, Dawson Street, Dublin 2 (671 0029).*
O'Connell's Pharmacy *Henry Street, Dublin 1 (873 1077); O'Connell Street, Dublin 1 (873 0427); 17 Westmoreland Street, Dublin 2 (677 8440), Grafton Street, Dublin 2 (679 0467).*
Spectra Photo *Jervis Street, Dublin 1 (878 1980) & 73 Grafton Street, Dublin 2 (679 6045).*

Disabled visitors

The Irish service industry is slowly coming around to the idea that potential customers are made up of all types of people. More and more places are now providing facilities for the disabled, so the easiest way to keep up to date is to telephone ahead first and see if a venue is accessible and amenable. For using public transport *see below* **Getting Around.**

The following numbers may also be helpful:
Catholic Institute for the Deaf *(830 0522).*
Cerebral Palsy Ireland *(269 5355).*
Cystic Fibrosis Association of Ireland *(496 2433).*
Irish Deaf Society *(872 5748).*
Irish Wheelchair Association *24 Blackheath Drive, Dublin 3 (833 5366).*

Getting to Dublin

By air

Dublin has one airport, about eight miles north of the city. It has a great range of duty free, but the mark-up on food products is high, so buy your cheeses, whiskey marmalade and soda bread in Dublin. All flight information is available on Teletext (see Aertel pp 570-575 for details).

Dublin airport is managed by Aer Rianta, and you can contact their Airport Information Centre on 704 4222.

Useful telephone numbers include:
Bus Coach & Rail Information *(677 1871).*
Duty & Tax Free pre-order shopping *(1800 747 747).*
Greencaps Left Luggage & Porterage *(704 4633).* Cost £2 per item per day.

Dublin airport is not serviced by rail, so the easiest way to get into the city centre is by bus or taxi. Airport taxis are notoriously expensive, since, apart from all the extra payments, there's a charge of £1.30 automatically added to your bill

when you get a cab at the airport (with cabs going *to* the airport there's no charge). Getting into town will probably cost at least £10, but if it's above £15, start asking questions.

Airlink
Dublin Bus runs a direct coach link from the airport to the city centre, stopping at Busáras *(Store Street, Dublin 1)* and Heuston Station. The journey takes around 20 minutes. Tickets from the airport to Busáras are £2.50 (adult) and £1.25 (child), and to Heuston Station £3 (adult), and £1.50 (child). Buy tickets from the driver. It's a fairly frequent service; the first bus leaves the airport at 6.40am, and the last bus at 11pm (and only goes as far as Busáras). Timetables are available from **Dublin Bus Head Office**. Four other city centre buses also service the airport: 41, 41A, 41B, 41C. These are fine if you're not in a hurry, and, because they're not express, the fare is only £1.10 to get into town. The timetables are displayed at the bus stops outside the airport's Arrivals area.

Major airlines
Aer Lingus *(head office 705 2222/flight information 705 6705/reservations for Ireland & UK 844 4777/other reservations 844 4747).* **Open** 7.30am-9.30pm daily

except Christmas Day. **Credit** AmEx, DC, MC, V.
Alitalia *4-5 Dawson Street, Dublin 2 (677 5171).* **Open** 9am-5.30pm Mon-Fri. **Credit** AmEx, DC, MC, V.
British Airways *(24-hour reservations/enquiries 1800 62 67 47).* **Credit** AmEx, DC, MC, V.
British Midland *(flight information 704 4259/reservations 283 8833).* **Open** 8am-8pm Mon-Fri; 8am-6pm Sat; 9am-6pm Sun. **Credit** AmEx, DC, MC, V.
Ryanair *(reservations 609 7800).* Line open 8am-9pm Mon-Fri; 9am-6pm Sat; 10am-7pm Sun.
Dublin Airport *(844 4400/flight information 1550 200 200, calls cost 58p per minute).* **Credit** AmEx, DC, MC, V.
Virgin Atlantic *30 Lower Abbey Street, Dublin 1 (873 3388).*
City Jet *(flight information 844 5577/reservations 844 5566).* **Open** 8am-8pm Mon-Fri; 9am-5.30pm Sat; 10am-6.30 Sun. **Credit** AmEx, DC, MC, V.

By coach

Travelling by coach is far cheaper than by rail, although you do have to contend with Irish country roads. The largest nationwide coach service is run

by Bus Éireann out of Busáras (opposite Connolly Station).
Bus Éireann *Head Office, Broadstone, Dublin 7 (830 2222).* **Passenger information only** *836 6111.*
Other private coach companies offer similar services, but they won't be as comprehensive.
Academy Travel Services *(671 5333).*
Nestor Coaches Express Travel *(832 0094).*
Rapid Express *(679 1549).*

By train

All national main lines run from either Connolly Station or Heuston Station. As a quick guide, Connolly services Belfast, Rosslare and Sligo; Heuston services Galway, Westport, Tralee, Kildare, Cork, Ennis and Waterford.

For details of the InterCity lines contact **Iarnród Éireann Head Office** *Connolly Station, Dublin 1 (836 3333).*

By ferry

The two main companies are Irish Ferries and Stena Line, both of which run from Dublin Port to Holyhead. Irish Ferries also run from Rosslare-Pembroke, Rosslare-Roscoff, and Cork-Roscoff, Cherbourg and Le Havre.
Irish Ferries *2-4 Merrion Row, Dublin 2 & 16 Westmoreland Street, Dublin 2 (passenger bookings & enquiries 661 0511).* **24-hour information service** *661 0715.* **Credit** AmEx, DC, MC, V.
Stena Line *Ferry Terminal, Dun Laoghaire Harbour & 15 Westmoreland Street, Dublin 2 (reservations & enquiries 204 7777).* **Credit** AmEx, DC, MC, V. Stena Line also operate from Dun Laoghaire-Holyhead, Rosslare-Fishguard and Belfast-Stranraer.

Disabled travellers

Buses are completely out of the question, and most stations weren't designed with

wheelchairs in mind. Iarnród Éireann tries to accommodate disabled travellers, and if you telephone ahead they will get staff to meet you at the station and accompany you to the train. They can also arrange car parking space and set up portable ramps.

If you intend to remain in your wheelchair for the journey, give them notice and they'll remove a seat for you. The dining cars of all InterCity trains now have areas specifically intended for easy access.

For a leaflet containing the easiest access to stations nationwide, call in to any DART station or train station and ask for the InterCity Guide for Mobility Impaired Passengers. For further information, contact the **Department of Transport** *44 Kildare Street, Dublin 2 (670 7444).*

Getting around

Dublin is downright cosy compared to cities such as London or New York. Normally, if you're told some place is 'right the other side of town', you immediately get on a bus or train. However, in Dublin, 'the other side' is never more than a 25-minute walk away.

Although northside and southside sprawl for miles, the core of the city is very small. The main markers are O'Connell Street, Trinity College and St Stephen's Green, and it takes at most 25 minutes to stroll from one end to the other. In Dublin, everyone walks everywhere: the main shopping areas (Grafton Street, Henry Street and Temple Bar) are pedestrianised, and the city is ideal for meandering through. So, what you need transport for is getting into town in the first place.

Public transport

There are two types of public transport in Dublin – train and bus. Iarnród Éireann runs the DART (electric rail) and Suburban Rail services. Bus Átha Cliath (Dublin Bus) is responsible for all the city bus services. There are several kinds of ticket available covering both bus and train, so figure out where and how you want to travel, and see what suits best.

Dublin Bus

Head Office, 59 Upper O'Connell Street, Dublin 1 (872 0000/ passenger information & customer services 873 4222). **Open** 8.30am-5.30pm Mon; 9am-5.30pm Tue-Fri; 9am-1pm Sat.
Bus stops basically look like long green lollipops. The numbers at the top show which buses stop there – 'set down only' means that the bus only lets passengers off there, so don't hang around waiting. There are about 900 buses on the road, serving well over 100 different routes. This means that

there's bound to be a bus stop close by, although the frequency of buses is something else. Buses on popular routes are ten-20 minutes apart, but for others you could be waiting over an hour, and the majority of stops don't have shelters. Timetables at bus stops are often defaced, so your best bet is to pick up all the ones you need at the Head Office on O'Connell Street. Buses keep somewhat loosely to their schedules; sometimes they leave early or don't show up, so if you have to be somewhere, leave plenty of extra time, especially in rush hour. Also, Dubliners seem to start their weekend early, and on Fridays, traffic is heavy from about lunch-time. Fares depend on the number of bus stops contained in the journey.
Adult 1-3 stages 55p; 4-7 stages 80p; 8-13 stages £1; more than 13 stages £1.10. **Children** (under 16) 1-7 stages 35p; more than 7 stages 55p. Tickets are bought from the driver, and you should try to have the exact fare ready. They certainly won't accept £10 for a £1 fare, and they sometimes refuse to break a fiver. To pay the driver, get up on the left-hand side of the entrance – the right-hand side is for pre-paid tickets, which are quicker, easier and cheaper (*see below*).

Pre-paid tickets

Adult Bus & Rail Short Hop
Allows unlimited bus, suburban rail
& DART travel: £4.50 (daily); £15.50
(weekly); £58 (monthly).
Adult Bus Travel Wide
Unlimited bus travel: £3.30 (daily);
£13 (weekly); £50 (monthly).
Ten Journey Tickets
For adults, these allow ten single bus
trips: £5.50 (for ten bus trips when
cash fare is 55p); £8 (80p); £9.50 (£1);
£10.50 (£1.10); £11.50 (£1.25).

Daily tickets

Family Bus Travel Wide
Unlimited bus travel – £5.50.
Family Bus & Rail Short Hop
Unlimited travel on bus, suburban
rail & DART – £6.50.
Four Day Explorer Four days
unlimited off peak bus, suburban rail
& DART travel – £10.
Transfer Ninety Citizone Allows
two trips within the Citizone area, as
long as they occur within 90 minutes
of each other – £1.50.

Weekly tickets

Adult Bus Citizone Unlimited
travel in the Citizone area – £11.
**Adult Bus & Rail Medium, Long
& Giant Hop** Depending on zone,
these cost between £20-£30.
Student Bus Travel Wide
Unlimited bus travel – £10.
Student Bus Citizone Unlimited
bus travel in the Citizone area – £9.

Monthly tickets

Adult Bus Citizone Unlimited bus
travel in the Citizone area – £50.
**Adult Bus & Rail Medium, Long
& Giant Hop** Depending on zone,
these start at £58.
Student Bus & Rail Short Hop
Unlimited travel on bus, suburban
rail & DART – £41.
For student tickets *(see below
Students)*, you need a valid USIT ID
card with a CIE Travelsave stamp,
which you buy at USIT (19 Aston
Quay). For adult weekly and monthly
tickets, you need a Dublin Bus adult
photo ID, which you get at 59
O'Connell Street. All tickets can be
purchased from the Head Office,
USIT, the Tourist Office (Suffolk
Street), and from a range of
newsagents throughout the city.
Some of the more prominent ones are:
Reynolds (Lower Abbey Street),
Front Page (109 Grafton Street),
Reads (Nassau Street), Colemans
(Westmoreland Street) and the Dame
(Dame Street). All have signs outside
saying Dublin Bus Ticket Agent, so
keep an eye out.

Nitelink

The last buses leave Dublin around
11.30pm, which means a taxi for
anyone clubbing or drinking late in
town. However, there is a late-night

Express bus – Nitelink – which runs
every Thur, Fri and Sat (and nightly
over the Christmas period). It goes
from the city centre to suburbs along
15 routes. Departures are from
D'Olier Street, Westmoreland Street
and College Street, at midnight, 1am,
2am and 3am. Price £2.50 (but route
P to Maynooth costs £4). For further
information contact 873 4222.

Iarnród Éireann

The DART & Suburban Rail lines
provide a cleaner and faster
alternative to buses. However,
they're crammed during rush hour,
and not for the claustrophobic.
Several stations offer connecting bus
services, including one between
Connolly and Heuston stations, so if
there's a station a few miles away
from your accommodation, there may
well be a bus link. Apart from
Connolly and Heuston, the other city
stations are Tara Street and Pearse
Street. Iarnród Éireann's Head Office
is located in *Connolly Station, Dublin
1 (836 3333)*, and for passenger
information phone 836 6222.

Fares

There are several special-offer tickets
covering bus and rail travel *(see
above)*. Tickets are available from all
DART/Suburban Rail stations and
from the **Rail Travel Centre** *35
Lower Abbey Street, Dublin 1 (836
6222)*. The rail-only tickets are:
Weekly rail ticket £10.50 (adult);
£5.50 (child). **Monthly rail ticket**
£40 (adult).
When purchasing a single/return
ticket you need to specify the exact
destination, so that the ticket will be
validated for the Feeder Bus if
necessary. Bikes aren't allowed on
DART trains, but you can bring
them on diesel trains – ask where
you should store them because
regulations change depending on the
train. The rates for transporting
bikes range between £4-£12,
depending on how far you're going:
0-56 km £2 single; £4 return.
57-108 km £3 single; £6 return.
109-137 km £4 single; £8 return.
over 138 km £6 single; £12 return.

Taxis

Taxis in Dublin are not cheap,
and are usually reserved for
mammoth shopping sprees, getting home from nightclubs, and
having to travel with a bad
head (public transport is not
good for the tender heads of the
hungover). The minimum
charge is £1.80, which covers
the first half-mile or four

minutes. Each additional 1/8
mile or one minute is 10p.
There are extra payments for
additional passengers (40p
each) and animals (40p). If you
put your luggage in the boot of
the cab you have to pay 40p per
item, so keep it with you if you
can. There's an additional
charge of 40p for unsocial
hours (8pm-8am Mon-Sat and
all day Sunday), and if you hire
a taxi between 8pm on the
night before a public holiday
and 8am on the morning after
then you pay an extra 80p (this
is apart from the 'unsocial
hours' charge).
  If you're getting a taxi at
night, remember most clubs finish around the same time, so
it's worth leaving a bit early to
avoid the queues. Over the
Christmas period, taxis are
nearly impossible to come by,
and an hour's wait is common.
Since the city is so small, it's
easier to walk to the nearest
rank rather than trying to hail a
taxi. The following taxi ranks
are 24-hour:
*Aston's Quay, Dublin 2;
College Green, Dublin 2;
Eden Quay Dublin 1;
O'Connell Street Upper, Dublin 1;
O'Connell Street Lower, Dublin 1;
Westland Row Station, Dublin 2;
St Stephen's Green, Dublin 2;
St Stephen's Green North, Dublin 2;
Lansdowne Road, Dublin 4.*

Phone cabs

There are loads of taxi
companies, so if you don't
fancy waiting at a rank, then
just order one. The pick up
charge is £1.20. Some areas
have local services that offer
fixed rates for certain journeys
– these don't charge a pick up
fee. Here are some of the larger
companies:
Co-Op Taxis *(676 6666)*.
City Cabs *(872 2688)*.
ABC Taxis *(285 5444/284 6666)*.
Black Cab Company *(872
2222/844 5844)*.
Access & Metro Cabs *(668
3333)*.
Pony Cabs *(661 2233)*.
If your have any complaints or
queries about the taxi service,
contact the Irish Taxi Federation on
836 4166.

Transport hire

Car hire

Cars are worth hiring if you're going travelling, or just exploring the rest of the country. Public transport is relaxed with regard to timetables at the best of times, and it's far less frequent outside the city, so a car is pretty much essential for touring. The major companies are set up at the airport, and others are available in the city centre. All advise pre-booking during the summer months, which means giving at least 24 hours' notice.

Hertz *Arrivals Hall, Dublin Airport (844 5466) & 149 Upper Leeson Street, Dublin 4 (660 2255).* **Credit** AmEx, DC, MC, V.

Avis Rent A Car *Arrival Hall, Dublin Airport (605 7500) & 1E Hanover Street, Dublin 2 (605 7555).* **Credit** AmEx, DC, MC, V.

Eurodollar *Arrivals Hall, Dublin Airport (844 4162).* **Credit** AmEx, MC, V.

Budget Rent A Car *Arrivals Hall, Dublin Airport (844 5919) & 151 Lower Drumcondra Road, Dublin 9 (837 9802).* **Credit** AmEx, DC, MC, V.

Chauffeur service

City West Executive Cars *(459 8623).*

Execkars *(830 5148).*

The Limousine Company *(872 3003).*

Metro Limousine & Saloon Hire *(667 0955).*

Bike hire

By far the biggest problem with cycling in Dublin is neither air pollution nor mad drivers, but finding a safe place to keep your bicycle. The railings in Dublin are filled with single wheels dangling from locks, so unless you have a place to park indoors, think twice.

Expect to pay around £7 per day for a bike; weekly rates and group discounts will reduce the price.

C Harding for Bicycles *Raleigh Rent A Bike Agent, 30 Bachelors Walk, Dublin 1 (873 2455).*

Dublin Bike Hire *27 North Great George's Street, Dublin 1 (878 8473).*

Women's Dublin

Although Ireland has undergone tremendous progress in terms of its economy, change in the fundamentally patriarchal social structure has been much more gradual, and women's issues are badly neglected. The number of women in Irish politics is gradually increasing, no doubt thanks in part to Mary Robinson's ground-breaking presidency. There has been a tremendous increase in awareness of women's rights over the last decade, but the legal system is slow to change, and government funding for women's aid is scarce. Divorce is newly legal, and so far the predicted collapse of the marriage institution has not come to pass.

Abortion is still illegal in Ireland, and a highly inflammatory subject. Its prohibition became part of Ireland's constitution in 1983, but debate raged once more in 1992 with the infamous 'X case'. A young girl, pregnant as a result of rape, was restrained from leaving the country to procure an abortion. The Dublin Supreme Court eventually decided that she did have the right to travel, and the pro-life movement responded with a fanatical campaign to have three new clauses legislated: that abortion was illegal, that pregnant women would have no right to leave the country if they intend to have an abortion overseas, and that the dissemination of information concerning abortion was illegal. The referendum resulted in the acceptance of the first clause and the rejection of the other two. Ireland is not exactly the ideal country in which to have an unwanted pregnancy.

Health/contraception

For anything relating to contraception or women's health, contact one of the **Well Woman Centres**. They offer a range of services including breast examination, PAP smears, pregnancy counselling, contraceptive advice and the morning-after pill. No appointment is necessary, and the centres are located at:

73 Leeson Street Lower, Dublin 2 (661 0086).

35 Liffey Street Lower, Dublin 1 (872 8051).

Alternatively, contact one of the following organisations:

Marie Stopes Reproductive Choices *10 Merrion Square, Dublin 2 (676 7852).*

Other useful addresses include:

Albany Women's Clinic *Clifton Court, Fitzwilliam Street Lower, Dublin 2 (661 2222).*

Baby Matters Breastfeeding Clinic *1 The Vale, Wood Farm Acres, Palmerstown, Dublin 20 (623 2886).*

Breast Clinic *46 Eccles Street, Dublin 7 (830 2870).*

Institute of Women's Health *9 Herbert Place, Dublin 2 (676 6717).*

Women's Medical Clinics *34 Main Street, Blackrock, Co Dublin (288 4943) & Mart House, Leopardstown Road, Dublin 18 (289 8585).*

Women's support

Aoibhneas *(842 2377).* Women's refuge.

Counselling Line *(1800 778 888).*

Haven House *(873 2279).* Women's night shelter.

Rape Crisis Centre *70 Lower Leeson Street, Dublin 2 (661 4911).* Open 24 hours daily.

Women Entering Business *(459 0223).*

Women in the Home *(490 6778).*

Women's Aid Helpline *(1800 341 900).*

Women's Refuge *(496 1002).*

Women's Support Project *(451 7500).*

Accommodation

YWCA of Ireland *64 Baggot Street Lower, Dublin 2 (662 4463).*

Students

With the amount of language schools, business colleges and universities in Dublin, the student population is considerable. It's also diverse: during the summer, thousands of people come to Dublin to brush up on their English, and for the rest of the year, colleges are filled with students from 'the land of saints and scholars' and the rest of the world. EU citizens don't require a student visa to study in Ireland. If you're from outside the EU, contact the Department of Justice (visa enquiries 678 9466).

For the low-down on student life in Dublin, contact the Union of Students in Ireland (USI), in the heart of Temple Bar – *Aston Place, D2 (671 0088)*. Here, those over 18 years of age can get tourist information, accommodation advice, and avail themselves of a wide range of services. The Student Entertainment Centre offers cheap Internet and e-mail facilities, pool tables and video games. You can also stock up on student concessions for Dublin clubs, including Kitchen, PoD, and the Mean Fiddler.

But what would a student centre be without a pub: Club USI has possibly the cheapest beer in Dublin, and is open late at weekends (*see below*). There are free events organised here almost every day: music and table quizzes, discos and screenings of live football games. Definitely a place to check out.

USI will also take care of your travel needs. Contact Union of Students in Ireland Travel (USIT). They handle all student travel arrangements, so wherever you're going, they can tell you the cheapest way to get there. USIT is very much a meeting of the ways – its noticeboards are filled with

details of flatshares, language tuition, jobs and cheap flights. You'll probably have plenty of time to browse through the small ads while you're waiting to be served – allow for at least 30 minutes' loitering.

To avail yourself of student travel discounts in Ireland you need to have a USIT International Student Card with a travel save stamp. Bring student identification with you to USIT at the address below; you can also try International Student Travel (*see below*). *See also above* **Getting around**.

If you happen to be planning a large party, exhibition, concert or conference, contact the National Student Centre (*see below*).

Club USI *Aston Place, Dublin 2 (671 0433).* **Open** noon-11.30pm Mon-Thur; noon-12.30am Fri, Sat; 4-11pm Sun.
Union of Students in Ireland Travel (USIT) *19 Aston Quay, Dublin 2 (677 8117).* **Open** 9am-6pm Mon-Wed, Fri; 9am-8pm Thur; 10am-5.30pm Sat. **Credit** AmEx, V, DC, MC.
National Student Centre *1 Aston Place, Dublin 2 (671 0433).* **Open** noon-midnight Mon-Sat. Just around the corner from USIT, this is a lively bar, hooked up to the Internet. DJs on Thur, Fri and Sat evenings.
International Student Travel *5 Merrion Row, Dublin 2 (676 4386).* **Open** 9am-6pm Mon-Fri. **Credit** AmEx, DC, MC, V.

Accommodation

Rents have risen sharply in the last decade, and the days of a roomy, clean house share for £25 a week are dead and gone. Expect to pay upwards of £40 a week for a reasonable place. The renting business gets cut-throat from September, when all the students return to Dublin to sort out lodgings for the next academic year, so the summer is the best time to move in and catch those bargains. The *Evening Herald* is probably the best paper to

use, and keep an eye out for ads in USIT. If you're affiliated with a college, you can use their accommodation service and figure out your rights as a future tenant. If you're unaffiliated, you can probably just wander through and sneak a look at the noticeboards for flats and houseshares.

Also, consider going through a letting agency. It may require a fee, but it can save a great deal of legwork.

Letting agencies
Home Bureau *6 Grafton Street, Dublin 2 (679 2222).*
Home Locators *35 Dawson Street, Dublin 2 (679 5233).*
Relocators *38 Dame Street, Dublin 2 (679 3511).*

Hostels

Meanwhile, to keep you going until you find a more permanent abode, hostels present a cheap choice.
Backpackers Ireland Hostel *80-81 Lower Gardiner Street, Dublin 1 (836 4900).*
Dublin International Youth Hostel *61 Mountjoy Street, Dublin 7 (830 4555).*
ISAAC's Hostel *2 Frenchman's Lane, Dublin 1 (855 6215).*
Temple Bar Hostel *18-21 Anglesea Street, Dublin 2 (671 1822).*

Colleges

The three biggies are as follows:
Dublin City University *Glasnevin, Dublin 9 (student services 704 5165/ accommodation office 704 5344).*
Trinity College Dublin *Dublin 2 (students' union 677 6545/ accommodation office 608 1177).*
University College Dublin *Belfield, Dublin 4 (student accommodation office 269 3244/ students' union general office 269 3244).*
Other schools and colleges include:
Dublin Institute of Technology. There are eight DITs in the city area, offering a wide range of courses, including architecture, music, engineering and tourism. The students' union is in *Cathal Brugha Street, Dublin 1 (874 1768).*

American College Dublin *2 Merrion Square, Dublin 2 (676 8939).*
Dublin Business College *64 Mount Street Lower, Dublin 2 (661 9811).*
Griffith College Dublin *South Circular Road, Dublin 8 (454 5640).*

Language schools

There are countless language schools in Dublin. It might well be worth your while going and chatting to a couple of schools before you sign up with one, because with the amount currently open, you can afford to be choosy.
American College Dublin *2 Merrion Square, Dublin 2 (676 8939).*
Centre of English Studies *31 Dame Street, Dublin 2 (671 4233).*
Dublin School of English *11 Westmoreland Street, Dublin 2 (677 3322).*
Language Centre of Ireland *45 Kildare Street, Dublin 2 (671 6266).*
English Language Institute *99 St Stephen's Green, Dublin 2 (475 2965).*

Other language schools

Gael-linn (Irish) *26 Merrion Square, Dublin 2 (676 7283).*
Alliance Française *1 Kildare Street, Dublin 2 (676 1732).*
Spanish Cultural Institute (Instituto Cervantes) *58 Northumberland Road, Dublin 4 (668 2024).*
German Institute (Goethe Institute) *62 Fitzwilliam Square, Dublin 2 (661 8506).*

Libraries

Colleges often allow foreign students a temporary reader's pass to use the library facilities. You'll need student identification, and if possible bring a letter of introduction from your college. Ask at the students' union for details.

In addition, Dublin Corporation libraries are located at:
Central Library *ILAC Centre, Henry Street, Dublin 1 (873 3996).*
Community & Youth Information Centre *Sackville House, Sackville Place, Dublin 1 (878 6844).*

Dublin Corporation Library *138-142 Pearse Street, Dublin 2 (677 2764).*
Gilbert Library *138 Pearse Street, Dublin 2 (677 7662).*

Eating & socialising

The large student presence means that there is a range of inexpensive places to eat out, and a wealth of fast-food chains. Thursday is the big night out for third-level students, because so many go 'down the country' (anywhere in Ireland, bar Dublin) on Friday evenings. All the cheaper restaurants listed in the **Eating & Drinking** chapters are a good bet. Pubs vary as to universities and faculties, but favourite city centre haunts include The Stag's Head (Dame Court), Neary's (Chatham Street), The Long Stone (Townsend Street), O'Neill's (Pearse Street & Suffolk Street), and basically anywhere in Temple Bar.

Business

Information/libraries

BTIS Business & Technical Information Service *University of Limerick (061 202 781).*
Business Information Centre *ILAC Centre, Henry Street, Dublin 1 (873 3996).*
CFI Online *14-15 Parliament Street, Dublin 2 (679 4479).* Information on Irish Companies and trade names.
Chamber of Commerce of Ireland *22 Merrion Square, Dublin 2 (661 2888).*
Dublin Chamber of Commerce *7 Clare Street, Dublin 2 (661 4111/ 676 4291).*
European Commission *18 Dawson Street, Dublin 2 (662 5113).*
Forbairt Information Centre *Glasnevin, Dublin 9 (808 2325).*
Inter Company Comparisons *17 Dame Street, Dublin 2 (679 6477).*
Irish Architectural Archive *73 Merrion Square, Dublin 2 (676 3430).*
Irish Stock Exchange *28 Anglesea Street, Dublin 2 (677 8808).*
Law Library *Four Courts, Dublin 7 (872 0622).*

Stock Market Journal *Strand Road, Portmarnock (846 1833).* Stock Market advice.

Services

Auditors & accountants

Accounting & Costing Services *21 Wicklow Street, Dublin 2 (679 4970).*
Arthur Andersen *Andersen House, International Financial Service Centre (IFSC), Dublin 1 (670 1000).*
Association of Chartered Certified Accountants *9 Leeson Park, Dublin 6 (491 0466).*
Craig Gardner/Price Waterhouse *Gardner House, Wilton Place, Dublin 2 (662 6000).*
Cremin McCarthy & Co *28 Harcourt Street, Dublin 2 (454 2766).*
Ernst & Young *Ernst & Young Building, Harcourt Centre, Harcourt Street, Dublin 2 (475 0555).*

Corporate solicitors

Clifford Sullivan & Co *31 Westland Square, Dublin 2 (670 4022).*

Damien Hughes & Co *2 Fitzwilliam Street Upper, Dublin 2 (661 2134).*
Duncan Grehan & Partners *24 Suffolk Street, Dublin 2 (577 9078).*
HJ Roundtree *25 Upper Mount Street, Dublin 2 (662 3011).*

Financial services

Acorn Group *13 St Stephen's Green, Dublin 2 (677 3233).*
Bank of Ireland Asset Management *26 Fitzwilliam Place, Dublin 2 (661 6433).*
Byron & Woods Financial Services *61 Dame Street, Dublin 2 (677 3085).*
Corporate Link Ltd *7 Sidmonton Court, Bray, Co Wicklow (282 9930).*
Farrell Grant Sparks *Molyneux House, Bride Street, Dublin 8 (475 8137).*
Gandon Capital Markets *Andersen House, 1 Harbour Master Place, International Financial Service Centre, Dublin 1 (670 1300).*
Guardian Financial Services *33 Westland Square, Dublin 2 (677 1411).*
Larchmont Trading *Dublin Exchange Facility, International Financial Service Centre, Dublin 1 (829 1607).*

Louis Fitzgerald & Associates
*13 Adelaide Street, Dun Laoghaire,
Co Dublin (284 2916).*
NCB Group Ltd *48-53 Lower
Mount Street, Dublin 2 (661 4977).*

Business accommodation

See also chapter Accommodation.
The Berkeley Court *Lansdowne
Road, Dublin 4 (660 1711).*
The Burlington *Leeson Street
Upper, Dublin 4 (660 5222).*
Conrad Hilton *Earlsfort Terrace,
Dublin 2 (676 5555).*
Gresham Hotel *Upper O'Connell
Street, Dublin 1 (874 6881).*
The Shelbourne *27 St Stephen's
Green, Dublin 2 (676 6471).*
The Westbury *Grafton Street,
Dublin 2 (679 1122).*

Conference organisers

Incentive Conference Ireland *1
Pembroke Place, Ballsbridge, Dublin
4 (667 1711).*
International Conference
Management *2 Kildress House,
Pembroke Row, Dublin 2 (676 4595).*
Marketing By Design *62
Pembroke Road, Dublin 4 (660
0511).*
PM Management *95 Haddington
Road, Ballsbridge, Dublin 4 (660
9011).*

Aircraft charter

The following operations are all
Dublin-based:
Celtic Helicopters *(890 1349).*
International Airline Charters
(661 3757).
Irish Air Transport *(844 4159).*
Westair Aviation *(1800 560 504).*

Couriers

DHL Worldwide Express *(1800
725 725).*
Fastrack Express Parcel
Service *(1850 767 676).*
Federal Express *(1800 535 800).*
Pony Express *(Ireland 661 0101/
international 676 7766).*

Freight forwarders

Aer Lingus Cargo *(export 705
6688/import 705 2916).*
Irish Shipping & Transport
(1800 437 344).
Stafford Freight *(475 1021).*
United Cargo Services *(890
1009).*

Mobile &
car telephones

Allstat *5-7 Westland Square, Pearse
Street, Dublin 2 (679 9033).*
Carphone Warehouse *30 Grafton
Street, Dublin 2 (670 5265).*
Eircell *6-8 College Green, Dublin 2
(790 1234).*
NEC *15-17 Eden Quay, Dublin 1
(873 1233).*
One Stop Phone Shop *67 Dame
Street, Dublin 2 (679 1313).*

Computers

Apple Computer Centre *35
Dame Street, Dublin 2 (679 8011).*
Beyond 2000 *Chatham Row,
Dublin 2 (677 7633).*
Budget Computer Services *120
Malahide Road, Dublin 3 (833 2358).*
The Computer Shop *120 Upper
Dorset Street, Dublin 1 (830 7282).*
IBM *2 Burlington Road, Dublin 4
(660 3744/1800 205 205).*

Desktop publishing &
computer graphics

Apple Computer Centre *35 Dame
Street, Dublin 2 (679 8011).*
The Computer Picture
Company *38 Fenian Street, Dublin
2 (661 2697).*
Professional Presentations *21
Mespil Road, Dublin 4 (660 2260).*

Document disposal
service

Confidential Document
Destruction *(450 5475).*
Information Security
Management *(842 2944).*
Shreddit *(1800 747 333).*

Office facilities

Abbey House Serviced Offices
*15-17 Abbey Street Upper, Dublin 1
(872 4911).*
Capital House *10-13 Amiens
Street, Dublin 2 (855 8100).*
Heritage House *23 St Stephen's
Green, Dublin 2 (676 6333).*
Merrion Business Centre *20
Merrion Street Upper, Dublin 2 (676
1044).*
Orania House *97 St Stephen's
Green, Dublin 2 (475 1891).*

PR & marketing

Dimension Adsell Public
Relations *70 Leeson Street Upper,
Dublin 4 (667 3222).*
Financial & Corporate
Communications *15 Clanwilliam
Terrace, Grand Canal Quay, Dublin
2 (676 0158).*
GCAS Profile *Fitzwilliam Business
Centre, 26-27 Upper Pembroke
Street, Dublin 2 (661 4406).*
Maguire & Associates *31
Schoolhouse Lane, Dublin 2 (676
3521).*

Photocopying

Chroma Colour Imaging *7
Pembroke Street Lower, Dublin 2
(661 0451).*
Colour Copy Centre *33 Lower
Hatch Street, Dublin 2 (661 2066).*
McGowans *Adelaide Road Corner,
Harcourt Street, Dublin 2 (475
1311).*
One Hour Photo *110 Grafton
Street (677 4472); 5 St Stephen's
Green (671 8578); Ilac Centre, Henry
Street (872 8824).*
Reads *24 Nassau Street, Dublin 2
(679 6011).*

Printing

Action Print & Design
*International Financial Services
Centre, Dublin 1 (836 0063).*
Baggot Print & Design *38
Upper Baggot Street, Dublin 4
(660 9777).*
Johnston Print & Design *73
Leeson Street Lower, Dublin 3 (676
7091).*
SNAP Printing *20 Lower Ormond
Quay, Dublin 1 (872 5077); 25
Exchequer Street, Dublin 2 (677
0230); 33-34 Dame Street, Dublin 2
(679 1333).*
VT Print & Design *Merchants
House, Merchants Quay, Dublin 8
(679 0612).*

Secretarial services

ALISEC Secretarial Services
*Basement 7, Upper Fitzwilliam
Street, Dublin 2 (661 3824).*
Beck 'n' Call *10 Abbey Street
Lower, Dublin 1 (874 2826).*
The Business Bureau *30-31
Wicklow Street, Dublin 2 (679
7588).*
Firstaff Personnel Consultants
*85 Grafton Street, Dublin 2 (679
7766).*
Top Secretaries *63 Fitzwilliam
Square, Dublin 2 (676 6777).*

Telephone
answering service

Abbey House *15-17 Abbey Street
Upper, Dublin 1 (872 4911).*
Conduit House *2 Clanwilliam
Place, Dublin 2 (1800 222 200).*
Nelson House *50 Pembroke Road,
Dublin 4 (660 9222).*
Tran Send *14 South Frederick
Street, Dublin 2 (677 8180).*

Translation &
interpreters

Globelink Language Services
*32 Blackhall Place, Dublin 7 (671
3821).*
Quid *68 Fitzwilliam Square, Dublin
2 (676 1389).*
Words Language Services *70
Baggot Street Lower, Dublin 2 (661
0240).*

Conference centres

AMEV House Conference &
Training Centre *AMEV House,
Temple Road, Blackrock, Co Dublin
(283 2488).*
Berkeley Court Hotel *Lansdowne
Road, Dublin 4 (660 1711).*
Burlington Hotel *Leeson Street
Upper, Dublin 4 (660 5222).*
Dublin Castle Conference
Centre *Dublin Castle, Dublin 2 (679
3713).*
Marino Institute of Education
*Griffith Avenue, Dublin 9 (833
5111).*
Westbury Hotel *Grafton Street,
Dublin 2 (679 1122).*

Further Reading

Drama & poetry

Samuel Beckett *Waiting for Godot*
The metaphysical limits of procrastination.
Brendan Behan *The Quare Fellow*
Shocking dramatisation of pre-execution period in prison.
Seamus Heaney *Selected Poems, 1965-1975*
The Nobel Laureate at his most powerful.
Patrick Kavanagh *The Great Hunger*
Bleak poet turns his wrathful phrase towards the Famine.
Frank McGuinness *Observe the Sons of Ulster Marching Towards the Somme*
Sean O'Casey *Collected Plays*
Issues of morality and political activity in 1920s Ireland.
George Bernard Shaw *Selected Plays*
Fabian, feminist, socialist 'immoralist and heretic' genius.
JM Synge *The Playboy of the Western World*
Less than admiring of Irish nationalism, it caused a riot.
Oscar Wilde *Plays, Prose, Writings and Poems*
Great, witty and weighty: the omnibus edition.
WB Yeats *Collected Poems*
Iconoclast poet of Ireland's mytho-political landscape.
YB Yeats *Selected Plays*
Cuchulain, Cathleen and more from master playwright.

Fiction

Samuel Beckett *Dream of Fair to Middling Women*
Absurdist king's first novel lampooning Dublin elders.
Samuel Beckett *Molloy/Malone Dies/The Unnamable*
Black sunshine lighting on recognisable Dublin haunts.
Brendan Behan *Borstal Boy*
Autobiographical novel of childhood in Dublin slum.
Maeve Binchy *Circle of Friends*
Rural types brave big, bad Dublin.
Maeve Binchy *Dublin 4*
Decadence among the city sophisticates.
Dermot Bolger (et al) *Finbar's Hotel*
Bolger, Doyle and others' joint effort paints complex city.
Dermot Bolger *The Journey Home*
Hard-hitting account of life lived on the edge.
Dermot Bolger *Night Shift*
Rock fans making ends meet in Dublin's twilight world.
Emma Donoghue *Hood*
Mourning not melancholia: seven days of widowhood.
Emma Donoghue *Stir-fry*
Wry lesbian love story makes for fine fictional début.
JP Donleavy *The Ginger Man*
High japes at TCD; as banned by the Catholic Church.
Roddy Doyle *The Commitments*
Band of Dublin wannabes chase fame and fortune.
Roddy Doyle *Paddy Clarke Ha Ha Ha*
Booker-winning tale of boy's suburban adolescence.
Roddy Doyle *The Snapper*
A fateful encounter leads to pregancy… and problems.
Roddy Doyle *The Van*
Have knackered old burger-van, will travel.
Jeffrey Gantz (trans) *Early Irish Myths and Sagas*
Iron Age yarns whose themes recur in later Irish fiction.
Henry Glassie (ed) *Penguin Book of Irish Folktales*
Fairies, leprechauns and big potatoes.
Seamus Heaney *Sweeney Astray/Buile Suibhne*
Crazy King Sweeney updated in modern translation.
William Hope Hodgson *The House on the Borderland*
Mind-bending fantasy set in the west of Ireland.
James Joyce *A Portrait of the Artist as a Young Man*
Cuts through all sources of superstition like a knife.
James Joyce *Dubliners*
Polished, intuitive short stories from the master at work.
James Joyce *Finnegans Wake*
'Riverrun…' The Liffey personified as Anna Livia.
James Joyce *Ulysses*
A day – June 16, 1904 – in the life of Leopold Bloom.
Edna O'Brien *The Country Girls*
Bawdy girlish fun which predictably roused clerical ire.
Flann O'Brien *At-Swim-Two-Birds*
Breathtakingly funny novel about man writing novel.
Flann O'Brien *The Poor Mouth*
Satire on traditional Gaelic prose.
Liam O'Flaherty *The Informer*
Tense social comment from civil war veteran.
Liam O'Flaherty *Insurrection*
Hero inadvertantly caught up in Easter Uprising.
Chris Petit *The Psalm Killer*
Belfast- rather than Dublin-set, nail-biting political thriller.
Iain Sinclair *Radon Daughters*
Sinclair's off-the-wall sequel to William Hope Hodgson's *The House on the Borderland* reaches its climax in the Burren.
Edith Somerville and Martin Ross *The Irish RM*
Witty Anglo Irish hunting yarns.
Bram Stoker *Dracula*
Enduring vampire yarn with roots in Dublin Gothic.
Jonathan Swift *Gulliver's Travels*
Political satire from the giant of Anglo-Irish penmanship.
Colm Tóibín *The Heather Blazing*
An elderly city judge forced to confront history.
William Trevor *The Ballroom of Romance*
Short stories of rural Ireland.

Non-fiction

John Ardagh *Ireland and the Irish*
Acute look at present-day Ireland.
Douglas Bennett *Encyclopaedia of Dublin*
Packed with vital information.
Tim Pat Coogan *The IRA*
Well-balanced take on shady paramilitary organisation.
RF Foster *Paddy and Mr Punch*
Media-savvy study of modern nation's 'Irishness'.
Oliver St John Gogarty *As I Was Going Down Sackville Street*
The original Buck Mulligan's riposte to *Ulysses*.
Robert Kee *The Green Flag*
Recommended three-volumed Irish nationalist history.
Robert Kee *The Laurel and the Ivy*
Parnell, Gladstone and the fraught history of Home Rule.
Máire & Conor Cruise O'Brien *A Concise History of Ireland*
Deals thoroughly with the convolutions of Irish history.
Jacqueline O'Brien & Desmond Guinness *Dublin – A Grand Tour*
Useful guide to the Irish capital.
Nuala O'Faolain *Are You Somebody?*
Dublin memories from Ireland's cult columnist.
Seán O'Fáolain *The Great O'Neill*
Elizabeth I, Hugh O'Neill and the battle of Kinsale.
Cecil Woodham-Smith *The Great Hunger*
The definitive study of the 1845-51 potato famine.

Index

Advertisers' Index

Please refer to the relevant sections for
addresses/telephone numbers

Maps

Street Index

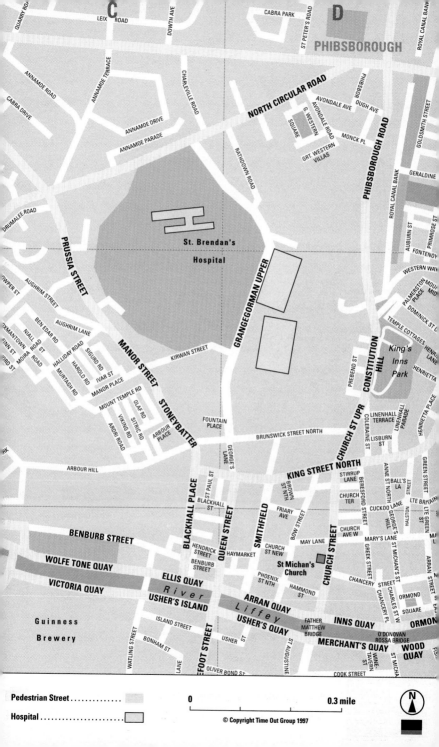

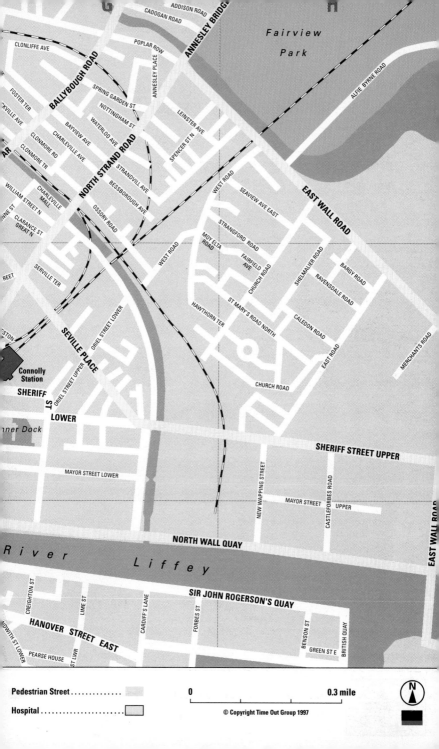

Fairview Park

ADDISON ROAD
CADOGAN ROAD
CLONLIFFE AVE
POPLAR ROW
ANNESLEY BRIDGE
SPRING GARDEN ST
BALLYBOUGH ROAD
NOTTINGHAM ST
FOSTER TER
ANNESLEY PLACE
LEINSTER AVE
BAYVIEW AVE
WATERLOO AVE
CHARLEVILLE AVE
SPENCER ST N
CLONMORE RD
CLONMORE TR
NORTH STRAND ROAD
STRANDVILL AVE
EAST WALL ROAD
WILLIAM STREET N
CHARLEVILLE MALL
BESSBOROUGH AVE
WEST ROAD
SEAVIEW AVE EAST
ALFIE BYRNE ROAD
CLARANCE ST GREAT N
OSSORY ROAD
STRANGFORD ROAD
MOY ELTA ROAD
SHELMALIER ROAD
BARGY ROAD
SERVILLE TER
SERVILLE TER
WEST ROAD
FAIRFIELD AVE
RAVENSDALE ROAD
STREET
CHURCH ROAD
CALEDON ROAD
SEVILLE PLACE
ORIEL STREET LOWER
HAWTHORN TER
ST MARY'S ROAD NORTH
EAST ROAD
MERCHANTS ROAD
Connolly Station
ORIEL STREET UPPER
CHURCH ROAD
SHERIFF ST
LOWER
SHERIFF STREET UPPER
Inner Dock
MAYOR STREET LOWER
NEW WAPPING STREET
MAYOR STREET UPPER
CASTLEFORBES ROAD
NORTH WALL QUAY
River Liffey
EAST WALL ROAD
CREIGHTON ST
LIME ST
CARDIFF'S LANE
FORBES ST
SIR JOHN ROGERSON'S QUAY
BENSON ST
BRITISH QUAY
HANOVER STREET EAST
ST LWR
GREEN ST E
PEARSE HOUSE
DWITH ST LOWER

Pedestrian Street ....
Hospital ....

0   0.3 mile
© Copyright Time Out Group 1997

N

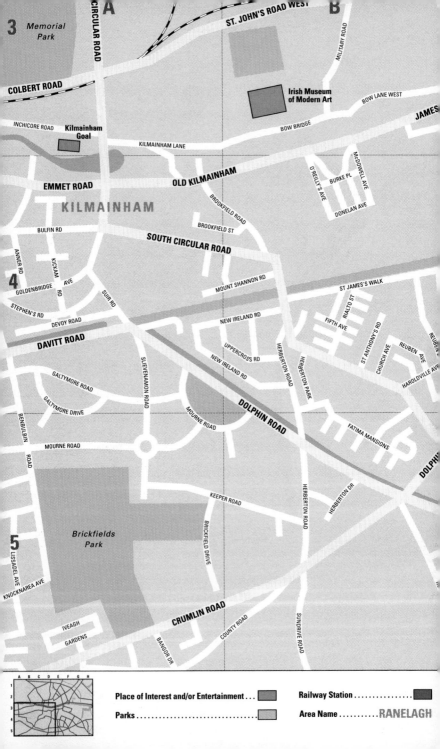

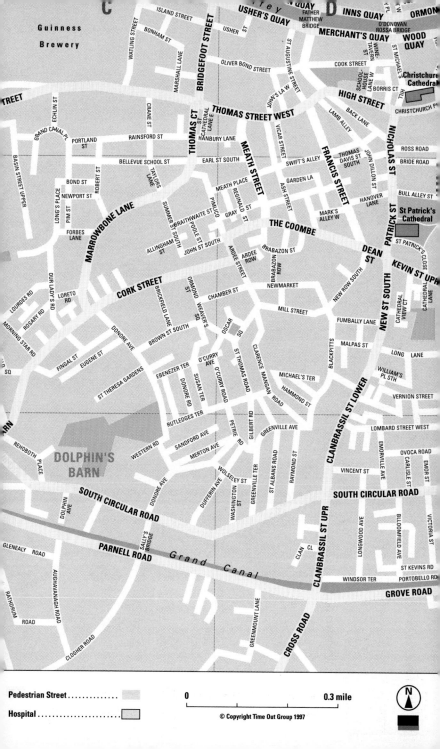

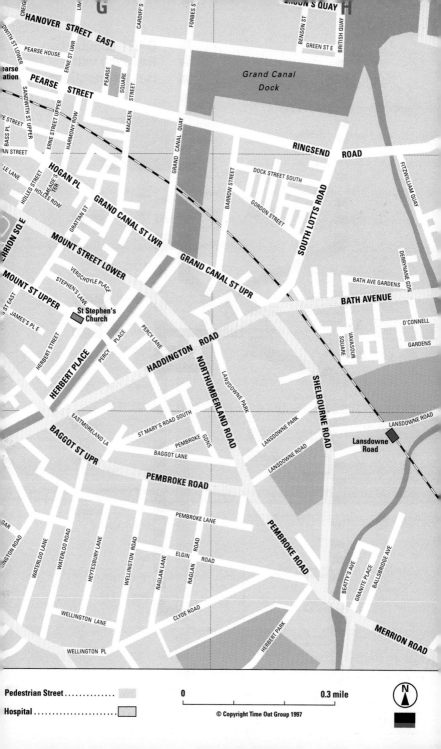

Pedestrian Street . . . .

Hospital . . . .

0

0.3 mile

© Copyright Time Out Group 1997

N

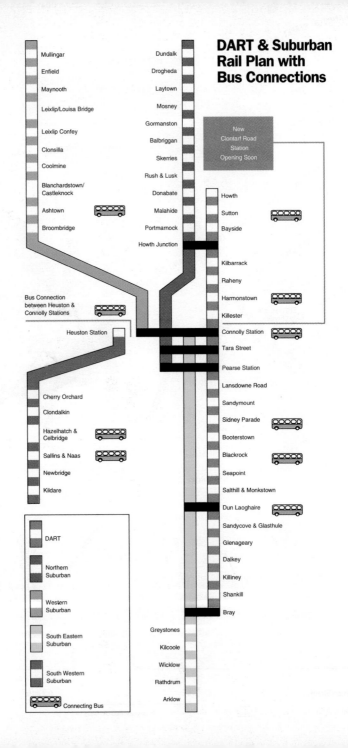

DART & Suburban Rail Plan with Bus Connections

Dublin Overview

To Douglas
To Holyhead
To Holyhead
To Holyhead

6 Km

© Copyright Time Out Group 1997

0

N11

Bray ↓

Dublin Bay

Dalkey Island

Howth

North Bull Island

Dun Laoghaire

Dalkey

Monkstown

Coolock

Clontarf

Blackrock

Artane

Stillorgan

Foxrock

Drumcondra

DUBLIN

p 278-285

Rathmines

Santry

Finglas

Dundrum

FINGAL

Stepaside

Crumlin

Enniskerry ↓

Airport

Phoenix Park

Tallaght

Killakee

M50

Mulhuddart

Royal Canal

Clonsilla

River Liffey

Grand Canal

Newcastle

Rathcoole

N81

MEATH

Dunboyne

Leixlip

Celbridge

KILDARE

M4

N7

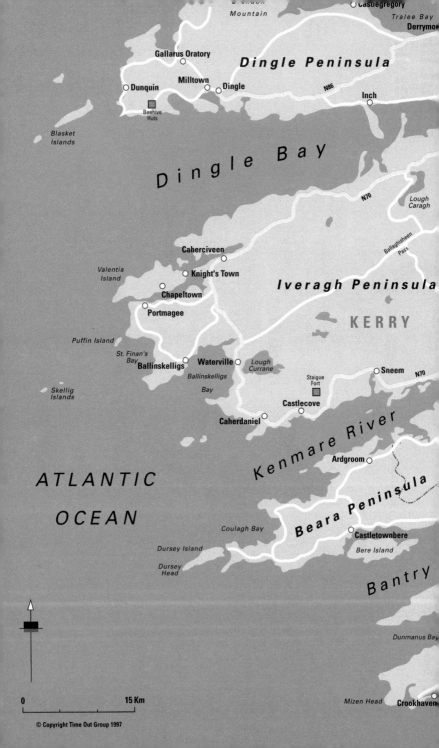

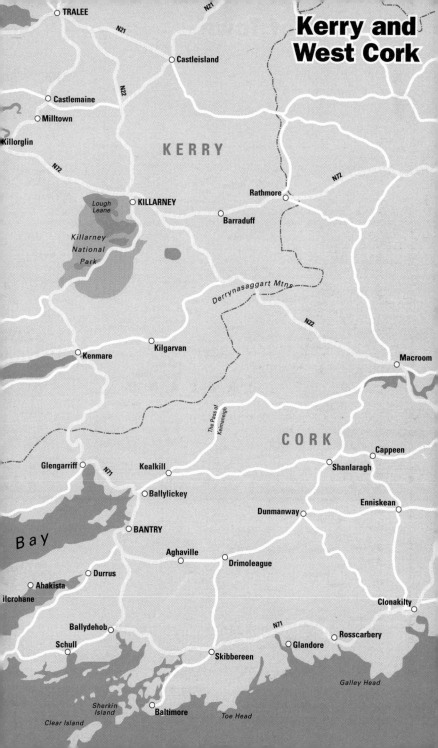

Kerry and West Cork

Trips Out of Town

NORTHERN
IRELAND

Giants
Causeway

Rathlin Is.

Dunfanaghy

Aran Is.

Londonderry
Coleraine

ANTRIM

Letterkenny
Londonderry

DONEGAL
LONDONDERRY

Larne

Glencolumbcille

Donegal

TYRONE

Ballymena

Belfast
Internl.

Killybegs

Ballyshannon

Omagh

BELFAST
Donag

Donegal
Bay

L. Lough
Erne

Enniskillen

Harbour
Airport

Lough
Neagh

N15

LEITRIM

FERMANAGH

Armagh

Portadown

Ballina

Sligo

U. Lough
Erne

Monaghan

ARMAGH

DOWN

Achill Is.

Lough Conn

SLIGO

Lough
Allen

Cavan

MONAGHAN

Newry

Dundalk

Clare Is.

MAYO

Castlebar

Carrick-on-
Shannon

CAVAN

LOUTH

Dundalk
Bay

Clew
Bay

Westport

ROSCOMMON

Longford

N3

Drogheda

Lough
Mask

Roscommon

LONGFORD

N4

Kells
(Ceanannas Mor)

MEATH

See Dublin
Overview M

Clifden

Connemara

Tuam

Lough Ree

Athlone

WESTMEATH

Mullingar

Dublin

Oughterard

GALWAY

Lough Corrib

Ballinasloe

N4

DUBLIN

Galway

N6

OFFALY

Tullamore

KILDARE

N7

Dun Laoghaire
Bray

Aran
Islands

Galway Bay

I R E L A N D

Birr

Kildare

Wicklow
Mtns

Doolin

The
Burren

Port Laoise

Wicklow

Cliffs of
Moher

CLARE

Lough
Derg

Roscrea

LAOIS

Athy

WICKLOW

Ennis

Shannon

N7

Roscrea

Carlow

Arklow

Limerick

N24

Thurles

Kilkenny

CARLOW

N11

LIMERICK

TIPPERARY

KILKENNY

WEXFORD

I R I S
S E A

KERRY

N20

Tipperary

N25

Tralee

Wexford

Great
Blasket
Is.

Dingle
Killorglin

Kerry County

Rosslare

Dingle Bay

Lough
Leane

Killarney

Mallow

WATERFORD

Waterford

Valentia
Is.

Cahirciveen

Kenmare

Macroom

CORK

N25

Dungarvan

Waterford

Sneem

N22

Cork

Youghal

Dursey Is.

Bear Is.

Glengarriff

Bantry

N22

Cork

Kinsale

Bantry Bay

Clonakilty

ST GEORGE'S CHANNEL

Skibbereen

Clear Is.

See Kerry and
West Cork Map

0   50   100 Km

© Copyright Time Out Group 1997